ACKNOWLEDGMENTS

This book was designed as a guide for teachers of Organization Development. It is fitting, then, to dedicate it to all of our own OD teachers — that is, our professors and trainers, colleagues, clients, and students who have helped us learn about OD and have been the source of much of the material contained in this book. Specifically, we would like to acknowledge the contributions of Irv Rubin, as teacher, colleague, and friend — and coauthor of some of the material in Chapters 2, 5, 13, 14, 15, 16, and 18 that has been adapted for use in this book.*

Thanks also to all the people who contributed to the seemingly endless typing, editing, and retyping of this material, including Louise Janhunen, Joann Clark, Carol Sullivan, Regina O'Rourke, Retta Holdorf, and Marian Hogue.

Finally we acknowledge the support and understanding of our families and friends who provided the "space" we needed to produce this book.

* I. Rubin, M. Plovnick, and R. Fry, *Managing Human Resources in Health Care Organizations,* 1978, pp. 88–93, 154–161, 182–189, 236–243, 289–308. Reprinted with permission of Reston Publishing Co., a Prentice-Hall Company, 11480 Sunset Hills Road, Reston, Va. 22090.

CONTENTS

Part II
Readings / 173

INTRODUCTION

This book consists of class session descriptions, teaching materials, and coordinated readings designed to provide an educational package for students in courses, workshops, or training programs in Organization Development.

Interest in Organization Development (OD) as a field is increasing, yet OD is still very much in its adolescence — still growing and still searching for its identity. As difficult as it is to define or characterize OD precisely, it is even more difficult to prescribe how it should be taught. It is not the intention of this book to define the field or to suggest that there is a best way to teach OD. Rather, this book represents a collection of readings and classroom activities that provide a comprehensive sampling from the field, which, it is hoped, will aid instructors who are struggling with the same definitional and instructional problems as the authors.

Who Is This Book For?

This book takes the perspective of the change agent — providing knowledge, skills, and techniques to help individuals facilitate change in organizations. In focusing on the change agent, the intent is not to limit the use of the book to those interested in being external consultants to organizations. Rather, the term *change agent* is meant to include internal consultants, managers, trainers, or anyone else interested in changing the way organizations function. However, the authors, who have performed primarily in the role of external change agents, accept responsibility for any bias in the selection and organization of teaching materials.

The materials in this book were designed primarily to be used in a school setting (for example, an M.B.A. program) meeting weekly in 2 to 3 hour sessions. However, the format can be used in, or adapted to, other contexts including in-house organization training and development programs and extended (2–3 day) workshops.

Organization and Use of This Book

This book can be used independently or in conjunction with any of the OD texts currently available (see the chart on p. ix). The book is organized into two parts: Classroom Activities and Readings. Classroom Activities consists of three sections each containing one or more chapters (that is, class sessions) focusing on a particular

OD content or skill area. There are a total of 19 chapters from which an instructor can choose.

Part I: Classroom Activities

SECTION ONE: INTRODUCTION TO ORGANIZATION DEVELOPMENT

This section contains three chapters concerned with understanding the field of OD. In addition to a session on defining OD, this section includes chapters on basic organization change concepts and skills (such as action research and force-field analysis) and demonstrations of various models of the change agent role.

SECTION TWO: DIAGNOSTIC THEORIES AND TECHNOLOGIES

The three chapters in this section focus on two aspects of organization diagnosis — theories of organization effectiveness and techniques for collecting and using data in organization change projects.

SECTION THREE: INTERVENTION THEORY AND METHODS

This section has 13 chapters demonstrating a variety of OD intervention techniques. These techniques range from large-system change (for example open-systems planning) to intergroup change (intergroup mirroring) to group change (team building) to individual change (career planning) and appear in that order. This intervention section also includes a chapter on getting started in an intervention, and a final chapter integrating issues of diagnosis, intervention, and the consultant-client relationship.

Each Classroom Activities chapter contains instructions and materials for running a class and refers to associated readings found in the readings section of the book. Generally a chapter describes activities that can be completed in one 2½–3 hour block of class time. For two chapters (4 and 5), two 3 hour sessions are possible, and one (Chapter 6) requires three sessions to complete.

Each chapter consists of the following sections:

I. Objectives
II. Preclass Preparation
   This includes required readings from this book as well as any written assignment necessary before the class session begins. Any required preclass readings are contained in this book.
III. Supplementary Readings
   This includes additional readings relevant to the subject matter of the chapter that interested students can read in preparation for the session or as follow-up after the session.
IV. Introduction
   The introduction generally reviews the conceptual material required for the class session or provides some perspective for the required readings. In addition, the introduction contains instructions for preclass written assignments. The introduction also contains an overview describing the in-class activities.

Correlation of Chapters in Major OD Texts with Teaching Materials in Plovnick, Fry, and Burke

		Burke[a]	French and Bell[b]	Huse[c]	Beer[d]
Section One	**Introduction to Organization Development**				
Chapter 1	Defining Organization Development	1,2,3,	1,2,3,4,	1,2,3,4,	1,2,3,
Chapter 2	Theories and Models of Planned Change	8,11,	5,6,7,8,	5,6,14	4,7
Chapter 3	Models of Change Agentry	17	9,17		
Section Two	**Diagnostic Theories and Technologies**				
Chapter 4	Theory Orientations in Organization Development	4,5,6,			
Chapter 5	Models for Diagnosing Systems	7,8,9,	8,13,18	3,8	5,6,8
Chapter 6	Diagnostic Technologies: Group-on-Group Action Research				
Section Three	**Intervention Theories and Methods**				
	Getting Started				
Chapter 7	Entry and Contracting	8,11,17	17	14	4,5
	Large System Techniques				
Chapter 8	Open-Systems Planning	4,15	5	3	12
Chapter 9	Organization Design	15	14	7	10
Chapter 10	Confrontation Meeting	15	13	8	8,13
Chapter 11	Intergroup Mirroring	14	11	11	12
Chapter 12	Quality of Work Life	12	14	9,10	10
	Group Techniques				
Chapter 13	Team Building	13	10	11	9
Chapter 14	Role Negotiation	13	10	10	9
Chapter 15	Decision Charting	13	10	10	9
Chapter 16	Process Consultation	13	12	11	9
	Individual Techniques				
Chapter 17	Career Planning and Development	12	12,16	12	11
Chapter 18	Values Clarification: Exploring Change Agent Ethics	12,17	4,12,17	6,14	11
	Finale				
Chapter 19	Integrating Change Agent Skills	8,15,18	15,17	13	12

[a] W. W. Burke, *Organization Development: Principles and Practices* (Boston: Little, Brown, 1982).
[b] W. French and C. Bell, *Organization Development,* 2nd ed. (Englewood Cliffs, N.J.: Prentice-Hall, 1978).
[c] E. Huse, *Organization Development and Change,* 2nd ed. (St. Paul, Minn.: West, 1980).
[d] M. Beer, *Organization Change and Development* (Santa Monica, Calif. Goodyear, 1980).

V. Procedure for Class Session

The classroom activities are described step by step with estimates of time required for each step. Additional materials, such as cases, are also often contained in this section. Classroom activities include exercises, simulations, role plays, small- and large-group discussions, case analyses, and minireadings (which can be done as lectures by the instructor).

VI. Summary

This contains a brief review of the significance of the material covered in the session, and a discussion of where it fits in organization development.

Instructor's Manual

Additional notes on how to run the sessions, including options for structuring classes, assignments, discussions, and so on, are included in an instructor's manual available from the publisher. This manual also contains answers to the various cases and problems included in the sessions.

Use of Learning Teams

Many of the class sessions described in the various chapters are designed to take advantage of *permanent* subgroups created at the beginning of the course or training program in which the book is being used.* These subgroups, referred to as *learning teams,* are useful in a variety of ways. First, they provide convenient, easily identifiable groups to perform the many group tasks that are assigned both in and outside of class. More important, the learning teams develop into real task groups that can then be utilized to demonstrate the OD techniques addressed by the classroom activities. Many of these activities require the use of real groups and live issues in order to structure meaningful demonstrations of the OD techniques involved. Because of the usefulness of these learning teams, we strongly advise their creation and use throughout the course, if at all possible.

Final Advice

Most important, this book is meant to help an instructor design a course in OD — not to constrain the instructor. Therefore, users should feel free to add, delete, or modify materials as they see fit to enhance the educational value of their program.

---

* Procedures for establishing these learning teams are included in Chapter 1.

PART I

Classroom Activities

INTRODUCTION TO ORGANIZATION DEVELOPMENT

CHAPTER 1

Defining Organization Development

I. OBJECTIVES

A. To understand how OD is defined by several noted practitioners.
B. To become more aware of your own and others' values and beliefs about how individuals and organizations change.
C. To begin formulating a working definition of OD for yourself.

II. PRECLASS PREPARATION

A. Read the introduction to Chapter 1.
B. Fill out Personal Beliefs Sheet on page 6.
C. Read M. Miles and R. Schmuck, ''The Nature of Organization Development,'' in this book, pages 176–179.
D. Read W. French, ''Organization Development: Objectives, Assumptions, and Strategies,'' in this book, pages 180–192.

III. SUPPLEMENTARY READING

Beckhard, R. *Organization Development: Strategies and Models*. Reading, Mass.: Addison-Wesley, 1969.
French, W.; Bell, C.; and Zawacki, R., eds. *Organization Development: Theory, Practice, and Research*. Dallas, Tex.: Business Publications, 1978.

IV. INTRODUCTION

Organization Development (OD) is concerned with exactly what the words imply. First, OD deals with the *organization* and all the critical factors and resources that constitute an organization. But one cannot touch, feel, or speak to an organization. Thus OD deals in particular with the major element through which one does relate to an organization—its people as individuals, groups, or groups of groups. Second, OD is concerned with *development,* or change. Merely defining or describing organizations is insufficient. The label *development* implies a focus on effectiveness, improvement, learning, and problem solving.

OD has been defined in many ways by individuals acknowledged as OD practitioners. You will see these differences in this class session. For now, it is perhaps most useful to consider the practice of Organization Development. Even though specific definitions of OD differ, there appears to be wide agreement about its application and the principles underlying the use of various OD strategies, tools, and techniques. The practice of OD is most characterized by:

5

1. *A method of inquiry:* Techniques and skills associated with OD (and presented in this workbook) are heavily influenced by a strategy that emphasizes the collection of valid information about some issue or problem and the mutual understanding of that data by both those who gave it and those who collected it. From this mutual inquiry into the meaning of some new knowledge or information come action steps, or plans to change something. (This action-research process will be covered in more detail in Chapters 2 and 3.)

2. *A focus on the change agent:* The practice of OD is concerned with the *relationship* between the change agent, consultant, facilitator, or helper and the client that has a problem or otherwise seeks to improve itself. All OD efforts require attention to the working relationship between the helper and those being helped. (This theme will be dealt with specifically in Chapters 3 and 7.)

3. *Humanistic values:* All OD technologies and strategies reflect a concern for the health of the individual in a large social system. Practitioners may differ over whether the collective needs of the organization ultimately come first. Yet the practice of OD has grown from, and continues to advance, the general value that individuals will be both more productive and more personally enriched if they are given the greatest possible opportunity to have a say in what they do and how they conduct themselves in a work setting. You will experience this value stance as you go through this workbook and are given increasing opportunities to decide what is best for your own learning and use of time.

The authors believe the most useful way to begin to understand what OD is and is not is to begin to relate others' definitions to one's own experience and beliefs. Thus, in preparation for the upcoming session in which you will compare different definitions of OD, fill out the Personal Beliefs Sheet. This information will be used to:

1. identify you in a meaningful way to your classmates;
2. form the basis for a comparison with the beliefs of OD practitioners;
3. help create an information base from which you can begin to create a working definition of OD for yourself.

My Personal Beliefs

Complete the following phrases with whatever comes to mind as something you believe to be true from your experience.

All people in organizations

Organizations definitely change when

People are most productive in organizations when

I change my behavior when

OVERVIEW OF UPCOMING CLASS SESSION	Step One:	Introduction to Course and Instructor	(time as needed)
	Step Two:	Forming Learning Groups Around Personal Beliefs	(30 minutes)
	Step Three:	Individual Reading: Practitioner Definitions of Organization Development	(15 minutes)
	Step Four:	Small-Group Discussion	(45 minutes)
	Step Five:	Presentations and Large-Group Discussion of OD	(40 minutes)
	Step Six:	Summary: Individual Learning Agendas	(10 minutes)

V. PROCEDURE FOR CLASS SESSION

Step One: Introduction to Course and Instructor (time as needed)

If this is the first session of the course, the instructor may wish to spend some time clarifying course objectives, logistics, and so on. If there has not been preclass time to read the Introduction and fill out the Personal Beliefs Sheet, that time should be taken now.

Step Two: Forming Learning Groups Around Personal Beliefs (up to 30 minutes)

The purpose of this part of the session is to form discussion groups of five to seven persons. These groups may remain as permanent learning groups, depending on the instructor's design for the course.

If these are to be permanent groups, the following procedure is recommended:

1. Class members form pairs and share each other's answers to the Personal Beliefs Sheet.
2. After 5–10 minutes, class members should form trios. Share your Personal Beliefs Sheets again. Class members may also want to share work backgrounds and particular reasons for taking this course.
3. After 5–10 minutes, trios should divide or add in order to form quartets. Again, members should share relevant information about their beliefs, backgrounds, and learning goals.
4. Now the class should form itself into groups of five, six, or seven. (The instructor will specify the limit if necessary.)

Step Three: Individual Reading: Practitioner Definitions of Organization Development (15 minutes)

Read the following definitions from noted OD professionals and be prepared to discuss in your group the one(s) you liked most and why.

Definitions of OD
by the Experts *

Richard Beckhard, MIT:
An effort (1) planned, (2) organization-wide, and (3) managed from the top, to (4) increase organization effectiveness and health through (5) planned interventions in the organization's "processes," using behavioral-science knowledge.

Robert Blake and Jane Mouton, Scientific Methods, Inc.:
Organization Development emphasizes the "O" in every sense of the word. It means

* Reprinted with permission from D. Warrick, ed., *The Academy of Management OD Newsletter* (Winter 1978).

development of the entire organization or self-sustaining parts of an organization from top to bottom and throughout. True Organization Development is theory-based, team-focused, and undertaken by means of self-help approaches which place a maximum reliance upon internal skills and leadership for development activities. It is top led, line managed, and staff supported. Development activities focus on the ''system,'' those traditions, precedents, and past practices which have become the culture of the organization. Therefore, development must include individual, team, and other organization units rather than concentrating on any one to the exclusion of others. Organization Development is thus this comprehensive approach which integrates the management sciences, business logic, and behavioral systems of an organization into an organic, interdependent whole.

Leland Bradford, National Training Laboratories:
Work, and the organizational structure in which work usually takes place, can provide a number of very important human needs: goal achievement, affirmation, belongingness to a work group, organization or cooperative project—all leading to a sense of usefulness, self-esteem, and ready potential for creativity necessary for the present and future (postretirement) well-being of the person. Generally as these needs are met, productivity for the organization increases.

Conversely, when the work task, for whatever reason, prevents feelings of personal satisfaction, achievement, and contribution, pathways for affirmation are closed off; when insensitive supervision or management unconcern dehumanizes the worker; or the purposes and values of the organization's top management are totally contrary to those of the individual, production, both qualitatively and quantitatively, tends to decrease.

It would appear, then, that the purpose of OD efforts should be to effect a perfect correspondence between organizational goals, purposes, and values on the one hand and the satisfaction of such human needs as belongingness, achievement, affirmation and self-esteem.

But such perfect correspondence in our imperfect world; with hierarchical structures containing built-in conflict; with often profound differences between organizational goals and individual desires; with overpowering resistances to basic changes, becomes impossible.

Warner Burke, Teachers College, Columbia University:
Organization development is a process of change in an organization's culture through the utilization of behavioral science technology, research and theory. More specifically, for an intervention in an organization to be OD, it must (1) respond to a felt need on the part of the client, (2) involve directly and collaboratively the client in the planning and implementing of the intervention, and (3) lead to change in the organization's culture.

Wendell French, University of Washington:
For the present I would like to stay with the definition of Organizational Development as given in French and Bell . . . ''Organization development is a long-range effort to improve an organization's problem-solving and renewal processes, particularly through a more effective and collaborative management of organization culture—with special emphasis on the culture of formal work teams—with the assistance of a change agent, or catalyst, and the use of the theory and technology of applied behavioral science, including action research.''

It seems to me that a definition of organization development should include or imply at least the following features: (1) a . . . collaborative management of team and organizational culture; (2) extensive use of participant action research; (3) an extensive focus on intact work teams; (4) extensive focus on group and organizational processes; (5) the use of a systems point of view; and (6) the use of the facilitation role.

Robert Golembiewski, University of Georgia:
In intent, OD constitutes a value-loaded, theory-based set of interventions that seek a simultaneous, multiple pay-off: meeting individual and group needs, while contributing to the long-run efficiency and effectiveness of large systems. The value-bases have been ex-

pressed in various converging forms, as by Tannenbaum and Davis, which in common imply either that the directionality of desirable human development can be specified in two ways, which can be mutually reinforcing: by imputing from observation a set of gyroscopic needs in individuals that in effect imply preferred pathways of healthy human development; and/or by refining ideals for life from our normative and ethical traditions.

In actuality extant OD knowledge/experience approaches that intent as a jagged profile approaches a straight-line limit. Specifically, some OD designs with substantial predictability generate intended effects, especially in what may be called "limited-purpose contracts." Consider third-party consultation, confrontation designs, and so on. Specifically, also, OD knowledge/experience is less complete in the case of broad and basic systemic change.

Larry Greiner, University of Southern California:
A process of intervention in an organization to influence its long-term development through a: (a) focus on behavioral processes (b) emphasis on a broad range of humanistic values (c) concern for coping ability in solving problems and exploring opportunities for growth.

Gordon Lippitt, George Washington University:
OD is the application of the planning, development, and problem-solving process to the overall functioning of the organization in such a way that it strengthens the physical, financial, and human resources; improves the process of interface; helps the organization mature; and is responsive to the environment of which the organization is a part.

I also use the word Organization Renewal rather than OD. My definition of OR is: Organization Renewal is the pro-active process of revitalizing the organization through synthesizing individual, group, and organizational goals so as to provide effective service to the client and community while furthering a quality of product and worklife.

Jay Lorsch, Harvard University:
My definition of Organizational Development is any steps taken by managers to improve the effective and efficient functioning of the organization. In using the terms effective and efficient, I am thinking about them as Chester Barnard used them. For me, then, Organizational Development is synonymous with the fresh organizational improvement. The means used to achieve these objectives go beyond the traditional and interpersonal and group process techniques which others define as the domain of Organizational Development.

Craig Lundberg, Oregon State University:
In pondering many definitions of OD, a classification seemed to appear: on one axis I have "process" and "structure"; on the other axis I have "organizational achievement/effectiveness," "quality of work life," "enables organization to positively affect its environment." My current definition of OD is: "OD proactively facilitates the design of inter and intra-organizational congruency and adaptability over time."

You'll immediately see that I have to say something like this to cover all the cells in the classification mentioned above. "Proactive" simply means consciously, actively. "Facilitate" refers to style of change agent work and implies that change agents do not do the work for the clients. "Design" encompasses all sorts of units of analysis, process and structure and hopefully carries an intentional connotation.

Newton Margulies, University of California at Irvine:
Organizational Development is a *process* (and an associated technology) directed at organizational improvement. The process and the technology are value based, e.g. they reflect a particular normative view about organizations and people in organizations. While organizational development does not prescribe specific organizational configurations it does imply movement toward an organizational culture which is both productive and "healthy" for those who live and work in organizations.

William Reddin, International Publications Limited–Bermuda:

My definition of OD is operating on the interfaces to optimize the system. This definition is useful because it distinguishes sharply organization development from management development which deals with the individual as the change target. It is also useful because it is nonideological. It accepts the system on its own terms and is interested only in making the system more effective by using its internal resources.

Edgar Schein, MIT:

OD is all the activities engaged in by managers, employees, and helpers that are directed toward building and maintaining the health of the organization as a total system.

OD is for the total organization what group building and maintenance is for small groups. How it is done, by whom, and by what means will vary. What defines it is the *goal* of a healthy organization.

OD should *not* be associated with what consultants and helpers do. A healthy organization can develop itself; its managers are the primary practitioners of OD. But just as healthy individuals or groups need help in maintaining their health, so organizations need help in maintaining their system health, and such help can come from internal or external consultants.

OD experts should therefore be experts at helping. They should *not* get caught up with any particular technique such as survey feedback, team building, etc., but should stay focused on how to help.

Robert Tannenbaum, UCLA:

Whatever OD is, I personally hold that among other attributes, it should be centrally characterized by three things: (1) Humanistic values; (2) personal, interpersonal, organizational, and inter-organizational processes deeply rooted in such values; and (3) the possibility of growth (development, unfolding) of individuals and of all other social entities towards ends widely and poignantly yearned for within each entity.

Step Four: Small-Group Discussion (45 minutes)

Each subgroup formed in step two should now meet to discuss the definitions above. A suggested agenda is as follows:

1. Share each member's preferred definition and reasons (because it seemed to match your personal beliefs about organizations, change, and so on).
2. Spend the rest of your time identifying the key factors or issues that seem to differentiate some definitions from others.
3. Prepare a spokesperson to summarize your group's position on items 1 and 2 in the upcoming large-group discussion.

Step Five: Presentations and Large-Group Discussion of OD (40 minutes)

The entire class should reconvene to hear each group's report on how the OD definitions differed, which were preferred, and why. As the presentations are heard, key points or issues should be recorded on the blackboard or newsprint.

After each group has been heard, the class should discuss what they think OD is and is not. The following questions are intended to guide such a discussion:

1. How does OD appear to differ from other approaches for changing or improving organization functioning?
2. How would you respond to the statement, "OD looks like one more slick scheme that top management can use to manipulate employees to do their bidding"?

3. Do any of the definitions imply assumptions about people, groups, or organizations that do not match your personal beliefs about the way things work in the "real world"?

Step Six: Summary—Individual Learning Agendas (10 minutes)

The purpose of the exercise you just participated in was not to evolve a consensus definition of OD for this class. Rather, the intent was to stimulate in each learner some new questions or curiosity about this thing, Organizational Development, that you are about to explore.

In the space that follows, note any such ideas, questions, or dilemmas that have come to mind during this session that you particularly wish to learn more about during this course. If time permits, the class may wish to share everyone's Personal Learning Agendas, or the instructor may collect copies of them to incorporate into the course design.

Personal Learning
Agendas for
this Course

VI. SUMMARY

You might ask why the authors have not chosen a single definition of OD around which to orient this workbook. There are two primary reasons. First, those who practice in the field are not totally in agreement, as you have seen in this past class session. In fact, the field of OD is characterized by constant exploration of means of improving organization effectiveness by seeking to understand new dilemmas, to work with different groups and levels of the organization, and to form new organizational structures for experiment with ideas or concepts. Running throughout all this is a concern for humanistic values and education, but even these common threads are not static.

Second, the authors believe that rather than viewing OD as something you fit yourself into (or the OD practitioner as someone you become), it is more appropriate to work toward assimilating those concepts, tools, and strategies associated with OD to your own beliefs, style, and interests. One does not memorize everything in this workbook and then become an OD professional. Rather, readers of this workbook are already experienced in surviving in organizations (like school) and in developing themselves. It is the authors' intent to offer new experiences to supplement readers' repertoires of personal and managerial skills and understanding of organizational phenomena.

Thus, if you do ultimately get involved in OD, the field becomes whatever you do. And the only relevant definition of OD is the one you have formulated for yourself to guide your efforts and create new learning experiences for yourself and your coworkers.

Theories and Models
of Planned Change

I. OBJECTIVES

    A. To review some models of how organizations change.

    B. To learn some skills and techniques useful in diagnosing the need for change and in planning strategies for overcoming resistance to change.

    C. To apply these skills and techniques to an actual case of organization change.

II. PRECLASS PREPARATION

    A. Read the introduction to Chapter 2.

    B. Read A. Zander, "Resistance to Change—Its Analysis and Prevention," in this book, pages 193–196.

III. SUPPLEMENTARY READING

Schein, E. "Mechanisms of Change." In W. Bennis, K. Benne, and R. Chin, eds., *Planning of Change,* pp. 98–167. New York: Holt, Rinehart and Winston, 1969. (The rest of this book is also recommended.)

Lippitt, R.; Watson, J.; and Westley, B. *The Dynamics of Planned Change.* New York: Harcourt, Brace and World, 1958.

Hornstein, H., et al., eds. *Social Intervention.* New York: Free Press, 1971.

IV. INTRODUCTION

The Process of Change

In our modern society, change has become the rule rather than the exception. The effectiveness of many of the changes we are witnessing is often less a function of the soundness of the new idea itself than the result of the way in which the change is managed. One of the fundamental assumptions of Organization Development is that there are two criteria for planning change effectively: (1) the logic or soundness of the change and (2) acceptance of the change and commitment to its implementation by those who must carry it out. In fact, the second criterion, acceptance, is generally more essential to a successful change process.

    Influencing people's acceptance of a change necessitates understanding how people, and therefore systems, change. One general model of change, originally developed by Kurt Lewin, was expanded by Edgar Schein to explain the process of change in individual behavior (see E. Schein, "Mechanisms of Change," in the supplementary reading list). This model, which can be applied to organizations and large systems as well, suggests that change has three stages:

Stage 1, Unfreezing: creating motivation to change.
Stage 2, Changing: developing new responses based on new information.
Stage 3, Refreezing: stabilizing and integrating the changes.

UNFREEZING

In stage 1, the object is to develop in the target population a felt need or stimulus to change. Generally, people must become dissatisfied with the status quo; they must be made to feel that the way things are is bad or at least not good enough. In individuals this often occurs through some form of failure (such as doing poorly on an exam) or other critical feedback. Similarly, in organizations evidence must be presented that current conditions are unacceptable (for example, a drop in sales or a threatened strike).

Less drastic measures for unfreezing an organization include data collection and feedback mechanisms that point up problems in the system before they become crises. This can be done through meetings (gripe sessions or planning meetings) or through organization surveys using questionnaires or interviews. The value of these techniques is that the data are generated by the organization itself and therefore are less likely to be rejected or rationalized away. Similarly, it is most useful if the data generated by these techniques can be used by the organization members themselves to diagnose a problem. In this way the organization's unfreezing and its commitment to change are maximized and resistance minimized (see A. Zander's article in this book for elaboration of this point).

CHANGING

In stage 2, changing, the unfrozen system seeks to rectify the situation that led to its unfrozen state. In order to change, the target system must have some model of a better way to function. Mere awareness of a problem does not guarantee change unless the system can see a direction toward which to change. For example, when individuals change their attitudes, values, or behavior, it is often toward the attitudes, values, or behavior of some other person(s)—a role model. This process is called *identification*. Similarly, groups or organizations need some image of a better or different way to function to direct the energy released through unfreezing. This image can take the form of new goals or priorities, new means of achieving existing objectives, new structures, and so on. The desired directions may be modeled after those of another organization or may simply develop internally in response to the changing environment that brought about the unfreezing in the first place.

Second, for the target system to change, the path to the new way must be seen as achievable and not more threatening than doing nothing at all. For example, plans to redesign an organization's structure may at first seem overwhelming and raise fears in some organization members about such things as reporting relationships and loss of authority. Some smaller, less threatening first steps may need to be outlined to allow the system to begin changing (for example, a seminar on new ideas in organization structure).

It may be useful in helping people understand why a change is needed and what changes would be most beneficial to involve those affected by the change in the problem-solving and planning discussions. This approach tends to minimize people's resistance to the proposed changes (since some resistance comes from misunderstanding) and to maximize commitment to the changes.

REFREEZING

In stage 3, refreezing, the changes engaged in during the second stage are internalized by the system. That is, the changes are integrated into the system's standard operating procedures, and appropriate steps are taken to maintain them. Many efforts at change fail at this stage because appropriate support systems for the initial changes are not developed. For example, individuals who are "cured" of drug addiction and then sent back to the original environment that contributed to their addiction often revert to addiction. Although the individual has changed, the support system has not; the resulting incongruity may lead back to drug use. Similarly, changes in some organizational procedures may necessitate other changes to reinforce the new system. For example, if supervisors are trained in new leadership styles but their bosses are not, it may be difficult for the supervisors to use their new styles, since they view their bosses as role models and as part of the organizational reward system. If the supervisors' bosses practice a style different from that suggested in the training program, the newly trained supervisors will generally continue to behave in what they perceive as the accepted style.

In addition, it may be necessary to provide training for in-house personnel to develop new skills necessary to manage the changed system (some organization structures, like the matrix, require more sophisticated management techniques than do others).

Although refreezing does not mean becoming rigid in the new or changed situation, it does mean developing systems that allow the organization to integrate and internalize the desired changes.

Identifying Obstacles to Change

Many of the points made in the unfreezing-changing-refreezing model of change have been summarized in a formula that can be applied to specific problems. The formula identifies factors affecting a system's readiness and capability for changing.

DETERMINING READINESS AND CAPABILITY FOR CHANGE *

Readiness as stated here means either attitudinal or motivational energy concerning the change. Capability means the physical, financial, or organizational capacity to make the change. These are separate but interdependent variables.

In determining readiness for change, there is a formula developed by David Gleicher of Arthur D. Little that is particularly helpful. The formula can be described mathematically as $C = abd > R$, where C = change, a = level of dissatisfaction with the status quo, b = clear or understood desired state, d = practical first steps toward a desired state, and R = cost of changing. In other words, for change to be possible and for commitment to oc-

* Excerpted with permission of the publisher, from R. Beckhard, "Strategies for Large System Change," *Sloan Management Review* 16, no. 2 (1975): 45. Copyright © 1975 by The Sloan Management Review Association. All rights reserved.

cur, there has to be enough dissatisfaction with the current state of affairs to mobilize energy toward change. There also has to be some fairly clear conception of what the state of affairs would be if and when the change were successful. Of course, a desired state needs to be consistent with the values and priorities of the client system. There also needs to be some client awareness of practical first steps, or starting points, toward the desired state.

An early diagnosis of which of these conditions does not exist, or does not exist in high strength, may provide direct clues concerning where to put early intervention energy. For example, if most of the system is not really dissatisfied with the present state of things, then early interventions may well need to aim toward increasing the level of dissatisfaction. On the other hand, there may be plenty of dissatisfaction with the present state, but no clear pictures of what a desired state may be. In this case, early interventions might be aimed at getting strategic parts of the organization to define the ideal or desired state. If both of these conditions exist but practical first steps are missing, an early intervention strategy may well be to pick some subsystem, e.g., the top unit or a couple of experimental groups, and to begin improvement activities.

As the formula indicates, the strength of a (dissatisfaction or unfreezing) $\times$ b (image of desired state) $\times$ d (concrete first steps) must be greater than the perceived cost of change, R. R can be thought of as *resistance* to change. Resistance to change consists of all the personal (such as fear of the unknown), organizational (such as poor communications), and environmental (such as governmental regulation) issues that may be seen as obstacles to a successful change effort. However, most of these obstacles can themselves be changed as part of an overall strategy. For example, if poor communications among staff members is getting in the way of introducing organizational changes, a first step in a change strategy might be setting up meetings at which the staff can discuss common issues.

Before employing any strategies to overcome obstacles to change, however, it is necessary to identify the obstacles or resistances to change. A systematic identification of the obstacles and an evaluation of what can be done about each are the first steps in a change process, ultimately leading to a change strategy. A simple technique known as *force-field analysis,* developed by K. Lewin and refined by R. Beckhard, can be used to help identify obstacles to change as well as factors that are encouraging the system towards change.

Force-Field Analysis *

One way to think about a change is to regard it as a product of forces working in opposite directions. Although in actual situations the forces at work operate from many different directions, at different strengths, and with varying degrees of interrelationships, one can simplify the analysis of a situation by thinking of the forces as operating in opposite directions—those forces operating to improve or change the situation (*abd* in Gleicher's formula) and those operating against improvement or change (R in Gleicher's formula). In physics there is a concept that a body is at rest when the sum of all the forces operating on it is zero. The body will move in a direction determined by the unbalancing of these forces. This concept can be applied to a situation involving human factors. For example, the production level of work teams in a factory is often constant (within small limits) around a certain level. The level

* The force-field analysis discussion is adapted from a teaching note by R. Beckhard.

stays constant because the forces tending to raise the level are just counteracted by forces tending to lower the level.

The forces tending to raise the level (the change forces) might include:

A. pressures from the supervisors to produce more;
B. the desire of some team members to earn higher incentive payments;
C. the team's desire to compete with other teams.

These forces and others like them will be called the *increasing forces*.

The forces that tend to lower the level of production or resist a change (the *restraining forces*) include:

D. lack of interest in working harder;
E. dissatisfaction of team members with supervisors;
F. poor maintenance of machinery.

As in the example from physics, the balance of increasing and restraining forces determines the production level of the factory work teams, even though here the bodies acted on are human beings—the performance of a group of people. Forces need not be of the same magnitude. As can be seen from the following diagram, the level of production in a factory work team can be analyzed in terms of a series of opposing forces of varying strength (represented by varying lengths of the arrows). The letters correspond to those given the forces just described on the list of increasing and decreasing forces.

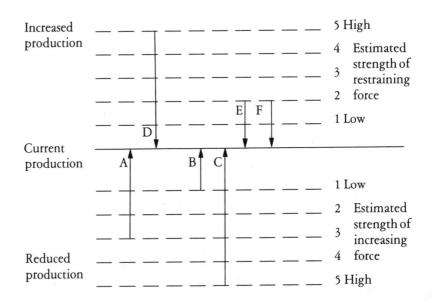

Such a diagram is called a *force-field diagram*. Note that although there is no limit on the number of forces on either side, their sum will have to be zero if performance is to remain static, positive (in an upward direction) if performance is to increase, and negative (in a downward direction) if performance is to decrease.

This kind of analysis can be applied to a wide range of situations involving human behavior. For example, suppose you are a member of a group in which another member remains silent and uncommunicative. In an effort to understand his or her behavior better, you might make up a problem analysis that might look like the following illustration.

The increasing forces might include:

A. pressure from other group members;
B. rewards given for amount of participation;
C. relevant topics he or she knows about.

The restraining forces might be:

E. desire to avoid hurting other members;
F. fear of retaliation if he or she does talk;
G. anxiety about exposing him- or herself.

Just as in the production case, of course, there could be any number of forces of varying intensities. As long as the total strength of the restraining forces exceeds that of the increasing forces, however, the group member will reduce the amount of talking he or she does. The member will maintain the rate of talking if the forces match exactly, and increase the rate if the increasing forces outweigh the restraining. The following illustration shows a situation in which increasing forces outweigh restraining forces:

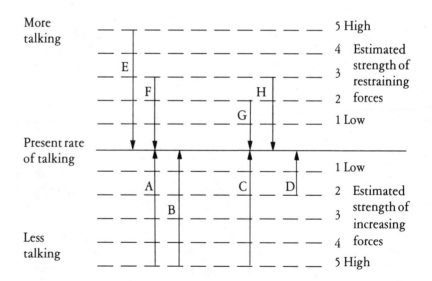

TYPES OF FORCES

Although specific forces are numerous, they tend to fall into one of three categories:

1. *self:* things that have to do with me (or us) as an individual(s);
2. *other:* things that have to do with other people or groups;
3. *environment:* things of a nonpersonal nature (such as physical facilities).

For example, in diagnosing a group's productivity the supervisor might list the following three increasing forces:

1. attempts to motivate my subordinates (self);
2. pressure from sales for higher volume (others);
3. new automatic equipment (environment).

People have a strong tendency, when diagnosing problems, to play down (or ignore) their own relevance in the situation. When "self" forces are included, they appear most often as increasing forces. Others and the environment are seen as the major restraining forces. People are less likely to recognize the roles they themselves play in hindering a problem solution.

CHANGE STRATEGIES INVOLVING FORCE–FIELD ANALYSIS

To facilitate change it is necessary to explore two change strategies, or alternative ways of solving the problem. One method is to increase the strength of the increasing forces. This has the predictable effect of increasing tension in the system because there will be a tendency for an equal but opposite force to develop on the restraining side. An example is the supervisor who puts more pressure on his or her subordinates and gets higher productivity in the short run but at the expense of morale, turnover, and lower commitment.

A second strategy is to eliminate or reduce the strength of the restraining forces. In this way the equilibrium level will rise to a higher point without the negative consequences that accompany the first method.

This phenomenon helps to explain people's hesitancy to include themselves as restraining forces when diagnosing problems. If the most efficient way to solve a problem is to eliminate the restraining forces, and an individual finds that his or her behavior, attitudes, or assumptions are a significant barrier to the solution, then he or she must change in order for the problem to be solved.

REAL VERSUS POTENTIAL FORCES

Finally, there is a tendency when using force-field analysis to find that every force has a mirror image (increasing force is my desire to help; decreasing force is my lack of desire to help). However, this is true only in the abstract. In reality one of the two forces usually is stronger and thus outweighs the other. If the tool is to be useful in diagnosing a particular problem, it is important to deal with the forces that actually are operating in the specific situation.

PLANNING A CHANGE STRATEGY

As suggested earlier, it is often more useful in developing a change strategy to focus on reducing obstacles or restraining forces rather than on strengthening the increasing forces. However, generating a list of obstacles to change and deciding on strategies to alter these obstacles can lead to the identification of a great many things for a potential change agent to do. A way is needed to assign priorities to these plans so that energy can be focused on the obstacles with the highest payoff.

A series of criteria have been identified that can help identify the obstacles to change that should be dealt with first:

1. *Readiness* for change: To what extent is the obstacle unfrozen and prepared to consider change? The more ready, the better to focus on it.
2. *Capability* of changing: To what extent is the person or obstacle free to change? Are there other people or factors that preclude that obstacle from changing? For example, a person who is going through a political struggle in an organization may be unwilling to risk any dramatic changes at that time. The less capable, the lower the likelihood of success.
3. *Accessibility* of the obstacle: To what extent is the resisting force accessible to the change agent(s)? For example, is the change agent on good terms with the resistant person? The more accessible, the better the return on investment of the change agent's time.
4. *Leverage* of the obstacle on other obstacles: To what extent does the obstacle in question influence other obstacles? If a person, is he or she a high-level manager who can exert pressure on others? The more leverage a force has, the more important it is.

These four criteria can be used to determine an appropriate starting point from among a list of obstacles and resisting forces. As an aid in remembering these four criteria, keep in mind the acronym CARL (*C*apability, *A*ccessibility, *R*eadiness, *L*everage).

In the upcoming class session you will be asked to use the tools of force-field analysis and the CARL criteria to plan an organization change.

OVERVIEW OF UPCOMING CLASS SESSION		
Step One:	An Example of Force-Field Analysis	(30 minutes)
Step Two:	Diagnosis/Planning Case	(90 minutes)
Step Three:	Subgroup Presentations	(30 minutes)
Step Four:	Total-Group Critique and Discussion	(20 minutes)

V. PROCEDURE FOR CLASS SESSION

Step One: An Example of Force-Field Analysis (30 minutes)

The instructor can take this opportunity to help the class work through an example of force-field analysis (including application of the CARL model). One problem that can be used is how to reduce the amount of smoking in America.

Step Two: Diagnosis/Planning Case (90 minutes)

Subgroups of four to six people should meet to work on the case assignment. The instructor should clarify the problem (for example, to increase the learning effectiveness of the XYZ M.B.A. Program). Groups should use force-field analysis to diagnose the organization being reviewed. Then apply the CARL planning criteria to develop a strategy for increasing the effectiveness of the organization in question. Subgroups should appoint a spokesperson who will make a presentation of their diagnosis and change strategy during step three.

Step Three: Subgroup Presentations (30 minutes)

Subgroup spokespersons should present the force-field analysis and change strategy their groups have developed. After each group's presentation questions of clarification should be entertained. However, discussion of subgroup analyses and strategies should be postponed until all presentations are completed.

If more than four subgroups have been working, three or four groups should be chosen at random (perhaps by drawing lots) to present their work.

Step Four: Total-Group Critique and Discussion (20 minutes)

After all presentations have been completed, the class should discuss how force-field analysis and strategy planning were used by the various subgroups. The following questions may be useful in this discussion:

1. Was there agreement among subgroups about the relevant forces and their relative strength?
2. Did the forces identified include self, other, and environmental issues?
3. Did the strategies developed adequately reflect the CARL principles? Which principle(s), if any, dominated strategy development?
4. Did the strategies developed include concerns for process (involvement of individuals in key decision making, safe first steps, and so forth)?
5. Do you think these techniques are useful in thinking about planned change? Why or why not?

VI. SUMMARY

Organization Development as a field is unique in its focus on *how* things change as well as on *what* changes should be made. Much of the technology of OD has been developed to take into account the principles of the change process discussed in this chapter. In the chapters on diagnostic and intervention techniques you will see many of these principles put into practice.

For now, it is important to remember that organization change is a process—both a human and a systems process. A key to being an effective change agent is to develop strategies or steps that follow the natural process of change.

OD practitioners occasionally become overly enamored of particular intervention techniques (such as sensitivity training or career planning) and lose sight of the total change process. The conscientious use of models such as force-field analysis and CARL can help you avoid this problem.

Models of Change Agentry

<table>
<tr><td>I. OBJECTIVES</td><td>A. To understand some of the dynamics associated with facilitating the process of change.
B. To begin experiencing the role of the change agent.
C. To practice being a helper.</td></tr>
<tr><td>II. PRECLASS PREPARATION</td><td>A. Read M. Frohman, M. Sashkin, and M. Kavanagh, "Action-Research as Applied to Organization Development," in this book, pages 197–208.
B. Read the introduction to Chapter 3.</td></tr>
<tr><td>III. SUPPLEMENTARY READING</td><td>Fry, R. "The Change Agent: An Approach or a Methodologist?" Forum (Fall–Winter 1978): 18–21.
Kolb, D., and Frohman, A. "An Organization Development Approach to Consulting." Sloan Management Review 12 (1970): 51–65.</td></tr>
<tr><td>IV. INTRODUCTION</td><td>Why focus on change agentry? If we know some steps for bringing about change, such as those described in Chapter 2, then why not just jump in and do them? As noted in Chapter 1, one of OD's major characteristics is a concern for change agentry, or the relationship between client and consultant throughout the planned change effort. This concern arises from some basic assumptions about changes in social systems:</td></tr>
</table>

1. that people change only when they want to;
2. that people commit themselves to a course of action only when they have understood it and had the opportunity to influence it;
3. that changes remain only if those who change learn how they have changed and what it takes to maintain the change.

If one accepts these assumptions, it becomes clear that the people or groups in question need to be treated in particular ways so that they develop a personal need to change, a commitment to the course of action, and the skills to maintain that course once implemented. Traditional management consulting often fails on one or all of these accounts, with its assumption that if you simply tell people what the experts think, their rational response will be to do it. Although this is true in some cases, it is not in many others, as evidenced by the expensive consultant reports gathering dust on executives' shelves.

The Medical Model of Consultation

Schein highlights the difference in styles or modes of consultation by defining two extreme models.* The *medical model* of facilitation is more representative of the traditional, expert-oriented, management consultant approach. As in a doctor-patient relationship, there is some mutual cooperation in diagnosing the problem; but after that decisions and methods are left to the consultant, who is expected always to know what is best. Again, this is appropriate in situations where the patient or client clearly lacks the necessary knowledge or skill to solve the problems. But a major flaw in the overall medical model is exemplified by the person who stops using or refilling a prescription because he or she is no longer in pain. The patient could be dying inside but not know it because the real problem was never fully understood; the patient merely obeyed the doctor for awhile and was not committed to the course of action.

The Process Model

As an alternative Schein describes the *process model* of facilitation, which characterizes much of what OD practitioners do with clients. He defines it as "a set of activities on the part of the consultant which help the client to perceive, understand, and act upon process events which occur in the client's environment."† This approach assumes that, among other things:

1. Managers often experience symptoms, not causes, and need help in diagnosing their problems.
2. Most people and organizations can be more effective if they learn to diagnose their own strengths and weaknesses.
3. A consultant can seldom, if ever, spend enough time and energy to learn enough about a particular organization or culture to recommend reliable courses of action. Therefore, he or she must work jointly with members of the organization who do know that culture and how to survive or flourish in it.
4. To be committed to a new course of action or remedy, the client must be actively involved in generating that solution.
5. It is a prime responsibility of the consultant to pass on to the client skills in diagnosing problems and in establishing helping relationships with others, so that future problems can be resolved.‡

* E. Schein, *Process Consultation: Its Role in Organization Development* (Reading, Mass.: Addison-Wesley, 1969), pp. 3–9.

† *Ibid.*, p. 9.

‡ Although many of these assumptions are not typically accorded patients, it is interesting to note that the current trend in health care toward viewing the patient more as manager of his or her body is more in tune with this set of assumptions.

This process consultation model, then, reflects an overall concern for involvement with the client: a mutual effort to understand, define, discover, or do something together. This theme is also apparent in the article by Frohman, Sashkin, and Kavanagh in this book. Their description of the action-research process depicts different kinds of activities (data collection, diagnosis, action planning, evaluation) that consultant and client engage in jointly. To move from one stage in the process to another requires helping. Given the foregoing assumptions, the consultant cannot decide by him- or herself what to do next. Neither can the client, or else he or she would not have needed help in the first place. Thus we can look at the client-consultant relationship in an OD effort as a helping situation.

This class session will enable you to experience helping and being helped in different ways. You will have a chance to experiment with both the medical and process models to help you realize how you like to give and get help.

OVERVIEW OF UPCOMING CLASS SESSION	Step One: Total-Group Discussion	(up to 20 minutes)
	Step Two: Organizing for the Consulting Exercise	(10 minutes)
	Step Three: Round One of Role Plays: Medical Model	(30 minutes)
	Step Four: Round Two of Role Plays: Process Model	(30 minutes)
	Step Five: Round Three of Role Plays (Optional)	(time as needed)
	Step Six: Small-Group Analyses of Consulting Models	(30 minutes)
	Step Seven: Total-Group Discussion	(30 minutes)

V. PROCEDURE FOR CLASS SESSION

Step One: Total-Group Discussion (up to 20 minutes)

The class, together with the instructor, should review the models and concepts presented in the assigned reading for this session. Before moving on to the exercise on different styles of consulting, everyone must be clear about the kinds of things clients and consultants work on during the action-research process.

Step Two: Organizing for the Consulting Exercise (10 minutes)

The class should break down into trios for this and steps three, four, and five. The members of every trio will play a client, a consultant, or an observer.

Each trio should designate now who will play each role in round one (step three), round two (step four), and round three (step five). Each round will last 30 minutes. After the consultant and client have interacted on their own for 20 minutes, the observer shares his or her observations and leads a discussion around them. The observer will act as the timekeeper.

Once you know your role for the first round, read the suggested guidelines on the following pages (for your role only), and prepare for what you intend to do.

CLIENT ROLE: ALL ROUNDS

You are to be yourself! You have the next 20 minutes to get help on any issue, concern, or problem you may be experiencing. Try not to pick a problem that is obviously too big or complex even to begin to explore in 20 minutes. Suitable issues might relate to course work (understanding concepts) or to previous problems with class members or with school in general. Try not to think about making things easy or hard for the helper. Just try to get some counsel or guidance to improve your ability to understand or handle the problem.

OBSERVER ROLE: ALL ROUNDS

Your task is to observe the interaction between client and consultant using the Observer Sheet on this page. After 20 minutes of discussion, you should stop the process and share your observations. Then lead a short discussion to get the client's and consultant's views about the interaction that took place.

CONSULTANT ROLE: ROUND ONE

Try to help the client solve his or her problem. In doing so, assume that you were called on to give advice. Tell what you would do if you were he or she. Tell the client what you think he or she is doing incorrectly. Don't be hesitant to give your opinion—you're there to help. Be as confident as you can. Try to define the problem clearly right away. Try to envision the client as a "patient" coming to you, the "doctor," for help.

Observer Sheet

Notes for discussion with the participants after the discussion:

1. What was the atmosphere of the discussion?
   a. supportive _____ defensive
   b. free _____ constricted
   c. helping _____ judging
2. How well did the helper "hear" the client?
   a. List evidence of effective or ineffective listening.
3. Did the helper perceive the problem as:
   a. the client's problem?
   b. the helper's problem (how do I help?)?
   c. a mutual problem?
   Check how each participant perceived it at the end of the interview.
4. In making plans for dealing with the problem:
   a. Who made them?
   b. Was the client passive or active in determining next steps?
5. How important were the effects of the consultant role on the discussion (assumptions about how a consultant should act)?
   a. made a significant difference;
   b. made some difference;
   c. didn't seem to have any effects on the discussion.
6. Other observations:

CONSULTANT ROLE: ROUND TWO

Try to help the client understand what he or she could do to better deal with the problem. Listen and paraphrase back to the client what you hear him or her saying so that he or she can say if that's really the way he or she feels. Ask the client what he or she wants to do about something. Don't say what you would do unless specifically asked. If in doubt about what to say or do, ask, "How can I help you right now?" Try to help the client to better understand the problem by him- or herself. Envision yourself more as a mirror or reflector enabling the client to see him- or herself better. Be a helper, not an answer giver.

CONSULTANT ROLE: ROUND THREE (OPTIONAL)

Try to help the client in any way you feel appropriate. Try to integrate what you believe to be the best aspects of the previous two roles into an overall helping or consulting style. Above all, be yourself.

Step Three: Round One of Role Plays—Medical Model (30 minutes)

In each trio the client and consultant try to get and give help for 20 minutes. For the last 10 minutes, the observer shares his or her observations and leads a discussion.

Step Four: Round Two of Role Plays—Process Model (30 minutes)

In each trio, rotate assignments, read the appropriate guidelines, and conduct another 30-minute session as in step three.

Step Five: Round Three of Role Plays (Optional) (time as needed)

If time permits, this round can be a chance to integrate the experiences of the first two rounds. Rotate roles in each trio one more time. Read the appropriate guidelines for your role and conduct a 30-minute session as in step three.

Step Six: Small-Group Analyses of Consulting Models (30 minutes)

Learning groups (or random groups of five to seven persons if permanent groups are not being used) should convene to discuss the pros and cons of the medical and process-oriented models of consultation. Each group should be prepared to share with the class the following:

1. What was most useful about the medical model (round one)? Least useful?
2. What was most useful about the process model (round two)? Least useful?
3. What, if any, key behavioral differences did you see between the two approaches?

Step Seven: Total-Group Discussion (30 minutes)

The entire class should reconvene to discuss reactions to and questions about their experiences during the role plays. Possible questions for discussion are:

1. Which style (medical or process) was most beneficial to the consultant? For what kind of problem?
2. Which style was most beneficial to the clients? For what kind of problem?
3. Would an emphasis on one style over the other be more appropriate in working with the client at each of the following stages of the action-research model:
   a. Scouting
   b. Entry
   c. Data collection
   d. Data feedback
   e. Diagnosis
   f. Action planning
   g. Action implementation
   h. Evaluation
4. In the role plays, a peer (student-student) relationship was present. How would the process and medical models compare in a situation in which a boss was helping a subordinate? An outside consultant was helping a manager? An internal consultant was helping a manager?

VI. SUMMARY

This chapter has focused on the interpersonal process that is part of any planned change effort. No matter what stage of the action-research process you are in, the client or target group is also involved with you. In OD, unlike the traditional medical model, the client not only helps in the data collection as a patient would with a doctor, but also helps in the defining and understanding of the problem, in determining of action plans, and so on. The assumption is that clients or helpers will be more committed to changing what they regard as their own problems.

Thus most OD consultants prefer the process orientation to the medical. However, this is not to say that the OD practitioner is never evaluative, direct, prescriptive, or opinionated. In practice, both models tend to operate to varying degrees. The process model makes the consultant primarily a methodologist, always attending to *how* the client is working, feeling, interacting. The medical model makes the consultant focus on determining *what* is wrong, right, or next. Thus, if one viewed OD consultation on a methodologist-to-advocate continuum, a rule of thumb might be to try to remain a methodologist at least 51 percent of the time (see article by R. Fry in Supplementary Readings).

Judging whether to be an advocate or methodologist requires sensitivity to the process going on between consultant and client. What does he or she need right now? What do I need right now? Are we working in a manner that will elicit our mutual needs and concerns? This kind of focus tends to separate the change agent in an OD effort from any other kind of consultant, expert resource, facilitator, or catalyst.

SECTION TWO

DIAGNOSTIC THEORIES AND TECHNOLOGIES

Theory Orientations in Organization Development*

I. OBJECTIVES

A. To become familiar with several foundation theories of organization behavior and change
B. To compare and contrast the usefulness of these different theories
C. To identify students' orientations with respect to these theories.

II. PRECLASS PREPARATION

A. Fill out the Theory Orientation in Organization Development questionnaire, pages 30–33.
B. Read the introduction to Chapter 4.
C. Read W. Warner Burke, ''Conceptual and Theoretical Underpinnings of Organization Development,'' in this book, pages 210–222.

III. SUPPLEMENTARY READING

Argyris

Argyris, C. *Management and Organizational Development*. New York: McGraw-Hill, 1971.
Argyris, C. *Intervention Theory and Method*. Reading, Mass.: Addison-Wesley, 1970.

Bion

Bion, W. R. *Experiences in Groups*. New York: Basic Books, 1959.
Rioch, M. The work of Wilfred Bion on groups. *Psychiatry* 33 (February 1970): 56–66.

Herzberg / Maslow

Herzberg, F.; Mausner, B.; and Snyderman, B. *The Motivation to Work*. New York: Wiley, 1959.
Maslow, A. *Motivation and Personality*, 2nd ed. New York: Harper and Row, 1970.
Maslow, A. *Eupsychian Management*. Homewood, Ill.: Richard D. Irwin, 1965.

* This chapter is designed to be completed in two separate class sessions.

Lawrence and Lorsch

Lawrence, P. R., and Lorsch, J. *Developing Organizations: Diagnosis and Action.* Reading, Mass.: Addison-Wesley, 1969.

Lawrence, P. R., and Lorsch, J. *Organization and Environment: Managing Differentiation and Integration.* Boston: Graduate School of Business Administration, Harvard University, 1967.

Lewin

Deutsch, M. "Field Theory in Social Psychology." In G. Lindzey and E. Aronson, eds., *The Handbook of Social Psychology,* 2nd ed., vol. 1.

Lewin, K. *Field Theory in Social Science.* New York: Harper, 1951.

Lewin, K. *Resolving Social Conflicts.* New York: Harper, 1948.

Lewin, K. "Group Decision and Social Change." In T. Newcomb and E. Hartley, eds., *Readings in Social Psychology,* pp. 330–344. New York: Henry Holt, 1947.

Likert

Likert, R. *The Human Organization.* New York: McGraw-Hill, 1967.

Skinner

Skinner, B. F. *Beyond Freedom and Dignity.* New York: Knopf, 1971.

Skinner, B. F. *Contingencies of Reinforcement: A Theoretical Analysis.* New York: Appleton-Century-Crofts, 1969.

Levinson

Levinson, H. *Organizational Diagnosis.* Cambridge, Mass.: Harvard University Press, 1972.

"Oedipus in the Board Room" (interview with Harry Levinson), *Psychology Today* (December 1977).

Levinson, H. *Executive Stress.* New York: Harper and Row, 1970.

Levinson, H. "The Clinical Psychologist as Organization Diagnostician." *Professional Psychology* 3 (Winter 1972): 34–40.

Theory Orientation in Organization Development

Instructions: Using a 10-point scale where 10 denotes "most characteristic" (I believe or do this consistently) and 1 "least characteristic" (I rarely, if ever, believe or do this), rate each of the forty items as they characterize your belief, behavior, or general orientation as an Organization Development consultant.

_____ 1. As a consultant, I base much of my diagnosis on quantitative data and address the organization primarily in systems terms—organizational structure, information flow from one unit to another, and so on.

_____ 2. As a consultant, I believe in sharing my knowledge and expertise about behavioral-science theory, research, and practice with my client.

_____ 3. When I consult with a work group, I prefer to use questionnaire data to form my diagnosis rather than to rely on the interpretation of underlying, perhaps unconscious issues in the group.

_____ 4. All organizations act out the basic family structure in our culture; therefore, as a consultant I pay attention to the symbolic role of the top manager as parent and the next lower level of managers as siblings.

_____ 5. My approach to understanding morale as well as productivity in an organization is to make sure that I discern the difference between decisions that seem to be imposed and those, if any, that are participative.

_____ 6. As a consultant, I encourage my management clients to emphasize positive reinforcement of competent performance and to pay significantly less attention to employees' mistakes.

_____ 7. In diagnosis I particularly want to know to what extent the needs and potentials of the people making up the organization are not being fulfilled or capitalized on for the benefit of both the individuals and the organization.

_____ 8. As a consultant, I help my client devise ways to praise and reward organization members who perform well.

_____ 9. As a consultant, I stress the need for meaningful work for employees by helping my client to become more aware of this need and to design jobs that provide for more responsibility and authority and, often, for greater complexity.

_____ 10. In diagnosis I pay particular attention to how conflict, especially intergroup conflict, is handled in the organization.

_____ 11. As a consultant, my approach to OD intervention is to change certain norms to which people conform rather than to change individual patterns of behavior or personality structure.

_____ 12. In diagnosis I pay attention to power dynamics, more in terms of who attributes power to whom rather than of who has authority for what.

_____ 13. As a consultant, I generally lean toward the advocacy of participative management.

_____ 14. I value a client's attacks toward and mistrust of me as serving an important client need and as useful points of departure.

_____ 15. In diagnosing organizational behavior, I pay particular attention to whether people state their ideas, opinions, and feelings in an open and forthright manner.

_____ 16. As a consultant, I pay considerable attention to an organization's history, from its founding to the present.

_____ 17. As a consultant, I look for organizational blocks or hindrances to individual motivation.

_____ 18. I feel most comfortable when using research-based forms to collect data, thereby providing a sound base for analysis.

_____ 19. Diagnostically, I look for the location of the pain in the organization: with no pain there's no problem, and with no problem there's no action.

_____ 20. In diagnosis I particularly want to know the nature of the organization's reward system.

_____ 21. In diagnosis I especially consider organizational structure, particularly in terms of the provision made for the effectiveness of vertical linkage.

_____ 22. In diagnosing group (team) behavior, I assume that a group is like an individual: it has needs both conscious and unconscious and will behave rationally and irrationally, creatively and uncreatively, and so on.

_____ 23. In diagnosis I look carefully at the organization's structure and design, paying considerable attention to the degree of interdependence that exists between and among organizational units.

_____ 24. Since I believe that an organization, like a person, has a personality, I typically analyze an organization's management, for example, in such terms as paternalistic, maternalistic, benevolent, or authoritarian.

_____ 25. As a consultant, I pay considerable attention to the mental health of organizational members, especially the degree of stress they experience and how they cope with it.

_____ 26. As a consultant, I especially urge my management clients to develop processes whereby their employees can realize more of their potential.

_____ 27. In diagnosing group or team behavior, I believe that a group's functioning, like an individual's, is influenced by unconscious dynamics.

_____ 28. A central part of my diagnosis involves understanding the level of organizational members' complaints—that is, whether they largely complain about working conditions or about lack of appropriate recognition for outstanding performance.

_____ 29. In diagnosis I pay particular attention to organizational structure and to whether there is an effective match of structure (organizational chart) with the organization's environment (market demands).

_____ 30. When an organizational group (team) resists self-diagnosis, self-study, and related efforts, I assume that the group is in a "fight or flight" mode.

_____ 31. In diagnosis I believe the most important dynamic to understand is the organization's unique pattern of norms—that is, those rules or standards of conduct to which organizational members conform.

_____ 32. As a consultant, I encourage the use of incentive systems.

_____ 33. Underlying my diagnosis of organizational behavior is the belief that human relationships, whether for work or social purposes, have an irrational quality that is just as important to understand as their more rational dynamics.

_____ 34. In an Organization Development sense, I believe a system will not change unless the behavior of the top management group changes.

_____ 35. As a consultant, I am *not* necessarily an advocate of participative management since I believe managerial style should be contingent on the situation.

_____ 36. As a consultant, I am particularly interested in which factors in the organization are rewarding for organizational members and which are punitive.

_____ 37. In team diagnosis I pay particular attention to ways in which group members relate to their leader—for example, whether they are overly dependent, passively hostile or aggressive, and so on.

_____ 38. When it comes to Organization Development, I believe it is more important to remove restraints than to provide forces that will induce people to change.

_____ 39. I believe certain organizational structures, especially those based on participative group problem solving and decision making, are better than others.

_____ 40. I believe it is essential that the data I collect become the basis for a conceptual map that sets the course for action steps that will lead to organizational change.

IV. INTRODUCTION

The field of Organization Development can be said to have evolved from two distinct theoretical origins. One set of foundation theories is concerned with management and organizational effectiveness. These theories compare the characteristics of healthy, productive organizations with those of less well managed systems and suggest areas in which a manager or consultant might improve organizational functioning. Many of the theories of this type are included under such general headings as organization behavior, organization theory, management theory, and organization psychology.

Within OD there is another related but nonetheless distinct set of theories that is concerned with the process and technologies of organization change. These theories suggest that understanding *what* to change to make systems more effective is only part of the problem: successful attempts to improve organization functioning also require skill in the implementation of change, or *how* to change.

The questionnaire you just completed contains elements of both types of theories found in OD. The questions reflect eight different theoretical orientations to organization development and are designed to measure the similarity of your orientation to each of those reflected in the questionnaire. You will be scoring your questionnaire in the upcoming class session. The article by W. Warner Burke assigned for reading before the class session contains brief descriptions of each of the eight theories (and associated theorists). These theoretical orientations will be discussed in greater detail during the next class.

OVERVIEW OF
UPCOMING CLASS
SESSIONS
SESSION ONE

Step One:	Scoring Theoretical Orientations	(10 minutes)
Step Two:	Review and Discussion of Eight Theories	(2 hours)
Step Three:	Taking a Census of Orientations	(20 minutes)
Step Four:	Group Assignments for Future Session	(10 minutes)
Step Five:	Subgroups Develop Presentations	(time as needed)

SESSION TWO

Step One:	Subgroup Presentations	(2 hours)
Step Two:	Total-Group Discussion	(45 minutes)

Theory Orientation in Organization Development: Scoring Form	Theorist	Item Number	Points per Item	Total Points per Theorist
	Argyris	2	___	
		14	___	
		15	___	
		34	___	
		40	___	___
	Bion	22	___	
		27	___	
		30	___	
		33	___	
		37	___	___
	Herzberg / Maslow	7	___	
		9	___	
		17	___	
		26	___	
		28	___	___
	Lawrence / Lorsch	1	___	
		10	___	
		23	___	
		29	___	
		35	___	___
	Lewin	5	___	
		11	___	
		12	___	
		31	___	
		38	___	___
	Likert	3	___	
		13	___	
		18	___	
		21	___	
		39	___	___
	Skinner	6	___	
		8	___	
		20	___	
		32	___	
		36	___	___
	Levinson	4	___	
		16	___	
		19	___	
		24	___	
		25	___	___

V. PROCEDURE FOR CLASS SESSION
SESSION ONE

Step One: Scoring Theoretical Orientations (10 minutes)

Use scoring sheet on page 34 to score the Theory Orientation in Organization Development questionnaire.

Step Two: Review and Discussion of Eight Theories (2 hours)

Instructor and class should review each of the eight theories measured by the questionnaire. This discussion, which should focus on clarifying and elaborating each orientation, can also raise the following questions:

1. Does the theory in question focus on criteria for organization effectiveness, the change/consulting process, or both?
2. How relevant or useful does each theory seem to you? Can you think of situations in which it has been or could be a useful working theory?
3. What concerns would you have in working from each theoretical perspective?

Step Three: Taking a Census of Orientations (20 minutes)

Using blackboard or flip-chart paper, create a chart on which class participants can enter their questionnaire scores and thereby determine the conceptual orientations of the group. Discuss briefly the reasons for class scores and their implications for the practice of Organization Development.

Step Four: Group Assignments for Future Session (10 minutes)

1. Four or eight work groups should be identified to develop presentations for a class session to be scheduled some two to three weeks hence. (If permanent learning teams are being used in this course, use them for this assignment.)
2. Each work group should be assigned one or two of the theoretical orientations discussed in this session. If two orientations are assigned to each group, the following is a suggested list of good match-ups:
     Herzberg/Maslow and Bion
     Lewin and Levinson
     Skinner and Argyris
     Likert and Lawrence/Lorsch
3. Each group should take the perspective of its assigned theoretical orientation(s) and perform an analysis of the Local Health Center (LHC) case that follows. If two orientations are assigned to groups, two separate analyses must be prepared. The presentations should (1) review the particular theoretical orientation; and (2) show how a practitioner having that orientation would diagnose and intervene in the case.
4. Each group should prepare its analyses for presentation to the class. Each theoretical orientation should take approximately 15 minutes.

Step Five: Subgroups Develop Presentations (time as needed)

Local Health Center (LHC) Case

In a recent conversation, the director of the LHC described his major problems as follows:

> Health care is delivered to the families in the community through health teams composed of physicians, nurses, and community-based and center-trained family-health workers. We are having a lot of difficulties in the operation of the health teams.
>
> We have problems with the role of the public-health nurse on the teams. She is assigned as the coordinator and leader of the health team but this is a very unfamiliar role for her.
>
> We have difficulties in communication between the community-oriented family-health workers and the professionally trained physicians and nurses.
>
> We are having a number of problems with supervisors, particularly first-line supervisors, most of them community residents whom we have trained.
>
> We're having a lot of difficulty with information flow and record keeping. Patient records are often incomplete and misplaced. A number of referrals get lost between departments and between the center and the hospital.
>
> Another problem for me is that the top team doesn't function very much as a team. The head at each functional department, such as pediatrics, has his functional counterparts on the delivery team reporting to him and naturally tends to be more concerned with his own functional area than with the overall management of the center. This makes it difficult to get the best decisions for the whole organization.
>
> We're pretty sure that we're not properly organized structurally to manage this operation, but we don't know exactly how we should change our organization.

Background

The LHC began operations four years ago for the purpose of providing comprehensive family-centered health care services for the inhabitants of a neighborhood in which low-income families represent the significant element of the population. The particular area served by the LHC centers around a ghetto of a major city inhabited primarily by blacks, Puerto Ricans, and elderly Jews. At present there are 12,000 families in the area, a total of 45,000 people to be served.

The social innovation that distinguishes the LHC is the utilization of health teams as the primary vehicle for providing "comprehensive family-centered health care." The crucial element in the LHC philosophy of health teams is that an entire family is the patient. For example, Mrs. Jones comes to the center because she thinks she is pregnant. In addition to attending to the pregnancy, the health team does a complete diagnosis (medical, social, economic, and so on) of the entire Jones family. The Jones family with all its problems now becomes the concern of the health team.

The Health Team

Generally a health team consists of approximately twelve people. The three salient roles within a health team are doctor, nurse, and family health worker (FHW). A team would consist of one internist, one pediatrician, three nurses, six FHWs, and the part-time services of a psychiatrist and dentist. Obstetrics-gynecology is a backup service for all teams, located within the center but not represented on teams.

The typical FHW is a black or Puerto Rican female who resides in the neighborhood served by the LHC. In many ways she resembles the average resident—married, with two or three children and little, if any, formal education. In preparation for her role as FHW she received six months of formal training as a generalist in home nursing, health education, and the like. FHWs have no separate supervisor at the LHC and thus report to the nursing director.

The typical nurse is an unmarried white female in her middle to late twenties who is a graduate of a degree program in nursing education. In addition to being responsible for supervising the FHW, practicing well-baby care, pre- and postnatal care, and so on, she is at present the *team coordinator*. In this role she is theoretically responsible for pulling together all of the team's efforts with all of its families. Nurses at the LHC report to the nursing director.

The typical physician (internist, pediatrician) has been hospital trained to deal with acutely ill patients. Thus his orientation toward the center is not one of extreme idealism: "the poor people of the world need medicine." For some minority physicians (female, foreign trained, and so on) employment at the LHC is one of the better opportunities available. Overall, they are paid well, though certainly not as well as the "Fifth Avenue practitioner." Each type of physician (internist, pediatrician, psychiatrist) at the LHC reports to his or her specialty chief.

This basic team, of which there are presently eight serving 1,500 families each, is backed up by necessary support services. Six teams are housed in the LHC. The remaining two teams are housed at a satellite center not far from the main complex.

Two teams form a unit and share a team office to save space. While one team is having clinic hours, the other team members are involved in outreach, record keeping, and follow-up. A family record is kept, with each note recorded sequentially according to problem. All material referring to the family is kept in the inner leaf of the family folder, which contains all the individual folders. The nurses and physicians practice side by side in the center. One-quarter of the nurse's time is spent on home visits. The nurse and family-health worker meet daily. Informal communication occurs throughout the day in the team office, the team area, over the telephone, or in the cafeteria.

Once a week all team members meet for one and a half hours over lunch. The team conference was originally intended to review the health plan of all families, to review multiproblem or prototypical families, or to deal with organizational or administrative issues. In addition to the team conference, the internists, pediatricians, nurses, and FHWs hold their own weekly meetings.

The delivery of comprehensive health care (the center's mission) through this concept of health teams (the social innovation) does not fit any existing models of traditional medical care. For example, doctors, given their hospital experiences, are unused to dealing with family and social issues. Their primary reference group may be fellow doctors, not the team. Doctors are trained to work as loners; when not alone, they have come to expect to be in charge. But on an LHC health team, in some areas of work a doctor must report to a nurse. Reversals like these may give doctors a form of culture shock.

Nurses, too, are trained in hospitals. Unlike doctors, however, they have been trained to be submissive. Even though those attracted to LHC have presumably rejected the authoritarian structure of the hospital, coordinating doctors is not part of their background. Further, supervising FHWs, who tend to be older women with children, from very different social and ethnic backgrounds, who understand the community far better than the nurses do, only adds to the difficulties of the nurse's role on a health team.

The Center's Organizational Structure

The structure of the total organization in which these eight health teams live is described in Figure 4.1.

FIGURE 4.1
LHC Organization Chart

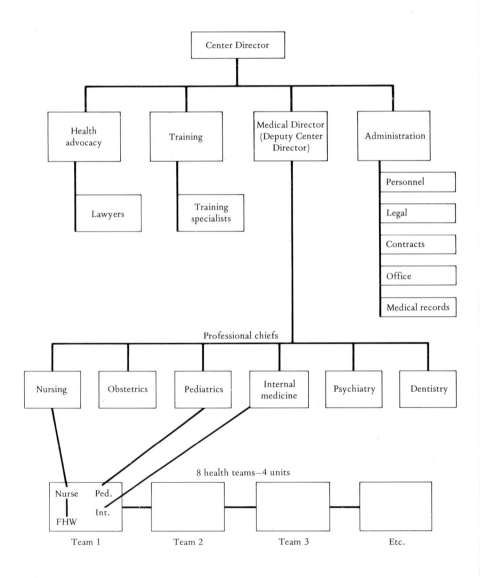

SESSION TWO

Step One: Subgroup Presentations (2 hours)

Each group should make its presentations to the class, limiting the time to 15 minutes per theory. Some questions and comments can be entertained by the groups after each presentation, although discussion time should be limited to approximately 5 minutes per theory.

Step Two: Total-Group Discussion (45 minutes)

After all presentations are completed, the following questions can be addressed by the group:

1. What were the major differences and similarities in the analyses and recommendations of the various presentations?
2. Did these similarities and differences reflect the similarities and differences of the theories discussed?
3. Is there anything about the case that made one or more of the theories more relevant than the others?
4. How do you feel now, overall, about the usefulness of the various theoretical orientations?

VI. SUMMARY

The eight theories presented in this chapter represent some of the more significant theoretical underpinnings of organization development. It is important that OD practitioners have a thorough understanding of the theoretical roots of the field to help ensure the validity of their diagnoses and the efficacy of their interventions. No one of the theories presented is sufficient for effective OD practice; it is important for a practitioner to be aware of the diversity of perspectives within OD. And it is important for a practitioner to be aware of his or her own theoretical biases.

CHAPTER **5**

Models for Diagnosing Systems*

I. OBJECTIVES

   A. To become familiar with several different conceptual models used in diagnosing organizational effectiveness.

   B. To develop your own diagnostic model.

   C. To design a data collection instrument, such as a questionnaire or an interview approach, that incorporates your diagnostic model.

   D. To use the tool designed to assess a live system.

II. PRECLASS PREPARATION

   A. Read the introduction to Chapter 5.

   B. Fill out the preclass assignment beginning on page 41.

   C. Read M. Weisbord, "Organizational Diagnosis: Six Places to Look for Trouble with or without a Theory," in this book, pages 223–234.

   D. Read D. Nadler and M. Tushman, "A Model for Diagnosing Organizational Behavior," in this book, pages 235–248.

III. SUPPLEMENTARY READING

Bouchard, T. S., Jr. "Field Research Methods: Interviewing, Questionnaires, Participant Observations, Unobtrusive Measures." In M. Dunnette, ed., *Handbook of Industrial and Organizational Psychology*. Chicago: Rand McNally, 1976.

Katz, D., and Kahn, R. *The Social Psychology of Organizations,* 2nd ed. New York: Wiley, 1978.

IV. INTRODUCTION

Each of us has his or her own image of an effective organization. Some people have quite explicit ideas that represent a well-developed theory or model of proper organizational functioning. Others, although they may lack such a clearly thought-out organizational diagnostic model, may still have an intuitive sense of what is right and what is wrong in an organization.

As managers, consultants, or students of organizations, however, you should be able to be as explicit as possible about your personal theories of organization

* This chapter may require more than one class session to complete.

behavior, since these notions dictate your own observations, behavior, and recommendations regarding the organizations you are involved with. In order to follow your ideas and suggestions, your colleagues, subordinates, superiors, or clients must understand and share the underlying principles or concepts that led to them. Further, in order to maximize his or her effectiveness, a consultant or manager must have a theory of organizations that is both comprehensive and valid. The only way to know whether yours meets these criteria is to describe and review it.

This session focuses on developing a model for diagnosing organization effectiveness that can be used in conjunction with Organization Development activities. The preclass assignment is designed to help you articulate your own theory of organizational effectiveness. In the class session itself you will have the opportunity to compare your theoretical model with those of others. Together you will attempt to determine a common model that will form the basis for evaluating the performance of an actual organization.

Individual Preclass Assignment

In the exercise that follows, it is useful to have a particular organizational context or image in mind. This could be an organization you are currently working in, one you recently worked in, or one you would like to consult with. In two or three brief sentences, describe this organization:

Now suppose you have been asked by the chief executive officer of the organization you have just described to: (1) diagnose the effectiveness of the organization, and (2) recommend changes in areas in which effectiveness is less than desirable. Your efforts to respond to these two requests would be guided by your personal theory. The following steps are designed to enable you to begin to articulate the major elements in your personal theory of organization effectiveness.*

Step One: In the space below list the five or six most important questions you would ask that individual about his or her organization.

Step Two: From the following list, check off those variables that your five or six questions would address. Add any variables not listed that would be addressed by your questions.

* This activity is an adaptation of the "Tichy-Hornstein Organizational Model Building Exercise." See N. Tichy et al., "Participative Organization Diagnosis and Intervention Strategies: Developing Emergent Pragmatic Theories of Change," *Academy of Management Review* 1, no. 2 (1976): 109–120.

Variable List

1. ____ Formal authority structure
2. ____ Informal reward system
3. ____ Span of control
4. ____ Work process: technology and organization of tasks
5. ____ Informal groupings
6. ____ Relation of system to external factors: market and government
7. ____ Formal reward system
8. ____ Selection of staff
9. ____ Training
10. ____ Organizational culture: norms and values of system members
11. ____ Fiscal characteristics: assets, profits
12. ____ Turnover
13. ____ Satisfaction of members with their jobs
14. ____ Performance evaluation: individuals

15. ____ Performance evaluation and appraisal of organizational units
16. ____ Satisfaction of members with interpersonal relationships
17. ____ Goals of system
18. ____ Resource limitations
19. ____ Information channels
20. ____ Political leadership
21. ____ Informal leadership
22. ____ Control systems
23. ____
24. ____
25. ____
26. ____
27. ____
28. ____
29. ____
30. ____

Step Three: Arrange the variables you have checked into *categories*. Look over the items you checked to see whether they fall into groupings. In the spaces provided, place those that seem to you to belong together. Finally, give each grouping a descriptive name in the space provided.

1. Category name:

   (variables)

   Briefly state why items fall in this group.

2. Category name:

   (variables)

   Briefly state why items fall in this group.

3. Category name:

   (variables)

   Briefly state why items fall in this group.

4. Category name:

   (variables)

   Briefly state why items fall in this group.

Step Four: This section is designed to help you understand the relationships among the categories you have just created. First, list each category in the appropriately numbered space in the left-hand column of the following table. Then imagine that the elements of Category 1 underwent major change. Assign each of the other categories (write in the category number) to one of the three spaces to the right of Category 1 to indicate what you feel would be the likely effects. Do the same for all the remaining categories you have listed. (Use category numbers below.)

	Likely to show a great deal of change	Likely to show moderate change	Likely to show little or no change
Category 1			
Category 2			
Category 3			
Category 4			
Category 5			
Category 6			
Category 7			
Category 8			

Step Five: You can now depict your personal theory graphically by drawing a picture of the causal relationships between the categories. For each category, draw a circle and write the name of the category in the circle. Then draw arrows between the various circles to represent the direction of influence between them. For example, if Category 1 is likely to cause great change in Category 2, it might look as follows:

If only moderate change is likely to occur, draw a dotted line between categories.

Now arrange all the circles and arrows in a way that most clearly depicts the relationships described in step four. As an example, your model might look something like the illustration on top of the next page. Bring this model to class with you.

OVERVIEW OF UPCOMING CLASS SESSION

Step One:	Sharing Personal Theories	(45 minutes)
Step Two:	Creating a Group Theory	(60 minutes)
Step Three:	Presentations of Diagnostic Models	(30–40 minutes)
Step Four:	Assignment of Diagnostic Target System and Report Back	(5 minutes)
Step Five:	Implementing the Diagnostic Models	(time as needed)
Step Six:	Reporting Results	(time as needed)

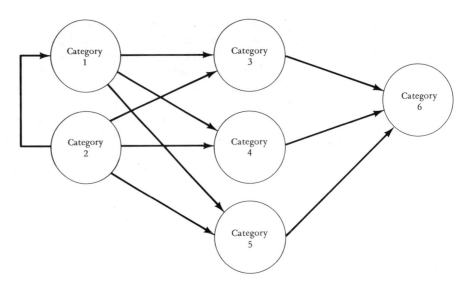

V. PROCEDURE FOR CLASS SESSION

Step One: Sharing Personal Theories (45 minutes)

Subgroups of five or six persons should meet to share their personal theories. Each subgroup member should describe the diagnostic model he or she developed as a result of the preclass work. Other group members should be sure they understand each model. Long debates about the validity or usefulness of the models should be postponed until all members of the group have presented their work.

Step Two: Creating a Group Theory (60 minutes)

The group should now try to blend the various personal theories into one cohesive model of organizational effectiveness. In the interests of efficiency, not every component of every theory may need to be incorporated into the group model. However, a good diagnostic model does need to be comprehensive. Someone in the group should be designated as spokesperson to present the model to the class.

Step Three: Presentations of Diagnostic Models (30–40 minutes)

Each group should present its diagnostic model to the class. The audience should ask questions for clarification and comment on areas each model may be missing or mistreating.

Step Four: Assignment of Diagnostic Target System and Report Back (5 minutes)

At this time the instructor should review step five and assign the target systems to the various groups, as well as whatever requirements for reporting back have been determined.

Step Five: Implementing the Diagnostic Models (time as needed)

For homework the subgroups should meet to do the following:

1. Review and revise your diagnostic model as necessary, based on class feedback.
2. Develop a method (such as a questionnaire, observation guide, or interview) for implementing your diagnostic model. In developing your methodology, keep in mind the constraints of the system you are diagnosing. In some cases, for example, the organization may not want to take the time to complete a lengthy questionnaire or interview. You may want to negotiate with the target system before you develop your instrument(s).
3. Implement your diagnostic approach with the target system.

Step Six: Reporting Results (time as needed)

Groups should report on their diagnosis using whatever mechanism the instructor has assigned (such as in-class presentation or written report).

VI. SUMMARY

The practice of Organization Development necessitates an understanding of the factors that contribute to organization health and effectiveness. In particular, a change agent must have a clear picture of these organizational variables, since his or her success depends both on addressing the right factors and on enlisting the client system's understanding and commitment to addressing these factors. In working on your personal theories of organizational effectiveness in this session, you should have developed a clearer awareness of your current diagnostic notions and of other models that are available, as well as some skills in operationalizing those models for use with actual organizations.

The models you designed in this session may be of use again in Chapter 6, in which the focus will be on developing a diagnostic and planning strategy for a live consulting experience.

Diagnostic Technologies: Group-on-Group Action Research *

I. OBJECTIVES

A. To review several methods available for gathering diagnostic information in organizations.
B. To compare the usefulness of these methods.
C. To develop and practice skills in designing diagnostic approaches.
D. To examine the functioning of the class learning groups and develop plans to enhance their effectiveness.

II. PRECLASS PREPARATION

A. Because this activity requires the equivalent of three 3-hour class sessions, everyone should read the entire chapter beforehand to become completely familiar with the activities planned.
B. Read D. Nadler, "Techniques for Data Collection," in this book, pages 249–256.
C. Read M. Frohman, M. Sashkin, and M. Kavanagh, "Action Research as Applied to Organization Development," in this book, pages 197–208.

III. SUPPLEMENTARY READING

Bouchard, T. J., Jr. "Field Research Methods: Interviewing, Questionnaires, Participant Observation, Unobtrusive Measures." In M. D. Dunnette, ed., *Handbook of Industrial and Organization Psychology*. Chicago: Rand McNally, 1976.

Bowers, E., and Franklin, J. *Survey-Guided Development: Data Based Organizational Change*. Ann Arbor, Mich.: Institute for Social Research, 1976.

Heller, F. A. "Group Feedback Analysis as a Change Agent." *Human Relations* 23 (1970): 319–333.

McElvaney, C. T., and Miles, M. B. "Using Survey Feedback in Consultation." In R. A. Schmuck and M. B. Miles, eds., *Organization Development in Schools*. La Jolla, Calif.: National Press Books, 1971.

Nadler, D. A. *Feedback and Organization Development: Using Data Based Methods*. Reading, Mass.: Addison-Wesley, 1977.

---

* This chapter requires several class sessions to complete.

IV. INTRODUCTION

Most theories of organization address the content aspects of diagnosis: they describe the parameters of effective and ineffective systems. In Chapter 5 several different diagnostic models were discussed, and class participants worked on developing their own theories of organization effectiveness.

Consciously or not, all OD change agents work from some theory of organization in diagnosing system effectiveness. However, whatever content theory is used, in order to obtain the information necessary to assess an organization's capabilities and problems a change agent must use some data collection technique, such as interviews, questionnaires, or observations. The particular technique used should depend on a variety of factors, including the type of data sought (that is, the parameters of organizational effectiveness that are being considered); the size and nature of the target population; and the amount of time and resources available for the change. The article by D. Nadler included in the preclass preparation discusses in greater detail the pros and cons of several alternative data collection strategies.

In OD, however, data collection techniques must take into account factors other than the data themselves. Any data collection approach in and of itself represents an organization intervention. For example, asking a client population to describe a supervisor's style may unleash a sense of dissatisfaction in interviewees that was not previously apparent. Because data collection represents an intervention into the client system, the data collection approach must be carefully planned as part of an overall intervention strategy.

Perhaps the most prevalent data collection strategy in OD interventions is represented by the action-research model (see Figure 6.1). In the action-research model, data collection is followed by data feedback, action planning, action implementation, and more data collection (evaluation). During data collection, information about the effectiveness of the target system is gathered through questionnaire, interview, observation, or other techniques. This information is summarized and reported back to the organization during the data feedback stage. Recipients of the summarized data work together to identify the most important problems and make plans to address these problems during the action-planning stage. In the following stage, these plans are implemented. Finally, an evaluation mechanism is established to monitor the success of the problem solving, requiring further data collection and recycling through the action-research model. If a change agent is involved, he or she generally performs the data collection and feedback and works closely with the system in the planning, implementation, and evaluation phases.

For the action-research strategy to be most effective, it is essential, for several reasons, that the data feedback and action-planning approach be planned at the same time as the data collection process is being developed. First, it enables the data

FIGURE 6.1
The Action-Research Model

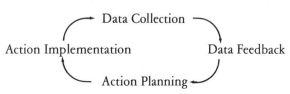

collector to communicate to the target population what will happen to the information gathered. This clarification of expectations tends to relax the client system and encourages the collection of more complete and valid information. An employee who is unsure of the use of the information he or she is sharing will often fear for his or her confidentiality or anonymity and will be more guarded in his or her inputs.

Another rationale for early planning of the entire process is to ensure consistency between the data collection approach and the feedback/planning process. For example, the group to be involved in feedback/planning is generally the same group that is the subject of the data collection. If data are to be collected from organization members who will not participate in the formal planning process, then some thought must be given to how to encourage them to give accurate and complete information (given that they are likely to be hesitant) and how to provide some feedback to them (lest they feel they have been used).

Finally, if the intervention is to be effective, it is important to involve the client system actively in the decisions about the data collection approach. In this sense the action-research model is preceded by scouting and entry, and the diagnostic strategy becomes a jointly planned organization intervention (see Figure 6.2).

In summary, data collection is really part of a multistage intervention process that includes feedback, planning, and implementation. At a minimum the collection, feedback, and planning stages can and should be developed between change agent and target system before any systematic data collection is implemented. The overall plan should be clearly communicated to all those involved in the data collection before implementation of the process. These contracting, planning, and communication steps lay the groundwork for a smooth, effective intervention. If this preparation is done carefully, the action-research process should be clearly understood, committed to, and effectively carried out by the target system.

The Class Demonstration

This chapter is designed to provide the class participants with an opportunity to see and experience firsthand the dynamics involved in an action-research intervention.

FIGURE 6.2
Action-Research/Consulting Model

The learning teams that have been developed during the course will become the targets of a data collection–feedback process. The learning teams will also be the consultants in this intervention process. Thus each team will act as both a client group and a consultant group. As a consultant group, a learning team will consult with another learning team to assess the latter's effectiveness and will identify action plans to enhance effectiveness. Whether these action plans are actually carried out is up to the client group. Thus at a minimum each learning team must plan a strategy for data collection, data feedback, and action planning on its assigned target system—another learning team.

If there is an even number of teams, learning-team consultant-client assignments can be made in a round-robin fashion so that no two teams are both consultant and client to each other (unless there are only two teams). The consulting activities will always take place in two rounds. For example, if there are four learning teams:

Round 1: Learning Team A consults to Learning Team B.
Round 1: Learning Team C consults to Learning Team D.
Round 2: Learning Team B consults to Learning Team C.
Round 2: Learning Team D consults to Learning Team A.

If there is an odd number of learning teams, one team acts as an observer group and distributes itself among the consultant-client pairs to take notes on the effectiveness of the strategies used.

Since learning teams have by now been functioning together as task groups for some time, this activity represents a live intervention into an ongoing work group. It is hoped that the outcomes will include greater understanding of and skill in action-research interventions, as well as improvement in learning-team effectiveness.

OVERVIEW OF UPCOMING CLASS SESSIONS

SESSION ONE

Step One:	Review of Data Collection–Feedback Techniques	(30 minutes)
Step Two:	Assign Consultant-Client Pairings	(5 minutes)
Step Three:	Learning-Team Strategy Development	(time as needed)

SESSION TWO

Step Four:	Data Collection—Round 1	(60 minutes)
Step Five:	Learning Teams Regroup	(20 minutes)
Step Six:	Data Collection—Round 2	(60 minutes)
Step Seven:	Learning Teams Regroup Again	(time as needed)

SESSION THREE

Step Eight:	Data Feedback–Action Planning—Round 1	(45 minutes)
Step Nine:	Learning Teams Regroup	(15 minutes)
Step Ten:	Data Feedback–Action Planning—Round 2	(45 minutes)
Step Eleven:	Learning Teams Regroup	(15 minutes)
Step Twelve:	Total-Class Analysis and Discussion	(60 minutes)

V. PROCEDURE FOR CLASS SESSION
SESSION ONE

Step One: Review of Data Collection–Feedback Techniques (30 minutes)

The instructor should use this time to respond to any questions about the action-research approach, specific data collection techniques, or the organization and flow of the three session activities.

Step Two: Assign Consultant-Client Pairings (5 minutes)

Learning teams should be assigned as consultants and clients using the round-robin approach described earlier. No two teams should be consultant and client to each other, unless there are only two teams. If there is an odd number of teams, one team should be assigned to observe and evaluate the various pairings.

Step Three: Learning-Team Strategy Development (time as needed; use the remainder of the class session and any outside-class time necessary)

Learning teams should use as much time as they need to develop their consulting strategies. If there is an observer group, its members should use this time to determine criteria for evaluating the various activities they will be observing. The observer group will be responsible for presenting its assessment at the end of the consulting activities.

Consultant teams should be considering the following issues:

1. What data collection technique(s) or instrument(s) should be used?
2. What feedback procedures are most appropriate?
3. How can action planning be accomplished?
4. Do the answers to the first three questions fit together?
5. What contact with the client, if any, is necessary prior to data collection?

SESSION TWO

Step Four: Data Collection—Round 1 (60 minutes)

Half the learning teams implement their data collection strategy on their clients at this time.

Step Five: Learning Teams Regroup (20 minutes)

The groups that have just been consulting can now meet to assess their data collection process and discuss any implications for the next steps.

Groups that will be consultants in the next round can use this time for preparation.

Step Six: Data Collection—Round 2 (60 minutes)

The learning teams that are consultants in round 2 now implement their data collection strategies on their respective client systems.

Step Seven: Learning Teams Regroup Again (time as needed; use the remainder of the class session and any outside-class time necessary)

Learning teams regroup to assess the data collection process and prepare for feedback and action planning.

SESSION THREE

Step Eight: Data Feedback–Action Planning—Round 1 (45 minutes)

The learning teams in the consultant role in round 1 now implement their data feedback and action-planning strategies.

Step Nine: Learning Teams Regroup (15 minutes)

Learning teams meet individually to assess the data feedback and action-planning process. Those teams about to be consultants can do some last-minute strategy preparation.

Step Ten: Data Feedback–Action Planning—Round 2 (45 minutes)

The second set of consultant groups now implements their data feedback and action-planning strategies.

Step Eleven: Learning Teams Regroup (15 minutes)

Learning teams again meet individually to assess their feedback and planning process in preparation for total-group analysis.

Step Twelve: Total-Class Analysis and Discussion (60 minutes)

The class comes together to critique the consultant-client interactions that have occurred during the past three sessions. If an observer group has been used, it should present its observations and analysis first, according to whatever format it has developed (be sure to leave at least 30 minutes for total-group discussion).

The group discussion should be conducted as a helpful feedback session. Beware of intergroup competition between learning teams—the class will do that in another exercise in this book!

The following questions may help in the class discussion:

1. Which data collection, data feedback, and action-planning strategies seemed most appropriate to this particular intervention situation?
2. What factors in the situation influenced your choice of strategy? The effectiveness of your strategy?
3. What data collection instruments were used, and why? How appropriate were they?
4. What type of helping relationship evolved between consultant and client? How and why did it evolve? How did it affect the outcome of the intervention?
5. What factors will you need to consider more carefully in designing your next action-research intervention?

VI. SUMMARY

The action-research approach is one of the basic intervention models of Organization Development. It is useful in many types of situations and is reflected in many intervention approaches that go by other names (intergroup mirroring, confrontation meeting, team building, and so on). A change agent can go a long way using this model. Familiarity with the various strategic decisions that must be made in a data collection–feedback intervention is essential to effective intervention. It is hoped that the foregoing series of activities has familiarized you with some of the subtleties and intricacies of action research.

SECTION THREE

INTERVENTION THEORIES AND METHODS

CHAPTER **7**

Entry and Contracting

I. OBJECTIVES

A. To experience the dynamics associated with starting an OD effort.
B. To understand what constitutes an effective intervention.
C. To use intervention theory in a simulated client-consultant interaction.

II. PRECLASS PREPARATION

A. Read the introduction to Chapter 7.
B. Read C. Argyris, "The Primary Tasks of Intervention Activities," in this book, pages 264–271.
C. Read M. Weisbord, "The Organization Development Contract," in this book, pages 258–263.
D. Read R. Harrison, "Choosing the Depth of Organizational Intervention," in this book, pp. 272–281.

III. SUPPLEMENTARY READING

Argyris, C. *Intervention Theory and Method.* Reading, Mass.: Addison-Wesley, 1970.
Kaplan, R. "Stages in Developing a Consulting Relation: A Case Study of a Long Start." *Journal of Applied Behavioral Science* 14, no. 1 (1978): 43–60.

IV. INTRODUCTION

Getting started in an OD activity or planned change process involves the creation of a working relationship between the change agent and the client. The importance of establishing this relationship is evident from Table 7.1, in which three popular models of the change process are compared. The first action-research model by Frohman et al. has been discussed in Chapter 3. Both this and Kolb and Frohman's model of consultation emphasize the early scouting and entry phases. The emphasis in these phases is on establishing a collaborative, open practitioner-client relationship and clearly defining what each party expects of the other. Further, in Lippitt et al.'s model this early development of a change relationship seeks to agree on a mutually recognized need for help and a willingness to help and be helped on the part of practitioner and client. Taken together, these models emphasize the importance of creating a psychological contract between client and change agent very early

TABLE 7.1
Models of Working Relationships During a Planned Change Effort

Phases of Action Research (Frohman, Sashkin, Kavanagh)[a]	*Phases of Consulting (Kolb, Frohman)*[b]	*Phases of Planned Change (Lippitt, Watson, Westley)*[c]
Scouting	Scouting	Developing a need for change
Entry	Entry	Establishing a change relationship
Data collection		
Data feedback	Diagnosis	
Diagnosis		Working toward change
Action planning	Planning	
Action implementation	Action	Generalization and stabilization of change
Evaluation	Evaluation	
	Termination linkage	Achieving a terminal relationship

[a] See M. Frohman, M. Sashkin, and M. Kavanagh, "Action Research as Applied to Organization Development," in this book, pp. 197–208.
[b] D. Kolb and A. Frohman, "An OD Approach to Consulting," *Sloan Management Review* 12 (1970): 51–65.
[c] R. Lippitt, J. Watson, and B. Westley, *The Dynamics of Planned Change* (New York: Harcourt, Brace and World, 1958).

in any change effort, before any techniques are implemented or any action taken to change something.

As the reading by M. Weisbord for this session illustrates, this contract is not merely a legal document to be negotiated and signed. The primary purpose of a contract is to share and agree on:

1. a clear, mutual understanding of the problem or need;
2. some clear next steps;
3. clear expectations of client and consultant or facilitator;
4. clear commitments regarding time, money, people; and
5. when and how the next evaluation or replanning will occur.

While this is being done, the parties are also engaged in deciding whether they want to work together. Does each have something to gain? Does each offer enough commitment so that the other will take risks? Is there mutual respect or acceptance?

Importance of Contracting

Many OD failures can be traced to faulty or ambiguous contracts. It is natural for people to resist or even sabotage change if they are taken by surprise during the process or do not understand the rationale behind someone else's request at some point during the effort. In Chapter 6, for example, you may have felt like resisting the other group's help when they fed back their diagnosis of your group's functioning, or you may have felt resistance from the group you were trying to help because there was no contract. Since that learning exercise was imposed, neither party had any formal choice about how—or whether—to be helped. Thus the best intentions of the group collecting and feeding back the data may have met with less than total support because there was little or no contracting: discussing what the client group would like to learn about, how group members would like the data fed back, how they wished to participate in the feedback meeting, and so forth. In that class session, as in change efforts in actual organizations, contracting would have helped to:

1. further define the problem and the client or client group that needs help (decide specifically what clients want to learn about themselves or issues they want to address, and who wants to learn);
2. clarify work to be done (agree on expectations of time involved in interviewing, responsibility of client group in feedback session, and so forth);
3. avoid unnecessary work or work on the wrong problem (such as deciding whether consultant needs to worry about anonymity in collecting data or whether numerical data have to be averaged or displayed in a certain manner);
4. provide change agent and client with freedom and parameters within which to act (agree to a specific time for review and replanning of the intended process, for talking about the worst scenario, and so on);
5. give both parties an experience in working together and a feeling of comfort with each other.

Contracting as an Intervention

An *intervention* is any behavior that stops or interferes in the ongoing social processes of an organization. Obvious interventions would be meetings, presentations, workshops, and so on, intended to create new awareness, change structure, modify plans, set goals, define tasks, and the like. Less obvious, but just as crucial, is contracting itself. Simply sitting down with a manager to try to reach a mutual understanding of a problem can interrupt the normal ongoing processes of the setting.

The initial contracting efforts of OD activities are not always viewed as interventions in themselves. The result may be less than ideal if the change agent is looking ahead to the intervention he or she has in mind and forgets to think about, plan, and attend to the early interactions with the client. The client is likely to feel pressure and lack of concern that can make him or her less committed and sometimes even unwilling to proceed.

Given that contracting is as important an intervention as is the application of some technology (such as survey feedback or team building), there are some important factors to consider in choosing how one goes about this start-up phase: what you say, how much you probe, how much you question the client, and so on. Harrison in his article in this book considers the level at which one intervenes (or speaks) with the client or client group. One level to which an intervention can be directed involves changing work behavior or working relationships. Defining job responsibilities, negotiating role expectations, changing meeting procedures, setting goals, designing new structures, and collecting information about these kinds of things are all examples of interventions aimed at an instrumental or nonpersonal level. A deeper level to which interventions can be directed is that of interpersonal relationships. This could include conflict resolution, supervisor-subordinate relationships, and collection of data that focus on an individual's often hidden feelings, attitudes, or perceptions. Finally, interventions can be aimed at an intrapersonal level. This includes attempts to reveal the individual's deeper attitudes, values, and conflicts regarding his or her functioning in life.

Any level of intervention may be appropriate to initiate change for a given situation. There has been a tendency, however, for the change agent to err on the side of intervening at too deep a level too soon. This is particularly risky in the contracting phase. Harrison suggests two rules of thumb:

1. Intervene at a level no deeper than that required to produce enduring solutions to the problems at hand (that is, just what needs to be resolved at the contracting stage).
2. Intervene at a level no deeper than that at which the energy and resources of the client can be committed to problem solving and to change (that is, contracting for every imaginable detail or contingency may make the client fearful and immobilize him or her).

Thus two fundamental tasks of contracting are ascertaining (1) what the client perceives the problems at hand to be and (2) what kinds of skills, time, commitment, and so on the client could give to the resolution or further investigation of the problem(s).

The reading by C. Argyris in this book further describes criteria for effective interventions. Argyris suggests that in order to stay on track with the client, from contracting through the later phases of consultation, the change agent or helper must always seek to maximize three things when intervening:

1. the validity of information being generated or dealt with;
2. the internal commitment of the client to own the problem or need to change; and
3. the freedom of choice for either consultant or client to terminate their relationship at any time.

Your Intervention Style

In the upcoming class session you will have an opportunity to role play a meeting with a prospective client to achieve a contract to do further work. You will have a chance to intervene with someone else, so the class session will focus first on what characterizes effective interventions in this class organization. In preparation for this, ask yourself the following: "When, during our learning group activities (or other class discussions or exercises), have I tried to change or alter what was going on, and succeeded?" Use the following space to describe what you remember saying or doing and the consequences.

A successful intervention in my group (or class) occurred when I . . .

Now, recall an instance in which you tried to alter the course of action and thought your effort failed:

An unsuccessful intervention in my group (class) occurred when I . . .

These notes will be discussed in your learning group in the upcoming session in order to test and explore Harrison's and Argyris's ideas further.

Note that in the upcoming class session you will be trying out your intervention skills in the contracting phase of an OD effort. Everyone will have a chance to be both the intervenor—the change agent—and the client. This will be an opportunity to take all the theoretical models and constructs covered in previous chapters and to decide for yourself, "How can I (as an OD practitioner) help this person or facilitate this situation?" You will get the most out of the learning experience if you do not read the role play instructions for the case until they have been assigned to everyone.

OVERVIEW OF UPCOMING CLASS SESSION	Step One: Small-Group Discussion of Intervention Styles	(30 minutes)
	Step Two: Preparing for Contracting Role Plays	(15 minutes)
	Step Three: Round One of Contracting Role Plays	(30 minutes)
	Step Four: Individual Reading: Contracting as a Helping Relationship	(5 minutes)
	Step Five: Rounds Two and Three (if time permits) of Contracting Role Plays	(60 minutes)
	Step Six: Large-Group Critique and Discussion	(30 minutes)

V. PROCEDURE FOR CLASS SESSION

Step One: Small-Group Discussion of Intervention Styles (30 minutes)

The class should break into small groups to share the notes you made at the end of the introduction to this chapter. This is an opportunity to clarify further the readings and discussion of interventions by considering your successful and unsuccessful attempts to intervene. Some questions for this discussion might include:

1. What do people take as indicators of successful or unsuccessful interventions?
2. What was the depth of successful versus unsuccessful interventions?
3. Did successful interventions tend to focus more on information or data that were known to others or verified by others (as opposed to being based on hearsay, supposition, your interpretation, and so on)?

Step Two: Preparing for Contracting Role Plays (15 minutes)

The remainder of this class session will be devoted to experiencing the contracting process. Each learning group should form trios or quartets. (In groups of four there will be two observers for each round, and each person will not be able to experience all three roles: client, consultant, and observer.)

Within each trio (or quartet) you need to decide who will play what role in each round. For example, one member may be the consultant in round one, observer in round two, and client in round three. Once the roles for round one have been selected, each party should read the following guidelines and their selected role description. Note that for the best learning experience, the consultant and the client should *not* read each other's role descriptions.

Guidelines

Client Role

You are in the position of needing some kind of help. The role description that follows is intended to give you a basis from which to start. Your concerns in this first meeting with the consultant are:

Is this person someone you can work with?
Does this person have something to offer?
Exactly what are you going to do if you do work together?

Read your role description for this round on the following pages and prepare for your interpretation of that role in round one.

Consultant Role

Your job is to meet with the potential client to see whether you can and want to work with this person. Although you will not have enough time to accomplish everything, remember the overall goals of the contracting phase:

a clear, mutual understanding of the problem;
some clear next steps;
clear expectations of each other;
some sense that the client is committed enough to go ahead; and
an initial agreement on when the first evaluation replanning of the contract will occur.

Read your role description for this round and prepare for your intervention to develop a good working relationship with this client.

Observer Role

Your job during the role play is to look for certain factors that contribute to or detract from the effectiveness of the interaction. Using the observer guide in this chapter, take notes and be prepared to share your observations with the two role players after they have met for awhile. Once you have shared your perceptions of the meeting, get the role players to join with you in a discussion so that they can also give their reactions.

Client Role Descriptions

Round One

You are the day shift production supervisor for the soap-packing department in a large soap and cleanser manufacturing plant. Your staff includes a chemical engineer (for quality control) and three foremen, each of whom is responsible for a production line (soap forming, stamping, and wrapping and boxing).

Recently, there has been pressure on you (subtle, but nonetheless obvious) from your plant manager to work more closely with your subordinates. There is a big push on throughout the plant for more meetings, more open communication, and so on, to help reduce grievances, absenteeism, and moves to unionize. You really don't see how this sort of thing can help.

Personally, you don't care for this approach. You went to a communication skills workshop last year and felt it was a waste of your own and the company's time.

You do believe that things could be better on the floor. Production could be increased if only you could do it yourself, but how can you be held responsible for the young, lazy people they're hiring these days? Your solution would be to tell the foremen to handle more of the squabbles that now always seem to come to you. Then you could be free to go out and stand over people more so they would work. That's the other problem—these young college graduates who are the foremen just don't know how to supervise!

Now you've agreed (you had no choice, really) to talk to someone from the personnel department who sponsors that communication skills workshop. You'll listen, but this person better not try to tell you how to run a shop floor, not after your twelve years in the company.

Round Two

You are the account manager of a creative advertising staff in an advertising agency. There are four others working with you to serve one of your firm's biggest clients. Things have been going well, but recently that client has been implying to your agency's leaders that you should be more creative.

You and your group are all good friends. You meet often both on and off the job, joke with each other, and generally enjoy working together. You are less than satisfied, however, with the results of many meetings. The results are fuzzy and sometimes are not implemented. Staff members do not use each other's resources as well as you would like.

You attended a public workshop on Organization Development and believe that some kind of diagnosis and action planning could help your group. You doubt, however, that your staff would accept it. They seem pleased with the way things are going and would be suspicious of anyone looking into their personalities. You really don't see yourself as part of the problem. Perhaps if the staff members went to that seminar, they would see a need to change in order to be more creative. But this is a fickle industry, and these are highly sensitive people who are also your friends.

Your secretary has arranged an appointment with one of the leaders of the seminar on OD, who has agreed to explore with you the possibility of doing something to help you out. You are anxious to get help but wary of what you may have to do or say with your group.

Round Three

You are the regional superintendent of a countywide secondary school system. Your staff includes five headmasters (school principals).

Lately, everything is a problem for you. Parents are criticizing the quality of education, SAT results for your graduates are below the national average, your budget is frozen in the state legislature, your headmasters will not talk with each other or share resources, teachers in four of the schools are unhappy because they were not assigned to the new school that was just built, and so on. You could talk forever about these problems and many more.

You meet with your headmasters as a group each month, but this meeting typically turns into a finger-pointing argument. Each calls you daily to complain about the others or to try to get you to okay requests for funds and so on.

You believe some kind of training or help with improving teamwork is necessary, and you definitely include yourself among those who need it. You are very much aware that you lack some of the leadership and managerial skills to get yourself out of this situation. You are receptive to anyone's help as long as the person makes you feel that he or she knows what it's like to be in your shoes. You are then willing to go ahead, depending on him or her to show you what to do, how, and when. You are suspicious of any "quick and dirty" solutions; on the other hand, you sometimes wish someone would just tell you the best thing to do.

An active member of the PTA is a close friend of yours and of the organization consultant you are about to meet. You scheduled the appointment at this friend's urging.

Consultant Role Descriptions

Round One

You have been asked to talk with this client about a problem. You were contacted by the secretary of the department head and have not spoken directly with the client. You are part of the corporate personnel staff, which is in charge of management and Organization Development.

The client is the day shift production supervisor for the soap-packing department in a large soap and cleanser manufacturing plant. His or her staff includes a chemical engineer (for quality control) and three foremen, each of whom is responsible for a production line. You are aware that he or she has attended a communication skills workshop run by your group. Your colleagues remember him or her as one of the "old, hard-boiled types."

You are meeting to determine what the client's problem is, how and whether you can help, and what the first step should be.

Round Two

You have been asked to talk with this client about a problem he or she is having. You were contacted by the secretary and have not spoken directly with this client since you met him or her at a two-day public workshop you gave on Organization Development.

The client is the product manager of a creative advertising staff in an advertising agency. He or she has four people working with him or her to serve one of the firm's biggest clients.

You are meeting to determine what the client's problem is, whether and how you can help, and what the first step should be.

Round Three

The client is the regional superintendent of a countywide secondary school system. His or her staff includes five school principals.

You have been asked to talk with this client about a problem he or she is having. Your appointment was arranged by a mutual friend who is an active parent in the school system. You are an external consultant from a management-consulting firm.

You are meeting to determine what the client's problem is, whether and how you can help, and what the first step should be.

Observer Guide for Contracting Role Plays

As you observe, focus on the interaction between the consultant and the client. Use the following points, but do not limit your observations to them. At the end of the role play, share your observations and encourage the client and consultant to give theirs.

1. Did the consultant discover and understand the client's real problem? Were the crucial facts identified?
2. How did the consultant deal with resistance from the client?
   A. By probing?
   B. By competing—lecturing, trying to be "one up" on the client?
   C. By avoiding—going on to other issues?
3. Who used the most air time? What were the implications?
4. To what degree were the client and consultant really engaged during the consultation?

Disinterested	Moderate	Highly engaged

5. What were the behaviors that helped the client and consultant to move closer together (to build a relationship) or further apart?
   Consultant behaviors:

   Client behaviors:

6. Did they discuss feelings—that is, how were they feeling and how others involved in the problem felt?
7. Did the consultant bring into the open areas of agreement, areas of disagreement, and sensitive issues?

General Discussion Questions	1. How did the consultant and the client feel about the consulting interaction? 2. Would both parties continue working together? Why? Why not? 3. Was there agreement on the next step?

Step Three: Round One of Contracting Role Plays (30 minutes)

Time schedule: Consultant and client meet for 20 minutes. Observer feedback and discussion: 10 minutes. The observer should act as timekeeper.

Step Four: Individual Reading—Contracting as a Helping Relationship (5 minutes)

One thing that can help a contracting meeting go smoothly is the realization that the client and the change agent are interdependent. Neither can achieve his or her goal without the other. In other words, this is a "helping relationship."*

The key to developing a helping relationship is to find or define the mutual need or problem. Thus the consultant does not immediately act as an expert or a teacher until or unless he or she and the client have both decided that is necessary. Otherwise, either the expert or teacher mode can threaten the client and arouse his or her own needs for power ("Don't tell me how to run a shop floor") or affiliation ("I don't need answers; I just need someone to understand my dilemma and to be supportive of me in my efforts").

In a helping relationship, both parties need to feel accepted by and able to influence the other before they will have enough trust to work together toward a common goal. A key still in contracting is the ability to hear the client's message when he or she appears to challenge your expertise or interpretation of something. The person really may be testing whether he or she can influence you or whether you will accept him or her as a peer, where challenges would be appropriate.

During the next two rounds of contracting, keep in mind this view of the contracting process. See whether such an attitude set from the beginning helps or hinders your ability to create a working relationship.

Step Five: Rounds Two and Three of Contracting Role Plays (60 minutes)

Switch roles in each trio or quartet, read the appropriate role descriptions, and conduct the contracting meeting for the round two case.

If time permits, switch roles again and do the round three case.

Step Six: Large-Group Critique and Discussion (30 minutes)

The class should reconvene to share members' insights about the contracting process. The following questions might guide the discussion:

---

* See also D. Kolb and R. Boyatzis, "On the Dynamics of the Helping Relationship," in D. Kolb et al., eds., *Organizational Psychology: A Book of Readings,* 3rd ed. (Englewood Cliffs, N.J.: Prentice-Hall, 1979), pp. 303–319.

1. Across all the cases, what kinds of consultant behavior seemed to make the client comfortable, willing to disclose more, and interested in going ahead?
2. How were specific instances of client resistance handled by consultants?
3. How did stereotypes of what a consultant should do and how a client would behave get in the way of just talking with each other, person to person?
4. Of what use is the concept of contracting to a manager and his or her subordinates? Is it appropriate only for consultants or facilitators?

VI. SUMMARY

The contracting process can make the difference between success and failure in any planned change effort. In our experience, a major cause of ineffective or aborted contracting is the tendency to play a role rather than being oneself. We often tend to imagine what a consultant ought to be or sound like and, with that in mind, plunge ahead without listening either to the client or to our own emotions. Thus, for example, you may propose a complete program for change when all the client needs is a better understanding of his or her problem. Or you may push the client to do something with his or her subordinates (perhaps because you know exactly what you could do with them) when what the client really needs is help in standing up to his or her own boss. The following is a summary of suggested guidelines for the contracting process.

1. *Do not accept any final contract without gathering some data on views of other parts of the organization.* Test the client's view by getting a broader base of data than just discussions with the client before establishing a plan. This produces more valid data for everyone to work with.
2. *Don't be an agent.* Being an agent means carrying messages from one part of the organization to another. This does not build into the organization the ability of one part of the organization to communicate with or confront the other. Acting as an agent allows the client to remain less committed since he or she does not have to own and manage information.
3. *Know what you will and will not do.* Do not get trapped into performing services you do not want to do either for ethical reasons or because they are bad consulting practices or things you dislike doing or know you do not do well. From the start, exercise your freedom of choice to work where you believe you can help.
4. *Do not challenge every assumption the client makes.* If you do so, you will not make much progress during the contracting session. You will tend to get involved in the actual consultation needed when there isn't time or when it does not meet the client's expectations. If you question the validity of his or her perceptions, you should work on getting that defined as a problem and learning how you can help collect additional information.
5. *Contracts should be renewable at any time by either party.* It is often during the renewal of contracts that a more specific and more suitable contract for both parties is established.
6. *Confront the client if you are unsure about what he or she is thinking or what the contract is.* Confrontation ranges from presenting the goals of OD, telling anecdotes about successful work, or assessing the client's situation, to providing direct feedback to the client. You may need to confront the client on a personal level to determine his or her commitment.

7. *Be clear who the client is.* The client may be an individual, a total organization, or a group. Knowing who the client is helps to keep problem solving and interventions focused rather than dispersed. In the round one case, for instance, the real client was the supervisor's boss, who had urged him or her to see the consultant.

The next several chapters will address specific steps or interventions that could result from contracting. Depending on the mutual definition of the problem and the part of the organization involved, interventions in the system (Chapters 8 to 12), in groups or teams (Chapters 13 to 16), or with individuals (Chapters 17 to 18) could be used. Remember that the earlier chapters on data collection and feedback methods also constitute interventions that are often decided on as the result of contracting.

CHAPTER **8**

Open-Systems Planning

<table>
<tr>
<td>I. OBJECTIVES</td>
<td>

A. To understand some of the issues involved in organizational planning and goal setting.

B. To explore the appropriateness and usefulness of alternate organizational planning processes.

C. To apply the open-systems planning technique in the context of an organization familiar to the class.

</td>
</tr>
<tr>
<td>II. PRECLASS PREPARATION</td>
<td>

A. Read the introduction to Chapter 8.

B. Read R. Fry, "Improving Trustee, Administrator, and Physician Collaboration Through Open Systems Planning," in this book, pages 282–292.

C. Do Individual Preparation in this chapter.

</td>
</tr>
<tr>
<td>III. SUPPLEMENTARY READING</td>
<td>

Jayaram, G. E. "Open Systems Planning." In W. Bennis, K. Benne, R. Chin, and R. Corey, eds., *The Planning of Change.* New York: Holt, Rinehart and Winston, 1976.

Krone, C. "Open Systems Redesign." In J. D. Adams, ed., *Theory and Method in Organization Development: An Evolutionary Process.* Arlington, Va.: NTL Institute for Applied Behavioral Science, 1974.

McCaskey, M. "A Contingency Approach to Planning: Planning with Goals and Planning Without Goals." *Academy of Management Journal* 17, no. 2 (1974).

</td>
</tr>
<tr>
<td>IV. INTRODUCTION</td>
<td>

Many organizations these days appear to be characterized by a crisis orientation toward management. Amid pressures to respond to day-to-day demands, monthly fluctuations in the economy, quarterly earnings reports, and the like, energy is seldom invested in long-range planning or goal setting. Thus situations can develop that seem to catch the organization off guard: hospitals appear unable to adapt to increasing regulation and consumer pressure to cut costs, automobile companies "suddenly" try to catch up to their Japanese competitors, and so on. The crisis atmosphere that develops ("Drop everything and come up with a plan to cut 10 per-

</td>
</tr>
</table>

cent of the white-collar labor force within thirty days'') further drains time and energy needed to run the organization. In the face of increased pressure brought on by the crisis, even less time and effort are available for long-range planning and crisis prevention.

It is not hard to see how such a situation can create a self-fulfilling prophecy: a crisis-management orientation minimizes attention to long-range plans and thereby creates more crises that demand immediate attention. This session will focus on a process that enables organizations to step out of this self-defeating cycle in order to plan and set goals in a way that prevents rather than promotes crises.

Planning Versus Goal Setting

Nearly all organization theorists recognize that having goals is a defining criterion of organizations. Although it is true that every organization has a purpose—that is, exists to achieve some goal or goals—it is much less clear how an organization should define its goals. M. McCaskey (1974; see Supplementary Reading) has described two different basic processes organizations use to accomplish planning:

1. *Goal Setting:* The most common and more traditional method is to plan to meet specific goals—that is, to set targets that are measurable in some specific way and then to create strategies, policies, and plans to reach these targets. Zero-Based Budgeting, Management by Objectives, PERT charts, and Behavioral Objectives are all representative of this approach. This planning-toward-goals orientation tends to be most appropriately applied in situations in which:
   a. the organization is at a stage at which it wishes to narrow its focus (product line, geographical market area, specialized services);
   b. the environment surrounding the firm is relatively stable and predictable; and
   c. severe time or resource limitations exist, and the only way to preserve unprogrammed tasks (strategic planning) is to build them into short-term goals and priorities.

2. *Directional or thrust planning:* An alternative to this process (though the two are not necessarily mutually exclusive) can be characterized as planning for directions, as opposed to goals. Here planners are concerned with defining directions or domains to guide an organization member's styles of perceiving and doing things. The focus shifts from carefully formulating a goal to be accomplished to considering the major thrust of the individual, group, or system in conjunction with the environmental factors that will affect that area of work. Such a planning orientation appears more suitable to conditions in which:
   a. it is too early to set specific goals: the person or system has not yet decided what it is or should be doing (plant start-ups, new coalitions, new ventures or programs);
   b. the environment is changing and uncertain: there is little sense in planning to reach specific goals in twelve months if the firm will be subject to major regulatory, economic, technological, or other changes during that period; and

c. when key actors in the system are unable to build enough trust or agreement to decide on a specific, common goal, as R. Fry describes in the required reading for this chapter.

This latter approach to planning for direction would appear more and more useful, given the current state of the economy and the increasing complexity that characterizes organization-environment interfaces. Consumer movements, economic reforms, ecological conservation, and international markets all contribute to these three conditions. The implication is that there is an increased need to help organizations view themselves as open systems that need to do less goal setting before acting and more acting in relation to the environment in order to discover which goals or directions to pursue. Viewing oneself or one's organization as an open system necessitates focusing on the environment, however unstable or uncertain, *before* attempting to set specific goals. The following procedure helps planners to do this and can be used by OD practitioners to help organizations reach consensus on directions they wish to emphasize.

Open-Systems Planning Process*

Open-systems planning (OSP) is intended to help planners and managers move from crisis-management into more directional planning by making them more explicitly aware of the demands of today's environment, their current responses, likely future trends and demands, and their desired future state. The OSP process comprises the following steps:

PHASE ONE: DEFINING A CORE MISSION

What is the basic purpose or reason for being of the enterprise? In a manufacturing organization, for example, is it to maximize profits, produce socially useful products at a profit, provide a high-quality place for people to work, or maximize return to stockholders?

PHASE TWO: ANALYSIS OF CURRENT DEMAND SYSTEMS

After defining and agreeing on a core mission, the next step is to take a "snapshot" of the present conditions. To do this, one first identifies those domains that make demands on the present system. In our manufacturing example, such domains might include organized labor groups, the local community, consumer values, stockholders, international governments, OSHA, competitors, and so on.

Once the domains have been identified, determine for each the key demands being made; for example, "We (organized labor) want you (the firm) to keep our jobs, above all, in the current recession."

PHASE THREE: ANALYSIS OF CURRENT RESPONSE TO DEMANDS

The response of the present system to each demand identified in phase two should be clarified. In the case of the demand from organized labor, the firm could be responding in one of several ways: by ignoring it, by involving union representatives in deci-

* Adapted with permission from a teaching note by R. Beckhard.

sions involving loss of jobs, by listening to them but being unable to meet the demand, by satisfying them, and so on.

PHASE FOUR: PREDICTED FUTURE DEMANDS

Once the current state has been set out in phases two and three, the focus shifts to the future, again starting with the environment. Projecting over a relevant period (two to five years), and using the domains identified in phase two, predict what demands are likely to exist if your current response continues and if changes or trends from other sources occur as anticipated: ''Given our present stance and whatever else we realistically expect to happen, they (the domain) are likely to be urging us to . . .'' In the labor example, a prediction might be: ''Given a current response to ignore them and some improvement in the economy over the next three years, they could be threatening us with a strike.''

PHASE FIVE: DESIRED FUTURE DEMANDS

Considering the same set of domains from phase two, the ideal scenario is now identified: ''What would we like each domain to be asking (demanding) of us three to five years from now?'' The core mission from phase one may help in achieving consensus on this. In the labor example, the desired state might be: ''We would like them to be saying, 'Tell us how we can help you get our people involved in quality control to improve productivity, profits, and hence job security.' ''

PHASE SIX: ANALYSIS OF GAPS BETWEEN ACTUAL AND IDEAL

After predicting the consequences of current response modes and anticipating external changes or trends (phase four), and after determining the desired state (phase five), the next step is to identify and prioritize a list of gaps or major differences between where the firm is headed and where it wants to be. This process clarifies which current directions or thrusts are unlikely to lead the organization toward its desired state.

PHASE SEVEN: ACTION PLANNING

What are the first steps in shifting current response or heading off likely external forces in order to increase the chances of realizing the ideal state? This step often involves prioritizing which trends or gaps are most costly if not addressed and often necessitates another look at the core mission, thus cycling back to phase one (see the article by R. Fry in the required reading).

This process may appear logical and straightforward. As the reading for this chapter indicates, however, it can also be difficult. It tends to be long and often ambiguous because there is always incomplete information. It can be frustrating to the extent that the process leads, not to specific goals, but rather to new directions or thrusts. On the other hand, the situation facing the organization may offer no other choice. OSP forces one to learn about, and proactively anticipate the consequences of, the environment of the system in question. It requires key actors in the organization to learn, predict, and develop future scenarios together. Finally, it minimizes the likelihood of the organization's being completely surprised or caught off guard by some external factor.

Individual Preparation: Defining a Core Mission

In the upcoming class session you will experience parts of each phase in the open-systems planning process. The focal system or organization will be the school or educational program in which you are currently enrolled.* In preparation for phase one, use the following space to jot down your perception of what the core mission of this school should be: As I see it, the core mission or basic reason for being of _____ _____ is to:

OVERVIEW OF UPCOMING CLASS SESSION

Step One:	Creating Planning Groups	(5 minutes)
Step Two:	Defining a Core Mission	(25 minutes)
Step Three:	Identifying Domains in the Demand System	(10 minutes)
Step Four:	Open-Systems Planning in Subgroups	(60 minutes)
Step Five:	Planning-Group Reports and Discussion	(30 minutes)
Step Six:	Large-Group Discussion/Critique of OSP Process	(20 minutes)

V. PROCEDURE FOR CLASS SESSION

Step One: Creating Planning Groups (5 minutes)

The class should divide into planning groups of five or six members each. If permanent learning teams for the course have been created, they should be used as planning groups for this session.

Step Two: Defining a Core Mission (25 minutes)

The instructor will lead class discussion to define a core mission statement for the system on which you are about to do OSP. As time allows, class members can discuss their individual perceptions of a core mission statement.
   Once a mission statement has been defined, go on to step three.

Step Three: Identifying Domains in the Demand System (10 minutes)

The class as a whole should agree on the key domains in the environment that create demands on the present system. If the focal system is, for example, a graduate school of business, relevant domains might include faculty, students, employers, alumni, and applicant pool. Each planning group should be assigned one domain to focus on during step four.

* The course instructor may have already defined a more specific system (such as a department or degree program) or another outside organization for you to consider.

Step Four: Open-Systems Planning in Subgroups (60 minutes)

In order to experience the OSP process, each planning group should go through the remaining phases of the process, focusing only on the domain assigned to that group.*

The steps you should go through are as follows:

1. Identification of current demands: What does your domain currently expect from or demand of the system? (estimated time: 15 minutes)
2. Current response: For one or two of the major demands, what is the system's current response—whether action or inaction? (estimated time: 10 minutes)
3. Future demands: Considering the current response and whatever other changes or trends you think are likely to occur over the next two years, what are the key demands from your domain going to be two years from now? (estimated time: 10 minutes)
4. Ideal state: Imagine two years from now; what kinds of expectations or demands would you like to see coming from the domain you are analyzing? (estimated time: 10 minutes)
5. Identifying gaps and action planning: Compare and contrast the results of items 3 and 4. What gaps exist between current anticipated demands given current directions, and ideal demands? Choose one gap and suggest some first step the system could take to alter its current course. (estimated time: 15 minutes)

Note that you have one hour to go through these five phases. You will have to manage your time carefully. At each step, focus on only one or two items. Normally, a client group could spend days on each. A spokesperson should be ready to present a 5-minute summary of the group's work in step five.

Step Five: Planning-Group Reports and Discussion (30 minutes)

A spokesperson from each group should take no more than 5 minutes to summarize what that group discovered, discussed, and concluded about the domain it examined. Any suggestions for action should be listed on the board or flip chart.

If time permits, each spokesperson should also describe how his or her group's discussion proceeded. Which topics were harder? Which phases took longer? What unexpected issues arose?

Step Six: Large-Group Discussion of OSP Process (20 minutes)

The class should now reflect and discuss the OSP process just completed. It may be difficult to drop the content at this point, but it is important to share your insights about the tool itself. The following are suggested discussion questions:

1. If you were the dean of this school (or head of whatever system you examined), would you adopt a process like this one? Why?

---

* This obviously simplifies the complex issue of having to consider demands from multiple domains at the same time, but it should still give you a taste of what OSP is like for a client group.

2. Considering the time OSP can take and the immense amount of information it can generate (as evidenced in the required reading for this session and in your group reports), what benefits do you see coming out of OSP that make it worth the investment?
3. What other kinds of organizations or situations would you see as likely candidates for OSP? Which ones should not use it?
4. What kinds of things could a facilitator or OD practitioner have done in your planning groups to make your work more effective?

VI. SUMMARY

OSP is not a panacea for all organizations. A significant investment of time and energy is required. In addition, the OSP process may involve a great deal of stress and ambiguity. However, OSP is one tool that can enable organizations to manage pro-actively their responses to ambiguous and often conflicting environmental demands. The resulting directions and action plans can provide the coherent sense of direction and control that organizations need to function effectively in a complex and changing environment.

OSP can be used as a tool to help managers or planners do long-range planning and as a method to help organizations achieve consensus around their mission and plans. For example, OSP can be used to mediate intergroup conflicts, as shown in the trustee-administrator-physician situation in the required reading for this chapter. It can also be the overriding framework for job redesign or new plant design, as C. Krone has suggested (1974; see Supplementary Reading). In most cases OSP requires group effort, often with a newly formed group or a group unfamiliar with long-range planning. Hence the use of OSP necessitates helping a group to work well together. Techniques and approaches for doing this are covered in Chapters 13 through 16.

CHAPTER 9

Organization Design

I. OBJECTIVES

A. To become familiar with some principles involved in designing an organization's structure.
B. To understand the implications of organization structure for intervening into organizational functioning from an OD perspective.
C. To apply organization design principles to a particular organization involved in an OD effort.

II. PRECLASS PREPARATION

A. Read the introduction to Chapter 9.
B. Read M. Jelinek, "Organization Structure: The Basic Conformations," in this book, pages 293–303.
C. Read J. Galbraith, "Organization Design: An Information Processing View," in this book, pages 304–311.
D. Read the Metropolitan Judicial Alternative Program case in this chapter.

III. SUPPLEMENTARY READING

Galbraith, J. *Organization Design*. Reading, Mass.: Addison-Wesley, 1977.
Jelinek, M.; Litterer, J.; and Miles, R., eds. *Organization Design: Theory and Practice*. Plano, Tex.: Business Publications, Inc., 1981.
Lawrence P., and Lorsch, J. *Developing Organizations: Diagnosis and Action*. Reading, Mass.: Addison-Wesley, 1969.
Plovnick, M. "Structural Interventions in Health Systems Organization Development." In N. Margulies and J. Adam, eds., *Organization Development in Health Care Organizations*. Reading, Mass.: Addison-Wesley, 1981.

IV. INTRODUCTION

In recent years Organization Development practitioners have become increasingly aware of the impact of organization structure on the behavior of organizational members and the resulting implications of changes in structure for OD. From an OD point of view, organization design issues take three forms:

1. What organization structures are necessary to support organization functioning in a given organization?

2. What organization structures are necessary to reinforce organization changes resulting from other OD efforts?
3. What strategies and procedures can be used to effect changes in organization structure?

The Design Question

Organization structure, including such elements as job descriptions, authority relationships, reward systems, and information and control systems, represents the context within which organizational life takes place. If the structure does not support necessary behaviors among organizational members, organizational effectiveness is diminished. For example, if various members of the organization must collaborate to produce a particular program or project (for example, representatives from marketing, finance, production, and engineering), yet each member reports to a different boss, it is possible that the required collaboration will be inhibited by conflicting demands from the members' superiors.

The Interaction Between Organization Structure and OD

Many OD interventions are aimed at enhancing the collaboration among various organization members, departments, and so on. To the extent that the organization structure does not reinforce OD efforts at building collaboration, the OD effort is unlikely to succeed. As an illustration, in the foregoing example an OD attempt at team building with the project group described clearly would be inhibited by the potentially conflicting demands experienced by group members. It is crucial that OD practitioners pay careful attention to the structures of the organizations they work with in order to effect lasting change.

Strategies for Structural Change

The principles of organization structure and design, as outlined in the articles by M. Jelinek and J. Galbraith that are required reading for this chapter, can serve as guidelines for evaluating what structures are appropriate for a particular organization, as well as for understanding how structure can help or hinder an OD effort. Where an organizational diagnosis suggests that a change in organization structure may be necessary, such changes should be approached through the same OD principles and strategies outlined in previous sections of this book. In designing organization structures there is a great temptation to act as an expert who presents the system with a revised organization chart. This approach can result in the same sort of resistance encountered in other so-called expert interventions. Like other organization changes, structural changes typically benefit from the involvement of those who will be affected directly by the reorganization. This involvement can take the form of providing information to help in the construction of the best possible design, and ideas and opinions about the preferred method or plan for implementing the structural change.

In some cases, however, changes in organization structure cause changes in the perceived status or importance of various organization members. When this is the case, it may be difficult to involve these people effectively in joint decision making about the ultimate change. However, it is both possible and valuable to organize the intervention to maximize the participation, as information sources, of all those affected by the structural changes, while reserving final decision-making authority for a more detached and objective level in the system.* For instance, assume that in the previous example of the project group it became evident that the representatives from marketing, finance, production, and engineering should be established as a separate department within the organization with its own group manager. The department managers of finance, marketing, production, and engineering might perceive this change as a loss of their resources and importance. The ultimate decision to reorganize therefore might be difficult for those department managers alone to make and might need the involvement and backing of a higher-level manager.

Organization Structure Application

In the upcoming class session you will be asked to apply the principles of organization design to help analyze an OD case situation. In preparation for this class, read the required articles by M. Jelinek and J. Galbraith, as well as the Metropolitan Judicial Alternative Program Case, which follows.

The Metropolitan Judicial Alternative Program Case

The Metropolitan Judicial Alternative Program (MJAP) is an organization whose mission is to provide a rehabilitative program for young-adult first offenders as an alternative to the standard judicial process for felons. Located in a large northeastern city, MJAP works with 17-to-22-year-olds accused of nonviolent felonies such as auto theft. The program is voluntary for the defendant and is recommended at the discretion of the presiding judge after the defendant's arrest and arraignment. A defendant who enters and successfully completes the MJAP can avoid the normal judicial process of trial and sentencing (if found guilty) and does not acquire a criminal record. The idea is (1) to keep the courtroom census down and (2) to provide a second chance for youths able to be rehabilitated.

The Program

MJAP provides psychological counseling, vocational guidance, and career placement functions for its clients. MJAP serves thirteen different courts within the central city and surrounding towns. The program is seen as being fairly successful, establishing a far lower recidivism rate than any version of the normal judicial system, including various forms of suspended sentencing, parole, and so on. MJAP is funded by a combination of federal and state grants and contracts from the counties and municipalities served.

MJAP is organized into four major departments (counseling/advocacy, screening, orientation, and career development), which, along with a regional coordinator and an office manager, all report to a director of operations, who in turn reports to the

---

* A specific OD technology to help the client and/or OD practitioner to decide who should be involved in decisions such as this, and how they should be involved, is presented in Chapter 15 on decision charting.

FIGURE 9.1
MJAP Organization Chart

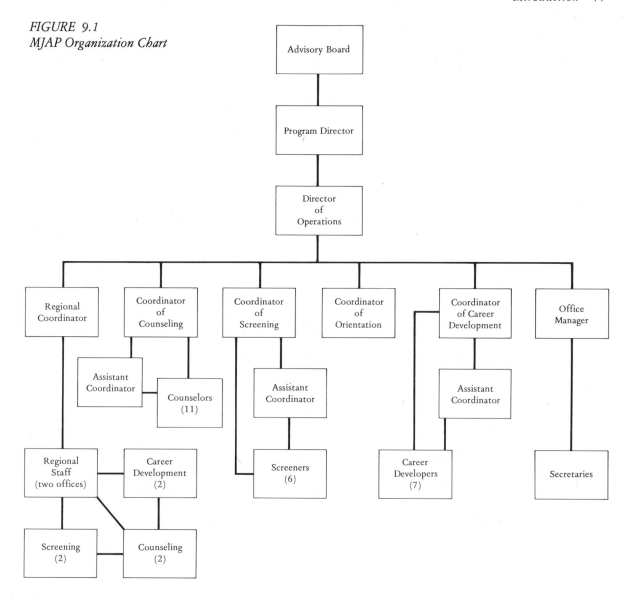

program director (see Figure 9.1). A description of MJAP's activities and services follows.

SCREENING

1. A screener is normally assigned to each court in which the program operates. In some cases, however, a screener may cover more than one court if the schedules of the courts involved or the client flow from those courts make such a procedure feasible.

2. The screener's most crucial functions are to develop and maintain positive relationships with court staff, probation and police officers, district attorneys, and public defenders, and to serve as daily liaison between the program and the court of assignment.

3. The screener arrives at his or her court assignment at 9:00 A.M. to review daily court arraignment lists and to identify potential clients. The screener then confers with probation officers, arresting officers, and assistant district attorneys for the offender's records and other background information that might be helpful in determining program eligibility.

4. If the objective data indicate eligibility, the screener interviews the potential client in order to explain the program, gather background data, and form an opinion about the potential client's interest in and receptivity to program services. If the foregoing conditions are satisfied, the screener then appears with the potential client at arraignment, indicates evidence of eligibility to the judge, and requests a 14-day continuance for purposes of assessment.

5. With the concurrence of the judge and upon the granting of the continuance, the screener makes an appointment for the potential client with the coordinator of counseling on one of the two days scheduled by the program for intake. The screener also makes sure that the potential client knows the location of the program office and how to get there by public transportation.

ASSESSMENT

1. The potential client is interviewed by the coordinator of counseling, who again explains the program and the mutual expectations between the potential client and the program, and who assigns the client to a staff team—the advocate/counselor and career developer who, in his or her opinion, are best suited to meet the needs of the particular client.

2. The assigned advocate/counselor conducts the first interview with the potential client. He or she again explains the program's goals and objectives and general mutual expectations between the client and the program, and sets the ground rules for that particular counselor-client relationship.

3. The other responsibilities of the counselor during the assessment period include arranging a regular schedule for individual counseling; arranging for group counseling if warranted; visiting the client in his or her home in order to assess the environment, introducing him- or herself and the program to the parents, and determining the sources of support he or she may draw on and the possible negative influences he or she will have to contend with.

4. The other team member, the career developer, conducts the second interview. The career developer's job includes: gathering information about work, school history, and career interests, and familiarizing the potential client with industry, training programs, social-resource agencies, and the local job market. Subsequently, the career developer verifies the data given by the potential client and makes a determination about his or her job readiness.

5. An appointment is made for the client to attend orientation. This is mandatory unless there is a conflict with his or her work or school schedule. Orientation is conducted by the coordinator of orientation in a group setting for 2 or 3 hours on several consecutive days. The first day's orientation is concerned with informing

the potential client of the history, staff, and purpose of the program, and the client's role in it. It elicits background data, including family background, the client's present situation, and the circumstances leading to it. It also focuses on the requisites for independence—that is, employment, responsibility, and issues of financial planning and management.

6. Before the end of the assessment period, there is an intake disposition attended by the counseling coordinator, the assigned counselor, the coordinator of orientation, the career developer, the screener, and when possible the client. They analyze all the data that have been obtained about the potential client. Together they determine (1) whether or not to accept the client; (2) if he or she is accepted, what services are required; and (3) the priority of those services.

7. The advocate then writes a letter notifying the court whether or not the client is acceptable. If he or she is acceptable, the letter also contains the proposed plan of service.

8. If the program finds the potential client acceptable, the screener, on behalf of the client, with the advice and consent of defense counsel, petitions the court for a 90-day continuance to allow the client to participate in the program and to allow the program to implement the service plan.

SERVICE DELIVERY

1. The first service normally delivered is a physical examination, which is provided under contract with one of the local hospitals.

2. The services of the counselor for individual and group therapy counseling, motivation, reinforcement, and support—including availability to accompany the client on initial visits to educational, employment, training, and supportive services—are also continual.

3. The services of the career developer for career counseling—including interest and aptitude testing and the evaluation and development of resources in education, employment, training, and supportive services—are also continual.

4. As long as the client complies with program guidelines and structures, and exerts a reasonable effort toward the completion of his or her service plan, the program staff is available to assist him or her.

5. Should a client fail to comply with the program guidelines and structures, he or she is terminated; the court is notified in writing (only of the noncompliance, not of specifics that might prejudice the case); and the normal court process of trial and disposition takes place.

6. If it is determined that reasonable progress is being made but that more time is necessary for the completion of the service plan, the program will request of the court an additional continuance of 30 to 90 days to allow for the completion of the service plan.

7. If the client has successfully completed the service plan or has made substantial progress toward it, the program will recommend that the court dismiss the criminal charges against him or her.

8. In any event, the results of the exit disposition and accompanying recommendation are presented to the court in writing at the end of the 90-day period. The program's recommendation is followed in more than 90 percent of the dispositions.

9. If it is decided at the exit disposition that the program will recommend dismissal, the counselor will arrange an exit interview with the client at which he will make the client aware of the continuing program services and explain the follow-up procedures.

FOLLOW–UP

1. Obtaining a dismissal does not end a client's relationship with the program. The services of the advocate and career developer, through the personal relationships they have established, are always available to the client. Program services are formally available for one year.
2. Aside from a diminishing schedule of follow-up counseling sessions, formal follow-up evaluations occur at three-, six-, and twelve-month intervals after dismissal. These evaluations concentrate principally on rearrest data and evidence of employment stability and career advancement.

OTHER ROLES

1. The regional coordinator is responsible for coordinating orientation, screening, counseling, and career development activities in court districts that are geographically distant (20 t 25 miles) from the central city. These outlying courts are divided into two service areas, each served by a regional office. Each regional office has a career developer, a screener, a counselor/advocate, and clerical support.
2. The office manager is responsible for day-to-day coordination of typists and clerical help.
3. The operations manager coordinates all internal staff functions on a day-to-day basis.
4. The program director is the major policy setter; he or she approves all hire/fire decisions and provides MJAP's liaison to the various governmental, judicial, and community groups on whose support MJAP depends.

Problem Areas

In an effort to improve services further and to enhance organizational efficiency in the light of pending cutbacks in funding, MJAP's operations manager has contacted a management-consulting group to address several organizational issues. These were described as follows.*

FIRST CONCERN: CLEAR LINES OF AUTHORITY

Problem: Confusion in lines of authority is caused by differing organizational structures within the organization. The central office is structured around the three main job functions: screening, counseling, and career development. The regional offices (RO) are organized around client service delivery and the courts. To oversimplify somewhat, the conflict appears to be between specialization and generalization: the RO organizations don't fit into the central office organization.

Example: It is not clear whether the screener in a regional office should take direc-

* Excerpted from MJAP internal memo.

tion from the senior advocate, the RO administrator, or the screening unit director: For example, forms and procedures developed by the screening unit director are imposed on the RO screener. Who should evaluate the RO screener? These two situations have led to controversy over promotions, communications breakdowns, and lack of coordination within the program. The same condition exists in the counselor and career development units.

SECOND CONCERN: EFFECTIVE SERVICE DELIVERY

Problem: MJAP's major objective should be to deliver high-quality services to clients coming through the district courts. To accomplish this objective, we should be organized around the client and the court rather than according to specialized skills, as at present. As MJAP has grown, the skill-oriented components have become the focus rather than a team effort. The objective has become to be the best component or the best staff member of a component. This has fostered competition both between and within components.

Example A: Some courts require individual monthly client reports. Who should write these monthly reports? A great deal of client business falls outside of actual job descriptions, and lines of authority are unclear. Clients are scattered throughout the MJAP organization, making up partial caseloads of counselors. There is no one definable person to do the reports. At present the screener assembles the forms, because he or she is able to identify the clients, and distributes them to the counselors. Counselors, however, do not consider these reports a priority, do not feel the pressure of the court, and therefore do not complete the forms. The screener is not in a position to demand that they do so. The line of authority would take the forms from the screening coordinator to the director of operations to the counselor coordinator, who would have the authority to demand a response from the counselors. The reverse procedure would return the forms to the screener.

Example B: Why are there so many terminations when clients are transferred from one counselor to another? If a screener wishes to remain in contact with a client whom he or she has screened into the program, it may be necessary to contact up to thirteen counselors. As a result, screeners and the screening director often lose contact with clients. Similarly, a counselor–career developer team may have clients from up to thirteen courts. Hence they may lose sensitivity to the court and the problems that are peculiar to each neighborhood represented by the court. The client tends to become isolated. A problem in one court affects the whole program.

THIRD CONCERN: MANAGEABLE ADMINISTRATIVE CONTROL

Problem: As MJAP is now structured, the administrative span of control is stretched to unreasonable limits and indiscriminately assigned. The coordinator of orientation has no staff, the career development coordinator has seven staff members, and the counselor supervisor has eleven. This places all decisions in the hands of a few administrators. The tendency toward crisis decision making rather than planned decision making increases as the program grows.

Example: Major client decisions are made at meetings known as case conferences, which include the counselor coordinator, counselor, screener, and career developer. An estimated time for a good case conference is 3 hours once a week, covering a number of clients. If the counselor coordinator and his or her assistant share the job, these administrators each would spend 18 hours a week on case conferences alone. This ties up a full administrative week (36 hours) on case conferences. As a result, limited case conferences can only touch on client problems. There is also an additional problem. Since career developers (CDs) participate in case conferences, does the career development coordinator or assistant have to participate to direct the CDs as the counselor coordinator directs the counselors? Can a counselor be directed by the career development coordinator, and vice versa? Expansion compounds this problem.

FOURTH CONCERN: STAFF UPWARD MOBILITY

Problem: As MJAP grows, staff opportunities to advance are diminished. If there is one coordinator plus one assistant for components that could contain up to twenty-five staff members, the ratio of administrative opportunities is two to twenty-five. Add to this the problem of isolating line staff by function, which creates a situation of specialists supervised by specialists, limiting the opportunity to develop general administrative skills or to learn other jobs.

Example: How does the director of operations identify promotable staff members? Can a screener become the counselor coordinator without any skill training? Can the screening coordinator move from his or her isolated job to become the director of operations? Isolated functions are hard to translate into good program overview. It is difficult for these individuals and other component specialists to compete for jobs in components other than those in which they work.

Case Assignment

In class, groups of students will be asked to analyze the MJAP. In preparation for the class session, you should spend some time thinking about the following questions. Assume you were the consultant group contacted by MJAP:

1. What changes in organizational structure do you think are needed?
2. What strategies would you suggest to get MJAP to implement necessary changes?

OVERVIEW OF UPCOMING CLASS SESSION

Step One:	Creating Consultant Teams	(5 minutes)
Step Two:	Case Analysis	(90 minutes)
Step Three:	Subgroup Presentation	(30 minutes)
Step Four:	Total-Group Discussion	(25 minutes)
Step Five:	Discussion of Actual Changes at MJAP	(10 minutes)

V. PROCEDURE FOR CLASS SESSION

Step One: Creating Consulting Teams (5 minutes)

Class should divide into management-consulting groups of five or six members each. These groups will perform the MJAP case analysis as described at the end of the case description.

Step Two: Case Analysis (90 minutes)

Management-consulting groups should perform the MJAP case analysis, focusing on organizational structure changes necessary in MJAP and on OD strategies to achieve these changes.

Step Three: Subgroup Presentations (30 minutes)

Three or four of the management-consulting groups identified should take 10 minutes each to present their case analyses to the class. Questions of clarification from the class are all right at this time, but further critique or discussion should be deferred until all the presentations are completed.

Step Four: Total-Group Discussion (25 minutes)

After all the presentations are completed, the total class should critique and discuss the various alternatives presented. The following questions may be useful:

1. What different organizational forms were suggested? How do these forms address organizational differentiation? Integration?
2. What information-processing techniques (see J. Galbraith's article in this book) are represented in the structural changes suggested?
3. What new problems are created by the structural improvements suggested?
4. Did the groups develop OD strategies that would help them get their structural changes implemented? How do their strategies deal with issues of organizational commitment? At what levels?
5. Will the strategies identified lead to the changes needed? Why or why not?

Step Five: Discussion of Actual Changes at MJAP (10 minutes)

Instructor should review, discuss, and critique with the class the actual changes and change strategies that were implemented at MJAP.

VI. SUMMARY

Organization design interventions are different from many other OD interventions in the sense that they do not seem to focus directly on people and interpersonal relationships. Yet organizational structure indirectly affects all behavior in most systems. As the MJAP case demonstrates, interventionists must be aware of some of the structural causes of undesirable behavior. The further paradox is that although structural interventions do not seem to focus on interpersonal issues in an organization, these interventions often fail because change agents overlook the process issues involved in structural change and thus encounter resistance from organization members affected by the change in structure.

The Confrontation Meeting

I. OBJECTIVES

    A. To learn a useful technique—the confrontation meeting—for assessing the state of an organization and determining action plans to address organizational problems.

    B. To use this technique in analyzing the class (course, program, or other system) as a learning organization.

II. PRECLASS PREPARATION

    A. Read R. Beckhard, "The Confrontation Meeting," in this book, pages 312–318.

    B. Read the introduction to Chapter 10.

III. INTRODUCTION

The confrontation meeting is a form of total-system intervention that can focus an organization on its problems and possible solutions in a relatively quick and uncomplicated fashion. Although there are several possible variations on the steps described by R. Beckhard for the confrontation meeting format, the basic model should follow the four steps of the action-research model, involving (1) data collection, (2) data feedback, (3) action planning, and (4) implementation and evaluation.

Although Beckhard indicates that a total organization must be the target of a confrontation meeting, it is often used with a definable subsystem such as a division or department. In this class session the class will actually experience the confrontation meeting by becoming the focal organization for such an intervention. The instructor can be seen as the chief executive officer, groups of students (learning teams if they are being used) as departments or divisions, and learning-team leaders or facilitators (if they are being used) as members of the top team.

Although Beckhard has outlined many of the advantages and limitations of the confrontation meeting, several points should be kept in mind for the class session:

1. The confrontation meeting approach focuses on problems in the organization. It does not give a balanced view by also emphasizing things that are going well. As a result it can give a very negative impression. However, it must be remembered that the objective of this intervention is to identify and resolve problems quickly

and efficiently. Participants should keep this in mind during the meeting and try not to become overly defensive or anxious in reaction to the data generated.

2. As in any experiential activity, the learning is enhanced to the extent that participants take it seriously. Also, as in any intervention activity, the problem-solving outcomes are maximized to the extent that everyone is open and truthful about the factors influencing organizational (in this case, class) effectiveness.

3. There is a tendency in activities of this type to consider others (instructors, group leaders, and so on) the major problems. Class participants are reminded to look closely at their own responsibility for learning effectiveness.

4. Finally, the confrontation meeting steps here have been shortened considerably to fit into one class session. To expedite the meeting, it is important for class members to read the Beckhard article and the class procedure carefully before class in order to minimize the time required for explanation of activities.

Although this may be an emotionally draining session for many participants, class members should realize that it usually feels much "heavier" to an actual client organization, in which jobs and careers may hang in the balance. In this sense the class exercise is a good vehicle to help class members develop empathy for systems with which they may want to use the confrontation meeting in the future.

OVERVIEW OF UPCOMING CLASS SESSION		
Step One:	Review of Confrontation Meeting Principles	(15 minutes)
Step Two:	Organizing the Class for a Confrontation Meeting	(5 minutes)
Step Three:	Setting the Organizational Climate	(5 minutes)
Step Four:	Information Collection by Heterogeneous Groups	(40 minutes)
Step Five:	Information Sharing in the Total Class	(30 minutes)
Step Six:	Learning-Team Action Planning	(40 minutes)
Step Seven:	Organizational Action Planning	(30 minutes)
Step Eight:	Commitment to Follow-Up by Top Team and Learning Teams	(5 minutes)
Step Nine:	Climate Recheck	(5 minutes)
Step Ten:	Progress Review	(15 minutes—next session)

IV. PROCEDURE FOR CLASS SESSION

Step One: Review of Confrontation Meeting Principles (15 minutes)

Instructor and class should briefly review and discuss any questions about the confrontation meeting as an intervention tool. This review may cover such areas as confrontation meeting objectives, procedures, possible applications, limits, advantages, and disadvantages.

Step Two: Organizing the Class for a Confrontation Meeting (5 minutes)

Instructor and class should clarify the class organizational structure for the purposes of the confrontation meeting. If learning teams have not been used up to now, several organizational "departments" should be created for this activity. If there is an appropriate ''top team,'' it should be identified. (If none already exists, there is no need to create one for this exercise.)

Step Three: Setting the Organizational Climate (5 minutes)

As indicated in the Beckhard format, the instructor should take this opportunity to remind the class of the objectives for this activity and the expectations regarding openness, opportunity for real course improvement, and instructor policy about recriminations. The instructor may also want to review the steps for the meeting (the agenda).

Step Four: Information Collection by Heterogeneous Groups (40 minutes)

Three or four heterogeneous groups of students should be formed from the learning teams or the arbitrarily designated departments. If there is a top team, it should meet as a separate group. The heterogeneous groups should meet in separate rooms, if possible, to create lists of ''factors inhibiting the effectiveness of this class as a learning organization.'' These lists should be written on large sheets of newsprint so that they can be posted. Factors identified can include anything about the course, the instructor, the students, or the external environment (for example, the school). A reporter should be identified by each group to present its list to the total class.

Step Five: Information Sharing in the Total Class (30 minutes)

Each heterogeneous group returns to the meeting room and posts its list. The class should have about 5 minutes to scan the lists. Then the reporters for each group should in turn read through each group's list, elaborating on the items and responding to questions of clarification where appropriate. This is not the time to debate the validity of any issue. After the lists have been reviewed, the consultant should, if possible, categorize the items mentioned into four to six areas (environmental, teacher style, course structure, learning-team performance, student behavior, and so on). This categorization may facilitate action planning in the next step.

Step Six: Learning-Team Action Planning (40 minutes)

Learning teams (or the arbitrarily formed departments) should now regroup and meet in separate rooms (if possible). If there are learning-team leaders or facilitators who have been meeting as the top team, they should now meet with their learning teams. The assignment for the learning teams is to:

1. identify and discuss those issues generated in the problem sharing that the learning team should take action on;
2. identify and prioritize those issues that the learning team feels are top management's responsibility; and
3. if time permits, determine action steps the learning team will take to address issues identified in item one.

Again, a reporter should be selected to review the outcomes of this meeting with the total class, and the outcomes should be placed on newsprint.

Step Seven: Organizational Action Planning (30 minutes)

Each learning team (or ad hoc department) in turn should share with the class the outcomes of its meeting, responding to questions of clarification. The instructor should then react to the lists of items the learning teams have allocated to the top team. Several responses are possible:

1. "O.K., we'll take that one on."
2. "That's nonnegotiable for the following reason(s): _____ ."
3. "I think that one is really the responsibility of _____ for the following reasons: _____ ."

The second and third responses may require further discussion and negotiation with the class. These discussions should be scheduled to occur as soon as possible.

Step Eight: Commitment to Follow-Up by Top Team and Learning Teams (5 minutes)

The instructor and learning teams now commit themselves to take on the issues and action steps to which they have agreed. Both top management and the learning teams should meet outside of class before the next session to write up brief reports outlining solutions or steps they have identified to address their issues.

If additional negotiation sessions are needed between class and instructor, these should be scheduled now, before the class is dismissed.

Step Nine: Climate Recheck (5 minutes)

Before breaking up, the class should take a couple of minutes to review its reactions to the confrontation meeting, both in terms of the meeting's perceived relevance as an OD activity and in terms of the class's personal feelings about progress made at this session.

Step Ten: Progress Review (15 minutes—next session)

At the beginning of the next class session the top management team and the learning teams should distribute their planning reports and discuss them briefly.

V. SUMMARY

The confrontation meeting, as you may have experienced, can be a powerful OD tool. Some observers have suggested that it relies very heavily on the charisma and expertise of the consultant or facilitator.[*] However, we have found it very useful as a structured intervention for many types of interventionists, as long as there is commitment from top management to dealing with organizational issues. For this reason, the contracting phase with top management is particularly crucial to the success of the intervention.

The confrontation meeting does seem to work more effectively when some outside facilitator, other than the group manager, runs the meeting. This takes some

[*] C. Argyris, *Intervention Theory and Method* (Reading, Mass.: Addison-Wesley, 1970), p. 53.

pressure off the manager and enables him or her to focus on understanding the data. The exact steps and timing of the meeting can be varied to some extent to fit the target system, as was the case in the class session. Also as in the class session, the intervention need not be restricted to an entire organization or even to the top level of an organization, although this is often the case. It is essential, however, that the target system be able to be defined readily and its boundaries drawn, as is the case in a division, a department—or a class.

It is hoped that the class involvement in this intensive problem-solving activity has accomplished the multiple objectives of demonstrating a type of intervention, sensitizing individuals to target system reactions to this type of intervention, and enhancing the learning potential for participants in this learning organization.

Intergroup Mirroring

I. OBJECTIVES

A. To learn a useful technique for assessing and managing relations among two or more potentially conflicting groups in an organization.

B. To apply this technique to an analysis of intergroup relations in this class.

II. PRECLASS PREPARATION

A. Read W. Burke, "Managing Conflict Between Groups," in this book, pp. 319–326.

B. Read the introduction to Chapter 11.

III. SUPPLEMENTARY READING

Brown, D. "Managing Conflict Among Groups." In D. Kolb et al., eds., *Organizational Psychology: A Book of Readings,* 3rd ed., pp. 377–389. Englewood Cliffs, N.J.: Prentice-Hall, 1979.

Shonk, J. "Improving Interdepartmental Coordination." In J. Adams and N. Margulies, eds., *Approaches to Improving Health Care Organizations Using Organization Development.* Reading, Mass.: Addison-Wesley, 1981.

IV. INTRODUCTION

Conflict among groups in organizations is commonplace and, in fact, can be a healthy sign. Creative ideas come from the clash of conflicting notions. Sound reasoning or accurate planning comes from scrutinizing one's position repeatedly and even aggressively. Such conflict is the reason that different groups are formed in organizations: to present a particular perspective on a particular issue and weigh it against another, different perspective. Such intergroup conflict often gets out of hand, however. It can become dysfunctional. Instead of agreeing to compete with one another in order to improve everyone's lot (that is, to get the best idea out of conflicting points of view in order to beat the other company to the marketplace), such originally friendly competition often evolves into a win-lose (as opposed to win-win) situation, in which each group is competing, not to improve everyone's lot, but to enhance its own position at another's expense. Thus one department may hold up project approval, another division may fail to cooperate in cross-divisional transfer policies, still another area may not get its work to your department on time or in the fashion you expect, and so on—even after repeated attempts to persuade them by pointing out "We're all in this together."

Mirroring

Intergroup mirroring is a technique used to help bring to the surface the root cause(s) of conflict between two groups and to create conditions under which a win-win attitude can prevail and mutual problem solving can occur. The mirroring process involves three major phases:

1. *Imagery:* Each group develops an image of itself and of the other group. One reason for this first step is to elicit the stereotypes and untested assumptions that naturally exist about "them" and "us." Often, just reducing myths about each other can bring groups closer together.
2. *Confrontation:* Each group admits its uniqueness and difference(s) from the other. The aim here is specifically to define those differences that are accepted as valid and are causing conflict. Without this clarification and labeling of just what is in conflict (given our real images), no meaningful resolution is likely. Smoothing over or avoiding conflict would be more likely.
3. *Bonding:* Groups experiencing irresolvable conflict with one another can begin to collaborate and address problems mutually as they become more alike in their perceptions of:
   a. the injustices (false image) each has endured;
   b. the motivation of each group to do well;
   c. the competency or resource each has to offer (mutual respect); and
   d. a need to work together or to depend on one another.

While these phases are occurring, the mirroring process increasingly creates opportunities for face-to-face contact between groups, which has been shown to be a key factor in improving intergroup relations (see article by D. Brown in the Supplementary Reading).

Preconditions for Conflict Resolution

Organization mirroring can fail in any given intergroup conflict situation. In fact, the very best OD practitioner may conduct a perfect session but fail miserably because certain preconditions did not exist. Walton* has identified two of the more important factors that must exist as givens for intergroup relations to improve:

1. Both groups must have a positive motivation to improve the situation. If one group likes or enjoys the current impasse or stalemate, it is rational for that group to continue its present behavior.
2. Both groups must have power parity. If a group perceives that it has nothing to gain, but everything to lose, or that it holds all the cards and will win eventually, then one cannot expect that group to change its behavior. Each group must believe it can gain something through collaborating. If a third-party facilitator

---

*R. E. Walton, *Interpersonal Peacemaking: Confrontations and Third-Party Consultation* (Reading, Mass.: Addison-Wesley, 1969).

diagnoses a power imbalance, he or she may work with the underdog first to build that group's skill base, resources, self-identity, cohesiveness, and so on, so that it can confront the other group from a feeling of parity.

Assumptions Behind Conflict Resolution Interventions

In addition to the preconditions just mentioned, anyone intending to use an intervention such as mirroring must also understand some basic assumptions underlying its design. The first of these is the belief that both parties in conflict are acting with integrity and good intentions. If one honestly believes otherwise—that people willfully wish to harm, punish, or humiliate each other, or in other ways benefit at another's loss—then there can be no resolution of differences.

The other basic assumption is that the responsibility for the present state of affairs between the groups in conflict lies with both groups. The responsibility can be unequal, but it must be shared.

The upcoming class session is an opportunity to experience a mirroring intervention in your class. As you go through the process, also keep in mind the preconditions and assumptions discussed here. Do you perceive them to exist in most people's minds, or not, and what are the consequences of either perception on your behavior and that of others?

OVERVIEW OF UPCOMING CLASS SESSION		
Step One:	Orientation to Class Session and Definition of Groups	(5 minutes)
Step Two:	Generating Images: Homogeneous Groups	(20 minutes)
Step Three:	Sharing and Clarifying Perceptions	(20 minutes)
Step Four:	Identifying Discrepancies: Homogeneous Groups	(20 minutes)
Step Five:	Sharing and Prioritizing Discrepancies	(20 minutes)
Step Six:	Problem Solving: Heterogeneous Groups	(45 minutes)
Step Seven:	Large-Group Sharing and Action Planning	(30 minutes)
Step Eight:	Critique	(20 minutes)

V. PROCEDURE FOR CLASS SESSION

Step One: Orientation to Class Session and Definition of Groups (5 minutes)

A decision should be made about what groups will be mirroring each other. For the sake of clarity, the remaining instructions for this session will assume that male and female groups have chosen to mirror one another. The same suggested procedures would apply for different learning groups, undergraduates and graduates, organization behavior majors and others, full-time and part-time students, and so on.

Everyone should read through and be familiar with the entire class agenda.

Step Two: Generating Images—Homogeneous Groups (20 minutes)

Each group should meet and generate answers or responses to the following cues on large pieces of newsprint:

1. Things about the others: "Men (women) in this class _____
_____ .''

2. Things about us: "Women (men) in this class _____ ."

Note that brainstorming or going around the group at first will help elicit ideas. Try, however, to reach a consensus on whatever you intend to share as your group output. If opinion is clearly split on an item, note this next to that item.

Step Three: Sharing and Clarifying Perceptions (20 minutes)

The total class should reconvene to hear what each group has said. This is a time for clarification and understanding, not debate.

A useful way to manage the data at this point is for one group, say the women, to share their list for the men first. Then the men share their list for themselves so that all the data about men are out first. Then repeat for data about women.

Step Four: Identifying Discrepancies—Homogeneous Groups (20 minutes)

Each subgroup should convene to examine what it said about itself and what was said about it.

On a piece of newsprint, list the discrepancies between "how we viewed ourselves" and "how we are viewed by others."

Step Five: Sharing and Prioritizing Discrepancies (20 minutes)

The total class should meet again to share each group's list of discrepancies. Similar ones should be combined. A decision then should be made as to the top two to four discrepancies the class would like to work on.

Step Six: Problem Solving—Heterogeneous Groups (45 minutes)

Mixed subgroups made up of members from each of the original groups should discuss and problem-solve issues identified in step five. Each mixed group should work on a different issue. Each group should try to prepare some recommendation(s) to be considered by the entire class in step seven.

Option: An alternative, particularly in the case in which one or two discrepancies stand out above the rest, is to form one mixed group to discuss and problem-solve an issue while another mixed group silently observes the discussion. After 25 to 30 minutes, the observers sit in the inner set of chairs (the original discussants now sit on the outside as observers) and discuss how male-female perceptions were operating in the discussion they just watched and listened to.

Step Seven: Large-Group Sharing and Action Planning (30 minutes)

The total class should reconvene to decide which, if any, recommendations from step six should be adopted or tried out. One procedure would be to put up on newsprint any agreed-on responses to the statement "Men (women) in this class will _____ _____ ."

Step Eight: Critique (20 minutes)

This last part of the class should be devoted to discussing the usefulness of this kind of design to deal with intergroup issues in organizations.

1. When would you recommend this kind of intervention? When not?
2. If you have already completed Chapter 10, how is mirroring different from the confrontation meeting?
3. If the groups mirroring each other were interdependent task groups (such as personnel staff and a plant management staff they service), how would you alter the design to help each group set more realistic goals?

VI. SUMMARY

It is hoped that this class session has suggested how intergroup mirroring can be useful in eliciting and exploring general attitudes and feelings groups hold toward each other. The article by J. Shonk (see Supplementary Readings) also suggests that the mirroring process can be used to get at specific procedural problems that have arisen between groups who need each other to get their work done. An important element of that case description is the emphasis on training as part of the overall intervention strategy. As you may have discovered during this past session, it is far easier to generate perceptions and even to identify discrepancies than to agree to change them. It is very common that as part of a strategy utilizing mirroring, the OD practitioner will contract for some training time to prepare members of both groups and to deal with the data collaboratively. As you go on to Chapters 13 to 16, which focus on interventions to facilitate working in groups, you will experience some of the techniques one might use in such training.

Quality of Work Life

I. OBJECTIVES

A. To become familiar with some of the issues involved in improving job satisfaction.
B. To apply the Job Diagnostic Survey to an actual work setting in order to determine the need for improvement.
C. To develop and critique strategies to bring about improved quality of work life in the job(s) studied through the Job Diagnostic Survey.

II. PRECLASS PREPARATION

A. Read the introduction to Chapter 12.
B. Read J. Drexler and E. Lawler, "A Union-Management Cooperative Project to Improve the Quality of Work Life," in this book, pages 327–335.
C. Administer the Job Diagnostic Survey found in this chapter.

III. SUPPLEMENTARY READING

Hackman, J. R., and Oldham, G. R. *Work Redesign.* Reading, Mass.: Addison-Wesley, 1980.

Pasmore, William A. "Turning People on to Work," in D. A. Kolb et al., eds., *Organizational Psychology: A Book of Readings,* 3rd ed., pp. 101–115. Englewood Cliffs, N.J.: Prentice-Hall, 1979.

IV. INTRODUCTION

In recent years increasing attention has been given to assisting managers and their organizations in enhancing the quality of work life of employees. The techniques used to turn people on to their work have ranged from autonomous work groups to flexi-time, from Japanese quality circles to worker ownership of the firm, from removing time clocks to painting and carpeting locker rooms. Quality of work life (QWL) has come to symbolize any effort to improve productivity and quality by increasing the employee's interest, satisfaction, or morale with respect to his or her job.

Strategies for Improving QWL

Pasmore (1979; see Supplementary Reading) has suggested three basic strategies for improving QWL: data feedback methods, job enrichment techniques, and sociotechnical system interventions. Each of these is oriented toward fulfilling a basic human need at work, but each taken alone also has its shortcomings.

DATA FEEDBACK METHODS

These are strategies that center around the OD action-research model discussed in Chapter 3. The emphasis is on getting employees involved in the organizational-change process by involving them first in the organizational (or subsystem) data collection and then including them in problem-solving groups to determine the meaning of the data and the action steps to be taken. In Drexler and Lawler's required reading for this chapter, the joint labor-management thrust stems from this data feedback strategy. The idea is that those who will be most affected by the data analysis should be involved in the collection, feedback, and action planning stemming from the analysis. The action-research process is widely used in OD intervention, but it has been particularly instrumental in QWL efforts, as evidenced by the labor-management projects discussed by Drexler and Lawler and the increasing mention of organizational efforts at employee involvement.

The basic assumption behind a data feedback strategy is that the more employees can be involved in the design of their work and associated reward systems, the more internally motivated they will be to achieve organizational goals. The strength of data feedback approaches lies in their ability to get people involved and to engender worker commitment to changing the immediate context in which work takes place (work group norms; supervisor-subordinate interactions; physical surroundings, and so on). The weakness of this strategy is that even with employee involvement, a boring job may still be a boring job. That is, change in the nature of the work itself is not a necessary outcome of this strategy.

JOB ENRICHMENT

These are efforts, based primarily on the motivational theories of McGregor, Herzberg, and Maslow, that focus on increasing the level of responsibility, variety, autonomy, and feedback associated with a particular job. The underlying assumption is that greater degrees of such job characteristics are typical of the more interesting and satisfying jobs in organizations.

The process of job enrichment typically involves initiating changes in the content of a job through (1) combining tasks and forming natural work groups to increase skill variety, task identity, and task significance; (2) giving each worker more responsibility so as to increase his or her sense of autonomy; and (3) opening up channels for immediate feedback to employees concerning their performance in order to increase their knowledge of the actual results of their work.

Compared with data feedback strategies, job enrichment strategies tend to be less participative or involving for workers and typically focus only on a narrowly defined job or task. Nevertheless, various studies have demonstrated the effectiveness of job enrichment as a strategy for improving quality, attitudes, absenteeism levels, and overall productivity measures.[*] Even with its documented success, job enrichment is often criticized because of its lack of attention to the context or environment surrounding the work being changed and because the changes are often controlled or mandated exclusively by management and do not involve worker inputs.[†]

[*] See, for example, S. Srivastva et al., "Job Satisfaction and Productivity," Department of Organizational Behavior, Case Western Reserve University, Cleveland, Ohio, 1975.

[†] J. Hackman, "On the Coming Demise of Job Enrichment," Report no. 9, Department of Administrative Sciences, Yale University, 1974.

SOCIOTECHNICAL SYSTEM INTERVENTIONS

These strategies focus on changing the basic technology of work or the way work is processed in order to better meet the needs of employees. These efforts begin, as in job enrichment, by trying to increase the variety, autonomy, responsibility, and feedback involved in the work itself. Beyond this, however, attempts are made to change the surrounding work organization, context, or climate. This often results in the formation of autonomous work groups, quality circles, and the like.*

As with job enrichment, sociotechnical strategies are typically nonparticipative, although they may well result in changes that require more employee involvement (for example, Quality Circles). The research on sociotechnical interventions is limited but nonetheless promising. A large percentage of the studies document improvements in productivity, costs, quality, and attitudes as a result of this type of strategy.[†]

QWL and OD

It is clear from the foregoing discussion that no one method of changing work or people's attitudes toward work is recommended for all situations. The factors taken into consideration in a successful QWL effort appear to include employee involvement, change in the actual work, and changes in the environment within which the work takes place. These are all factors included in most definitions of OD. Thus OD may serve as an umbrella concept for QWL approaches within which the concern for participative processes (such as in the Drexler and Lawler reading) and changes in social and technical systems are included. The upcoming class session is designed to view QWL under such an umbrella.

Preclass Preparation: The Job Diagnostic Survey

In preparation for the class session in this chapter, your learning group (or subgroup assigned by the instructor) will use the Job Diagnostic Survey (JDS) reproduced in this chapter.[‡] You will be assigned a particular job or task in a particular organization for analysis. Generally there will be several employees performing this job or task. Unless otherwise instructed, you may either observe the job being performed and complete the JDS based on your own perceptions or administer it to actual employees if they are willing to participate. Your objective is to come to class with a composite, data-based view of the particular job or role you are studying. After individually observing and filling in the JDS yourself, or after administering it to all or some employees, your group must meet to (1) score everyone's questionnaires according to the Scoring Key that follows the JDS, (2) summarize the results, and (3) develop a format for presenting the results to the class. In class you will develop

---

* For more information, see Pasmore, W. and Sherwood, J. *Sociotechnical Systems: A Sourcebook* (La Jolla, California, University Associates, 1978).

† Srivastva et al., ''Job Satisfaction and Productivity.''

‡ From J. R. Hackman and G. Oldham, *Work Design* (Reading, Mass.: Addison-Wesley, 1980). Development of the Job Diagnostic Survey was funded by Manpower Administration, U.S. Department of Labor (Research & Development Grant No. 21–09–74–14 to Yale University, 1974).

strategies to make changes in specific jobs and in the job context. The JDS data will aid you in diagnosing the degree of responsibility, variety, identity, feedback, and so on inherent in the present situation.

Make sure that your group comes to class with a summary perspective of the job you used the JDS to assess, and that someone is prepared to share the summarized data with the rest of the class.

| Job Diagnostic Survey: Short Form | This questionnaire was developed as part of a Yale University study of jobs and how people react to them. The questionnaire helps to determine how jobs can be better designed, by obtaining information about how people react to different kinds of jobs. The questions are designed to obtain your perceptions of your job and your reactions to it. There are no trick questions. Your individual answers will be kept completely confidential. Please answer each item as honestly and frankly as possible. |

Section One

This part of the questionnaire asks you to describe your job as objectively as you can.

Please do *not* use this part of the questionnaire to show how much you like or dislike your job. Questions about that will come later. Instead, try to make your descriptions as accurate and as objective as you possibly can.

A sample question is given below.

A. To what extent does your job require you to work with mechanical equipment?

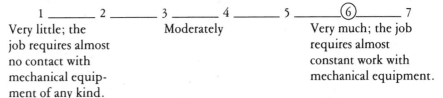

1	2	3	4	5	(6)	7
Very little; the job requires almost no contact with mechanical equipment of any kind.		Moderately			Very much; the job requires almost constant work with mechanical equipment.	

You are to circle the number that is the most accurate description of your job. If, for example, your job requires you to work with mechanical equipment a good deal of the time—but also requires some paperwork—you might circle the number six, as was done in the example above.

1. To what extent does your job require you to work closely with other people (either clients or people in related jobs in your own organization)?

1	2	3	4	5	6	7
Very little; dealing with other people is not at all necessary in doing the job.		Moderately; some dealing with others is necessary.			Very much; dealing with other people is an absolutely essential and crucial part of doing the job.	

2. How much autonomy is there in your job? That is, to what extent does your job permit you to decide on your own how to go about doing the work?

1 _____ 2 _____ 3 _____ 4 _____ 5 _____ 6 _____ 7

| Very little; the job gives me almost no personal say about how and when the work is done. | Moderate autonomy; many things are standardized and not under my control, but I can make some decisions about the work. | Very much; the job gives me almost complete responsibility for deciding how and when the work is done. |

3. To what extent does your job involve doing a whole and identifiable piece of work? That is, is the job a complete piece of work that has an obvious beginning and end? Or is it only a small part of the overall piece of work, which is finished by other people or by automatic machines?

1 _____ 2 _____ 3 _____ 4 _____ 5 _____ 6 _____ 7

| My job is only a tiny part of the overall piece of work; the results of my activities cannot be seen in the final product or service. | My job is a moderate-sized chunk of the overall piece of work; my own contribution can be seen in the final outcome. | My job involves doing the whole piece of work, from start to finish; the results of my activities are easily seen in the final product or service. |

4. How much variety is there in your job? That is, to what extent does the job require you to do many different things at work, using a variety of your skills and talents?

1 _____ 2 _____ 3 _____ 4 _____ 5 _____ 6 _____ 7

| Very little; the job requires me to do the same routine things over and over again. | Moderate variety | Very much; the job requires me to do many different things, using a number of different skills and talents. |

5. In general, how significant or important is your job? That is, are the results of your work likely to affect significantly the lives or well-being of other people?

1 _____ 2 _____ 3 _____ 4 _____ 5 _____ 6 _____ 7

| Not very significant; the outcomes of my work are *not* likely to have important effects on other people. | Moderately significant | Highly significant; the outcomes of my work can affect other people in very important ways. |

6. To what extent do managers or coworkers let you know how well you are doing on your job?

1 _____ 2 _____ 3 _____ 4 _____ 5 _____ 6 _____ 7

| Very little; people almost never let me know how well I am doing. | Moderately; sometimes people may give me feed-back; other times they may not. | Very much; managers or coworkers provide me with almost constant feedback about how well I am doing. |

7. To what extent does doing the job itself provide you with information about your work performance? That is, does the actual work itself provide clues about how well you are doing—aside from any feedback coworkers or supervisors may provide?

1 _____ 2 _____ 3 _____ 4 _____ 5 _____ 6 _____ 7

| Very little; the job itself is set up so I could work forever without finding out how well I am doing. | Moderately; sometimes doing the job provides feedback to me; sometimes it does not. | Very much; the job is set up so that I get almost constant feedback as I work about how well I am doing. |

Section Two

Listed below are a number of statements that could be used to describe a job. You are to indicate whether each statement is an accurate or an inaccurate description of your job. Once again, please try to be as objective as you can in deciding how accurately each statement describes your job—regardless of whether you like or dislike your job.

Write a number in the blank beside each statement, based on the following scale: *How accurate is the statement in describing your job?* 1, very inaccurate; 2, mostly inaccurate; 3, slightly inaccurate; 4, uncertain; 5, slightly accurate; 6, mostly accurate; 7, very accurate.

____ 1. The job requires me to use a number of complex or high-level skills.

____ 2. The job requires a lot of cooperative work with other people.

____ 3. The job is arranged so that I do not have the chance to do an entire piece of work from beginning to end.

____ 4. Just doing the work required by the job provides many chances for me to figure out how well I am doing.

____ 5. The job is quite simple and repetitive.

____ 6. The job can be done adequately by a person working alone—without talking or checking with other people.

____ 7. The supervisors and coworkers on this job almost never give me any feedback about how well I am doing in my work.

____ 8. This job is one where a lot of other people can be affected by how well the work gets done.

_____ 9. The job denies me any chance to use my personal initiative or judgment in carrying out the work.

_____ 10. Supervisors often let me know how well they think I am performing the job.

_____ 11. The job provides me the chance to finish completely the pieces of work I begin.

_____ 12. The job itself provides very few clues about whether or not I am performing well.

_____ 13. The job gives me considerable opportunity for independence and freedom in how I do the work.

_____ 14. The job itself is not very significant or important in the broader scheme of things.

Section Three

Now please indicate how you personally feel about your job. Each of the statements below is something a person might say about his or her job. You are to indicate your own personal feelings about your job by marking how much you agree with each of the statements.

Write a number in the blank for each statement, based on this scale: *How much do you agree with the statement?* 1, disagree strongly; 2, disagree; 3, disagree slightly; 4, neutral; 5, agree slightly; 6, agree; 7, agree strongly.

_____ 1. My opinion of myself goes up when I do this job well.

_____ 2. Generally speaking, I am very satisfied with this job.

_____ 3. I feel a great sense of personal satisfaction when I do this job well.

_____ 4. I frequently think of quitting this job.

_____ 5. I feel bad and unhappy when I discover that I have performed poorly on this job.

_____ 6. I am generally satisfied with the kind of work I do in this job.

_____ 7. My own feelings generally are not affected much one way or the other by how well I do on this job.

Section Four

Now please indicate how satisfied you are with each aspect of your job listed below. Once again, write the appropriate number in the blank beside each statement, based on this scale: *How satisfied are you with this aspect of your job?* 1, extremely dissatisfied; 2, dissatisfied; 3, slightly dissatisfied; 4, neutral; 5, slightly satisfied; 6, satisfied; 7, extremely satisfied.

_____ 1. The amount of job security I have.

_____ 2. The amount of pay and fringe benefits I receive.

_____ 3. The amount of personal growth and development I get in doing my job.

_____ 4. The people I talk to and work with on my job.

_____ 5. The degree of respect and fair treatment I receive from my boss.

_____ 6. The feeling of worthwhile accomplishment I get from doing my job.

_____ 7. The chance to get to know other people while on the job.

_____ 8. The amount of support and guidance I receive from my supervisor.

_____ 9. The degree to which I am fairly paid for what I contribute to this organization.

_____ 10. The amount of independent thought and action I can exercise in my job.

_____ 11. How secure things look for me in the future in this organization.

_____ 12. The chance to help other people while at work.

_____ 13. The amount of challenge in my job.

_____ 14. The overall quality of the supervision I receive in my work.

Section Five

Listed below are a number of characteristics that could be present on any job. People differ about how much they would like to have each one present in their own jobs. We are interested in learning how much you personally would like to have each one present in your job.

Using the scale below, please indicate the degree to which you would like to have each characteristic present in your job.

Note: The numbers on this scale are different from those used in previous scales.

4 _____ 5 _____ 6 _____ 7 _____ 8 _____ 9 _____ 10

Would like having   Would like   Would like having
this only a moderate   having this   this extremely much.
amount (or less).   very much.

_____ 1. High respect and fair treatment from my supervisor.

_____ 2. Stimulating and challenging work.

_____ 3. Chances to exercise independent thought and action in my job.

_____ 4. Great job security.

_____ 5. Very friendly coworkers.

_____ 6. Opportunities to learn new things from my work.

_____ 7. High salary and good fringe benefits.

_____ 8. Opportunities to be creative and imaginative in my work.

_____ 9. Quick promotions.

_____ 10. Opportunities for personal growth and development in my job.

_____ 11. A sense of worthwhile accomplishment in my work.

Scoring Key for the Short Form of the Job Diagnostic Survey	Each variable measured by the JDS short form is listed below, along with (1) a one- or two-sentence description of the variable and (2) a list of the questionnaire items that are averaged to yield a summary score for the variables.

I. Job Dimensions: Objective Characteristics of the Job Itself

A. *Skill variety:* The degree to which a job requires a variety of different activities in carrying out the work, which involve the use of a number of different skills and talents of the employee. Average the following items (reversed scoring—that is, subtract the number entered by the respondent from 8):

Section One   4

Section Two   1

           5

B. *Task Identity:* The degree to which the job requires the completion of a whole and identifiable piece of work—that is, doing a job from beginning to end with a visible outcome. Average the following items (reversed scoring):

Section One   3
Section Two   11
               3

C. *Task significance:* The degree to which the job has a substantial impact on the lives or work of other people—whether in the immediate organization or in the external environment. Average the following items (reversed scoring):

Section One   5
Section Two   8
               14

D. *Autonomy:* The degree to which the job provides substantial freedom, independence, and discretion to the employee in scheduling his or her work and in determining the procedures to be used in carrying it out. Average the following items (reversed scoring):

Section One   2
Section Two   13
               9

E. *Feedback from the job itself:* The degree to which carrying out the work activities required by the job results in the employee obtaining information about the effectiveness of his or her performance. Average the following items (reversed scoring):

Section One   7
Section Two   4
               12

F. *Feedback from agents:* The degree to which the employee receives information about his or her performance effectiveness from supervisors or from coworkers. (This construct is *not* a job characteristic per se and is included only to provide information supplementary to construct E above.) Average the following items (reversed scoring):

Section One   6
Section Two   10
               7

G. *Dealing with others:* The degree to which the job requires the employee to work closely with other people (whether other organization members or organizational clients). Average the following items (reversed scoring):

Section One   1
Section Two   2
               6

II. Affective Response to the Job

The affective reactions or feelings an employee gets from working on his or her job.

A. *General satisfaction:* An overall measure of the degree to which the employee is satisfied and happy in his or her work. Average items 2, 4, and 6 from Section Three (reversed scoring).

B. *Internal work motivation:* The degree to which the employee is *self*-motivated to perform effectively on the job. Average items 1, 3, 5, and 7 from Section Three (reversed scoring).

C. *Specific satisfactions:* These short scales tap several specific aspects of the employee's job satisfaction.

1. Pay satisfaction: Average items 2 and 9 of Section Four.
2. Security satisfaction: Average items 1 and 11 of Section Four.
3. Social satisfaction: Average items 4, 7, and 12 of Section Four.
4. Supervisory satisfaction: Average items 5, 8, and 14 of Section Four.
5. Growth satisfaction: Average items 3, 6, 10, and 13 of Section Four.

III. Individual-Growth Need Strength

This scale taps the degree to which an employee has a strong desire to obtain growth satisfactions from his or her work. Average the following six items from Section Five. Before averaging, subtract 3 from each item score; this will result in a summary scale ranging from 1 to 7. The items are 2, 3, 6, 8, 10, and 11.

IV. Motivating Potential Score

A score reflecting the potential of a job for eliciting positive internal work motivation on the part of employees (especially those with high desire for growth need satisfaction) is given below:

$$\text{Motivating Potential Score (MPS)} = \left[\frac{\text{Skill Variety} + \text{Task Identity} + \text{Task Significance}}{3}\right] \times \left[\text{Autonomy}\right] \times \left[\text{Feedback from the Job}\right]$$

OVERVIEW OF UPCOMING CLASS SESSION			
	Step One:	Subgroups Report Results of Diagnostic Surveys	(30 minutes)
	Step Two:	Formation of Strategy Teams	(5 minutes)
	Step Three:	Developing Strategies for Improving Quality of Work Life	(60 minutes)
	Step Four:	Strategy Team Reports	(30 minutes)
	Step Five:	Total-Group Discussion	(25 minutes)

V. PROCEDURE FOR CLASS SESSION

Step One: Subgroups Report Results of Diagnostic Surveys (30 minutes)

Each subgroup or learning team should share with the total class the results of the Job Diagnostic Survey (JDS) for the job or task it was assigned.

Each report should last no more than 5 minutes. It will be helpful if summary data can be displayed on large easel pads or handed out to each class member for easy reference in step three.

When all reports are completed, the total class should have before it a composite view of the quality of work life, as measured by the JDS, for the key tasks or jobs in the organization under study.

Step Two: Formation of Strategy Teams (5 minutes)

The class should form into two or three new teams made up of representatives from each of the subgroups that reported in step one. These new strategy teams will remain together for steps three and four that follow. Each team will develop and present a strategy for improving the quality of work life for an area of the organization under study. The target area can be one the group chooses as most needy or one that is assigned by the instructor.

Step Three: Developing Strategies for Improving Quality of Work Life (60 minutes)

Each strategy team should spend the next hour designing an overall strategy to improve the quality of work life for the particular job, task, or group of jobs it has been assigned.

The strategies should be data based, that is, they should emerge from an assessment of the data presented in step one. Unless otherwise instructed, each team must decide which aspects of the job(s) appear most in need of improvement and how one would go about an improvement effort. The following points are useful to consider in developing an overall strategy:

1. Who in the organization will be responsible for the overall strategy?
2. What additional data should be collected, and from whom?
3. To whom will the data be fed back, and what will they do with it?
4. Where should the strategy be focused: on worker involvement, job redesign, job enrichment, or some other area?
5. What are the likely sources of resistance to the strategy you have developed?

A spokesperson from each strategy team should be prepared to present a summary of the group's strategy to the total group.

Step Four: Strategy Team Reports (30 minutes)

Each strategy team should report its overall plan or scheme to improve QWL in the organization under study. Time should be allocated during each report for questions of clarification.

Step Five: Total-Group Discussion (25 minutes)

The total class should compare, contrast, and critique the strategies presented in step four. The following questions are intended as guides to this discussion:

1. To what extent did any strategy emphasize employee involvement, actual change of work, or changes in the area or context surrounding the work? Are there any consequences of emphasizing any one of these over the others?
2. What new groups, if any, need to be formed as a result of any of the strategies? What consequences would this have for the organization's structure or current policies and power distribution?
3. For any strategy, what might be the positive or negative impact on others not directly involved in it?
4. What roles for a third-party consultant or change agent are implied in any of the strategies (who would collect data, and so forth)?

VI. SUMMARY

This session has attempted to introduce participants to some of the factors underlying the nature of work and to the complexity of issues involved in trying to change the quality of life at work. OD methodology can be useful in combining the elements of a scientific job diagnosis, as with the JDS, and employee participation through survey feedback to achieve an effective change effort. It should be noted, however, that this chapter has emphasized only one route toward improving overall productivity at work. J. R. Hackman and G. R. Oldham (1980; see Supplementary Reading) have called this route that of fitting jobs to people. Another route they suggest that is neither more nor less appealing in terms of research to date is that of fitting people to jobs. OD can also be useful in implementing this approach. Up to now OD probably has been used more in this area through management training and development programs and other educational interventions designed to better equip people to function in the roles they occupy.

One further point to note is that QWL is not just a concept for blue-collar or hourly employees. It applies to the executive suite as much as to the job shop. Although it is currently used to characterize many union-management situations, there is also a growing interest in the QWL of salaried, professional, and executive personnel. Making work inherently more meaningful and satisfying appears to be a universal issue.

CHAPTER **13**

Team Building

I. OBJECTIVES

A . To understand the factors that influence effective work group functioning.
B. To know what is meant by *teams* and *team development*.
C. To practice using a diagnostic model to determine the need for team development.
D. To begin to assess your learning groups as teams.

II. PRECLASS PREPARATION

A. Read the introduction to Chapter 13.
B. Read R. Beckhard, ''Optimizing Team Building Efforts'' in this book, pages 336–342.
C. Read the Metric Division case in this chapter.

III. SUPPLEMENTARY READING

Beckhard, R., and Lake, D. ''Short- and Long-Range Effects of a Team Development Effort.'' In H. Hornstein et al., eds., *Social Intervention: A Behavioral Science Approach,* pp. 421–439. New York: Free Press, 1971.

Dyer, W. *Team Building: Issues and Alternatives.* Reading, Mass.: Addison-Wesley, 1971.

Fry, R.; Rubin, I.; and Plovnick, M. ''Dynamics of Groups That Manage or Execute Policy.'' In R. Payne, and C. Cooper, eds., *Groups at Work.* New York: Wiley, 1980.

IV. INTRODUCTION

A *team* is any group of two or more persons who must coordinate with each other in order to complete some task or accomplish some mission. Although this is a very general definition, it is important to understand that it means that teams should only exist when there is some task that requires the resources of two or more persons in order to be done properly (for example, plan a budget, do open heart surgery, play football, or run a factory). If a job can be done effectively and efficiently by one person, a team is not necessary and is in fact a waste of the organization's resources.

It is a fact of modern organizational life, however, that fewer and fewer jobs can be performed by one person alone. Teams exist everywhere. They may or may not be officially designated as staffs, task forces, project teams, or the like. Rather than merely focusing on these formal teams, the OD practitioner is often called on to facilitate situations in which people are *interdependent*—they must work together—regardless of the label or title of their group. The following are examples of teams and the kinds of interdependence that bring them together:

Types of coordination or interdependence *	Groups that would be teams with respect to certain tasks
Pooled	
Must influence each other on the use and allocation of shared or scarce resources	Legal office or group medical practice
Sequential	
Must depend on one another for necessary input or information to their specific task performance	Assembly line group
Mutual/Reciprocal	
Must influence each other to make key decisions to accomplish primary task(s)	Project teams/task forces Plant manager and staff Interdisciplinary or cross-functional groups

Any team may in fact have all these types of interdependence. The foregoing list is intended to illustrate only the kinds of issues or tasks that require teamwork. All teams like those listed tend to experience certain obstacles to coordination that exist precisely because they are a collection of interdependent people—a team. These issues can be summarized as follows.

Goals†

The effective coordination of a team's resources rests in part on the ability to specify the goals or objectives one is trying to achieve. For example, on the top management staff of a body parts manufacturing division of a large U.S. automobile company, there is continual debate over emphasizing ''getting iron out the door'' as the main goal as opposed to balancing productivity with increased safety measures. Conflict can be expected over how much time and energy should be allocated to various tasks or projects (for example, eliminating scrap as opposed to developing new tooling) because of these different views of the primary mission or team goal. Much time and energy is wasted if (1) the mission is not clearly understood and agreed on or (2) priorities are not clearly agreed on. This latter issue is particularly important because different people will have different priorities, and choices must be made. It

---

* J. D. Thompson, *Organizations in Action* (New York: McGraw-Hill, 1967), pp. 54–57.
† The remaining discussion is adapted from M. Plovnick, R. Fry, and I. Rubin, ''New Technologies in Organization Development: Programmed Team Development,'' *Training and Development Journal* 29, no. 4 (1975). Used by permission.

is unlikely that there will ever be sufficient resources to do everything at the same level of quality.

Roles

The question of who should be doing what can be handled only in part by a priori formal written job descriptions. Job descriptions cannot and should not be relied on to cover the day-to-day contingencies that arise as an interdisciplinary team struggles to accomplish a task.

Many problems arise in this area simply because people are not clear and specific about what they expect of each other. In addition to role ambiguity, three types of role conflicts frequently arise. First, the expectations others have of a person may be in conflict with that person's expectation of him- or herself (a self-other conflict). Second, the expectations two or more people hold of the same person can be incompatible (an other-other conflict). Finally, the sum total of all the expectations held of a person may require more time and energy than is feasible in a given workday (an overload conflict). Much energy is wasted because people do not have the mechanisms needed to develop clear and agreed-on role definitions or allocations of responsibility.

Procedures

Whereas the focus in the first two categories was on "what" (goals) and "who" (roles), the focus in this category is on "how." Effective teamwork requires clear and agreed-on procedures in several areas: How will decisions be made? How are conflicts resolved? How are problems solved? Will there be team meetings? Who should attend? How should meetings be conducted? Generally, then, procedures are mechanisms for sharing information or making decisions and protocols designed to guarantee coordinated activity.

In some teams, such as work groups in manufacturing plants or job shops, the answers to the foregoing kinds of questions are often clear and specifiable before the fact (that is, they are standard operating procedures). In other teams, such as a new-ventures planning group, answers to these questions must be developed. Tested procedures that fit in one task circumstance cannot be forced onto the unique demands of new or different tasks. Many coordination problems can be traced to the lack of an agreed-on set of appropriate work procedures for the key interdependent tasks a team faces.

Interpersonal Relations

Any group of people who must work closely together to achieve a task will develop feelings toward each other. The extent to which people trust, support, respect, and feel comfortable with one another can influence the way they work together. The negative consequences of bad feelings are clear in verbal or nonverbal behavior. People avoid one another, snipe at each other (either directly or in a backbiting fashion), and find working together exasperating. In these instances one hears about personality clashes and "bad chemistry."

Although a given team may exhibit elements of several of the foregoing categories, this four-factor framework (goals, roles, procedures, and interpersonal relations) can help in a variety of ways. First, it can help team members to better understand the "nature of the beast." The framework can help provide some conceptual clarity and keep individuals from feeling overwhelmed ("There are so many problems, I wouldn't know where to begin").

Effective categorization of issues is also important in improving teamwork. Appropriate or feasible solution alternatives are in part a function of the particular category or problem. A role-related problem would be addressed in a different manner than a goal-related one, and so on.

Team Development

Team development or team building is any planned activity that helps a team to manage the goal, role, procedural, and interpersonal issues cited previously. The word *manage* is used because it is unrealistic to expect that all conflicts will ever be totally resolved (particularly those that are truly interpersonal). Since these issues are givens when two or more people are trying to work together, team development is merely the act of attending to them specifically instead of just letting things develop as they may. Getting involved in a team development activity is akin to saying that teams do not merely develop into effective work groups by chance, fate, or over time—it takes practice. A football team will practice for 20 or 30 hours just to perform for 2½ hours. Yet many management teams hardly ever step back to practice or develop into good teams.

Although team development can be done by a manager or the team itself, it is a type of work often performed by outside facilitators. In the upcoming case you will be able to take the perspective of a change agent or OD practitioner who has been asked in to help a team develop into a better-functioning unit.

The Metric Division Case *

You are a member of the corporate OD staff of a large conglomerate of companies manufacturing household hardware goods. As is typical of your work, you have been asked to make a presentation to a management team in one of the companies concerning the different kinds of management development programs and activities that the corporation offers. The contact in this case comes from the personnel manager of the Metric Division. This division has recently been reorganized so that it is now totally responsible for an entire product line. The top management staff has been in place for five months, and the division president is interested in the available options for management development of his subordinates. Joan, the personnel manager, has also shared with you her perception that Joe, the division head, wants to get off to a good start in the new structure and is looking for "perks" for his people: programs they can attend to increase their knowledge, skills, and so on.

At a staff meeting of Metric Division management you presented the various kinds of training programs, consultation services, and so on that your corporate group offers. The presentation covered individual skill-oriented programs as well as on-site action-research or OD interventions, including team development. During a

---

* This case is adapted with permission from a teaching case developed by James Shonk, President, J. H. Shonk & Associates, Ridgefield, Connecticut.

Metric Division Organization Chart

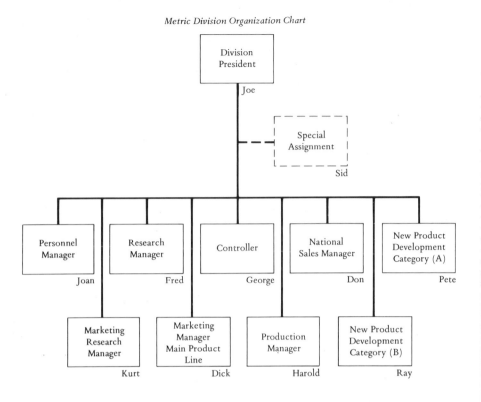

brief discussion of the kinds of things that enhance team effectiveness, the national sales manager, Don, commented that some of the ideas you were covering might be helpful to his staff. You discussed the need to do some diagnosis before launching into a developmental program. Don further stated that he thought it would be very helpful to have someone interview all the members of the staff to determine what could be done to help them work together more effectively. A more general discussion ensued; everyone, including Joe, agreed verbally to have you conduct a diagnosis to help them decide whether some special developmental effort was warranted.

You proceeded to interview each member of the staff for about one to one and a half hours each over the next ten days. Your contract around the interviews included:

1. *Anonymity:* They should use names only if it was all right for others to see that name in some paraphrase of their comments.
2. *Feedback:* You would provide a summary of the interview data for the team to look at together in order to decide collectively whether there was sufficient need to spend future time on particular issues to improve their functioning.
3. *Action planning:* The staff has agreed to one 3-hour session to look at your feedback summary and to decide whether or not to go ahead with any developmental efforts.

It is now three days before the scheduled feedback meeting.

The following information is the summary of the interviews with each staff member, including Joe. Your task is to outline the following:

1. What are the major issues you think this team is facing?
2. What would you do next with the data? Who would see them? In what form?
3. What do you think this team would do if they reviewed the data as they are?
4. Assuming the team agreed, what course of action or next steps would you recommend after the feedback meeting?

In the upcoming class session, your learning group will have about 1 hour to arrive at a consensus on these four points to present to the rest of the class.

Staff Interview Notes

Summary of verbatim responses to questions:

What does this staff do well as a team?

Not a team yet but does have common thread of loyalty to Joe—don't function as a team on group decision, however. We don't listen, though we talk a hell of a lot and say little. In crisis we band together. One-on-ones don't contribute to team concept.

Share information well. Have mutual and high regard for one another.

Not too much as a team yet—mainly a source of information from each other. Effective in information sharing.

Cope fairly well with business situations, such as profit position—good willingness to recognize others' problems.

Bring keen interest and desire to do well, but not that many things done well as a team. There's a question of functional as opposed to division responsibility.

What does this staff not do well as a team?

Nothing really as a team—"Don't really know what we do well."

Identify and solve or decide on issues of divisional nature (things like examining ourselves as a division—how we operate, how we function as management group within a division). Not agreed as a staff that we should even do that.

Might be unreal, but I don't feel the staff does very well at solving problems. We don't address issues, clarify data, or go for resolution very well. All problems are treated alike, and we need ground rules for the kinds of problems to be solved by the group at the right time and by the right people. We're less effective as a team than we are in pairs or in one-to-one situations.

Where we have tried to problem-solve, I think we've been less effective than we could have been—not too much practice at it.

Deal in abstract matters—tendency not to resolve such issues but rather to let them disappear. We're a business-oriented group that deals best with dollars and things.

We don't question one another—don't feel we're open to looking at each other's worlds—don't have overriding sense of owning divisionwide problems—still some functionalism present. Look to Joe for decisions.

As a team, we haven't come to grips with anything of great relevance to the business decision-making process—probably have avoided it.

Haven't learned to resolve issues quickly and provide input to areas outside our area.

We don't routinely as a group discuss division problems, only in a crisis when we're trying to put out a fire. Do a lot of one-on-one in staff meeting, especially sales and marketing, while rest of us sit there not knowing what's going on or how to contribute. Subjects get so specific you're out in center field. We don't discuss business needs like development—we as staff don't know what's going on in any depth.

We debate and discuss a subject forever—for example, name tags discussion. Joe lets discussion ramble. Someone ought to be process observer and pull us up short if wasting time.

How effective do you feel staff meetings are?

Semieffective—information mode—do well. However, when a specific problem arises, we don't do as well. Don't attack a problem in an orderly way. We would like a more systematic approach. Must utilize staff time more effectively.

Don't feel everyone's on board. Issues of new versus old still present and get in the way. We are more just a group of functional heads around the table. Staff meeting not effective at all. Question about how to conduct a staff meeting—never complete an agenda. What should these meetings be—information sharing, decision making, or what? What does Joe really want?

Meetings seem to be a waste of time in terms of moving the business ahead, but helpful as a learning device. There's not a lot of building, and we talk to Joe rather than each other. Heavy loading of marketing people probably skews perspective of staff. Must decide on how we want to use the staff. Are we really going to be a problem-solving group, or just an information-sharing team? We should agree to define our role if we are serious about it.

Not very effective if you expect problem solving or decision making, but effective as information sharing—depends on question of role. I'd like it to be a problem-solving group for division—size might make it difficult.

Compared with my previous experiences, I think they're more effective; however, we seem unable to generate agenda items and deal with them.

Staff meetings are pretty ineffective. No one questions why we're there.

Relatively ineffective. Misapplication of time for majority of people there. We wait for our issue to come up. We should deal with issues that transcend total division—convene relevant staff on business issues.

We confirm previously made decisions and disguise this as decision making.

We don't discriminate between major and minor issues; we handle them the same way—from a million-dollar problem to name tags for a sales meeting.

Staff expertise could be productive if applied to bigger, longer-range problems instead of this being done by individuals.

Staff meetings ramble. Joe likes everyone to have an opportunity to talk. I like meetings crisp and to the point; we are better organized with agendas and minutes and follow-up. Size of staff affects this also—in long run we should reduce size.

How effective do you feel the organization structure of the division is in facilitating getting the work done?

Has some problems—the untraditional marketing organization gives me some concerns. I don't see any real negatives though.

Very effective. We've gotten along very well as a division in an operating business fashion. Feel more strongly about our unit as opposed to former structure.

My only other comment would be about the number of marketing people on the staff, which may risk tilting the direction toward marketing too much.

Reasonably effective.

I'm pleased with it. We do fundamental things well, but administratively we're not that effective (except controller's function).

Not bad. Some communication problem between operations and marketing. Size of staff might make forming a team more difficult.

We're set up the way we should be, but having nine people report to Joe may preclude us from dealing with things as a staff. We might have to trim the number to operate truly as a staff team.

We should improve interaction of staff—not confine to staff meetings—and improve productive exchange between members.

We should (1) identify people relevant to decision; (2) clearly identify others as resource; (3) get primary options out quickly; (4) avoid continual competitiveness and dwelling on minor aspects, such as name tags.

If I had responsibility for all aspects of business and could get all people working together as a team, I'd do even a better job.

We should be organized to maximize development, and I don't think we are. Development is not fully coordinated, but is going on in several separate areas.

In the long run, the division should be organized around our businesses. Our division should be organized so that a person responsible for a given product line should have all aspects: research, operations, marketing, and so forth.

With three marketing jobs, I have concern we have too many people on staff—eleven people cut air time for each. I have to deal with three guys instead of one to get job done, which takes time.

Present structure requires several people in each function to zero in on work direction, and this is time consuming.

What are the goals or priorities of this staff, and how do you feel about them?

None that explicit. Implicit goals to learn how to function under this kind of structure. What is our role? We could use explicit goals and priorities.

What goals? We still don't have the clear-cut goals I'd like to see.

We have some clear-cut goals and priorities as a division, and each function is contributing separately. Staff should help achieve them in a synergistic fashion.

We don't have goals as a group, but individually we probably do. One commonly shared goal might be to move staff meetings along more expeditiously.

No specific set of goals for staff aside from business objectives.

Not come to grips yet—no list, but a goal could be the establishment of process (climate) and relationship that would lead to accomplishment of our business objectives.

Absence of goals and priorities linked to plan and to how we solve issues. As raw materials costs rise, goals should be defined. Everybody keeps asking what the goals and objectives are. They want the boss to restate them: (1) to achieve the

Profit Objectives—most important; (2) make products *x* and *y* successful new businesses; (3) increase the profitability of business; (4) weave us into an effective operating division.

Goals have not been communicated to staff accurately and emphatically enough. We develop strategies for top management, but we don't discuss them. They are developed between marketing and Joe. We don't develop them jointly and therefore have to run to find out what they are.

We don't talk in staff about priorities—we decide in our own minds. Joe never says exactly what we are going to do. Joe should go off and lay out plan and come back and we will critique; instead, it's taken for granted. Joe's a great guy, however; don't get me wrong.

Goals and priorities not fully coordinated—for example, where we stand on the new generation of products. Is anyone working on them, and if not, shouldn't we be?

What helps you get your job done?

The learning part of my job has clearly been helped by the staff, and exposure to individuals has helped me to work more effectively with them.

They're still bringing me on board. Very helpful efforts to bring me up to date. Willingness to help has been gratifying.

Fair exchange of information among ourselves, facilitated by personal respect.

Posting from staff is important—extent to which they get involved in my work is important.

Timely provision of information in an easily disgested form capable of being passed on—"completed staff work"—we're getting better but I'm still rewriting a lot. Lack of organizational status; for example, when marketing doesn't dominate the business to an unhealthy degree.

When staff involves and uses me as a resource and they do it early enough.

Complete confidence of boss, accessibility of other levels within organization and other functions (point of relevant information), plus effective support of other functions. Resource application from other functional heads is very important, and that deployment is critical.

Staff's commitment to giving me resources to do my job. They have restraints.

Pete, Dick—less exchange or help from them. They are too into their own bag. We could counsel each other better, but we don't.

If division does well and I don't, I suffer. If division does not do well and I do, I suffer.

Support of staff to make new products division successful is very helpful.

Joe is a leader and very supportive, is trusting and stays cool in face of problems. Without that kind of boss my job would be twice as difficult.

Helps—knowing what total decision is and knowing Joe's on board so I can go ahead with money, time, and so on, knowing I have authority once decision is made.

Joe's saying that you have authority and responsibilities—he does not nitpick things. He leaves you on your own to run your job.

Question is how to make my organization to fit into overall operation of division.

What gets in the way of getting your job done?

Not having it clear in our minds what our individual roles and responsibilities are— "Where should we be getting into the act?"

One-to-one decisions as opposed to those that have impacts on other areas—time restraints, schedules, time demands. Inability to sit down and make decisions together quickly.

Tendency of senior marketing personnel to delegate market research could create problems for me. Question of trust and respect of market research professionalism raises a concern.

Not enough interaction between functions; for example, development guys across units don't interchange their knowledge and take advantage of individual capabilities.

Not getting into a situation until it's cast in concrete—it becomes more difficult to be of constructive help then.

What would you like your boss to do more or less of?

Continue leaning on me for input—more leadership in staff meetings and more decisiveness when there are disagreements among us. Less detail orientation on some items, as it could be a waste of his time.

Be more available to each of the functions. Work at continuing interface relationships. Fewer one-on-one decisions where decision makes impact on my area.

Get himself away from details of day-to-day business. Ask more often, ''What do you need or want from me?'' Keep himself oriented to how business is operating and just trust staff more for their functional expertise. He gets problems transferred to him.

Apply decisive leadership abilities more—he's hedging to be nice right now. More appreciation/involvement in developing aspects of business and in long-term issues transcending all groups. Less orientation to brand detail.

Boss—as a resource; give more of his time. Less of sending signals to rest of organization (my area of organization) without touching base with me first, for example, discussing with agency what he feels is working with our advertising program. Express where he thinks business is capable of going—his assessment. What he thinks we can and should be doing.

Joe must recognize that president's job is different; principal function is to mold different functions together toward common objective. Need to find his philosophy and express to group what the role of president is.

Could reach out more to staff to do and define his job. Perhaps staff should tell him how we see his role.

What would you like your peers to do more or less of?

I wish the staff as a totality would become less sensitive to people running across functional lines to get information from individuals directly involved. We're too compartmentalized.

Would like group to be more sensitive to the sales organization situation and help us to become more effective as a line function. In other words, use us more. I would hope individuals would resolve possible disagreements before meetings to avoid taking up others' time.

Make me more aware of their planning needs earlier. Be less independent of each other.

Set climate in their organization that would allow all expertise regardless of level to surface. Give their people more lead time.

Help discipline staff to allocate appropriate amount of time to big versus little issues.

Give me more time to discuss my business with them.

Like more opportunity to participate in their business and broader aspects of business; for example, I'd like to feel people are tapping me for my expertise in technical research and development.

Express goals and strategies for businesses and functional areas more. Not in detail, but overview.

More working as team and less perpetuating one-on-one interaction, especially when subject cuts across many functions.

Which, if any, of your relationships with members of this staff do you feel could be improved? How would you start to do this?

Relations with production could be worked on. Communications between functions at plant levels could be improved. Division professional services, too—have started discussions on this with Don. We're defining the problem now.

We've done some fence mending with Harold and are off to a good start with technical research, financial, and sales. Have innate rivalries with new-products development group, and Pete and I would have to work on and set the right climate. Could be sharing of ideas and data that we are both developing.

Harold and I have good work-a-day relationship. George and I still sorting out our different styles—I'm too loose and we're in process of bending. Don's fine, still fending his way—Dick and I have good relationship, he keeps me aware and involved but doesn't always respond to things I'd like to see done; he must keep me aware of things I need to know—Pete and I still working on relationship, I think he believes I intrude into nuts and bolts too much. Ray believes I don't spend enough time with him and his function. Fred and I have clear understanding. I have little contact with Kurt and would like more participation and counseling in staff meetings. Pleased with relationship with Joan—would like a stronger functional voice at times.

Relationship between Dick and me one of standard politeness; don't get along, contribute little to each other.

My best relationship is with Fred.

I could improve my relationship with George. I have to get his confidence that I'm not managing the numbers to make them look better than they are.

Harold and I have a good relationship. He makes it clear that I should handle relationships with his subs through him. We could keep each other posted more.

Dick—slightly strained relationship. We are hesitant to give each other advice. I get the feeling of a competitive relationship.

Joan and I are fine, and George and Don also.

Initially, there was an old guard and new guard feeling with Dick and Sid, who have been with the company for years—I believe that's going away.

Dick is obviously smart and ambitious; he's willing to speak long and articulately on any and all subjects. I feel he overwhelms organization and shuts off many because it turns into a philosophical discussion between Joe and Dick. Pete is not about to let Dick be crown prince and throws in his points also; this cuts off air time for others. They love to debate. Don also takes his share of air time.

Pete's feeling of competition and of being alone in getting new product off the ground getting in way.

Sid undecided about whether or not he is coming back and so on is getting in way.

Dick has fine connections and pushes through decisions. Sid always plays it cagy.

OVERVIEW OF UPCOMING CLASS SESSION

Step One:	Groups Analyze Metric Division Case	(60 minutes)
Step Two:	Presentations and Discussion in Large Group	(30 minutes)
Step Three:	Individual Reading: What Happened with Metric?	(10 minutes)
Step Four:	Large-Group Discussion	(15 minutes)
Step Five:	Learning Groups Discuss Their Goals as Teams	(45 minutes)
Step Six:	Large-Group Sharing and Discussion	(20 minutes)

V. PROCEDURE FOR CLASS SESSION

Step One: Groups Analyze Metric Division Case (60 minutes)

Each learning group (or assigned study groups for this session) should meet to discuss the case and prepare a spokesperson to present the group's opinions and recommendations.

Step Two: Presentations and Discussion in Large Group (30 minutes)

Each group's spokesperson, in turn, should take 5 to 7 minutes to summarize his or her group's position(s) (large newsprint with main ideas would be helpful).

Step Three: Individual Reading—What Happened with Metric? (10 minutes)

After sharing and discussing your groups' solutions to the case, everyone should read the following.

What Happened with Metric *

The first step in improving the effectiveness of a team is to diagnose correctly where it needs help. The potential power and usefulness of the goals, roles, procedures, and interpersonal (GRPI) model you used to analyze the Metric Division case is enhanced when one considers the following points.

Symptoms Versus Causes

Most people see the causes of poor teamwork as existing in the interpersonal area. If this were true, the options for solution would be few and of limited value—either a change in personnel or some form of true personality change.

Extensive experience with this model supports an alternative assumption. The *causes* of poor teamwork stem mainly from one of the other three areas: goals, roles,

---

* The instructor will share the summary of what happened in the actual case after this reading.

or procedures. The interpersonal feelings people experience are real; but they are usually *symptoms,* not causes, of poor teamwork and coordination of resources.

If, for example, two people have very different ideas about the priority of goals and do not deal with this as a goal difference, sooner or later they will conclude they have a personality clash. Consider, for example, an instance in the Metric staff example wherein Ray or Pete (new-product development) and Dick argue and eventually fail to listen to each other because each one defends his vested interests as absolutely necessary to the future of the business. They will tend (as most people in those positions do) to see each other as uncooperative persons unless they can be led to agree that they are both on the team and should work together to develop the best plans and priorities for the entire division, not to make a case for their own constituents at the expense of others. Similarly, if a role problem goes unaddressed and unresolved initially, sooner or later two people will avoid talking to each other or working together, creating what looks like an interpersonal conflict.

In the overwhelming majority of cases, the bad feelings disappear when the root cause of the problem is successfully addressed. People feel better about working together because they have found a way to eliminate the task-related (as opposed to personality-related) reasons for their difficulty in the first place.

Hierarchy of Factors Influencing Team Effectiveness

Stemming from the foregoing is a general principle concerning the strategy for improving team effectiveness. There is a hierarchy or order in which the inherent obstacles to coordination ought to be addressed. "Who should do what?" (a roles question) should be postponed until the "What?" (goals question) has been addressed. The procedural question ("How?") should be considered after the issues of goals and roles have been addressed.

These points can be summarized graphically in the following manner:

Interdependent Task
(Defines the team)
↓
Goals[a]
(Core mission; priorities; outcomes)
↓
Roles[b]
(Who is expected to contribute what?)
↓
Procedures[b]
(How will the work be organized?)
↓
Interpersonal Relationships[b]
(How people feel about each other)

[a] An example of an intervention to help a team manage goal issues is the final step in this session.

[b] In future chapters you will practice methods to help teams manage these issues: Chapter 14—roles; Chapter 15—decision-making procedures; Chapter 16—meeting procedures.

In the Metric Division case, this GRPI model would result in the following sequence of focal issues:

1. What are we, as a team, trying to do? What output should we have as a result of our meeting? Why are we meeting?
2. Who is in charge of what? Who should make what inputs?
3. How will we make decisions? How will follow-up be handled? How am I expected to participate (as an advisor, just to be informed, or as a collaborative problem solver)?

Many of the apparently petty personal feelings you may have read in the data probably could be traced to these questions. When you stop to think about it, they probably had little to do with the personalities of other members involved per se.

This is not meant to minimize the importance of personality issues altogether. The issue of interpersonal relationships requires more explanation. Goal conflicts, role conflicts, and procedural issues do in fact manifest themselves in interpersonal relationships. In this sense interpersonal relationships are present throughout the GRPI model. If a team has worked through its goals, roles, and procedures and still finds itself with a member or members who are not on board, a basic value conflict may exist. This is often essentially an *intra*personal issue: an individual finds him- or herself unable to accept and work within the constraints dictated by the task and agreed on by the team, including him or her. A mismatch between person and job exists, and the only viable remaining alternative may be to seek a more personally congruent job situation (such as a transfer or a new position).

Finally, one should keep in mind that these issues of goals, roles, procedures, and interpersonal relationships are inevitable in a team situation. Each factor exists as a natural result of bringing two or more persons together to do a job. They have the potential to drain time and energy away from accomplishing a task unless they are managed proactively. Thus every team should learn to pay attention to its own needs for team development in order to maintain itself as a smoothly functioning unit.

Step Four: Large-Group Discussion (15 minutes)

The total class should discuss the previous reading and the instructor's summary in the context of the Metric case. Some discussion guides include:

1. What examples of the hierarchical GRPI model did people sense from the data? Was there a role conflict between managers because of unshared or unclarified goals or hidden agendas?
2. In terms of the diagnosis itself, in what other ways might you have collected data? Would you have collected different data?
3. What problems, if any, do you think the Metric team will have in determining its goals or purpose for being?

Step Five: Learning Groups Discuss Their Goals as Teams (45 minutes)

Each learning group should convene to discuss the question, "When are we a team?" Using the GRPI model, the first step in improving your effectiveness is to clarify your purpose. One way to do this is to share each other's ideas about why or when you are interdependent. This should clarify the issue of when you are in fact a team. Try to reach a consensus on what you are trying to accomplish as a learning team in this course.

Step Six: Large-Group Sharing and Discussion (20 minutes)

Each learning group should share a summary of its discussion in step five so that the entire class can compare and contrast. This is also an opportunity for groups to get new ideas from other groups' ideas about what they could be doing as teams.

VI. SUMMARY

Team development or team building is a basic OD technique. Since groups in organizations are nearly always the targets of or means to change, it is common for the change agent to be facilitating the growth and development of group effectiveness. Different practitioners have tended to focus on particular issues in working with teams. Beer has reviewed and categorized these orientations toward goal-setting interventions, role-clarifying interventions, and interpersonally oriented intervention. * The GRPI model presented in this chapter actually integrates all these approaches into a task-oriented approach; see Fry, Rubin, and Plovnick (1980; in Supplementary Reading). The next four chapters will introduce specific interventions to help teams manage role, procedural, and interpersonal issues that tend to occur in work groups. As you go through these chapters, keep in mind that each of these techniques (including the goal defining you did in this chapter) is seldom used without the others. That is, a team development program usually consists of multiple meetings or sessions that may cover more than one of the G, R, P, and I areas.

It should also be remembered that teams in organizations do not exist in a vacuum. There is always a larger system or environment within which the team functions. Thus it is quite possible that even if a team has learned to manage its G, R, P, and I issues successfully, it is still ineffective because the organization or groups it must work with do not cooperate, reward teamwork, agree on goals, and so on. In these cases, the interventions discussed in earlier chapters in Part III (confrontation meeting, intergroup mirroring, and so on) are often applied to the system around the team to reinforce effective team functioning.

Finally, task-oriented team development, as presented here, is only one of several options or choices managers have in dealing with work groups. Managers often prefer to let things ride or to let time heal all wounds. Even if team development were the ideal, the fact is that all teams do not get developed in formal, planned ways. An underlying assumption of the authors and other OD practitioners, however, is that it takes more than just time and fate for teams to work well. In other words, teams and individuals can learn skills that make them more effective in working together than those who lack such skills.

---

* M. Beer, "The Technology of Organization Development," in M. Dunnette, ed., *Handbook of Industrial and Organizational Psychology* (Chicago: Rand McNally, 1976), pp. 955–961.

Role Negotiation

I. OBJECTIVES

A. To understand the concept of roles and its relevance to organizational functioning.

B. To become aware of some of the causes and consequences of role conflicts in a real situation (this class).

C. To practice using a conflict resolution technique called *role negotiation.*

II. PRECLASS PREPARATION

A. Read the introduction to Chapter 14.

B. Read R. Harrison, "Role Negotiation: A Tough Minded Approach to Team Development," in this book, pages 343–351.

C. Write practice role messages, as discussed in this chapter.

III. SUPPLEMENTARY READING

Kahn, R., et al. "A Theory of Role Dynamics." In *Organizational Stress: Studies in Role Conflict and Ambiguity,* chap. 2. New York: Wiley, 1964.

Sherwood, J. J., and Glidewell, J. C. "Planned Renegotiation: A Norm-Setting O.D. Intervention." In W. Bennis et al., eds., *Interpersonal Dynamics,* 3rd ed. Homewood, Ill.: Dorsey Press, 1973.

IV. INTRODUCTION

The Concept of Roles

Popular usage of the word *role* often refers to someone who is playing a part and hence is being a phony or not his or her real self: "He's just acting like a tough guy," or, "She's playing the role of a mother hen." This is not the connotation of *role* as used in this text. Here the word represents a set of expectations about good or appropriate behaviors that people hold for someone in a particular position in a social space. Hence *husband* connotes a position for which there exists a set of role expectations, as do *superstar, boss, wife, plant manager, team leader,* and so on.

Each individual usually occupies more than one position in his or her social space; the same person can be wife, mother, artist, friend, and student. As the occupant of a given position, a person is often subject to the expectations of several others. We also have expectations for ourselves that are based on a variety of influences (family, history, television images, movies, job descriptions, and so on).

Role Set

These points can be summarized graphically using what has been called a *role set* or *role map*. For example:

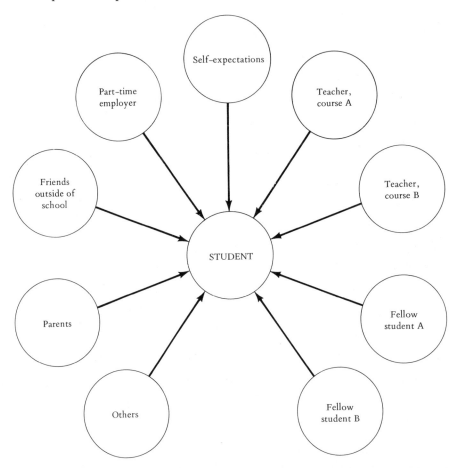

Our individual role sets, in other words, are made up of those demand systems whose expectations significantly influence our sense of what constitutes good or appropriate behavior in a particular position. (This model is analogous to the open-systems planning model discussed in Chapter 8, but it is applied at the individual rather than at the organizational level.) Finally, for each of the role positions a person occupies, a different (but perhaps overlapping) role set could be drawn.

Types of Role-Related Problems

Using the graphic image of a role set, one begins to get a clearer idea of the kinds of role problems people can and do experience. The first type of problem is that of ambiguity. *Role ambiguity* arises when we are not clearly told what another expects of us, or when we misinterpret what that person intended to communicate. Once a person is at all unclear about what others expect of him or her, the likelihood of meeting their expectations is seriously reduced.

Beyond role ambiguity, there can also be a legitimate *role conflict*. This can take three forms:

1. Between self and another: Something I expect to do as part of my role is in conflict with what some other person expects me to do. For example, I expect to ask a lot of questions in class to help me learn, but the instructor never allows time for it.
2. Between others: Two or more other people expect me to do things that are in conflict with each other. For example, my instructor likes us to point out weaknesses in others' arguments, but my peers don't want to feel put down by me or another classmate.
3. Overload: The total of my expectations and those of everyone else is just too much—they cannot all be met within the constraints of time, energy, and so on. For example, the time required for homework in my courses, plus my part-time job, leaves me no time to sleep.

Before considering how to resolve role ambiguity and conflict (the major focus of the class session), it is important to understand how these conditions are created and manifested in work settings.

Role Expectations and the Process of Work*

The relationship between role problems and the way work gets done between individuals can be seen in the following model of a work relationship between two persons or between a person and an organization. The model is cyclical and involves four major phases:

1. *Expectation sharing:* When persons initially establish a working relationship, they exchange information about themselves and job expectations, both implicit and explicit, about how each is to behave vis-à-vis others (job description). Once enough information is exchanged to reduce ambiguity to an acceptable level, there is mutual agreement to proceed and the beginnings of commitment to these shared expectations.

2. *Commitment:* As commitment to a set of shared expectations takes place, a person's role becomes defined. He or she knows for the most part what is expected of him or her and what he or she can expect of others. The more commitment, the more stability and feeling that the role is set.

3. *Stability and productivity:* Although stability of role relationships does not guarantee productivity, it is necessary for productive work to occur. Knowing that you are doing what is expected and that you can count on others to do the same frees up more time and energy for other things (creativity, accomplishing more tasks, and so on).

* The points here are adapted primarily from J. J. Sherwood and J. C. Glidewell, "Planned Renegotiation: A Norm-Setting O.D. Intervention," in W. W. Burke (Ed.), *Contemporary Organization Development: Conceptual Orientations and Interventions.* Washington, D.C.: NTL Institute, 1972, pp. 35–46. © Sherwood and Glidewell, 1971. By permission.

4. *Disruption:* Sooner or later a violation of expectations occurs, regardless of the degree of stability and commitment. This is inevitable because (1) information is never completely shared during the initial sharing of expectations, and (2) most organizations are open systems—that is, they change as a consequence of their environment (new laws, new technology, new consumer pressures, and so forth). Thus disruptions can be external in origin—a new hire, a budget cut, a new task allocation, a new job title, or a reorganization. Or they may be internal in origin, stemming from new information made available by someone that was not known earlier when expectations were shared. Once previously shared expectations are disrupted, uncertainty follows. The people involved become increasingly anxious. Depending on the severity of the disruption, the length of the period of uncertainty, and the frequency with which disruptions have been occurring, one of three things usually happens:

1. *Return to the way we were:* This is often the quickest way to reduce uncertainty and all the negative feelings that accompany it. A handshake, apology, or mutual acceptance of blame allows a return to the stability of the past. The danger here is that what led to the disruption is forgotten or avoided, so that new information that could provide the basis for productive change is lost.

2. *Renegotiation:* If new information—whatever caused the disruption—is allowed to enter the relationship and is treated in a problem-solving rather than an accusatory manner, it can provide the basis for negotiating new expectations for the relationship. This new relationship is more likely to be in line with the realities of the situation (particularly if the disruption was externally oriented) than if things had reverted to the way they were.

3. *Termination:* Constructive reallocation of resources is a possible outcome of a problem-solving renegotiation. It is more likely to be destructive and to result in the loss of effective resources if the disruption is explosive, the system is rigid and inflexible, or the persons involved have little or no previous experience in adjusting to or changing conditions.

Planned Renegotiation: The Ideal

In order to avoid hasty and costly terminations or the avoidance of necessary change by reverting to old behaviors, it is desirable to renegotiate role expectations whenever there is a disruption. This is best done by introducing a controlled problem-solving process in anticipation of a disruption and renegotiating expectations in advance. This is analogous to preventing an illness in order to avoid the risks of major surgery. This planned renegotiation is initiated whenever someone notices a "pinch"—any indication or signal that a disruption is possible.

The role problems discussed earlier—role ambiguity and role conflict—are typical conditions that result in pinches. The dynamic quality of the model presented here is that it recognizes the fact that changes are to be expected in any work relationship and that therefore it is necessary for the parties involved to be able to renegotiate in some controlled, problem-solving manner.

Although formal job descriptions can provide the broad outlines of one's role responsibilities, it is unlikely that they can—or ever should—be expected to be either specific or complete enough to cover all the contingencies that will develop in situations as complex as most jobs today. What is needed is a framework and procedure that will enable people to deal with the pinches they will invariably experience in their work roles. The required reading by R. Harrison for this chapter describes such a procedure: role negotiation. The development and application of this problem-solving technique is the major focus of the upcoming class session.

Harrison's Role Negotiation Technique

Harrison describes a *planned renegotiation process* that is the necessary ingredient of ongoing, productive role relationships in a work setting. This Role Negotiation Model is shown below. The suggested classroom activities that follow are designed to help you try out a negotiating process similar to that described by Harrison. To do this, you will first practice identifying pinches and sending a role message. Then you will engage in some real role negotiations based on pinches felt by members of this class.

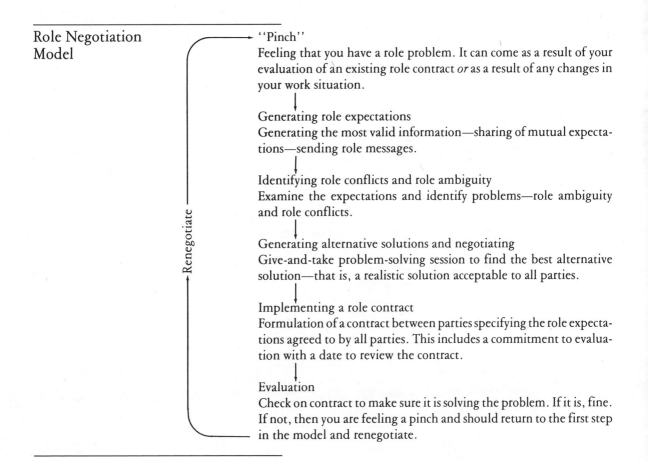

Role Negotiation Model

Renegotiate

"Pinch"
Feeling that you have a role problem. It can come as a result of your evaluation of an existing role contract *or* as a result of any changes in your work situation.

↓

Generating role expectations
Generating the most valid information—sharing of mutual expectations—sending role messages.

↓

Identifying role conflicts and role ambiguity
Examine the expectations and identify problems—role ambiguity and role conflicts.

↓

Generating alternative solutions and negotiating
Give-and-take problem-solving session to find the best alternative solution—that is, a realistic solution acceptable to all parties.

↓

Implementing a role contract
Formulation of a contract between parties specifying the role expectations agreed to by all parties. This includes a commitment to evaluation with a date to review the contract.

↓

Evaluation
Check on contract to make sure it is solving the problem. If it is, fine. If not, then you are feeling a pinch and should return to the first step in the model and renegotiate.

It is useful to remember a few key assumptions as you go through this class session:

1. This entire model concerning roles is based on the belief that disruptions (resulting from ambiguity or conflicts) of stable role relationships are naturally bound to occur in today's complex and changing organizations.
2. The effective manager or change agent is one who has the skill to identify potential disruptions or "pinches" early on and to treat these as new inputs that will change his or her system in a constructive, problem-solving manner.

3. *Negotiation,* as used in this session, is not intended to connote the stereotype of union-management deliberations. Role negotiation is not like a poker game, where you hold your cards "close to the chest." Rather, it is a mutual, give-and-take process, conducted openly. If one party asks another to change his or her behavior, that person should be willing to attempt to comply.

The most important part of this exercise is probably the final class discussion, in which you have the opportunity to challenge or expand on these assumptions, having had the chance to try out the role negotiation process for real.

The first step in role negotiation is effectively identifying and communicating your "pinch" or role message. In order to prepare for the upcoming class, you are going to write some practice messages. First, however, the specific face-to-face role negotiation process is shown to acquaint you with what happens to a message during the process. This is not a trivial point. If you are to use this technique with a client group, they should know exactly what is going to be done with the data collected through role messages before they write them.

Role Negotiation Procedure

1. Role message is sent (or given).
2. Receiver clarifies the message with the sender.
   "As I understand it, in order for you to _____

   _____

   you want me to _____

   _____
3. Sender reexplains the message if not satisfied with receiver's interpretation. (Steps two and three are repeated until both parties agree on what the message says and means.)
4. Receiver responds in one of three ways:
   a. "That's a good idea, I can do it. Let's write up a contract."
   b. "I can do that, but only if you (or someone else) can do _____
      _____ to help me."
   c. "I can't do that, but I can probably do something else that will help solve your problem, like _____ ."
5. Negotiation: Sender and receiver collaboratively attempt to solve whatever problem(s) exist.
6. Contract is written in the form of:
   a. Problem definition: _____
   b. Person A will do _____

    c. Person B will do   _____

    d. Person C will do   _____

    e. Etc.

    f. We will check back on this on (date) _____.

Individual Preparation

Think for a minute of your "role set" in your learning group for this class. (If permanent learning groups have not been in use, write a message to any significant other in any of your role sets.) Then, using the Sample Role Message Form that follows, practice writing a message to some other member or to all the members of your group. You will not actually negotiate these messages in the class. They are just for practice unless you and your group decide to negotiate them outside of class.

    Note that for a role message to be effective, it is helpful to think about three criteria:

1. Is the "why" portion clear? How could it be framed differently to gain the message receiver's commitment?
2. Is the "what" portion specific? Would the receiver know exactly what to do differently tomorrow if he or she accepted the message as is?
3. Would the message as worded make the receiver overly defensive?

Sample Role Message Form

To: _____ (name of person to whom you are sending the message)

From: _____ (your name as sender of the message)

In order to help me (you fill in the "why") _____

_____

I need you to:

1. More of (you fill in the "what"):

2. Same of (you fill in the "what"):

3. Less of (you fill in the "what"):

    Note that you must use at least one of these three categories (more, less, or the same). You may have more than one message for a particular person. It is possible that in addition to messages in the "more" or "less" categories, you could still send a message in the "same" category, thus indicating your support for some things the person is doing or expecting you to do.

OVERVIEW OF UPCOMING CLASS SESSION

Step One: Clarifying the Role Negotiation Process   (time as needed)
Step Two: Sharing and Critiquing Practice Messages   (5–10 minutes)
Step Three: Large-Group Sharing/Discussion   (10 minutes)
Step Four: Individual Reading: Setting the Stage
              for Negotiation   (5 minutes)
Step Five: Identifying Pinches or Disruptions   (20 minutes)
Step Six: Formulating Priority Role Messages   (15 minutes)
Step Seven: Preparing for a Role Negotiation   (15 minutes)
Step Eight: Conducting and Critiquing an Actual
              Role Negotiation   (30–45 minutes)
              (Repeat step eight with a second negotia-
              tion if time permits.)
Step Nine: Total-Group Discussion   (20 minutes)

V. PROCEDURE FOR CLASS SESSION

Step One: Clarifying the Role Negotiation Process (time as needed)

The entire class should spend this time reviewing the major points in the Introduction and in the reading by R. Harrison, and addressing any questions people may have about the negotiation process, the role message, the rationale for the process, and so on.

Step Two: Sharing and Critiquing Practice Messages (5–10 minutes)

In learning groups (or in pairs) class members should exchange their practice message with someone *other* than the person to whom it was addressed. The receiver should give the sender feedback on the three criteria for effective messages:

1. Is it clear why the message is being sent?
2. Is the "what" portion specific? Would the intended receiver know what to do differently tomorrow if he or she accepted the message as it is?
3. Does the message, as now worded, tend to make the receiver defensive?

Discuss briefly if and how the message might be reworded to be heard and understood more accurately.

Step Three: Large-Group Sharing/Discussion (10 minutes)

The class should convene as a whole group to share examples of poor messages that were changed as a result of step two and good messages that meet the foregoing three criteria. Since *clarity* and *specificity* mean different things to different people, it is useful to try to get some general class consensus around a few examples of good messages.

Step Four: Individual Reading—Setting the Stage for Negotiations (5 minutes)

Let us focus for a moment on the classroom setting in which you are a participant. Although it may not seem so at first, you are in fact a member of an organization—a learning organization. This learning organization—the class—is subject to many of the dynamic processes that affect any other organization.

Think back to the first day of class. In some manner, the people in this class went through the first three phases of the process described in the Introduction. Information was shared either before or during the first class, and students did some testing or probing by asking questions, checking expectations, and so on. Although it may have been very crude, one-sided, and ambiguous, a "psychological contract" was formed between and among the students and the faculty. The first three or four class sessions represented an opportunity to test the initial psychological contract. How did it stand up against the test of time and reality? It would be surprising indeed if no disruptions or pinches have been experienced.

The occurrence of disruptions or pinches is to be expected. If this organization is much like every other organization, however, these disruptions tend to be ignored or dealt with only indirectly (for example, by complaining to other students about a particular session but never confronting the instructor). Role negotiation is designed to be a set of steps—a tool—that can be used to deal with pinches and disruptions more directly and productively.

In previous and future class sessions you have been and will be working on external case situations and doing role play simulations. During the upcoming class session, your own real experiences together as a learning organization will be the data you work with—you will be your own case situation. The pinches identified will be real ones that people feel. The conflicts you identify and work to resolve—through the role negotiation process—will be real conflicts with real consequences. This here-and-now focus gives you an opportunity to practice using role negotiations under real conditions and to enjoy the gains (from successful resolution of differences) in your own learning organization.

All members of this classroom organization—faculty and students—will participate actively in the steps that follow. For example, in completing steps five and six, the entire class will split up into small subgroups. The faculty members responsible for the course are expected to form a subgroup of their own (this may be a one-person "group").

The focus during step five will be on the formulation of pinches or disruptions individuals have experienced or are now experiencing as members of this classroom organization. These pinches must in some way be relevant to the core mission of this organization—learning. Some examples of issues that could create specific pinches in a learning organization such as a classroom might be: (1) *student to teacher*—ambiguity over the reward system (how grades are determined), ambiguity over subject matter (request for more lectures or summaries), and so on; (2) *student to student*—uneven classroom participation (some people always ask irrelevant questions that prolong discussions), tardiness of class members (the class generally starts 20 minutes late), and so on; (3) *teacher to student*—some people are always requesting extensions in class assignments, some people expect answers rather than struggling to find their own; (4) *group to group*—some groups always take too long to report on their work.

This session represents a unique opportunity (as did Chapter 10 on the confrontation meeting) to practice using a specific tool—role negotiation—while at the same time improving this learning organization. Since these negotiations will be real, you may well experience some feelings of discomfort and anxiety in the process. Experiencing these feelings and learning to cope with them is an essential part of preparing to use such a technique as an OD practitioner.

Step Five: Identifying Pinches or Disruptions (20 minutes)

The entire class should split up into your learning groups or subgroups of five to seven persons. Faculty person(s) should form a separate group. Each subgroup should identify and list on a piece of newsprint the major pinches or disruptions they have experienced or are now experiencing as members of the class. Students should list peer pinches (student to student) as well as any teacher-directed or other group-directed pinches they may have experienced.

List all these relevant pinches/disruptions on a piece of newsprint.

Step Six: Formulating Priority Role Messages (15 minutes)

Each subgroup should now review their pinch list and identify one or two priority pinches. A priority pinch is one that (1) several people feel strongly about, and (2) represents an issue that, if not addressed, would continue to have dysfunctional consequences on people's desire and ability to learn (the mission of this organization).

A role message sheet must be created on a piece of newsprint for each priority pinch. The format is as follows:

To: (Name of person(s) to whom you are sending the message)
From: (Your name(s) as the sender of the message)
In order to help us to (you fill in the "why"), we need you to do:

1. More of (specific change in behavior requested—the "what").
2. Same of (tells someone to keep up the good work).
3. Less of (specific change in behavior requested—the "what").

Write these priority role messages on newsprint.

The entire class should come back together, and each subgroup (including faculty) should post its role message sheets where they can be seen by everyone.

Step Seven: Preparing for a Role Negotiation (15 minutes)

It will not be possible to deal with all the role messages on everyone's lists within the format of a formal role negotiation. Therefore, the class should choose one priority message it wishes to negotiate and select appropriate class members to be involved in the negotiation.

Do not spend a lot of time debating which issue to choose. It is most important to get started around any issue for which there is energy and concern.

To prepare for the first negotiation, therefore:

1. a message sender(s) (two or more subgroups can have the same priority message to negotiate) and message receiver(s) volunteer to conduct the first negotiations and take seats in front of the entire class;
2. one person volunteers to be a third-party helper; and
3. everyone reviews the tips for role negotiating that follow.

**Tips for
Role Negotiation**

A. Message senders
   1. Can you be more specific in the messages you sent?
      a. Can you tell the receiver exactly how you would like him or her to behave differently starting tomorrow?
      b. Can you tell the receiver more specifically how what you want will help you?
   2. Can you offer ways to help the other person change his or her behavior (do more or less of something)?
   3. Can you tell him or her what you need and why you need it without "pointing a finger" and making him or her defensive?
   4. Are you sure that the final contract is one you can live with—or at least experiment with?

B. Message receivers
   1. Can you agree that the "why" part of the message is important? Do you understand how it relates to the goals you have in common? If you can't, you are unlikely to be very committed to changing your behavior.
   2. Are you sure you understand exactly what behavior you are being asked to change? Do you know how you would like to behave differently starting tomorrow?
   3. Can you frame your initial response into one of the following three categories:
      a. "That's a good idea, I'll do it."
      b. "I can do that if you (or some other team member) can do something to help me."
      c. "I can't do that, but I can do something else that will help solve your problem."
   4. Are you sure that the final contract is one you can live with—or at least experiment with?

C. Third-party helpers
   1. Try to help them be as specific as possible with questions such as:
      a. "Can you explain why this is important to you?"
      b. "How will it help you?"
      c. "How, specifically, do you want the person's behavior to change? Can you give examples?"
   2. Be sure they arrive at a written statement of their solution—a contract—indicating behavioral changes to which each person has agreed. They may resist this step because it feels awkward and unnecessary, but it is crucial to the ultimate clarity and success of the negotiations.
   3. Try to help them confront rather than avoid conflicts. Watch for "forcing" or unrealistic acceptance (smoothing) by the parties; for example, "Are you sure this is a contract that is acceptable to you?"
   4. Where you sense hesitancy, try to encourage participation. Remember, your role is to facilitate the process of the negotiation. The actual solution (the content) must come from the negotiating parties.

Step Eight: Conducting and Critiquing an Actual Role Negotiation
(30–35 minutes)

The structure for this step is exactly as follows. Remember to do a critique of your negotiation (10–15 minutes). This is very important. Also, if time permits, it is useful to conduct and critique a second role negotiation.

Role Negotiation Procedure	

1. Role message is sent (or given).
2. Receiver clarifies the message with the sender.
   "As I understand it, in order for you to _____
   you want me to _____ ."
3. Sender reexplains the message if not satisfied with receiver's interpretation. (Steps 2 and 3 are repeated until both parties agree on what the message says and means.)
4. Receiver responds in one of three ways:
   a. "That's a good idea; I can do it. Let's write up a contract."
   b. "I can do that, but only if you (or someone else) can do _____ _____ to help me."
   c. "I can't do that, but I can probably do something else that will help solve your problem, like _____ ."
5. Negotiation: Sender and receiver collaboratively attempt to solve whatever problem(s) exist.
6. Contract is written in the form of:
   a. Problem definition: _____
   b. Person A will do _____
   c. Person B will do _____
   d. Person C will do _____
   e. Etc.
   f. We will check back on this on: (date) _____ .

Step Nine: Total-Group Discussion (20 minutes)

The complete pinch lists that people identified should be collected. They represent an evaluation of how things are going from both students and faculty. If time permits during the actual class session, or future sessions, they can be examined and discussed together.

The following points will serve to guide a total-group discussion of the process of role negotiation:

1. What parts of the role negotiation process were hardest or most uncomfortable to implement?
2. What parts seemed to be easier or more comfortable to implement?
3. How could everyone work to ensure that the gains achieved today do not wither away over time? How can the entire class work to minimize backsliding?
4. What new insights or thoughts do people have about the real world use of a process like role negotiation?
5. How was the third-party role useful? Is this necessary for role negotiation to work?

VI. SUMMARY

On the surface, role negotiation looks like a very simplistic tool. Many people who read over the steps react by saying or thinking: "This isn't so new," or, "We do this all the time," or, "It's just basic human communications." This is true. Role negotiation is a rather simple set of steps. But effective application of these steps in real situations in which real feelings are involved is not—as many of you may now realize—such a simplistic process.

The experiences we and others have had with this tool in OD efforts have followed this same pattern: initial surprise at its simplicity followed by an even greater surprise at how powerful a tool it really is. Interdependent work (project groups, staffs, task forces, and so on) is inherently fraught with many points of conflict over who does what, when, and how in relation to others. Rather than smoothing over such conflict or treating it as a personality clash, role negotiation can be an effective means to: (1) increase everyone's understanding of what is expected of them; and (2) resolve or manage true conflicts at a level that deals with work-related issues, not personalities. This is why so much importance is given to the form of the role message—having to relate your expectation to a specific objective or goal (the "why" portion of the message). Remember that the premise for doing role negotiation in the first place is *interdependency*. If you, your classmates, and the instructor did not need each other in order to learn effectively, there would be no basis for you to ask another to change to suit your needs, or vice versa.

CHAPTER **15**

Decision Charting

IV. INTRODUCTION

Organization Development as a field has focused a great deal of attention on group processes, particularly group decision making. Dissatisfaction with the decisions that are made, how they are made, and by whom, are issues that work teams often identify as obstacles to their effectiveness. These problems may be characterized as issues of *leadership style.* A variety of tools and techniques have been developed to help managers resolve some of these questions. Two such techniques designed to aid managers in assigning responsibility for decision making are discussed in this chapter. Before proceeding to the decision-making cases that follow, read the article by V. Vroom in this book. Then use Vroom's model to do the preclass assignment that follows.

    To illustrate how Vroom's model might be applied in some actual situations, three case situations have been described in the following pages. In preparation for the upcoming class, analyze each of these cases, indicating which management decision-making style you think is most appropriate (AI, AII, CI, CII, GII), and what route on Vroom's decision tree should be used to arrive at your answer.

Bring your analyses to class.

Decision-Tree Cases[*]

Case I

You are general foreman in charge of a large gang laying an oil pipeline. It is now necessary to estimate your expected rate of progress in order to schedule material deliveries to the next field site.

You know the nature of the terrain you will be traveling and have the historical data needed to compute the mean and variance in the rate of speed over that type of terrain. Given these two variables, it is simple to calculate the earliest and latest times at which materials and support facilities will be needed at the next site. It is important that your estimate be reasonably accurate. Underestimates result in idle foremen and workers, and overestimates result in tying up materials for a period of time before they are to be used.

Progress has been good, and the five foremen and other members of the gang stand to receive substantial bonuses if the project is completed ahead of schedule.

Case II

You are the head of a staff unit reporting to the vice-president of finance. He has asked you to provide a report on the firm's current portfolio to include recommendations for changes in the selection criteria currently employed. Doubts have been raised about the efficiency of the existing system in the current market conditions, and there is considerable dissatisfaction with prevailing rates of return.

You plan to write the report, but at the moment you are quite perplexed about the approach to take. Your own specialty is the bond market, and it is clear to you that a detailed knowledge of the equity market, which you lack, would greatly enhance the value of the report. Fortunately, four members of your staff are specialists in different segments of the equity market. Together, they possess a vast amount of knowledge about the intricacies of investment. However, they seldom agree on the best way to achieve anything when it comes to the stock market. While they are obviously conscientious as well as knowledgeable, they have major differences when it comes to investment philosophy and strategy.

You have six weeks before the report is due. You have already begun to familiarize yourself with the firm's current portfolio and have been provided by management with a specific set of constraints that any portfolio must satisfy. Your immediate problem is to come up with some alternatives to the firm's present practices and select the most promising for detailed analysis in your report.

[*] These cases are excerpted, by permission of the publisher, from Vroom, *Organization Dynamics*, 1973, 1(4), © 1973 by AMACOM, a division of American Management Associations. All rights reserved.

Case III

You are on the division manager's staff and work on a wide variety of problems, of both an administrative and technical nature. You have been given the assignment of developing a universal method to be used in each of the five plants in the division for manually reading equipment registers, recording the readings, and transmitting the scorings to a centralized information system. All plants are located within a relatively small geographical region.

Until now there has been a high error rate in the reading and/or transmittal of the data. Some locations have considerably higher error rates than others, and the methods used to record and transmit the data vary between plants. It is probable, therefore, that part of the error variance is a function of specific local conditions rather than anything else and that this will complicate the establishment of any system common to all plants. You have the information on error rates but no information on the local practices that generate these errors or on the local conditions that necessitate the different practices.

Everyone would benefit from an improvement in the quality of the data, as they are used in a number of important decisions. Your contacts with the plants are through the quality-control supervisors who are responsible for collecting the data. They are a conscientious group, committed to doing their jobs well, but are highly sensitive to interference on the part of higher management in their own operations. Any solution that does not receive the active support of the various plant supervisors is unlikely to reduce the error rate significantly.

OVERVIEW OF UPCOMING CLASS SESSION	Step One: Discussion of Decision-Tree Cases	(30–40 minutes)
	Step Two: Presentation of Textbook Choices	(5 minutes)
	Step Three: Discussion of Textbook Analyses	(15 minutes)
	Step Four: Individual Reading: Decision Charting	(15 minutes)
	Step Five: Decision-Charting Case Analysis	(40–50 minutes)
	Step Six: Total-Class Discussion of Case Analyses	(20 minutes)
	Step Seven: Discussion of Furnace Team: Actual Results	(15 minutes)

V. PROCEDURE FOR CLASS SESSION

Step One: Discussion of Decision-Tree Cases (30–40 minutes)

This step can be done with the total class. Student responses to each of the three case situations should be recorded where everyone can see them. When this distribution of responses has been collected, the class should focus on the following discussion questions:

1. Within a particular case situation, explore the reason(s) for any differences of opinion that exist about the most appropriate decison-making style to use.
2. Within each case situation, what were the major situational attributes (Vroom's seven rules) that influenced people's analyses?
3. What were the major situational differences among the three case situations?

Step Two: Presentation of Textbook Choices (5 minutes)

The instructor should take a moment to review the ''theoretically most appropriate'' managerial decision-making style for each situation, as indicated by Vroom.

Step Three: Discussion of Textbook Analyses (15 minutes)

The ''textbook'' answers represent Vroom's interpretations of the decision-tree analysis. It is important to emphasize that some subjectivity is involved in making assumptions in each case situation. As class members review these textbook responses and contrast them with their own choices, the following questions will serve to focus the discussion:

1. Where a discrepancy existed between the majority choice among class members and the textbook choice, what seemed to be the causes of the discrepancy (for example, difficulty in understanding particular diagnostic questions; disagreement over what were facts and what were opinions in the case description)?
2. What personal concerns or reservations would individuals have in implementing the most appropriate textbook choice (for example, personal styles and needs; assumptions about what subordinates really want or need; pressure from superiors for a fast decision)?

Step Four: Individual Reading—Decision Charting (15 minutes)

This section is intended to explain a basic but powerful tool—decision charting—that builds on the Vroom model by identifying differences in the ways different people on a work team can participate in any given managerial decision. This is particularly important in interdisciplinary groups (those including representatives of marketing, finance, production, and so on), where each member's responsibilities may vary depending on the issue being considered by the team. Decision charting is essentially a graphic way of helping a manager avoid common pitfalls in decision making. There are three basic categories of pitfalls, which will be presented in question format. These questions can then be used as checkpoints prior to managerial decision making.

1. *What, exactly, am I (or we, if a group is involved) trying to decide?* Considerable inefficiency can occur in decision making because of a lack of specificity about the precise nature of the decision. Typically, a manager will say that the objective is to ''solve the problem.'' Although this is true, ultimately, it is very important to distinguish among the various phases in a problem-solving process: (1) assessment (identifying the problem); (2) analysis (generating solution alternatives); (3) choice (selecting the one best alternative); (4) action (implementing the choice); and (5) evaluation (following up with evaluation of the implemented solution).

At each stage of a problem-solving process, as well as in moving from one stage to the next, decisions are made. This is the connection between decision making and problem solving: every decision is the result of a problem. If there were no problems, no choices would be necessary and no decisions required.

Consequently, when a manager answers this first question, it is necessary to be specific about ''what.'' The ''what'' could be a definition of the problem or of the range of alternatives, and so on. If several phases of the problem-solving process are involved at one time (for example, a single meeting), several specific decisions ("whats") are in fact going to be made.

2. *Who should be involved?* Two factors contribute to answering the "who" question. One is informational and directly affects the logical soundness of any decision. Who has valid and necessary inputs into the assessment, the generation of alternatives, the selection of the best alternative, and so forth? The second question is procedural and directly affects commitment to the decision. If person A has no direct informational inputs into the assessment but must be involved in the implementation, he or she therefore needs to understand and be committed to the decision. Often, however, person A may have very good inputs about the logical soundness of a decision because he or she is the one who will implement it.

These two factors, "what" and "who," represent a simplification of Vroom's seven diagnostic questions. However, in decision charting, unlike Vroom's model, not all participants are necessarily involved equally, or at all.

3. *How should people be involved?* This question is important because it helps to differentiate among members of a team or group. For a given decision, it is possible that some are involved in actually making the decision (a GII decision), whereas others are consulted (a CI or CII decision) and still others in that same group need only to be informed (an AI or AII decision). Thus it is possible for people to be involved in the following ways:

1. Directly involved in the decision: This is the person or persons who actually make(s) the choice or decision.
2. Consulted on a decision: These are people who are consulted before the fact because they lend particular expertise to the problem or because they are in a position to judge the likelihood of implementing certain alternatives. These persons can be consulted individually (AII or CI mode) or in groups (CII mode).
3. Informed about the decision: Some persons need only to be told after the fact that a decision has been made (as in Vroom's AI mode). They are willing to abide by the decision without having to make it (be directly involved) or offer any opinions about it (be consulted).

A decision chart is simply a graphical tool for organizing and recording responses to these three diagnostic questions. It looks like this:

What \ Who		How	How	How		
1.						
2.						
3.						

One: First identify exactly *what* decision or decisions must be made. Enter these down the left-hand column.

Two: Then list the names of all persons (where feasible, always identify specific names) *who* must be involved in any way with the decision. Try not to list groups.

Three: Next, a role must be assigned to each and every name across the top so that everyone knows *how* he or she will be involved. Any person can have only one role, either: D—directly involved in making the decision; or C—consulted prior to the decision being made; or I—informed about the decision.

Consider an example from a personnel department. The vice-president for personnel had to choose one of three training programs available on affirmative action to be used throughout the company's four divisions. Each division has its own personnel manager, each of whom is on the vice-president's staff along with the training director, corporate compensation manager, affirmative action officer, and recruiting director. The staff must decide how to organize itself to reach an effective decision. The decision chart looked as follows:

Who / *What*	*V.P. Personnel*	*Affirmative Action Officer*	*Compensation Manager*	*Recruiting Director*	*Training Director*	*Personnel Manager 1*	*Personnel Manager 2*	*Personnel Manager 3*	*Personnel Manager 4*
Choosing an affirmative action training program	D	D	I	I	D	C	C	C	C

Although other groups may have come up with a different allocation of responsibilities, this example illustrates how decision charting can be used. Several important points can be made using this example.

1. If more than one D is assigned, then a group decison-making session is *required*. Procedures for conflict resolution and decision making will need to be worked out.
2. The nature of involvement of the consultants must be specified. Will they be included in the group discussion, or will their inputs be solicited beforehand?
3. The vice-president will need to be careful not to allow his or her D to become the most important or only D. If this happens in a group, the value of the decision-charting technique will be nullified because the team will perceive it as an insincere effort.

Step Five: Decision-Charting Case Analysis (40–50 minutes)

Class should break into small groups of five or six people. Each individual should analyze the Furnace Team case in this chapter and fill out a decision chart for it (a chart has been provided). The group members should then compare their analyses and discuss similarities and differences in their charts and the rationale behind their answers. The group should develop one chart to be presented to the total class.

Step Six: Total-Class Discussion of Case Analyses (20 minutes)

Three or four subgroups should present their analyses to the total class. After all the presentations are complete, the class should discuss and critique the different approaches.

Step Seven: Discussion of Furnace Team—Actual Results (15 minutes)

The instructor should present and discuss with the class the actual analysis done by the furnace team, keeping in mind that it is not necessarily the "right" or only answer.

The Furnace Team Case

The Aluminum Ingot Company (AIC) produces aluminum ingot for use by a variety of manufacturing concerns in the United States and abroad. Huge bars of aluminum ingot are produced by melting and molding large quantities of aluminum waste material (residue from an aluminum foil mill) in giant furnaces.

The ingot plant contains several furnaces, each operated by a five-man crew including a furnace crew foreman. The furnaces are operated around the clock, on three eight-hour shifts, each with its own foreman.

The ingot plant has two maintenance departments, electrical and mechanical, each run by a foreman who is responsible for both routine maintenance and breakdown repairs to furnaces. It is necessary to take a furnace off line for repairs when the ingot being produced contains too many impurities, when pollution from the stacks becomes excessive, or when safety hazards are evident. A plant metallurgist is responsible for maintaining ingot quality and pollution control standards.

The so-called furnace team consists of all the shift foremen responsible for all plant furnace operations, the plant metallurgist, the plant mechanical-maintenance foreman, and the plant electrical-maintenance foreman. The team has been meeting to establish better coordination and management of plant production.

One issue that has arisen concerns who is responsible for making the decision to shut down a given furnace for maintenance—either scheduled routine maintenance or repair work. The issue primarily involves the two maintenance foremen, the metallurgist, and all the furnace foremen. The maintenance foremen feel they need to control all maintenance-related decisions in order to maximize the efficiency of utilization of their maintenance crews. The metallurgist feels the decision to shut down operation of a furnace should be his since he is responsible for both quality control and pollution control. The furnace foremen feel they should have total control over their furnace operations. The furnace foremen feel very strongly about this issue since their performance is rated by furnace output during their shift, and a furnace taken off line during their shift hurts the foreman's production statistics. Unfortunately, their tendency has been to put off maintenance as long as possible in hopes that the next shift will take care of it. This practice results in more serious furnace breakdowns later on.

The problem, then, is who should be responsible for decisions to shut down in order to perform maintenance.

Decision Chart

Those Who Should Be Involved

What needs to get done: specific decisions to be made								
·								

* Types of involvement:
  D—directly makes the decision.
  C—consulted prior to the decision.
  I—informed of the decision.

VI. SUMMARY

Both the decision-tree analysis and decison-charting techniques provide useful models to help managers and groups think about decision making. The decision-charting technique in particular has also been extremely useful as a team-building tool. There are basically two ways that these techniques can be used. In the first, an individual manager can use the models to allocate responsibility in decision making for a given problem. The second use is more of an OD approach in which team members each analyze a particular decision from the team using the technique much as the class did in the furnace team case. Individual answers are then shared and discussed as the team attempts to reach consensus about the allocation of responsibilities for the decision(s) in question. The outcome is a common understanding of and commitment to a protocol for resolving the decision(s) being discussed. A by-product is a better understanding of the needs of team members and a better sense of how responsibility should be allocated to team members in general.

Decision charting represents a contingency approach to decision making. It does not assume that all decisions are made by everyone. In this sense decision charting appeals to many managers who have been put off by the more normative assumptions behind many OD techniques and practitioners that stress democratic management. The decision-charting technique has been used very successfully with a wide variety of teams and is a useful addition to the repertoire of an OD practitioner.

Process Consultation

I. OBJECTIVES

A. To understand the concept of *group process* and its relevance to group and organizational functioning.
B. To learn what to observe in groups.
C. To diagnose the type of group process(es) currently occurring in the class.
D. To experience and practice interventions aimed at improving small-group functioning.

II. PRECLASS PREPARATION

A. Read the introduction to Chapter 16.
B. Read E. Schein, ''Intervention,'' in this book, pages 363–367.
C. Complete the individual assignment in this chapter by filling out your assessment of how your learning group is fulfilling its task and maintenance needs.

III. SUPPLEMENTARY READING

Benne, K., and Sheats, P. ''Functional Roles of Group Members.'' *Journal of Social Issues* 4, no. 2 (1948).

Schein, E. *Process Consultation: Its Role in Organizational Development*. Reading, Mass.: Addison-Wesley, 1969.

IV. INTRODUCTION

As a generalization, it is probably safe to conclude that people often find their experiences in groups less than satisfying or productive. The old cliché ''A camel is a horse put together by a committee'' typifies this feeling.

Yet, as you may have discovered during recent classes (Chapters 13, 14, and 15), groups are a fact of organizational life. Certain tasks or problems require the collaborative inputs of several different people. In Vroom's terms, these are GII and CII decisions (see the required reading by V. Vroom in Chapter 15). More than one person often must be involved in the decision-making process to ensure the ultimate acceptance of that decision, as well as its quality. An example is seen in the use of a decision chart, also from the previous chapter, where more than one D occurs and thus a decision-making meeting is required, or when the person with a D role seeks the collective advice of two or more Cs.

These are typical situations in which groups must function well to make a decision(s). Unfortunately, knowing when to use groups is only the first step. Conducting an effective group meeting is not just an art. It takes an understanding of what is called *group dynamics,* as well as skills in behaving in ways that foster good group functioning.

Since the OD practitioner is always working with a group (he or she and the client constituting the smallest possible group, of two persons) a major resource this person can contribute is the ability to understand what is going on in the group and to intervene in ways that both enhance the present group's functioning and help the client or client group to learn how to monitor and change group functioning in the absence of the OD facilitator. The upcoming class session will provide opportunities for your learning group to diagnose how it is operating in order to improve your effectiveness, and for you to take on the role of a consultant or facilitator to another group in order to help them learn about and, where necessary, change the ways they operate.

The Concept of Group Process*

If you ask, "*What* is a group doing?" this is a question of *content.* The content of a meeting includes its objective, agenda, topics for discussion, and so on. The content defines the reason that the group got together in the first place.

You could also ask, "*How* is a group functioning?" How does the group achieve its objectives, move through its agenda, discuss necessary topics, and so forth? These are questions of a group's *process.* The focus is on how the group goes about doing what it is trying to do.

What Do You Look for When You Ask "How?"

There are two basic kinds of behavior to look for in answering this question: task-oriented behavior and maintenance-oriented behavior.

Task-Oriented Behavior (TOB)

1. *Initiating.* In order for a group to accomplish or make progress on its tasks (the content) there must be some initiating behavior. Examples of initiating behavior include stating the objective or definition of the problem, offering alternatives for working on or solving the problem, setting time limits, building an agenda, and so on.

2. *Information and Opinion Seeking and Giving.* Communication is the essential process by which the group accomplishes its tasks. Information seeking and giving, and opinion seeking and giving, are therefore important TOBs. "What more do we know about the problem?" "I've got some more data that may help." "What do people think about these alternatives?" "My opinion of that issue is such and such."

---

* Much of what follows is an abbreviated summary of an excellent discussion of this concept by Edgar Schein, *Process Consultation,* © 1969, Addison-Wesley, Reading, Massachusetts, pp. 32–41. Used with permission.

3. *Clarifying and Elaborating*. The reason for calling the group together in the first place rests on the assumption that no individual has "the" answer. Clarifying and elaborating are therefore important examples of TOB. Clarification helps to sharpen everyone's understanding of the specifics involved. Elaborating on someone else's inputs is the essence of collaboration. By asking for clarification and by building on the ideas of others, a group moves toward creative solutions to complex problems that are beyond any single individual's capability.

4. *Summarizing*. To further help a group operate with full information, effective summarization is an important function. Reviewing the points that have been covered, the ideas up for consideration, the decisions made and pending, and so on, can help a group clarify where it has been, where it is, and where it needs to go.

5. *Consensus Testing*. A final dimension is consensus testing. Checking to see whether the group is close to a decision is important task-oriented behavior. Even if the group is not ready for a decision, testing can still serve the important function of reminding the group that it is there to achieve some objective and within some time constraint. This is a productive form of time keeping.

The major elements of TOB are summarized as follows:

Major Elements of Task-Oriented Behavior	1. Initiating
	2. Information and opinion seeking and giving
	3. Clarifying and elaborating
	4. Summarizing
	5. Consensus testing

Maintenance-Oriented Behavior (MOB)

A second class of behaviors that are essential for effective group functioning are maintenance-oriented behaviors. Whereas TOBs deal primarily with what people say or do to get something done, MOBs deal primarily with how people behave toward each other in performing the task, and ultimately with how cohesive the group members feel toward one another.

1. *Gatekeeping*. Often some group members behave in ways that makes it difficult for others to make their own contributions. For example, repeatedly interrupting a person and taking away the floor can create a situation in which he or she just stops contributing. Gatekeeping (regulating the communication gates) ensures that everyone has at least the opportunity (an invitation) to contribute.

2. *Encouraging*. Encouraging, as an MOB, can serve a function similar to that of gatekeeping. For various reasons some individuals do not jump in as quickly as others. They may need some encouragement if they are to be willing and able to make a contribution, or to continue making contributions if their first attempts fall flat, sound disorganized, or are immediately discounted by others.

3. *Harmonizing and Compromising*. Two other important MOBs are harmonizing and compromising. Their utilization and value must, however, be carefully examined in each particular situation. When used too hastily, they can actually detract from the group's effectiveness. In some situations it may be very important first to

confront the fact that a serious disagreement does exist, and to strive to find a creative, integrative solution, before resorting to a compromise or next best solution. When used as mechanisms to avoid real differences of opinions, harmonizing and compromising result in a state of false security.

The major elements of MOB are summarized as follows:

Major Elements of Maintenance-Oriented Behavior	1. Gatekeeping 2. Encouraging 3. Harmonizing and compromising

Who Is Responsible for TOB and MOB?

TOB and MOB can be viewed as functions that must be available and used in a group when appropriate. The word *function* has been emphasized because it is rare to find situations in which any one person is skilled at providing the entire range of behaviors required. It is quite common, however, to expect the formal boss or senior person in a peer group to do all these things. It is essential that the needed behaviors be fulfilled, and effective groups are most often those in which various members share the responsibility for TOB and MOB.

Several distinctions are therefore important in thinking about group process. One of these has to do with a leader or leadership. People often assume that is is solely the leader's responsibility to lead the group. Viewing TOB and MOB as necessary functions, however, suggests that in order to operate effectively a group needs many acts of leadership. A person is assuming leadership when he or she exhibits any one or several of the TOBs and/or MOBs the group needs in order to function properly. It is, in fact, dangerous to assume that only one person—the leader—can or should perform all these vital leadership functions. Given such an overwhelming responsibility, even the best of people can "burn out" trying to do all this. OD consultants themselves have been known to fall into this trap. If the client becomes dependent on you, expecting you to manage TOB and MOB in your relationship, you may end up unable to address yourself to anything else.

Another distinction has to do with the relationship between *leadership* and *membership*. In situations in which a directive, unidirectional form of leadership is appropriate, the required membership skills are relatively simple: listen carefully and follow directions. The membership skills—TOBs and MOBs—required to make participative leadership effective are vastly different from and more sophisticated than those required under directive leadership. It is important to reemphasize that a group needs both kinds of behavior—in varying degrees at various times—in order to function effectively.

Although TOB and MOB sound straightforward on paper, they are quite complex and interrelated in actual group settings. This is one reason that most managers and administrators tend not to worry about process in their staff meetings, task forces, and so on—it's hard work. This session will allow you to experience this phenomenon from two perspectives: as a watcher and as a doer.

In the upcoming class session, you will have an opportunity to:

1. sharpen your diagnostic skills by being able to observe these TOB and MOB issues in a live, small-group decision-making process;
2. practice your intervention skills by using the foregoing observations to help another group function more effectively; and
3. become more aware of your behavior in groups by giving and receiving feedback on who fulfills TOB and MOB in your learning group.

To some extent you will be on stage for the benefit of others—the observers or consultants—at some point during the class session. But remember that the purpose is to help you learn about yourself and that the feedback you get (and give when you are an observer or consultant) is intended to be constructive.

Preclass Assignment

In part of the upcoming class session, your learning group (if you are using learning groups) will be stopping to examine how well its TOB and MOB functions are being fulfilled. To prepare for this discussion, use the Individual Assessment form provided to answer the questions: What kinds of TOB and MOB functions are being performed adequately, and which functions are either inadequately performed or missing altogether?

1. For each behavior listed, think of the person(s) who, in your opinion, seem(s) to perform that behavior particularly well—it is one of their strengths.
2. Enter the name of that person(s) in the space provided for each category.
3. Enter your name in the space provided for any category you see as one of your strengths.

Note that it is useful to keep several things in mind while doing this task.

1. *Focus on specific behaviors:* Enter a person's name if you have seen that person behave in the specified way. Do not give the benefit of doubt because you feel he or she could do it if he or she wanted to or was asked to.
2. *Do not worry about open space:* It is quite possible that for some categories no one in particular will come to mind. That's all right. The purpose of looking at these data will be to uncover such areas, if they exist, and to decide what to do about them.
3. *Avoid balancing:* Resist the natural temptation to make sure every team member's name appears at least once. The purpose of this data will be to discover *team* strengths and weaknesses, not to determine the relative strengths of members. A person who may not appear to have contributed greatly to TOB or MOB may never have been given a chance to by the group, regardless of what he or she may actually have to offer.

Complete your assessment on the form provided, and bring it to the next class session.

Individual Assessment of How Well the Learning Team Is Meeting Its Needs for TOB and MOB	*TOBs*	*Individuals in the Learning Group Who Perform These Functions Very Well*
	1. Initiating	_____
	2. Information giving	_____
	3. Opinion seeking	_____
	4. Clarifying and elaborating	_____
	5. Summarizing	_____
	6. Consensus testing	_____

	MOBs	*Individuals in the Learning Group Who Perform These Functions Very Well*
	1. Gatekeeping	_____
	2. Encouraging	_____
	3. Harmonizing	_____
	4. Compromising	_____

OVERVIEW OF UPCOMING CLASS SESSION

Step One:	Review Flow of Events for Class Session	(5 minutes)
Step Two:	Preparing for the Fishbowl Process	(15 minutes)
Step Three:	Round One of Process Consultation	(45 minutes)
Step Four:	Discussion and Feedback to Consultants	(15 minutes)
Step Five:	Round Two of Process Consultation	(45 minutes)
Step Six:	Discussion and Feedback to Consultants	(15 minutes)
Step Seven:	Total-Class Discussion	(20 minutes)
Step Eight:	Small-Group Action Plans	(15 minutes)

V. PROCEDURE FOR CLASS SESSION

Step One: Review Flow of Events for Class Session (5 minutes)

Instructor and class should review briefly the purpose and steps for this session. Learning groups should pair off and select which group will act as the client first while the other group observes and consults.

Step Two: Preparing for the Fishbowl Process (15 minutes)

Members of each group should review with one another the following tasks for the fishbowl exercise:

CLIENT GROUP (INNER GROUP)

You will have a 45-minute period to share and discuss your perceptions of TOB and MOB in your group. The purpose of this discussion is to decide whether more or less TOB or MOB would improve your group effectiveness. A suggested agenda would be:

1. Create a composite team profile on large newsprint by going around the group to learn who put what names in each category. (See the example of a team profile sheet that follows.)
2. Discuss meaning of the composite data:
   a. In what areas are we doing all right?
   b. In what areas are we overdoing it?
   c. In what areas are we underrepresented?
3. Discuss individual roles:
   a. Who needs clarification on why he or she was mentioned or not included in some area?
   b. Who appears to be carrying too much responsibility?
   c. Who could help out in an underrepresented area?
4. Try to agree on next steps: specific things certain members will try to do more or less of or to continue doing in future group meetings.

OBSERVER/CONSULTANT GROUP

Your job is to observe and facilitate the process of the other group's meeting. You should look for examples of TOB and MOB that occur and your perception of the consequences of these actions: did they help, divert, confuse, and so on? Use the observer rating form that follows to help capture your observations.

BOTH GROUPS: PROCESS CONSULTATION

In addition to observing, your job is to comment on the client group's current process in terms of TOB, MOB, and so on, in such a way as to help them understand what is going on and whether or not it is appropriate. A useful way to envision this is to see it as "stopper" behavior that is ultimately everyone's responsibility but that OD facilitators often model for groups they work with.

As the stopper, you share your perception of a dilemma, problem, or pinch the group is experiencing. You need not have the answer to resolve the issue, but raising the question or sharing your view can help the group to stop and look at its own process.

A stopper might go like this:

Assessment: "It looks as though only a few of you are really interested in this discussion." "Some of you look bored" (you think they have a pinch), or "It would make me angry if I didn't have a chance to get my opinion in" (you have a pinch).
Standard testing: "Do you agree with that perception?" "Do those of you who weren't talking feel like saying anything now?"

Standard testing: "What does the group want to do about this?" "What could any-one do differently in the future to prevent . . . ?"

While the inner group is discussing its TOB and MOB data, one extra chair should be placed in the circle. This is for the process consultant (PC) who can be anyone from the outside group. The job of the PC is to intervene during the discussion to help the client group be most effective. The type of intervention should be as just described above (stopper behavior).

Members of the outside group can take turns being in the "PC chair" during the discussion. Someone should always be in the chair, even if there is nothing to be said.

Composite Profile Team View of Our TOB and MOB Behavior		*(Enter below names of all those mentioned in each category. Also check below when you are mentioned by someone else, and jot down any examples or comments given.)*
	TOB	
	1. Initiating	_____
	2. Information giving	_____
	3. Opinion seeking	_____
	4. Clarifying and elaborating	_____
	5. Summarizing	_____
	6. Consensus testing	_____
	MOB	
	1. Gatekeeping	_____
	2. Encouraging	_____
	3. Harmonizing	_____
	4. Compromising	_____

Observer Form	*Behavior* *TOB*	*What Was Said/Done by Whom*	*Consequences*
	Initiating	_____	
	Information or opinion seeking	_____	

Information or opinion
   giving   _____

Clarifying   _____

Elaborating   _____

Summarizing   _____

Consensus taking   _____

MOB

Gatekeeping   _____

Encouraging   _____

Harmonizing   _____

Compromising   _____

Step Three: Round One of Process Consultation (45 minutes)

Once the chairs have been set and someone has agreed to start in the PC chair, the inner client group should begin its work. The observer or consultant group should sit around the outside of the client group and alternate the PC role among its members as they wish. Someone should be a timekeeper to stop the discussion after 45 minutes.

Step Four: Discussion and Feedback to Consultants (15 minutes)

Both groups (inner and outer) should join together to discuss what has just taken place. Some suggested questions are:

1. What consultant comments or interventions were particularly helpful? Why?
2. What was the impact on the client group of knowing someone was watching your process?
3. What was it like for each observer to take the empty seat or to share his or her perceptions with the client? Did you feel appreciated?
4. What types of TOB or MOB helped or hindered the interaction between clients and consultants? (This is a time to share more observations if appropriate.)

Step Five: Round Two of Process Consultation (45 minutes)

In each pair of groups, reset the seats, switch positions (inner group becomes observer/consultant group, and so on), select the first PC, and begin the next 45-minute period as in step three.

Step Six: Discussion and Feedback to Consultants (15 minutes)

Both groups should join together to discuss what has taken place in round two. Additional questions might be:

5. What (if anything) did the consultant group for this round try to do differently from round one? What was the consequence?
6. Comparing both rounds, what types of interventions seemed to be received well and/or to have a positive impact on the client group? Which did not? Why?

Step Seven: Total-Class Discussion (20 minutes)

The total class should join together with the instructor to share impressions of the fishbowl exercise. Although the tendency may be to continue debating the usefulness of a particular consultant intervention from some discussion in step six, it is useful at this point to focus on more global issues:

1. How did each group find the actual collection and sharing of TOB and MOB data? Was it useful as a structured intervention? How could it have been more useful?
2. How did each group feel about having a person(s) there to observe and comment on their "process"?
3. In relation to other intervention techniques studied in previous chapters, when would a focus on group process be most useful? When would you not recommend such a focus?

Step Eight: Small-Group Action Plans (15 minutes)

Each learning group should reconvene for a short while to get closure on any issues about its own functioning. Since your discussions about TOB and MOB data were cut off arbitrarily, you may need this time to agree to meet again outside of class, to make a decision about changing the way you work, and so on.

VI. SUMMARY

Groups with the very best of intentions are often less than effective because they forget to pay attention to their process: how they go about their work. Process consultation, therefore, is a common and valuable OD technology to enhance group productivity. Groups often resist such help because stopping to look at what is going on in terms of MOB or TOB means taking time away from the immediate work at hand. But although a totally content-oriented group (that is, one with all TOB focus) may succeed in the short run, those who do not feel support, involvement, or commitment and who have not had an opportunity to raise these concerns soon will begin to withdraw or resist the rest of the group. Thus over the long run their resources are underutilized or lost unless some attention is paid to the process.

Some balance of TOB and MOB appears to be ideal for group functioning. Just what balance is appropriate is up to each group to decide, but no group can even raise this question without MOB: the ability to stop and discuss how the group is doing, just as you did in this class session. Such "stopper" behavior should be everyone's responsibility. Students often leave this session feeling frustrated because although they can now detect the presence of task- or maintenance-oriented behavior (or lack of it) in groups, they do not yet feel well skilled in what to do about it if they feel a change is necessary. In the role of the process consultant, for instance, they may ask, "What should I say or do when I think I see a need for something?" One answer is just to raise the question: ask the group whether they also see such a need or agree with your observation. This is like saying, "I feel like something's wrong or about to go wrong (a pinch), so I'll check on it by asking others." Not only will you thus redirect the group's attention to its process (at least for a moment), but you will also be modeling for them what they can do or say themselves.

Finally, you may have experienced in this class session an added consequence of focusing on process: it is a useful way to help people in a group learn more about how they perceive and are perceived by others. In giving and receiving TOB or MOB feedback, you should learn more about how you behave in groups and what impact different behaviors have on others.

CHAPTER **17**

Career Planning and Development

I. OBJECTIVES

A. To become familiar with the rationale for career planning and development activities.
B. To review some different types of career planning and development interventions.
C. To participate in a demonstration of several techniques useful in career-planning efforts.

II. PRECLASS PREPARATION

A. Read the introduction to Chapter 17.
B. Read D. T. Hall and M. A. Morgan, "Career Development and Planning," in this book, pages 368–385.

III. SUPPLEMENTARY READING

Hall, D. *Careers in Organizations.* Santa Monica, Calif.: Goodyear, 1976.
Jelinek, M. *Career Management.* Chicago: St. Clair, 1979.
Kotter, J.; Faux, V.; and McArthur, C. *Self-Assessment and Career Development.* Englewood Cliffs, N.J.: Prentice-Hall, 1978.
Schein, E. *Career Dynamics: Matching Individual and Organizational Needs.* Reading, Mass.: Addison-Wesley, 1978.

IV. INTRODUCTION

In recent years Organization Development practitioners have become increasingly involved in the area of career development. Career development interventions can be broadly defined as any activity or activities designed to enhance an individual's knowledge of, satisfaction with, or performance in his or her current or future job, often through greater self-insight, better job knowledge, and more focused career-planning processes.

These activities can include such things as modifying the job to better meet employee needs (job enrichment), helping individuals plan their career paths in the organization, counseling individuals on their job strengths and weaknesses, developing organizational mechanisms to facilitate employee knowledge of career opportunities, and assisting employees in the transition to retirement or layoffs.

Organizations have become more interested in the career development of individuals for a variety of reasons. First, there is the belief that a better match between individuals and their jobs will lead to enhanced job satisfaction and performance. Many organizations also feel that an individual who has planned out a career path within the organization is more likely to develop the skills necessary to achieve his or her career goals, thereby benefiting the organization. Some organizations also hope that individuals who have planned their career paths within the organization will be more likely to remain in the organization. Finally, many of today's organizations recognize that they can provide a valuable service to employees by helping them integrate their work lives with their nonwork lives through thoughtful career-planning processes.

What's Involved

Most career development activities involve some form of:

1. individual assessment of interests, abilities, and career goals; combined with
2. the indentification of career opportunities; and
3. a planning process for developing strategies to achieve the individual's career objectives.

There are, however, several other factors that need to be addressed by an organization (and therefore presumably by the change agent) before such a career-planning process can be effectively implemented.

Feedback Mechanisms

In addition to the individual's self-assessment (utilizing one or more of the many tools available for this), there should be organizational procedures available for identifying an employee's strengths, weaknesses, and potentialities. These can include personal feedback—for example, from supervisors—or from more structured mechanisms such as psychological or behavioral testing. If supervisory feedback is to be used, managers will need to be trained to develop better skills in the areas of counseling. If testing is to be utilized, as in so-called assessment centers, a great deal of planning is involved in the establishment of these mechanisms.*

Career Information Systems

In order to make realistic career plans, employees need information about the types of career opportunities available within the organization and perhaps within alternative systems. To supply this information, the organization itself must know what types of opportunities are likely to develop in the organization, as well as within the

---

* *Assessment center* is the term used to describe the efforts of some organizations that involve employees in a battery of tests, both behavioral (for example, role play) and paper-and-pencil, to assess their managerial skill and potential. For more information on these approaches, see W. C. Byham, "Assessment Centers for Spotting Future Managers," *Harvard Business Review* (July–August 1970).

industry and beyond. This type of information necessitates the establishment of manpower planning and projection programs within the organization. It also requires a mechanism or mechanisms to make this information available to employees for planning purposes.

In addition, if career planning is to be seen as relevant, the criteria for advancement need to be made clear to organization members, as does the decision-making process for promotions and transfers. Techniques such as job posting are often useful in this regard.

Organization Culture

If any meaningful change is to occur in the organization's career-planning and development processes, there must be organizational norms and reward systems that reinforce the planning processes. For example, effective career planning requires accurate data on salary ranges, something many organizations diligently withhold from employees.

Another example concerns the supervisor's participation in feedback, planning, and developmental activities for subordinates. If the time required to attend to these activities is not regarded as valuable by the organization and hence is not suitably rewarded, it is unlikely that supervisors will voluntarily engage in these efforts. Perhaps most important, if there is no clear connection between planning, performance, and advancement (if promotion decisions, for example, are seen as politically motivated), then it is unlikely that employees will take career development programs very seriously.

Career-planning and development activities must consider and deal with all the organizational implications discussed above if they are to be genuinely seen as Organization Development interventions rather than personal-growth programs. However, the heart of most of these programs is still the basic self-assessment and planning activity. To give the class some sense of the nature of these activities, the upcoming class session provides participants with the opportunity to experience some typical self-assessment and career-planning techniques.

Many of the techniques designed to facilitate career planning require individuals to consider aspects of their lives outside of their formal organizational jobs. This reflects the perspective that effective career planning can only be done in a broader context. This life-planning approach to career development is widely practiced and is reflected in the activities described in the upcoming class session.

OVERVIEW OF UPCOMING CLASS SESSION	Step One: Setting the Tone for Career-Planning Activities	(5 minutes)
	Step Two: Developing "Who Am I" Lists	(10 minutes)
	Step Three: Rank Ordering	(10 minutes)
	Step Four: Developing a Fantasy	(15 minutes)
	Step Five: Sharing Fantasies	(60–90 minutes)
	Step Six: Reordering "Who Am I" Lists	(10 minutes)
	Step Seven: Planning	(time as needed)

V. PROCEDURE FOR CLASS SESSION

Step One: Setting the Tone for Career-Planning Activities (5 minutes)

If career planning is to be effective, it must be taken seriously. The following activities provide an opportunity for you to identify your own interests, values, or objectives and develop plans to achieve career satisfaction. Open, sincere exploration of these issues should prove to be a valuable experience. Instructors or participants may want to stress this point further at this time.

Step Two: Developing ''Who Am I'' Lists (10 minutes)

Each individual should cut or tear ten pieces of paper to approximately the size of index cards (3″ × 5″). On each piece of paper write a one- or two-word completion to the sentence, ''I am _____ .'' Fill in the blank with nouns (student, athlete, and so on) or phrases that serve as nouns (for example, hard worker).

Step Three: Rank Ordering (10 minutes)

Each individual should now rank order his or her list by determining which items are, at this point in your life, most characteristic of you (1 = most characteristic of you now; 10 = least characteristic of you now). Write the rank you assign each item on the pieces of paper.

Step Four: Developing a Fantasy (15 minutes)

Each individual should now focus on writing down a fantasy projection of what you would like your life to be like in the future. In order to do this, three different techniques are suggested:

1. Write your own *eulogy,* assuming you live a long and full life.
2. Write a *newspaper clipping* about yourself some twenty years from now.
3. Write a description of a *day in your life* some twenty years from now.

Step Five: Sharing Fantasies (60–90 minutes)

Participants should form trios to meet and share the fantasies they have developed. In the trios each individual should read his or her fantasy. The other two members of the group should help the reader focus on the themes, goals, interests, values, and so on that the fantasy seems to suggest. The trio should then compare these themes with the ten rank-ordered ''Who Am I'' lists the reader developed previously, identifying areas of difference or potential conflict. Note that any individual not wishing to share this information with others should feel free to engage in this step alone. It is strongly recommended, however, that this step be done with others, as the information generated tends to be richer and more insightful when it is shared.

Step Six: Reordering ''Who Am I'' Lists (10 minutes)

Each individual should now review his or her ''Who Am I'' list and make the following changes based on an analysis of his or her fantasy exercise:

1. Delete any items that do not appear relevant to the future.
2. Add any items that should be included.
3. Rerank items according to their long-term relevance or importance.

Step Seven: Planning (time as needed)

This activity can be done either individually or in groups. If time is running out, it can be completed at home, perhaps involving additional friends or family.

Each individual should note discrepancies between the first "Who Am I" list, which pertains to the present, and the new list focusing on the future. These discrepancies raise the question, "How do I get from here to there?" Identify the obstacles that must be overcome to achieve the second "Who Am I" list. Then list steps that can be taken to help overcome those obstacles. Finally, try to place dates or deadlines next to the various steps you have identified. The following chart may help you organize this planning activity.

Life/Career Planning Chart

"Who Am I?" Discrepancy	Obstacles to Overcome	Steps to Take	Target Date for Step Completion
I.	a.	1. 2. 3.	1. 2. 3.
	b.	1. 2. 3.	1. 2. 3.
	c.	1. 2. 3.	1. 2. 3.
	d.	1. 2. 3.	1. 2. 3.
II.			
III.			

VI. SUMMARY

Career development activities are aimed at better integrating the individual and the workplace. Although career development programs have important implications for changes in organizational structure, control, and culture, most career development interventions focus on an individual's self-knowledge, awareness of career options, and personal planning and development activities. It should be noted here that, like most organization development activities, career development cannot be treated as a one-shot program. For a planning process to be effective, there must be continuous monitoring and updating.

The activities described during this class session can help to develop initial awareness, objective setting, and planning. As change agents implementing career development programs in organizations, you will need to encourage organizations to build in ongoing assessment and planning activities. Similarly, participants in this class are strongly encouraged to review the plans they developed during this session in the future, in order to assess their progress and the relevance of their projections.

Values Clarification: Exploring Change Agent Ethics

I. OBJECTIVES

A. To explore some personal values related to Organization Development and change.
B. To be more aware of assumptions you hold about others' values.
C. To explore the potential sources of value conflicts and their impact on effective interpersonal transactions.
D. To experience one technique for clarifying values.

II. PRECLASS PREPARATION

A. Read the introduction to Chapter 18.
B. Do the case analyses in this chapter.
C. Read D. Bowen, "Values Dilemmas in Organization Development," in this book, pages 386–394.

III. SUPPLEMENTARY READING

Tannenbaum, R., and Davis, S. "Values, Man, and Organizations." *Industrial Management Review* 10, no. 2 (1969): 56–83.
Tichy, N., and Nisberg, J. "Change Agent Bias: What They View Determines What They Do." *Group and Organization Studies* 1, no. 3 (1976): 286–301.
Walton, R., and Warwick, D. "The Ethics of Organization Development." *Journal of Applied Behavioral Science* 9, no. 6 (1973): 681–698.

IV. INTRODUCTION

A very simple but powerful formula concerning human behavior states that Behavior = $f(P,E)$. An individual's behavior in a given situation is the result of two sets of forces: aspects of the person's personality (P) and aspects of the enivronment in which that person finds him- or herself at the moment (E). The overall objective of this class session is to begin to understand the potential sources and organizational consequences of interpersonal differences (P factors) that may exist between clients and consultants or between individuals in organizations. The specific focus of this class session will be on the concept of values. A related objective is to demonstrate a technique, values clarification, which can be used to help organizations clarify and manage value conflicts among employees that can inhibit organizational effectiveness.

Values are strong beliefs people hold about what is right and wrong, good and bad, appropriate and inappropriate in a variety of situations. They represent personal rules of thumb that become activated particularly in choice situations. For example, a person's need to make a job choice will stimulate thought about numerous value issues: family versus career, personal monetary gain versus social responsibility, and so on.

Types of Values

The values we hold can be arranged on a sort of continuum of concreteness or levels. The continuum measures our awareness of the existence of the value and the extent to which we consciously act on this value rather than merely talk or think about it.

LEVEL 1

Many of the values we hold may be buried in our unconscious. They influence our behavior but not in ways we are aware of.

LEVEL 2

Other values are in our state of conscious awareness but remain very private. These beliefs undoubtedly influence our behavior in some ways, but we never talk about them explicitly. Because they are kept private, we tend to assume they do not influence our behavior in day-to-day interactions.

LEVEL 3

At Level 3 we find ourselves talking about our values with others. We make firm statements such as, "I believe _____ ," or, "People should _____ ." The differentiation within Level 3 has to do with the nature of the public with whom we are sharing our values. At one extreme there is the "cab driver syndrome"—some people will share anything with a cab driver. At the other extreme, a person might share his or her values verbally only with close friends or family.

LEVEL 4

The fourth level of concreteness is the behavioral level. At this level a person consciously acts in ways he or she believes to be expressive of his or her more important values. There is a significant jump from Level 3 to Level 4. Many of us are willing to talk about certain of our values, but the discrepancy between what we say and what we do is often very marked.

Value Conflicts

This discrepancy between what one says and what one does represents an internal inconsistency and can be viewed as one form of value conflict. A second form of internal value conflict (within one person) arises when two or more values are inconsistent. Still another form of conflict can arise between two or more persons who find that they hold different values.

In a work situation the important points in this respect are: (1) to make certain that a conflict really does exist and is not merely perceived to exist on the basis of stereotypes or assumptions, and (2) to test the extent to which the value conflict is related to the work to be done. Two people can be very different in certain value areas without having this difference spill over to create work-related difficulties.

A final type of value conflict can arise from a discrepancy between an individual's values and the demands of the environment in which he or she works. For example, a conscientious objector is a person whose own values are incompatible with the demands of a fighting military unit. An OD practitioner with strong personal feelings against abortion might be hard pressed to function effectively in an organization committed to providing prospective mothers with full information about all options. Individuals caught in such situations are in a different dilemma. Their values (aspects of personality, P) lead them to behave in one way, but the organizational mission (aspect of the environment, E) leads them to behave in an opposite manner.

During the upcoming class you will have an opportunity to experience a technique—values clarification—to help you explore and clarify some of your own values, to examine the kinds of values you believe others hold, and to discuss the kinds of values you believe are enhanced or dampened in the practice of OD.

Changing Values

There is no presumption that anyone should (or could) change his or her basic values. It is assumed, however, that: (1) people's values differ, (2) people hold assumptions and stereotypes about other people's values that may or may not be true, and (3) people's values and their assumptions and stereotypes about others' values do influence their behavior. Helping organization members to recognize their values or stereotypes and their impact can, therefore, help them to sort out what is going on and behave in more appropriate ways. In addition, this awareness and ability to sort out stereotypes and false assumptions is particularly important in the situations of conflict or difference that often characterize the relationships between change agents and clients or client systems. Thus the purpose of this class session is both to demonstrate a technique useful in Organization Development and to explore some of the value dilemmas frequently experienced by OD practitioners.

Individual Preclass Assignment

On the following pages a situation is described that involves a difficult personal choice. Read and respond to each of these situations, and bring your responses with you to class.

Situation 1

Mr. C is a senior engineering project manager. You are consultant F and have just completed a successful team-building effort with the executive vice-president of engineering and his staff, of which Mr. C is a long-standing member. On the basis of that experience, Mr. C has asked you to do a diagnosis of his project team. You have completed in-depth interviews and have organized the data for a feedback meeting with Mr. C and his team. They have committed themselves to a two-day off-site retreat just to deal with these data. It turns out that much of the data and sentiment of the team members are focused on changing Mr. C's leadership style: they are not happy with it. You have "contracted" with C at length, and he repeatedly assures you that he wants to help his team improve in any way it can. You know from the previous team building that C dearly wants to succeed in his work. You also know him to be fairly rigid, a "good old boy" who is accustomed to doing things his way. You also wish to have a successful retreat, not one that could blow up unpredictably.

Imagine you are consultant F. The following is a list of several probabilities that Mr. C will react defensively and dysfunctionally to any negative feedback at the retreat.

PLEASE CHECK HOW SURE YOU NEED TO BE THAT C WILL NOT REACT DEFENSIVELY (THE LOWEST PROBABILITY) IN ORDER TO GO AHEAD WITH THE RETREAT.

_____ The chances are 0 in 10 that C will react negatively to the feedback (that is, he is sure to be helpful at the retreat).
_____ The chances are 1 in 10 that C will react negatively to the feedback.
_____ The chances are 2 in 10 that C will react negatively to the feedback.
_____ The chances are 3 in 10 that C will react negatively to the feedback.
_____ The chances are 4 in 10 that C will react negatively to the feedback.
_____ The chances are 5 in 10 that C will react negatively to the feedback.
_____ The chances are 6 in 10 that C will react negatively to the feedback.
_____ The chances are 7 in 10 that C will react negatively to the feedback.
_____ The chances are 8 in 10 that C will react negatively to the feedback.
_____ The chances are 9 in 10 that C will react negatively to the feedback.
_____ The chances are 10 in 10 that C will react negatively to the feedback (that is, he is sure to disrupt the retreat).

Situation II

Consultant R has been working with Ms. S, a project manager, for the past six months. The project involves recommending whether or not the corporation should undertake a new venture opportunity. It has been fraught with difficulties in gaining acceptance, meeting deadlines, getting project team members to show up, and so on since its inception. Nevertheless, consultant R and Ms. S have formed a good relationship and have been able to jump each hurdle as it has appeared. In a recent meeting of another management group that consultant R was facilitating (S was not present), the president of the corporation shared his opinion that Ms. S's career in the corporation would be riding on the new venture project should it be implemented: "If we go ahead, it's up or out for S." Consultant R is now concerned that if further complications arise in the project, S could stand to lose her job.

Imagine you are Consultant R. The following is a list of several probabilities that no further complications will occur during the project. CHECK THE LOWEST PROBABILITY OF OCCURRENCE OF NO ADDITIONAL COMPLICATIONS

THAT YOU WOULD CONSIDER ACCEPTABLE TO ADVISE MS. S TO ALLOW
THE PROJECT TO CONTINUE.

_____ The chances are 0 in 10 that further complications will not arise (that is, it is certain that further complications will arise).
_____ The chances are 1 in 10 that further complications will not arise.
_____ The chances are 2 in 10 that further complications will not arise.
_____ The chances are 3 in 10 that further complications will not arise.
_____ The chances are 4 in 10 that further complications will not arise.
_____ The chances are 5 in 10 that further complications will not arise.
_____ The chances are 6 in 10 that further complications will not arise.
_____ The chances are 7 in 10 that further complications will not arise.
_____ The chances are 8 in 10 that further complications will not arise.
_____ The chances are 9 in 10 that further complications will not arise.
_____ The chances are 10 in 10 that further complications will not arise (that is, it is
certain that further complications will not arise).

Situation III	Mr. A is a 55-year-old senior technical staff advisor with thiry years in the company. He has been passed over twice for a promotion into a managerial position that would represent a substantial increase in salary and retirement benefits, additional opportunities for promotion, and increased influence in the company. A management consultant to the chief executive officer and his staff has advised Mr. A that the only way he can get the job is to develop new skills and attitudes toward interpersonal relations and managing others. Further, the consultant told Mr. A that there was a type of management training called a t-group that might help Mr. A become more self-aware and skilled interpersonally. At the same time, the consultant told Mr. A that, based on her experience as a t-group trainer, the training might be emotionally painful, uprooting, and generally risky for a person in A's career and life situation.

Imagine you are Mr. A. The following is a list of several probabilities or odds that
the t-group experience would be a successful one for you (that you would become
more aware of how you come across to others, more skilled in giving and receiving
personal feedback, and more accepting of differences; that any emotional strain
caused by feedback you receive of issues you deal with in the t-group would be
manageable and, in the end, useful; and that your self-image would not be in any
way lessened).

PLEASE CHECK THE LOWEST PROBABILITY THAT YOU WOULD CON-
SIDER ACCEPTABLE FOR YOU TO ENROLL IN THE T-GROUP.

_____ The chances are 0 in 10 that the t-group will be a success (that is, the t-group is
certain to be a failure).
_____ The chances are 1 in 10 that the t-group will be a success.
_____ The chances are 2 in 10 that the t-group will be a success.
_____ The chances are 3 in 10 that the t-group will be a success.
_____ The chances are 4 in 10 that the t-group will be a success.
_____ The chances are 5 in 10 that the t-group will be a success.
_____ The chances are 6 in 10 that the t-group will be a success.

_____ The chances are 7 in 10 that the t-group will be a success.

_____ The chances are 8 in 10 that the t-group will be a success.

_____ The chances are 9 in 10 that the t-group will be a success.

_____ The chances are 10 in 10 that the t-group will be a success (that is, the t-group is certain to be a success).

OVERVIEW OF UPCOMING CLASS SESSION	Step One: Individual Reading: Orientation to Sharing Case Responses	(5 minutes)
	Step Two: Discussion of Individual Values	(30–40 minutes)
	Step Three: Assumptions About Others' Values	(30 minutes)
	Step Four: Identifying Potential Conflicts and Their Impact on Getting Work Done	(30 minutes)
	Step Five: Sharing of Small-Group Output	(20 minutes)
	Step Six: Total-Group Discussion	(45–60 minutes)

V. PROCEDURE FOR CLASS SESSION

Step One: Individual Reading—Orientation to Sharing Case Responses (5 minutes)

The discussion you are about to begin should be a lively and productive one. It is important to emphasize that there are no right or wrong responses to the case situations you prepared for homework. In the small-group discussions that follow, the primary objective is to maximize clarity and understanding—not to convince somebody that their values are wrong. Case responses will be discussed from three perspectives.

PERSPECTIVE ONE: SELVES

In responding to the cases, each individual in some sense puts him- or herself into the particular situation. Initial discussions will therefore focus on what you can see and learn about your own personal values from the choices you made in each case situation. What personal values were in conflict as you weighed your choice?

PERSPECTIVE TWO: ASSUMPTIONS OF OTHERS

Two major roles are presented in the case situations: change agents or consultants, and managers or professional employees. During the second set of discussions, you will be asked to step away from yourself (perspective one) and to look at what you may be saying about values you believe are associated with each of these roles (that is, values others hold).

PERSPECTIVE THREE: POTENTIAL CONFLICTS

During this phase you will be asked to focus on the work-related consequences that might result when these roles and the values associated with them interact. In other words, to what extent are value differences a cause of interpersonal tensions and conflict in working relationships?

Step Two: Discussion of Individual Values (30–40 minutes)

1. Each learning group should create a simple matrix for displaying its own data in which each person enters his or her probability assessment.

	Situation I	*Situation II*	*Situation III*
Person 1			
Person 2			
Person 3			
Person 4			
Person 5			
Person 6			

2. Each person should take a few moments to think and share out loud with his or her small group how he or she came to a particular assessment. What were the factors in the case situation (the facts of the case) and in themselves as persons (their own backgrounds, experiences, and so on) that had the most impact on their assessment? Were you aware of conflicts among your own values in making your choice?

Note that the objective of this discussion is for each individual to become more clear about his or her own personal values.

Step Three: Assumptions About Others' Values (30 minutes)

The focus during step two was on your personal values and beliefs—*I* feel, *I* believe, *I* think, and so on. During this step you should shift your perspective to what you believe to be true about others' values. The group should address the following:

1. Strongly held values we think managers or professionals hold;
2. Strongly held values we think consultants or change agents hold;
3. Strongly held values we think are held in client-consultant relationships.

Note that every individual is in some sense unique. It is also true that (1) certain values do characterize certain groups of persons, and (2) people believe that certain values characterize certain groups of persons. Someone should record the group's position on these three issues because the information will be used in step four.

Step Four: Identifying Potential Conflicts and Their Impact on Getting Work Done (30 minutes)

Your previous discussions may have pointed to many areas in which managers, employees, and change agents or consultants are perceived to have different values. Clearly, within an OD effort these roles must frequently interact around work issues. Therefore, it is important to understand which differences have a potential impact on getting work done.

Using the following format, each subgroup should identify potential value conflicts and their impact on getting work done. These conflicts could come from your analysis in step three or your experiences elsewhere. Use a large piece of newsprint so that your output can be shared with the rest of the class.

Relationships Between Managers and Employees	Two or Three Significant Value Differences	Impact on Getting Work Done
	1.	1.
	2.	2.

Relationships Between Clients and Consultants	Two or Three Significant Value Differences	Impact on Getting Work Done
	1.	1.
	2.	2.

Step Five: Sharing of Small-Group Output (20 minutes)

This can be accomplished by having a representative from each small group read out his or her group's output. If the class is very large, each group can simply post its sheets of newsprint for others to read.

The focus during this activity is on clarity of understanding and not on agreeing or disagreeing.

Step Six: Total-Group Discussion (45–60 minutes)

This discussion is intended to focus on the more general values or value conflicts one could envision experiencing in an OD effort.

1. In his definition of OD, Golembiewski has said, "OD constitutes a *value-laden* [sic], theory-based set of interventions. . . ."* Do you agree? What are these values?
2. Are some values or beliefs more suitable to the practice of OD than others?
3. In what kinds of situations would you consider an intervention designed to elicit individual values and value differences (like this class session) to be beneficial?
4. Is it better for a change agent to have values congruent with those of the client or client system? When, if ever, would a value stance in conflict with the client's be useful?

VI. SUMMARY

The subject of values is clearly very complicated. In one brief class session one can only scratch the surface. The values clarification techniques demonstrated here can be useful in addressing problems resulting from value conflicts. Some people may have reacted to the implicit focus during this class on the client-consultant relationship: "You're creating a conflict where one doesn't exist." The intent of the classroom activity was certainly not to create a conflict between two central figures in

* See Chapter 1, page 8.

an OD effort. On the other hand, our own and others' experiences confirm the perception that such relationships are generally characterized by some tension and conflict. Therefore a major purpose of this class session was to put that conflict and tension into a more manageable and acceptable context. Some of the value differences that may exist are in fact necessary to the overall functioning of the entire organization. Managers need to value status quo and caution in risk taking; change agents need to push for alternative paradigms, new ways, and so on. At times these two value perspectives will come into conflict. This is inevitable. For each person to define the other as the adversary will do nothing but add fuel to the fire. One way to minimize such labeling is to be able at all times to articulate one's values explicitly. For the OD practitioner, this means being aware of the values implicit in his or her use of various data collection techniques and interventions.

CHAPTER **19**

Integrating Change Agent Skills

I. OBJECTIVES

A. To practice using diagnostic and planning skills in a large-system analysis.
B. To practice the behavioral skills involved in scouting and entry.
C. To integrate skills from both the content and process areas of Organization Development.

II. PRECLASS PREPARATION

A. Read the introduction to Chapter 19.
B. Read the Local Health Center case in this chapter.
C. Read I. Rubin, M. Plovnick, and R. Fry, "The Role of the Consultant in Initiating Planned Change: A Case Study in Health Care Systems," in this book, pages 395–406.

III. SUPPLEMENTARY READING

Weisbord, M. "Why Organization Development Hasn't Worked (So Far) in Medical Centers." *Health Care Management Review* 1, no. 2 (1976): 17–28.
Wise, H.; Beckhard, R.; Rubin, I.; and Kyte, A. *Making Health Teams Work*. Cambridge, Mass.: Ballinger, 1974.

IV. INTRODUCTION

In this session students will be asked to role play consultants brought in to work with the director of the large health center described in Chapter 4. This consultant-client interaction requires the consultant to utilize a wide range of change agent skills, including those of diagnosis, contracting, planning, and relationship building. Note that the skills required are both cognitive and behavioral—or *content* and *process,* as they are often referred to in Organization Development. In this sense this exercise represents the integration of many of the concepts and skills dealt with in previous chapters. The discussion by Rubin, Plovnick, and Fry of consultant assumptions and roles, in the assigned readings, as well as previous readings on contracting and large-system change, can serve as a useful guideline for some of the issues that must be addressed in a meeting of this type.

First, read the Local Health Center case introduction that follows.

The Local Health Center Case

Harvey Smart, M.D., is the director of a large neighborhood health center. In addition to fee-for-service revenues, the center is funded by several government agencies as well as by several grants from private foundations. The project officer at one of the private foundations, Ms. Mary Murphy, has suggested to Dr. Smart that he might want to speak with a friend of hers, Richard Johnson, about some of the problems Smart is having at the center. Johnson, according to Ms. Murphy, is a highly respected Organization Development consultant. Although Johnson's consulting experience to date has been primarily in business and government, Murphy thinks that much of that experience may be translatable to health care organizations. In addition, Murphy suggests that if Smart finds Johnson to be a helpful resource, the foundation is prepared to underwrite consultant expenses for any resulting projects or programs.

As a result of his conversation with Ms. Murphy, Dr. Smart contacts George Johnson and Associates, Johnson's consulting firm, and arranges for Johnson to visit the center and spend some time with Smart discussing the center's problems and how Johnson might be able to help. In addition to the phone call, Smart sends Johnson some background material. The information found in the Local Health Center case on pages 36–38 in Chapter 4 represents everything Johnson knows about the Local Health Center prior to his visit.

Class Assignment

In the upcoming class several consulting teams will be formed. These teams will role play George Johnson and Associates in the meeting with Dr. Harvey Smart at the LHC. Smart will be played by the instructor.

There will be three distinct rounds of discussion between George Johnson and Associates and Smart, each lasting 10 minutes. A different consultant team will role play the consultant(s) in each 10-minute round, picking up where the previous team has left off (in other words, the new team does not start all over again, although changes in direction, strategy, and so on are possible). There will be a 5-minute strategy period for teams between each 10-minute round. The consultant teams should not know which team will participate in the upcoming round until immediately prior to the round. Thus all teams will have to plan as though they were the next up. Someone should be designated to keep time during the consultant-client interviews and to interrupt the meetings at the 10-minute point.

Consultant teams are free to design any strategy and should consider such issues as which and how many people will actually participate in the meeting.

The following agenda illustrates the role-play format:

1. consultant teams develop strategies;
2. first consultant team chosen;
3. first 10-minute interview;
4. 5-minute consultant team meeting;
5. second consultant team chosen;
6. second 10-minute interview;

7. 5-minute consultant team meeting;
8. third consultant team chosen;
9. third 10-minute interview;
10. 5-minute consultant team meeting;
11. total-class critique.

OVERVIEW OF UPCOMING CLASS SESSION

Step One:	Creation of Consultant Teams	(5 minutes)
Step Two:	Consultant Teams Develop Strategies	(20 minutes)
Step Three:	Consultant-Client Role Plays, Three Rounds	(60 minutes)
Step Four:	Critique of Role Plays	(40 minutes)
Step Five:	Review of Actual Results of Johnson-Smart Meetings	(10 minutes)

V. PROCEDURE FOR CLASS SESSION

Step One: Creation of Consultant Teams (5 minutes)

Class should divide into consultant groups of no more than six persons each.

Step Two: Consultant Teams Develop Strategies (20 minutes)

Consultant teams should meet to analyze the LHC case and develop a strategy for the upcoming meeting with Dr. Smart.

Step Three: Consultant-Client Role Plays, Three Rounds (60 minutes)

Consultant teams meet with Dr. Smart according to the format outlined in the class assignment. Selection of teams for each of the role plays should be done just prior to each round in order to maintain the suspense for consultant teams. If more than three teams have been formed, some team(s) may not actually get to role play an interview. However, all teams should take notes during each round, critiquing the consultant-client interaction, in order to facilitate the summary discussion.

Step Four: Critique of Role Plays (40 minutes)

Instructor leads critique of preceding consultant-client role plays. The discussion should review positive aspects of the interviews as well as things that were not done or that could have been done more effectively. The following questions may be helpful as discussion guides:

1. Did the consultant(s) set clear expectations for objectives for the meeting?
2. Did the consultant(s) focus on understanding and responding to the client's concerns and needs? Were they flexible?
3. Was the problem or problems explored and clearly understood before solutions were discussed?
4. Did the consultant(s) utilize a facilitator style, expert style, or any other style?
5. Were clear next steps identified before the meeting ended?
6. Did the client seem committed to the outcomes of the meeting?

Step Five: Review of Actual Results of Johnson-Smart Meetings (10 minutes)

Instructor presents the actual scenario that developed between Johnson and Smart, discussing differences between Johnson's approach and those of the consultant teams and focusing on the advantages and disadvantages of each.

VI. SUMMARY

This exercise required the integration of a variety of skills necessary for effective OD intervention. These include skills in diagnosing organizational needs, planning intervention strategies, and developing client-consultant relationships.

It is often difficult to utilize all these skills at the same time since they require very different intellectual and psychosocial abilities. The diagnostic and planning modes are detached and analytic in nature, whereas developing a good relationship requires interpersonal involvement and sensitivity. Because it is difficult to do all these things simultaneously, it is important to practice them and to get feedback in activities similar to the role play in this session.

PART **II**

Readings

INTRODUCTION TO ORGANIZATION DEVELOPMENT

The first section of the readings of this volume consists of four articles. The first two articles, by Miles and Schmuck and French, define organization development from differing perspectives. Since the field is difficult to define, these perspectives help to clarify and identify the unique characteristics of OD. The brief article by Zander introduces the concept of resistance to change. Although he does not address organization development as such, his analysis of how to prevent resistance incorporates some of the fundamental principles and practices of OD. As noted in most textbooks of organization development, action-research as a model for data collection, feedback, and change is the conceptual and applied frame of reference for OD practice. In the final article of this introductory section, Frohman, Sashkin, and Kavanagh explain the action-research model as it applies to OD.

The Nature of Organization Development

Matthew B. Miles and Richard A. Schmuck

Definition of OD

OD can be defined as a planned and sustained effort to apply behavioral science for system improvement, using reflexive, self-analytic methods. Let us examine each element of this definition in detail.

SYSTEM IMPROVEMENT

The emphasis of OD is on the system, rather than the individual, as the target of change. In this respect the approach differs from "sensitivity training" and "management development." "System" may mean either an entire organization or a subsystem such as an academic department or team of teachers. The emphasis, however, is always on improving both the ability of a *system* to cope and the relationships of the system with subsystems and with the environment. Individuals, of course, often gain insights and new attitudes during such improvement processes, but the primary concern of OD is with such matters as adequate organizational communication, the integration of individual and organizational goals, the development of a climate of trust in decision making, and the effect of the reward system on morale.

REFLEXIVE, SELF-ANALYTIC METHODS

OD involves system members themselves in the assessment, diagnosis, and transformation of their own organization. Rather than simply accepting diagnosis and prescription from an outside "technocratic" expert, organization members themselves, with the *aid* of outside consultants, examine current difficulties and their causes and participate actively in the reformulation of goals, the development of new group

process skills, the redesign of structures and procedures for achieving the goals, the alteration of the working climate of the system, and the assessment of results.

PLANNED AND SUSTAINED EFFORT

OD involves deliberately planned change, as contrasted with system "drifts." Unlike an innovative project or program, it is generally not limited to a specific period of time. To implement OD, an organizational subsystem (such as a Department of Organization Development) is created and charged with the specific responsibility for planning, managing, and evaluating the continuous process of organizational self-renewal. Members of such a subsystem act as inside change agents or OD development specialists . . . and usually link with outside consultants to carry out their mission. The essential concept is that some fraction of an organization's resources is devoted to continuous organizational maintenance, rebuilding, and expansion. Such a concept is familiar to managers in the field of plant and equipment maintenance but is much less widely known and accepted in the maintenance of the human organization.

Organizations are not easily or quickly transformed. The available evidence[1] suggests that in large organizations two to three years of OD effort is typical before the completion of serious and self-sustaining change. In addition, it must be borne in mind that an organization is never transformed permanently. Instead, institutionalized, built-in OD functions must continually be involved in facing the dilemmas and vicissitudes of organizational renewal.

Reprinted from Richard A. Schmuck and Matthew B. Miles, Eds., *Organization Development in Schools* (San Diego, Ca.: University Associates, 1976), pp. 2–3 and 7–10. Used with permission.

[1] See, for example, P. C. Buchanan, "Laboratory Training and Organization Development," *Administrative Science Quarterly* 14 (1969): 466–480.

APPLIED BEHAVIORAL SCIENCE

OD relies strongly on concepts from the behavioral sciences: primarily social psychology but also psychology and sociology. Such concepts are used to diagnose an organization's problems, to equip organization members with a conceptual language for talking about phenomena they are facing, to redesign unsatisfactory structures and procedures, and to provide a basis for evaluation of OD interventions and processes.

How OD Works

A typical sequence of events in the initiation and development of an OD program is as follows:

1. Middle or top management of an organization becomes interested in OD and feels that the organization has problems which can be met through training. Initial interest is often developed after a manager's personal attendance at a T-group laboratory.
2. Management invites an outside OD consultant to visit the organization.
3. After the consultant's entry and contact with a variety of organization roles and groups, the organization works out a contract with the consultant, specifying the nature of the projected relationship and its goals and general procedures.
4. The consultant, working with insiders, collects data about the organization via interviews, questionnaires, and observations.
5. These data form the basis of a joint diagnosis of the points of difficulty in the organization and, if appropriate, between the organization and its environment. Goals for change are explicitly identified.
6. A first "intervention" (usually an intensive meeting involving several key roles, a group, or more than one group) is planned. The data collected earlier are often fed back and discussed. Exercises for training in communication skills or group functioning are often used as constructive vehicles for discussing the data. (For a delineation of the range of interventions employed, see below.)
7. The intervention is evaluated following a new collection of data. Often the future success of the ef-

fort depends on the degree to which key figures have been "freed up" to be more open, concerned, and creative about organizational improvement.

8. Subsequent steps in intervention are planned on the basis of these data, and the process continues.

The usual primary effect of the early stages of an OD training program is to change the "culture" of the organization: it becomes more open, trusting, collaborative, self-analytical, and inclined to take risks. As a program proceeds, structural changes become more typical as outcomes; reorganizations, the development of new roles and groups, and new forms of work flow are planned and set into motion. Typical additional steps in the OD program which occur at this later stage are as follows:

9. The OD function itself becomes institutionalized within the organization. An OD department or group is formed and takes central responsibility for continuing the OD process, drawing on outside resources as needed.
10. The internal OD specialists become increasingly professionalized and responsible for their own development via such bodies as NTL and networks of other professionals. They may at times serve as outside change agents to other organizations.

Technology of OD

The OD cube in Figure 1 displays the typical interventions employed in OD training. At the left are the *problems diagnosed* by the inside/outside change team; they may include difficulties in goal-setting and planning, communication, climate, and other matters. These problems may occur either in *existing* units, or in such *new* units as those created during the start-up phase of a new organization, those developed during the course of mergers with or acquisitions of other organizations, and those emerging during the course of the major reorganization of a firm. For clarity, the three additional "cubes" for start-ups, mergers, and reorganizations are not shown here. The interventions used in such new systems often differ substantially from those used in existing systems.

The diagonal edge of the cube identifies the *focus*

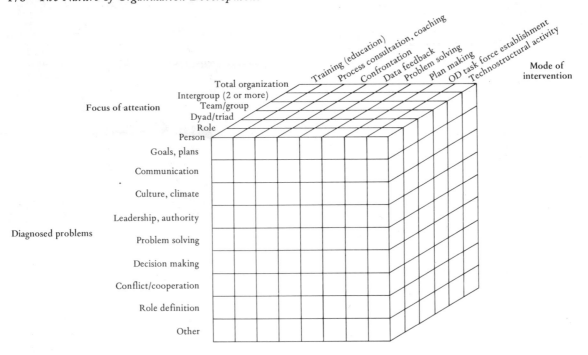

FIGURE 1

The OD Cube: A Scheme for Classifying OD Interventions

of attention of the forthcoming intervention. The intervention may be focused essentially on a change in persons (individuals), in roles, in dyads or triads (two- or three-person groups), in work teams, in the relations between two or more groups, or in the organization as a whole. OD training most frequently focuses on key roles, teams, relationships between groups, and the total organization.

The modes of intervention which can be employed are as follows:

1. Training or education: procedures involving direct teaching or experience-based learning. Such technologies as lectures, exercises, simulations, and T-groups are examples.
2. Process consultation: watching and aiding ongoing processes and coaching to improve them.
3. Confrontation: bringing together units of the organization (persons, roles, or groups) which have previously been in poor communication: usually accompanied by supporting data.
4. Data feedback: systematic collection of information, which is then reported back to appropriate

organizational units as a base for diagnosis, problem solving, and planning.
5. Problem solving: meetings essentially focusing on problem identification, diagnosis, and solution invention and implementation.
6. Plan making: activity focused primarily on planning and goal setting to replot the organization's future.
7. OD task force establishment: setting up ad hoc problem-solving groups or internal teams of specialists to ensure that the organization solves problems and carries out plans continuously.
8. Technostructural activity: action which has as its prime focus the attention of the organization's structure, work flow, and means of accomplishing tasks.

These intervention modes flow into each other and are not mutually exclusive. They range roughly from "soft" (person-changing) to "hard" (task-oriented or structure-changing) in emphasis. A strong OD program will typically involve all eight components at one time or another.

Any particular OD intervention can be classified according to problem, focus of attention, and mode of intervention. For example, an intervention might be aimed at increasing problem-solving and decision-making skills in an existing team—a plant manager and his seven subordinate division heads, for example. Its mode might be process consultation: the outside change agent watches the group work and provides feedback from time to time on their process (*how* they are proceeding, who is and is not listened to, whether the boss's word always holds sway, etc.). For another example, an intervention might focus on the entire faculty of a new junior high school to increase its ability to solve problems. The modes of the intervention could be training in communication skills, followed by training in problem solving, and then process consultation during real-life problem solving at faculty meetings.

As the latter example shows, the OD process is further complicated by the fact that most training interventions sequence various modes in unique ways. As one considers the complexities of OD design, the number of combinations involving all three of these dimensions becomes very large. Research as yet tells us little about optimal sequencing of interventions directed toward specific targets and problems over a period of years, but such strategic planning is the central stock-in-trade of the OD specialist.

Organization Development Objectives, Assumptions, and Strategies

Wendell L. French

Organization development refers to a long-range effort to improve an organization's problem-solving capabilities and its ability to cope with changes in its external environment with the help of external or internal behavioral scientist–consultants, or –change agents, as they are sometimes called. Such efforts are relatively new but are becoming increasingly visible within the United States, England, Japan, Holland, Norway, Sweden, and perhaps in other countries. A few of the growing number of organizations which have embarked on organization development (OD) efforts to some degree are Union Carbide, Esso, TRW Systems, Humble Oil, Weyerhaeuser, and Imperial Chemical Industries Limited. Other kinds of institutions, including public school systems, churches, and hospitals, have also become involved.

Organization development activities appear to have originated about 1957 as an attempt to apply some of the values and insights of laboratory training to total organizations. The late Douglas McGregor, working with Union Carbide, is considered to have been one of the first behavioral scientists to talk systematically about and to implement an organization development program.[1] Other names associated with such early efforts are Herbert Shepard and Robert Blake who, in collaboration with the Employee Relations Department of the Esso Company, launched a program of laboratory training (sensitivity training) in the company's various refineries. This program emerged in 1957 after a headquarters human relations research division began to view itself as an internal consulting group offering services to field managers rather than as a research group developing reports for top management.[2]

Objectives of Typical OD Programs

Although the specific interpersonal and task objectives of organization development programs will vary according to each diagnosis of organizational problems, a number of objectives typically emerge. These objectives reflect problems which are very common in organizations:

1. To increase the level of trust and support among organizational members.
2. To increase the incidence of confrontation of organizational problems, both within groups and among groups, in contrast to "sweeping problems under the rug."
3. To create an environment in which authority of

Wendell French, © (1969) by the Regents of the University of California. Reprinted from *California Management Review*, vol. 12, no. 2, pp. 23–34, by permission of the Regents.

This article is largely based on the second edition of my *The Personnel Management Process: Human Resources Administration* (Boston: Houghton Mifflin Company, 1970), Chap. 28.

[1] Richard Beckhard, W. Warner Burke, and Fred I. Steele, "The Program for Specialists in Organization Training and Development," mimeographed, NTL Institute for Applied Behavioral Science, December 1967, p.ii; and John Paul Jones, "What's Wrong with Work?" in *What's Wrong with Work?* (New York: National Association of Manufacturers, 1967), p. 8. For a history of NTL Institute for Applied Behavioral Science, with which Douglas McGregor was long associated in addition to his professorial appointment at M.I.T. and which has been a major factor in the history of organization development, see Leland P. Bradford, "Biography of an Institution," *Journal of Applied Behavioral Science*, vol. 3, no. 2 (1967), pp. 127–43. While we will use the word "program" from time to time, ideally organization development is a "process," not just another new program of temporary quality.

[2] Harry D. Kolb, Introduction to *An Action Research Program for Organization Improvement* (Ann Arbor: Foundation for Research in Human Behavior, 1960), p. 1.

assigned role is augmented by authority based on knowledge and skill.

4. To increase the openness of communications laterally, vertically, and diagonally.

5. To increase the level of personal enthusiasm and satisfaction in the organization.

6. To find synergistic solutions[3] to problems with greater frequency. (Synergistic solutions are creative solutions in which 2 + 2 equals more than 4, and through which all parties gain more through cooperation than through conflict.)

7. To increase the level of self and group responsibility in planning and implementation.[4]

Difficulties in Categorizing

Before describing some of the basic assumptions and strategies of organization development, it would be well to point out that one of the difficulties in writing about such a "movement" is that a wide variety of activities can be and are subsumed under this label. These activities have varied all the way from inappropriate application of some "canned" management development program to highly responsive and skillful joint efforts between behavioral scientists and client systems.

Thus, while labels are useful, they may gloss over a wide range of phenomena. The "human relations movement," for example, has been widely written about as though it were all bad or all good. To illustrate, some of the critics of the movement have accused it of being "soft" and a "handmaiden of the Establishment," of ignoring the technical and power systems of organizations, and of being too naively participative. Such criticisms were no doubt warranted in some circumstances, but in other situations may not have been at all appropriate. Paradoxically, some of the major insights of the human relations movement, e.g., that the organization can be viewed as a social system and that subordinates have substantial control over productivity, have been assimilated by its critics.

In short, the problem is to distinguish between appropriate and inappropriate programs, between effectiveness and ineffectiveness, and between relevancy and irrelevancy. The discussion which follows will attempt to describe the "ideal" circumstances for organization development programs, as well as to point out some pitfalls and common mistakes in organization change efforts.

Relevancy to Different Technologies and Organization Subunits

Research by Joan Woodward[5] suggests that organization development efforts *might be more relevant to certain kinds of technologies and organizational levels, and perhaps to certain work force characteristics, than to others.* For example, OD efforts may be more appropriate for an organization devoted to prototype manufacturing than for an automobile assembly plant. However, experiments in an organization like Texas Instruments suggest that some manufacturing efforts which appear to be inherently mechanistic may lend themselves to a more participative, open management style than is often assumed possible.[6]

However, assuming the constraints of a fairly narrow job structure at the rank-and-file level, organization development efforts may inherently be more productive and relevant at the managerial levels of the organization. Certainly OD efforts are most effective when they start at the top. Research and development units—particularly those involving a high degree of interdependency and joint creativity among group members—also appear to be appropriate for organization development activities, if group members are currently experiencing problems in communicating or interpersonal relationships.

---

[3] Cattell defines synergy as "the sum total of the energy which a group can command." Daniel Katz and Robert L. Kahn, *The Social Psychology of Organizations* (New York: John Wiley & Sons, Inc., 1966), p. 33.

[4] For a similar statement of objectives, see "What Is OD?" *NTL Institute: News and Reports from NTL Institute for Applied Behavioral Science,* vol. 2 (June 1968), pp. 1–2. Whether OD programs increase the overall level of authority in contrast to redistributing authority is a debatable point. My hypothesis is that both a redistribution and an overall increase occur.

[5] Joan Woodward, *Industrial Organization: Theory and Practice* (London: Oxford University Press, 1965).

[6] See M. Scott Myers, "Every Employee a Manager," *California Management Review,* vol. 10 (Spring 1968), pp. 9–20.

Basic Assumptions

Some of the basic assumptions about people which underlie organization development programs are similar to "Theory Y" assumptions[7] and will be repeated only briefly here. However, some of the assumptions about groups and total systems will be treated more extensively. The following assumptions appear to underlie organization development efforts.[8]

ABOUT PEOPLE

Most individuals have drives toward personal growth and development, and these are most likely to be actualized in an environment which is both supportive and challenging.

Most people desire to make, and are capable of making, a much higher level of contribution to the attainment of organization goals than most organizational environments will permit.

ABOUT PEOPLE IN GROUPS

Most people wish to be accepted and to interact cooperatively with at least one small reference group, and usually with more than one group, e.g., the work group, the family group.

One of the most psychologically relevant reference groups for most people is the work group, including peers and the superior.

Most people are capable of greatly increasing their effectiveness in helping their reference groups solve problems and in working effectively together.

For a group to optimize its effectiveness, the formal leader cannot perform all of the leadership functions in all circumstances at all times, and all group members must assist each other with effective leadership and member behavior.

[7] See Douglas McGregor, *The Human Side of Enterprise* (New York: McGraw-Hill Book Company, 1960), pp. 47–48.

[8] In addition to influence from the writings of McGregor, Likert, Argyris, and others, this discussion has been influenced by "Some Assumptions about Change in Organizations," in notebook "Program for Specialists in Organization Training and Development," NTL Institute for Applied Behavioral Science, 1967; and by staff members who participated in that program.

ABOUT PEOPLE IN ORGANIZATIONAL SYSTEMS

Organizations tend to be characterized by overlapping, interdependent work groups, and the "linking pin" function of supervisors and others needs to be understood and facilitated.[9]

What happens in the broader organization affects the small work group and vice versa.

What happens to one subsystem (social, technological, or administrative) will affect and be influenced by other parts of the system.

The culture in most organizations tends to suppress the expression of feelings which people have about each other and about where they and their organizations are heading.

Suppressed feelings adversely affect problem solving, personal growth, and job satisfaction.

The level of interpersonal trust, support, and cooperation is much lower in most organizations than is either necessary or desirable.

"Win-lose" strategies between people and groups, while realistic and appropriate in some situations, are not optimal in the long run to the solution of most organizational problems.

Synergistic solutions can be achieved with a much higher frequency than is actually the case in most organizations.

Viewing feelings as data important to the organization tends to open up many avenues for improved goal setting, leadership, communications, problem solving, intergroup collaboration, and morale.

Improved performance stemming from organization development efforts needs to be sustained by appropriate changes in the appraisal, compensation, training, staffing, and task-specialization subsystem—in short, in the total personnel system.

Value and Belief Systems of Behavioral Scientist–Change Agents

While scientific inquiry, ideally, is value-free, the applications of science are not value-free. Applied behavioral scientist–organization development consultants tend to subscribe to a comparable set of

[9] For a discussion of the "linking pin" concept, see Rensis Likert, *New Patterns of Management* (New York: McGraw-Hill Book Company, 1961).

values, although we should avoid the trap of assuming that they constitute a completely homogenous group. They do not.

One value, to which many behavioral scientist–change agents tend to give high priority, is that the needs and aspirations of human beings are the reasons for organized effort in society. They tend, therefore, to be developmental in their outlook and concerned with the long-range opportunities for the personal growth of people in organizations.

A second value is that work and life can become richer and more meaningful, and organized effort more effective and enjoyable, if feelings and sentiments are permitted to be a more legitimate part of the culture. A third value is a commitment to an action role, along with a commitment to research, in an effort to improve the effectiveness of organizations.[10] A fourth value—or perhaps a belief—is that improved competency in interpersonal and intergroup relationships will result in more effective organizations.[11] A fifth value is that behavioral science research and an examination of behavioral science assumptions and values are relevant and important in considering organizational effectiveness. While many change agents are perhaps overly action-oriented in terms of the utilization of their time, nevertheless, as a group they are paying more and more attention to research and to the examination of ideas.[12]

The value placed on research and inquiry raises the question as to whether the assumptions stated earlier are values, theory, or "facts." In my judgment, a substantial body of knowledge, including research on leadership, suggests that there is considerable evidence for these assumptions. However, to conclude that these assumptions are facts, laws, or principles would be to contradict the value placed by behavioral scientists on continuous research and inquiry. Thus, I feel that they should be considered theoretical statements which are based on provisional data.

This also raises the paradox that the belief that people are important tends to result in their being important. The belief that people can grow and develop in terms of personal and organizational competency tends to produce this result. Thus, values and beliefs tend to be self-fulfilling, and the question becomes "What do you choose to want to believe?" While this position can become Pollyannish in the sense of not seeing the real world, nevertheless, behavioral scientist–change agents, at least this one, tend to place a value on optimism. It is a kind of optimism that says people can do a better job of goal setting and facing up to and solving problems, not one that says the number of problems is diminishing.

It should be added that it is important that the values and beliefs of each behavioral scientist–change agent be made visible both to himself and to the client. In the first place, neither can learn to adequately trust the other without such exposure—a hidden agenda handicaps both trust building and mutual learning. Second, and perhaps more pragmatically, organizational change efforts tend to fail if a prescription is applied unilaterally and without proper diagnosis.

---

[10] Warren G. Bennis sees three major approaches to planned organizational change, with the behavioral scientists associated with each all having "a deep concern with applying social science knowledge to create more viable social systems; a commitment to action, as well as to research . . . and a belief that improved interpersonal and group relationships will ultimately lead to better organizational performance." Warren G. Bennis, "A New Role for the Behavioral Sciences: Effecting Organizational Change," *Administrative Science Quarterly*, vol. 8 (September 1963), pp. 157–58; and Herbert A. Shepard, "An Action Research Model," in *An Action Research Program for Organization Improvement*, pp. 31–35.

[11] Bennis, "A New Role for the Behavioral Sciences," p. 158.

[12] For a discussion of some of the problems and dilemmas in behavioral science research, see Chris Argyris, "Creating Effective Relationships in Organizations," in Richard N. Adams and Jack J. Preiss, Eds., *Human Organization Research* (Homewood, Ill.: The Dorsey Press, 1960), pp. 109–23; and Barbara A. Benedict, et al., "The Clinical Experimental Approach to Assessing Organizational Change Efforts," *Journal of Applied Behavioral Science* (November 1967), pp. 347–80.

Strategy in Organization Development: An Action-Research Model

A frequent strategy in organization development programs is based on what behavioral scientists refer to as an "action-research model." This model involves extensive collaboration between the consultant (whether an external or an internal change agent) and the client group, data gathering, data discussion, and planning. While descriptions of this model vary from

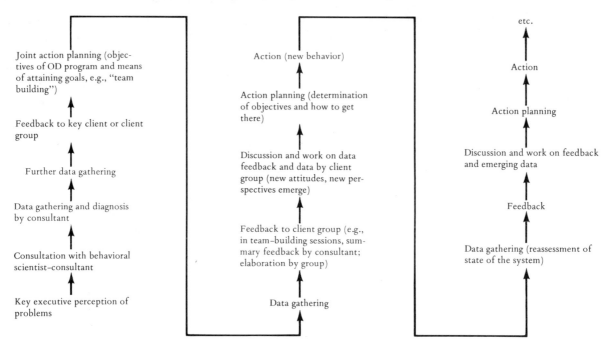

FIGURE 1

An Action-Research Model for Organization Development

author to author, the dynamics are essentially the same. [13]

Figure 1 summarizes some of the essential phases of the action-research model, using an emerging organization development program as an example. The key aspects of the model are *diagnosis, data gathering, feedback to the client group, data discussion and work by the client group, action planning, and action.* The sequence tends to be cyclical, with the focus on new or advanced problems as the client group learns to work more effectively together. Action research should also be considered a process, since, as William Foote Whyte says, it involves "... a continuous gathering and analysis of human relations research data and the feeding of the findings into the organization in such a manner as to change behavior." [14] (Feedback we will define as nonjudgmental observations of behavior.)

Ideally, initial objectives and strategies of organization development efforts stem from a careful *diagnosis* of such matters as interpersonal and intergroup problems, decision-making processes, and communication flow which are currently being experienced by the client organization. As a preliminary step, the behavioral scientist and the key client (the president of a company, the vice president in charge of a division, the works manager or superintendent of a plant, a superintendent of schools, etc.) will make a joint initial assessment of the critical problems which need working on. Subordinates may also be interviewed in order to provide supplemental data. The diagnosis may very well indicate that the central problem is technological or that the key client is not at all willing or ready to examine the organization's problem-solving ability or his own managerial behavior. [15] Either could be a reason for postponing or moving

[13] For further discussion of action research, see Edgar H. Schein and Warren G. Bennis, *Personal and Organizational Change through Group Methods* (New York: John Wiley & Sons, Inc., 1966), pp. 272–74.

[14] William Foote Whyte and Edith Lentz Hamilton, *Action Research for Management* (Homewood, Ill.: Richard D. Irwin, Inc., 1964), p. 2.

[15] Jeremiah J. O'Connell appropriately challenges the notion that there is "one best way" of organizational change and stresses that the consultant should choose his role and intervention strategies on the basis of "the conditions existing when he enters the client system." *Managing Organizational Innovation* (Homewood, Ill.: Richard D. Irwin, Inc., 1968), pp. 10–11.

slowly in the direction of organization development activities, although the technological problem may easily be related to deficiencies in interpersonal relationships or decision making. The diagnosis might also indicate the desirability of one or more additional specialists (in engineering, finance, or electronic data processing, for example) to simultaneously work with the organization.

The initial diagnosis, which focuses on the expressed needs of the client, is extremely critical. As discussed earlier, in the absence of a skilled diagnosis, the behavioral scientist–change agent would be imposing a set of assumptions and a set of objectives which may be hopelessly out of joint with either the current problems of the people in the organization or their willingness to learn new modes of behavior. In this regard, it is extremely important that the consultant *hear and understand* what the client is trying to tell him. This requires a high order of skill.[16]

Interviews are frequently used for *data gathering* in OD work for both initial diagnosis and subsequent planning sessions, since personal contact is important for building a cooperative relationship between the consultant and the client group. The interview is also important since the behavioral scientist–consultant is interested in spontaneity and in feelings that are expressed as well as cognitive matters. However, questionnaires are sometimes successfully used in the context of what is sometimes referred to as survey feedback, to supplement interview data.[17]

Data gathering typically goes through several phases. The first phase is related to diagnosing the state of the system and to making plans for organizational change. This phase may utilize a series of interviews between the consultant and the key client or between a few key executives and the consultant. Subsequent phases focus on problems specific to the top executive team and to subordinate teams (see Figure 2).

Typical questions in data gathering or "problem sensing" would include: What problems do you see in your group, including problems between people, that are interfering with getting the job done the way you would like to see it done?; and what problems do you see in the broader organization? Such open-ended questions provide wide latitude on the part of the respondents and encourage a reporting of problems *as the individual sees them*. Such interviewing is usually conducted privately, with a commitment on the part of the consultant that the information will be used in such a way as to avoid unduly embarrassing anyone. The intent is to find out what common problems or themes emerge, with the data to be used constructively for both diagnostic and feedback purposes.

Two- or three-day offsite *team-building or group problem-solving sessions* typically become a major focal point in organization development programs. During these meetings the behavioral scientist frequently provides *feedback* to the group in terms of the themes which emerged in the problem-sensing interviews.[18] He may also encourage the group to determine which items or themes should have priority in terms of maximum utilization of time. These themes usually provide substantial and meaningful data for the group to begin work on. One-to-one interpersonal matters, both positive and negative, tend to emerge spontaneously as the participants gain confidence from the level of support sensed in the group.

Different consultants will vary in their mode of behavior in such sessions but will typically serve as *"process" observers and as interpreters of the dynamics of the group interaction* to the degree that the group expresses a readiness for such intervention. They also typically encourage people to take risks, a step at a time, and to experiment with new behavior in the context of the level of support in the group. Thus, the trainer–consultant(s) serves as a stimulant to new behavior but also as a protector. The climate which I try to build, for example, is: "Let's not tear down any

[16] For further discussion of organization diagnosis, see Richard Beckhard, "An Organization Improvement Program in a Decentralized Organization," *Journal of Applied Behavioral Science,* vol. 2 (January–March 1966), pp. 3–4; "OD as a Process," in Jones, *What's Wrong with Work?*, pp. 12–13.

[17] For example, see Floyd C. Mann, "Studying and Creating Change," in Timothy W. Costello and Sheldon S. Zalkind, Eds., *Psychology in Administration—A Research Orientation* (Englewood Cliffs, N.J.: Prentice-Hall, Inc., 1963), pp. 321–24. See also Delbert C. Miller, "Using Behavioral Science to Solve Organization Problems," *Personnel Administration,* vol. 31 (January–February 1968), pp. 21–29.

[18] For a description of feedback procedures used by the Survey Research Center, University of Michigan, see Mann and Likert, "The Need for Research on the Communication of Research Results," in Adams and Preiss, Eds., *Human Organization Research*, pp. 57–66.

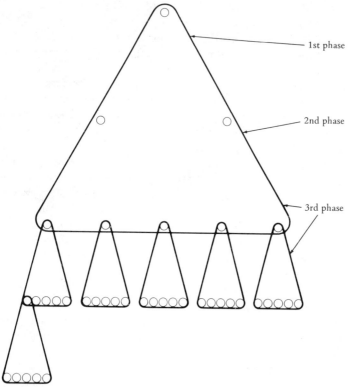

1st Phase. Data gathering, feedback, and diagnosis—consultant and top executive only.

2nd Phase. Data gathering, feedback, and revised diagnosis—consultant and two or more key staff or line people.

3rd Phase. Data gathering and feedback to total top executive team in "team-building" laboratory, with or without key subordinates from level below.

4th and Additional Phases. Data gathering and team-building sessions with second or third-level teams.

Subsequent Phases. Data gathering, feedback, and interface problem-solving sessions across groups.

Simultaneous Phases. Several managers may attend "stranger" T-Groups; courses in the management development program may supplement this learning.

FIGURE 2
Organization Development Phases in a Hypothetical Organization

more than we can build back together."[19] Further, the trainer–consultant typically works with the group to assist team members in improving their skills in diagnosing and facilitating group progress.[20]

It should be noted, however, that different groups will have different needs along a task-process continuum. For example, some groups have a need for intensive work on clarifying objectives; others may have the greatest need in the area of personal relationships. Further, the consultant or the chief consultant in a

team of consultants involved in an organization development program will play a much broader role than serving as a T-group or team-building trainer. He will also play an important role in periodic data gathering and diagnosis and in joint long-range planning of the change efforts.[21]

[19] This phrase probably came from a management workshop sponsored by NTL Institute for Applied Behavioral Science.

[20] For a description of what goes on in team-building sessions, see Beckhard, "An Organization Improvement Program," pp. 9–13; and Newton Margulies and Anthony P. Raia, "People in Organizations—A Case for Team Training," *Training and Development Journal*, vol. 22 (August 1968), pp. 2–11. For a description of problem-solving sessions involving the total management group (about 70) of a company, see Richard Beckhard, "The Confrontation Meeting," *Harvard Business Review*, vol. 45 (March–April 1967), pp. 149–55.

[21] For a description of actual organization development programs, see Paul C. Buchanan, "Innovative Organizations—A Study in Organization Development," in *Applying Behavioral Science Research in Industry* (New York: Industrial Relations Counselors, 1964), pp. 87–107; Sheldon A. Davis, "An Organic Problem-Solving Method of Organizational Change," *Journal of Applied Behavioral Science*, vol. 3, no. 1 (1967), pp. 3–21; Cyril Sofer, *The Organization from Within* (Chicago: Quadrangle Books, 1961); Alfred J. Marrow, David G. Bowers, and Stanley E. Seashore, *Management by Participation* (New York: Harper & Row, Publishers, 1967); Robert R. Blake, Jane S. Mouton, Louis B. Barnes, and Larry E. Greiner, "Breakthrough in Organization Development," *Harvard Business Review*, vol. 42 (November–December 1964), pp. 133–55; Alton C. Bartlett, "Changing Behavior as a Means to Increased Efficiency," *Journal of Applied Behavioral Science*, vol. 3, no. 2 (1967), pp. 381–403; Larry E.

Laboratory Training and Organization Development

Since organization development programs have largely emerged from T-group experience, theory, and research, and since laboratory training in one form or another tends to be an integral part of most such programs, it is important to focus on laboratory training per se. As stated earlier, OD programs grew out of a perceived need to relate laboratory training to the problems of ongoing organizations and a recognition that optimum results could occur only if major parts of the total social system of an organization were involved.

Laboratory training essentially emerged around 1946, largely through a growing recognition by Leland Bradford, Ronald Lippitt, Kenneth Benne, and others that human relations training which focused on the feelings and concerns of the participants was frequently a much more powerful and viable form of education than the lecture method. Some of the theoretical constructs and insights from which these laboratory training pioneers drew stemmed from earlier research by Lippitt, Kurt Lewin, and Ralph White. The term "T-group" emerged by 1949 as a shortened label for "basic skill training group"; these terms were used to identify the programs which began to emerge in the newly formed National Training Laboratory in Group Development (now NTL Institute for Applied Behavioral Science).[22] "Sensitivity training" is also a term frequently applied to such training.

Ordinarily, laboratory training sessions have certain objectives in common. The following list, by two internationally known behavioral scientists,[23] is probably highly consistent with the objectives of most programs:

Greiner, "Antecedents of Planned Organization Change," *Journal of Applied Behavioral Science,* vol. 3, no. 1 (1967), pp. 51–85; and Robert R. Blake and Jane Mouton, *Corporate Excellence through Grid Organization Development* (Houston: Gulf Publishing Company, 1968).

[22] From Bradford, "Biography of an Institution." See also Kenneth D. Benne, "History of the T-Group in the Laboratory Setting," in Leland P. Bradford, Jack R. Gibb, and Kenneth D. Benne, Eds., *T-Group Theory and Laboratory Method* (New York: John Wiley & Sons, Inc., 1964), pp. 80–135.

[23] Schein and Bennis, *Personal and Organizational Change through Group Methods,* p. 37.

Self Objectives

Increased *awareness* of own feelings and reactions, and own impact on others.

Increased *awareness* of feelings and reactions of others, and their impact on self.

Increased *awareness* of dynamics of group action.

Changed attitudes toward self, others, and groups, i.e., more respect for, tolerance for, and faith in self, others, and groups.

Increased *interpersonal competence,* i.e., skill in handling interpersonal and group relationships toward more productive and satisfying relationships.

Role Objectives

Increased *awareness* of own organizational role, organizational dynamics, dynamics of larger social systems, and dynamics of the change process in self, small groups, and organizations.

Changed attitudes toward own role, role of others, and organizational relationships, i.e., more respect for and willingness to deal with others with whom one is interdependent, greater willingness to achieve collaborative relationships with others based on mutual trust.

Increased *interpersonal competence* in handling organizational role relationships with superiors, peers, and subordinates.

Organizational Objectives

Increased *awareness* of, *changed attitudes* toward, and increased *interpersonal competence* about specific organizational problems existing in groups or units which are interdependent.

Organizational improvement through the training of relationships or groups rather than isolated individuals.

Over the years, experimentation with different laboratory designs has led to diverse criteria for the selection of laboratory participants. Probably a majority of NTL–IABS human relations laboratories are "stranger groups," i.e., involving participants who come from different organizations and who are not likely to have met earlier. However, as indicated by the organizational objectives above, the incidence of special labs designed to increase the effectiveness of persons already working together appears to be growing. Thus terms like "cousin labs," i.e., labs involving people from the same organization but not the same subunit, and "family labs" or "team-building" sessions, i.e., involving a manager and all of his subordinates, are becoming familiar. Participants in labs designed for organizational members not of the same unit may be selected from the same rank level ("horizontal slice") or selected so as to constitute a heterogeneous grouping by rank ("diagonal slice"). Further, NTL–IABS is now encouraging at least two members from the same organization to attend NTL Management Work Conferences and Key Executive Conferences in order to maximize the impact of the learning in the back-home situation.[24]

In general, experienced trainers recommend that persons with severe emotional illness should not participate in laboratory training, with the exception of programs designed specifically for group therapy. Designers of programs make the assumptions, as Argyris states them,[25] that T-group participants should have:

1. A relatively strong ego that is not overwhelmed by internal conflicts.
2. Defenses which are sufficiently low to allow the individual to hear what others say to him.
3. The ability to communicate thoughts and feelings with minimal distortion.

As a result of such screening, the incidence of breakdown during laboratory training is substantially less than that reported for organizations in general.[26] However, since the border line between "normalcy" and illness is very indistinct, most professionally trained staff members are equipped to diagnose severe problems and to make referrals to psychiatrists and clinical psychologists when appropriate. Further, most are equipped to give adequate support and protection to participants whose ability to assimilate and learn from feedback is low. In addition, group members in T-group situations tend to be sensitive to the emotional needs of the members and to be supportive when they sense a person experiencing pain. Such support is explicitly fostered in laboratory training.

The duration of laboratory training programs varies widely. "Micro-labs," designed to give people a brief experience with sensitivity training, may last only one hour. Some labs are designed for a long weekend. Typically, however, basic human relations labs are of two weeks' duration, with participants expected to meet mornings, afternoons, and evenings, with some time off for recreation. While NTL Management Work Conferences for middle managers and Key Executive Conferences run for one week, team-building labs, from my experience, typically are about three days in length. However, the latter are usually only a part of a broader organization development program involving problem sensing and diagnosis, and the planning of action steps and subsequent sessions. In addition, attendance at stranger labs for key managers is frequently a part of the total organization development effort.

Sensitivity training sessions typically start with the trainer making a few comments about his role—that he is there to be of help, that the group will have control of the agenda, that he will deliberately avoid a leadership role, but that he might become involved as both a leader and a member from time to time, etc. The following is an example of what the trainer might say:

> This group will meet for many hours and will serve as a kind of laboratory where each individual can increase his understanding of the forces which influence individual behavior and the performance of groups and organizations. The data for learning will be our own behavior, feelings, and reactions. We begin with no definite structure or organization, no agreed-upon procedures, and no specific agenda. It will be up to us to fill the vacuum created by the lack of these familiar elements and to study our group as we evolve. My role will be to help the group to learn from its own experience, but not to act as a traditional chairman nor to suggest how we should organize, what our procedure should be, or exactly what our agenda will include. With these few comments, I think we are ready to begin in whatever way you feel will be most helpful.[27]

[24] For further discussion of group composition in laboratory training, see Schein and Bennis, *Personal and Organizational Change through Group Methods*, pp. 63–69. NTL–IABS now includes the Center for Organization Studies, the Center for the Development of Educational Leadership, the Center for Community Affairs, and the Center for International Training to serve a wide range of client populations and groups.

[25] Chris Argyris, "T-Groups for Organizational Effectiveness," *Harvard Business Review*, vol. 42 (March–April 1964), pp. 60–74.

[26] Based on discussions with NTL staff members. One estimate is that the incidence of "serious stress and mental disturbance" during laboratory training is less than one percent of participants and in almost all cases occurs in persons with a history of prior disturbance (Charles Seashore, "What Is Sensitivity Training," *NTL Institute News and Reports*, vol. 2 [April 1968], p. 2).

[27] Ibid., p. 1.

The trainer then lapses into silence. Group discomfort then precipitates a dialogue which, with skilled trainer assistance, is typically an intense but generally highly rewarding experience for group members. What goes on in the group becomes the data for the learning experience.

Interventions by the trainer will vary greatly depending upon the purpose of the lab and the state of learning on the part of the participants. A common intervention, however, is to encourage people to focus on and own up to their own feelings about what is going on in the group, rather than to make judgments about others. In this way, the participants begin to have more insight into their own feelings and to understand how their behavior affects the feelings of others.

While T-group work tends to be the focal point in human relations laboratories, laboratory training typically includes theory sessions and frequently includes exercises such as role playing or management games.[28] Further, family labs of subunits of organizations will ordinarily devote more time to planning action steps for back on the job than will stranger labs.

Robert J. House has carefully reviewed the research literature on the impact of T-group training and has concluded that the research shows mixed results. In particular, research on changes as reflected in personality inventories is seen as inconclusive. However, studies which examine the behavior of participants upon returning to the job are generally more positive.[29] House cites six studies, all of which utilized control groups, and concludes:

> All six studies revealed what appear to be important positive effects of T-Group training. Two of the studies report negative effects as well . . . all of the evidence is based on observations of the behavior of the participants in the actual job situations. No reliance is placed on participant response; rather, evidence is collected from those having frequent contact with the participant in his normal work activities.[30]

John P. Campbell and Marvin D. Dunnette,[31] on the other hand, while conceding that the research shows that T-group training produces *changes in behavior*, point out that the usefulness of such training in terms of *job performance* has yet to be demonstrated. They urge research toward "forging the link between training-induced behavior changes and changes in job-performance effectiveness."[32] As a summary comment, they state:

> . . . the assumption that T-Group training has positive utility for organizations must necessarily rest on shaky ground. It has been neither confirmed nor disconfirmed. The authors wish to emphasize . . . that utility for the organization is not necessarily the same as utility for the individual.[33]

At least two major reasons may account for the inconclusiveness of research on the impact of T-group training on job performance. One reason is simply that little research has been done. The other reason may center around a factor of cultural isolation. To oversimplify, a major part of what one learns in laboratory training, in my opinion, is how to work

[28] For a description of what goes on in T-groups, see Schein and Bennis, *Personal and Organizational Change through Group Methods*, pp. 10–27; Bradford, Gibb, and Benne, *T-Group Theory and Laboratory Method*, pp. 55–67; Dorothy S. Whitaker, "A Case Study of a T-Group," in Galvin Whitaker, Ed., *T-Group Training: Group Dynamics in Management Education*, A.T.M. Occasional Papers (Oxford: Basil Blackwell, 1965), pp. 14–22; Irving R. Weschler and Jerome Reisel, *Inside a Sensitivity Training Group* (Berkeley: University of California, Institute of Industrial Relations, 1959); and William F. Glueck, "Reflections on a T-Group Experience," *Personnel Journal*, vol. 47 (July 1968), pp. 501–4. For use of cases or exercises based on research results ("instrumented training"), see Robert R. Blake and Jane S. Mouton, "The Instrumented Training Laboratory," in Irving R. Weschler and Edgar H. Schein, Eds., *Five Issues in Training* (Washington, D.C.: National Training Laboratories, 1962), pp. 61–76; and W. Warner Burke and Harvey A. Hornstein, "Conceptual vs. Experiential Management Training," *Training and Development Journal*, vol. 21 (December 1967), pp. 12–17.

[29] Robert J. House, "T-Group Education and Leadership Effectiveness: A Review of the Empiric Literature and a Critical Evaluation," *Personnel Psychology*, vol. 20 (Spring 1967), pp. 1–32. See also Dorothy Stock, "A Survey of Research on T-Groups," in Bradford, Gibb, and Benne, *T-Group Theory and Laboratory Method*, pp. 395–441.

[30] House, "T-Group Education and Leadership Effectiveness," pp. 18–19.

[31] John P. Campbell and Marvin D. Dunnette, "Effectiveness of T-Group Experiences in Managerial Training and Development," *Psychological Bulletin*, vol. 70 (August 1968), pp. 73–104.

[32] Ibid., p. 100.

[33] Ibid., p. 101. See also the essays by Marvin D. Dunnette and Campbell and Chris Argyris in *Industrial Relations*, vol. 8 (October 1968), pp. 1–45.

more effectively with others in group situations, *particularly with others who have developed comparable skills*. Unfortunately, most participants return from T-group experiences to environments including colleagues and superiors who have not had the same affective (emotional, feeling) experiences, who are not familiar with the terminology and underlying theory, and who may have anxieties (usually unwarranted) about what might happen to them in a T-group situation.

This cultural distance which laboratory training can produce is one of the reasons why many behavioral scientists are currently encouraging more than one person from the same organization to undergo T-group training and, ideally, *all* of the members of a team and their superior to participate in some kind of laboratory training together. The latter assumes that a diagnosis of the organization indicates that the group is ready for such training and assumes such training is reasonably compatible with the broader culture of the total system.

Conditions and Techniques for Successful Organization Development Programs

Theory, research, and experience to date suggest to me that *successful* OD programs tend to evolve in the following way and that they have some of these characteristics (these statements should be considered highly tentative, however):

There is strong pressure for improvement both from outside the organization and from within.[34]

An outside behavioral scientist–consultant is brought in for consultation with the top executives and to diagnose organizational problems.

A preliminary diagnosis suggests that organization development efforts, designed in response to the expressed needs of the key executives, are warranted.

A collaborative decision is made between the key client group and the consultant to try to change the culture of the organization, at least at the top initially. The specific goals may be to improve communications, to secure more effective participation from

subordinates in problem solving, and to move in the direction of more openness, more feedback, and more support. In short, a decision is made to change the culture to help the company meet its organizational goals and to provide better avenues for initiative, creativity, and self-actualization on the part of organization members.

Two or more top executives, including the chief executive, go to laboratory training sessions. (Frequently, attendance at labs is one of the events which precipitates interest in bringing in the outside consultant.)

Attendance in T-group program is voluntary. While it is difficult to draw a line between persuasion and coercion, OD consultants and top management should be aware of the dysfunctional consequences of coercion (see the comments on authentic behavior below). While a major emphasis is on team-building laboratories, stranger labs are utilized both to supplement the training going on in the organization and to train managers new to the organization or those who are newly promoted.

Team-building sessions are held with the top executive group (or at the highest point where the program is started). Ideally, the program is started at the top of the organization, but it can start at levels below the president as long as there is significant support from the chief executive, and preferably from other members of the top power structure as well.

In a firm large enough to have a personnel executive, the personnel–industrial relations vice president becomes heavily involved at the outset.

One of two organizational forms emerges to coordinate organization development efforts, either (*a*) a coordinator reporting to the personnel executive (the personnel executive himself may fill this role), or (*b*) a coordinator reporting to the chief executive. The management development director is frequently in an ideal position to coordinate OD activities with other management development activities.

Ultimately, it is essential that the personnel–industrial relations group, including people in salary administration, be an integral part of the organization development program. Since OD groups have such potential for acting as catalysts in rapid organizational change, the temptation is great to see themselves as "good guys" and the other personnel people as "bad

---

[34] On this point, see Larry E. Greiner, "Patterns of Organization Change," *Harvard Business Review*, vol. 45 (May–June 1967), pp. 119–30.

guys'' or simply ineffective. Any conflicts between a separate organization development group and the personnel and industrial relations groups should be faced and resolved. Such tensions can be the ''Achilles heel'' for either program. In particular, however, the change agents in the organization development program need the support of the other people who are heavily involved in human resources administration and vice versa; what is done in the OD program needs to be compatible with what is done in selection, promotion, salary administration, appraisal, and vice versa. In terms of systems theory, it would seem imperative that one aspect of the human resources function such as any organization development program must be highly interdependent with the other human resources activities including selection, salary administration, etc. (TRW Systems is an example of an organization which involves top executives plus making the total personnel and industrial relations group an integral part of the OD program.[35])

Team-building labs, at the request of the various respective executives, with laboratory designs based on careful data gathering and problem diagnosis, are conducted at successively lower levels of the organization with the help of outside consultants, plus the help of internal consultants whose expertise is gradually developed.

Ideally, as the program matures, both members of the personnel staff and a few line executives are trained to do some organization development work in conjunction with the external and internal professionally trained behavioral scientists. In a sense, then, the external change agent tries to work himself out of a job by developing internal resources.

The outside consultant(s) and the internal coordinator work very carefully together and periodically check on fears, threats, and anxieties which may be developing as the effort progresses. Issues need to be confronted as they emerge. Not only is the outside change agent needed for his skills, but the organization will need someone to act as a ''governor''—to keep the program focused on real problems and to urge authenticity in contrast to gamesmanship. The danger always exists that the organization will begin to

punish or reward involvement in T-group kinds of activities per se, rather than focus on performance.

The OD consultants constantly work on their own effectiveness in interpersonal relationships and their diagnostic skills so they are not in a position of ''do as I say, but not as I do.'' Further, both consultant and client work together to optimize the consultant's knowledge of the organization's unique and evolving culture and structure and web of interpersonal relationships.

There needs to be continuous audit of the results, both in terms of checking on the evolution of attitudes about what is going on and in terms of the extent to which problems which were identified at the outset by the key clients are being solved through the program.

As implied above, the reward system and other personnel systems need to be readjusted to accommodate emerging changes in performance in the organization. Substantially improved performance on the part of individuals and groups is not likely to be sustained if financial and promotional rewards are not forthcoming. In short, management needs to have a ''systems'' point of view and to think through the interrelationships of the OD effort with the reward and staffing systems and the other aspects of the total human resources subsystem.

In the last analysis, the president and the ''line'' executives of the organization will evaluate the success of the OD effort in terms of the extent to which it assists the organization in meeting its human and economic objectives. For example, marked improvements on various indices from one plant, one division, one department, etc., will be important indicators of program success. While human resources administration indices are not yet perfected, some of the measuring devices being developed by Likert, Mann, and others show some promise.[36]

Summary Comments

Organization development efforts have emerged through attempts to apply laboratory training values and assumptions to total systems. Such efforts are organic in the sense that they emerge from and are

[35] See Davis, ''An Organic Problem-Solving Method.''

[36] See Rensis Likert, *The Human Organization: Its Management and Value* (New York: McGraw-Hill Book Company, 1967).

guided by the problems being experienced by the people in the organization. The key to their viability (in contrast to becoming a passing fad) lies in an authentic focus on problems and concerns of the members of the organization and in their confrontation of issues and problems.

Organization development is based on assumptions and values similar to "Theory Y" assumptions and values but includes additional assumptions about total systems and the nature of the client–consultant relationship. Intervention strategies of the behavioral scientist–change agent tend to be based on an action-research model and tend to be focused more on helping the people in an organization learn to solve problems rather than on prescriptions of how things should be done differently.

Laboratory training (or sensitivity training) or modifications of T-group seminars typically are a part of the organizational change efforts, but the extent and format of such training will depend upon the evolving needs of the organization. Team-building seminars involving a superior and subordinates are being utilized more and more as a way of changing social systems rapidly and avoiding the cultural distance problems which frequently emerge when individuals return from stranger labs. However, stranger labs can play a key role in change efforts when they are used as part of a broader organization development effort.

Research has indicated that sensitivity training generally produces positive results in terms of changed behavior on the job, but has not demonstrated the link between behavior changes and improved performance. Maximum benefits are probably derived from laboratory training when the organizational culture supports and reinforces the use of new skills in ongoing team situations.

Successful organization development efforts require skillful behavioral scientist interventions, a systems view, and top management support and involvement. In addition, changes stemming from organization development must be linked to changes in the total personnel subsystem. The viability of organization development efforts lies in the degree to which they accurately reflect the aspirations and concerns of the participating members.

In conclusion, *successful organization development tends to be a total system effort; a process of planned change—not a program with a temporary quality; and aimed at developing the organization's internal resources for effective change in the future.*

Resistance to Change—Its Analysis and Prevention

Alvin Zander

In order to derive the benefits from research in industrial relations, someone must plan a program of action to apply them. When one begins implementing, he must change the social system in some way. The creation of this change can cause the development of resistance in those influenced by the change.

First, we shall look at what resistance is; second, the conditions that appear to be associated with its development; and third, some means whereby resistance may be prevented or decreased.

Nature of Resistance

Let us look at some examples of resistance growing out of administrative changes.

A large number of foremen in a company were given training in how to treat their men like human beings. They liked the course and were eager to apply their learnings on the job. The company found, however, that relatively few of the foremen were really behaving any differently on the job. They know their stuff but do not use it.

In one of the paper-shuffling government agencies a new data form was developed which all admitted was briefer, more logical, and easier to use. Yet, this department found that the employees often omitted much of the data needed on this form, their speed of work decreased, and they objected to it on many significant grounds.

Our favorite example of resistance was furnished by a farmer in the TVA area. He assured us that he knew all about contour plowing, the rotation of crops, and the use of what he called "phosaphate" for improving

the soil. He allowed as how these were good ideas, "But," he said, "I don't do it that way."

These examples have one common denominator which might serve here as a definition of resistance. They describe behavior which is intended to protect an individual from the effects of real or imagined change. This reaction might be to either real or imagined change since the resister might be reacting to things that were really not changed but he thinks were, or fears that they might be. If a person believes a change has been made, or fears potential change, it makes no difference whether or not it is true in fact. He will act as though there has been a change.

How can one recognize when resistance is working? Unfortunately, there is no list of typical behavior which can be described as the symptoms of resistance, which, if present, indicate that one is dealing with this phenomenon. It is the protective function which the behavior is providing which determines whether or not a person is resisting, rather than the kind of thing he does. By the same token, all behavior which opposes change is not necessarily resistance. Some opposition to change may be perfectly logical and grounded on well supported reasons. The behavior must be attempting to protect the person against the consequences of the change in order for it to be resistance. This may be clearer if we look at the origin of the concept.

The Hostility Pattern

The term and the concept we are using here has been borrowed from psychotherapy. When a therapist is attempting to change the behavior of the patient, he expects resistance from him. The therapist takes the position that the pattern of behavior used by the patient (which makes him a "sick" person) is a means to some satisfaction for him even though it also may make him ineffective or unhappy. Resistance occurs in the patient when the process of change (therapy here) comes close to being successful. When faced with the unpleasant necessity of giving up the behavior he does not like, but somehow needs, he begins to balk. He becomes silent, blushes, changes the subject, tells fibs, comes late to appointments, becomes angry with the therapist, or any of a number of similar things. The therapist watches for the context in which these signs of resistance occur since these indicate the crucial problems in the way the patient sees and deals with his world.

For the administrator, resistance may occur under fairly similar conditions. When he attempts to create a change the administrator may develop, unintentionally, many threats to the person or groups with whom he works. The behavior used by the resister may take many forms.

It may take the form of hostility either openly expressed or obliquely implied. The aggression may be directed against the change itself or against the administrator. What is done depends on how the person can safely resist without further endangering himself in that situation. Other symptoms of resistance may be sloppy effort after the change has been made, or fawning submissiveness which is a hybrid of apple-polishing and apathy. It can occur by lowering the level of aspiration to an inefficient degree, discouragement, or the development of unhappy cliques and outspoken factions. It is important however, to remind ourselves that it is the function which such actions are performing for the person that makes them resistant rather than what they look like.

Where Resistance Starts

It will be helpful if we look at a few conditions conducive to resistance.

1. Resistance can be expected if the nature of the change is not made clear to the people who are going to be influenced by the change. In one of the largest government agencies, a change required one department, which originally had the responsibility of processing paper involved in contacts with certain industries, to share this task with another office. An-

nouncement of the change was issued in a brief statement. The immediate reaction was violent objection, even though some of the workers privately admitted that it was a wise and necessary move. They were reacting to incomplete information. Many people fear incomplete information about changes which influence them. It is more comfortable to know exactly where one stands.

There is some evidence to support the hypothesis that those persons who dislike their jobs will most dislike ambiguity in a proposed change. They want to know exactly what they must do in order to be sure to avoid the unpleasant aspects of their jobs. Some administrators may attach too much importance to the value of information itself. Apparently they reason that people "ought not" to resist the way they do because the administrator has told them everything he thinks is important for them to know about the impending change.

2. Different people will see different meanings in the proposed change. Some of the resistant reaction described above came about because some workers saw the change as an indication that they had been doing a poor job, others assumed it meant their office would soon be abolished, still others were troubled since they were losing some of the power they had formerly controlled. We tend to see in our world the things that we expect to see. Complete information can just as readily be distorted as incomplete information, especially if the workers have found discomfort and threats in their past work situation.

3. Resistance can be expected when those influenced are caught in a jam between strong forces pushing them to make the change and strong forces deterring them against making the change.

4. Resistance may be expected to the degree that the persons influenced by the change have pressure put upon them to make it, and will be decreased to the degree that these same persons are able to have some "say" in the nature or direction of the change. In a garment factory a change was required. The switch meant that workers would be asked to change their jobs and, in many cases, to develop working relationships with new people. An experiment was made in which three different styles of introducing this change were tried out. One group of workers were simply in-

formed about the change and were allowed to ask questions. They developed the most resistance as measured by turnover, absenteeism, and slowness in learning the job. Resistance was *less* in those groups who sent representatives to a meeting in which the nature of the change was discussed and all persons present made plans to carry out the change.

Resistance was *least* in the groups in which those to be affected discussed the nature of the change, laid plans for making it, and as a total group made decisions which were satisfactory to the entire group. In this latter group everyone participated. They had an opportunity to develop their own motivation instead of making the change only on the basis of orders from the boss. The fact that they were able to develop their own understanding of the need for the change and their own decisions about how to do it reduced resistance most effectively.

5. Resistance may be expected if the change is made on personal grounds rather than impersonal requirements or sanctions. A supervisor posted the following notice:

> I have always felt that promptness is an important indicator of an employee's interest in his job. I will feel much better if you are at your desk at the proper time.

Employees responded to this notice by appointing a committee to get information which would justify their late arrival at the office. Many administrators can expect trouble in establishing a change if it is requested in terms of what ''I think is necessary,'' rather than making the request in the light of ''our objectives,'' the rules, the present state of affairs, or some other impersonal requirement.

6. Resistance may be expected if the change ignores the already established institutions in the group. Every work situation develops certain customs in doing the work or in the relations among the workers. The administrator who ignores institutionalized patterns of work and abruptly attempts to create a new state of affairs which demands that these customs be abolished without further consideration will surely run into resistance.

These are a few of the conditions in which resistance might be expected to occur. There probably are many others.

Decreasing Resistance

Some procedures on the part of the administrator might be useful in preventing or decreasing the resistance which arises in a changed situation. Let us look at a major principle in preventing resistance and some of its basic implications:

> Resistance will be prevented to the degree that the changer helps the changees to develop their own understanding of the need for the change, and an explicit awareness of how they feel about it, and what can be done about those feelings.

This principle implies that the administrator can use resistance as an important symptom. Specifically, he can use the nature of the resistance as an indicator of the cause of the resistance. It will be most helpful to him as a symptom if he diagnoses the causes for it when it occurs rather than inhibiting it at once. The same resistant behavior, for example, may indicate that one person feels that he has lost prestige by the change, to another it may mean that he has lost power over an area of influence which he formerly controlled, and to still another it may mean that he fears that his friends will think less well of him. An administrator must know what the resistance means in order that he may effectively lessen it by working on the causes instead of the symptom.

There has been a good deal of experience in recent years in staff meetings and in work conferences like the National Training Laboratory for Group Development with the use of a group observer. This observer gives to the group, and the leaders, information about the group and the nature of any resistance. In these cases, the data about itself is made common group property for all members to discuss and to use in planning better work relations.

This communication must go in both directions. If two-way communication is not maintained, negative attitudes created during resistance will tend to persist.

Restoring Understanding

In a utility company a new office was formed with a new set of supervisors. The entire staff of supervisors called the workers together and scolded them for shortcomings in their performance. The tone used by the supervisors was so aggressive that the employees found it difficult thereafter to discuss anything with them except those topics directly related to the effectiveness of production. The workers kept themselves at a distance from the supervisors and the supervisors made no move to close the gap. The result was that distance between these two groups made it impossible for them to come to any new understanding of each other. This mounting hostility was lessened only when the personnel department advised a number of "gripe-sessions" with small groups of workers in which the two levels developed a new understanding of each other.

Another implication in the above principle is that there is value in blowing off steam. The psychologists call this a "catharsis." There is good evidence that new attitudes can be accepted by a person only if he has a chance to thoroughly air his original attitude. Resistance to accepting the rigid, and often apparently meaningless, rules of military life showed itself in flagrant violation of the rule, often in a most aggressive manner. Punishment only increased the resistance. Relief was provided by group sessions in which men were able to thoroughly gripe. After this relief of tension, they were able to turn to a reasonable discussion about what they could do to learn to live in terms of these requirements. It is as though new air can be put in the tire only after the old air is released.

A third implication of the earlier expressed principle is that resistance may be less likely to occur if the group participates in making the decisions about how the change should be implemented, what the change should be like, how people might perform in the changed situation, or any other problems that are within their area of freedom to decide. The experiment in which three ways of introducing a change were tried out showed that the workers, who had a chance to make a group decision about the ways in which the change should be made, developed much less resistance than did those who were simply called together to be told about the change and have all of their questions answered. What is important here is that the workers feel that they have a chance to discuss

the major factors involved in the change, a chance to understand the nature of the fears they have in facing this change, and a chance to plan what they will do to calm their fears.

Self-Diagnosis Gets Action

Still another implication is that resistance will be less likely to develop if facts which point to the need for change are gathered by the persons who must make the change. A number of high-level supervisors in a utility industry came to feel that the workers had many negative attitudes about their jobs which were due to poor supervisory practices. Each supervisor, quite naturally, felt that other supervisors were at fault. Top management set up a number of study groups in which the supervisors first learned how they could diagnose the causes of these negative attitudes. Each supervisor then returned to his own work place and gathered facts that would be necessary for him to analyze the causes of negative attitudes he could spot among his workers. Later the supervisors came together to report their findings. At this meeting their enthusiasm for change in their own practices was high because they had participated in gathering the facts which best described their problems. People will be more likely to act in terms of information they gather themselves than in terms of information gathered by others and delivered to them. If it is clear that a change is indicated in a given state of affairs but the people who must abide by the change are resisting the shift, they can come to see it themselves by obtaining the facts which properly "case" the situation.

To summarize, we have said that resistance is a problem which any person who is responsible for social change must face. Even though it is strange and unexpected behavior, there are causes for the development of this phenomenon. These causes may be understood, and resistance may be prevented, if the administrator will help the changees develop their own understanding of the need for change and explicit awareness of how they feel about it and what can be done about those feelings.

Action-Research as Applied to Organization Development

Mark A. Frohman, Marshall Sashkin, and Michael J. Kavanagh

The field of organization development (OD) has gained increasing popularity in recent years. Certain "prepackaged" OD programs, such as Grid OD (Blake and Mouton, 1968), recent variants of MBO (Beck and Hillmar, 1972), and laboratory training programs (Schein and Bennis, 1965), have attained particular prominence and use, for at least four reasons. First, some OD practitioners may have a favorite development technique; therefore, they do not consider using other action strategies. For example, a particular OD consultant may have had experiences which lead him to conclude that all organization members need to receive training in openness, self-examination of assumptions and values, and feedback of others' perceptions of them. As a result, he may consistently prescribe sensitivity training to improve the operation of an organization.

A second reason is based on the desire of some OD consultants to specialize in certain specific OD activities. Thus, one consultant may concentrate on the application of team training in situations where some diagnosis has indicated the need for such a program.

Third, extensive diagnosis of an organization takes time, and a client—feeling some degree of pain and, therefore, pressure for help and action—is often unwilling to accept any delay in action. Thus, the client may call upon a management consultant who will promptly analyze the problem and provide immediate recommendations for its solution.

Finally, the client may argue that he *knows* what the problem is and does not require the investment of time, money, and manpower to undertake diagnostic

From *Organization and Administrative Sciences*, vol. 7, nos. 1 and 2 (Spring/Summer 1976), pp. 129–42. By permission of The Kent State University Press.

research for purposes of action planning; after all, a consultant is called in to help "improve" the organization, not to spend time "researching" what is already known.

These arguments all have some merit. As a result of the demands, needs, and resources of the consultant or the client, a direct application of some prepackaged OD program may be decided upon. Furthermore, this may achieve satisfactory results. However, several potentially negative outcomes are associated with the reasoning presented above.

One negative consequence is that many people view OD in a very limited way. The notion that a weekend sensitivity session or a one-week Grid program comprises the entire OD effort seems ingrained in many executives. As a result of this limited management perspective, many OD programs are doomed to failure from the beginning in that the OD effort is approached piecemeal, or nonsystemically. For example, many Grid programs and laboratory training sessions are run for a limited number of persons, excluding either whole departments or the top-management levels of an organization (Sykes, 1962). Nonsystemic OD efforts show a clear pattern of failure (Greiner, Leitch, and Barnes, 1968), and their effects seem to quickly "wash out" (Fleishman, 1953).

A second negative consequence is a tendency toward overconcern with the *content* of the organizational change to the exclusion of the *processes* involved. For example, members of the organization may be enthralled by the Managerial Grid diagram and consequently ignore the important interpersonal and task behaviors being subjected to the change activity; or, a top-management group planning a major reorganization may focus on the quality and elegance of the new organizational structure chart and ignore

197

the implications of the change relative to the interrelationships and role perceptions of the people in the organization.

A final consequence of the prepackaged approach is that many OD efforts are *nonadaptive;* that is, once a commitment is made to use a specific OD technique or program, the organization may retain it even though the effects of the attempted change may be minimal or, even worse, in a negative direction. This lack of flexibility in many OD programs results from approaching the organization as a static rather than a dynamic entity. Even though the organization itself may change over time as the result of an OD effort, many prepackaged programs are not designed to change with the changing circumstances in the organization.

This paper will describe a model of organizational development called action-research OD. It is aimed at correcting the above deficiencies (a nonsystemic approach, overemphasis on content, and lack of adaptive flexibility). The reader is, therefore, cautioned that the present report is *not* aimed at a comparative analysis of the processes and outcomes of different OD approaches. There is a great need for such information, of course. Sashkin, Morris, and Horst (1973) have provided a theoretical analysis, and Bowers (1973) has presented some research data; however, little work has yet been accomplished in this area.

In presenting the action-research OD approach, it will be necessary to first define action-research and its application to the field of organization development. The stages and processes involved in action-research OD will then be identified and examined in terms of studies involving this approach.

Action-Research

The term "action-research" is not new. Historically, it can be traced to the work of Collier (1945), and of Lewin (1946) and his students (Lippitt, 1950). Others (Corey, 1953; French and Bell, 1973) have provided historical descriptions of the development of the action-research model. Action-research describes a particular process model whereby behavioral science knowledge is applied to help a client (usually a group or social system) solve real problems and not inciden-

tally learn the processes involved in problem solving. At the same time, it generates further knowledge in the field of applied behavioral sciences. Collier (1945), discussing Indian affairs in the United States, described action-research as follows:

> . . . in the ethnic field, research can be made a tool of action essential to all other tools, indeed, . . . it ought to [be] the master tool. But we had in mind a particular kind of research, or if you will, particular conditions. We had in mind research impelled from central areas of needed action. . . . Since the findings of the research must be carried into effect by the administrator and the layman, and must be criticized by them through their experience, the administrator and the layman must themselves participate creatively in the research, impelled as it is from their own area of need. (p. 275)

The action-research model is based on collaboration between the behavioral scientist–researcher and the client. They collaborate in exploring problems and generating valid data concerning the problems (research activity); in examining the information to understand the problems and develop action plans for their solution; in actually implementing these plans; and in generating data regarding the effects of the action. Thus, the accurate evaluation of results can be accomplished. Evaluation of results may (and generally would) be followed by further problem diagnosis, action, planning, action implementation, and evaluation. By means of repetitions of this cycle, real problems are resolved and the client learns to use a science-based model of problem solving.

There is, however, a second aspect to the research process defined by the model, as noted by Lewin (1946). In addition to providing effective solutions to specific client problems and developing new problem-solving skills for the client, a successful action-research project generates new behavioral science knowledge which is fed back into the professional bank of information and used by other behavioral scientists. This new knowledge is obtained through the research activity of the applied behavioral scientist. It may deal with general laws about human behavior, or the type of problems with which the client is confronted, or the process of consultant-client collaboration. In any case, it addresses issues broader than the specific problems faced by the client.

Action-Research and Organization Development

There are a variety of approaches to organization development. We disagree with French and Bell (1973), who state that the action-research model is basic and common to all effective OD efforts. Action-research OD is one of a variety of OD approaches. In general, OD involves the application of behavioral science knowledge in organizations, through client-consultant collaboration, for the purpose of creating effective and lasting changes in the system (i.e., adaptive responses to organizational problems). While there is some overlap between our descriptions of action-research and OD, there are also some elements present in one but not the other. Table 1 summarizes these similarities and differences.

Let us now see how the approaches described in Table 1 might be united, or how action-research can be tied to an OD approach. The action-research approach as applied to OD involves data collection interventions by an OD practitioner in collaboration with the client. Thus, working together they can obtain useful information which will enable them to jointly: develop and implement action plans for change in the client system; evaluate the effects and effectiveness of these action plans; and based on these evaluations, create and implement further action plans. The ultimate aims of the changes are increased organizational effectiveness and the development of internal organizational resources for creating adaptive, problem-solving change. The total process is based on the interlocking, interdependent, and interactive processes of research (data collection and evaluation) and action (directed intervention and implementation of change).

PHASES OF ACTION-RESEARCH OD

We have described action-research as a cyclical-sequential model, proceeding through several phases of research and action. These phases are briefly listed and defined, in the context of OD practice, in Table 2. In some respects, our phases are similar to other models (e.g., Lippitt, Watson, and Westley, 1958). We will discuss each phase in some detail.

Scouting. As Lippitt, Watson, and Westley (1958) note, the change agent, consultant, or OD practitioner generally has an implicit "descriptive-analytic theory," a frame of reference (or bias) which he uses to arrange and interpret information about the organiza-

TABLE 1
Comparison of Descriptive Factors in Action-Research and in Organization Development

Organization Development	Both	Action-Research
May involve data-based diagnosis of organization problems	Involve the planned application of behavioral science knowledge based on consultant-client collaboration	Emphasizes data-based diagnosis of system problems
Is aimed at producing effective and lasting system change	Involve the use of groups	Is aimed at solving system problems as a means of improving problem-solving skills of the client
Often involves application of a preplanned "package" of actions	Recognize that any action with respect to a client system is an intervention and may have some effect on the client system	Rarely involves application of a preplanned "package"; specific actions generally are developed on the basis of specific problems
May involve training the client in the application of effective processes of change		
May or may not include evaluation of results—effects and effectiveness of efforts—in concrete terms		Emphasizes training the client in effective problem-solving skills and procedures
Often does not result in new behavioral science knowledge		Usually does result in new behavioral science knowledge

TABLE 2
Summary of Phases in Action-Research

Action-Research Phase	Emphasis	Aim
Scouting	Research	Arriving at a decision of whether or not to enter
Entry	Action	Establishing a collaborative relationship, initial problem exploration, and selecting data collection/feedback
Data collection	Research	Developing measures of organization variables and processes
Data feedback	Action	Returning data to the client system for discussion and diagnosis
Diagnosis	Research	Understanding the state of the system and problems
Action planning	Action	Developing specific action plans, including determining who will implement the plans and how the effects will be evaluated
Action implementation	Action	Implementing specific change plans
Evaluation	Research	Determining effects and effectiveness of action implementation, leading to further efforts or to termination

tion and which has implications regarding the interventions he will choose to make in the client system. It is important that the OD practitioner consciously understands his own analytic framework, and equally important that the elements of the framework which are of significance to the client be made explicit to the client. Thus, the practitioner-client relationship is collaborative from the beginning. The practitioner exposes his assumptions, biases, and values and receives feedback from the client about how the above factors fit or fail to fit the frame of understanding of the client system members. The concept of scouting is drawn from a model developed by Kolb and Frohman (1970). In the scouting phase, the OD practitioner develops an initial "fix" on the significant characteristics and problems of the client system. He then makes an initial application of his "descriptive-analytic theory" to organize and understand these facts. The general information of interest to the OD practitioner at this point includes various characteristics of the client system (e.g., product or service, structure, size, technology, demographic char-

acteristics of organization members, types of customers, external environmental relationships, prior OD experience) and descriptions of the problem(s) initially perceived by the client. Obtaining these data constitutes the major work of the scouting phase. Such data will play a major role in the client and consultant mutually deciding whether they will enter into a formal relationship and, if so, at what point in the organization the entry will be made.

Entry. The process of establishing a collaborative and open OD practitioner-client relationship and clearly defining the expectations of the parties (Frohman, 1968) is the major focus of the entry phase. The major emphases at this point are establishing the credibility of the OD practitioner and making certain that those in power positions in the client system openly sanction the OD activity. The lack of such open sanction is a nearly certain guarantee that the OD effort will fail (Clark, 1972). In such an event, any OD actions which occur are likely to be carried out in a nonsystemic manner.

Data Collection. The "prediagnostic" examination of problems during scouting and entry is collaborative in nature and useful for exploring the implications of collecting data about the client system and the problems it faces. Note that such prediagnosis during the first two phases is primarily the product of the OD practitioner. The third phase, data collection, involves client system members to a greater extent—first, in selecting a method and deciding how it will be used, and second, in the actual collection of information (which will inevitably involve client system members via interviews, questionnaire responses, and observations of their behavior, or some combination of these methods). French and Bell (1973) provide a set of excellent reference tables on data gathering for diagnosis, typologized by system level and by the organizational process of major concern, and including types of information which should be obtained and common methods for doing so.

The first three phases are focused primarily on research activities but, nonetheless, involve certain action interventions which may have some impact on the client system. Some research data, which will be reviewed (Frohman and Waters, 1969), suggest that entry and data collection in and of themselves have little, if any, impact on the client system. These early phases are within the broader phase of social-system change that Lewin (1947) called "unfreezing," or developing a need for change and establishing a client-consultant change relationship (Lippitt, Watson, and Westley, 1958). These are necessary (but not sufficient) conditions for effective organizational change.

Data Feedback. If diagnosis of problems and action planning are to be collaborative activities (as prescribed by the action-research model), the OD practitioner must fully share with the client the data which are gathered. There are a variety of options for accomplishing this, which we will not detail here. Most, however, involve some form of group or work-team meeting. It is during the data feedback phase that interventions may have some real impact on the client system (Bowers, 1971b; A. L. Frohman, 1970), although such effects do not seem to be of major significance.

Feedback provides the client with information about the client system, information which is useful in determining the strengths and weaknesses of that system. Therefore, this fourth phase, data feedback, is intimately tied with the next phase, diagnosis. It is quite artificial to treat them separately; however, there are two reasons for doing so. First, the feedback of data to the client is the first activity of the OD practitioner which is *primarily an action intervention* in the client system, as opposed to the phases described earlier and the next phase, which primarily involve research activities (Brown, 1972). Second, we want to describe the action-research OD process as clearly as possible, and this separation may aid the reader in following and understanding the nature and logic of the model. In practice, data feedback and diagnosis often occur at the same time.

The artificiality of the clear-cut separation of phases is further highlighted by considering the interdependent and interactive nature of the phases. Data collection and data feedback are obviously interdependent; one must collect data if one is to share those data with the client. The phases are also interactive; hence, the feedback targets will, in part, determine the types of data to be collected, while the data obtained will, in part, determine the best presentation or feedback methods.

Diagnosis. The focus of the process shifts back to research as the client system members and the OD practitioner jointly use the data to define and explore organizational problems and strengths. This diagnostic process is very different from the general meaning of "diagnosis." The medical-clinical model defines diagnosis as an activity by the consultant (or physician), who is solely responsible for the specific diagnostic conclusions. In action-research OD, diagnosis is a joint activity of the consultant and the client (Sashkin, 1973). Note that this collaborative diagnosis is no less data based than the traditional form—it is the collaborative nature of the process that is critically different.

An adequate diagnostic process will lead directly to implications for the actions needed to resolve the problems. However, a conclusion that further data are needed for accurate diagnosis is quite possible, in which case the action-research process will "recycle" to the data collection phase. Finally, this research phase of diagnosis is directly and interactively linked to the subsequent action phase (action planning), just as the research phase of data collection is closely linked to the following action-oriented phase (data feedback).

Action Planning. This and the next phase shift the focus of the action-research OD model back to action. The involvement of the client is increased during this phase in that the client participates in planning change activities. At this point, the role of the OD practitioner becomes one of a process helper and a trainer, rather than a consultant-expert. If the OD practitioner solves the client's problems as an "expert," an effective change might take place; but the client will learn little of the skills or processes involved in dealing with problems in the organization—a major goal of many OD programs. Thus, it is at this point that the OD practitioner's aim of developing internal problem-solving skills and resources becomes operationalized.

In accomplishing this aim, the OD practitioner walks a tightrope: he must help in the presentation (feedback), interpretation (diagnosis), and exploration (action planning) of specific data, but he must avoid being cast in the role of expert problem solver. Specific action plans must be created by the client with the assistance of the OD practitioner, not presented to the client by the expert-consultant.

Action Implementation. This and the preceding two phases fall within the broader phase of social-system change that Lewin (1947) called "moving." By altering certain social forces and removing or introducing others, the social system may be moved toward a new state or "quasi-stationary equilibrium," in Lewin's terms.

The action implementation phase involves the most actively directed OD efforts. One cannot, however, be very specific as to the actual content of the changes. This is because the content of the action implementation phase, the specific actions taken and changes made, depends on the situation and the nature of the problems diagnosed. Thus, the variety of possible action steps is wide in range. Some OD practitioners have produced catalogs of action interventions which can serve as useful reference sources (Fordyce and Weil, 1971; Pfeiffer and Jones, 1970, 1971, 1972a,

1972b); however, the specific plan chosen must be based on situational determinants. Regardless of the content chosen, the primary concern here is with the process of implementation. In this process, the model again specifies active collaboration between client and OD practitioner.

The actions taken may depend greatly on the skills and resources of the OD practitioner or may be developed almost entirely by the client. Essentially, this means that the professional action-oriented resources of the OD practitioner are not ignored; but the decision to use the change agent in specific ways is reached jointly, by the client *and* the consultant. Thus the OD practitioner may develop and implement a team-training laboratory for certain groups in the client system. A decision to do so, however, would be based on *collaborative* diagnostic and action-planning activities; such action would not be taken on the basis of a consultant recommendation, but rather on the basis of mutual problem exploration, need definition, and examination of various alternative actions. An example of an action implementation carried out primarily by the client would be the decision to institute weekly cross-department coordination and problem-solving meetings. The consultant might offer assistance in conducting such meetings, but the primary action would be accomplished by the client. The decision to implement this specific action would have been made in the same way as the earlier example—through a process of client-consultant collaboration.

The development of action plans requires attention to two major factors. The first is that the action plan must contain an adequately detailed description of what is to be done, who is to do what part, and when. The second factor, too often omitted in OD practice, is that there must be *continual monitoring* of the effects of the action intervention. This must be done throughout the action-research OD process and most particularly with regard to the specific problem-solving actions planned and implemented in this and the preceding phases of the process. Thus, the model ends with a direct link back to research—the evaluation phase.

Evaluation. The action plan should specify, in detail, evaluation procedures to be implemented during and followng the preceding phase. All too often consultants and OD practitioners seem satisfied with little more than guesses as to the effects and effectiveness of actions in and on the client system. But thorough evaluation is an absolute necessity for both the consultant and the client for several reasons. First, a data-based evaluation will indicate to the consultant whether the specific change efforts have been successful. Second, the same data will be needed by the client system as a basis for further diagnosis and action planning (recycling). Third, the empirical data will help the client and the OD practitioner determine when it is appropriate that their relationship be ended. And finally, only a well-designed evaluation phase can determine whether and when the primary, overall goal of the OD effort has been achieved: the development of internal client system resources with skills for creating effective, adaptive, problem-solving change in the future.

"Refreezing" (Lewin, 1947) has been one term used to describe this primary goal. Unfortunately, it carries the connotation of a fixed, unchanging, and unchangeable end state. Moreover, Lewin's use of the term was in reference to the attainment and continuation of specific changes, rather than to the development of increased and more effective adaptability on the part of the client system. A. L. Frohman's (1970) term, "integration," seems more appropriate but lacks descriptive detail. Lippitt, Watson, and Westley's (1958) term, "stabilization and generalization of change," is more descriptive but omits the focus on evaluation and recycling. An extension of this term to "stabilization of specific, effective changes and generalization of the action-research OD process" seems to best describe the desirable end-state of action-research OD.

ACTION-RESEARCH OD PROCESSES

The reader should be aware that the preceding discussion on the phases of action-research OD repesents the content of this approach. Earlier, one possible general deficiency of organization development activities was identified as a concern with content to the exclusion of process. The OD practitioner could, for example, follow the phases outlined but still fail to use the action-research OD model because he omitted the critical processes or attended to these processes without possessing the required skills to do so effectively. The real strength of the action-research OD approach is its emphasis on the processes involved in the client-consultant relationship. Thus, the identification of critical processes characteristic of action-research OD is perhaps more important than a comparison or integration of the elements of the two approaches described in Tables 1 and 2.

There are five processes or methods of operation basic to and continuous throughout the application of the action-research model. These are not tied to a specific time or phase, but all five share a common element—a *problem-solving orientation*. Even though the processes can be identified clearly and discussed independently, it is obvious that in practice they do not operate independently. The commonality of problem orientation binds them to one another. Each process will be briefly defined, but no order or priority is implied by the listing.

Client-Consultant Collaboration. The previous descriptions of the phases consistently emphasized the process of collaboration between client and consultant in each phase and in all activities. This process is most critical in diagnosis and action planning, where older models prescribed decision making primarily by the consultant. Of course, this is where the OD practitioner may most easily fall into the trap of becoming the expert problem solver on content issues, rather than the process trainer. The OD practitioner, through this close client collaboration, aims not only to help the client solve immediate problems but, more significantly, to help the client learn a generally useful problem-solving process. To some extent, the OD practitioner is a model for the client. Acceptance of his behavior as desirable to model is facilitated by collaboration between the two parties. In other words, effective internalization of modeled behavior (Kelman, 1958) depends upon a base of referent power (French and Raven, 1959), which is developed and enhanced through the collaborative relationship.

In addition to the reasons previously discussed relative to the phases of the action-research OD model, the collaborative process is also crucially important in establishing client system involvement in the OD effort. While involvement is necessary to attain the overall aims of the OD effort, it is also required to successfully accomplish many of the specific activities of each phase. For example, the OD effort must respond to relevant demands and characteristics of the client system. This requires collecting accurate and adequately detailed data about the client system, an activity greatly facilitated by client involvement.

Client Learning for Internal Resource Development. By helping the client understand the action-research OD approach, the OD practitioner becomes a trainer. Through this training, the client learns to use the action-research OD model and develops the internal skills for effective use of the model on a continuing basis. Client learning is an important process element in each phase of the model. To a large extent, the OD practitioner trains by *modeling,* although other learning approaches are also likely to be involved (conceptual instruction, guided skill practices, etc.). In the broadest sense, the client system learns to use the action-research OD approach by *doing;* this is an experiential learning process. It is important to note that this client-learning process has its major emphasis on problem solving and is not merely an academic exercise or an attempt to make "sensitivity trainers" of the organization's membership.

Monitoring and Evaluation. Action-research is data based, which means that "tracking"—empirical monitoring and evaluation of the effort—is continuous throughout, not just limited to the evaluation phase. The particular problems and objectives generated as a result of the client-consultant collaboration provide the focus for the monitoring and evaluation. In terms of client learning, this continuous evaluation provides data-based feedback, a requirement for effective learning. Furthermore, this evaluation demonstrates to the client, in specific, concrete terms, the value (or lack of value) of the OD effort or any specific portion of the program. The monitoring and evaluation function is useful for the consultant as well, for through it he learns more about the action-research OD process and its application and generates information which may be added to the bank of professional knowledge (academic and applied).

Interaction and Link Between Research and Action. It has been previously noted that there is an interdependence and interaction among the various phases of the action-research OD process. This reflects the fact that the model, by genesis oriented toward solving problems in the client system (Collier, 1945), is based on the reciprocal interlinking of research and action interventions. This makes explanation of the model difficult, particularly in separating the phases and processes for definition and discussion. Scientific methods of data gathering and analysis are tied to reality with the persistent questions, "What does this information mean, and what implications does it have in terms of *actions?*" The interventions of the OD practitioner may be seen as primarily research or primarily action oriented; however, the effects of research as action are not ignored (Brown, 1972), and actions invariably contain a research element in the design for evaluating their effects.

Flexibility. Finally, the action-research OD approach is characterized throughout by a high degree of flexibility, of ready modifiability. This process is obviously related to the prior two processes and is aimed at resolving one of the deficiencies of many OD efforts (described earlier as a lack of adaptability). For example, recycling is one aspect of flexibility. Data gathering may yield information which implies a need to return to the client in order to modify the feedback plan or to obtain further data which will better fit the initial feedback model. The feedback process may result in a request for further or different data analysis or presentation. Diagnostic discussion may identify a need for more or other data, or for further feedback using the same or a different feedback model. It should be clear that recycling can occur at any point in the process, thus requiring a high degree of flexibility in the application of the model.

Flexibility also means that the range of research methods and action interventions open to the OD practitioner is essentially unlimited. Survey, interview, and observational research methods are all among the options; none is automatically excluded or prescribed. In a similar manner, many different actions are possible—so many, in fact, that it is not feasible to itemize here even those which are part of the

OD practitioner's standard repertoire. We might note, however, that actions could even involve the application of a specific OD program, such as Grid OD (Blake and Mouton, 1968), sensitivity training (Bradford, Gibb, and Benne, 1964), or management by objectives (Beck and Hillmar, 1972). Again, the "problem-centeredness" of the model, applied to the organization as a dynamic entity, requires flexibility in its application.

To this point, we have dealt with three major questions: (*a*) What is action-research?, (*b*) What is action-research OD?, and (*c*) What are the critical processes in action-research OD which differentiate it from other OD models? However, the most important question must still be addressed: Do OD efforts have better prospects of success when they are based on and conducted using the action-research model? This question could be approached deductively, since it is evident that any OD program could be selected and implemented within the context of the action-research model. Therefore, action-research would seem to offer a higher probability of satisfactory results as compared with prepackaged programs. However, as with all logical answers to practical questions, the next, more significant questions must be: (*a*) Does the model operate as described in this paper? and (*b*) Does it really work (i.e., yield effective results) in OD applications?

To answer these final questions we must turn to some empirical research. Rather than reporting and discussing the numerous older studies involving action-research, only some of which have an organizational focus, the following review will concentrate on recent research, examining four studies conducted in the past five or six years. All of these studies involved, to some extent, a particular form of research data-gathering and feedback methodology known as the "survey feedback" approach. It seems worthwhile, then, to briefly review one large-scale study examining the effects of the survey and feedback methodology as the basis of an OD approach, compared with several other packaged OD programs. This will help us understand how survey and feedback methods operate when implemented as a means of data gathering and data feedback within the action-research OD approach.

Research on the General Impact of Survey and Feedback

The impact of survey and feedback on work groups relative to other strategies has been investigated by Bowers (1971a, 1971b, 1973). Using data from longitudinal multicompany studies, he compared changes (on leadership and climate variables) associated with five different OD programs. The condition of these variables was measured by questionnaire before and after the action plans were implemented. The five OD strategies compared were: (*a*) survey feedback; (*b*) interpersonal process consultation; (*c*) sensitivity training; (*d*) task process consultation; and (*e*) data handback. For each action strategy, about 100 or more work groups were studied.

No full and current description of the survey and feedback method is easily accessible, although several reference sources exist (Bowers and Franklin, 1972; Mann, 1957; Neff, 1965; Taylor and Bowers, 1972). In brief, the approach, as currently used (Bowers and Franklin, 1972; Taylor and Bowers, 1972), involves the application of fairly sophisticated survey research methods in the development and use of an organizational survey throughout a client system. The data are analyzed, summarized, and fed back to the client in a series of small-group discussions. In these discussions, the change agent assists the manager or supervisor in conducting a discussion of the data and the problems they indicate and in exploring relevant issues in greater detail. In this way, all members of the client system will eventually be exposed to the data gathered and will participate in the problem diagnosis.

Thus, the survey feedback OD package used by Bowers (1973) is, in effect, a data-based diagnostic package. The survey instrument is essentially standardized (Taylor and Bowers, 1972), and this particular data-gathering and feedback model is applied to a client without consideration of alternative methods. We must be clear, then, that the present discussion is for the purpose of examining this particular methodology in comparison with other packaged options; the survey feedback model, as used here, is not an example of action-research OD.

We need spend little time describing the sensitivity training approach; it is well known, and standard reference sources are available (Bradford, Gibb, and Benne, 1964; Schein and Bennis, 1965). Interpersonal process consultation (Schein, 1969) emphasizes developing the ability of groups within the client system to work together and handle their own interpersonal relationship problems and concerns effectively.

Task process consultation focuses almost singularly on task objectives. Extensive exploration of the job-related strengths and weaknesses in a group is the major thrust of the consultant. A premise of this OD technique is that interpersonal processes and dynamics are relevant only as they relate to task accomplishment. This method seems related to (or an extension of) the operations research approach (Bennis and Peter, 1966). The last technique, data handback, is actually no treatment at all. As Bowers (1971a, 1971b) describes it, surveys were taken and written reports were sent to the client, but no consultant activity occurred. Therefore, this fifth condition served as a baseline comparison for the other four.

Based on a detailed analysis comparing changes stemming from these five techniques, Bowers (1971a) concludes: "treatments differ in their productive potency. Interpersonal process consultation and those treatments which are data-based, particularly survey feedback, seem to have an advantage over either laboratory training or a more task-oriented form of process consultation" (p. 52). Later he notes, "Data handback, while generally positive in impact, seems to have had little capability for handling the climate change problem and suffers somewhat as a result" (p. 53).

Thus, using a variety of statistical methods, Bowers found that a survey and feedback technique ranked high in overall effectiveness in prompting change in climate conditions and leadership behavior, as compared with four alternate approaches. Again, we emphasize that *none* of the OD efforts described by Bowers can be considered action-research OD in the sense that we have defined it. "Each setting consisted of a more or less universal application of an intervention package" (Bowers, 1971b: 55). In no case was any meaningful diagnostic activity undertaken to determine the type of OD action most appropriate. Bowers' reports are, of course, of great value, representing the only large-scale comparative study of differing OD methods ever conducted. Much knowledge has thus been gained regarding both the general application of packaged OD programs and their comparative utilities, including the particular value of survey and feedback as a diagnostically oriented packaged program. Bowers' work, however, tells us little about the part that survey feedback methodology may play in the context of the action-research model. The following studies interspersed among the references are more clearly directed toward this issue.

References

Beck, A. C., Jr., and Hillmar, E. D. (Eds.) *A Practical Approach to Organization Development Through MBO*. Reading, Mass.: Addison-Wesley, 1972.

Beer, M., and Huse, E. F. "A Systems Approach to Organizational Development," *Journal of Applied Behavioral Science*, 1972, 8, 79–101.

Bennis, W. G. *Organization Development: Its Nature, Origins, and Prospects*. Reading, Mass.: Addison-Wesley, 1969.

Bennis, W. G., and Peter, H. W. "Applying Behavioral Science for Organizational Change." In H. W. Peter, Ed., *Comparative Theories of Social Change*. Ann Arbor, Mich.: Foundation for Research on Human Behavior, 1966.

Blake, R. R., and Mouton, J. S. *Achieving Corporate Excellence through Grid Organization Development*. Houston: Gulf, 1968.

Bowers, D. G. "Development Techniques and Organizational Change: An Overview of Results from the Michigan Inter-Company Longitudinal Study." *Technical Report to the U.S. Office of Naval Research*. Ann Arbor, Mich.: Center for Research on Utilization of Scientific Knowledge, Institute for Social Research, University of Michigan, 1971. (a)

Bowers, D. G. "Development Techniques and Organizational Climate: An Evaluation of the Comparative Importance of Two Potential Forces for Organizational Change." *Technical Report to the U.S. Office of Naval Research*. Ann Arbor, Mich.: Center for Research on Utilization of Scientific Knowledge, Institute for Social Research, University of Michigan, 1971. (b)

Bowers, D. G. "OD Techniques and Their Results in 23 Organizations: The Michigan ICL Study," *Journal of Applied Behavioral Science*, 1973, 9, 21–43.

Bowers, D. G., and Franklin, J. L. "Survey Guided Development: Using Human Resources Measurement in Organizational Change," *Journal of Contemporary Business,* 1972, *1*, 43–55.

Bradford, L. P., Gibb, J. R., and Benne, K. D. *T-Group Theory and Laboratory Method.* New York: Wiley, 1964.

Brown, L. D. " 'Research Action': Organizational Feedback, Understanding, and Change," *Journal of Applied Behavioral Science,* 1972, *8*, 697–712.

Clark, A. W. "Sanction: A Critical Element in Action Research," *Journal of Applied Behavioral Science,* 1972, *8*, 713–731.

Collier, J. "United States Indian Administration as a Laboratory of Ethnic Relations," *Social Research,* 1945, *12*, 275–276.

Corey, S. M. *Action Research to Improve School Practices.* New York: Bureau of Publications, Teachers College, Columbia University, 1953.

Fleishman, E. A. "Leadership Climate, Human Relations Training, and Supervisory Behavior," *Personnel Psychology,* 1953, *6*, 205–222.

Fordyce, J. K., and Weil, R. *Managing with People.* Reading, Mass.: Addison-Wesley, 1971.

French, J. R. P., Jr., and Raven, B. "The Bases of Social Power." In D. Cartwright, Ed., *Studies in Social Power.* Ann Arbor, Mich.: Institute for Social Research, University of Michigan, 1959.

French, W. L., and Bell, C. H., Jr. *Organization Development.* Englewood Cliffs, N.J.: Prentice-Hall, 1973.

Frohman, A. L. "The Development of Impact of a Joint Goal Setting Technique for Conflict Resolution." Unpublished doctoral dissertation. Cambridge, Mass.: Sloan School of Management, Massachusetts Institute of Technology, 1970.

Frohman, M. A. "Conceptualizing a Helping Relationship." Mimeographed paper. Ann Arbor, Mich.: Center for Research on Utilization of Scientific Knowledge, Institute for Social Research, University of Michigan, 1968.

Frohman, M. A. "An Empirical Study of a Model and Strategies for Planned Organizational Change." Unpublished doctoral dissertation, Ann Arbor, Mich.: University of Michigan, 1970.

Frohman, M. A., and Waters, C. A. "Building Internal Resources for Organizational Development." Paper presented before the staff of the Institute for Social Research. University of Michigan, Ann Arbor, Michigan, Nobember 1969.

Frohman, M. A., Weisbord, M. R., and Johnston, J. "Turnover Study and Action Program." Unpublished report. Merion Station, Pa.: Organization Research and Development Co., 1971.

Greiner, L. E., Leitch, D. P., and Barnes, L. B. "The Simple Complexity of Organizational Climate in a Governmental Agency." In R. Taguire and G. H. Litwin, Eds., *Organizational Climate.* Boston: Division of Research, Graduate School of Business Administration, Harvard University, 1968.

Havelock, R. G., Guskin, A., Frohman, M. A., Havelock, M., Hill, M., and Huber, J. *Planning for Innovation.* Ann Arbor, Mich.: Center for Research on Utilization of Scientific Knowledge, Institute for Social Research, University of Michigan, 1969.

Kelman, H. C. "Compliance, Identification, and Internalization: Three Processes of Attitude Change," *Journal of Conflict Resolution,* 1958, *2*, 51–60.

Kolb, D. A., and Frohman, A. L. "An Organization Development Approach to Consulting," *Sloan Management Review,* 1970, *12*, 51–65.

Leavitt, H. J. "Applied Organizational Change in Industry: Structural, Technological, and Humanistic Approaches." In J. G. March, Ed., *Handbook of Organizations.* Chicago: Rand McNally, 1965.

Levinson, H. "The Clinical Psychologist as Organizational Diagnostician," *Professional Psychology,* 1972, *3*, 34–40.

Lewin, K. "Action Research and Minority Problems," *Journal of Social Issues,* 1946, *2*, 34–36.

Lewin, K. "Frontiers in Group Dynamics," *Human Relations,* 1947, *1*, 5–42.

Likert, R. *New Patterns of Management.* New York: McGraw-Hill, 1961.

Likert, R. *The Human Organization.* New York: McGraw-Hill, 1967.

Lippitt, R. "Value-Judgment Problems of the Social Scientist Participation in Action-Research." Paper presented at the annual meeting of the American Psychological Association, September 1950.

Lippitt, R., Watson, J., and Westley, B. *The Dynamics of Planned Change.* New York: Harcourt, Brace & World, 1958.

Mann, F. C. "Studying and Creating Change: A Means to Understanding Social Organization." In C. Arensberg, Ed., *Research in Industrial Human Relations.* Publication no. 17. New York: Industrial Relations Research Association, 1957.

McElvaney, C. T., and Miles, M. B. "The School Psychologist as a Change Agent: Improving a School System through Survey Feedback Methods." In G. B. Gottsegan and M. G. Gottsegan, Eds., *Professional School Psychology.* New York: Grune & Stratton, 1969.

McElvaney, C. T., and Miles, M. B. "Using Survey Feedback and Consultation." In R. A. Schmuck and M. B. Miles, Eds., *Organization Development in Schools.* Palo Alto, Calif.: National Press, 1971.

Miles, M. B., Hornstein, H. A., Calder, P. H., Callahan, D. M., and Schiavo, R. S. "The Consequence of Survey Feedback: Theory and Evaluation." In W. G. Bennis, K. D. Benne, and R. Chin, Eds., *The Planning of Change* (2d ed.). New York: Holt, Rinehart and Winston, 1969.

Neff, F. W. "Survey Research: A Tool for Problem Diagnosis and Improvement in Organizations." In A. W. Gouldner and S. M. Miller, Eds., *Applied Sociology*. New York: The Free Press, 1965.

Pfeiffer, J. W., and Jones, J. E. *A Handbook of Structured Experiences for Human Relations Training,* vol. 2. Iowa City: University Associates Press, 1970.

Pfeiffer, J. W., and Jones, J. E. *A Handbook of Structured Experiences for Human Relations Training,* vol. 3. Iowa City: University Associates Press, 1971.

Pfeiffer, J. W., and Jones, J. E. *A Handbook of Structured Experiences for Human Relations Training* (rev. ed.), vol. 1, Iowa City: University Associates Press, 1972. (a)

Pfeiffer, J. W., and Jones, J. E. *The 1972 Annual Handbook for Group Facilitators,* Iowa City: University Associates Press, 1972. (b)

Roethlisberger, F. J., and Dickson, W. J. *Management and the Worker*. Cambridge, Mass.: Harvard University Press, 1939.

Sashkin, M. "Organization Development Practices," *Professional Psychology,* 1973, *4*, 187–194 ff.

Sashkin, M., Morris, W. C., and Horst, L. "A Comparison of Social and Organizational Change Models: Information Flow and Data Use Processes," *Psychological Review,* 1973, *8c*, 510–526.

Schein, E. H. *Process Consultation: Its Role in Organization Development*. Reading, Mass.: Addison-Wesley, 1969.

Schein, E. H., and Bennis, W. G. *Personal and Organizational Change through Group Methods*. New York: Wiley, 1965.

Sykes, A. J. M. "The Effect of a Supervisory Training Course in Changing Supervisors' Perceptions and Expectations of the Role of Management," *Human Relations,* 1962, *15*, 227–243.

Taylor, J. C., and Bowers, D. G. *The Survey of Organizations: A Machine-Scored, Standardized Questionnaire Instrument*. Ann Arbor, Mich.: Institute for Social Research, University of Michigan, 1972.

Waters, C. A. "Building Internal Resources for Organization Development." In Executive Study Conference, *Managing Organizational Effectiveness*. Princeton, N.J.: Educational Testing Service, 1969.

Weisbord, M. R., Frohman, M. A., and Johnston, J. "Action-Reseach on Turnover as an OD Entry Strategy." Paper presented at the fall 1971 meeting of the OD Network, Minneapolis, Minn.

SECTION TWO

DIAGNOSTIC MODELS AND TECHNIQUES

The four articles in this section of the readings provide three categories of coverage. First, in the article by Burke, are the summaries of the primary theories that underlie OD practitioners' conceptual and value orientations toward understanding and changing organizations. The next two articles cover models for organization diagnosis: the six-box model developed by Weisbord and the congruence or component-fit model developed by Nadler and Tushman. The final article by Nadler covers the third category—techniques of data collection and analysis for the diagnosis phase of OD consultation.

Conceptual and Theoretical Underpinnings of Organization Development

W. Warner Burke

The Individual Perspective

Psychologists have taken two major approaches to the understanding of human motivation: need theory and expectancy theory. One of the early proponents of need theory was Murray; later representatives were Maslow and Herzberg. Expectancy theory, a more recent approach to understanding human motivation, is usually associated with Lawler and Vroom. Applications of need theory in organizations have centered around job design, career development, and certain aspects of human relations training, whereas expectancy theory has been applied with respect to both needs and reward systems. I shall focus first on need theory and some of its applications, since Maslow and Herzberg have probably been the most influential historically.

NEED THEORY—MASLOW AND HERZBERG

According to Maslow (1954) human motivation can be explained in terms of needs that people experience to varying degrees all the time. An unsatisfied need creates a state of tension, which releases energy in the human system and, at the same time, provides direction. This purposeful energy guides the individual toward some goal that will respond to the unsatisfied need. This process—an unsatisfied need for providing energy and direction toward some goal—is how Maslow defined motivation. Thus, only unsatisfied needs provide the sources of motivation; a satisfied need creates no tension and therefore no motivation.

Briefly, the foundation of Maslow's theory is his arrangement of human needs into a hierarchical system. The hierarchy consists of five levels, beginning with

From W. W. Burke, *Organization Development: Principles and Practices,* Chapter 2 (Boston: Little, Brown, 1982). Copyright © 1982 by W. W. Burke. Reprinted by permission of the publisher.

the basic or physiological needs, such as the needs for oxygen, food, and water. Next in the hierarchy are the safety or security needs—the needs for a secure environment, order, predictability, and the like. Third in the hierarchy is the need for belonging—a person's desire to be accepted by significant others. The fourth level is an individual's ego-status need. At this level a person wants to be recognized by others as unique, as having special talents, as having achieved important objectives, and so forth. For this need and the need for belonging to be met, the individual is dependent on others. For the fifth and final level of need, the need for self-actualization, the person is not dependent on others. At this level one has a need to realize one's potential, to prove oneself *to* oneself. Realizing this need is acquiring a sense of personal growth and development, stretching to one's full potential. The fifth need level completes the hierarchy. One final key point, however, is that Maslow used the term *hierarchy* because he believed that a person would not experience a next-higher level of need until the previous level or levels had been satisfied.

To discuss motivation more fully in regard to Maslow, we must also consider the particular goals associated with each level of need. The following chart depicts the kinds of goals or goal objects that are associated with each need level in an organizational context:

Need Level	Goal Objects
Self-actualization	Autonomy on the job, opportunity to determine criteria for job and for effectiveness
Ego-status	Title, carpet on the private office floor, promotions, salary
Belonging	Being part of work team, playing on company's softball team

Need Level	Goal Objects
Safety and security	Seniority, salary, fringe benefits
Basic (physiological)	Clean, safe air to breathe, proper ventilation, hazard-free environment

In summary, Maslow contended that we progress through this five-level need system in a hierarchical fashion and that we do so one level at a time. The hierarchy represents one continuum from basic needs to self-actualization.

It is on this last point, a single continuum, that Herzberg parts company with Maslow. Herzberg (1966; Herzberg, Mausner, and Snyderman 1959) maintains that there are two continua, one concerning dissatisfaction and the other concerning satisfaction. It may be that the two theorists are even more fundamentally different in that Herzberg's approach has more to do with job satisfaction than with human motivation. The implications and applications of the two are much more similar than they are divergent however.

Specifically, Herzberg argues that only the goal objects associated with Maslow's ego-status and self-actualization needs provide motivation or satisfaction on the job. Meeting the lower-order needs simply reduces dissatisfaction; it does not provide satisfaction. Herzberg calls the goal objects associated with these lower-order needs (belonging, safety, and basic) hygiene or maintenance factors. Providing fringe benefits, for example, prevents dissatisfaction and thus is hygienic, but this provision does not insure job satisfaction. Only motivator factors, such as recognition, opportunity for achievement, and autonomy on the job insure satisfaction.

Herzberg's two categories, motivator factors and maintenance or hygiene factors, do not overlap. They represent qualitatively different aspects of human motivation. We can depict Herzberg's theory graphically as shown in Figure 1.

It is important to note one other point of Herzberg's. He states that not only does the dimension of job dissatisfaction differ psychologically from job satisfaction, but it is also associated with an escalation phenomenon, or what some have called the principle of rising expectations—that the more people

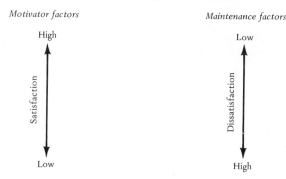

FIGURE 1
Herzberg's Continua of Need Theory

receive, the more they want. This principle applies only to job dissatisfaction. Herzberg uses the example of a person who received a salary increase of $1,000 one year and then receives only a $500 increase the following year. Psychologically, the second increase is a cut in pay. Herzberg maintains that this escalation principle is a fact of life and that we must live with it. Management must continue to provide, upgrade, and increase maintenance factors—good working conditions, adequate salaries, and competitive fringe benefits—but should not operate under the false assumption that these factors will lead to greater job satisfaction.

Job enrichment, a significant intervention within OD and a critical element of quality-of-work-life projects, is a direct application of Herzberg's theory and at least an indirect one of Maslow's.

EXPECTANCY THEORY—LAWLER AND VROOM

Expectancy theory (Lawler 1973; Vroom 1964) has yet to have the impact on organization development that need theory has had, but it is gaining in acceptance and popularity. This approach to understanding human motivation focuses more on outward behavior than on internal needs. The theory is based on three assumptions:

1. People believe that their behavior is associated with certain outcomes—the performance-outcome expectancy. People may expect that, if they accomplish certain tasks, they will receive certain rewards.

2. Outcomes or rewards have different values (valence) for different people. Some people, for

example, are more attracted to money as a reward than others are.

3. People associate their behavior with certain probabilities of success—the effort-performance expectancy. People on an assembly line, for example, may have high expectancies that, if they try, they can produce 100 units per hour, but their expectancies may be very low that they can produce 150 units, regardless of how hard they may try.

Thus, people will be highly motivated when they believe (1) that their behavior will lead to certain rewards, (2) that these rewards are worthwhile and valuable, (3) that they are able to perform at a level that will result in the attainment of the rewards.

The theory further states that, given that people believe their behavior will lead to certain outcomes or rewards, the extent to which they will be motivated is a function of the multiplicative relationship between the value the reward holds for them and the perceived probability that their effort will result in the reward. The multiplicative relationship means that one without the other results in zero—no motivation. People may value the potential reward, but if they do not expect that their efforts will lead to the obtainment of the reward, they will not be motivated. If people believe that their efforts will lead to the reward but do not care for the reward, they will not be motivated. There are degrees of mixture of these two factors, of course, and the mixture will determine the amount of motivation. The amount of motivation a person will have is equal to $E \times V$, the expectancy times the valence of the reward.

Research has shown that high-performing employees believe that their behavior, or performance, leads to rewards that they desire. Thus, there is evidence for the validity of the theory. Moreover, the theory and the research outcomes associated with it have implications for how reward systems and work might be designed and structured.

JOB SATISFACTION—HACKMAN AND OLDHAM

Hackman and Oldham's (1980) work design model is grounded in both need theory and expectancy theory. Their model is more restrictive in that it focuses on the relationship between job or work design and worker satisfaction. Although their model frequency leads to

what is called job enrichment, as does the application of Herzberg's motivator-hygiene theory, the Hackman and Oldham model has broader implications. Briefly, Hackman and Oldham (1975) contend that there are three primary psychological states that significantly affect worker satisfaction: (1) experienced meaningfulness of the work itself, (2) experienced responsibility for the work and its outcomes, and (3) knowledge of results, or performance feedback. The more that work is designed to enhance these states, the more satisfying the work will be.

POSITIVE REINFORCEMENT—SKINNER

The best way to understand the full implications of the applications of B. F. Skinner's (1971, 1953) thinking and his research results is to read his novel, *Walden Two* (1948). The book is about a utopian community designed and maintained according to Skinnerian principles of operant behavior and schedules of reinforcement. A similar application was made in an industrial situation in the Emery Air Freight case ("At Emery" 1973). By applying Skinnerian principles, which are based on numerous research findings, Emery quickly realized an annual savings of $650,000. (The Emery case is discussed more fully later in this section.)

Skinner is neither an OD practitioner nor a management consultant, but his theory and research are indeed applicable to management practices and to organizational change. For Skinner, control is key. If one can control the environment, one can then control behavior. In Skinner's approach, the more the environment is controlled, the better, but the necessary element of control is the rewards, both positive and negative. This necessity is based on a fundamental of behavior that Skinner derived from his many years of research—a concept so basic that it may be a law of behavior—that people (and animals) do what they are rewarded for doing. Let us consider the principles that underlie this fundamental of behavior.

In the famous case of Pavlov's dog, after continuously pairing food with the sound of a bell, Pavlov eventually elicited a salivation response from the dog with the bell sound only. The key word here is *elicited*. Skinner believes most behavior is *emitted*. He agrees that Pavlovian, or classical, conditioning is real but believes that it proves only that reflexes can be conditioned to various stimuli. Most behavior is more a result of an active process by a person than of a passive, reflexive response to certain stimuli in the environment. For Skinner, then, the primary subject matter of psychology is the study of emitted responses and their consequences. When we emit a response—that is, do something, such as writing a book—we tend to increase this response when it is followed by reinforcement. When the consequence of a certain behavior is reinforcement or reward, the behavior tends to be repeated. Absolutely identical behavior will not necessarily be repeated, but similar acts having essentially the same effect will certainly occur. Moreover, the act does not have to be continuously reinforced for it to be repeated. One of the most dramatic findings of psychological research has been the principle of partial reinforcement. In a comparison of behavior that has been reinforced all the time with the same behavior of a similar organism that has been reinforced only occasionally after all reinforcement for both has stopped, the behavior of the partially reinforced respondent will last significantly longer than that of the continuously reinforced respondent. (This explains, of course, why many people continue to go to the golf course on weekends even though they may hit only one beautiful shot out of about every twenty attempts.)

The first phase of learned behavior is called shaping, the process of successive approximations to reinforcement. When children are learning to walk, they are reinforced by their parents' encouraging comments or physical stroking, but this reinforcement typically follows only the behaviors that lead to effective walking. Programmed learning, invented by Skinner, is based on this principle. To maintain the behavior, a schedule of reinforcement is applied, and, generally, the more variable the schedule is, the longer the behavior will last.

Skinner therefore advocates positive reinforcement for shaping and controlling behavior. Often, however, when we consider controlling behavior, we think of punishment—"If you don't do this, you're gonna get it!" According to Skinner, punishment is no good. His stance is not based entirely on his values or whims, however. Research clearly shows that, although punishment may temporarily stop a certain behavior, negative reinforcement must be admin-

istered continuously for this process to be maintained. The principle is the opposite of that for positively reinforced behavior. There are two very practical concerns here. First, having to reinforce a certain behavior continuously is obviously not very efficient. Second, although the punished behavior may be curtailed, it is unlikely that the subject will learn what to do; all that is learned is what *not* to do.

Thus, the way to control behavior according to Skinnerian theory and research is to reinforce the desirable behavior positively and, after the shaping process, to reinforce the behavior only occasionally. An attempt should be made to ignore undesirable behavior and not to punish (unless, perhaps, society must be protected) but, rather, to spend time positively shaping the desired behavior. The implications of Skinner's work for organizations is that a premium is placed on such activities as establishing incentive systems, reducing or eliminating many of the control systems that contain inherent threats and punishments, providing feedback to all levels of employees regarding their performance, and developing programmed-learning techniques for training employees.

The application of Skinner's work to OD did not occur systematically until the 1970s. Thus, his influence is not as pervasive as Maslow's is, for example. Skinner's behavior-motivation techniques as applied to people also raise significant questions regarding ethics and values: Who exercises the control, and is the recipient aware? Thus, it is not a question of whether Skinner's methodology works, but rather how and under what circumstances it is used.

The Emery Air Freight example, mentioned at the beginning of this section, illustrates how and under what circumstances Skinner's methodology may be applied in an organizational setting. At Emery supervisors were taught to use positive reinforcement, but not punishment, as a motivational tool. In keeping with Skinnerian principles, two main supervisory practices were stressed: recognition coupled with rewards and feedback. In a workbook provided for supervisors, as many as 150 types of recognition and rewards were suggested, ranging from a smile with an encouraging nod to detailed praise for excellent work. Praise and recognition were applied to specific behavior as soon as possible after the act had occurred.

For the behavior to be shaped at Emery, supervisors used praise and recognition at least twice a week during the early weeks and months and then tapered off, providing praise only occasionally and never at a predictable time. Supervisors were also instructed to provide concrete and specific feedback to workers regarding their performance. Supervisors let the worker know specifically what was being rewarded; for example, a supervisor would say, "Mac, I liked the initiative you showed in getting those crates into the large containers. You're performing consistently now at 98 percent of standard." As workers were able to see more clearly, by this specific feedback, which behavior was being rewarded, they began to associate the feedback with reward—what Skinner refers to as "noncontrived reinforcers." The more workers associated the specific feedback they received with the recognition and praise, the more the feedback itself became a reward. Even when the workers' performance feedback came to them in the form of written reports, such as computer printouts listing workers' rates of production compared with the standard, the form itself became a reward.

At Emery the behavior to be shaped was first identified—for example, putting more crates into each container. As workers packaged more crates per container, this behavior was recognized and rewarded by the supervisor, frequently at first and less frequently and intermittently later. In the process, the supervisor also indicated, by feedback to workers, the specific behavior that was associated with the desired direction or standard. Gradually, the feedback became a positive reinforcer.

The Group Perspective

THE GROUP AS THE FOCUS OF CHANGE—LEWIN

The theorist among theorists, at least within the scope of the behavioral sciences, is Kurt Lewin. His thinking has had a more pervasive impact on organization development, both direct and indirect, than any other person's. It was Lewin who laid the groundwork for much of what we know about social change, particularly in a group and by some extrapolation in an organization. Lewin's interest and, easily determined by implication, his values have also influenced OD.

As a Jew who escaped Hitler's Germany in the 1930s, it was not coincidental that Lewin was intensely interested in the study of autocratic versus democratic behavior and matters of influence and change (Marrow 1969). Thus, his own and his students' research findings regarding the consequences of such variables as participative leadership and decision making have had considerable impact on the typical objectives of most if not all OD efforts.

According to Lewin (1951, 1948), behavior is a function of a person's personality, discussed primarily in terms of motivation or needs, and the situation or environment in which the person is acting. The environment is represented as a field of forces that affect the person. Thus, a person's behavior at any given moment can be predicted if we know that person's needs and if we can determine the intensity and valence (whether the force is positive or negative for the person) of the forces impinging on the person from the environment. Although Lewin borrowed the term *force* from physics, he defined the construct psychologically. Thus, one's perception of the environment is key, not necessarily reality. An example of a force, therefore, could be the perceived power of another person. Whether or not I will accomplish a task you want me to do is a function of the degree to which such accomplishment will respond to a need I have and how I perceive your capacity to influence me—whether you are a force in my environment (field).

Lewin made a distinction between imposed or *induced* forces, those acting on a person from the outside, and *own* forces, those directly reflecting the person's needs. The implications of this distinction are clear. Participation in determining a goal is more likely to create own forces toward accomplishing it than is a situation in which goal determination is imposed by others. When a goal is imposed on a person, his or her motives may match accomplishment of the goal, but the chances are considerably more variable or random than if the goal is determined by the person in the first place. Typically, then, for imposed or induced goals to be accomplished by a person, the one who induced them must exert continuous influence or else the person's other motives, not associated with goal accomplishment, will likely determine his or her behavior. This aspect of Lewin's theory helps to explain the generally positive consequences of participative management and consensual decision making.

Another distinction Lewin made regarding various forces in a person's environment is the one between *driving* and *restraining* forces. Borrowing yet another concept from physics, quasi-stationary equilibria, he noted that the perceived status quo in life is just that—a perception. In reality, albeit psychological reality, a given situation is a result of a dynamic rather than a static process. The process flows from one moment to the next, with ups and downs, and over time gives the impression of a static situation, but there actually are some forces pushing in one direction and counterbalancing forces that restrain movement. The level of productivity in an organization may appear static, but sometimes it is being pushed higher—by the force of supervisory pressure, for example—and sometimes it is being restrained or even decreased by a counterforce, such as a norm of the work group. There are many different counterbalancing forces in any situation, and what is called a force-field analysis is used to identify the two sets of forces.

Change from the status quo is therefore a two-step process. First, a forcefield analysis is conducted, and then the intensity of a force or set of forces is either increased or decreased. Change can occur by adding to or increasing the intensity of the forces Lewin labeled driving forces—that is, forces that push in the desired direction for change—or by diminishing the opposing or restraining forces. Lewin's theory predicts that the better of these two choices is to reduce the intensity of the restraining forces. By adding forces or increasing the intensity on the driving side, a simultaneous increase would occur on the restraining side, and the overall tension level for the system—whether it is a person, a group, or an organization—would intensify. The better choice, then, is to reduce the restraining forces.

This facet of Lewin's field theory helps us to determine not only the nature of change but how to accomplish it more effectively. Lewinian theory argues that it is more efficacious to direct change at the group level than at the individual level.

If one attempts to change an attitude or the behavior of an individual without attempting to change the same behavior or attitude in the group to which the individual belongs, then the individual will be a deviate and either will come under pressure from the group to get back into line or will be rejected entirely. Thus, the major leverage point for change is at the group level—for example, by modifying a group norm or standard. According to Lewin (1958):

> As long as group standards are unchanged, the individual will resist change more strongly the farther he is to depart from group standards. If the group standard itself is changed, the resistance which is due to the relation between individual and group standard is eliminated. (p. 210)

Adherence to Lewinian theory involves viewing the organization as a social system, with many and varied subsystems, primarily groups. We look at the behavior of people in the organization in terms of (1) whether their needs jibe with the organization's directions, usually determined by their degree of commitment; (2) the norms to which people conform and the degree of that conformity; (3) how power is exercised (induced versus own forces); and (4) the decision-making process (involvement leading to commitment).

CHANGING VALUES THROUGH THE GROUP—ARGYRIS

It is not possible to place the work of Chris Argyris in one category, one theory, or one conceptual framework. He has developed a number of mini theories, whose relationship and possible overlap are not always apparent. He has always focused largely on interpersonal and group behavior, however, and he has emphasized behavioral change within a group context, along the same value lines as McGregor's (1960) Theory Y. The work described in *Management and Organizational Development: The Path from XA to YB* (Argyris 1971) best illustrates this emphasis. Since Argyris has made many theoretical contributions, we shall briefly cover his work chronologically, discussing it as early, middle, and recent Argyris work.

Argyris's early work (1962) may be characterized as emphasizing the relationship of individual personality and organization dynamics. His objective was to look for ways in which this relationship could be satisfied; that is, that the person and the organization both might compromise so that each could profit from the other—*satisfied* meaning that there is an improvement but that it is less than optimal for each party. Although the relationship may never be optimal for both parties, it could still be better for both. For this relationship between the individual and the organization to be achieved, the organization must adjust its value system toward helping its members to be more psychologically healthy—less dependent on and controlled by the organization—and the individuals must become more open with their feelings, more willing to trust one another, and more internally committed to the organization's goals.

Argyris has always believed that organizations, especially pyramidally structured ones, tend to stifle people, to overcontrol them, and to treat them as children, thus making them something less than their projected potential. It is not surprising, therefore, that Argyris was captured by the early thrust of sensitivity or T-group training in the 1950s. He wrote the article "T Groups for Organizational Effectiveness" (Argyris 1964). It was also during this period and within the same behavioral framework that Argyris developed his three-facet theory of interpersonal competence. He postulated that an interpersonally competent individual is one who *owns up,* openly expressing what he or she thinks and feels; *expresses feelings* to others when experiencing an emotion; and *experiments,* trying new behaviors and seeking to learn from these attempts. Thus, one who is interpersonally competent relates with others openly and seeks greater self-awareness and growth through risk taking.

In this thinking, research, and writing during the late 1960s and early 1970s, Argyris became more closely associated with organization development. His thrust of this middle period was in (1) theorizing about competent consultation, and especially about the nature of an effective intervention, and (2) operationalizing organizational change in behavioral terms by McGregor's Theory Y. Regarding the first aspect, Argyris (1970) contends that, for any intervention into an organization-social system to be effective, it must generate valid information, lead to free, informed choice on the part of the client, and provide internal commitment by the client to the choices taken. More on this aspect of Argyris's work is provided in Chapter 10. For the second aspect, Argyris connects behaviors (he calls them Pattern A) with McGregor's Theory X and Theory Y (Pattern B).

Argyris specifies the behavioral manifestations of someone who holds either of the sets of assumptions about human beings in organizations that were postulated earlier by McGregor (1960). Pattern A behaviors are characterized as predominantly intellectual rather than emotional, conforming rather than experimenting, individually oriented rather than group-oriented, involving closed rather than open communications, and generally mistrusting rather than trusting. This pattern is the opposite of interpersonally competent behavior. Thus, Pattern B is an extension of Argyris's earlier facets of interpersonal competence.

More recently, Argyris has turned his attention to the gaps in people's behavior between what they say (he calls it espoused theory) and what they do (theory in action). People may say that they believe that McGregor's Theory Y assumptions about human beings are valid, for example, but they may act according to Pattern A. Argyris goes on to argue that as people become more aware of these gaps between their stated beliefs and their behavior, they will be more motivated to reduce the differences, to be more consistent. In one project, Argyris tape-recorded managerial staff meetings, analyzed the recorded behaviors, and then showed the managers where their actions were not consistent with their words (Argyris 1973). More recently, in collaboration with Don Schön, Argyris studied and elaborated the learning process involved in obtaining greater self-awareness and organizational awareness about human effectiveness (Argyris and Schön 1978). Argyris and Schön argue that most organizations accomplish no more than "single loop learning," that problems are solved or fixed and a single loop of learning is accomplished. For significant organizational improvement and for insuring long-term survival and renewal, however, change must occur in more fundamental ways. Although problems must be solved in a single loop, new ways of learning *how* to solve problems must be learned as well. Another loop is thus added to the learning cycle—what Argyris and Schön refer to as "double loop learning."

THE GROUP UNCONSCIOUS—BION

Most people believe that everyone has an unconscious; Freud has clearly had an effect. Wilfred Bion believes, as others do, that there is also a group unconscious—a collective unconscious that is more than the sum of the individual unconsciouses—and he gives compelling but complex arguments (Bion 1961; Rioch 1970).

Bion believes that every group is actually composed of two groups, the work group and the basic-assumption group; that is, every group *behaves* as if it were two groups, one concerned with group accomplishment and rational actions, the other concerned with activity that stems from the unconscious and is irrational. Bion does not mean simply that a group is both rational and irrational. He goes far beyond this commonly accepted dichotomy.

The work group is the aspect of group functioning that is concerned with accomplishing what the group is composed to do, the task at hand. The work group is aware of its purpose, or at the outset knows that its initial task is to establish clarity of purpose. The work group is sure about, or quickly becomes sure about, roles and responsibilities in the group. The work group is also clearly conscious of the passage of time and the procedures and processes needed to accomplish the task.

How many times have you been a member or leader of a group that fit such a description? I suspect that it has not been very often, if ever. Bion states that groups do not behave in this clearly rational and sensible way because there is always another group operating simultaneously—the basic-assumption group.

Bion theorizes that all groups function according to basic assumptions, that groups operate as if certain things are inevitable. Perhaps an analogy will help to explain. In the early days of automobiles, many people made the basic assumption that no motorized vehicle could go faster than a horse, and these people acted accordingly. In fact, some of them eventually lost money because they bet heavily on their assumption. The point is that they acted as if their belief were true and inevitable.

There are three types of basic-assumption groups: the dependency group, the fight-flight group, and the pairing group. The dependency group assumes that the reason the group exists is to be protected and to be assured of providence by its leader. The group members act immaturely, childishly, and as if they know little or nothing as compared with the leader. The leader is all-powerful and wise. In the dependency group, the leader is typically idolized. We mortals are neither omnipotent nor omniscient,

however, and the group members soon realize that they must seek a "new messiah." The cycle then repeats itself with a new leader.

The fight-flight group assumes that it must preserve itself, that its survival is at stake, so group members act accordingly. Taking action is the key to survival, as in the proverbial Army command: "Do something even if it's wrong!" It is the *group* that must be preserved, so individuals may be sacrificed through fight or abandonment (flight). The leader's role in this basic-assumption group is clear: to lead the group into battle or retreat. The best leader is one who acts in a paranoid manner, assuming that "They're out to get us, gang!" Eventually and inevitably the leader will not meet all the group's demands, at which point the group panics and searches for a new leader.

In the pairing group the assumption is that the group's purpose is to give birth to a new messiah. The leader in this case is purely incidental, and the group must quickly get on with the business of bringing forth the new savior. Two members therefore pair off to procreate. The two may be both male, both female, or male and female, but the basic assumption is that, when two people pair, the pairing is sexual in nature, even though it takes the innocent form of establishing a subcommittee. Although new life and hope may be provided, the new messiah, as the Christian Messiah, will soon be done away with. All the basic-assumption groups behave as if the leader must be replaced or, to use Bion's more dramatic and graphic terminology, as if the leader must be crucified.

Although the work group and the basic assumption group are functioning simultaneously, their degree of activity varies. At times the work group is predominant and at other times the basic assumption group holds sway.

Another Bion concept is his idea of valency. With this construct, he accounts for individual differences in groups. He contends that some people have a greater tendency to enter into (collude with) a basic-assumption group than others do. The comparison is in the work group; some people are more cooperative than others. The difference is that cooperative behavior in the work group is a conscious, deliberate effort, whereas valency for the basic-assumption group is exclusively an unconscious process.

Bion has never been an OD practitioner; he is a psychotherapist. His theory, however, is applicable to interventions with teams, consultation with leaders, and diagnosis of possible processes of collusion. For a direct application and extension of the latter group or organizational dynamic, see Harvey's "Abilene Paradox" (1974), an extension of Bion's theory that explains collusive behavior on the part of members of a group.

For the OD practitioner serving as a consultant to an organizational team, Bion's theory is particularly useful for diagnosing internal problems, especially those concerning team members' relationships with the leader.

The Total System Perspective

PARTICIPATIVE MANAGEMENT, THE ONE BEST WAY—LIKERT

Likert is best known for two concepts: the linking pin notion of management and the four-system model of organizations. He is also known for his unequivocal advocacy of participative management as *the* approach to be taken by managers, regardless of organizational type. Likert's method for organization development is survey feedback. I shall cover each of these concepts in turn.

Likert's (1961) idea of the linking pin originated from his desire to design organizations in a more decentralized form without eliminating the hierarchical structure. He also wanted to incorporate more opportunity for group activity, especially group decision making, in the managerial process. Thus, each manager is simultaneously a member of two groups, one in which he or she manages and is the leader and one in which he or she is a subordinate and follows the leadership of a boss. By being a member of both these hierarchical groups, the person becomes a key *link* within the vertical chain of command. This linkage manifests itself primarily in activities involving communication and resolution of conflict. The manager-subordinate, therefore, is the primary conduit for information and facilitates the resolution of conflict, by virtue of the linking position, when there are differences between the two vertically connected organizational groups. An organization chart is drawn so that groups overlap vertically rather than in the more traditional way, as separate boxes connected

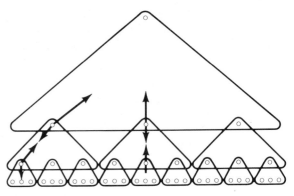

The arrows indicate linking pin function.

FIGURE 2

Likert's Linking Pin Design of Organizational Structure and Managerial Role.

Source: Likert, R. *New Patterns of Management.* New York: McGraw-Hill, 1961. Used by permission.

only by lines. Figure 2 shows this concept of organizational structure.

Likert (1967) has described four major models or systems of organization design: the autocratic, the benevolent autocratic, the consultative, and the participative. He uses seven organizational functions to describe the four models differentially: leadership, motivation, communication, interaction and influence, decision making, goal setting, and control. His "Profile of Organizational Characteristics," a diagnostic questionnaire, is organized according to these seven functions and four models. Organizational members' answers to the questionnaire provide a perceptual profile of the organization. The profile is derived from the respondent's views of how the seven functions are managed and depicts which of the four systems seems to be predominant, at least in the eyes of the respondents.

The autocratic model—System 1 in Likert's terminology—is characterized by strictly top-down management, with little or no leeway for subordinates to affect decisions. Communication is one-way, starting from the top, motivation is by use of the stick, and control is tight and concentrated at the top. System 2, benevolent autocracy, is less punitive and uses the carrot rather than the stick; people are treated more humanely, and top management will listen to subordinates, but it is always clear who ultimately controls the organization. In consultative management, System 3, managers not only listen to subordinates but genuinely want their ideas. Managers *consult* with their subordinates in the decision-making process but reserve the right to make the final decisions themselves. Communication is more two-way, motivation is mostly by carrot rather than stick, subordinates have influence on their own organizational goals, and control is more decentralized. Participative management, System 4, is at the opposite end of the spectrum from the autocratic model. In a System 4 organization, leadership is participative, motivation is developed according to Maslow's higher-order needs, communication is always two-way and open, influence and interpersonal relations are cooperative and trusting, decisions are frequently made in groups and by consensus, goals are mutually established, and control is highly decentralized and widespread. As indicated earlier, Likert advocates System 4. Thus, he is a normative theorist, declaring one best way, rather than a contingency theorist. In his book *The Human Organization* (1967), he provides research evidence to support his position.

Likert not only argues that there is one best way to manage, he also espouses one best way to conduct an organization development effort. His method is survey feedback, the survey instrument being his "Profile of Organizational Characteristics" and the feedback being organized and analyzed according to the four-system model of organizational management. In an organization development effort, then, Likert's approach is highly data-based, but the diagnosis is largely limited to the functions he deems important. Once the survey data are collected, they are given back in profile form to organizational family units—to a boss and his or her team. This group then considers the data in light of their particular situation and organizational mandate, then decides on a plan for changes they want to make, and finally takes the necessary action for implementing the plan. Approximately a year later, the organization should take another survey to check progress and to plan and implement further changes.

Although organizational change agents may be uncomfortable with Likert's one best way and may prefer an approach that is more contingent and perhaps more flexible, they can be very sure of the direction and the objectives of the change effort.

IT ALL DEPENDS—LAWRENCE AND LORSCH

For an organization to operate efficiently and effectively, one person cannot do everything, and every organizational member cannot do the same thing. In any organization, therefore, there is a division of labor. Lawrence and Lorsch (1969, 1967) call this *differentiation*. In an organization with many divisions, some people must provide coordination, so that what the organization does is organized in some fashion. Lawrence and Lorsch label this process *integration*. This approach is sometimes referred to as a theory of differentiation-integration. A more appropriate label, however, and the one they prefer, is *contingency* theory. They believe that how an organization should be structured and how it should be managed depend on several factors, primarily the organization's environment, or its marketplace. The central elements of the Lawrence and Lorsch contingency theory are differentiation, integration, the organization-environment interface, interunit relations, and the implicit contract between the employees and management.

Differentiation means dividing up tasks so that everything that needs to be done is accomplished. To determine the degree of differentiation in an organization, Lawrence and Lorsch consider four variables: (1) goal certainty—whether goals are clear and easily measured or ambiguous and largely qualitative; (2) structure—whether the structure is formal, with precise policy and procedure, or loose and flexible, with policy largely a function of current demands; (3) interaction—whether there is considerable interpersonal and intergroup communication and cooperation or very little; and (4) timespan of feedback—whether people in the organization see the results of their work quickly or it takes a long time. The more that units within an organization differ from one another along these four dimensions, the more differentially structured the organization is. Some units may be very sure of their goals while others are not so sure, and some units may follow strict and precise work procedures while other units are still trying to formulate working procedures. It should be clear, therefore, that highly differentiated organizations are more difficult to coordinate. In a pyramidal organization, the coordination and the resolution of conflict are handled by the next higher level of management. When organizations are simultaneously highly differentiated and decentralized with respect to management, Lawrence and Lorsch argue that integrator roles are needed, that certain people must be given specific assignments for coordinating and integrating diverse functions. These people may or may not be in key decision-making positions but they ensure that decisions are made by someone or by the appropriate group.

How should an organization be structured, differentiated, and centralized (pyramidal) or decentralized? We already know the answer—that it depends—but on what does it depend? Lawrence and Lorsch argue that it depends primarily on the organization's environment, on whether the environment is complex and rapidly changing, as in the electronics industry, or relatively simple (one or two major markets) and stable (raw materials forthcoming and predictable and market likely to remain essentially the same in the foreseeable future). The more complex the environment, the more decentralized and flexible management should be. Lawrence and Lorsch's reasoning is that, the more rapidly changing the environment, the more necessary it is that the organization have people monitoring these changes, and the more they should be in a position to make decisions on the spot. When the organization's environment is not particularly complex and when conditions are relatively stable, management should be more centralized, since this way of structuring is more efficient.

Lawrence and Lorsch consider matters of conflict resolution because conflicts arise quickly and naturally in a highly differentiated organization, and the management of these conflicts is critical for efficient and effective organizational functioning. Moreover, if the organization is highly differentiated *and* decentralized, conflict is even more likely.

Finally, how well an organization operates is also a function of the nature of the interface between management and employees. Lawrence and Lorsch recognize the importance of individual motivation and effective supervision. They tend to view motivation in terms of expectancy, believing that employee's motivation (and morale) is based on the degree to which their expectations about how they should be treated are actually met by management in the work environment.

In summary, Lawrence and Lorsch are known as contingency theorists. They advocate no single form of organizational structure or single style of management. The structure and the style depend on the business of the organization and its environment—how variable or how stable it is.

Currently, Lawrence and Lorsch are among the most influential theorists for OD practitioners. There is something appealing about the idea of considering contingencies before acting.

THE ORGANIZATION AS A FAMILY—LEVINSON

Harry Levinson believes that an organization can be psychoanalyzed and that an organization operates like a family, with the chief executive officer as the father. According to Levinson, all organizations "recapitulate the basic family structure in a culture." Thus, the type of organization Levinson understands best, of course, is the family-owned business, and his theory about organizations and how they operate and change has its roots in Freudian psychoanalytic theory (Levinson 1972*a*, 1972*b*).

Levinson does not look at organizations exclusively through psychoanalytic glasses, however. He is well aware that structure, the type of business, the kinds of people who are attracted to the organization as employees, and the outside environment affect the internal behavioral dynamics of organizations. More important for Levinson's diagnosis of an organization, however, is the nature of the organization's personality (we might call it culture). He believes that an organization has a personality, just as an individual does, and that the health of an organization, like that of a person, can be determined in terms of how effectively the various parts of the personality are integrated. He refers to this process as maintaining equilibrium. Levinson also believes that implicit psychological contracts exist between management and employees, based on earlier experiences from family life. If the employees behave themselves (are good boys and girls), the parents (management) will reward them appropriately. Thus, the psychological contract is characterized by dependency. Note that this aspect of Levinson's theory is similar to Argyris's theory.

Continuing the psychoanalytic paradigm, Levinson

theorizes that the chief executive officer represents the ego ideal for the organizational family and that this ideal, for better or for worse, motivates the kinds of people who are attracted to the organization in the first place, the interaction patterns among people in the organization, especially in matters of authority, and the kinds of people who are promoted. If a chief executive officer stays in office for a long time, the personality of the organization slowly crystallizes over the years; those who aspire to the ego ideal stay in the organization, and those who do not leave. Accordingly, Levinson believes that history is a critical factor in diagnosing an organization.

Levinson is a clinical psychologist who became more interested in organizational health than in individual psychodynamics as a result of his work at the Menninger Clinic. He has applied the principles of individual clinical therapy to his consulting practice with organizations. His approach as a consultant is (1) to immerse himself as deeply as possible in the psychodynamics of the organization; (2) to take a thorough history of the organization, just as a clinician would in the initial session with a patient; (3) to work predominantly with top management, since they tend to shape the personality of the organization and are therefore in the best position to change it; and (4) to pay particular attention to the stress factors in the organization and to how organizational members cope. In regard to this last point, Levinson is considered the "great worrier" among OD theorists. He worries about executive stress (Levinson 1975) and about the incidence in an organization of such variables as psychosomatic illnesses, absenteeism, and business pressures, such as the all-out emphasis many organizations place on meeting the so-called bottom line. Levinson is very interested in what people do with their energy, in whether human energy in the organization is directed toward goal accomplishment or toward coping with stress.

In summary, as a consultant, Levinson uses the clinical case method in diagnosis, intervenes primarily at the top of an organization, and bases his theory on psychoanalysis. In his own words:

> You've got to take into account all the factors in an organization, just as you gather all the main facts of a person's life in taking a case history. But you need a comprehensive theory like psychoanalysis to make sense of all the facts, to make it hang together in a useful way. (1972a; p. 126)

Summary

At the risk of oversimplification, I have summarized ten theorists by categorizing them according to their perspectives and emphases and according to potential applications of their theoretical approaches. A summary of these factors is given in Table 1. Keep in mind

TABLE 1

Summary of Primary OD Theorists According to Their Perspectives, Emphases, and Applications

Perspective	Theorist	Emphasis	Application
Individual	Maslow and Herzberg	Individual needs	Career development, job enrichment
	Vroom and Lawler	Individual expectancies and values	Reward system design, performance appraisal
	Hackman and Oldham	Job satisfaction	Job and work design, job enrichment
	Skinner	Individual performance	Incentive systems, reward system design
Group	Lewin	Norms and values	Changing conformity patterns
	Argyris	Interpersonal competence and values	Training and education
	Bion	Group unconscious, psychoanalytic basis	Group behavior diagnosis
System	Likert	Management style and approach	Change to participative management
	Lawrence and Lorsch	Organizational structure	Change contingent on organizational environment
	Levinson	Organization as a family, psychoanalytic basis	Diagnosis of organization according to familial patterns

that there is no single, all-encompassing theory for organization development. What we have are several mini theories that help us understand certain aspects of organizational behavior and OD. Taken together and comparatively, they become more useful to the practitioner who must cope with an ever-changing, complex, total organization.

Thus, organization development comes from many sources and has its roots in more than one methodology and in a variety of theories and concepts. The background provided in this chapter, though varied, nevertheless has commonality. The trunk from these roots might be expressed as the attempt to improve an organization with methods that involve people and to create conditions whereby the talents of these people are used more effectively.

References

Argyris, C. 1973. "The CEO's Behavior: Key to Organizational Development." *Harvard Business Review* 51(2): 55–64.

———. 1971. *Management and Organizational Development*. New York: McGraw-Hill.

———. 1970. *Intervention Theory and Method*. Reading, Mass.: Addison-Wesley.

———. 1964. "T Groups for Organizational Effectiveness." *Harvard Business Review* 42(2): 60–74.

———. 1962. *Interpersonal Competence and Organizational Effectiveness*. Homewood, Ill.: Dorsey Press.

Argyris, C., and Schön, D. A. 1978. *Organizational Learning: A Theory of Action Perspective*. Reading, Mass.: Addison-Wesley.

"At Emery Air Freight: Positive Reinforcement Boosts Performance." *Organizational Dynamics* 1(3): 41–67.

Bion, W. R. 1961. *Experience in Groups*. New York: Basic Books.

Hackman, J. R., and Oldham, G. R. 1980. *Work Redesign*. Reading, Mass.: Addison-Wesley.

Hackman, J. R., and Oldham, G. R. 1975. "Development of the Job Diagnostic Survey." *Journal of Applied Psychology* 60: 159–70.

Harvey, J. B. 1974. "The Abilene Paradox: The Management of Agreement." *Organizational Dynamics* 3 (Summer): 63–80.

Herzberg, F. 1966. *Work and the Nature of Man*. Cleveland: World.

Herzberg, F.; Mausner, B.; and Snyderman, B. 1959. *The Motivation to Work*. New York: Wiley.

Lawler, E. E., III. 1973. *Motivation in Work Organizations*. Monterey, Calif.: Brooks/Cole.

Lawrence, P. R., and Lorsch, J. W. 1969. *Developing Organizations: Diagnosis and Action*. Reading, Mass.: Addison-Wesley.

Lawrence, P. R., and Lorsch, J. W. 1967. *Organization and Environment: Managing Differentiation and Integration*. Boston: Division of Research, Harvard Business School.

Levinson, H. 1975. *Executive Stress*. New York: Harper.

———. 1972a. *Organizational Diagnosis*. Cambridge, Mass.: Harvard University Press.

———. 1972b. "The Clinical Psychologist as Organizational Diagnostician." *Professional Psychology* 3: 34–40.

Lewin, K. 1958. "Group Decision and Social Change." In *Readings in Social Psychology*, ed. E. E. Maccoby, T. M. Newcomb, and E. L. Hartley, pp. 197–211. New York: Holt, Rinehart and Winston.

———. 1951. *Field Theory in Social Science*. New York: Harper.

———. 1948. *Resolving Social Conflicts*. New York: Harper.

Likert, R. 1967. *The Human Organization*. New York: McGraw-Hill.

———. 1961. *New Patterns of Management*. New York: McGraw-Hill.

McGregor, D. 1960. *The Human Side of Enterprise*. New York: McGraw-Hill.

Marrow, A. J. 1969. *The Practical Theorist*. New York: Basic Books.

Maslow, A. H. 1954. *Motivation and Personality*. New York: Harper and Brothers.

Rioch, M. J. 1970. "The Work of Wilfred Bion on Groups." *Psychiatry* 33: 56–66.

Skinner, B. F. 1971. *Beyond Freedom and Dignity*. New York: Knopf.

———. 1953. *Science and Human Behavior*. New York: Macmillan.

———. 1948. *Walden Two*. New York: Macmillan.

Vroom, V. 1964. *Work and Motivation*. New York: Wiley.

Organizational Diagnosis:
Six Places to Look for Trouble
With or Without a Theory

Marvin R. Weisbord

No single model or conceptual scheme embraces the whole breadth and complexity of reality, even though each in turn may be useful in particular instances. This is why management remains an art, for the practitioner must go beyond the limits of theoretical knowledge if he is to be effective (Tilles, 1963).

For several years I have been experimenting with "cognitive maps" of organizations. These are labels that would help me better describe what I saw and heard and understand the relationships among various bits of data. I started this endeavor when I realized that though I knew many organization theories, most were either (1) too narrow to include everything I wished to understand or (2) too broadly abstract to give much guidance about what to do.

This article represents a progress report on my efforts to combine bits of data, theories, research, and hunches into a working tool that anyone can use. It is one example of a process I believe goes on among practitioners that is neither well documented nor well understood (Weisbord, 1974a). The process does not take place in a mode consistent with the protocols of social science research. It is not tied to any particular theory, nor is it subject to easy translation into research instruments. It is not intended to prove or disprove hypotheses. Rather, it represents what Vaill (1975; Friedlander and Brown, 1974) calls a "practice theory"—a synthesis of knowledge and experience into a concept that bears "some relation to public, objective theories about organizational situations, but in no sense (is) identical to them."

Reprinted from J. E. Jones and J. W. Pfeiffer (Eds.), *Group & Organization Studies*, Volume 1, Number 4. San Diego, Ca.: University Associates, December 1976. Used with permission.

I think this accurately describes what I have been calling, for want of a more elegant name, the "six-box model." This model (Figure 1) has helped me rapidly expand my diagnostic framework from interpersonal and group issues to the more complicated contexts in which organizations are managed. It provides six labels, under which can be sorted much of the activity, formal and informal, that takes place in organizations. The labels allow consultants to apply whatever theories they know when doing a diagnosis and to discover new connections between apparently unrelated events.

We can visualize Figure 1 as a radar screen. Just as air controllers use radar to chart the course of aircraft—height, speed, distance apart, and weather—those seeking to improve an organization must observe relationships among the boxes and not focus on any particular blip.

Organizational "process" issues, for example, will show up as blips in one or more boxes, signaling the blockage of work on important organizational tasks. (Process issues relate to *how* and *whether* work gets done, rather than *what* is to be done.)

Unfortunately, such issues too often are seen as the result of someone's personality. For example, the failure of a group to confront its differences may be diagnosed as the inability of one or two people to assert themselves. Yet, if the consultant were to look closely, he might find that no one in the organization confronts, independent of the assertion skills they may have. Those who do confront may be considered deviant and may be tolerated only to the extent that they have power.

From a management standpoint, it is probably more useful to think of process issues as systemic, that

223

FIGURE 1
The Six-Box Organizational Model

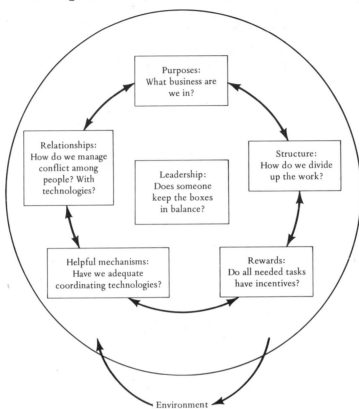

is, as part of the organization's management culture. This culture can be described as:

1. "Fit" between *organization* and *environment*—the extent to which purposes and structure support high performance and ability to change with conditions; and/or
2. "Fit" between *individual* and *organization*—the extent to which people support or subvert formal mechanisms intended to carry out an organization's purposes.

The relationship between individual and organization is the basis for many important books in the organizational literature. McGregor (1960) argued that a better fit might be attained under Theory Y assumptions (people like to work, achieve, and be responsible) than Theory X assumptions (people are passive, dependent, and need to be controlled). Blake and Mouton (1964) devised elaborate change strategies (variations of "Grid" theory) based on the notion that productivity and human satisfaction need not be mutually exclusive.

Maslow (1971) struggled in his last years to reconcile employee self-actualization—personal growth and creativity—with an organization's needs for structure, order, and predictability. Argyris has written extensively on the potential incompatibilities of individuals and organizations and the threat that bureaucratic structures pose to self-esteem (Argyris, 1957).

In the last ten years, both managers and consultants have become much more conscious of organizations as open systems in which structure and behavior are heavily influenced by environment. Lawrence and Lorsch (1967) compared high- and low-performance businesses in terms of structural requirements—based largely on rate of change in business technology and environment—and came up with a contingency theory: The way subunits of an organization are structured depends not only on their functions but on environmental factors, which results in different policies and procedures for different organizations.

Sociotechnical theorists such as Trist (1969) have tried to reconcile structured technologies and work systems with people's individual and social needs, theorizing that high performance equals an optimum balance between technology (''task'') and people (''process'').

Each of the possible frameworks highlights important organizational issues; each has been the basis for useful interventions in the organization development repertoire. Yet, none is an adequate tool for the management of an entire organization without an expansion of concepts.

Management needs a view simple enough, and complete enough, to improve the quality of its decisions. What follows is a description of how the six-box organizational model can be used to put into perspective *whatever* theories and concepts a consultant already knows along with *whatever* problems present themselves in diagnosing an organization's problems.

The circle in Figure 1 describes the boundaries of an organization to be diagnosed. *Environment* means forces difficult to control from inside that demand a response—customers, government, unions, students, families, friends, etc. It is not always clear where the boundaries are or should be. Although such a system can be characterized accurately as ''open,'' its rationality depends on partially closing off infinite choices. Deciding where the boundary lies is an act of

reason wed to values, for there are no absolutes (Vickers, 1965).

The consultant may find it necessary to set boundaries arbitrarily so that a diagnosis can proceed. I do this by picking a unit name (i.e., XYZ Company, ABC Department, QUR Team) and listing groups or individuals inside the boundary by virtue of dollar commitments, contract, or formal membership. Within the boundaries, the boxes interact to create what is sometimes called an input-output system, whose function is to transform resources into goods or services. Figure 2 illustrates the six-box organization/environment using input-output terms. Given that organizations function or do not function depending on what is going on in and between each of the six boxes, a consultant has a basis for doing an organizational diagnosis.

Formal and Informal Systems

Within each box are two potential trouble sources—the formal system that exists on paper and the informal system, or what people actually do. Neither system is necessarily better, but both exist. In doing a diagnosis, it helps to identify blips in each system and to attempt to define the relationships among them.

Diagnosing the formal system requires some informed guessing, based on knowledge of what the organization *says*—in its statements, reports, charts, and speeches—about how it is organized. The guessing comes after comparing its rhetoric with its environment and making a judgment about whether everything fits—whether society will value and underwrite

FIGURE 2

The Six-Box Organizational Model Using Input-Output Terms

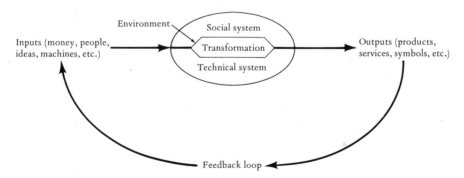

an organization with such a purpose and such a means of organizing itself. Much expert consultation is aimed at bringing organizational rhetoric into better harmony with the outside world.

However, in every organization there is another level of behavior—what people actually do. Diagnosing these informal systems is sometimes called "normative" diagnosis (Clapp, 1974). It focuses on the frequency with which people take certain actions in relation to how important these actions are for organizational performance. Normative behavior usually determines whether otherwise technically excellent systems succeed or fail, because normative behavior indicates the degree to which the system as designed meets the needs of the people who have to operate it. Sometimes norms cannot be changed informally, so there is a need to study relationships *between* the two levels of analysis. By persisting in such an inquiry, a consultant discovers some of the reasons why the input-transformation-output stream is not flowing as smoothly as it could.

How to Collect Data

Collecting data on which to base a diagnosis can be as simple as brainstorming or as complex as a "grand design" research methodology involving hypotheses, instruments, and computer analysis. Complexity aside, there are four ways to collect data:

1. *Observation.* Watch what people do in meetings, on the job, on the phone, etc.
2. *Reading.* Follow the written record—speeches, reports, charts, graphs, etc.
3. *Interviews.* Question everyone involved with a particular project.
4. *Survey.* Use standard questionnaires or design your own. Surveys are most useful when they ask for information not readily obtainable in any other way, such as attitudes, perceptions, opinions, preferences, beliefs, etc.

All four methods of data collection can be used to isolate the two major kinds of discrepancy—between what people say (formal) and what they do (informal) and between what is (organization as it exists) and what ought to be (appropriate environmental fit). The trick is not to use any particular methods, but to

sort the evidence of one's senses into some categories that encourage sensible decisions.

Where to Start

There are two main reasons why one might want to diagnose an organization: to find out systematically what its strengths and weaknesses are or to uncover reasons why either the producers or consumers of a particular output are dissatisfied. Because the latter reason is most often the trigger for corrective actions, I suggest starting a diagnosis by considering one major output. Tracing its relationship to the whole system will result in an understanding of the gaps in the organization between what is and what ought to be.

Let us look at one output—say a single product or service—and determine how satisfied the *consumers* are and how satisfied the *producers* are. The central assumption behind this activity is that consumer acceptance, more than any other factor, determines whether an organization prospers or fades. Satisfied consumers generally indicate a good fit with the environment at one major contact point. Without satisfied consumers, producer satisfaction is likely to be unstable. If neither group is satisfied, an organization is in serious trouble. If one group is happy and the other is not, trouble is forthcoming. Either way, the situation can be diagnosed by tracing the dissatisfactions through each box, looking for a likely intervention point.

Purposes

People have all sorts of feelings (mainly anxiety) about work, which cannot be addressed rationally if an organization's goals remain obscure. Thus, the two critical factors in this box are goal clarity and goal agreement (Steers and Porter, 1974). They must both be present.

In part the environment (what will society support?) and in part managers and members, who succeed to the extent that they read the environment right in relation to themselves, decide an organization's purposes. Purposes can be seen as a sort of psychological negotiation between "what we have to do" (for survival) and "what we want to do" (for growth, self-expression, idealism, etc.). The outcome of this negotiation is called "priorities." Effective organizations translate priorities into programs, projects, and products aimed at particular consumers.

Ill-defined or overly broad purposes may increase anxiety and strain relations among producers and consumers alike. Considerable conflict exists when purposes are unclear or when people disagree on what the priorities should be, although such conflict may serve certain people. In universities, medical centers, and some industrial staff groups, for example, competition is so high, interdependence is so low, and goals are so diffuse, that the only way individuals keep control, and thus maintain self-esteem, is by resisting efforts to focus organizational resources. Without concentration, organizations cannot be made to perform, according to Drucker (1974a).

Hence a diagnosis first should examine *goal "fit."* (Are this organization's purposes ones that society values and will pay for?) It should also consider *goal clarity.* (How well articulated are these goals in the formal system, both for producers and consumers?) Finally, the informal (process) issue is *goal agreement.* (To what extent do people understand and support the organization's purposes?) Some organizations have inherent low goal clarity because their concerns are so global or all encompassing that each member defines them in his own personal way. Certain policy institutes, foundations, and universities, for instance, have such a spectrum of possibilities that priorities are unclear; commitment, therefore, is spotty.

Structure

In organizations, as in architecture, form follows function. Every structure is good for something, no one is good for everything. There are three main ways to organize:

1. By function—specialists work together
2. By product, program, or project—multiskilled teams work together
3. A mixture of both—two homes for everyone (Gulick, 1937)

None of these structures is trouble free, but each does result in different problems. In the *functional* organization (see diagram), for instance, division of labor, budgets, promotions, and rewards are all based

FUNCTIONAL ORGANIZATION

```
                  ┌─────────────────┐
                  │ General Manager │
                  └─────────────────┘
         ┌─────────────┼─────────────┐
   ┌──────────┐  ┌────────────┐  ┌────────┐
   │  Sales   │  │ Production │  │  R&D   │
   └──────────┘  └────────────┘  └────────┘
```

on special competence. Functional bosses have the most influence on decisions and they seek to maximize their own goals, not the organization's as a whole. The drawbacks are that intergroup conflict is more predictable; big decisions pile up at the top; few members have the overall picture; and it is difficult to shift directions rapidly.

On the good side are support for in-depth competence; people at each level who speak the same language; freedom to specialize while others worry about coordination; and a chance for people to maximize whatever they do well. Functional organizations are stable and work best where environment and technologies change slowly, where quick response is not essential, and where in-depth competence is necessary. They resist rapid change. Functionalism and bureaucracy make fine marriage partners.

By contrast, the *product-line* or program or project-team organization works better in fast-changing environments. In product-line organizations, people do multiple tasks and integrate skills around one output. (See diagram below.) In this structure, coordination with other teams is minimal, cutting down intergroup conflict. Rewards, promotions, and influence go to those who can integrate resources to innovate, produce, and deliver a product or service quickly.

On the other hand, in-depth competence erodes rapidly in each specialty, for generalists cannot keep up with everything and specialists become harder to

PRODUCT ORGANIZATION

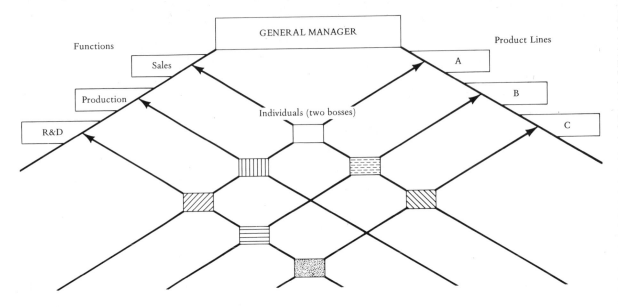

attract. Innovation is restricted to existing areas. Groups may compete for pooled resources such as computers or for staff functions such as purchasing. Internal task conflicts may emerge, making division of labor on each team a salient issue.

When organizations decentralize, they often change from functional to product structure, improving the informal system at an eventual cost to formal needs.

Therefore, some organizations try to have it both ways. This gives rise to the *matrix* or mixed model (see diagram), which grew up in the aerospace industry, where projects required both diverse state-of-the-art expertise and focused effort on each project. In the matrix model, people have two or more formal locations on the chart.

No organization could neatly arrange itself this way from top to bottom. It might better be called a *mixed model,* in which some units of a company, university, or medical center may be functional and some programmatic; some people may wear two hats and some only one, based on the various environments surrounding each subunit (Weisbord, 1974b).

A mixed model provides maximum flexibility, for it can shrink or expand with need. It provides multiple career paths, rewarding both special and integrative skills. However, these plusses are offset by serious drawbacks that might be summarized as "human limitation." Ambiguity is high. Conflict management requires considerable time and effort, for conflict is rife and built in.

To be wholly effective, practically and psychologically, a mixed organization needs two budget lines, contracts with two bosses, dual reward systems, and so on. Such mechanisms are expensive. Moreover, they are not well understood. None of us has had much experience, in school or at work, to prepare us for such a set of relationships.

People who try mixed models find that they must invent or discover new procedures and norms to support their goals. This is very hard to do and seems justified only when the stakes are high (saving lives, landing on the moon). It is hardly worth the energy if simpler forms will serve, for it greatly complicates relationships (Kingdon, 1973).

In diagnosing structure, a consultant must look for the fit between the goal (output) and the structure producing it (formal system), then attend to how the work is *actually* divided up and performed and how people use or subvert the organization chart.

Relationships

Three types of work relationship are the most important:

1. Between people—peers or boss-subordinate
2. Between units doing different tasks

3. Between people and their technologies (i.e., systems or equipment)

In the formal system, the consultant should diagnose such relationships in terms of how much interdependence is required to get the work done. There are two possible dysfunctions:

1. People need to work together and do not do it well.
2. People do not need to work together, but try to force collaboration (i.e., in the name of "good human relations" or because they "should").

A second level of relationship diagnosis relates to the degree of built-in conflict. Some units (sales and production, for example) may fight with each other as willingly as they eat. Such conflict is legitimate, because each unit needs to see things differently to do good work. This conflict is potentially useful and ought to be managed rather than suppressed (Lawrence and Lorsch, 1967). Quality of relations between units (or people) matters more to an organization's performance the more the units must work together to achieve results.

How conflict is managed is an issue for normative diagnosis. Some people fight openly for what they want. Others manipulate, deceive, pull strings, or do everything but burn down the building to gain their objective, thus helping themselves and probably hurting the organization. Here is a simple classification of conflict management norms:

1. *Forcing.* Allow more powerful people to have their way.
2. *Smoothing.* Reduce differences by pretending there are none. Organize all units the same way whether it helps them do a good job or not.
3. *Avoiding or suppressing.* Make it disloyal to raise disagreements openly.
4. *Bargaining.* Negotiate differences, hold some cards in the hole, narrow the issues, and play for maximum advantage.
5. *Confronting.* Open all issues and data to inspection by both parties. Create mechanisms to surface all aspects of disagreement and initiate problem solving.

A consultant needs to diagnose first for required interdependence, then for *quality of relations,* and finally for modes of conflict management (Lawrence et al., 1973).

Rewards

Having a reward system (formal) in no way guarantees that people will feel and act as if they are rewarded (informal). Maslow (1954) explained the problem in terms of a "hierarchy of needs," which, once satisfied, become essential. Herzberg et al. (1959) showed that meeting basic needs ("hygiene factors") was necessary for morale but not sufficient for the motivation to carry out creatively the tasks an organization needs to have done. Figure 3 shows the relationship between Maslow's theory and Herzberg's research findings.

Both reinforce the point that the fit between person and organization improves when there is a chance for growth, responsibility, and achievement. A reward system that pays off in fringe benefits and salary alone is inadequate unless people also value their work and see in it a chance to grow.

The trick is translating reward theory into organizational practice. Some managers still believe salary and fringe benefits motivate, although there is considerable evidence to support the idea that once a need is satisfied it no longer motivates. Thus, salary and benefits stimulate performance only when given as symbols of worthy work that is needed and valued by the organization (recognition).

A second important issue is "equity" or fairness among members of an organization. Informal feelings or beliefs determine whether or not people *act* as if rewarded, independent of how much they actually receive. Herbert Meyer has made a convincing argument that merit pay may undermine self-esteem and reduce commitment to the work itself, because most of us feel we *always* are worth more than our supervisors judge, especially in comparison to others (Meyer, 1975).

Moreover, especially in industrial systems where incentive pay is based on individual production, the informal norm of peer approval frequently outweighs the economic benefits of rate breaking. This functions to hold down production to a level below what people are capable of doing (Whyte and Miller, 1957).

In white collar work, the problem is even more complex. For example, finding rewards for teaching that

FIGURE 3
The Relation Between Maslow's Need Hierarchy and Herzberg's Research *

Maslow's Needs Hierarchy	Herzberg's Factors	
Personal growth	Motivators	Work itself (achievement)
Esteem		Advancement (recognition)
Belongingness	Hygiene Factors	Interpersonal and supervisory relationships
Safety		Technical supervision Working conditions Company policy and administration
Physiological		Salary

* This integration was called to my attention by Dr. Robert Maddox of RCA Staff, who used it in a 1965 Professional Personal Programs notebook on motivation.

are as psychologically potent as the rewards for research is a critical dilemma in universities.

Thus, before making the diagnosis, the consultant should take into account questions such as the following:

1. What does the organization need to do (fit)?
2. What does it pay off for, both actually and psychologically (formal system)?
3. What do people *feel* rewarded or punished for doing (informal system)?

Leadership

Much leadership theory focuses on interpersonal style—the informal system. Likert (1967) placed behavior on an autocratic-democratic continuum. He found that "System 4" managers (participative) exhibited high support, had high standards, and used group methods. They were also more productive than "System 1" autocrats. Blake and Mouton (1964) hypothesized that the best managers are those who can emphasize production or people, as the situation requires.

Both theories suggest development through training. Pseudodemocrats can learn to stop asking others for answers they already have and be more decisive; autocrats can learn to collect more data before proceeding. Both can learn to solicit and use feedback.

Fiedler (1967) took a different approach. He sorted leaders by task or relationship orientation; he concluded that each style is good in some situations, neither is good in all, and changing one's orientation is difficult to do. Rather than training, Fiedler recommended either (a) fitting leaders to the task or situation or (b) changing the task to fit the leader's style.

Although this notion takes in so many contingencies that it is not easy to use, it does highlight an issue that is not very well understood, especially in nonindustrial organizations: the growing evidence that interpersonal skills are most functional in unstructured, ambiguous, and/or high-anxiety situations. Although a leader can use such skills to smooth ruffled feathers, the skills contribute little to organizational performance in the absence of goal clarity and goal agreement.

No one can be sure what is required for good leadership in every situation. The best a manager can do is try to understand his organization and its requirements and then judge how much his leadership norms contribute to or block progress and how easily new skills can be learned if needed.

One formal dimension of leadership may make the difference between an organization that "works" and one that does not. Selznick (1957) names four leadership *tasks,* which, if not done, seriously undermine organizations:

1. Defining purposes.
2. Embodying purposes in programs.
3. Defending institutional integrity.
4. Ordering internal conflict.

Much turmoil in organizations—especially among administrative employees—results from a failure of leadership to define, embody, and defend purposes and to manage internal conflict. A unique task of leadership, then, independent of task and relationship skills, might be to take responsibility for scanning the six-box radar screen, looking for blips both formal and informal, and doing something about them. This task can be shared, but it cannot be delegated. This is especially true in functional organizations, in which, if specialists look out for their *own* tasks, they cannot be expected to be responsible for the total organization.

I do not believe that leaders should know and do everything, but they should know where the trouble spots are and how these affect the whole organization. This requires them to systematically monitor and initiate corrective action (interventions) whenever the radar reveals a blip that threatens performance.

The main leadership dilemma is persuading others to share the risk. They will not be willing if they think a leader has defective vision, for normative behavior tends to be reinforced from the top down. Few people get out ahead of the boss.

Leadership requires, in addition to behavioral skill, an understanding of the environment and a will to focus purposes, especially if there is a problem in one of the six boxes. A leader's precise understanding of his role and the extent to which this understanding results in his using mechanisms designed to keep formal and informal systems in balance are the main components of a successful leadership style. No one can achieve exactly the proper balance; to the extent that it is not achieved, a formal organization may, in practice, be (informally) leaderless.

Helpful Mechanisms

Mechanisms have proven to be a useful way to think about the cement that binds an organization together to make it more than a collection of individuals with separate needs. Helpful mechanisms are related to the contents of all the other boxes. Mechanisms are the procedures, policies, meetings, systems, committees, bulletin boards, memos, reports, meeting rooms, space, information, and so on that facilitate concerted efforts. Problems with such mechanisms are most easily understood by observing the flow of work on all sides and the points at which it seems clogged.

An effective organization continually revises its mechanisms, eliminating some or adding others, as the need arises. If a gap between what is and what ought to be is identified, it is often found that no mechanism exists for closing it, which often leads to much informal discussion over coffee and little movement toward a solution. The deliberate creation of new mechanisms is essential for the identification and closing of gaps.

All good managers and effective consultants provide structured procedures, meetings, and ground rules for diagnosis and action and know how to create problem-solving vehicles that did not previously exist.

In addition, there are four other processes that require helpful mechanisms,[1] which every organization must attend to in some fashion. Each has the potential for helpful (formal intent) or unhelpful (informal result) outcomes. The processes are planning, budgeting, control, and measurement (information). Without helpful mechanisms in each of these areas, organizations will act more like rudderless ships than purposeful men-of-war. Thus, the first diagnostic question for a consultant is whether an organization does have some formal helpful mechanisms.

The second set of questions (informal) is how these systems actually are used; to what extent quantitative data are fed back to employees so that they can make better course corrections; to what extent relevant others are involved in planning and budgeting; and to what extent control is used as a safety and alert system to educate rather than to punish.

A consultant must watch for two situations in particular when diagnosing helpful mechanisms. One is the lack of any rational planning, budgeting, control, or measurement systems. In this case, no amount of interpersonal or group process work will "improve" an organization. Second, and worse, is the organization that has budgeting and controls, but no goals that

---

[1] These processes are covered in many standard management texts. For a source that integrates them in a behavioral context, see Kast & Rosenzweig (1970).

FIGURE 4
Matrix for Survey Design or Data Analysis

	Formal System (work to be done)	*Informal System* (process of working)
1. Purposes	Goal clarity	Goal agreement
2. Structure	Functional, program, or matrix?	How work is actually done or not done.
3. Relationships	Who should deal with whom on what? Which technologies should be used?	How well do they do it? Quality of relations? Modes of conflict management?
4. Rewards (Incentives)	Explicit system. What is it?	Implicit, psychic rewards. What do people *feel* about payoffs?
5. Leadership	What do top people manage? What systems in use?	How? Normative "style" of administration?
6. Helpful Mechanisms	Budget system Management information (measures?) Planning Control	What are they actually used for? How function in practice? How are systems subverted?

Diagnostic questions may be asked on two levels:
1. How big a gap is there between formal and informal systems? (This speaks to the fit between individual and organization.)
2. How much discrepancy is there between what is and what ought to be? (This highlights the fit between organization and environment.)

the people doing the work agree are *organizationally relevant* (for them). The latter describes some universities and medical centers, for example, in which financial control systems provide an illusion of rationality that, like beauty, is only skin deep (Drucker, 1974b).

OD in such situations is not an *organization* development process at all. The best than a consultant can do is help members make more rational decisions about their own careers, thereby contributing to their personal growth. Certainly there is no interdependency to be negotiated in the absence of agreement about the ends toward which the organization is being managed (Weisbord, 1976).

The six-box organization model is a useful "early-

warning system" for a consultant who is trying to decide where and whether to take corrective action. There are three levels of diagnosis that provide clues to appropriate interventions:

1. Does the organization fit its environment? If not, it cannot be developed until the fit can be rationalized and supported.
2. Is the organization structured to carry out its purposes? If not, work on structure is required before an examination of interpersonal and group processes can take on meaning other than personal growth.
3. Are the organization's norms out of phase with its intent? How much discrepancy exists between for-

mal and informal systems? If this is the main problem (as it often is in otherwise successful businesses), most of the management and organization development interventions will apply.

Any diagnostic questions a consultant asks about any of the boxes will yield useful data. Figure 4 summarizes the important questions about both formal and informal systems. There are as many ways to use these ideas as there are managers. I have offered this practice theory as the basis for starting new teams, tasks forces, and committees, or for helping existing teams decide what they need to do next. Others have adapted the six-box model to screen prospective employers, evaluate the management literature in terms of which issues it illuminates, write job descriptions, and organize research findings. It is also a useful teaching tool in comparing various types of organizations.

Finally, the six-box organization model provides an easy way of testing the extent to which an intervention seems right. I have used it both to explain and to anticipate my failures and have found that more anticipating means less explaining. In my experience, all interventions that ''fail'' eventually do so for one of three reasons (Bowers et al., 1975):

1. The intervention is inappropriate to the problem or organization. (A T-group may improve relationships without surfacing serious deficiences of purpose, structure, or technology.)
2. The intervention deals with the wrong (less salient) blip on the radar screen. (When the pressing problem is ineffective leadership, a new reward system, no matter how desirable, may not make a difference.)
3. The intervention solves the identified problem, thus heightening issues in other boxes it was *not* designed to solve. An organization can be restructured to better fit its environment without changing norms and relationships that require other interventions.

References

Argyris, C. *Personality and Organization: The Conflict Between System and the Individual.* New York: Harper & Row, 1957.

Blake, R. R. and Mouton, J. S. *The Managerial Grid.* Houston, Tex.: Gulf, 1964.

Bowers, D. G., Franklin, J. L., and Pecorella, P. A. Matching problems, precursors, and interventions in OD: A systemic approach. *Journal of Applied Behavioral Science,* 1975, *11* (4), 391–409.

Clapp, N. W. Work group norms: Leverage for organizational change, I-theory, II-application. *Organization development reading series* (No. 2). Plainfield, N.J.: Block Petrella Associates, 1974.

Drucker, P. F. The Dimensions of Management. In P. F. Drucker, *Management: Tasks, Responsibilities, Practices.* New York: Harper & Row, 1974. (a)

Drucker, P. F. Why Service Institutions Do Not Perform. In P. F. Drucker, *Management: Tasks, Responsibilities, Practices.* New York: Harper & Row, 1974. (b)

Fiedler, F. E. *A Theory of Leadership Effectiveness.* New York: McGraw-Hill, 1967.

Friedlander, F., and Brown, L. D. Organization development. *Annual Review of Psychology,* 1974, *25,* 319.

Gulick, L. Notes on the Theory of Organizations. In L. Gulick and L. F. Urwick (Eds.), *Papers on the Science of Administration.* Columbia University, Institute of Public Administration, 1937.

Herzberg, F., Mausner, B., and Snyderman, B. *The Motivation to Work.* New York: Wiley, 1959.

Kast, F. E., and Rosenzweig, J. E. *Organization and Management: A Systems Approach.* New York: McGraw-Hill, 1970.

Kingdon, D. R. *Matrix Organization: Managing Information Technologies.* London: Tavistock, 1973.

Lawrence, P. R., and Lorsch, J. W. *Organization and Environment.* Boston: Harvard University, Graduate School of Business Administration, 1967.

Lawrence, P. R., Weisbord, M. R., and Charns, M. P. *Academic Medical Center Self-Study Guide.* Washington, D.C.: Report of Physicians' Assistance Branch, Bureau of Health, Manpower Education, National Institutes of Health, 1973.

Likert, R. *The Human Organization: Its Management and Value.* New York: McGraw-Hill, 1967.

Maslow, A. H. *Motivation and Personality.* New York: Harper, 1954.

Maslow, A. H. Synergy in the Society and in the Individual. In A. H. Maslow, *The Farther Reaches of Human Nature.* New York: Viking Press, 1971.

McGregor, D. *The Human Side of Enterprise.* New York: McGraw-Hill, 1960.

Meyer, H. H. The pay-for-performance dilemma. *Organizational Dynamics,* 1975, *3*(3), 39–50.

Selznick, P. *Leadership in Administration.* New York: Harper & Row, 1957.

Steers, R. M., and Porter, L. W. *The Role of Task Goal Attributes in Employee Performance* (Report No. TR-24). Washington, D.C.: Office of Naval Research, April 1974.

Tilles, S. The manager's job: A systems approach. *Harvard Business Review,* 1963, *41*(1), 73–81.

Trist, E. L. On Socio-Technical Systems. In W. G. Bennis, K. D. Benne, & R. Chin, *The Planning of Change* (2nd ed.). New York: Holt, Rinehart and Winston, 1969.

Vaill, P. B. Practice Theories in Organization Development. In J. D. Adams (Ed.), *New Technologies in Organization Development: 2.* La Jolla, Calif.: University Associates, 1975.

Vickers, G. *The Art of Judgment.* New York: Basic Books, 1965.

Weisbord, M. R. The gap between OD practice and theory—and publication. *Journal of Applied Behavioral Science,* 1974, *10*(4), 476–484. (a)

Weisbord, M. R. A Mixed Model for Medical Centers: Changing Structure and Behavior. In J. Adams (Ed.), *Theory and Method in Organization Development: An Evolutionary Process.* Arlington, Va.: NTL Institute for Applied Behavioral Science, 1974. (b)

Weisbord, M. R. Why organization development hasn't worked (so far) in medical centers. *Health Care Management Review,* April 1976, 17–28.

Whyte, W. F., and Miller, F. B. Industrial Sociology. In J. B. Gittler (Ed.), *Review of Sociology: Analysis of a Decade.* New York: Wiley, 1957.

A Model For Diagnosing
Organizational Behavior

David A. Nadler and Michael T. Tushman

Management's primary job is to make organizations operate effectively. Society's work gets done through organizations and management's function is to get organizations to perform that work. Getting organizations to operate effectively is difficult, however. Understanding one individual's behavior is challenging in and of itself; understanding a group that's made up of different individuals and comprehending the many relationships among those individuals is even more complex. Imagine, then, the mind-boggling complexity of a large organization made up of thousands of individuals and hundreds of groups with myriad relationships among these individuals and groups.

But organizational behavior must be managed in spite of this overwhelming complexity; ultimately the organization's work gets done through people, individually or collectively, on their own or in collaboration with technology. Therefore, the management of organizational behavior is central to the management task—a task that involves the capacity to *understand* the behavior patterns of individuals, groups, and organizations, to *predict* what behavioral responses will be elicited by various managerial actions, and finally to use this understanding and these predictions to achieve *control*.

How can one achieve understanding and learn how to predict and control organizational behavior? Given its inherent complexity and enigmatic nature, one needs tools to unravel the mysteries, paradoxes, and apparent contradictions that present themselves in the everyday life of organizations. One tool is the conceptual framework or model. A model is a theory that indicates which factors (in an organization, for example) are most critical or important. It also shows how these factors are related—that is, which factors or combination of factors cause other factors to change. In a sense then, a model is a roadmap that can be used to make sense of the terrain of organizational behavior.

The models we use are critical because they guide our analysis and action. In any organizational situation, problem solving involves the collection of information about the problem, the interpretation of that information to determine specific problem types and causes, and the development of action plans accordingly. The models that individuals use influence the kind of data they collect and the kind they ignore; models guide people's approach to analyzing or interpreting the data they have; finally, models help people choose their course of action.

Indeed, anyone who has been exposed to an organization already has some sort of implicit model. People develop these roadmaps over time, building on their own experiences. These implicit models (they usually are not explicitly written down or stated) guide behavior; they vary in quality, validity, and sophistication depending on the nature and extent of the experiences of the model builder, his or her perceptiveness, his or her ability to conceptualize and generalize from experiences, and so on.

We are not solely dependent, however, on the implicit and experience-based models that individuals develop. Since there has been extensive research and theory development on the subject of organizational behavior over the last four decades, it is possible to use scientifically developed explicit models for analyzing organizational behavior and solving organizational problems.

We plan to discuss one particular model, a general model of organizations. Instead of describing a specific phenomenon or aspect of organizational life (such as a model of motivation or a model of organizational design), the general model of organization attempts to provide a framework for thinking about the organization as a total system. The model's major premise is that for organizations to be effective, their subparts or components must be consistently structured and managed: they must approach a state of congruence.

In the first section of this article, we will discuss the basic view of organizations that underlies the model—that is, systems theory. In the second section, we will present and discuss the model itself. In the third section, we will present an approach to using the model for organizational problem analysis. Finally, we will discuss some of the model's implications for thinking about organizations.

A Basic View of Organizations

There are many different ways of thinking about organizations. When a manager is asked to "draw a picture of an organization," he or she typically draws some version of a pyramidal organizational chart. This is a model that views the stable, formal relationships among the jobs and formal work units as the most critical factors of the organization. Although this clearly is one way to think about organizations, it is a very limited view. It excludes such factors as leadership behavior, the impact of the environment, informal relations, power distribution, and so on. Such a model can capture only a small part of what goes on in organizations. Its perspective is narrow and static.

The past two decades have seen a growing consensus that a viable alternative to the static classic models of organizations is to envision the organization as a social system. This approach stems from the observation that social phenomena display many of the characteristics of natural or mechanical systems. In particular, as Daniel Katz and Robert L. Kahn have argued, organizations can be better understood if they are considered as dynamic and open social systems.

What is a system? Most simply, a system is a set of interrelated elements—that is, a change in one ele-

ment affects other elements. An *open system* is one that interacts with its environment; it is more than just a set of interrelated elements. Rather, these elements make up a mechanism that takes input from the environment, subjects it to some form of transformation process, and produces output. At the most general level, it should be easy to visualize organizations as systems. Let us consider a manufacturing plant, for example. It is made up of different related components (a number of departments, jobs technologies, and so on). It receives inputs from the environment—that is, labor, raw material, production orders, and so on—and transforms these inputs into products.

As systems, organizations display a number of basic systems characteristics. Some of the most critical are these:

1. *Internal interdependence.* Changes in one component or subpart of an organization frequently have repercussions for other parts; the pieces are interconnected. Again, as in the manufacturing plant example, changes made in one element (for example, the skill levels of those hired to do jobs) will affect other elements (the productiveness of equipment used, the speed or quality of production activities, the nature of supervision needed, and so on).

2. *Capacity for feedback*—that is, information about the output that can be used to control the system. Organizations can correct errors and even change themselves because of this characteristic. If in our plant example plant management receives information that the quality of its product is declining, it can use this information to identify factors in the system itself that contribute to this problem. However, it is important to note that, unlike mechanized systems, feedback information does not always lead to correction. Organizations have the potential to use feedback to become self-correcting systems, but they do not always realize this potential.

3. *Equilibrium*—that is, a state of balance. When an event puts the system out of balance the system reacts and moves to bring itself back into balance. If one work group in our plant example were suddenly to increase its performance dramatically, it would throw the system out of balance. This group would be making increasing demands on the groups that supply it with the information or materials it needs; groups that work with the high-performing group's output would

feel the pressure of work-in-process inventory piling up in front of them. If some type of incentive is in effect, other groups might perceive inequity as this one group begins to earn more. We would predict that some actions would be taken to put the system back into balance. Either the rest of the plant would be changed to increase production and thus be back in balance with the single group, or (more likely) there would be pressure to get this group to modify its behavior in line with the performance levels of the rest of the system (by removing workers, limiting supplies, and so on). The point is that somehow the system would develop energy to move back toward a state of equilibrium or balance.

4. *Equifinality.* This characteristic of open systems means that different system configurations can lead to the same end or to the same type of input-output conversion. Thus there's no universal or "one best way" to organize.

5. *Adaptation.* For a system to survive, it must maintain a favorable balance of input or output transactions with the environment or it will run down. If our plant produces a product for which there are fewer applications, it must adapt to new demands and develop new products; otherwise, the plant will ultimately have to close its doors. Any system, therefore, must adapt by changing as environmental conditions change. The consequences of not adapting are evident when once-prosperous organizations decay (for example, the eastern railroads) because they fail to respond to environmental changes.

Thus systems theory provides a way of thinking about the organization in more complex and dynamic terms. But although the theory provides a valuable basic perspective on organizations, it is limited as a problem-solving tool. This is because a model systems theory is too abstract for use in day-to-day analysis of organizational behavior problems. Because of the level of abstraction of systems theory, we need to develop a more specific and pragmatic model based on the concepts of the open systems paradigm.

A Congruence Model of Organizational Behavior

Given the level of abstraction of open theory, our job is to develop a model that reflects the basic systems concepts and characteristics, but that is more specific and thus more usable as an analytic tool. We will describe a model that specifies the critical inputs, the major outputs, and the transformation processes that characterize organizational functioning.

The model puts its greatest emphasis on the transformation process and specifically reflects the critical system property of interdependence. It views organizations as made up of components or parts that interact with each other. These components exist in states of relative balance, consistency, or "fit" with each other. The different parts of an organization can fit well together and function effectively, or fit poorly and lead to problems, dysfunctions, or performance below potential. Our *congruence model of organizational behavior* is based on how well components fit together—that is, the congruence among the components; the effectiveness of this model is based on the quality of these "fits" or congruence.

The concept of congruence is not a new one. George Homans, in his pioneering work on social processes in organizations, emphasized the interaction and consistency among key elements of organizational behavior. Harold Leavitt, for example, identified four major components of organization as being people, tasks, technology, and structure. The model we will present here builds on these views and also draws from fit models developed and used by James Seiler, Paul Lawrence and Jay Lorsch, and Jay Lorsch and Alan Sheldon.

It is important to remember that we are concerned about creating a model for *behavioral* systems of the organization—the system of elements that ultimately produce behavior patterns and, in turn, organizational performance. Put simply, we need to deal with questions of the inputs the system has to work with, the outputs it must produce, the major components of the transformation process, and the ways in which these components interact.

INPUTS

Inputs are factors that, at any one point in time, make up the "givens" facing the organization. They're the material that the organization has to work with. There are several different types of inputs, each of which presents a different set of "givens" to the organization (see Figure 1 for an overview of inputs).

The first input is the *environment,* or all factors outside the organization being examined. Every orga-

FIGURE 1
Key Organizational Inputs

Input	Environment	Resources	History	Strategy
Definition	All factors, including institutions, groups, individuals, events, and so on, that are outside the organization being analyzed, but that have a potential impact on that organization	Various assets to which the organization has access, including human resources, technology, capital, information, and so on, as well as less tangible resources (recognition in the market, and so forth)	The patterns of past behavior, activity, and effectiveness of the organization that may affect current organizational functioning	The stream of decisions about how organizational resources will be configured to meet the demands, constraints, and opportunities within the context of the organization's history
Critical Features for Analysis	1. What demands does the environment make on the organization? 2. How does the environment put constraints on organizational action?	1. What is the relative quality of the different resources to which the organization has access? 2. To what extent are resources fixed rather than flexible in their configuration(s)?	1. What have been the major stages or phases of the organization's development? 2. What is the current impact of such historical factors as strategic decisions, acts of key leaders, crises, and core values and norms?	1. How has the organization defined its core mission, including the markets it serves and the products/services it provides to these markets? 2. On what basis does it compete? 3. What supporting strategies has the organization employed to achieve the core mission? 4. What specific objectives have been set for organizational output?

nization exists within the context of a larger environment that includes individuals, groups, other organizations, and even larger social forces, all of which have a potentially powerful impact on how the organization performs. Specifically, the environment includes markets (clients or customers), suppliers, governmental and regulatory bodies, labor unions, competitors, financial institutions, special interest groups, and so on. As research by Jeffrey Pfeffer and Gerald Salancik has suggested, the environment is critical to organizational functioning.

The environment has three critical features that affect organizational analysis. First the environment makes demands on the organization. For example, it may require certain products or services at certain levels of quality or quantity. Market pressures are particularly important here. Second, the environment may place constraints on organizational action. It may limit the activities in which an organization may engage. These constraints range from limitations imposed by scarce capital to prohibitions set by government regulations. Third, the environment provides opportunities that the organization can explore. When we analyze an organization, we need to consider the factors in the organization's environment and determine how those factors, singly or collectively, create demands, constraints, or opportunities.

The second input is the organization's *resources*. Any organization has a range of different assets to which it has access. These include employees, technology, capital, information, and so on. Resources can also include less tangible assets, such as the perception of the organization in the marketplace or a positive organizational climate. A set of resources can be shaped, deployed, or configured in different ways by an organization. For analysis purposes, two features are of primary interest. One concerns the relative quality of those resources or their value in light of the environment. The second concerns the extent to which resources can be reshaped or how fixed or flexible different resources are.

The third input is the organization's *history*. There is growing evidence that the way organizations function today is greatly influenced by past events. It is particularly important to understand the major stages or phases of an organization's development over a period of time, as well as the current impact of past

events—for example, key strategic decisions, the acts or behavior of key leaders, the nature of past crises and the organization's responses to them, and the evolution of core values and norms of the organization.

The final input is somewhat different from the others because in some ways it reflects some of the factors in the organization's environment, resources, and history. The fourth input is *strategy*. We use this term in its broadest context to describe the whole set of decisions that are made about how the organization will configure its resources against the demands, constraints, and opportunities of the environment within the context of its history. Strategy refers to the issue of matching the organization's resources to its environment, or making the fundamental decision of "What business are we in?" For analysis purposes, several aspects of strategy are important to identify. First, what is the core mission of the organization, or how has the organization defined its basic purpose or function within the larger system or environment? The core mission includes decisions about what markets the organization will serve, what products or services it will provide to those markets, and how it will compete in those markets. Second, strategy includes the specific supporting strategies (or tactics) the organization will employ or is employing to achieve its core mission. Third, it includes the specific performance or output objectives that have been established.

Strategy may be the most important single input for the organization. On one hand, strategic decisions implicitly determine the nature of the work the organization should be doing or the tasks it should perform. On the other hand, strategic decisions, and particularly decisions about objectives, determine the system's outputs.

In summary, there are three basic inputs—environment, resources, and history—and a fourth derivative input, strategy, which determines how the organization responds to or deals with the basic inputs. Strategy is critical because it determines the work to be performed by the organization and it defines desired organizational outputs.

OUTPUTS

Outputs are what the organization produces, how it performs, and how effective it is. There has been a lot of discussion about the components of an effective organization. For our purposes, however, it is possible to identify several key indicators of organizational output. First, we need to think about system output at different levels. In addition to the system's basic output—that is, the product—we need to think about other outputs that contribute to organizational performance, such as the functioning of groups or units within the organization or the functioning of individual organization members.

At the organizational level, three factors must be kept in mind when evaluating organizational performance: (1) goal attainment, or how well the organization meets its objectives (usually determined by strategy), (2) resource utilization, or how well the organization makes use of available resources (not just whether the organization meets its goals, but whether it realizes all of its potential performance and whether it achieves its goals by building resources or by "burning them up"), and (3) adaptability, or whether the organization continues to position itself in a favorable position vis-à-vis its environment—that is, whether it is capable of changing and adapting to environmental changes.

Obviously, the functioning of groups or units (departments, divisions, or other subunits within the organization) contribute to these oganizational-level outputs. Organizational output is also influenced by individual behavior, and certain individual-level outputs (affective reactions such as satisfaction, stress, or experienced quality of working life) may be desired outputs in and of themselves.

THE ORGANIZATION AS A TRANSFORMATION PROCESS

So far, we've defined the nature of inputs and outputs of the organizational system. This leads us to the transformation process. Given an environment, a set of resources, and history, "How do I take a strategy and implement it to produce effective performance in the organization, in the group/unit, and among individual employees?"

In our framework, the organization and its major component parts are the fundamental means for transforming energy and information from inputs into outputs. On this basis, we must determine the key components of the organization and the critical dynamic that shows how those components interact to perform the transformation function.

ORGANIZATIONAL COMPONENTS

There are many different ways of thinking about what makes up an organization. At this point in the development of a science of organizations, we probably do not know the one right or best way to describe the different components of an organization. The task is to find useful approaches for describing organizations, for simplifying complex phenomena, and for identifying patterns in what may at first blush seem to be random sets of activity. Our particular approach views organizations as composed of four major components: (1) the task, (2) the individuals, (3) the formal organizational arrangements, and (4) the informal organization. We will discuss each of these individually (see Figure 2 for overviews of these components).

The first component is the organization's *task*—that is, the basic or inherent work to be done by the organization and its subunits or the activity the organization is engaged in, particularly in light of its strategy. The emphasis is on the specific work activities or functions that need to be done and their inherent characteristics (as opposed to characteristics of the work created by how the work is organized or structured in this particular organization at this particular time). Analysis of the task would include a description of the basic work flows and functions with attention to the characteristics of those work flows—for example, the knowledge or skills demanded by the work, the kinds of rewards provided by the work, the degree of uncertainty associated with the work, and the specific constraints inherent in the work (such as critical time demands, cost constraints, and so on). Since it is assumed that a primary (although not the only) reason for the organization's existence is to perform the task consistent with strategy, the task is the starting point for the analysis. As we will see, the assessment of the adequacy of other components depends to a large degree on an understanding of the nature of the tasks to be performed.

A second component of organizations involves the *individuals* who perform organizational tasks. The issue here is identifying the nature and characteristics

FIGURE 2
Key Organizational Components

Component	Task	Individual	Formal Organizational Arrangements	Informal Organization
Definition	The basic and inherent work to be done by the organization and its parts	The characteristics of individuals in the organization	The various structures, processes, methods, and so on that are formally created to get individuals to perform tasks	The emerging arrangements, including structures, processes, relationships, and so forth
Critical Features for Analysis	1. The types of skill and knowledge demands the work poses 2. The types of rewards the work can provide 3. The degree of uncertainty associated with the work, including such factors as interdependence, routineness, and so on 4. The constraints on performance demands inherent in the work (given a strategy)	1. Knowledge and skills individuals have 2. Individual needs and preferences 3. Perceptions and expectancies 4. Background factors	1. Organization design, including grouping of functions, structure of subunits and coordination and control mechanisms 2. Job design 3. Work environment 4. Human resource management systems	1. Leader behavior 2. Intragroup relations 3. Intergroup relations 4. Informal working arrangements 5. Communication and influence patterns

of the organization's employees (or members). The most critical aspects to consider include the nature of individual knowledge and skills, the different needs or preferences that individuals have, the perceptions or expectancies that they develop, and other background factors (such as demographics) that may potentially influence individual behavior.

The third component is the *formal organizational arrangements*. These include the range of structures, processes, methods, procedures, and so forth that are explicitly and formally developed to get individuals to perform tasks consistent with organizational strategy. The broad term, organizational arrangements, encompasses a number of different factors. One factor is organization design—that is, the way jobs are grouped together into units, the internal structure of those units, and the coordination and control mechanisms used to link those units together. A second factor is the way jobs are designed within the context of organizational designs. A third factor is the work environment, which includes a number of factors that characterize the immediate environment in which work is done, such as the physical working environment, the available work resources, and so on. A final factor includes the organization's formal systems for attracting, placing, developing, and evaluating human resources.

Together, these factors create the set of formal organizational arrangements—that is, they are explicitly designed and specified, usually in writing.

The final component is the *informal organization*. Despite the set of formal organizational arrangements that exists in any organization, another set of arrangements tends to develop or emerge over a period of time. These arrangements are usually implicit and unwritten, but they influence a good deal of behavior. For lack of a better term, such arrangements are frequently referred to as the informal organization and they include the different structures, processes, and arrangements that emerge while the organization is operating. These arrangements sometimes complement formal organizational arrangements by providing structures to aid work where none exist. In other situations they may arise in reaction to the formal structure, to protect individuals from it. They may therefore either aid or hinder the organization's performance.

Because a number of aspects of the informal organization have a particularly critical effect on behavior, they need to be considered. The behavior of leaders (as opposed to the formal creation of leader positions) is an important feature of the informal organization, as are the patterns of relationships that develop both within and between groups. In addition, different types of informal working arrangements (including rules, procedures, methods, and so on) develop. Finally, there are the various communication and influence patterns that combine to create the informal organization design.

Organizations can therefore be thought of as a set of components—the task, the individuals, the organizational arrangements, and the informal organization. In any system, however, the critical question is not what the components are, but what the nature of their interaction is. This model raises the question: What are the dynamics of the relationships among the components? To deal with this issue, we must return to the concept of congruence or fit.

THE CONCEPT OF CONGRUENCE

A relative degree of congruence, consistency, or fit exists between each pair of organizational inputs. The congruence between two components is defined as "the degree to which the needs, demands, goals, objectives, and/or structures of one component are consistent with the needs, demands, goals, objectives, and/or structures of another component."

Congruence, therefore, is a measure of how well pairs of components fit together. Consider, for example, two components—the task and the individual. At the simplest level, the task presents some demands on individuals who would perform it (that is, skill/knowledge demands). At the same time, the set of individuals available to do the tasks have certain characteristics (their levels of skill and knowledge). Obviously, if the individual's knowledge and skill match the knowledge and skill demanded by the task, performance will be more effective.

Obviously, too, the individual-task congruence relationship encompasses more factors than just knowledge and skill. Similarly, each congruence relationship in the model has its own specific characteristics. Research and theory can guide the assessment of fit in each relationship. For an overview of the crit-

FIGURE 3
Definitions of Fits

Fit	Issues
Individual/Organization	How are individual needs met by the organizational arrangements? Do individuals hold clear or distorted perceptions of organizational structures? Is there a convergence of individual and organizational goals?
Individual/Task	How are individual needs met by the tasks? Do individuals have skills and abilities to meet task demands?
Individual/Informal organization	How are individual needs met by the informal organization? How does the informal organization make use of individual resources consistent with informal goals?
Task/Organization	Are organizational arrangements adequate to meet the demands of the task? Do organizational arrangements motivate behavior that is consistent with task demands?
Task/Informal organization	Does this informal organization structure facilitate task performance or not? Does it hinder or help meet the demands of the task?
Organization/Informal organization	Are the goals, rewards, and structures of the informal organization consistent with those of the formal organization?

ical elements of each congruence relationship, see Figure 3.

THE CONGRUENCE HYPOTHESIS

The aggregate model, or whole organization, displays a relatively high or low degree of system congruence in the same way that each pair of components has a high or low degree of congruence. The basic hypothesis of the model, which builds on this total state of congruence, is as follows: Other things being equal, the greater the total degree of congruence or fit between the various components, the more effective will be the organization—effectiveness being defined as the degree to which actual organization outputs at individual, group, and organizational levels are similar to expected outputs, as specified by strategy.

The basic dynamic of congruence sees the organization as most effective when its pieces fit together. If we also consider strategy, this view expands to include the fit between the organization and its larger environment; that is, an organization is most effective when its strategy is consistent with its environment (in light of organizational resources and history) and when the organizational components are congruent with the tasks necessary to implement that strategy.

One important implication of the congruence hypothesis is that organizational problem analysis (or diagnosis) involves description of the system, identification of problems, and analysis of fits to determine the causes of problems. The model also implies that different configurations of the key components can be used to gain outputs (consistent with the systems characteristic of equifinality). Therefore the question is not how to find the "one best way" of managing but how to find effective combinations of components that will lead to congruent fits among them.

The process of diagnosing fits and identifying combinations of components to produce congruence is not necessarily intuitive. A number of situations that lead to congruence have been defined in the research literature. Thus in many cases fit is something that can be defined, measured, and even quantified; there is, in other words, an empirical and theoretical basis for assessing fit. The theory provides considerable guidance about what leads to congruent relationships (although in some areas the research is more definitive and helpful than others). The implication is that the manager who wants to diagnose behavior must become familiar with critical aspects of relevant organizational behavior models or theories so that he or she can evaluate the nature of fits in a particular system.

The congruence model provides a general organizing framework. The organizational analyst will need other, more specific "submodels" to define high and low congruence. Examples of such submodels that might be used in the context of this general diagnostic model include the following:

1. The job characteristics model to assess and explain the fit between individuals and tasks as well as the fit between individuals and organizational arrangements (job design)
2. Expectancy theory models of motivation to explain the fit between individuals and the other three components
3. The information processing model of organizational design to explain the task-formal organization and task-informal organization fits
4. An organizational climate model to explain the fit between the informal organization and the other components

These models and theories are listed as illustrations of how more specific models can be used in the context of the general model. Obviously, those mentioned above are just a sampling of possible tools that could be used.

In summary, then, we have described a general model for the analysis of organizations (see Figure 4). The organization is seen as a system or transformation process that takes inputs and transforms them into outputs, a process that is composed of four basic components. The critical dynamic is the fit or congruence among the components. We now turn our attention to the pragmatic question of how to use this model for analyzing organizational problems.

A Process for Organizational Problem Analysis

The conditions that face organizations frequently change; consequently, managers are required to continually engage in problem-identification and problem-solving activities. Therefore, managers must gather data on organizational performance, compare the data with desired performance levels, identify the causes of problems, develop and choose action plans, and, finally, implement and evaluate these action

FIGURE 4
A Congruence Model for Organization Analysis

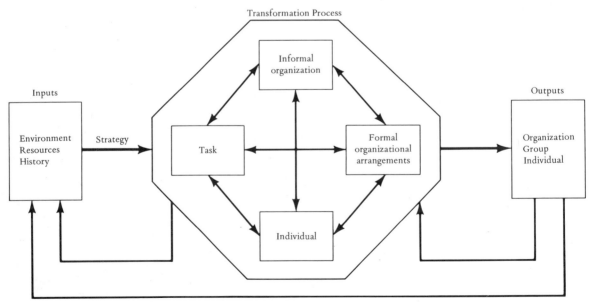

plans. These phases can be viewed as a generic problem-solving process. For long-term organizational viability, some type of problem-solving process must operate—and operate continuously.

Experience with using the congruence model for organizations for problem analysis in actual organizational settings has led to the development of an approach to using the model that's based on these generic problem-solving processes (see Figure 5). In this section, we will "walk through" this process, describing each step in the process and discussing how the model can be used at each stage. Here are the steps in the problem-analysis process.

1. *Identify symptoms.* In any situation, initial information (symptomatic data) may indicate that there are problems but not what the problems are or what the causes are. Symptomatic data are important because the symptoms of problems may indicate where to look for more complete data.

2. *Specify inputs.* Once the symptoms are identified, the starting point for analysis is to identify the system and the environment in which it functions. This means collecting data about the nature of environment, the type of resources the organization has, and the critical aspects of its history. Input analysis also involves identifying the overall strategy of the organization—that is, its core mission, supporting strategies, and objectives.

3. *Identify outputs.* The third step is an analysis of the organization's outputs at the individual, group, and organizational levels. Output analysis actually involves two elements: (1) defining the desired or planned output through an analysis of strategy that explicitly or implicitly defines what the organization wants to achieve in terms of output or performance indicators, and (2) collecting data that indicate the type of output the organization is actually achieving.

4. *Identify problems.* Symptoms may indicate problems—in this case, significant difference be-

FIGURE 5
Basic Problem Analysis Steps Using the Congruence Model

Step	Explanation
1. Identify symptoms.	List data indicating possible existence of problems.
2. Specify inputs.	Identify the system. Determine nature of environment, resources, and history. Identify critical aspects of strategy.
3. Identify outputs.	Identify data that define the nature of outputs at various levels (individual, group/unit, organizational). This should include desired outputs (from strategy) and actual outputs being obtained.
4. Identify problems.	Identify areas where there are significant and meaningful differences between desired and actual outputs. To the extent possible, identify penalties; that is, specific costs (actual and opportunity costs) associated with each problem.
5. Describe components of the organization.	Describe basic nature of each of the four components with emphasis on their critical features.
6. Assess congruence (fits).	Conduct analysis to determine relative congruence among components (draw on submodels as needed).
7. Generate and identify causes.	Analyze to associate fit with specific problems.
8. Identify action steps.	Indicate the possible actions to deal with problem causes.

tween desired or planned output and actual output. Such problems might be discrepancies (actual vs. expected) in organizational performance, group functioning, individual behavior, or affective reactions. These data tell us what problems exist, but they still don't tell us the causes. (Note: Where data are available, it is frequently also useful to identify the costs associated with the problems or the *penalties* the organization incurs by not fixing the problem. Penalties might be actual costs—increased expenses, and so on—or opportunity costs, such as revenue lost because of the problem.)

5. *Describe organizational components.* At this step the analysis to determine the causes of problems begins. Data are collected about the nature of each of the four major organizational components, including information about the component and its critical features in this organization.

6. *Assess congruence (fits).* Using the data collected in step 5 as well as applicable submodels or theories, an assessment is made of the positive or negative fit between each pair of components.

7. *Generate hypotheses about problem causes.* Once the components are described and their congruence assessed, the next step is to link together the congruence analysis with the problem identification (step 4). After analyzing to determine which are the poor fits that seem to be associated with, or account for, the output problems that have been identified, the patterns of congruence and incongruence that appear to cause the patterns of problems are determined.

8. *Identify action steps.* The final step in problem analysis is to identify possible action steps. These steps might range from specific changes to deal with relatively obvious problem causes to a more extensive data collection designed to test hypotheses about relatively more complex problems and causes.

In addition to these eight steps, some further steps need to be kept in mind. After possible actions are identified, problem solving involves predicting the consequence of various actions, choosing the course of action, and implementing and evaluating the impact of the chosen course of action. It is, of course, important to have a general diagnostic framework to monitor the effects of various courses of action.

The congruence model and this problem-analysis process outline are tools for structuring and dealing with the complex reality of organizations. Given the indeterminate nature of social systems, there is no one best way of handling a particular situation. The model and the process could, however, help the manager in making a number of decisions and in evaluating the consequences of those decisions. If these tools have merit, it is up to the manager to use them along with his or her intuitive sense (based on experience) to make the appropriate set of diagnostic, evaluative, and action decisions.

Future Directions

The model we have presented here reflects a particular way of thinking about organizations. If that perspective is significant, the model might be used as a tool for handling more complex problems or for structuring more complex situations. Some directions for further thought, research, and theory development could include these:

1. *Organizational change.* The issue of organizational change has received a good deal of attention from both managers and academics. The question is how to effectively implement organizational change. The problem seems to center on the lack of a general model of organizational change. It is hard to think about a general model of organizational change without a general model of organizations. The congruence perspective outlined here may provide some guidance and direction toward the development of a more integrated perspective on the processes of organizational change. Initial work in applying the congruence model to the change issue is encouraging.

2. *Organizational development over time.* There has been a growing realization that organizations grow and develop over time, and that they face different types of crises, evolve through different stages, and develop along some predictable lines. A model of organizations such as the one presented here might be a tool for developing typology of growth patterns by indicating the different configurations of tasks, individuals, organizational arrangements, and informal organizations that might be most appropriate for organizations in different environments and at different stages of development.

3. *Organizational pathology.* Organizational problem solving ultimately requires some sense of the types of problems that may be encountered and the kinds of patterns of causes one might expect. It is reasonable to assume that most problems encountered by organizations are not wholly unique but are predictable. The often expressed view that ''our problems are unique'' reflects in part the lack of a framework of organizational pathology. The question is: Are there basic ''illnesses'' that organizations suffer? Can a framework of organizational pathology, similar to the physician's framework of medical pathology, be developed? The lack of a pathology framework, in turn, reflects the lack of a basic functional model of organizations. Again, development of a congruence perspective might provide a common language to use for the identification of general pathological patterns of organizational functioning.

4. *Organizational solution types.* Closely linked to the problem of pathology is the problem of treatment, intervention, or solutions to organizational problems. Again, there is a lack of a general framework in which to consider the nature of organizational interventions. In this case, too, the congruence model might be a means for conceptualizing and ultimately describing the different intervention options available in response to problems.

Summary

This article has presented a general approach for thinking about organizational functioning and a process for using a model to analyze organizational problems. This particular model is only one way of thinking about organizations; it clearly [is] not the only model, nor can we claim it is definitely the best model. It is one tool, however, that may be useful for structuring the complexity of organizational life and helping managers create, maintain, and develop effective organizations.

Bibliography

For a comprehensive review and synthesis of research in organizational behavior, see Marvin Dunnette's *Handbook of Industrial and Organizational Psychology* (Rand McNally, 1976). Daniel Katz and Robert Kahn's seminal work on organizations as systems, *The Social Psychology of Organizations* (Wiley, 1966), has been revised, updated, and extended in their 1978 edition. See their new book for an extensive discussion of organizations as open systems and for a unique synthesis of the literature in terms of systems ideas.

For a broad analysis of organizational behavior, see David Nadler, J. Richard Hackman, and Edward E. Lawler's *Managing Organizational Behavior* (Little, Brown, 1979), and see Charles Hofer and Daniel Schendel's *Strategy Formulation: Analytical Concepts* (West, 1978) for a discussion of strategy.

For an extensive discussion of output and effectiveness, see Paul Goodman and Johannes Pennings's *New Perspectives on Organizational Effectiveness* (Jossey-Bass, 1977), and Andrew Van de Ven and Diane Ferry's *Organizational Assessment* (Wiley Interscience, 1980).

For more detail on organizational arrangements, see Jay R. Galbraith's *Designing Complex Organizations* (Addison-Wesley, 1973); on job design and motivation, see J. Richard Hackman and Greg Oldham's *Work Redesign* (Addison-Wesley, 1979); and on informal organizations, see Michael Tushman's ''A Political Approach to Organizations: A Review and Rationale'' (*Academy of Management Review,* April 1977), and Jeffrey Pfeffer's new book, *Power and Politics in Organizations* (Pittman Press, 1980).

Submodels corresponding to the various components of our congruence model would include: J. Richard Hackman and Greg Oldham's job design model; Victor Vroom and Edward Lawler's work on expectancy theory of motivation and decision making—see Vroom's *Work and Motivation* (Wiley, 1964) and Lawler's *Motivation in Work Organizations* (Wadsworth Publishing Co., 1973); Jay R. Galbraith, Michael Tushman, and David Nadler's work on information processing models of organizational design; and George Litwin and Robert Stringer's work on organization climate—see Litwin and Stringer's *Motivation and Organizational Climate* (Harvard University Graduate School of Business Administration, 1968).

David Nadler's ''Managing Organizational Change: An Integrated Perspective'' (*Journal of Ap-*

plied Behavioral Science 17, no. 2 (1981): 191–211) uses the congruence model to think about the general problems of organizational change and dynamics. Several distinct levers for change are developed and discussed. Other pertinent books of interest include: Jay R. Galbraith's *Organization Design* (Addison-Wesley, 1979); Jay R. Galbraith and Daniel A. Nathanson's *Strategy Implementation: The Role of Structure and Process* (West, 1978); George C. Homans's *The Human Group* (Harcourt Brace Jovanovich, 1950); Paul R. Lawrence and Jay W. Lorsch's *Developing Organizations: Diagnosis and Action* (Addison-Wesley, 1969); Harold J. Leavitt's ''Applied Organization Change in Industry'' in J. G. March's (Ed.) *Handbook of Organizations* (Rand McNally, 1965); Harry Levinson's *Organizational Diagnosis* (Harvard University Press, 1972); Harry Levinson's *Psychological Man* (Levinson Institute, 1976); Jay W. Lorsch and Alan Sheldon's ''The Individual in the Organization: A Systems View'' in J. W. Lorsch and P. R. Lawrence's (Eds.) *Managing Group and Intergroup Relations* (Irwin-Dorsey, 1972); David A. Nadler and Noel M. Tichy's ''The Limitations of Traditional Intervention Technology in Health Care Organizations'' in N. Margulies and J. A. Adams's (Eds.) *Organization Development in Health Care Organizations* (Addison-Wesley, 1980); Edgar H. Schein's *Organizational Psychology* (Prentice-Hall, 1970); and James A. Seiler's *Systems Analysis in Organizational Behavior* (Irwin-Dorsey, 1967).

Techniques for Data Collection

David A. Nadler

Data-based methods are essentially tools which change agents or managers can use to learn about and improve organizations. At the heart of the data-collection–feedback cycle is the feedback activity. At the same time, however, the other stages of planning, collection, and analysis are also important because they build toward feedback. . . . While process issues are important, so are the more concrete questions of methods and techniques. In order to use data-based methods, the change agent needs to know something about how data can be collected as well as what to do with the data once it is in hand.

This [article] is aimed at exploring a number of the basic techniques and methods for data collection. . . . (For a detailed discussion of these areas, see references at the end of this chapter.)

There are different ways of collecting data on how organizations function and how the people in them feel and behave. There are numerous specific techniques, but most of these fall into one of four broad categories—that is, interviews, questionnaires, observations, and a final category of secondary data and unobtrusive measures. (See Table 1 for a brief comparison of these methods.)

Interviews

. . . Members of an organization are valuable sources of data on how the organization functions and how they feel. . . . As informants, they can provide the consultant with information about how things work; they are descriptors of the organizational system. Members have judgments about what things are performing well and what things are performing poorly.

From David A. Nadler, *Feedback and Organizational Development: Using Data-Based Methods*, pp. 118–143. © 1977 Addison-Wesley, Reading, Massachusetts. Reprinted with permission.

If asked, they also are able to reveal the data that they have collected which led to these judgments. Members also have affective reactions to what goes on around them, positive or negative reactions such as feeling happy or dissatisfied, frustrated or complacent, etc. The people in the organization are therefore valuable sources of descriptive information, diagnostic evaluations, and affective reactions. . . .

TYPES OF INTERVIEWS

Interviews can be conducted in many different ways. (For a comprehensive discussion of interviewing, see Kahn and Cannell, 1967.) Interviews differ in their degree of structure. One type of interview is the *unstructured* interview, where the interviewer provides very little guidance to the respondent in terms of questions or possible answers. In this form of nondirective or client-centered interviewing, the interviewer is only interested in information which the respondent feels is important, and the interviewer attempts to provide only minimal guidance through stimulating discussion and getting the respondent to explore his or her feelings and perceptions in the areas that he or she chooses to. One consultant who uses unstructured interviews frequently begins his interviews with the following: "Tell me about this place. How did things get to be the way they are?" Starting with this general question, the consultant continues the interview by clarifying or summarizing what the respondent says, probing occasionally with questions. The interview thus can move in any number of directions.

Another type of interview is the *structured, open-ended* interview. In this case, the interviewer has predetermined questions covering certain topics, but the respondent is unconstrained in his answering. The interviewer may ask a question such as "How do you know when you are performing well or poorly?" and

TABLE 1
A Comparison of Different Methods of Data Collection

Method	Major Advantages	Major Potential Problems
Interviews	1. Adaptive—allows data collection on a range of possible subjects 2. Source of "rich" data 3. Empathic 4. Process of interviewing can build rapport	1. Can be expensive 2. Interviewer can bias responses 3. Coding/interpretation problems 4. Self-report bias
Questionnaires	1. Responses can be quantified and easily summarized 2. Easy to use with large samples 3. Relatively inexpensive 4. Can obtain large volume of data	1. Nonempathic 2. Predetermined questions may miss issues 3. Data may be overinterpreted 4. Response bias
Observations	1. Collects data on behavior rather than reports of behavior 2. Real-time, not retrospective 3. Adaptive	1. Interpretation and coding problems 2. Sampling is a problem 3. Observer bias/reliability 4. Costly
Secondary data/unobtrusive measures	1. Nonreactive—no-response bias 2. High face validity 3. Easily quantified	1. Access/retrieval possibly a problem 2. Potential validity problems 3. Coding/interpretation

then attempt to write down in as much detail as possible the respondent's answer to the question.

The most structured form of interview is the *structured, fixed-response* interview. Here the interviewer not only provides the questions but also provides a set of predetermined alternative responses. An example would be the following question:

Which one of the following statements best describes how you feel about your job?

Very satisfied
Satisfied
Neither satisfied nor dissatisfied
Dissatisfied
Very dissatisfied

Frequently this kind of question would be accompanied by a set of response cards, each card having one of the five responses written on it, enabling the respondent to pick the response which is most appropriate. This kind of interview is in many ways an orally administered questionnaire, but it permits options. For example, when an extremely negative or positive response occurs, the interviewer can ask "Why do you feel that way?". . .

ADVANTAGES AND DISADVANTAGES OF INTERVIEWS

Interviews have the major advantage of being adaptive. As the interviewer proceeds with the interview, he or she can modify the questions, choose an area to probe, or make other changes to adapt the interview to the situation. Thus the interview allows collection on a wide range of possible subjects, with the interviewer having the ability to change the interview to emphasize those subjects about which the respondent seems to have information. Open-ended interviews are a potentially rich source of data. The responses may contain detailed information about causes of problems as well as the symptoms. The respondent can explain *why* he or she is satisfied or dissatisfied, as opposed to just indicating *how* satisfied or dissatisfied he or she is, for example. Specific quotations or examples from interviews are often particularly useful during feedback to illustrate a finding or a pattern in the data.

As a collection device, an interview conducted by a good interviewer can be an empathic device. By communicating to the respondent that he or she understands the organization and the problems of being in the organization, the interviewer can communicate empathy with the respondent—an understanding of the respondent and his or her environment. Empathy can very frequently result in the respondent being more willing to open up and disclose possibly threatening information to the interviewer. (Alderfer and Brown, 1972, demonstrated this with questionnaires.) For example, where more empathic methods have been used, respondents seem to be less hesitant about making negative statements about themselves, their coworkers, their supervisors, or their working conditions. Similarly, the whole process of the interview can lead to increased rapport with members of the organization. This rapport can aid both the information collection in the interview itself and the future activities of the change agent in the system. People enjoy talking about their work, and the interview can be a pleasurable and meaningful experience if the respondent feels that the interviewer has listened, understood, and valued what has been said.

Interviews have some potential problems as data collection devices. First, interviews can be expensive. They can consume a great deal of the consultant's time. Second, while the interviewer can elicit responses from the respondent and adapt the interview, the interviewer can also bias the responses with his or her choice of questions to ask and pursue and with the nature of his or her interactions with the respondent, which may encourage or discourage certain responses. Similarly the interviewer's biases may creep into the data that are recorded or omitted. Thus there is the risk of the interview reflecting the biases of the interviewer rather than the perceptions, evaluations, and feelings of the respondent. Open-ended interviews pose a particular problem of coding and interpretation. In order to summarize the findings (either for feedback or analysis) over a number of interviews, some interpretation and category coding of responses is necessary. The process of coding is expensive and provides another possible source of bias (from the coder). Finally there is the basic problem of self-report biases. The interview does not provide direct information on behavior, rather it provides a report on an organization member of behavior and feelings. There are many sources of bias in self-report measures. (See Webb et al., 1966, for a listing of sources of error in self-report measures.) The respondent may have biased perceptions or incomplete information; the respondent may also give the interviewer what he or she thinks the interviewer wants to hear; or the respondent may feel threatened and thus withhold information.

While there are the problems of interviewer, coder, and respondent bias, the interview still remains perhaps the single most useful data collection tool in an organization. The disadvantages imply that the results of interviews should be validated and used with care, rather than always being accepted at face value. . . .

Questionnaires

Questionnaires are essentially self-administered interviews. A set of questions are given to the respondent in printed form. The respondent reads the questions and answers, either by writing in an answer or choosing from alternative predetermined responses. As a paper-and-pencil instrument that is not dependent upon a "live" interviewer being present, it allows simultaneous data collection from many people in an organization. With fixed-response questionnaires, quantitative analysis can be done in a short period of time, allowing for a relatively short turn-around time.

The underlying rationale for the questionnaire is similar to the interview. Information is obtained by directly asking the organization members for their perceptions, evaluations, and feelings. The major difference between an interview and a questionnaire is that the questionnaire is self-administered and, as used in organizations, generally tends to make use of fixed responses rather than open-ended responses to questions.

TYPES OF QUESTIONNAIRES

As with interviews, one of the options available in using a questionnaire is whether the responses are designed to be open-ended or fixed. Because of the problems of coding and a tendency of respondents not to want to write extensive or greatly descriptive answers, most organizational questionnaires are fixed-response. Of the many different types of questions and responses, the one most widely used is the Likert-type item. The respondent is asked to reply to a question or statement by checking a point on a scale of varying degrees of agreement or disagreement, satisfaction, etc. An example of this type of questionnaire item follows:

Below are some statements which describe jobs. How much do you agree or disagree with each statement as a description of your job?

	Strongly disagree	Disagree	Somewhat disagree	Neither agree nor disagree	Somewhat agree	Agree	Strongly agree
1. My job allows me to control my own work pace.	(1)	(2)	(3)	(4)	(5)	(6)	(7)
2. I can see the results of my own work.	(1)	(2)	(3)	(4)	(5)	(6)	(7)

Questions can also be constructed which ask the respondent to check a number indicating his or her position on a scale described by several descriptive statements, such as the following:

How much *variety* is there in your job?

(1)	(2)	(3)	(4)	(5)	(6)	(7)
Very little; I do pretty much the same things over and over, using the same equipment and procedures almost all the time.			Moderate variety			Very much; I do many things, using a variety of equipment and procedures.

Similarly, the respondent may be asked to check a response on a scale anchored only by two words, as follows:

How do you feel about your present life in general?

Boring	(1)	(2)	(3)	(4)	(5)	(6)	(7)	Interesting
Enjoyable	(1)	(2)	(3)	(4)	(5)	(6)	(7)	Miserable

These examples represent only a few of the many ways in which questions can be constructed, but they illustrate some of the possible alternatives.

Questionnaires can also vary in the scope of their coverage. One might put together a questionnaire that focuses on one particular issue (for example, group process) or one might want to use a questionnaire to get a very broad diagnostic picture of an entire organization.

Another difference in questionnaires is the degree to which they are standardized versus custom-constructed for a situation. Standardized questionnaires have a predetermined set of questions that are designed to be used in almost any situation. These questions have been developed and refined over a period of time, are based on a model of organizational functioning, and have been pretested. The format, responses, and administrative procedures for the questionnaires have also been tested and refined. A large number of standardized questionnaires have been developed and are in use, but they vary greatly in quality. An example of a comprehensive and thoroughly developed instrument can be seen in the *Survey of Organizations* (Taylor and Bowers, 1972), which has been used extensively for diagnostic and survey feedback purposes.

While standardized questionnaires exist, a consultant or a client may want to develop a survey specifically for an organization, adding new questionnaire items that are specific to that situation. A custom-designed survey may better fit the needs of a particular client. This questionnaire might be composed by the consultant or by the consultant along with his or her internal partners—for example, with a cross-sectional or labor-management group.

ADVANTAGES AND PROBLEMS
OF USING QUESTIONNAIRES

The fixed-response questionnaires have a number of distinct advantages for organizational work. The answers can easily be quantified because the fixed-response questionnaire actually has the respondent doing his or her own coding. The numerical responses can be summarized, aggregated, and subjected to statistical analysis with little or no coding, interpretation, or preparation. Questionnaires can be administered to more than one person at a time and the potentially quick turn-around time makes them easy to use with large samples of people (from several hundred to thousands). Once a questionnaire is developed, the cost of administering it is relatively low. The cost of conducting interviews may be at least three to five times more per respondent than the cost of using questionnaires. Also, with skillful question writing and formatting, a single questionnaire can be used to obtain from an individual a large amount of data on a whole range of topics and issues.

Questionnaires also have drawbacks as data-collection methods. First, questionnaires are nonempathic. A respondent may find it difficult to ''warm up'' to a questionnaire; it can be a relatively impersonal data-collection process. Questionnaires can be made to be more empathic by using the specific language of the organization, by communicating knowledge of the organization's problems, etc. When this is done, respondents seem more willing to answer questions openly (Alderfer and Brown, 1972). Obviously,

a completely standardized questionnaire provides the least empathic form.

Questionnaires by definition are prestructured, self-administered interviews. Since they are prestructured, they are not adaptive. If the questions are not appropriate for a specific respondent, they cannot be changed during the administration. Once the individual has been given the questionnaire, the questions are fixed. Questionnaires may therefore present questions to the respondent to which he or she cannot or will not respond, while disregarding other areas where the respondent may have a rich store of information.

Fixed-response questionnaires present problems in terms of interpretation and analysis. The consultant, his or her internal partners, or whoever does the interpretation and analysis has only the specific checked response alternative to work with on each question. If, for example, a person answered the second sample question on the list given previously (''I can see the results of my work'') by checking a [5] response, the analyst does not know why the [5] was checked, what specifically the [5] means, or whether the [5] is a good or bad response. Furthermore, it is not clear whether the [5] means the same thing to this respondent as it might mean to someone else. The data are inherently limited, and their easy quantification can lead one to interpretations that may not be valid.

Finally, questionnaires have in common with interviews the problems of self-report or response biases. Rather than collecting data about behavior itself, the questionnaire collects individuals' reports of behavior, and these reports may be biased (consciously or unconsciously) by the respondent. These biases may include such things as a tendency to answer questions that are next to each other in a similar manner, and a tendency to answer questions later in the questionnaire with less care than earlier questions (a fatigue effect), as well as the other forms of self-report bias mentioned in the discussion of interviews. . . .

Observations

One of the most obvious ways of collecting data about behavior in organizations is to observe the behavior as it occurs. Observation is particularly valuable because it removes one possible source of bias, the report of the respondent. It puts the data collector directly in touch with the activities about which data are being collected. Observational methods have been widely used in organizations. Many classic examples of organizational research have relied on the presence of an on-site observer, usually with the data collector as a participant-observer, having an actual role in the organization while systematically watching the behavior that occurred. (See examples and discussions of this method in Whyte, 1955; McCall and Simmons, 1969; or Schatzman and Strauss, 1972). While also making use of other kinds of data collection, this approach has been based largely on the observation of behavior as it occurs.

A basic question regarding observation is, "How can the observation be structured so that meaningful and useful data can be collected?" There are more things to be observed in an organization than any one consultant or group of consultants can possibly observe and note. Total observation would require large numbers of people being present at all times and in all parts of the organization, and this is usually not feasible. Thus the observations are structured through choices—that is, what to observe and what not to observe; when to observe and when not to observe; what to record and what not to record. Structuring may range from fairly explicit observation guidelines and instruments to frameworks which are not written or specified, but which the consultant uses as a guide while observing behavior in the organization.

The basic strength or weakness of observation as a tool is that the observer is the data-collection instrument (as opposed to the questionnaire or interview instrument). A sensitive observer making use of an effective structure for observation can be an effective data-collection tool. An observer who has little sensitivity and no guiding structure may spend hours observing, see nothing, and report no usable data.

TYPES OF OBSERVATION

Structure is an important factor in observation, and approaches to observation differ in the degree to which they structure both the watching and the recording. One approach, which might be labelled *structured* observation, uses instruments and procedures to direct the observer very specifically to what type of behavior he or she should be observing and to specify exactly how the observations will be recorded.

An example of this approach is seen in the Interaction Process Analysis (IPA) framework developed by Bales (1971) for observing and analyzing behavior in small groups. This scheme has the observer noting each interaction between individuals in a group. The observer records who initiated the interaction and to whom it was directed and codes the interaction according to its content, using a standard set of categories.

A second type of observation is the *semistructured* observation, where observation is only minimally structured but the recording is specified. An example of this can be seen in the standardized job-observation form (Jenkins, Nadler, Lawler, and Cammann, 1975) used for observing psychological characteristics of jobs. Using this procedure, the observer watches the employee perform his or her job for an hour. While there are some questions about the specifics of the job (e.g., where does the employee get his or her raw materials?), the hour is spent with relatively little structure being given to the observation other than watching the employee perform the job. The recording process, however, is highly structured. After the observation period is over, the observer fills out a 15-page instrument which requires that the observer rate the dimensions of the job using Likert-type items.

A third type of observation is *unstructured*. Here there are no specific directions regarding what should be observed and what should be recorded, or how. While unstructured observation (clinical or anthropological observation as it is frequently called) does not have an explicit structure, effective unstructured observation will usually have some kind of implicit underlying structure which at least directs the attention of the observer in general terms. Schein (1969), for example, in the first part of his book on process consultation provides a general framework for observing behavior in groups. By specifying the variables that should be considered (for example, communication and leadership), he provides a general structure for observation.

ADVANTAGES AND PROBLEMS OF OBSERVATION

The outstanding advantage of the observation process is it enables direct collection of data about behavior itself, rather than reports of behavior. As such, observational data have relatively high face validity. In other words, while people in the organization may doubt the validity of questionnaire responses and may attempt to deny the validity of interview data by arguing that people did not answer truthfully, well-documented observational data have a great deal of strength and believability.

Observation collects data about behavior, rather than reports of behavior. Observation therefore enables one to discover existing patterns of behavior, which are not known to the people in the organization. Because of a lack of awareness, these data might never be revealed in a questionnaire. In addition, observation is a real-time data-collection device rather than a retrospective collection device. Self-reports mostly describe behavior that has occurred in the past, while observation deals with behavior that is occurring in the present. Retrospective reports frequently involve distortion. People tend to reinterpret earlier events in the light of what occurred later.

Finally, observation is an adaptive method. In all but the most structured observation schemes, the observer can modify what he or she is observing as the situation requires.

While valuable, observations also have a number of inherent logistical problems. As observations move away from the more structured forms (such as the Bales IPA), interpretation and coding must frequently be done in order to use the data. As with interviews, this interpretation and coding is expensive, takes time, and can be a source of further bias. Another problem that is often overlooked is that of sampling. In a questionnaire or interview, sampling may be an issue but all it involves is deciding which respondents to pick and how many. Observations necessitate this sampling over people, but they also necessitate sampling over time (when should observations be done), sampling over space (where should the observer be located), and sampling over events (at what specific events in time should the observer be present). Less structured observation also has a tremendous potential for observer bias and thus a requirement that observers be adequately trained so that different observers will see the same things when viewing an event. When all of these factors are added up (training, sampling, coding, etc.), effective observation becomes a potentially expensive proposition. However, many times there is simply no substitute for having a trained observer on the scene. Many impor-

tant events or patterns of behavior cannot be understood without someone actually being present. . . .

Secondary Data and Unobtrusive Measures

Most of the methods that are used to gather data in organizations assume that data have not already been collected and thus must be obtained either by asking organizational members or by observation of events as they occur. In fact, organizations do an immense amount of data collection during the normal course of activities, and they therefore contain huge (but often hidden) "data banks," waiting to be used by the change agent. These data in general are called secondary data, since they are collected from secondary sources rather than directly from the respondent. All data collected from sources other than the subject fall directly into this category. Another label for this class of data is *unobtrusive measures*. (The term is taken from Webb, Campbell, Schwartz, and Sechrest, 1966.)

In organizations, perhaps the richest source of secondary data is archives—that is, the various documents, records, and written material in the possession of the organization. These sources can be particularly valuable to the data collector.

TYPES OF SECONDARY DATA
AND UNOBTRUSIVE MEASURES

There are numerous types of secondary data and they vary from organization to organization. Mentioning a few common kinds of data should provide a picture of the range and potential usefulness of these measures. Many organizations, for example, keep detailed records of certain kinds of behavior including records of absenteeism, lateness, turnover, accidents, grievances, etc. Many of these data are collected for legal purposes and are therefore always available. Another kind of data is that which the organization collects about the performance of work units. In particular, data about productivity, reject rates, repairs, costs, complaints, etc., all provide information about the performance of the organization. Similarly, correspondence files may provide information on the number of meetings that are held and the nature of contacts between people and groups, both inside and outside the organization. Other kinds of records such as electric light bills, phone bills, signin and signout sheets for after hours work, etc., also are potential sources of useful information. . . .

ADVANTAGES AND PROBLEMS WITH SECONDARY DATA AND UNOBTRUSIVE MEASURES

The advantages of secondary data are fairly obvious. Being unobtrusive, this type of data collection is relatively nonreactive. There is little chance for a response bias to occur due to the consultant's collection. In addition, archival data, especially those involving dollar figures, have extremely high face validity. As opposed to questionnaire, interview, or even most observational data, these data are ''real'' in the eyes of many people in the organization. Finally, most of these data are easily quantified and can thus be analyzed statistically.

The problems involved in using these data revolve around obtaining the data and assessing their validity. Access or retrieval is frequently a problem. An amazing number of organizations do not keep records of this kind in usable or retrievable form. . . .

A second problem involves the potentially poor quality of much archival data. While archival data are usually accepted at face value within the organization, experiences with these measures suggest that frequently they bear little relation to reality. A consultant attempting to assess the effects of his or her interventions on job performance in a cereal plant, for example, began to collect data from the productivity records of the plant and from job-ticket information filled out by employees. Only after much frustrating analysis did the consultant discover that employees tended to randomly choose numbers to put on these tickets and that the numbers did not reflect actual production at all. Much of this distortion was indeed response bias—not to the consultant but to the normal data collection that goes on in the organization. People frequently provide the organization with the information that they think it wants or information that will reflect well on them, rather than information that is valid. (See Cammann and Nadler, 1976, for a discussion of why this occurs.)

Finally, archival data may pose problems of coding and interpretation. It's not always clear, for example, what constitutes an incident of absenteeism or lateness. The data can be interpreted in several different ways. . . . In general, archival data and unobtrusive measures are underused by consultants. There is a tendency to rely on one type of data, usually interviews or questionnaires, and sometimes observations, and to ignore the existence of data that have already been collected by the organization. These sources could be used much more than they have been.

In summary, the choice of data collection methods is an important one and a whole set of advantages and disadvantages for each method must be weighed against one another. While one cannot avoid making choices among these methods, the use of multiple data sources will help to avoid some of the most obvious problems. . . .

References

Alderfer, C. P., and Brown, L. D. ''Questionnaire Design in Organizational Research,'' *Journal of Applied Psychology,* 1972, *56,* 456–460.

Bales, R. F. *Personality and Interpersonal Behavior.* New York: Holt, Rinehart, and Winston, 1971.

Bouchard, T. J., Jr. ''Field Research Methods: Interviewing, Questionnaires, Participant Observation, Unobtrusive Measures.'' In M. D. Dunnette (Ed.), *Handbook of Industrial and Organizational Psychology.* Chicago: Rand McNally, 1976, pp. 363–413.

Cammann, C., and Nadler, D. A. ''Fit Control Systems to Your Management Style,'' *Harvard Business Review,* 1976, *54*(1), 65–72.

Jenkins, G. D., Nadler, D. A., Lawler, E. E. III, and Cammann, C. ''Standardized Observations: An Approach to Measuring the Nature of Jobs,'' *Journal of Applied Psychology,* 1975, *60,* 171–181.

Kahn, R. L., and Cannell, C. F. *The Dynamics of Interviewing.* New York: Wiley, 1967.

McCall, G., and Simmons, J. *Issues in Participant Observation.* Reading, Mass.: Addison-Wesley, 1969.

Schatzman, L., and Strauss, A. *Field Methods.* Englewood Cliffs, N.J.: Prentice-Hall, 1972.

Schein, E. H. *Process Consultation: Its Role in Organization Development.* Reading, Mass.: Addison-Wesley, 1969.

Taylor, J., and Bowers, D. G. *The Survey of Organizations: A Machine Scored Standardized Questionnaire Instrument.* Ann Arbor: Institute for Social Research, 1972.

Webb, E. J., Campbell, D. T., Schwartz, R. D., and Sechrest, L. *Unobtrusive Measures: Nonreactive Research in Social Sciences.* Chicago: Rand McNally, 1966.

Whyte, W. F. *Money and Motivation: An Analysis of Incentives in Industry.* New York: Harper, 1955.

SECTION THREE

INTERVENTION THEORY
AND METHOD

Since most of OD practice involves an organizational intervention of one kind or another, the final part of the Readings section, which addresses the intervention phase of OD consultation, is the most extensive. The articles range in topics from the early phases of OD practice, such as contracting (reading by Weisbord) and planning (reading by Fry) interventions; to the overall role of an OD consultant (reading by Rubin, Plovnick, and Fry). In this group, the articles may be subcategorized into those that deal with the nature of OD interventions (Argyris and Harrison), those concerned with organizational design and structure (Jelinek and Galbraith), those designed to solve problems (Beckhard, Burke, and Drexler and Lawler), and those dealing with team building (Beckhard and Harrison). Still others address a variety of OD interventions—decision making (Vroom), process consultation (Schein), and career development and planning (Hall and Morgan). Organization development values are discussed by Bowen. This last and largest group of articles demonstrates the considerable diversity of OD practice as well as the underlying nature of this practice in terms of values and consultant role and function.

The Organization Development Contract

Marvin R. Weisbord

In OD consulting, the contract is central to success or failure. Most other kinds of contracts—employment, service, research, etc.—focus heavily on content, that is, the nature of the work to be performed, the schedule, and the money to change hands. Generally, these issues are negotiated through a proposal, which one party writes and the other accepts or rejects. The consulting contract most people are familiar with takes two forms: (1) You hire me to study the problem and tell you what to do; (2) You hire me to solve the problem for you. I call these "expert" consulting contracts. In either case the quality of the advice and/or the solution is the focus and the *consultant* is a central figure, whatever happens.

But in OD consulting, the *client* is the central figure. He hires me to consult to him while he is working on his problem, helping *him* to achieve a better diagnosis of what has happened and what steps he must take to improve things. This is a form of collaboration which, if successful, helps the client also to achieve better working relationships with others, for example peers, boss, and subordinates.

For that reason, in OD contracting, more so than other kinds, the *process* by which content issues are pinned down is critical. Unless this negotiation is a model of the consultant's values and problem-solving behavior, the contract, when it is tested, probably will not stand up. More about testing later.

What do I mean by contract? I mean an explicit exchange of expectations, part dialogue, part written document, which clarifies for consultant and client three critical areas:

From *OD Practitioner*, Vol. 5, No. 2, 1973, pp. 1–4. Reprinted by permission.

1. What each expects to get from the relationship
2. How much time each will invest, when, and at what cost
3. The ground rules under which the parties will operate

What Each Expects

Clients expect, and have a right to expect, change for the better in a situation that is making their lives hard. This situation, as my clients experience it, has three main components:

1. Organizational crises, i.e. people leaving; excessive absenteeism; too high costs; too little budget; unmanageable environmental demands; pressure from above; conflict between individuals or work groups
2. People problems, i.e. one or two or more "significant others" are singled out as particular sore spots
3. Personal dilemma, i.e. whether this job, or this career, is what I really want

The third component always grows in magnitude in direct proportion to the first two. Clients in a bind don't get much fun out of their work. They long for something simpler, better suited to their strengths, more consistent with their values. Above all, most clients long for outcomes. They want permanent "change" for the better, with no backsliding. I, on the other hand, see new outcomes as evidence the client is learning a better way of coping. From my point of view the process—gathering information, becoming aware of deeper meanings, making choices—is my most important product. While the client identifies three kinds of difficult situations he wants to work on, I keep in mind three levels of improvement he might achieve:

1. Solution of the immediate crisis—changing structures, policies, procedures, relationships.
2. Learning something about his own coping style—how he deals with crises, how he might do it better
3. Learning a process for coping better, continually becoming aware and making choices, about whatever issue presents itself

. . . The existing problem is a vehicle for learning more about how to manage organizational life better. I have no preferences for the kinds of problems clients have. . . . One issue will do as well as another.

However, clients rarely ask my direct help in cutting costs, reducing absenteeism, raising morale, or improving services. Instead, identifying me mainly with the "people" issue, they nearly always look for guidance in taking swift, painless, self-evidently correct actions toward the significant others who contribute to their misery. I always ask prospective clients to name what outcomes they hope to achieve by working with me.

Here are some typical replies:

Want others to understand our goals better
Better communications, fewer misunderstandings
_____ will shape up or ship out
Better meetings—more excitement, more decisions made

Notice that each of these statements is somewhat abstract, self-evidently "good," and very hard to measure. I never accept such generalities as adequate statements of a client's expectations. Instead, I push hard on outcomes. What would you see happening that would tell you communications are improving? How will you know when goals are clearer or morale has gone up? What will people do? Will you be able to watch them do it? When I push at this level, I get more realistic statements:

Pete will come to me with his gripes directly instead of going to Fred.
Deadlines will be taken seriously and met more often.
In meetings, decisions will be made, actions agreed upon, and names and dates put on them.

I will understand how to set up the _____ unit, and will have agreement on whatever way I decide.
We will have a new procedure for handling customer complaints.
I will make a decision whether to keep or fire _____ .

These statements are good short-run indicators of change. They are realistic expectations. Are changes like these worth the client's investment of time and money? Is there enough in it for him to go ahead? It is important that he be clear he is choosing to do whatever we do together because it is worth it to him (and not because it is this year's panacea, or somebody else tried it and liked it, or because he thinks his problems will go away). What does he want personally out of this? Easier life? What does *that* mean?

I expect some things too. Clients know I work mainly for money and want to be paid on time. However, I try also to indicate some of my secondary motives for working with them.

For example, I crave variety. I like learning about and using my skills in various "content" areas—manufacturing and service industries, medicine, law enforcement, public education. I like to try new technologies, to break new theoretical ground, to write and publish my experiences. The chance to do something new raises my incentive with any client. So does a client's ready acceptance of some responsibility for the crisis. If clients are well motivated to work on their problems, so am I—and I tell them so. In doing this, I am trying to say that each of us has a right to some personal benefits from our relationship, apart from any benefits the organization may derive.

Structuring the Relationship: Time and Money

OD, like much of life, is carried forward by a sequence of meetings between people. The central decision in any contract discussion is which people should sit in what room for how long and for what purpose. At some point it is essential to name those people, pick dates, and set a budget. The client has a right to know how much time I will invest in interviewing, or survey sampling, or whatever, and how long our meetings will require. If I need time in between to organize data, I estimate how much. Often the initial contract is diagnostic, to be completed at a face-to-face meeting where the data will be examined, a common diagnosis arrived at, and next steps decided upon. Always, I work to clarify the costs, time and money, of each next step. Generally, this information will be written down.

In addition, there are some things I will and will not do, money aside. I know what these things are and only mention them if the client does, on the premise that there is no point in solving a problem I do not have. For instance, I always turn down opportunities to work weekends. I will work morning, noon, and night on any scheduled day if necessary. On weekends my contract is with my family. In addition, I have a strong value that *when* you work on your organization indicates how important you consider it. People get themselves into crises during the week. If they do not have time to get out during the week, they are never going to get out by working weekends. That makes me the wrong consultant for them. (Incidentally, I have never lost a client because of this policy.)

Ground Rules

Ground rules speak to the process of our relationship. Sometimes I write them down, sometimes not. In any case, I try to get an understanding that includes these explicit agreements:

1. I supply methods, techniques, theory, etc., to help you understand and work better on your problems. You supply energy, commitment, and share responsibility for success. I do *not* study your problems and recommend expert solutions.

2. Part of my job is to raise sticky issues and push you on them. You have a right to say no to anything you do not want to deal with. If you feel free to say no, I will feel free to push.

3. Tell me if I do something puzzling or irritating, and give me permission to tell you the same.

4. I have no special preferences for how you deal with others. Part of my job is to make you aware of what you do and what possible consequences your actions have for me and for the people around you. My job is also to preserve and encourage your freedom of choice about what, if anything, you should do.

5. My client is the whole organization. That means

I intend not to be seen as an advocate for anybody's pet ideas, especially ones requiring your special expertise. However, I do advocate a certain process for problem solving and recognize that some people oppose my process. I accept that risk.

6. Any information I collect and present will be anonymous. I will never attach names to anything people tell me. However, in certain situations (e.g. team building) I do not *want* confidential information, meaning anything which you are unwilling for other team members to know, even anonymously.

7. All data belong to the people who supply them. I will never give or show them to anyone without their permission.

8. Either of us can terminate on 24 hours notice, regardless of contract length, so long as we have a face-to-face meeting first.

9. We evaluate all events together, face-to-face, and make explicit decisions about what to do next.

Contracting, like the seasons, is repetitive and continually renewable. If I have a long-term contract (e.g. 4 days a month for a year) I also have a separate contract for each meeting, which I present on a flipsheet and discuss at the outset. If I have a contract with a boss to help him build his team, I need to extend it to the team before we go to work. If I succeed with the team, and some members want to work with *their* teams, I need again to negotiate a new deal with the new people. Once, having worked with a team, I found the boss wanting to confront *his* boss. He wanted the whole team to do it with him, with me as consultant. I pointed out that that would require a temporary contract between me, him, and his boss. He set up a dinner meeting—the night before the confrontation—and his boss and I made a one-day contract which stood up very well next morning.

In short, I am never finished contracting. Each client meeting requires that I reexamine the contract. Does it cover everybody I am working with? Is it clear what we are doing now, and why?

Moreover, contracting—while it deals ostensibly and mainly with content issues—has a process side crucial to its success. Consider, in some detail, where and how an OD contract is made.

OD contracts usually begin with a phone call or letter. Somebody has heard about what I did somewhere else. They wonder whether I can do it for (or with or to) them. If I receive a letter, I respond with a phone call to the writer. If he calls first, I return his call at a time when I can spend 10 minutes or more discussing what he wants and whether or not it makes sense to meet. This initial contact is crucial to any contract. Each of us is trying—over the phone—to decide whether he likes the other well enough to proceed. I try not to prejudge the conversation. I want a face-to-face meeting *if* there's a chance of getting a solid contract. Here are some questions running through my mind:

1. How open is caller with me? I with him?
2. Is the caller window-shopping, maybe calling several consultants to find the "best deal" (whatever that means)? Does he really want me? Perhaps—as is often the case—he does not know what he wants. If that is so, I have a good chance to consult with him on the phone, helping him clarify what he is after.
3. To which of his problems am I the solution? How does he name the issue?
4. What does he see as the solution? Is it a workshop? A meeting? A series of meetings? Magic?
5. Is his mind made up? Has he diagnosed his troubles and prescribed something already, which I am to administer?
6. Does he have a budget? Is it adequate to his expectations? To mine? Is it likely to be worth my while to invest in a face-to-face meeting? I don't talk price on the phone, but do test whether a budget exists or could be got together. If the answer is no, I decide not to pursue it further.
7. Assume a budget and willingness on his part and mine to go forward. We need a meeting. Should anybody else be there? Who? Is the caller in a position to enter into a contract? If not, who is? His boss? Can he make the meeting? Is there another consultant I want to involve? If so, I ask whether I can bring an associate.

I end the phone call by clarifying that each of us intends to explore further whether there is a fit between the kinds of things my potential client needs help on and the skills and experience I have. I am investing up to a day at no fee. (If there are travel expenses involved, I test whether he will pay those.) At the end of that day, each of us will know whether to go further.

First Meeting

I arrive, greet my prospective client, introduce myself and associate to him and his associates. We have coffee and exchange pleasantries. Each of us is deciding, silently, privately, and maybe unconsciously, how much we like the other. We look for cues. We give cues. Early on, we get down to business—or appear to. The content issues might include:

1. Our backgrounds—potential client needs to know enough about me to feel I can help before he will put out major problems.
2. Issues bothering client system—Are they symptomatic of other things, which are not being discussed? I always ask for examples in terms of observable behavior. "Communications" or "decision making" are not issues you can see, feel, or pin down. Who needs to talk to whom? Why? What do they do now? What do people do when they disagree? What patterns of behavior do the people present see in the organization?
3. What changes would the people I am talking to like to see? What things would they observe happening that would tell them they are getting desired outcomes? This step in naming outcomes is important in reducing the level of fantasy around OD and what it can do.
4. What first event would be appropriate to moving the system in the desired direction? Nearly always, this event should be diagnostic. It should be an activity which will heighten the awareness of the people I am meeting with about how the issues they raise are seen by others in the system—colleagues, subordinates, customers, students, peers, etc.

If the system is ready, the budget exists, and my reading of the willingness to proceed is good, I may propose a workshop activity, based on interviews. Sometimes I propose that the workshop start with interviews of each person as a first step in agenda-building (okay if no more than 10 or 12 attend). Sometimes, it makes more sense to consult to a work group within the framework of their regular weekly or monthly meetings. Sometimes, a survey questionnaire provides a data base for a diagnostic meeting.

Whatever the event, we need a schedule, a place to meet, and a division of labor for organizing materials, sending out the agenda, etc. Sometimes these things can be decided in the first meeting. Sometimes I agree to write a formal proposal and proceed from there. Always I try to close on the next step—what I will do, what the client will do, and by what date.

The above considerations focus mainly on content. However, there are several process issues surrounding this meeting which I'm continually working on too:

1. First among these is, "Do I like this person?" If not a spark of fondness, or warmth, or empathy, then what *am* I feeling? Annoyance? Frustration? Wariness? Can I find *something* to like, respect, or admire about the other person? Usually, I can. Until I do, however, and until the other person finds it in me, I think our work on issues, possible next steps, logistics, etc., is largely fictional. It is a way of using the task at hand to help us get greater clarity about our relationship. Any time I am uncertain about a relationship, I believe my contract is in jeopardy, no matter what fine words are spoken or written on paper. Each time the relationship question is resolved, a little spark jumps. I watch for it.

2. The client's depth of commitment is an issue for me. Does he really want to change things? Does he accept responsibility—at least a little bit—for the way things are? If he says, "I want you to change them," and I say, "Okay, but how open are you to changing?," does he pull back, hem and haw? Or does he smile and admit the possibility? How open is he to understanding how what he does affects other people? My value about organizations improving themselves—that is, people learning to do things better with each other—is clear; I try to test how my client feels about that.

3. Part of client commitment is resources. Clients find money to do things they want to do. If money seems to be an insurmountable problem, I look to some other process issue—anxiety about failure, a boss who is negative about OD, fear of opening up "destructive issues," etc. Helping the client get in touch with these possibilities, if I can, is valuable for both of us, whether I work with him again or not. [It is done] by asking such questions as: What is the risk? What is the worst thing that could happen? How much exposure can you stand? I also ask what good things might happen and whether the possible outcomes are worth the price.

In some ways OD is like playing the market. Every intervention is a calculated risk. There are no guarantees. The client will have problems no matter what he does. So will I. The question I continually confront is: Which problems would you *rather* have? The ones you have now? Or the ones you *will* have if you try to solve the ones you have now? Once in a while, potential clients decide they would rather live with what they [have]. I support this insight. It is better that both of us know it sooner rather than later.

More often this process leads to greater clarity and commitment on both our parts to make an intervention successful. My value set goes something like this: I want to find out what is real, what the environment will support, what is possible in this relationship, and then learn how to live with it. Of course I want to sell my services. I want to try new interventions. More than that, I want to be successful. I am learning to spot conditions under which I fail. An unclear contract ranks high on the list.

I resist entering untenable contracts, for I know deep down that they are like airplanes without fuel. No matter how beautiful they look, they will not fly. The fuel for an OD contract is (1) client commitment, (2) a good relationship between us, and (3) a clear structure to that relationship, symbolized by our ability to agree on what services I will perform, when, and at what costs in time and money.

Structuring the Relationship

Item 3 brings us to the specific first intervention. It has several criteria:

1. It is responsive to the client's perceived problem. He must see it as helping him gain greater clarity, insight, and control over whatever issues are bugging him. It is not based on my need to use any particular trick in my bag.

2. It names the people who will come together, when, for how long, and why. "Why" is generally the client's to answer, in his own words, but I help him shape the language if he has trouble. I get clear that the boss will tell people why they are there, as he sees it, and I will tell them what I see as my contract with them. It is never my job to tell people why they are there.

3. It involves some form of diagnosis. That means some systematic information is collected which will heighten the clients' awareness and enlarge their freedom of choice. Sometimes this information fits some conceptual scheme, which I make explicit. Sometimes I help the client build a scheme from the information which will make sense to him. Always, data collection, as I see it, must be done in such a way that the people who supply the information will recognize it as critical to their lives together when I collate it and hand it back. The more interpreting or categorizing I do in advance, the less likely this is to happen.

I insure confidentiality and anonymity. Interpretation, I try to make clear, will result when people who supplied the information meet face-to-face to assign meaning to it. I try always to specify how much time people must give, what kinds of questions will be asked, and what will become of the answers. This structuring reduces anxiety and sets up reasonable expectations.

4. I establish that part of the contract is mutual feedback. I expect clients to confront me openly on my behavior when it does not make sense, to question anything I do, and to point out to me words or behavior that violate their sense of what is appropriate. In return, I expect to be open with them.

It is around this clause, I think, that all contracts are tested sooner or later. In a workshop the test may come in the form of protest that the activities are irrelevant to the agenda and a waste of time. In a one-to-one relationship the test may be something I did or said that really irritated the client. It takes some risk to let me know. In opening the issue, he is checking to see whether I am as good at handling deeds as I am at manipulating words.

I define testing the contract as an emotion-provoking exchange between me and the client in some risky situation. As a result our relationship will become more "real," more truly experimental, more like the action-research model which I advocate as an appropriate way to live. I do not expect the burden for testing to rest entirely on the client. I test, too, whenever the time seems right, usually around something the client is doing which affects our relationship. Once, I noticed a client would continually express disappointment in others and told him I was worried that one day—if not already—he was going to feel the same way about me. He owned up to the possibility and assured me I would be the first to know, which, when the time came, I was. The confrontation deepened our relationship and strengthened the contract. It might have ended it, too.

I welcome ending a contract explicitly by having it tested and found wanting. Better a clean death than lingering agony. It is time to test (and maybe end) a contract when:

The client keeps putting things off

Agreements are made and forgotten (by either side)

The consultant appears to have a higher emotional stake in the outcomes than the client does

The consultant asks for events or activities, which intensify the feeling of crisis and pressure without much prospect for eventual relief

The client looks to the consultant to do things which he, as manager of his own organization, should be doing—i.e., arranging meetings, sending out agendas, carrying messages, and getting other people to do everything the client always wanted them to do but was afraid to ask

The client is doing better and really doesn't need outside help

For me, a crisp, clean ending remains desirable but sometimes elusive. Going over 14 major contracts during the last four years, I find nine ended cleanly with no "unfinished business," three ended because the boss lacked commitment to continue, and two because organizational changes left a leadership vacuum and me uncertain who the client was.

Where the boss lacked commitment, the intended follow-up meetings never took place, and I let things alone, feeling, I suppose, relatively little commitment myself. In the cases of organizational changes, it became plain the interim leadership lacked either incentive or authority to keep up the contract, and I had other fish to fry.

It seems to me contracts have a natural life. Organizations eventually outgrow or tire of or cease needing a particular consultant and vice versa. It is better for me and my client that we recognize explicitly when it is time to part.

The Primary Tasks of
Intervention Activities

Chris Argyris

A Definition of Intervention

To intervene is to enter into an ongoing system of relationship, to come between or among persons, groups, or objects for the purpose of helping them. There is an important implicit assumption in the definition that should be made explicit: the system exists independently of the intervenor. There are many reasons one might wish to intervene. These reasons may range from helping the clients make their own decisions about the kind of help they need in coercing the clients to do what the intervenor wishes them to do. Examples of the latter are modern black militants who intervene to demand that the city be changed in accordance with their wishes and choices (or white racists who prefer the same); executives who invite interventionists into their system to manipulate subordinates for them; trade union leaders who for years have resisted systematic research in their own bureaucratic functioning at the highest levels because they fear that valid information might lead to entrenched interests—especially at the top—being unfrozen.

The more one conceives of the intervenor in this sense, the more one implies that the client system should have little autonomy from the intervenor; that its boundaries are indistinguishable from those of the intervenor; that its health or effectiveness are best controlled by the intervenor.

In contrast, our view acknowledges interdependencies between the intervenor and the client system but focuses on how to maintain or increase the client system's autonomy; how to differentiate even more

clearly the boundaries between the client system and the intervenor; and how to conceptualize and define the client system's health independently of the intervenor's. This view values the client system as an ongoing, self-responsible unity that has the obligation to be in control over its own destiny. An intervenor, in this view, assists a system to become more effective in problem solving, decision making, and decision implementation in such a way that the system can continue to be increasingly effective in these activities and have a decreasing need for the intervenor.

[A] critical question the intervenor must ask is, who is he helping—management or employees, black militants or Negro moderates, white racists or white moderates? . . . At this point, it is suggested that the intervenor must be concerned with the system as a whole even though his initial contact may be made with only a few people. He therefore focuses on those intervention activities that eventually (not necessarily immediately) will provide *all* the members' opportunities to enhance their competence and effectiveness. If any individual or subsystem wishes help to prevent other individuals or subsystems from having these opportunities, then the intervenor may well have to question seriously his involvement in the project.

Basic Requirements for Intervention Activity

Are there any basic or necessary processes that must be fulfilled regardless of the substantive issues involved, if intervention activity is to be helpful with any level of client (individual, group, or organizational)? One condition that seems so basic as to be defined axiomatic is the generation of *valid information*. Without valid information, it would be difficult for the client to learn and for the interventionist to help.

A second condition almost as basic flows from our assumption that intervention activity, no matter what its substantive interests and objectives, should be so designed and executed that the client system maintains its discreteness and autonomy. Thus *free, informed choice* is also a necessary process in effective intervention activity.

Finally, if the client system is assumed to be ongoing (that is, existing over time), the clients require strengthening to maintain their autonomy not only vis-à-vis the interventionist but also vis-à-vis other systems. This means that their commitment to learning and change has to be more than temporary. It has to be so strong that it can be transferred to relationships other than those with the interventionist and can do so (eventually) without the help of the interventionist. The third basic process for any intervention activity is therefore the client's *internal commitment* to the choices made.

In summary, valid information, free choice, and internal commitment are considered integral parts of any intervention activity, no matter what the substantive objectives are (for example, developing a management performance evaluation scheme, reducing intergroup rivalries, increasing the degree of trust among individuals, redesigning budgetary systems, or redesigning work). These three processes are called the primary intervention tasks.

Primary Tasks of an Interventionist

Why is it necessary to hypothesize that in order for an interventionist to behave effectively and in order that the integrity of the client system be maintained, the interventionist has to focus on three primary tasks, regardless of the substantive problems that the client system may be experiencing?

VALID AND USEFUL INFORMATION

First, it has been accepted as axiomatic that valid and useful information is the foundation for effective intervention. Valid information is that which describes the factors, plus their interrelationships, that create the problem for the client system. There are several tests for checking the validity of the information. In increasing degrees of power they are public verifiability, valid prediction, and control over the phenomena. The first is having several independent diagnoses suggest the same picture. Second is generating predictions from the diagnosis that are subsequently confirmed (they occurred under the conditions that were specified). Third is altering the factors systematically and predicting the effects upon the system as a whole. All these tests, if they are to be valid, must be carried out in such a way that the participants cannot, at will, make them come true. This would be a self-fulfilling prophecy and not a confirmation of a prediction. The difficulty with a self-fulfilling prophecy is its indication of more about the degree of power an individual (or subset of individuals) can muster to alter the system than about the nature of the system when the participants are behaving without knowledge of the diagnosis. For example, if an executive learns that the interventionist predicts his subordinates will behave (a) if he behaves (b), he might alter (b) in order not to lead to (a). Such an alteration indicates the executive's power but does not test the validity of the diagnosis that if (a), then (b).

The tests for valid information have important implications for effective intervention activity. First, the interventionist's diagnoses must strive to represent the total client system and not the point of view of any subgroup or individual. Otherwise, the interventionist could not be seen only as being under the control of a particular individual or subgroup, but also his predictions would be based upon inaccurate information and thus might not be confirmed.

This does not mean that an interventionist may not begin with, or may not limit his relationship to, a subpart of the total system. It is totally possible, for example, for the interventionist to help management, blacks, trade union leaders, etc. With whatever subgroup he works he simply should not agree to limit his diagnosis to its wishes.

It is conceivable that a client system may be helped even though valid information is not generated. Sometimes changes occur in a positive direction without the interventionist having played any important role. These changes, although helpful in that specific instance, lack the attribute of helping the organization to learn and to gain control over its problem-solving capability.

The importance of information that the clients can use to control their destiny points up the requirement that the information must not only be valid, it must be useful. Valid information that cannot be used by the clients to alter their system is equivalent to valid information about cancer that cannot be used to cure cancer eventually. An interventionist's diagnosis should include variables that are manipulatable by the clients and are complete enough so that if they are manipulated effective change will follow.

FREE CHOICE

In order to have free choice, the client has to have a cognitive map of what he wishes to do. The objectives of his action are known at the moment of decision. Free choice implies voluntary as opposed to automatic; proactive rather than reactive. The act of selection is rarely accomplished by maximizing or optimizing. Free and informed choice entails what Simon has called "satisficing," that is, selecting the alternative with the highest probability of succeeding, given some specified cost constraints. Free choice places the locus of decision making in the client system. Free choice makes it possible for the clients to remain responsible for their destiny. Through free choice the clients can maintain the autonomy of their system.

It may be possible that clients prefer to give up their responsibility and their autonomy, especially if they are feeling a sense of failure. They may prefer . . . to turn over their free choice to the interventionist. They may insist that he make recommendations and tell them what to do. The interventionist resists these pressures because if he does not, the clients will lose their free choice and he will lose his own free choice also. He will be controlled by the anxieties of the clients.

The requirement of free choice is especially important for those helping activities where the processes of help are as important as the actual help. For example, a medical doctor does not require that a patient with a bullet wound participate in the process by defining the kind of help he needs. However, the same doctor may have to pay much more attention to the processes he uses to help patients when he is attempting to diagnose blood pressure or cure a high cholesterol. If the doctor behaves in ways that upset the patient, the latter's blood pressure may well be distorted. Or, the patient can develop a dependent relationship if the doc-

tor cuts down his cholesterol—increasing habits only under constant pressure from the doctor—and the moment the relationship is broken off, the count goes up.

Effective intervention in the human and social spheres requires that the processes of help be congruent with the outcome desired. Free choice is important because there are so many unknowns, and the interventionist wants the client to have as much willingness and motivation as possible to work on the problem. With high client motivation and commitment, several different methods for change can succeed.

A choice is free to the extent the members can make their selection for a course of action with minimal internal defensiveness; can define the path (or paths) by which the intended consequence is to be achieved; can relate the choice to their central needs; and can build into their choices a realistic and challenging level of aspiration. Free choice therefore implies that the members are able to explore as many alternatives as they consider significant and select those that are central to their needs.

Why must the choice be related to the central needs and why must the level of aspiration be realistic and challenging? May people not choose freely unrealistic or unchallenging objectives? Yes, they may do so in the short run, but not for long if they still want to have free and informed choice. A freely chosen course of action means that the action must be based on an accurate analysis of the situation and not on the biases or defenses of the decision makers. We know, from the level of aspiration studies, that choices which are too high or too low, which are too difficult or not difficult enough, will tend to lead to psychological failure. Psychological failure will lead to increased defensiveness, increased failure, and decreased self-acceptance on the part of the members experiencing the failure. These conditions, in turn, will tend to lead to distorted perceptions by the members making the choices. Moreover, the defensive members may unintentionally create a climate where the members of surrounding and interrelated systems will tend to provide carefully censored information. Choices made under these conditions are neither informed nor free.

Turning to the question of centrality of needs, a similar logic applies. The degree of commitment to the processes of generating valid information, scanning, and choosing may significantly vary according to the centrality of the choice to the needs of the clients. The more central the choice, the more the system will strive to do its best in developing valid information and making free and informed choices. If the research from perceptual psychology is valid, the very perception of the clients is altered by the needs involved. Individuals tend to scan more, ask for more information, and be more careful in their choices when they are making decisons that are central to them. High involvement may produce perceptual distortions, as does low involvement. The interventionist, however, may have a greater probability of helping the clients explore possible distortion when the choice they are making is a critical one.

INTERNAL COMMITMENT

Internal commitment means the course of action or choice that has been internalized by each member so that he experiences a high degree of ownership and has a feeling of responsibility about the choice and its implications. Internal commitment means that the individual has reached the point where he is acting on the choice because it fulfills his own needs and sense of responsibility, as well as those of the system.

The individual who is internally committed is acting primarily under the influence of his own forces and not induced forces. The individual (or any unity) feels a minimal degree of dependence upon others for the action. It implies that he has obtained and processed valid information and that he has made an informed and free choice. Under these conditions there is a high probability that the individual's commitment will remain strong over time (even with reduction of external rewards), or under stress, or when the course of action is challenged by others. It also implies that the individual is continually open to reexamination of his position because he believes in taking action based upon valid information.

Implications of the Primary Tasks for Intervention Activity

CONGRUENCE BETWEEN EFFECTIVE INTERVENTION ACTIVITY AND EFFECTIVE CLIENT SYSTEMS

The first implication states there is little difference between the activities an ongoing client system requires for effective daily operation and those activities required to intervene effectively. A client system will be effective to the extent that it is able to generate valid information, free and informed choice, and internal commitment.

Effective intervention activity helps the client system learn not only how to solve a particular set of problems but how to operate more competently. Presumably, this greater degree of competence should help to decrease the probability that if the set of problems recur, it will be solved without the help of an outside interventionist.

The concept of competence places contraints upon the interventionist. He may not design change strategies, which even though they may bring about change, can also reduce free choice or internal commitment. Such strategies increase the client's dependence upon the interventionist and reduce the probability that the client system will become self-regulating. . . .

Another way to conceptualize the issue is to note that the processes of management are not separable from the substantive human problems of systems. Indeed, many of the human substantive problems arise because of the process of the management used in many pyramidal organizations. To attempt to alter the human substantive problem—say resistance to change—without altering the processes of management is comparable to making changes without getting at the basic causes. From a client's viewpoint, the only worse strategy is for the interventionist to articulate intervention values, as described, yet behave in a manner that is not congruent and be blind to his incongruence.

CHANGE NOT A PRIMARY TASK

A second implication states that change is *not* a primary task of the interventionist. To repeat, the interventionist's primary tasks are to generate valid information, to help the client system make informed and responsible choices, and to develop internal commitment to these choices. One choice that the clients may make is to change aspects of their system. If this choice is made responsibly, the interventionist may help the client to change. However, the point we are making is that change is not a priori considered good and no change considered bad.

This position may seem out of keeping with the emphasis in the literature. Change is described as the challenge of the future, the basic characteristic of the next decade, and the only certainty. These proclamations may be true and they may be, partially at least, self-fulfilling prophecies.

If an interventionist assumes that the client's biggest problems are related to change, he has already made a choice for the client. It may very well be that change is the most important problem or need facing the client. However, it is important that the decision not be prejudged by the interventionist, and, according to this framework, the client should be helped to make the decision. The interventionist can help the client by assisting him in obtaining valid and useful information. . . .

PRIMARY TASKS USED AS CRITERIA
FOR SELECTING CLIENT SYSTEMS

Defining the primary tasks as generating valid information, free and informed choice, and internal commitment may help to cast light on some difficult value questions regarding the choice of client systems. For example, should one help a system which has, in the eyes of the interventionist, undesirable goals? Would one help the Ku Klux Klan? Most interventionists would say no or at least hesitate for a long time before they would help an organization whose members had been accused of racial hatred and murder. Perhaps this is the organization that needs help more than many others. If members of the KKK have killed, have they killed more than the most optimistic estimates of the impact of the recent edict by Pope Paul on birth control upon children in the poorly developed countries?

If the interventionist keeps the three primary tasks in the forefront, it will be possible for him to help organizations that may be questionable in his eyes without implicating himself (or them) with his values or with change. What would happen if the KKK invited an interventionist to generate valid information about its internal system and to create conditions of informed and free choice for all who became part of its system? Why should it not be helped to accomplish these purposes? Might its successful accomplishment lead to new self-inquiry within the client system? If it does, an important step forward has been taken; if it does not, the intervenor can choose to leave without being charged with bias.

The latter statement leads to another interrelated issue. Should an interventionist be permitted to decide unilaterally which client system he will help and which he will not? Medical doctors and lawyers discovered many years ago that one way to keep their respective professions alive and viable in a society was to offer their aid to anyone who needed it. To be sure, there are medical doctors and lawyers who refuse to take lower class clients, but these refusals are subject to investigation by the local medical or legal professional societies. Such denial of help is not condoned by fellow professionals.

If an interventionist is not to be granted power of unilateral choice of clients, it seems important that he be able to offer initial aid to any system that will not tend to compromise his values. Adherence to the three primary tasks offers such aid without committing the interventionist to remain in the system in order to help it change or to maintain its present equilibrium.

The relationship between the interventionist and client system forms a system in itself. The primary objective of the intervention system is to introduce into, or build upon, the client system's capacity to generate valid information, free and informed choice, and internal commitment. For two reasons, this objective is a difficult one to achieve in most client systems. . . . Most client systems tend to be designed and managed in ways that minimize the probabilities of generating valid information (for critical decisions), free choice, and internal commitment. Moreover, in view of the small amount the client system may have of these three activities, the probability is quite high that it was reduced even further and that this fact was one reason an interventionist was invited.

In order to graft onto the client system significantly higher dosages of the capacity to generate valid information, free choice, and internal commitment, the intervention system requires all the assistance it can get. First, the client system must be open to and capable of learning. Client systems at any level of complexity that are closed and not capable of learning are not going to be helped very much by an intervention strategy based on valid information, free and informed choice, and internal commitment. This means that behavioral science intervention theory may be seriously limited in what it can do for client systems that cannot or do not want to be helped. . . .

Second, the intervention system should be linked

with the power points in the client system that are the keys to the problem being studied. In pyramidal organizations this usually means the top of the organization. Changes in attitudes, values, and behavior at the top can lead to changes in administrative controls, structure, and organizational policies. All of these combined can produce clear messages to those below of the willingness to change the system. . . .

ADHERENCE TO PRIMARY TASKS
MINIMIZES PROBABILITIES FOR CLIENT
AND INTERVENTIONIST MANIPULATION

Selecting a client system with these three criteria in mind tends to create the conditions which will minimize intentional or unintentional client manipulation of the interventionist or vice versa. Neither will be able to control the other because valid information is being produced, free choice encouraged, and internal commitment generated.

The probability of unintentional manipulation by the interventionist is not so infrequent that it may be dismissed. . . . The interventionist may have needs (of power and affiliation) and defenses (about authority and conflict) that may lead him to want to control and coerce the client into specific courses of action. . . .

One of the most frequent manipulations attempted by clients is to demand that the interventionist short-cut the three primary tasks and get on with change. Industrial organizations seeking help to overcome a crisis see little need for careful diagnosis. Governmental representatives giving money to help correct inner city problems focus on change, not on diagnosis. . . .

Finally, even if the client and interventionist have the best of motives, it is possible that the client system exists in such a turbulent environment that the interventionist cannot be of significant help. This state of affairs is most quickly diagnosed if valid information is generated and the clients are asked to make their own informed and free choices. . . .

PRIMARY TASKS RELATED TO ADVANCEMENT
OF BASIC KNOWLEDGE AS WELL AS PRACTICE

The requirement of obtaining valid information encourages the interventionist to add to the basic knowledge in his field. The existence of free choice and internal commitment increases the probability that clients will confront the interventionist, and he will confront himself, regarding the validity and usefulness of the information generated. Adherence to the three primary tasks, therefore, allows the interventionist to be better able to make some contributions to his field. . . .

The interventionist and the clients may then develop secondary tasks of change, increasing system stability, etc. An interventionist's decision to select or remain in a particular client system depends upon the client's capacities to fulfill the three primary tasks.

Three Types of Intervention Activity

The suggestion that intervention activities and research are congruent should not be interpreted to mean that all intervention activities must be studied systematically or that those coupled with research are necessarily the most helpful to the clients. There are at least three different intervention activities that may be identified.

1. There is a large cluster of problems common to different types of clients. Many client systems have problems of poor communication, lack of trust, and lack of internal commitment to certain organizational policies. As a result of many attempts to help clients with these problems, there has been built up a body of knowledge and experience in methods for dealing with such problems. The intervention will therefore tend to be based upon existing knowledge and technique. An already validated questionnaire, an already tested confrontation meeting, or a T-group approach may be used.

The advantage of using tested methods is that they tend to assure the client system relatively quick action with a respectable probability of success. This type of intervention activity is especially useful if there is little time available to resolve the problems or if the organization lacks the resources for a more comprehensive study. It is also useful if the interventionist has limited time to give to the client system.

Probably all interventionists engage, to some degree, in this first type of activity. The more they focus on this type of activity, the more their confidence in their interventions will be based upon others' innovations. If this becomes the primary style, the interventionist may become reluctant to explore innovations of his own. Such an interventionist could be of help to client systems whose problems have known solutions. However, the interventionist needs to be careful that he does not, unrealizingly, see all the clients' problems in terms of his own repertoire of solutions.

2. A second type of intervention activity in which an interventionist may engage involves the creative arrangement of existing knowledge. The development of the intergroup exercise which was based on the earlier work of Lewin, Sherif, and Moreno is an example. The danger of too strong an emphasis upon this type of activity is development of a compulsiveness to find a new twist, a new intervention technique in every client relationship. T-group methods and intergroup exercises are continually modified and experimented with in client relationships, without previous exploration or analytical study. Although these experiments may be helpful, there are many times on record when experiments with a new intervention have not worked. The modification was dictated more by the inner compulsiveness of the interventionist than by the needs of the client. The value of a tested intervention was glossed over and the new twist was regarded as creative. In many cases, the twist is only half a twist and the help it has produced is half what the already-known intervention could have produced. Failure of a new intervention is usually explained away by saying in effect, "Well, there was learning. We learned it didn't work and the clients learned how to confront us when they did not find us helpful." The danger in this explanation is that *any* learning may become valued as a contribution. A new client system may accept this assumption, especially when they are anxious about their present state of affairs, and any change seems heart-warming. If this strategy is repeated frequently enough and justified by the criterion that any learning is progress, the client may soon begin to feel let down. After all, it follows from this criterion that the client should feel good about his many errors if he has realized and learned from them.

The second type of intervention activity tends to be possible when the client system has adequate time available, adequate resources, an already existing state of health which permits experimentation, and an interventionist who is able to perceive accurately the potential of the system.

3. The third intervention activity is the rarest. The resources of the client system and the resources of the interventionist are joined together to conduct an intervention that helps the client understand the nature of its problem and adds to the basic theory of intervention activity. The objective of this intervention activity is to help the client system and simultaneously to develop new conceptual models that help to explain that particular case as well as others that may be identified in the future. . . .

There are several important advantages that accrue to a client when this type of intervention activity is used. First, the development of a model that takes a position as to the variables that are or are not relevant, the probable interrelationships of the variables, and the probable reaction under change is a very difficult process. It usually takes much time, with the models going through seemingly countless revisions. An interventionist who subjects himself to the intellectual challenge of model building will probably be more articulate with the client as to what he can and cannot accomplish. He will also be better prepared to take on confrontation, friendly or hostile, because he has thought through his position.

Moreover, an interventionist who values model building may tend to be more open to confrontation of his model by the client because it is one way to test its usefulness. He will find it intrinsically satisfying to fill in a gap and to make a modification because it will make his model more elegant.

The client will gain because he will be clearer as to what the interventionist can and cannot accomplish. He can make his choice of interventionists on a more informed basis. He can also describe more clearly to members of his system what are real and unreal expectations to hold about the entire project.

The interventionist who is conceptually clear about his primary tasks and strategies will tend to increase the probability of being trusted at the outset. Clients, especially top executives, tend to judge strength in others by their ability to articulate and their consistency in their position. Although the interventionist

Client's Diagnosis	*Interventionist's Conceptualization*
1. How can we introduce product planning and program review into the organization?	1. How can we institute a basic change in the living system?
2. How can we make product-planning meetings more effective?	2. How can we determine and increase group effectiveness?
3. How can we get other groups to cooperate with product planning?	3. How can we understand the relationship of small group dynamics to the large environment in which it is embedded? How can we overcome destructive intergroup rivalries?
4. How can management get more commitment from the employees?	4. What is the differential impact of various leadership styles upon the subordinates?

knows that cognitive clarity is only a part of the requirements for trust, he is not unwilling nor unable to start on his client's level and slowly help him move toward additional sources for trust.

Finally, one of the best assurances that the client system will get the highest quality work is to require the interventionist to add to basic theory and to publish his findings (with appropriate deletions to protect the client). If an interventionist knows that his work will be subject to public scrutiny of the top professionals, both in terms of its helpfulness to the client and its contribution to basic theory, he will be highly motivated to perform at his best. . . .

The value of translating practical problems into theoretical issues is not clearly understood by most clients and deserves further discussion. In one study, the client system described its problem as instituting and maintaining an effective product-planning and program-review activity. This was translated by the interventionist into four basic issues so that the problem, as the clients described it, became an empirical example of a more general theory (see table above).

The translation into basic theoretical issues is of value because the client's problems are related to a wealth of concepts and findings. For example, only several quite narrowly focused documents exist on the subject of introducing product-planning and program-review activities. These documents are primarily case studies of how different organizations handled this problem. Each description tends to be specific to each system. Unfortunately, there is little or no data given to help us understand (1) why the particular strategy was chosen, (2) what kinds of resistance were developed, (3) to what extent the developers of the

programs were unintentionally creating the resistance, or (4) how the changes actually had impact upon the organization.

Some possible answers to these questions could come to the interventionist's attention if he were familiar with the relevant literature. Moreover, the literature would tend to provide concepts found helpful in understanding the underlying dynamics of change. The knowledge that each system developed about their particular change could be conceptualized so that it would provide important information about the nature of resistance to change in that system. This knowledge, in turn, could become part of the administrative resources available for planning further changes in product planning, program review, or *any other change*. The knowledge could also serve as material for executive development programs within each firm. If the interventionist is able to develop a model of the underlying reaction to the introduction of new programs (giving the introduction of product planning and program reviews as an example), the material could then be useful to all managers of the system (and other systems).

From the client's point of view, all three types of intervention activities are important. If they can be helped effectively with type one or two, they will tend to be satisfied. Indeed, as has been pointed out, some problems, given client constraints, may best be solved by the first type of interventionist activity. From the point of view of adding to basic knowledge about intervention theory, type three activity is most relevant (although it may take much experience with type one activity to lead to the stage of research).

Choosing the Depth of Organizational Intervention

Roger Harrison

Since World War II there has been a great proliferation of behavioral science-based methods by which consultants seek to facilitate growth and change in individuals, groups, and organizations. The methods range from operations analysis and manipulation of the organization chart, through the use of grid laboratories, T-groups, and nonverbal techniques. As was true in the development of clinical psychology and psychotherapy, the early stages of this developmental process tend to be accompanied by considerable competition, criticism, and argument about the relative merits of various approaches. It is my conviction that controversy over the relative goodness or badness, effectiveness or ineffectiveness, of various change strategies really accomplishes very little in the way of increased knowledge or unification of behavioral science. As long as we are arguing about what method is better than another, we tend to learn very little about how various approaches fit together or complement one another, and we certainly make more difficult and ambiguous the task of bringing these competing points of view within one overarching system of knowledge about human processes.

As our knowledge increases, it begins to be apparent that these competing change strategies are not really different ways of doing the same thing—some more effective and some less effective—but rather that they are different ways of doing *different* things. they touch the individual, the group, or the organization in different aspects of their functioning. They require differing kinds and amounts of commitment on

the part of the client for them to be successful, and they demand different varieties and levels of skills and abilities on the part of the practitioner.

I believe that there is a real need for conceptual models which differentiate intervention strategies from one another in a way which permits rational matching of strategies to organizational change problems. The purpose of this paper is to present a modest beginning which I have made toward a conceptualization of strategies, and to derive from this conceptualization some criteria for choosing appropriate methods of intervention in particular applications.

The point of view of this paper is that the depth of individual emotional involvement in the change process can be a central concept for differentiating change strategies. In focusing on this dimension, we are concerned with the extent to which core areas of the personality or self are the focus of the change attempt. Strategies which touch the more deep, personal, private, and central aspects of the individual or his relationships with others fall toward the deeper end of this continuum. Strategies which deal with more external aspects of the individual and which focus upon the more formal and public aspects of role behavior tend to fall toward the surface end of the depth dimension. This dimension has the advantage that it is relatively easy to rank change strategies upon it and to get fairly close consensus as to the ranking. It is a widely discussed dimension of difference which has meaning and relevance to practitioners and their clients. I hope in this paper to promote greater flexibility and rationality in choosing appropriate depths of intervention. I shall approach this task by examining the effects of interventions at various depths. I shall also explore the ways in which two important organizational processes tend to make demands and to set limits upon the depth of intervention which can produce effective change in organizational functioning. These two processes are the autonomy of organization members and their own perception of their needs for help.

Before illustrating the concept by ranking five common intervention strategies along the dimension of depth, I should like to define the dimension somewhat more precisely. We are concerned essentially with how private, individual, and hidden are the issues and processes about which the consultant attempts directly to obtain information and which he seeks to influence. If the consultant seeks information about relatively public and observable aspects of behavior and relationship and if he tries to influence directly only these relatively surface characteristics and processes, we would then categorize his intervention strategy as being closer to the surface. If, on the other hand, the consultant seeks information about very deep and private perceptions, attitudes, or feelings and if he intervenes in a way which directly affects these processes, then we would classify his intervention strategy as one of considerable depth. To illustrate the surface end of the dimension let us look first at operations research or operations analysis. This strategy is concerned with the roles and functions to be performed within the organization, generally with little regard to the individual characteristics of persons occupying the roles. The change strategy is to manipulate role relationships; in other words, to redistribute the tasks, the resources, and the relative power attached to various roles in the organization. This is essentially a process of rational analysis in which the tasks which need to be performed are determined and specified and then sliced up into role definitions for persons and groups in the organization. The operations analyst does not ordinarily need to know much about particular people. Indeed, his function is to design the organization in such a way that its successful operation does not depend too heavily upon any uniquely individual skills, abilities, values, or attitudes of persons in various roles. He may perform this function adequately without knowing in advance who the people are who will fill these slots. Persons are assumed to be moderately interchangeable, and in order to make this approach work it is necessary to

design the organization so that the capacities, needs, and values of the individual which are relevant to role performance are relatively public and observable, and are possessed by a fairly large proportion of the population from which organization members are drawn. The approach is certainly one of very modest depth.

Somewhat deeper are those strategies which are based upon evaluating individual peformance and attempting to manipulate it directly. Included in this approach is much of the industrial psychologist's work in selection, placement, appraisal, and counseling of employees. The intervenor is concerned with what the individual is able and likely to do and achieve rather than with processes internal to the individual. Direct attempts to influence performance may be made through the application of rewards and punishments such as promotions, salary increases, or transfers within the organization. An excellent illustration of this focus on end results is the practice of management by objectives. The intervention process is focused on establishing mutually agreed-upon goals for performance between the individual and his supervisor. The practice is considered to be particularly advantageous because it permits the supervisor to avoid a focus on personal characteristics of the subordinate, particularly those deeper, more central characteristics which managers generally have difficulty in discussing with those who work under their supervision. The process is designed to limit information exchange to that which is public and observable, such as the setting of performance goals and the success or failure of the individual in attaining them.

Because of its focus on end results, rather than on the process by which those results are achieved, management by objectives must be considered less deep than the broad area of concern with work style which I shall term instrumental process analysis. We are concerned here not only with performance but with the processes by which that performance is achieved. However, we are primarily concerned with styles and processes of work rather than with the processes of interpersonal relationships which I would classify as being deeper on the basic dimension.

In instrumental process analysis we are concerned with how a person likes to organize and conduct his work and with the impact which this style of work has on others in the organization. Principally, we are concerned with how a person perceives his role, what he values and disvalues in it, and with what he works hard on and what he chooses to ignore. We are also interested in the instrumental acts which the individual directs toward others: delegating authority or reserving decisions to himself, communicating or withholding information, collaborating or competing with others on work-related issues. The focus on instrumentality means that we are interested in the person primarily as a doer of work or a performer of functions related to the goals of the organization. We are interested in what facilitates or inhibits his effective task performance.

We are not interested per se in whether his relationships with others are happy or unhappy, whether they perceive him as too warm or too cold, too authoritarian or too laissez faire, or any other of the many interpersonal relationships which arise as people associate in organizations. However, I do not mean to imply that the line between instrumental relationships and interpersonal ones is an easy one to draw in action and practice, or even that it is desirable that this be done.

Depth Gauges: Level of Tasks and Feelings

What I am saying is that an intervention strategy can focus on instrumentality or it can focus on interpersonal relationships, and that there are important consequences of this difference in depth of intervention.

When we intervene at the level of instrumentality, it is to change work behavior and working relationships. Frequently this involves the process of bargaining or negotiation between groups and individuals. Diagnoses are made of the satisfactions or dissatisfactions of organization members with one another's work behavior. Reciprocal adjustments, bargains, and trade-offs can then be arranged in which each party gets some modification in the behavior of the other at the cost to him of some reciprocal accommodation. Much of the intervention strategy which has been developed around Blake's concept of the managerial grid is at this level and involves bargaining and negotiation of role behavior as an important change process.

At the deeper level of interpersonal relationships the focus is on feelings, attitudes, and perceptions which organization members have about others. At this level we are concerned with the quality of human relationships within the organization, with warmth and coldness of members to one another, and with the experiences of acceptance and rejection, love and hate, trust and suspicion among groups and individuals. At this level the consultant probes for normally hidden feelings, attitudes, and perceptions. He works to create relationships of openness about feelings and to help members to develop mutual understanding of one another as persons. Interventions are directed toward helping organization members to be more comfortable in being authentically themselves with one another, and the degree of mutual caring and concern is expected to increase. Sensitivity training using T-groups is a basic intervention strategy at this level. T-group educators emphasize increased personalization of relationships, the development of trust and openness, and the exchange of feelings. Interventions at this level deal directly and intensively with interpersonal emotionality. This is the first intervention strategy we have examined which is at a depth where the feelings of organization members about one another as persons are a direct focus of the intervention strategy. At the other levels, such feelings certainly exist and may be expressed, but they are not a direct concern of the intervention. The transition from the task orientation of instrumental process analysis to the feeling orientation of interpersonal process analysis seems, as I shall suggest later, to be a critical one for many organization members.

The deepest level of intervention which will be considered in this paper is that of intrapersonal analysis. Here the consultant uses a variety of methods to reveal the individual's deeper attitudes, values, and conflicts regarding his own functioning, identity, and existence. The focus is generally on increasing the range of experiences which the individual can bring into awareness and cope with. The material may be dealt with at the fantasy or symbolic level, and the intervention strategies include many which are noninterpersonal and nonverbal. Some examples of this approach are the use of marathon T-group sessions, the creative risk-taking laboratory approach of Byrd (1967), and some aspects of the task group therapy approach of Clark (1966). These approaches all tend to bring into focus very deep and intense feelings about one's own identity and one's relationships with significant others.

Although I have characterized deeper interventions as dealing increasingly with the individual's affective life, I do not imply that issues at less deep levels may not be emotionally charged. Issues of role differentiation, reward distribution, ability, and performance evaluation, for example, are frequently invested with strong feelings. The concept of depth is concerned more with the *accessibility* and *individuality* of attitudes, values, and perceptions than it is with their strength. This narrowing of the common usage of the term *depth* is necessary to avoid the contradictions which occur when strength and inaccessibility are confused. For instance, passionate value confrontation and bitter conflict have frequently occurred between labor and management over economic issues which are surely toward the surface end of my concept of depth.

In order to understand the importance of the concept of depth for choosing interventions in organizations, let us consider the effects upon organization members of working at different levels.

The first of the important concomitants of depth is the degree of dependence of the client on the special competence of the change agent. At the surface end of the depth dimension, the methods of intervention are easily communicated and made public. The client may reasonably expect to learn something of the change agent's skills to improve his own practice. At the deeper levels, such as interpersonal and intrapersonal process analyses, it is more difficult for the client to understand the methods of intervention. The change agent is more likely to be seen as a person of special and unusual powers not found in ordinary men. Skills of intervention and change are less frequently learned by organization members, and the change process may tend to become personalized around the change agent as leader. Programs of change which are so dependent upon personal relationships and individual expertise are difficult to institutionalize. When the change agent leaves the system, he may not only take his expertise with him but the entire change process as well.

A second aspect of the change process which varies with depth is the extent to which the benefits of an intervention are transferable to members of the organization not originally participating in the change process. At surface levels of operations analysis and performance evaluation, the effects are institutionalized in the form of procedures, policies, and practices of the organization which may have considerable permanence beyond the tenure of individuals. At the level of instrumental behavior, the continuing effects of intervention are more likely to reside in the informal norms of groups within the organization regarding such matters as delegation, communication, decision making, competition and collaboration, and conflict resolution.

At the deepest levels of intervention, the target of change is the individual's inner life; and if the intervention is successful, the permanence of individual change should be greatest. There are indeed dramatic reports of cases in which persons have changed their careers and life goals as a result of such interventions, and the persistence of such change appears to be relatively high.

One consequence, then, of the level of intervention is that with greater depth of focus the individual increasingly becomes both the target and the carrier of change. In the light of this analysis, it is not surprising to observe that deeper levels of intervention are increasingly being used at higher organizational levels and in scientific and service organizations where the contribution of the individual has greatest impact.

An important concomitant of depth is that as the level of intervention becomes deeper, the information needed to intervene effectively becomes less available. At the less personal level of operations analysis, the information is often a matter of record. At the level of performance evaluation, it is a matter of observation. On the other hand, reactions of others to a person's work style are less likely to be discussed freely, and the more personal responses to his interpersonal style are even less likely to be readily given. At the deepest levels, important information may not be available to the individual himself. Thus, as we go deeper the consultant must use more of his time and skill uncovering information which is ordinarily private and hidden. This is one reason for the greater costs of interventions at deeper levels of focus.

Another aspect of the change process which varies with the depth of intervention is the personal risk and unpredictability of outcome for the individual. At deeper levels we deal with aspects of the individual's view of himself and his relationships with others which are relatively untested by exposure to the evaluations and emotional reactions of others. If in the change process the individual's self-perceptions are strongly disconfirmed, the resulting imbalance in internal forces may produce sudden changes in behavior, attitudes, and personality integration.

Because of the private and hidden nature of the processes into which we intervene at deeper levels, it is difficult to predict the individual impact of the change process in advance. The need for clinical sensitivity and skill on the part of the practitioner thus increases, since he must be prepared to diagnose and deal with developing situations involving considerable stress upon individuals.

The foregoing analysis suggests a criterion by which to match intervention strategies to particular organizational problems. It is *to intervene at a level no deeper than that required to produce enduring solutions to the problems at hand*. This criterion derives directly from the observations above. The cost, skill demands, client dependency, and variability of outcome all increase with depth of intervention. Further, as the depth of intervention increases, the effects tend to locate more in the individual and less in the organization. The danger of losing the organization's investment in the change with the departure of the individual becomes a significant consideration.

Autonomy Increases Depth of Intervention

While this general criterion is simple and straightforward, its application is not. In particular, although the criterion should operate in the direction of less depth of intervention, there is a general trend in modern organizational life which tends to push the intervention level ever deeper. This trend is toward increased self-direction of organization members and increased independence of external pressures and incentive. I believe that there is a direct relationship between the autonomy of individuals and the depth of intervention needed to effect organizational change.

Before going on to discuss this relationship, I shall acknowledge freely that I cannot prove the existence of a trend toward a general increase in freedom of individuals within organizations. I intend only to assert

the great importance of the degree of individual autonomy in determining the level of intervention which will be effective.

In order to understand the relationship between autonomy and depth of intervention, it is necessary to conceptualize a dimension which parallels and is implied by the depth dimension we have been discussing. This is the dimension of predictability and variability among persons in their responses to the different kinds of incentives which may be used to influence behavior in the organization. The key assumption in this analysis is that the more unpredictable and unique is the individual's response to the particular kinds of controls and incentives one can bring to bear upon him, the more one must know about that person in order to influence his behavior.

Most predictable and least individual is the response of the person to economic and bureaucratic controls when his needs for economic income and security are high. It is not necessary to delve very deeply into a person's inner processes in order to influence his behavior if we know that he badly needs his income and his position and if we are in a position to control his access to these rewards. Responses to economic and bureaucratic controls tend to be relatively simple and on the surface.

INDEPENDENCE OF ECONOMIC INCENTIVE

If for any reason organization members become relatively uninfluenceable through the manipulation of their income and economic security, the management of performance becomes strikingly more complex; and the need for more personal information about the individual increases. Except very generally, we do not know automatically or in advance what styles of instrumental or interpersonal interaction will be responded to as negative or positive incentives by the individual. One person may appreciate close supervision and direction; another may value independence of direction. One may prefer to work alone; another may function best when he is in close communication with others. One may thrive in close, intimate, personal interaction; while others are made uncomfortable by any but cool and distant relationships with colleagues.

What I am saying is that when bureaucratic and economic incentives lose their force for whatever reason, the improvement of performance *must* involve linking organizational goals to the individual's attempts to meet his own needs for satisfying instrumental activities and interpersonal relationships. It is for this reason that I make the assertion that increases in personal autonomy dictate change interventions at deeper and more personal levels. In order to obtain the information necessary to link organizational needs to individual goals, one must probe fairly deeply into the attitudes, values, and emotions of the organization members.

If the need for deeper personal information becomes great when we intervene at the instrumental and interpersonal levels, it becomes even greater when one is dealing with organization members who are motivated less through their transactions with the environment and more in response to internal values and standards. An example is the researcher, engineer, or technical specialist whose work behavior may be influenced more by his own values and standards of creativity or professional excellence than by his relationships with others. The deepest organizational interventions at the intrapersonal level may be required in order to effect change when working with persons who are highly self-directed.

Let me summarize my position about the relationship among autonomy, influence, and level of intervention. As the individual becomes less subject to economic and bureaucratic pressures, he tends to seek more intangible rewards in the organization which come from both the instrumental and interpersonal aspects of the system. I view this as a shift from greater external to more internal control and as an increase in autonomy. Further shifts in this direction may involve increased independence of rewards and punishments mediated by others, in favor of operation in accordance with internal values and standards.

I view organizations as systems of reciprocal influence. Achievement of organization goals is facilitated when individuals can seek their own satisfactions through activity which promotes the goals of the organization. As the satisfactions which are of most value to the individual change, so must the reciprocal influence systems, if the organization goals are to continue to be met.

If the individual changes are in the direction of increased independence of external incentives, then the influence systems must change to provide oppor-

tunities for individuals to achieve more intangible, self-determined satisfactions in their work. However, people are more differentiated, complex, and unique in their intangible goals and values than in their economic needs. In order to create systems which offer a wide variety of intangible satisfactions, much more private information about individuals is needed than is required to create and maintain systems based chiefly on economic and bureaucratic controls. For this reason, deeper interventions are called for when the system which they would attempt to change contains a high proportion of relatively autonomous individuals.

There are a number of factors promoting autonomy, all tending to free the individual from dependence upon economic and bureaucratic controls, which I have observed in my work with organizations. Wherever a number of these factors obtain, it is probably an indication that deeper levels of intervention are required to effect lasting improvements in organizational functioning. I shall simply list these indicators briefly in categories to show what kinds of things might signify to the practitioner that deeper levels of intervention may be appropriate.

The first category includes anything which makes the evaluation of individual performance difficult:

A long time span between the individual's actions and the results by which effectiveness of performance is to be judged.

Nonrepetitive, unique tasks which cannot be evaluated by reference to the performance of others on similar tasks.

Specialized skills and abilities possessed by an individual which cannot be evaluated by a supervisor who does not possess the skills or knowledge himself.

The second category concerns economic conditions:

Arrangements which secure the job tenure and/or income of the individual.

A market permitting easy transfer from one organization to another (e.g., engineers in the United States aerospace industry).

Unique skills and knowledge of the individual which make him difficult to replace.

The third category includes characteristics of the system or its environment which lead to independence of the parts of the organization and decentralization of authority such as:

An organization which works on a project basis instead of producing a standard line of products.

An organization in which subparts must be given latitude to deal rapidly and flexibly with frequent environmental change.

I should like to conclude the discussion of this criterion for depth of intervention with a brief reference to the ethics of intervention, a problem which merits considerably more thorough treatment than I can give it here.

THE ETHICS OF DELVING DEEPER

There is considerable concern in the United States about invasion of privacy by behavioral scientists. I would agree that such invasion of privacy is an actual as well as a fantasied concomitant of the use of organizational change strategies of greater depth. The recourse by organizations to such strategies has been widely viewed as an indication of greater organizational control over the most personal and private aspects of the lives of the members. The present analysis suggests, however, that recourse to these deeper interventions actually reflects the greater *freedom* of organization members from traditionally crude and impersonal means of organizational control. There is no reason to be concerned about man's attitudes or values or interpersonal relationships when his job performance can be controlled by brute force, by economic coercion, or by bureaucratic rules and regulations. The "invasion of privacy" becomes worth the cost, bother, and uncertainty of outcome only when the individual has achieved relative independence from control by other means. Put another way, it makes organizational sense to try to get a man to *want* to do something only if you cannot *make* him do it. And regardless of what intervention strategy is used, the individual still retains considerably greater control over his own behavior than he had when he could be manipulated more crudely. As long as we can maintain a high degree of voluntarism regarding the nature and extent of an individual's participation in the deeper organizational change strategies, these strategies can work toward adapting the organization to the individual quite as much as they work the other

way around. Only when an individual's participation in one of the deeper change strategies is coerced by economic or bureaucratic pressures, do I feel that the ethics of the intervention clearly run counter to the values of a democratic society.

Role of Client Norms and Values in Determining Depth

So far our attention to the choice of level of intervention has focused upon locating the depth at which the information exists which must be exchanged to facilitate system improvement. Unfortunately, the choice of an intervention strategy cannot practically be made with reference to this criterion alone. Even if a correct diagnosis is made of the level at which the relevant information lies, we may not be able to work effectively at the desired depth because of client norms, values, resistances, and fears.

In an attempt to develop a second criterion for depth of intervention which takes such dispositions on the part of the client into account, I have considered two approaches which represent polarized orientations to the problem. One approach is based upon analyzing and overcoming client resistance; the other is based upon discovering and joining forces with the self-articulated wants or "felt needs" of the client.

There are several ways of characterizing these approaches. To me, the simplest is to point out that when the change agent is resistance-oriented he tends to lead or influence the client to work at a depth greater than that at which the latter feels comfortable. When resistance-oriented, the change agent tends to mistrust the client's statement of his problems and of the areas where he wants help. He suspects the client's presentation of being a smoke screen or defense against admission of his "real" problems and needs. The consultant works to expose the underlying processes and concerns and to influence the client to work at a deeper level. The resistance-oriented approach grows out of the work of clinicians and psychotherapists, and it characterizes much of the work of organizational consultants who specialize in sensitivity training and deeper intervention strategies.

On the other hand, change agents may be oriented to the self-articulated needs of clients. When so oriented, the consultant tends more to follow and facilitate the client in working at whatever level the latter sets for himself. He may assist the client in defining problems and needs and in working on solutions, but he is inclined to try to anchor his work in the norms, values, and accepted standards of behavior of the organization.

I believe that there is a tendency for change agents working at the interpersonal and deeper levels to adopt a rather consistent resistance-oriented approach. Consultants so oriented seem to take a certain quixotic pride in dramatically and self-consciously violating organizational norms. Various techniques have been developed for pressuring or seducing organization members into departing from organizational norms in the service of change. The "marathon" T-group is a case in point, where the increased irritability and fatigue of prolonged contact and lack of sleep move participants to deal with one another more emotionally, personally, and spontaneously than they would normally be willing to do.

I suspect that unless such norm-violating intervention efforts actually succeed in changing organizational norms, their effects are relatively short-lived, because the social structures and interpersonal linkages have not been created which can utilize for day-to-day problem solving the deeper information produced by the invervention. It is true that the consultant may succeed in producing information, but he is less likely to succeed in creating social structures which can continue to work in his absence. The problem is directly analogous to that of the community developer who succeeds by virtue of his personal influence in getting villagers to build a school or a community center which falls into disuse as soon as he leaves because of the lack of any integration of these achievements into the social structure and day-to-day needs and desires of the community. Community developers have had to learn through bitter failure and frustration that ignoring or subverting the standards and norms of a social system often results in temporary success followed by a reactionary increase in resistance to the influence of the change agent. On the other hand, felt needs embody those problems, issues, and difficulties which have a high conscious priority on the part of community or organization members. We can expect individuals and groups to be ready to invest time, energy, and resources in dealing with their felt needs, while they will be relatively passive or even resistant toward those who attempt to help them with externally defined needs. Community developers have found that attempts to help with felt needs are met with greater receptivity, support, and integration within the structure and life of the community than are intervention attempts which rely primarily upon the developer's value system for setting need priorities.

The emphasis of many organizational change agents on confronting and working through resistances was developed originally in the practice of individual psychoanalysis and psychotherapy, and it is also a central concept in the conduct of therapy groups and sensitivity training laboratories. In all of these situations, the change agent has a high degree of environmental control and is at least temporarily in a high status position with respect to the client. To a degree that is frequently underestimated by practitioners, we manage to create a situation in which it is more unpleasant for the client to leave than it is to stay and submit to the pressure to confront and work through resistances. I believe that the tendency is for behavioral scientists to overplay their hands when they move from the clinical and training situations where they have environmental control to the organizational consulting situation, where their control is sharply attenuated.

This attenuation derives only partially from the relative ease with which the client can terminate the relationship. Even if this most drastic step is not taken, the consultant can be tolerated, misled, and deceived in ways which are relatively difficult in the therapeutic or human relations training situations. He can also be openly defied and blocked if he runs afoul of strongly shared group norms; whereas when the consultant is dealing with a group of strangers, he can often utilize differences among the members to overcome this kind of resistance. I suspect that, in general, behavioral scientists underestimate their power in working with individuals and groups of strangers, and overestimate it when working with individuals and groups in organizations. I emphasize this point because I believe that a good many potentially fruitful and mutually satisfying consulting relationships are terminated early because of the consultant's taking the role of overcomer of resistance to change rather than that of collaborator in the client's attempts at solving his problems. It is these considerations which lead me to suggest my second criterion for the choice of organization intervention strategy: *to intervene at a level no deeper than that at which the energy and resources of the client can be committed to problem solving and to change.* These energies and resources can be mobilized through obtaining legitimation for the intervention in the norms of the organization and through devising intervention strategies which have clear relevance to consciously felt needs on the part of the organization members.

Consultant's Dilemma: Felt Needs vs. Deeper Levels

Unfortunately, it is doubtless true that the forces which influence the conditions we desire to change often exist at deeper levels than can be dealt with by adhering to the criterion of working within organization norms and meeting felt needs. The level at which an individual or group is willing and ready to invest energy and resources is probably always determined partly by a realistic assessment of the problems and partly by a defensive need to avoid confrontation and significant change. It is thus not likely that our two criteria for selection of intervention depth will result in the same decisions when practically applied. It is not the same to intervene at the level where behavior-determining forces are most potent as it is to work on felt needs as they are articulated by the client. This, it seems to me, is the consultant's dilemma. It always has been. We are continually faced with the choice between leading the client into areas which are threatening, unfamiliar, and dependency-provoking for him (and where our own expertise shows up to best advantage) or, on the other hand, being guided by the client's own understanding of his problems and his willingness to invest resources in particular kinds of relatively familiar and nonthreatening strategies.

When time permits, this dilemma is ideally dealt with by intervening first at a level where there is good support from the norms, power structure, and felt needs of organizational members. The consultant can then, over a period of time, develop trust, sophistication, and support within the organization to explore deeper levels at which particularly important forces

may be operating. This would probably be agreed to, at least in principle, by most organizational consultants. The point at which I feel I differ from a significant number of workers in this field is that I would advocate that interventions should *always* be limited to the depth of the client's felt needs and readiness to legitimize intervention. I believe we should always avoid moving deeper at a pace which outstrips a client system's willingness to subject itself to exposure, dependency, and threat. What I am saying is that if the dominant response of organization members indicates that an intervention violates system norms regarding exposure, privacy, and confrontation, then one has intervened too deeply and should pull back to a level at which organization members are more ready to invest their own energy in the change process. This point of view is thus in opposition to that which sees negative reactions primarily as indications of resistances which are to be brought out into the open, confronted, and worked through as a central part of the intervention process. I believe that behavioral scientists acting as organizational consultants have tended to place overmuch emphasis on the overcoming of resistance to change and have underemphasized the importance of enlisting in the service of change the energies and resources which the client can consciously direct and willingly devote to problem solving.

What is advocated here is that we in general accept the client's felt needs or the problems he presents as real and that we work on them at a level at which he can serve as a competent and willing collaborator. This position is in opposition to one which sees the presenting problem as more or less a smoke screen or barrier. I am not advocating this point of view because I value the right to privacy of organization members more highly than I value their growth and development or the solution of organizational problems. (This is an issue which concerns me, but it is enormously more complex than the ones with which I am dealing in this paper.) Rather, I place first priority on collaboration with the client, because I do not think we are frequently successful consultants without it.

In my own practice I have observed that the change in client response is frequently quite striking when I move from a resistance-oriented approach to an acceptance of the client's norms and definitions of his own needs. With quite a few organizational clients in the United States, the line of legitimacy seems to lie somewhere between interventions at the instrumental level and those focused on interpersonal relationships. Members who exhibit hostility, passivity, and dependence when I initiate intervention at the interpersonal level may become dramatically more active, collaborative, and involved when I shift the focus to the instrumental level.

If I intervene directly at the level of interpersonal relationships, I can be sure that at least some members, and often the whole group, will react with anxiety, passive resistance, and low or negative commitment to the change process. Furthermore, they express their resistance in terms of norms and values regarding the appropriateness or legitimacy of dealing at this level. They say things like: "It isn't right to force people's feelings about one another out into the open"; "I don't see what this has to do with improving organizational effectiveness"; "People are being encouraged to say things which are better left unsaid."

If I then switch to a strategy which focuses on decision making, delegation of authority, information exchange, and other instrumental questions, these complaints about illegitimacy and the inappropriateness of the intervention are usually sharply reduced. This does not mean that the clients are necessarily comfortable or free from anxiety in the discussions, nor does it mean that strong feelings may not be expressed about one another's behavior. What is different is that the clients are more likely to *work with* instead of *against* me, to feel and express some sense of ownership in the change process, and to see many more possibilities for carrying it on among themselves in the absence of the consultant.

What I have found is that when I am resistance-oriented in my approach to the client, I am apt to feel rather uncomfortable in "letting sleeping dogs lie." When, on the other hand, I orient myself to the client's own assessment of his needs, I am uncomfortable when I feel I am leading or pushing the client to operate very far outside the shared norms of the organization. I have tried to indicate why I believe the latter orientation is more appropriate. I realize of course that many highly sophisticated and talented practitioners will not agree with me.

In summary, I have tried to show in this paper that the dimension of depth should be central to the conceptualization of intervention strategies. I have presented what I believe are the major consequences of intervening at greater or lesser depths, and from these consequences I have suggested two criteria for choosing the appropriate depth of intervention: first, *to intervene at a level no deeper than that required to produce enduring solutions to the problems at hand;* and second, *to intervene at a level no deeper than that at which the energy and resources of the client can be committed to problem solving and to change.*

I have analyzed the tendency for increases in individual autonomy in organizations to push the appropriate level of intervention deeper when the first criterion is followed. Opposed to this is the countervailing influence of the second criterion to work closer to the surface in order to enlist the energy and support of organization members in the change process. Arguments have been presented for resolving this dilemma in favor of the second, more conservative, criterion. The dilemma remains, of course; the continuing tension under which the change agent works is between the desire to lead and push, or to collaborate and follow. The middle ground is never very stable, and I suspect we show our values and preferences by which criterion we choose to maximize when we are under the stress of difficult and ambiguous client-consultant relationships.

References

Byrd, R. E. Training in a non-group. *J. Humanistic Psychol.*, 1967, 7(1), 18–27.

Clark, J. V. Task group therapy. Unpublished manuscript, University of California, Los Angeles, 1966.

Improving Trustee, Administrator, and Physician Collaboration Through Open Systems Planning

Ronald E. Fry

Consider the following statements by leaders of the three most influential groups at Seaside Hospital:

Hospital Director: "I'm tired of being told by the trustees to get the doctors to make choices among all the new expenditures they request each year. It puts administration in the middle. We're always the bad guys. How can we make choices for the doctors? . . . We try to make them aware of the increasing regulations and cost constraints we are facing, but it hasn't led to any more realistic requests each year."

Chief, Medical Executive Committee: "I think it's the job of the administration and trustees to make final budget allocations. They can't expect us to sacrifice quality medical care by eliminating certain requests. We only ask for what's needed to remain the premier teaching and acute care hospital in the area. They always say that monies are tighter, yet we always get just a little less than asked for. They should continue as in the past or tell us what to shut down and what to keep going."

Chairman, Board of Trustees: "Both the administration and the medical staff have to realize that we can no longer dip into our endowment each year to fund the long list of positions, equipment, and facilities the doctors request. We're not against quality care, but our responsibility is to safeguard the future of this hospital as well as the present. . . . I think they should face up to the

From *Organizational Development in Health Care Organizations,* ed. Newton Margulies and John D. Adams, © 1982 Addison-Wesley, Reading, Ma. Reprinted with permission.

tough choices and prioritize their requests so we have guidance to make our decisions. Otherwise, we'll try to please everyone, meaning each will get less than it deserves."

Can organization development technology help with this situation? Is a third-party intervention needed to resolve the conflict? Should there be a confrontation meeting between groups? Is team building of the Medical Executive Committee needed? Would role negotiation between these three leaders help? In this particular instance, none of these more common OD interventions were tried, and so their usefulness in this situation is unknown. What was attempted was a technology called open systems planning (OSP) (Jayaram, 1976; Beckhard and Harris, 1977). This article will describe the application of OSP in Seaside Hospital and discuss the critical issues—for both consultant and client—associated with its use. Finally, the suitability of OSP approaches to health care systems in general will be discussed.

Setting

Seaside Hospital is a 700 bed community hospital centrally located in a city of some 500,000 residents. It is the main teaching hospital for a nearby medical school and is considered the top tertiary care institution for the immediate area (50 mile radius). Along with its image as the best hospital in the metropolitan area, it enjoys the support of a large endowment relative to most hospitals of its size. At the time this author worked with the hospital, it was participating in a 3 year experimental reimbursement plan with third-party insurers. For the past 5 years, the trustees had funded deficit budgets by dipping into endowment principal.

Problem Diagnosis

The author was contacted by the Hospital Director to "help the three diverse groups come together around priorities so that we can survive the oncoming era of regulation and cost containment." After briefly meeting with the Chairman of the Board of Trustees and Chief of the Medical Executive Committee, where comments like those cited earlier were heard, the author met with the three leaders together. All were dissatisfied with the current planning process by which funds were allocated for growth and development above estimated operating expenditures. The process began in the medical staff, where proposals were presented to the Medical Executive Committee's planning subcommittee, which was composed of physicians. The subcommittee made recommendations, which were usually approved by the executive committee. These proposals, in an unprioritized list, would be sent to an administrative planning committee for final fiscal review. (Their input was usually requested earlier from medical chiefs and department heads.) The list, with administration's financial estimates, was then forwarded to the trustee planning committee for deliberation and final recommendation to the trustee board. Usually, however, the trustee planning committee would send the list back to the administration for prioritization and cutting. The requests always amounted to more than the endowment interest could support after inflation and allocations for operating budgets. Unable to resolve the physicians' differences, the administration would either drop items from the list or resubmit the list in much the same form as the original. The trustees were then left to fund either some portion of each request or all requests by reducing the endowment fund.

This situation was creating hostility among the three groups. It was suggested to the leaders that their inability to coordinate the process was a symptom of a failure to define priorities for the hospital in light of its changing environment. Each group was acting on what it thought to be the best interests of the system, but each, in turn, was reacting to only one perspective: the trustees were responding to inflation (protect endowment), administrators to regulations (contain costs), and physicians to medical technology (modernize equipment).

Given this analysis, the Chairman of the Board of Trustees decided to have the Hospital Director chair an ad hoc planning committee of members of all three groups to clarify hospital priorities and to develop a more effective planning mechanism.[1]

Prescription: Open Systems Planning

Open systems planning is one of several recent approaches that have emerged to help organizations situated in turbulent or demanding environments to plan aggressively in the face of incomplete and changing information about the future (Krone, 1974; Melin and Rabkin, 1977). It is basically a seven-phase process as follows (Beckhard and Harris, 1977):

1. *Determination of the organization's "core mission."* As opposed to objectives, this is the organization's primary reason for being. It is the belief in, and use of, this mission that guides the priorities in goal setting, resource allocation, and so on.

2. *Mapping the demand system.* Identification of all the significant other groups, agencies, competitors, institutions, laws, etc., that make demands upon the organization that must be responded to. After identification, there is a need to specify exactly what each demanding factor is asking or requiring of the organization.

3. *Describing current response system.* With respect to each demand in item 2, the organization's current response is specified. This allows for consideration of additional or alternative responses.

4. *Projecting a future demand system.* Identification of what will be the likely demands at some point (e.g., three to five years) in the future, including new demands not now in force and changes in those currently acting from item 2.

5. *Identifying a desired state.* Identification of what the organization would like the external conditions to be at some point in the future.

[1] The planning committee consisted of the three leaders plus two more trustees, two chiefs of service (Medicine and Pediatrics), the Comptroller, and an Assistant to the Director.

6. *Activity planning.* Identification of activities, organizational forms or procedures, investments, strategies, projects, etc., that will be necessary to reach the desired state.

7. *Assessing cost effectiveness.* Analysis of social and economic costs to action alternatives identified in item 6, leading to priorities for strategic planning.

As a first step toward planning, OSP forces an analysis both of external factors that impinge on an organization and of the organization's current response to these factors. Future environmental demands are projected so that the organization can reasonably predict whether external factors will dissolve, or increase or decrease in scope or influence. Finally, the organization members' ideals are considered in conjunction with estimates of what will be if the present response pattern remains unchanged. Differences between what will be if the organization continues on as is and what is desired then become potential targets for change and action planning. The core mission is used throughout the process to help choose which items, alternatives, responses, and so on are more important or relevant than others.

This author met with the planning committee, which agreed to apply OSP to the situation at Seaside Hospital.

DEFINING A CORE MISSION

The planning committee first undertook efforts to arrive at a core mission statement. Much debate centered around what is and what should be. It became apparent to the group that being the foremost tertiary care and teaching hospital in the area was central to the hospital's current mission. It also was felt by many that this was not the desired mission, but the group was unable to agree on what new core mission should be adopted. In essence, the lack of priorities, which was causing the current planning process to break down, was directly related to the lack of an agreed-on core mission.

At this point, the planning committee adopted a modified version of the seven-step OSP model (Table 1). The core mission became a desired output of the overall intervention. The purpose of an external analysis, response analysis, and so on would be to for-mulate a new core mission more appropriate to the changing environment in and around Seaside Hospital.

In the author's opinion, the ad hoc group was not capable, at this early stage, of arriving at a mutually satisfactory mission statement through continued group discussion. It seemed more appropriate to use the OSP process to define what the committee members were about rather than to use it to further a mission. Also, their energy was focused on the first course of action.

EXTERNAL ANALYSIS

The most salient environmental factors considered to be acting on Seaside Hospital were identified by the planning committee as the federal government, the state health planning association, the nearby medical school, third-party payers, the medical profession and medical science, and hospital workers' unions (Seaside is not currently unionized). In order to determine just what these forces were demanding now and how they would most likely be affecting the hospital in the future, it was decided to invite experts from each group to present their analyses to key hospital personnel at two full-day workshops.

Thus this phase took on an educational focus. All trustees, top and middle managers, physician chiefs, and department heads were invited. At each workshop mixed and homogeneous group discussions of the presentations were conducted, led by members of the planning committee, and a list of questions and issues was compiled to be presented to the guest speakers. The administration, trustees, and medical staff had never before met together. After the second workshop, the committee distributed a brief questionnaire to all participants, soliciting their opinions regarding the critical concerns facing the hospital in the next 5 years, the hospital's most and least needed departments or clinics, which residencies were most important and other issues posed by presenters of various environmental demands. The questionnaire results were summarized by the committee in the form of an External Forces Outline. Excerpts from that document are shown in Table 2. The document was distributed to workshop participants for review and written comments were invited.

The newness and success of two workshops raised a

TABLE 1
Seaside Hospital Planning Process

Phases	Steps
External analysis	Agree on summary of forces placing demands or constraints on the hospital
Internal analysis	For each external force:
	1. How is Seaside Hospital responding today?
	2. What effect if Seaside Hospital continues present response?
	3. What are optional responses?
Issue identification and scenario analysis	Identify compatible and mutually exclusive options from above
	Determine any "ideal" responses not currently being "demanded"
Alternative generation analysis and evolution of mission	Generate sets of alternative courses of action
	Determine core mission based on preferred courses
Creation of plan	Implement or move toward goals implied in core mission

lot of expectations, and that condition was perceived by the planning committee as threatening. The committee required direction, and so it was necessary for the change agent to review the overall process and particularly the next phase. Certain committee members were beginning to realize the time investment that the entire process might require and the paperwork that it could generate, but there was also a sense of having learned. Many key people had mutually inquired about their system and shared their reactions. In a sense, this was the diagnostic phase of an action-research process. Now it was time to consider the data for further action and implications.

INTERNAL ANALYSIS

The planning committee met several times to analyze Seaside's current responses to each of the external demands acting on it. In anticipation of the next phase (issue identification) in the overall process, it was decided to consider for each external force: (1) how the hospital was currently responding, (2) the likely effect if that response continued, (3) brainstorming to develop optional responses, and (4) a list of issues or questions raised from items 1 through 3. Table 3 is an example of the resulting summaries for one external demand area. The bulk of the committee's time was spent reviewing and discussing drafts of the summaries, which were prepared mainly by administrative staff. Final drafts of these documents

were sent to all participants of the first two workshops for review and comment.

The group quickly began to be burdened by too much data. Each external force was generating a dozen new issues to be considered by the planning committee members. The members' complaints of making "mountains out of molehills," while they truly were doing so, was in part a way for them to dodge real confrontation over fundamental differences among them. There was a tendency to want to resolve any one issue once it was raised. When reminded that other phases in the process would follow before real policies or plans could be set, the committee members expressed impatience. It was important that the consultant continue to emphasize that they were involved in a process of mutual fact-finding and inquire into what is and what will be if current responses are maintained. The ad hoc group also needed more process consultation at this point, to enhance the quality of their listening, their ability to identify conflict, and their aptitude in managing their time, as they began to engage one another in attempts to influence personal values and beliefs.

ISSUES IDENTIFICATION

The planning committee listed all issues generated from the internal analyses, in order to determine which ones were mutually exclusive, which were inter-

TABLE 2
External Forces Outline

Forces	Example Demands
Federal government	Take low cost from high cost systems
SSA	Increased comparison of hospital costs and more demands for justification of high costs and/or lowering of costs
	Limit health expenditures—less than 1% real growth for foreseeable future hospital expenditures
HEW	
Manpower	More primary care MDs
	Increase in hospital residencies (nationally)
	Decrease in specialty residencies (nationally)
Planning	New legislation—but unpredictable postponements/moratoriums
State Government	
Department of Health	Increasing pressure to plan *with* other hospitals/community agencies
State Budget Office	Will set caps—similar to federal government
Local medical school program	Wants Seaside Hospital to be in a multi-hospital system
	Wants Seaside Hospital to assume primary responsibility for pediatrics, radiation oncology, radiology, and surgical subspecialities
Blue Cross/Blue Shield	Likely to become more aggressive in order to protect selves
Community	Use Seaside Hospital resources to rehabilitate southern area of community
	Have more neighborhood health centers—may require our future support
Other hospitals/HMOs	Seaside Hospital should not get any bigger
Organized labor	Pay certain categories of employees more (in relation to other hospital contracts)
	Pressure for more say for professionals—even without unionization
External review agencies	
PSRO	Pressure from PSRO to reduce length of stay and possibly ancillary service volume
JCAH	Pressure from JCAH and others for upkeep of physical plant and employee safety

SSA – Social Security Administration; HMO – Health Maintenance Organization; PSRO – Professional Standards Review Organization; JCAH – Joint Commission on the Accreditation of Hospitals.

related, and which had to be addressed before others. Six key issues emerged. They were:

1. What should be the role of the hospital in the various service levels (primary, secondary, and tertiary)?
2. What should be the role of the hospital in higher health payoff services?
3. Should the hospital become more consumer-oriented and provide certain patient conveniences even though such an approval may require additional resources and additional changes?
4. Should the hospital become more community-oriented, actively support the neighborhood health centers, and emphasize the primary care role?
5. What should be the future use of endowment fund principal and interest?
6. How does the hospital deal with the increasing pressures for cost containment and with the perception and possible reality of the effect of cost containment on quality of care?

It was then decided to take these issues to both the

TABLE 3
Analysis of State and Federal Government Planning as an External Force

A. *How is Seaside Hospital responding today?*

Little, if any, joint planning. Some planning with community agencies and University, e.g., Home Care Association, alcoholism program; not, however, through our initiation.

Cooperating in committee on future planning. Outcome of this committee's discussions unknown at present.

Outcome of planning with others is regionalization or "dividing the pie." Present process of examining our role is a response to that pressure.

Actively conversant with federal and state regulations and supporting efforts to monitor Health Department activities.

Increasing awareness of the importance of planning on our part, e.g., current process.

B. *Effect if Seaside Hospital continues present response*

Lack of response in planning with others may influence the Health Department to take a more active, aggressive role in planning for the system.

Lacking a coordinated interinstitutional plan, available limited resources may be utilized by other institutions, which may not be consistent with our objectives.

C. *Preliminary optional responses*

Become more aggressive in developing corporate affiliations with other institutions.

Support planning arm of the State Hospital Association to coordinate/integrate the plans of various institutions.

Individually coordinate Seaside Hospital plans with others having mutual interests and develop agreements for sharing resources or services.

Continue to plan individually.

Support the formation and development of a consortium of the university-affiliated hospitals.

Continue to develop internal planning capabilities to keep abreast.

Allow the Health Department to create plans without input and minimize changes for successful implementation.

D. *Issues*

What should be the relationship for planning/resource allocation between Seaside Hospital and other health care providers?

Should the objectives of other institutions be integrated in some way into the process of determining our own objectives, and if so, how?

What should be our role in various service levels, i.e., primary, secondary, and tertiary, for the region?

Management Executive Committee and Medical Executive Committee for review and discussion. The former group met for a day while the latter allotted a 2 hour special session for their review. The tasks to each group were to: (1) offer their best solution to each issue now; (2) identify additional information they would like to have in order to make a better decision than they now can; and (3) raise other key issues they feel are either missing or that stem from the six offered. From the two meetings with administrators and physicians, the six issues were reduced by the planning committee to five questions concerning Seaside's role vis-à-vis care, education, and research:

1. What should be our role at primary, secondary, and tertiary care levels?
2. What residencies should be offered here?

3. What undergraduate education should be offered here?
4. Which departments should be developed as academic (as opposed to clinical) departments?
5. What kinds of basic or clinical research should we support?

For each question, the administrative group submitted a single recommendation, while the physician group merely voiced and documented varying points of view.

Throughout the stage of issue identification, planning committee members approached the issues having to do with roles with the most zeal. The five questions compiled implied battlegrounds for deciding, for example, who got to enlarge his or her program and who would have to cut back, or whether outpatient primary care would gain more importance and thus be allocated more resources at a loss to inpatient programs. The involvement of larger groups such as the Medical Executive Committee served to reconfirm interest in and hopes for what the planning committee was undertaking. Finally, as top-priority issues became more specifically defined, debate and confrontation were less easy to dodge. The committee, at this stage, was both anxious to proceed, as it was nearing the end of the process, and hesitant to move by itself.

ALTERNATIVE GENERATION AND
EVOLUTION OF CORE MISSION

The task before the planning committee was to propose solutions to the five role, or core mission, issues they identified. Several meetings were held at which draft position statements were read and deliberated. An agreed-on statement concerning Seaside's role in primary, secondary, and tertiary care was finally arrived at and distributed to trustee, administration, and physician groups for comment. A similar process was then completed for the remaining four issues. Among many basic issues resolved at these meetings were the following:

Primary care would become more central in the future.
Tertiary standing in the community would be maintained by keeping certain residencies and academic departments, but others would be dropped.
Only two of the present clinical departments would ever become academic if funds were available for their growth.
The hospital's primary care services would proactively compete with private doctors' offices in the community.

The trustee members of the planning committee were more active at these meetings than were any other members. They tended to offer compromises, make finalizing statements, and support the committee's work in general. While final decisions from the committee appeared to rest with the Chairman of the Board's position, in most cases consensus was sought and attained. The more it became clear that the trustees valued this work, the more members began checking for agreement rather than fighting one another. As documents became more finalized, concerns in the group switched to "selling" the ideas to their constituencies: "Where do we go next?" "How do we make all this really happen?" The nature of influence within the group was personal and serious. Said the chief of the medical staff at one point, "... although it's hard for me to swallow, let's not beat around the bush. We're saying that it is in the best future interests of this hospital to go into competition with my own private practice. I will support that, given what we see facing us, and to soft-pedal does no good at this point."

IMPLEMENTATION

A sixty-page document covering the overall process, external and internal analyses, issue analysis, and position statements regarding Seaside's care mission was submitted to all participants of the first two workshops. A one-day workshop was held to field concerns about, solicit response to, discuss, and generally sell the policy statements. Shortly thereafter, a final report was submitted and approved by the board.

At this time, the planning committee also considered mechanisms to achieve, enforce, and monitor the policy decisions they had made. It was decided to make a structural change whereby an expanded version of the planning committee became a standing Joint Planning Committee with trustee, administrative, and physician members. This committee replaced the three subcommittees that originally functioned to plan for institutional growth and development. Thus the board planning subcommittee, medical executive subcommittee for planning, and the management executive subcommittee for planning were all disbanded. The responsibilities of the new Joint Planning Committee included:

1. Continually interpreting the hospital's core mission
2. Recommending program changes
3. Informing staff of rationale for program decisions
4. Determining guidelines to enforce core mission as problem cases arise

An immediate action plan was derived for the Joint Planning Committee. It included systematic reviews of each department to establish whether resources have been and will be allocated in appropriate ways, given the hospital's new core mission; review of all requests for exempt positions; and review of all requests for capital expenditure in excess of $50,000.

The original planning committee finally experienced a strong sense of accomplishment. The willingness of each constituent group to restructure (i.e., disband a heretofore powerful committee of their own) and of individual trustees and physician chiefs to commit to serving on the new Joint Planning Committee seemed to indicate their ownership of the results. During the transition from OSP to implementation, there was a more realistic sense of the work to be done and a shared recognition that new resources had to be found to support the work and time required for the Joint Planning Committee to function. Those who expressed any doubts at this point were quickly reassured by members of other constituencies.

The entire process, from mission definition to implementation, lasted 15 months. A timetable is shown in Figure 1.

Issues in Using an Open Systems Process

From a change agent's perspective, several considerations concerning client reactions to OSP emerge from this experience at Seaside Hospital.

1. *Time and resources required.* If the organization intends to do an effective job of projecting and analyzing environmental demands, this is not an intervention to be used in a 1 or 2 day off-site workshop. Beyond basic time needed for groups to meet, there is much preparatory work, such as drafting working statements and collecting data to analyze a response, that is required at various stages. If the client system does not anticipate provision of resources to create time for key people or to provide support work, resistance may surface early to a process that is perceived as too burdensome.

2. *Documentation.* The feelings of the ad hoc planning committee that they were overloaded with data were created, in part, by their documentation of all the information collected in each phase of the process. Nevertheless, without written information to which participants can react, the process appears even more complex and abstract. The tendency then might

be to simply discuss a situation rather than to make a specific decision regarding it.

3. *Level of abstractness.* A key strength of the OSP process may be the ordering of issues to be addressed. Urging an analysis of what is before any consideration is given to what should be helps to maintain more factual and concrete discussions. As planners or planning processes are allowed to be abstract, it becomes easier for clients to avoid making decisions. A conflict at one level can be smoothed over at a higher level of abstraction. In the Seaside Hospital case, if the participants had not first derived an agreed-on summary of what the environment was like, many physicians would have tended to talk about ideals at such a level that disagreement was impossible or guilt-producing (i.e., quality of care; care for anyone who needed it; one class care). This was, in fact, exactly how they had colluded previously to avoid prioritizing each other's vested interests in the planning process.

4. *Planning process vs. content.* The real value of OSP may lie more in helping to develop a shared logic and ongoing management system for adapting or interacting with one's environment than in producing a master plan (Melin and Rabkin, 1977). While at Seaside a document was created, it was the evolution in the hospital's structure of a joint planning mechanism that has had the most long-term impact.[2] This mechanism is an observable change that reflects a logic about the system's concern with external forces and internal desires, a logic that is understood, if not shared, by many trustees, administrators, and physicians in the system. Had there been no visible change in the way things were done, most of the output (the document) would probably have become obsolete within months.

5. *Decision-making responsibility.* The OSP process does not dictate who decides what at various points along the way. A key role for the change agent is to help the client group members organize themselves as they see fit to anticipate and make choices at each phase. While ultimate veto was always within the power of the trustees at Seaside, the original planning

[2] In recent discussions with the client system, the Joint Planning Committee has been in successful operation for 2 years and is felt to be a major factor in increased coordination and utilization of resources.

FIGURE 1
Timetable of OSP Process at Seaside Hospital

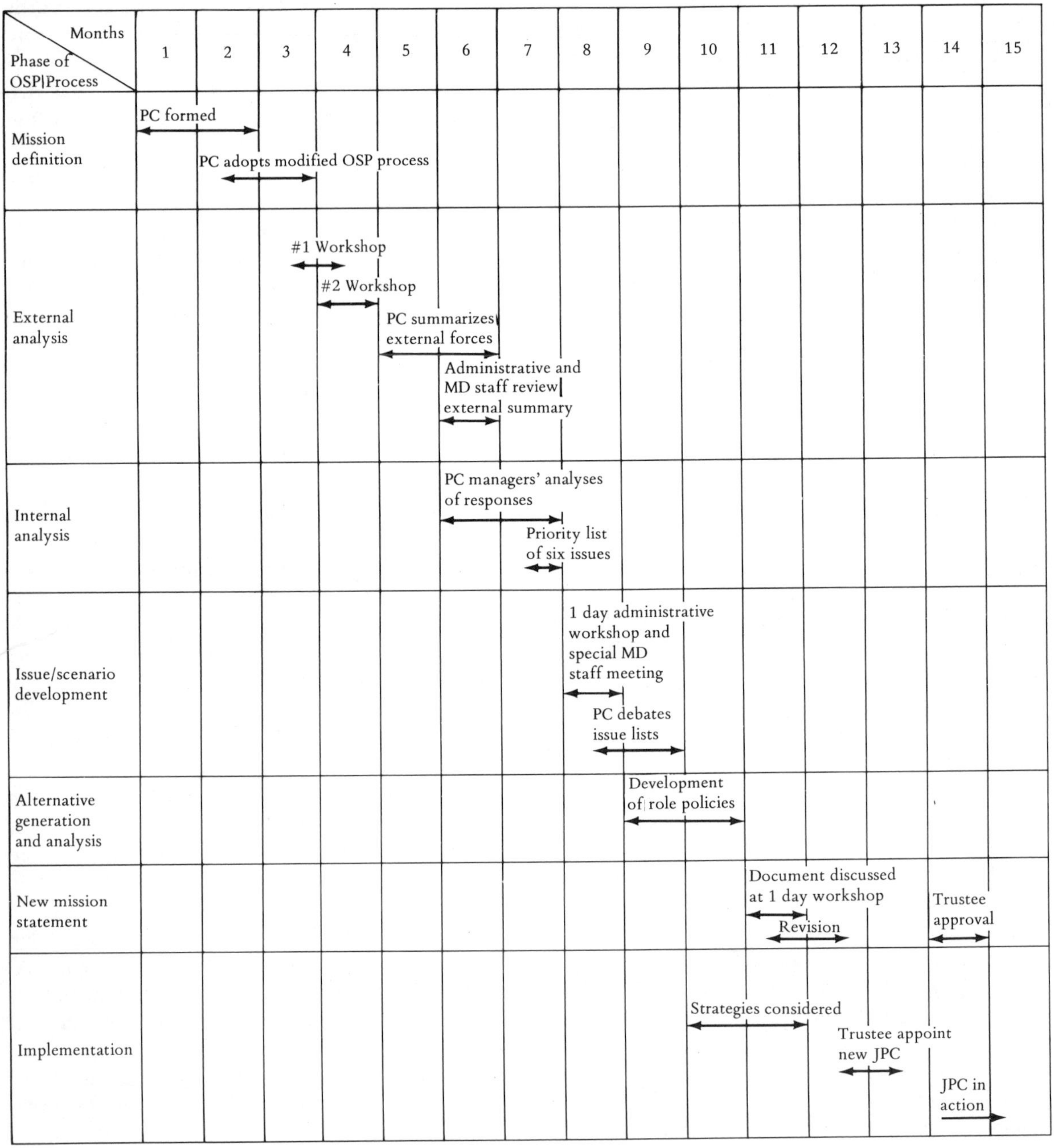

Phase of OSP|Process \ Months	1	2	3	4	5	6	7	8	9	10	11	12	13	14	15
Mission definition	PC formed →	PC adopts modified OSP process →													
External analysis			#1 Workshop →	#2 Workshop →	PC summarizes external forces →	Administrative and MD staff review external summary →									
Internal analysis						PC managers' analyses of responses →	Priority list of six issues →								
Issue/scenario development								1 day administrative workshop and special MD staff meeting → / PC debates issue lists →							
Alternative generation and analysis									Development of role policies →						
New mission statement											Document discussed at 1 day workshop → / Revision →			Trustee approval →	
Implementation										Strategies considered →		Trustee appoint new JPC →	JPC in action →		

PC – planning committee; JPC – Joint Planning Committee.

committee spent a good deal of time organizing itself and others with respect to: What decisions were to be made? Who should be involved (either directly in deliberations or advisory as in the workshops)? And who, specifically, will coordinate things to get everyone involved or informed at the right time?

6. *Internal forces.*   Several times during this case experience, members of the planning committee voiced concerns about not forgetting that they had staff problems, or about their eagerness to get to what each of them wanted. Certainly internal operational issues can not be avoided for 15 months while everyone plans. Nevertheless, OSP appears to be useful in making people step back and look at systemic causes and consequences of daily activities. At best it seems to be a necessary tug-of-war that may serve to keep the planning process results-oriented, not just at a pie-in-the-sky level.

Seaside's modified OSP process never did specifically devote attention to generating a desired set of environmental forces, yet when the OSP process reaches a stage of analyzing implications of current responses and future trends in demands, individuals inject their wishes through their analyses. By saying one force is more relevant than another or that, of all the possible responses, one is favored, the participants are expressing personal desires. It was a useful intervention at times to probe this point with the planning committee group members, to help them clarify *why* they favored a particular alternative or interpretation.

Relevance of OSP to Health Care Systems

The need for a process like OSP is a response to real environmental forces that hospitals are now experiencing (Mandel and Getson, 1979); there are increased pressures to effect long-term planning. More importantly, however, the nature of this particular process appears to comprise necessary ingredients for effective change in health care systems (Weisbord and Stoelwinder, 1979). These ingredients include:

1. *Joint problem solving.*   OSP requires collective effort. It can not be accomplished without input from key members of the system. It also fosters willingness to collaborate by addressing a need felt by many members of any health care system: that is, survival by adapting to or reacting proactively to an increasingly critical, hostile, and restraining environment. In other words, this process may succeed in fostering collaboration where others have failed because it addresses a system-level problem that everyone feels rather than an interpersonal or departmental problem that perhaps only some feel.

2. *Realistic orientation.*   In the Seaside Hospital case, OSP, by providing a methodical process to follow in order to collect, understand, and use information, served to reduce anxiety around how participants could possibly deal with all the changes occurring in their environment that affected them. The process accepts as a given that one will always have incomplete information about the future, but it nevertheless encourages best guesses based on what is and what could be.

3. *Self-esteem.*   The mutual inquiry mode of the external and internal analysis phases, in particular, facilitates exchange of ideas, opinions, and beliefs so that a better understanding among key members of the institution can occur. This enhances self-esteem and mutual respect. At Seaside, trustees and physicians, who had used administrators as a bridge between them, expressed that through the process they had grown to know and respect each other's views and commitment to the hospital.

4. *Understanding of the system.*   Learning to understand the system appears to be a particular strength of OSP, which, rather than immediately focusing on goal setting, forces an educationally oriented inquiry into what is going on right now so that participants can learn from the present to help predict the future.

5. *Total hospital view.*   OSP is particularly suited to meeting the planning needs of executive-level managers and professionals who run entire systems. It requires taking the perspective of the hospital's role rather than the administration's role, for example. The process stipulates tasks that require input from a range of influential parties in the typical hospital system. The trustee, administrator, or physician groups at Seaside could not have achieved and mutually accepted what they did in this case had they not collaborated and devoted themselves to the sys-

tem as a whole. Indeed, as time passed, the use of labels such as Doctor, Mister, and Your Honor (one trustee was a judge) diminished.

6. *Cost containment.* By focusing so much attention on external factors, it appears that OSP could not help but result in action plans that included or addressed cost containment.

In the Seaside Hospital case, the evolution of the new Joint Planning Committee, with its plan to review, monitor, and recommend allocation of funds for growth and expansion, symbolized the most direct impact of the overall process on daily operations and fiscal management.

To the extent that these six ingredients contribute to effective change and collaboration in today's health care settings, open systems planning appears to be very relevant to these settings. In addition, OSP offers a collaborative structure and method for organization members to discuss issues that are usually addressed by planners, who would then be charged with the responsibility of selling their ideas to trustees, physicians, and other vested interest groups.

Summary

This article has attempted to instruct the reader about open systems planning as a way of helping health care systems deal with their changing environments and as a method for increasing interchange and collaboration between typically uncooperative or competitive groups: in this case, trustees, administrators, and physicians.

For those who might consider using OSP in the future, a few final comments are in order. Do not be bound by the textbook model. If you or the client system feel modification is necessary, try it. OSP is a unique way of looking at future planning. Most clients expect to begin immediately with goal setting, but external and internal analyses of the present state are particularly important both for making any subsequent goals more realistic and for creating an atmosphere conducive to inquiry and education. Physicians in particular, who may tend to resist involvement in planning because it is a managerial task, tend to be attracted to learning more about the total system (their organizational worlds) so that they can assimilate that knowledge into their professional worlds. Finally, this author encourages the application of OSP because it attempts to help key actors in a health care setting to understand and to act to change things that impact on overall systems rather than on interpersonal relationships, a team, or two departments, for example. The most salient issues in hospitals today may well be at the system level and not at the levels more often addressed by OD efforts.

References

Beckhard, R., and Harris, R. *Organizational Transitions: Managing Complex Change.* Reading, Mass.: Addison-Wesley, 1977.

Jayaram, G. K. Open Systems Planning. In Bennis, W., et al. (Eds.), *The Planning of Change* (3rd ed.). New York: Holt, Rinehart and Winston, 1976, pp. 275–282.

Krone, C. Open Systems Redesign. In Adams, J. (Ed.), *Theory and Method in Organization Development: An Evolutionary Process.* Arlington, Va.: NTL Institute for Applied Behavioral Science, 1974, pp. 364–391.

Mandel, M., and Getson, J. Mandated long-range planning for hospitals—Where is it going and why? *Health Care Management Review* 4(1): 9, Winter 1979.

Melin, C., and Rabkin, M. Understanding the context for long-range planning in hospitals. *Health Care Management Review* 2(2): 13, Spring 1977.

Weisbord, M., and Stoelwinder, J. Linking physicians, hospital management, cost containment, and better medical care. *Health Care Management Review* 4(2): 7, Spring 1979.

Organization Structure:
The Basic Conformations

Mariann Jelinek

A key issue in organization design is the choice of the main structural conformation. There are varieties of each form and a range of possible styles within the forms. Nevertheless, the choice of one or another of the basic configurations is the selection of certain capabilities and benefits—and certain disadvantages and potential problems as well. The choice implies constraints of a fundamental nature.

What are the main options and what are their associated constraints? What are the forms' strengths and weaknesses and the trade-offs involved in choice of one as against another? These topics will be the subject of this paper. In passing, we shall also make reference to various dimensions of structure and other organizational factors, such as strategy and environment, which affect the organization designer's choice. We will deal with the basic organizational configurations as they evolved historically—although clearly no organization is compelled to repeat this historical sequence.

The Simple Organization or "Agency" Form

The simple organization is one with little or no structure; it typically consists of the boss (owner, leader, or manager) and the employees or workers. An example would be a workshop in which a master craftsperson supervised a number of apprentices or helpers. Direction or coordination is provided by personal supervision, and each worker acts as the *agent* or extension of the boss. More extensive examples would include most large organizations before the evolution of formal, bureaucratic means of organizing. For example,

kings directed extensive establishments personally, and each subordinate's authority and power derived directly from a relationship with the king, whose agent the subordinate was. More modern examples of the larger sort are difficult to identify, with the possible exception of some religious, cult, or political groups. Here, too, the subordinates' power and authority derive directly from the leader; it is as agents of the leader, doing whatever is required, that the subordinates act. Typically, such a subordinate owes responsibility only to the leader personally, rather than for a position, and duties are defined by the leader's requests.

Many organizations begin as simple organizations. An entrepreneur with an idea hires others to assist in its realization. Typically, each employee does what the entrepreneur directs and, particularly at initial stages, there is little or no formality. Anyone can be asked to do whatever needs doing, the work is the responsibility of all organization members, under the personal direction of the entrepreneur. As Mintzberg (1979) has pointed out, such organizations are flexible but decidedly limited in their capacity to cope with complexity. They tend to operate simple technologies in simple environments, in order that needed coordination can take place through the leader, whose capacity to process information is necessarily limited.

Dividing the Work

Most organizations quickly become more formalized than the simple agency model. As an early step in formalization, work is explicitly divided. Thus the interest of Adam Smith (1776) and Charles Babbage (1832) in the steps or functions that went into pin making—formally dividing the work and assigning different individuals responsibility for different parts, substitutes this structure for a portion of the control exercised by the leader in the agency or simple form. People no longer must be told what to do; instead they are assigned to do one specific portion of the work regularly. Their responsibility is limited to that portion of the work.

As Smith and Babbage noted, dividing the work permits significant advantages because it facilitates specialization. Among the results are increases in efficiency, speed, and expertise; reduced waste; less time to learn the job (because less must be learned and more frequent repetition speeds the process); and less time lost in changing from one tool or operation to another. The same advantages accrue whether the work to be subdivided is pin making, assembling an automobile or refrigerator, teaching, or engineering: specialization permits development of in-depth knowledge, experience, and facility *within a limited area.* Thus a large and complex task is often better accomplished by dividing it into smaller, more comprehensible pieces. In particular, where the range of skills required in a large task differ markedly, or where the strength or time requirements of different portions of the task differ, division of labor offers advantages.

The consequences of division of work are not wholly positive, however. Once the work is divided, people tend to orient themselves toward their portion of the work rather than toward other portions or toward the task as a whole. This orientation colors department members' perceptions, for instance, so that they quite naturally seek to make their own work easier and more meaningful, to acquire a larger share of resources, and to exercise more control over the flow of work to them and from them to others. Essentially, people behave in ways consistent with the structuring of tasks. Division of the work makes one portion of it central to them, and they proceed to behave in just that fashion—as if their portion of the work were central. These tendencies are called suboptimization, the optimizing of a portion of the work rather than the whole. They constitute one potentially dysfunctional consequence of dividing the work.

Functional Form

The systematic division of work, typically reflected in departments, is fairly obvious. Somewhat less obvious is the basis for dividing it. How should the work be divided? There are numerous ways of dividing the work and, given the potential consequences, the designer should choose knowledgeably from among the options. The basis on which work is divided will implicitly set the various departments' goals and define members' perceptions. If we note that function means a "portion of the tasks or activities necessary" (Litterer, 1973), we will have a starting place. By functional form, we mean an organizational structure that divides the work among departments or units, each responsible for a portion of it. Some common bases for dividing work among functional departments (see Figures 1 through 6) would include:

Business function.   Manufacturing, sales, personnel, R&D departments
Managerial function.   Controller, planning, operations
Technical function or process.   Painting, welding, stamping, assembly
Similar tools or techniques.   Typing, operations research, computer center
Time.   Day shift, evening shift
Shared product or purpose.   Maintenance, editorial department, police

FIGURE 1
Functional Departments—Manufacturing Firm

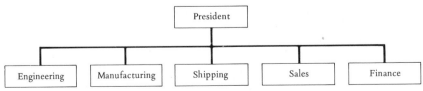

FIGURE 2
Functional Departments—School

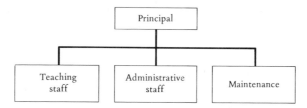

FIGURE 3
Functional Departments—Hospital

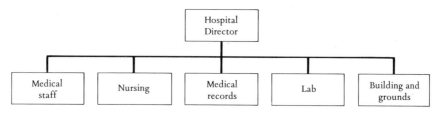

FIGURE 4
Departments by Managerial Function and Process

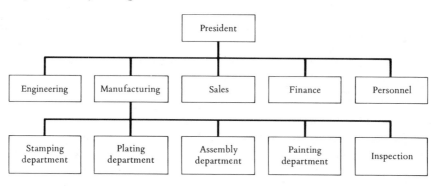

FIGURE 5
Departments by Process—City Government

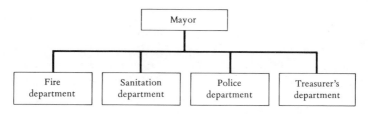

FIGURE 6
Departments by Clients Served

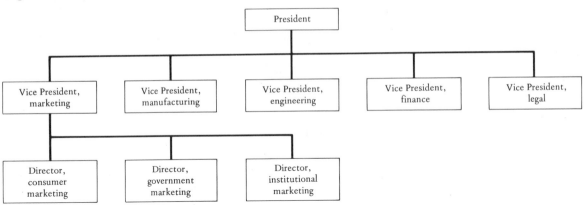

Geographic location.   Kalamazoo plant, New England region.

Client served.   Consumer sales, government contracts, industrial equipment

Some of these distinctions rest upon the activities of the manufacturing process, others on the output or client, still others on characteristics like time or location. It is important to note that the distinctions are not precise and mutually exclusive. Indeed, they are often used in combinations, particularly in more complex organizational forms. When someone refers to a functional organization structure, she or he means an organization in which each department performs only a portion of the needed activities of the organization, with coordination occurring at top levels. It is often provided by the president (as in Figures 1, 4A, and 4B, for instance), making the functional form a logical successor to the agency organization, for the top manager still maintains a large amount of control. Functional organization identifies key aspects of the task and clearly assigns responsibility for them. It permits and encourages specialization around these key tasks. Its disadvantages, beyond suboptimization, include potential difficulties in work flow between and among departments, and information overload as top managers become overwhelmed with too many coordinating decisions. This form of organization *specializes;* its main problem is *reintegration* of the specialized, differentiated activities.

Divisional Structure

While product departments were mentioned above, most typically product organization occurs in larger organizations that have evolved several distinctly different products or product lines. It usually implies product coordination at least one level *below* top management. Historically, the divisional structure evolved first at Du Pont and General Motors to meet a specific set of needs. Du Pont, which was reorganized from a cluster of family-owned predecessor firms in 1902, was soon expanded further by acquisition into the largest explosives manufacturing company in the United States. Du Pont had some thirty-one factories producing three main product lines—dynamite, black powder, and smokeless military gunpowder. The products were sufficiently different in raw materials, manufacture, and marketing to multiply complexities further. A great many new administrative mechanisms—like uniform and systematic information on costs and revenues, and rational allocation procedures—had to be evolved to make possible the coordination of so many activities.

Because of the differences in the product lines, the basic structure selected was organization into three operating departments, one for each product line. Within each, a functional structure was set up. The operating departments shared a common accounting system and a common system for evaluating unit performance (return on investment). Resources for investment were allocated from the top. It was clear from the outset, however, that running so large and so complex an organization would require more managerial capacity than just a single chief executive. To coordinate and manage the firm as a whole—in contrast to the individual departments within it—an executive committee made up of the operating department heads was formed. This structure explicitly recognized the need for both product line, or operating responsibilities, and for organizationwide, coordinative responsibilities. It was only thus, by explicitly monitoring and managing relationships among the product lines, that the company as a whole could avoid the inefficiencies that had plagued the predecessor companies. The explicit charge of the executive committee was to coordinate and integrate activities for the firm as a whole. (See Figure 7 for a simplified organization chart.) Over time, the distinction between product line operations and the overall management of the firm was more strongly drawn and more clearly reflected in structure by ensuring that the operating department heads were not the majority membership of the executive committee. Instead, corporate-level executives were appointed. This separation of tasks allowed the company to concen-

trate on new products, to allocate investment among the competing activities of the various product lines rationally, and to attend to financing new capital for expansion.

Du Pont's original structure made use of product-line form (the operating departments), functional departmentalization (within the main operating departments), and of staff as well as line managers. These innovations were essentially structural means to divide the work of management, distinguishing various product operations from corporate management and from the specialized ancillary support functions not concerned directly with operations. By providing structural legitimacy for all of these functions, Du Pont's divisional structure achieved a high order of performance in a vastly more complex business situation than had existed before.

General Motors

General Motors, too, evolved a divisional structure in response to product-line differences. However, the genesis was different from Du Pont's. GM was founded by William C. Durant, who assembled it from widely diverse companies manufacturing every-

FIGURE 7
Du Pont's Organization Prior to 1911 (much simplified)

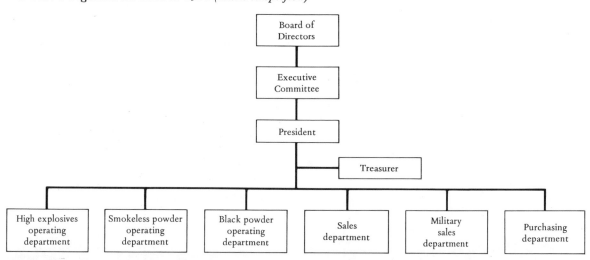

Source: Adapted from Alfred D. Chandler, Jr., and Stephen Salisbury, *Pierre S. Dupont and the Making of the Modern Corporation* (New York: Harper & Row, 1971).

thing from entire automobiles—such as Cadillac, Buick, Oakland, and even Cartercar—to components, tractors, an early refrigerator, and other things. Each had originally been an independent firm. There was no overall structure to begin with and no communication among different portions of the company. Aside from the name, the various factories shared little. In the absence of controls or coordination, the various lines competed with one another for financial resources not only within the firm but outside it in the marketplace as well.

GM's product line, even after some eliminations, contained ten car models and seven brands. All but two were losing money in 1921. Since the products competed directly (as smokeless powder and dynamite did not at Du Pont), coordination was even more essential. The problem at GM was to retain the advantages of decentralized independence—which permitted each division to specialize itself to concentrate on a specific market niche—while coordinating the whole

firm. The design problem was to combine centralized control on financial and policy matters (to coordinate among divisions) with decentralized operations (to ensure timely and adequate operating decisions). Under Durant, the executive committee had consisted of the heads of the operating divisions (much like Du Pont's first structure) and had exercised little or no control. After Durant's bankruptcy, the firm was reorganized with a new executive committee. The division heads were retained in an advisory capacity but were not executive committee members. A central financial staff, answerable to the executive committee, directed accounting and reporting procedures to ensure complete and comparable data. The divisions and their products were reduced, streamlined, and positioned so that each division was responsible for a single product line and a specific price range designated by the executive committee.

This basic structure reflected the philosophy of the company (see Figure 8): divisions should be autono-

FIGURE 8
Simplified Organization Chart, General Motors, 1924

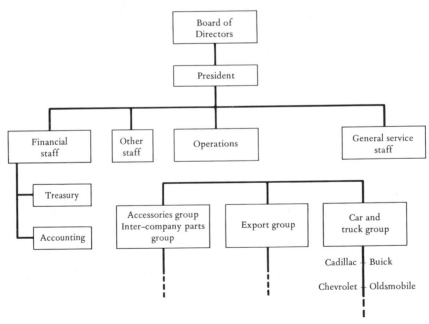

Source: Adapted from Alfred D. Chandler, Jr., and Stephen Salisbury, *Pierre S. Dupont and the Making of the Modern Corporation* (New York: Harper & Row, 1971).

mous and operate independently within broad policy boundaries laid down by the corporation. Policy should be a corporate responsibility, aimed at corporate coordination. The corporation would direct the reporting and accounting procedures and would allocate financial resources. This philosophy, and this structure, continues to the present day with relatively little change. GM grew to be the largest producer of automobiles in the world with this structure.

Administrative Structures

As organizations grew more complex, greater use was made of formal arrangements, written records and procedures, and explicit assignment of responsibilities. This formality offered many advantages, as Max Weber noted. Weber described a completely specified organization, which he called *bureaucracy* (from the French word for office, *bureau*). Weber's description was "an ideal type," or a model abstracted from the compromises required in the real world. By ignoring such compromises, the ideal type highlights the characteristics of bureaucracy. A bureaucracy, according to Weber, was rules based, in stark contrast to the earlier agency forms based on the leader's preference. As a result, the bureaucratic form provided a notable advance in efficiency, reliability, and predictability. The chief characteristics of the bureaucracy were:

1. Tasks are assigned to specific organization units and members as official duties, attached to *positions* (not individuals).
2. Authority is hierarchical, with higher positions holding greater authority, responsibility, and control. Power is concentrated at the top.
3. Formal rules govern behavior, ensuring uniformity in order to facilitate coordination.
4. Organization membership is a full-time commitment, typically a career for life.
5. Training and expertise are the basis for recruitment. There is a high degree of specialization.
6. Promotion is by seniority and merit.
7. Official activities are carefully segregated from private life; people act in accordance with their roles, not their preferences.
8. Files record and summarize all organizational activities.

Weber was aware of some drawbacks to this sort of organization, but he emphasized the advantages of the form in contrast to earlier methods of organizing. Predictability, reliability, increased output, lessened friction, discretion, and reduced material and personal costs were all advantages he cited as deriving from the technical superiority of the bureaucratic form.

The Degree of Formality

The advantages of bureaucracy are so great that virtually every modern organization is, to some degree, bureaucratic. This formality may be limited to an explicit division of labor, allowing and encouraging specialization, for instance. It may even be required by law: for example, hospitals are required to hire only specialists (medical doctors and trained nurses and technicians) to perform medical services. Even in private enterprises manufacturing proprietary materials for profit, such degrees of formality as explicit and accurate records of costs and revenues, payments and taxes, inspections and injuries are required. These are all examples of formality. Such measures as the number of specialist job categories differing from one another so that incumbents are not immediately interchangeable provide one indication of the degree of formality in an organization. Another measure is the degree to which procedures are specified in advance. If most activity within the organization is governed by protocol or procedure, and there is a set response to most situations, we can identify the organization as quite formal. Such organizations typically also have many levels of hierarchy and require that situations that fall outside the set rules of operation be referred upward, to superiors. So, too, with conflict or differences between different departments or units. Such an organization is often referred to as *mechanistic* (Burns and Stalker, 1961) because it is expected to operate like a machine.

At its extreme, the "machine bureaucracy" centralizes power and decision making, reserving them to the top executive. At the extreme, such an organization is rigid and highly formal—everything is specified and organization members are allowed virtually no discretion. The underlying assumption is that tasks, environment, and circumstances will always remain the same. Of course the extreme is far more rigid and specific than real-world organization structures would be. Nevertheless, it is clear that a range of bureaucratization is possible. To the degree that an organization does rely on rules, specify the duties of members, rely on specialists and so on, it is bureaucratic. To the extent that decision making is delegated downward, initiative is permitted or encouraged, and informal arrangements vary the procedures, the organization is less bureaucratic. Virtually every organization of any size, public or private, is to some degree bureaucratic. This ubiquity testifies loudly to the advantages that Weber noted. These benefits are counterbalanced by costs—"red tape," alienation, rigidity, inefficiency when rules fail to deal adequately with reality: in short, all that we imply by the stereotype "bureaucratic." The designer must recognize both costs and benefits.

In contrast to the highly bureaucratic, highly formal organization are informal or *organic* organizations (Burns and Stalker, 1961). These organizations rely on expertise and problem solving, rather than "the rules" or hierarchy, to accomplish tasks. People do what must be done, results matter more than rules, and tasks may frequently change, depending on the job at hand. Rather than relying on rules or procedures, such organizations may well rely on external training—as, for instance, when professional engineers, accountants, or architects are hired and then expected to work with relatively few formal rules. Instead, professional training and discretion are invoked. Of course, professional organizations are not the only organic organizations. Any organization that is relatively informal and operates in a flexible fashion may be identified as organic; professional organizations are merely one frequently encountered type of organic organization.

Organic, informal organization is very attractive to most of us. Many of us like to imagine ourselves operating with few rules or constraints. We see ourselves as capable and responsible organization members, easily able to choose appropriate actions and always in agreement with organizational goals. The difficulties of organic organizations are the obverse of those of bureaucracy: the informality and lack of rules that allow freedom of action also make for unpredictability, inefficiency, as people may

"reinvent the wheel," and inconsistency, as decisions are made one way this week and another the next. The lack of structure also fails to provide guidance for some who need direction. In short, organic organizations, too, have liabilities, and the designer must be aware of these as well as the undeniable advantages in choosing an appropriate degree of formality.

Line and Staff

Bureaucracy, with its carefully delineated hierarchy of authority and control, assumes that any higher organization member is more knowledgeable and has more responsibility than any lower member. Increasing complexity—as at Du Pont and GM—quickly led to the recognition of several sorts of authority, however. While some executives were directly responsible for operations, if the organization as a whole was to be coordinated and run effectively, various administrative mechanisms had to be explicitly managed. Thus, for instance, accounting procedures and reporting systems had to be designed, managed, maintained, and their results interpreted. This was clearly a specialist activity and just as clearly ancillary to the main activities of the firm. While essential to large-scale, complex operations, it was not part of operations. The solution was to divide the work—to specifically designate responsibility for the new technical requirements to specialists who held no other responsibility, while operating departments and members were designated as *line* activities. Organizationally, since support activity was all-pervasive yet not part of the central activity of manufacturing, these structural units were distinguished as *staff*.

Staff units are specialized support activities which are traditionally expected to advise (but not to command) line managers and members. In current organizations, this exclusively advisory role frequently breaks down—especially where staff units must approve budgetary expenses, for instance. Nevertheless, the traditional model is still typically invoked. Staff units are usually responsible for the development of specialized expertise and technical data, longer range activities concerning the coordination of the firm as a whole, and the like. The advantages of separating staff activities is akin to that of specialization in general—it encourages the development of greater expertise in the designated area. The disadvantages are also related to specialization. Because the staff unit concentrates only on its specialty, which may be quite arcane and esoteric to other organization members, staff personnel may become cut off from organizational reality and from other organization members. Difficulties include getting staff recommendations accepted by line personnel, ensuring realistic staff recommendations, and resolving jurisdictional disputes between line and staff.

These difficulties, and the need for greater responsiveness to both the needs of external environmental segments and internal coordination, led to the next organizational form, simultaneous organization.

Simultaneous Forms

The functional and divisional organizational forms were designed with an eye to separating the work into distinct pieces, generally eliminating overlap, and assigning relatively clear responsibility for activities along whatever underlying dimension was selected. In contrast, *simultaneous* organizational forms, of which the most familiar is the matrix, seek to design along multiple dimensions at the same time. The aim is to gain the benefits of several sorts of specialization, several emphases for attention at once. In order to do so, simultaneous organizations arrange people according to two (or occasionally more) basic divisions of work.

Simultaneous organization evolved first under the Defense Department and received major impetus at the National Aeronautics and Space Administration (NASA) and in the aerospace industry. The typical predecessor arrangements were functional departmentalization, with coordination occurring at the top (as in Figure 1). This structure did serve to encourage needed specialization and technical expertise by grouping technical specialists together. This grouping facilitated their communication with one another around work problems, thus providing a highly experienced technical resource pool. The structure was not adequate for coordinating the highly complex projects of aerospace work, however. The required communications across functional departments and technical specialties were not occurring smoothly, resulting in delays and increased costs. The design solution was to reorganize along both technical specialties and projects simultaneously. Project teams, drawn from numerous departments as needed, worked together on a given project. Meanwhile, all project members were still members of their functional departments, with access to their resources of technical expertise (see Figure 9). Each project member was responsible both to the functional

FIGURE 9

Matrix Organization in Manufacturing

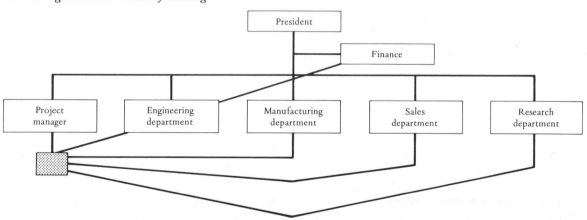

Note: Team members are drawn from various departments as needed and report to *both* the project manager and their home department head.

department head and to the project head; both evaluated the member.

Critical characteristics of the matrix form include simultaneous attention to two or more essential organizational tasks (here, the development and maintenance of specialized technical expertise and the coordination of diverse specialists around a common temporary task). Functional departments are oriented toward the acquisition, maintenance, and development of specialized *resources*—people and equipment, for instance. Project teams are oriented toward the production of *output*. As a result, relationships, authority patterns, and evaluation all become highly complex and usually negotiated, because there are no clear and simple answers. The multiple dimensions of organization foster an ongoing tension—which can be highly creative, if appropriately balanced—between the underlying *resource* orientation and the desired *output* orientation.

The matrix form encourages a far more useful view of organizational realities, because it legitimates the sort of bargaining and negotiation that is essential when many goals—for instance, both output and resources goals—are to be met at once. It also encourages a general managerial viewpoint well down in the organization, where members see these alternate dimensions interacting and begin quite early in their careers to understand the trade-offs required.

Matrix forms, like functional and departmental forms, evolve in response to the problems around them, as managers seek new answers. In the case of the matrix, the first step was temporary teams and temporary assignments. Later steps simply recognized that the organization faced an ongoing stream of such temporary projects. Thus while any individual project was temporary, another would take its place for firms involved in project work. For such organizations, a permanent project orientation (with projects changing) and a permanent functional organization (with appropriate resources maintained) were needed.

The advantages of simultaneous organizations like the matrix is their ability to maximize along several dimensions. Because project teams can be easily constituted and dissolved, the simultaneous form can be highly responsive to change as well. Because of this responsiveness, and because of the technical support the departmental structure provides, organization members often find they can "have their cake and eat it too," gaining benefits of motivation, involvement and worthwhile participation. Disadvantages include substantial managerial overhead, particularly in the early stages (which may last for two or three years) while participants learn to negotiate and bargain instead of referring all conflicts up to the hierarchy for resolution. The complexity and uncertainty of authority and responsibility lines can trouble some members, as can the need for high-order interpersonal skills.

Conclusions

Choice among organizational forms is contingent upon many factors. No single form—functional, product or geographic division, combination, or simultaneous—is best for all circumstances. The best choice is the one that best balances the costs and benefits for maximum gain, in the context of clear thinking about present and future organizational needs. Critical organizational dimensions must be addressed, as must the organization's ability to bear the costs and tolerate the disadvantages of any particular form. Stability is economically efficient but may impose heavy costs in terms of lost flexibility, creativity, and involvement. Innovative simultaneous organizations emphasize responsiveness but may impose substantial costs in terms of duplication, inefficiencies, and sheer complexity. Not all people tolerate well an ambiguous structure that requires multiple reporting relationships and bargaining. Each of the major design options—simple organizations, organization by functional components, by product, by division, mixed forms, and simultaneous forms—meets a particular set of needs. Each emphasizes some strengths at the price of some weaknesses. Design is the art of balancing these factors to choose appropriately.

References

Babbage, Charles. *On the Economy of Machinery and Manufacturers.* London: Charles Knight, 1832.

Burns, T., and Stalker, G. M. *The Management of Innovation.* London: Tavistock Publications, 1961.

Chandler, Alfred D. *Strategy and Structure.* Cambridge, Mass.: M.I.T. Press, 1962.

Chandler, Alfred D., and Salisbury, Steven. *Pierre S. Dupont and the Making of the Modern Corporation.* New York: Harper & Row, 1971.

Jelinek, Mariann. Organizational Design. In Don Hellriegel and John W. Slocum, Jr., *Organizational Behavior* (2nd ed.). St. Paul: West, 1979.

Litterer, Joseph A. *The Analysis of Organizations* (2nd ed.). New York: Wiley, 1973.

Mintzberg, Henry. *The Structuring of Organizations.* Englewood Cliffs, N.J.: Prentice-Hall, 1979.

Sloan, Alfred P. *My Years at General Motors.* Ed. by John McDonald and Catherine Stevens. Garden City, N.Y.: Doubleday Anchor, 1972.

Smith, Adam. *The Wealth of Nations.* London: Straham and Candell, 1776.

Organization Design:
An Information Processing View

Jay R. Galbraith

The empirical research of the last fifteen years on the structure of large organizations seems to confirm the hypothesis of Herbert Simon that human cognitive limits are a basic limiting factor in determining organization structures (Simon, 1957). This observation is derived from what is called modern contingency theory. A basic premise of this theory is that the most effective method of organizing is contingent upon some attributes of the organization's environment (Lawrence and Lorsch, 1967). While current research is devoted to discovering what these attributes are, there is a school of thought which suggests that the degree of uncertainty is the primary attribute. This paper takes that point of view and develops an explanation as to why that is the case. In so doing the organization design strategies for coping with cognitive limits are articulated.

Information Processing Model

The basic proposition is that the greater the uncertainty of the task, the greater the amount of information that has to be processed between decision makers during the execution of the task. If the task is well understood prior to performing it, much of the activity can be preplanned. If it is not understood, then during the actual task execution more knowledge is acquired which leads to changes in resource allocations, schedules, and priorities. All these changes require information processing *during* task performance. Therefore, *the greater the task uncertainty, the*

A revised version of Sloan School of Management Working Paper No. 425–69. Copyright 1969 by Jay R. Galbraith. Reprinted by permission.

greater the amount of information that must be processed among decision makers during task execution in order to achieve a given level of performance. The basic effect of uncertainty is to limit the ability of the organization to preplan or to make decisions about activities in advance of their execution. Therefore, it is hypothesized that the observed variations in organizational forms are variations in the strategies of organizations to (1) increase their ability to preplan, (2) increase their flexibility to adapt to their inability to preplan, or (3) to decrease the level of performance required for continued viability. Which strategy is chosen depends on the relative costs of the strategies. The function of the framework is to identify these strategies and their costs.

Mechanistic Model

The framework is best developed by keeping in mind a hypothetical organization. Assume it is large and employs a number of specialist groups and resources in providing the output. After the task has been divided into specialist subtasks, the problem is to integrate the subtasks around the completion of the global task. This is the problem of organization design. The behaviors that occur in one subtask cannot be judged as good or bad per se. The behaviors are more effective or ineffective depending upon the behaviors of the other subtask performers. There is a design problem because the executors of the behaviors cannot communicate with all the roles with whom they are interdependent. Therefore the design problem is to create mechanisms that permit coordinated action across large numbers of interdependent roles. Each of these mechanisms, however, has a limited range over which it is effective at handling the information requirements necessary to coordinate the interdependent roles. As the amount of uncertainty increases, and, therefore, information processing increases, the organization must adopt integrating mechanisms which increase its information processing capabilities.

COORDINATION BY RULES OR PROGRAMS

For routine predictable tasks, March and Simon have identified the use of rules or programs to coordinate behavior between interdependent subtasks (March and Simon, 1958, Chapter 6). To the extent that job-related situations can be predicted in advance and behaviors specified for these situations, programs allow an interdependent set of activities to be performed without the need for interunit communication. Each role occupant simply executes the behavior which is appropriate for the task-related situation with which he is faced.

HIERARCHY

As the organization faces greater uncertainty, its participants face situations for which they have no rules. At this point, the hierarchy is employed on an exception basis. The recurring job situations are programmed with rules while infrequent situations are referred to that level in the hierarchy where a global perspective exists for all affected subunits. However, the hierarchy also has a limited range. As uncertainty increases, the number of exceptions increases until the hierarchy becomes overloaded.

COORDINATION BY TARGETS OR GOALS

As the uncertainty of the organization's task increases, coordination increasingly takes place by specifying outputs, goals, or targets (March and Simon, 1958, p. 145). Instead of specifying specific behaviors to be enacted, the organization undertakes processes to set goals to be achieved and the employees select the behaviors which lead to goal accomplishment. Planning reduces the amount of discretion exercised at lower levels. Like the use of rules, planning achieves integrated action and also eliminates the need for continuous communication among interdependent subunits as long as task performance stays within the planned task specifications, budget limits, and

targeted completion dates. If it does not, the hierarchy is again employed on an exception basis.

The ability of an organization to coordinate interdependent tasks depends on its ability to compute meaningful subgoals to guide subunit action. When uncertainty increases because of introducing new products, entering new markets, or employing new technologies, these subgoals are incorrect. The result is more exceptions, more information processing, and an overloaded hierarchy.

Design Strategies

The ability of an organization to successfully utilize coordination by goal setting, hierarchy, and rules depends on the combination of the frequency of exceptions and the capacity of the hierarchy to handle them. As the task uncertainty increases, the organization must again take organization design action. It can proceed in either of two general ways. First, it can act in two ways to reduce the amount of information that is processed. And second, the organization can act in two ways to increase its capacity to handle more information. The two methods for reducing the need for information and the two methods for increasing processing capacity are shown schematically in Figure 1. The effect of all these actions is to reduce the number of exceptional cases referred upward into the organization through hierarchical channels. The assumption is that the critical limiting factor of an organizational form is its ability to handle the nonroutine, consequential events that cannot be anticipated and planned for in advance. The non-programmed events place the greatest communication load on the organization.

CREATION OF SLACK RESOURCES

As the number of exceptions begin to overload the hierarchy, one response is to increase the planning targets so that fewer exceptions occur. For example, completion dates can be extended until the number of exceptions that occur are within the existing information processing capacity of the organization. This has been the practice in solving job shop scheduling problems (Pounds, 1963). Job shops quote delivery times that are long enough to keep the scheduling problem within the computational and information processing

FIGURE 1
Organization Design Strategies

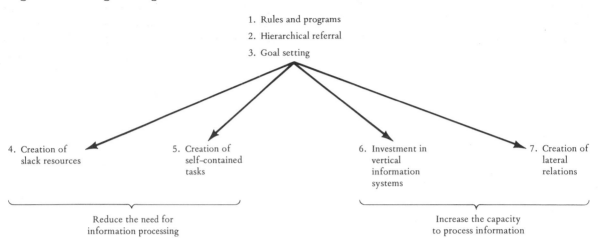

1. Rules and programs
2. Hierarchical referral
3. Goal setting

4. Creation of slack resources

5. Creation of self-contained tasks

6. Investment in vertical information systems

7. Creation of lateral relations

Reduce the need for information processing

Increase the capacity to process information

limits of the organization. Since every job shop has the same problem, standard lead times evolve in the industry. Similarly budget targets could be raised, buffer inventories employed, etc. The greater the uncertainty, the greater the magnitude of the inventory lead time or budget needed to reduce an overload.

All of these examples have a similar effect. They represent the use of slack resources to reduce the amount of interdependence between subunits (March and Simon, 1958; Cyert and March, 1963). This keeps the required amounts of information within the capacity of the organization to process it. Information processing is reduced because an exception is less likely to occur, and reduced interdependence means that fewer factors need to be considered simultaneously when an exception does occur.

The strategy of using slack resources has its costs. Relaxing budget targets has the obvious cost of requiring more budget. Increasing the time to completion date has the effect of delaying the customer. Inventories require the investment of capital funds which could be used elsewhere. Reduction of design optimization reduces the performance of the article being designed. Whether slack resources are used to reduce information or not depends on the relative cost of the other alternatives.

The design choices are among which factors to change (lead time, overtime, machine utilization, etc.) to create the slack and by what amount should

the factor be changed. Many operations research models are useful in choosing factors and amounts. The time-cost, trade-off problem in project networks is a good example.

CREATION OF SELF–CONTAINED TASKS

The second method of reducing the amount of information processed is to change the subtask groupings from resource (input)-based to output-based categories and supply each group with the resources it needs to supply the output. For example, the functional organization could be changed to product groups. Each group would have its own product engineers, process engineers, fabricating and assembly operations, and marketing activities. In other situations, groups can be created around product lines, geographical areas, projects, client groups, markets, etc., each of which would contain the input resources necessary for creation of the output.

The strategy of self-containment shifts the basis of the authority structure from one based on input, resource, skill, or occupational categories, to one based on output or geographical categories. The shift reduces the amount of information processing through several mechanisms. First, it reduces the amount of output diversity faced by a single collection of resources. For example, a professional organization with multiple skill specialties, providing service to three different client groups, must schedule the use of these specialties across three demands for their services and determine priorities when conflicts occur. But, if the organization changed to three groups, one for each client category, each with its own full complement of specialties, the scheduled conflicts across client groups disappear and there is no need to process information to determine priorities.

The second source of information reduction occurs through a reduced division of labor. The functional or resource specialized structure pools the demand for skills across all output categories. In the example above, each client generates approximately one-third of the demand for each skill. Since the division of labor is limited by the extent of the market, the division of labor must decrease as the demand increases. In the professional organization, each client group may have generated a need for one-third of a computer programmer. The functional organization would have hired one programmer and shared him across the groups. In the self-contained structure, there is insufficient demand in each group for a programmer, so the professionals must do their own programming. Specialization is reduced, but there is no problem of scheduling the programmer's time across the three possible uses for it.

The cost of the self-containment strategy is the loss of resource specialization. In the example, the organization foregoes the benefit of a specialist in computer programming. If there is physical equipment, there is a loss of economies of scale. The professional organization would require three machines in the self-contained form but only one large time-shared machine in the functional form. But those resources which have large economies of scale or for which specialization is necessary may remain centralized. Thus, it is the degree of self-containment that is the variable. The greater the degree of uncertainty, other things equal, the greater the degree of self-containment.

The design choices are the basis for the self-contained structure and the number of resources to be contained in the groups. No groups are completely self-contained or they would not be part of the same organization. But one product divisionalized firm may have eight of fifteen functions in the division while another may have twelve of fifteen in the divisions. Usually accounting, finance, and legal services are centralized and shared. Those functions which have economies of scale, require specialization, or are necessary for control, remain centralized and not part of the self-contained group.

The first two strategies reduced the amount of information by lowering performance standards and creating small autonomous groups to provide the output. Information is reduced because an exception is less likely to occur and fewer factors need to be considered when an exception does occur. The next two strategies accept the performance standards and division of labor as given, and adapt the organization so as to process the new information which is created during task performance.

INVESTMENT IN VERTICAL INFORMATION SYSTEMS

The organization can invest in mechanisms which allow it to process information acquired during task performance without overloading the hierarchical communication channels. The investment occurs according to the following logic. After the organization has created its plan or set of targets for inventories, labor utilization, budgets, and schedules, unanticipated events occur which generate exceptions requiring adjustments to the original plan. At some point, when the number of exceptions becomes substantial, it is preferable to generate a new plan rather than make incremental changes with each exception. The issue then is how frequently should plans be revised—yearly, quarterly, or monthly? The greater the frequency of replanning, the greater the resources—such as clerks, computer time, and input-output devices—required to process information about relevant factors.

The cost of information processing resources can be minimized if the language is formalized. Formalization of a decision-making language simply means that more information is transmitted with the same number of symbols. It is assumed that information processing resources are consumed in proportion to the number of symbols transmitted. The accounting system is an example of a formalized language.

Providing more information more often may simply overload the decision maker. Investment may be required to increase the capacity of the decision maker by employing computers, various man-machine combinations, assistants-to, etc. The cost of this strategy is the cost of the information processing resources consumed in transmitting and processing the data.

The design variables of this strategy are the decision frequency, the degree of formalization of language, and the type of decision mechanism which will make the choice. This strategy is usually operationalized by creating redundant information channels which transmit data from the point of origination upward in the hierarchy where the point of decision rests. If data are formalized and quantifiable, this strategy is effective. If the relevant data are qualitative and ambiguous, then it may prove easier to bring the decisions down to where the information exists.

CREATION OF LATERAL RELATIONSHIPS

The last strategy is to selectively employ joint decision processes which cut across lines of authority. This strategy moves the level of decision making down in the organization to where the information exists but does so without reorganizing around self-contained groups. There are several types of lateral decision processes. Some processes are usually referred to as the informal organization. However, these informal processes do not always arise spontaneously out of the needs of the task. This is particularly true in multinational organizations in which participants are separated by physical barriers, language differences, and cultural differences. Under these circumstances, lateral processes need to be designed. The lateral processes evolve as follows with increases in uncertainty.

1. *Direct Contact.*   This contact can be between managers who share a problem. If a problem arises on the shop floor, the foreman can simply call the design engineer and they can jointly agree upon a solution. From an information processing view, the joint decision prevents an upward referral and unloads the hierarchy.

2. *Liaison roles.*   When the volume of contacts between any two departments grows, it becomes economical to set up a specialized role to handle this communication. Liaison men are typical examples of specialized roles designed to facilitate communication between two interdependent departments and to bypass the long lines of communication involved in upward referral. Liaison roles arise at lower and middle levels of management.

3. *Task forces.*   Along with direct contact and liaison roles—like the integration mechanisms before them—task forces have a limited range of usefulness. They work when two managers or functions are involved. When problems arise involving seven or eight departments, the decision-making capacity of direct contacts is exceeded. Then these problems must be referred upward. For uncertain, interdependent tasks, such situations arise frequently. Task forces are a form of horizontal contact which is designed for problems of multiple departments.

The task force is made up of representatives from each of the affected departments. Some are full-time members; others may be part-time. The task force is a temporary group. It exists only as long as the problem remains. When a solution is reached each participant returns to his normal tasks.

To the extent that they are successful, task forces remove problems from higher levels of the hierarchy. The decisions are made at lower levels in the organization. In order to guarantee integration, a group problem-solving approach is taken. Each affected subunit contributes a member and, therefore, provides the information necessary to judge the impact on all units.

4. *Teams.*   The next extension is to incorporate the group decision process into the permanent decision processes. That is, as certain decisions consistently arise, the task forces become permanent. These groups are labeled teams. There are many design issues concerned in team decision making such as at what level do they operate, who participates, etc. (see Galbraith, 1973, Chapters 6 and 7). One design decision is particularly critical. This is the choice of leadership. Sometimes a problem exists largely in one department so that the department manager is the leader. Sometimes the leadership passes from one manager to another. As a new product moves to the marketplace, the leader of the new product team is first the technical manager followed by the production and then the marketing manager. The result is that if the team cannot reach a consensus decision and the leader decides, the goals of the leader are consistent with the goals of the organization for the decision in question. But quite often obvious leaders cannot be found. Another mechanism must be introduced.

5. *Integrating roles.*   The leadership issue is solved by creating a new role—an integrating role (Lawrence

and Lorsch, 1967, Chapter 3). These roles carry the labels of product managers, program managers, project managers, unit managers (hospitals), materials managers, etc. After the role is created, the design problem is to create enough power in the role to influence the decision process. These roles have power even when no one reports directly to them. They have some power because they report to the general manager. But if they are selected so as to be unbiased with respect to the groups they integrate and to have technical competence, they have expert power. They collect information and equalize power differences due to preferential access to knowledge and information. The power equalization increases trust and the quality of the joint decision process. But power equalization occurs only if the integrating role is staffed with someone who can exercise expert power in the form of persuasion and informal influences rather than exert the power of rank or authority.

6. *Managerial linking roles.* As tasks become more uncertain, it is more difficult to exercise expert power. The role must get more power of the formal authority type in order to be effective at coordinating the joint decisions which occur at lower levels of the organization. This position power changes the nature of the role which, for lack of a better name, is labeled a managerial-linking role. It is not like the integrating role because it possesses formal position power, but is different from line managerial roles in that participants do not report to the linking manager. The power is added by the following successive changes:

A. The integrator receives approval power of budgets formulated in the departments to be integrated.
B. The planning and budgeting process starts with the integrator making his initiation in budgeting legitimate.
C. The linking manager receives the budget for the area of responsibility and buys resources from the specialist groups.

These mechanisms permit the manager to exercise influence even though no one works directly for him. The role is concerned with integration but exercises power through the formal power of the position. If this power is insufficient to integrate the subtasks and creation of self-contained groups is not feasible, there is one last step.

7. *Matrix organization.* The last step is to create the dual authority relationship and the matrix organization (Galbraith, 1971). At some point in the organization, some roles have two superiors. The design issue is to select the locus of these roles. The result is a balance of power between the managerial-linking roles and the normal-line organization roles. Figure 2 depicts the pure matrix design.

The work of Lawrence and Lorsch is highly consistent with the assertions concerning lateral relations (Lawrence and Lorsch, 1967; Lorsch and Lawrence, 1968). They compared the types of lateral relations undertaken by the most successful firm in three different industries. Their data are summarized in Table 1. The plastics firm has the greatest rate of new product

TABLE 1

	Plastics	*Food*	*Container*
% New products in last 10 years	35%	20%	0%
Integrating devices	Rules	Rules	Rules
	Hierarchy	Hierarchy	Hierarchy
	Planning	Planning	Planning
	Direct contact	Direct contact	Direct contact
	Teams at 3 levels	Task forces	
	Integrating dept.	Integrators	
% Integrators/Managers	22%	17%	0%

(Adopted from Lawrence and Lorsch, 1967, pp. 86–138; and Lorsch and Lawrence, 1968.)

FIGURE 2
Pure Matrix Organization

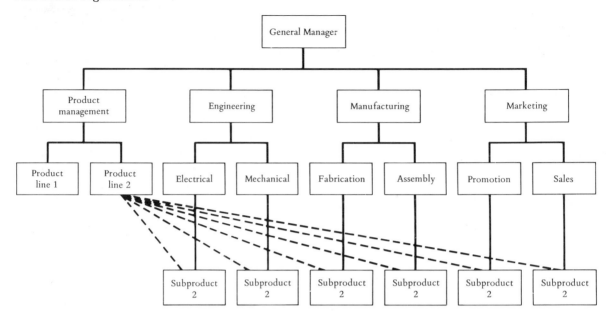

——— Technical authority over the product
——— Formal authority over the product (in product organization, these relationships may be reversed)

introduction (uncertainty) and the greatest utilization of lateral processes. The container firm was also very successful but utilized only standard practices because its information processing task is much less formidable. Thus, the greater the uncertainty, the lower the level of decision making and the integration is maintained by lateral relations.

Table 1 points out the cost of using lateral relations. The plastics firm has 22 percent of its managers in integration roles. Thus, the greater the use of lateral relations, the greater the managerial intensity. This cost must be balanced against the cost of slack resources, self-contained groups, and information systems.

Choice of Strategy

Each of the four strategies has been briefly presented. The organization can follow one or some combination of several if it chooses. It will chose that strategy which has the least cost in its environmental context. (For an example, see Galbraith, 1970.) However, what may be lost in all of the explanations is that the four strategies are hypothesized to be an exhaustive set of alternatives. That is, if the organization is faced with greater uncertainty due to technological change, higher performance standards due to increased competition, or diversifies its product line to reduce dependence, the amount of information processing is increased. *The organization must adopt at least one of the four strategies when faced with greater uncertainty.* If it does not consciously choose one of the four, then the first, reduced performance standards, will happen automatically. The task information requirements and the capacity of the organization to process information are always matched. If the organization does not consciously match them, reduced performance through budget overruns or schedule overruns will occur in order to bring about equality. Thus, the organization should be planned and designed simultaneously with the planning of the strategy and resource allocations. But if the strategy involves introducing new products, entering new markets, etc., then some provision for increased information must be made. Not to decide is to decide, and it is to decide upon slack resources as the strategy to remove hierarchical overload.

There is probably a fifth strategy which is not articulated here. Instead of changing the organization in response to task uncertainty, the organization can operate on its environment to reduce uncertainty. The organization, through strategic decisions, long-term contracts, coalitions, etc., can control its environment. But these maneuvers have costs also. They should be compared with costs of the four design strategies presented above.

Summary

The purpose of this paper has been to explain why task uncertainty is related to organizational form. In so doing, the cognitive limits theory of Herbert Simon was the guiding influence. As the consequences of cognitive limits were traced through the framework, various organization design strategies were articulated. The framework provides a basis for integrating organizational interventions, such as information systems and group problem solving, which have been treated separately before.

References

Richard Cyert and James March, *The Behavioral Theory of the Firm*. Englewood Cliffs, N.J.: Prentice-Hall, 1963.

Jay Galbraith, Environmental and Technological Determinants of Organization Design: A Case Study. In Lawrence and Lorsch (Eds.), *Studies in Organization Design*. Homewood, Ill.: Richard D. Irwin, 1970.

Jay Galbraith, Designing matrix organizations. *Business Horizons*, Feb., 1971, pp. 29–40.

Jay Galbraith, *Organization Design*. Reading, Mass.: Addison-Wesley, 1973.

Paul Lawrence and Jay Lorsch, *Organization and Environment*. Boston: Division of Research, Harvard Business School, 1967.

Jay Lorsch and Paul Lawrence, ''Environmental Factors and Organization Integration.'' Paper read at the Annual Meeting of the American Sociological Association, August 27, 1968, Boston, Mass.

James March and Herbert Simon, *Organizations*. New York: Wiley, 1958.

William Pounds, The Scheduling Environment. In Muth and Thompson (Eds.), *Industrial Scheduling*. Englewood Cliffs, N.J.: Prentice-Hall, 1963.

Herbert Simon, *Models of Man*. New York: Wiley, 1957, pp. 196–206.

The Confrontation Meeting

Richard Beckhard

One of the continuing problems facing the top management team of any organization in times of stress or major change is how to assess accurately the state of the organization's health. How are people reacting to the change? How committed are subordinate managers to the new conditions? Where are the most pressing organization problems?

In the period following a major change—such as that brought about by a change in leadership or organization structure, a merger, or the introduction of a new technology—there tends to be much confusion and an expenditure of dysfunctional energy that negatively affects both productivity and morale.

At such times, the top management group usually spends many hours together working on the business problems and finding ways of coping with the new conditions. Frequently, the process of working together under this pressure also has the effect of making the top team more cohesive.

Concurrently, these same managers tend to spend less and less time with their subordinates and with the rest of the organization. Communications decrease between the top and middle levels of management. People at the lower levels often complain that they are less in touch with what is going on than they were before the change. They feel left out. They report having less influence than before, being more unsure of their own decision-making authority, and feeling less sense of ownership in the organization. As a result of this, they tend to make fewer decisions, take fewer risks, and wait until the "smoke clears."

Reprinted by permission of the Harvard Business Review. "The Confrontation Meeting" by Richard Beckhard (HBR, March–April 1967). Copyright © 1967 by the President and Fellows of Harvard College; all rights reserved.

When this unrest comes to the attention of top management, the response is usually to take some action such as:

Having each member of the top team hold team meetings with his subordinates to communicate the state of affairs, and following this procedure down through the organization.

Holding some general communication improvement meetings.

Conducting an attitude survey to determine priority problems.

Any of these actions will probably be helpful, but each requires a considerable investment of time which is competitive with the time needed to work on the change problem itself.

Action Plans

Recently I have experimented with an activity that allows a total management group, drawn from all levels of the organization, to take a quick reading on its own health and—*within a matter of hours*—to set action plans for improving it. I call this a confrontation meeting.

The activity is based on my previous experience with an action-oriented method of planned change in which information on problems and attitudes is collected and fed back to those who produced it, and steps are taken to start action plans for improvement of the condition.

Sometimes, following situations of organizational stress, the elapsed time in moving from identification of the problem to collaborative action planning must be extremely brief. The confrontation meeting can be carried out in 4½ to 5 hours' working time, and it is designed to include the entire management of a large system in a joint action-planning program.

I have found this approach to be particularly practical in organization situations where there are large numbers in the management group or where it is difficult to take the entire group off the job for any length of time. The activity has been conducted several times with a one evening and one morning session, taking only 2½ hours out of a regular working day.

The confrontation meeting discussed in this article has been used in a number of different organization situations. Experience shows that it is appropriate where:

There is a need for the total management group to examine its own workings.

Very limited time is available for the activity.

Top management wishes to improve the conditions quickly.

There is enough cohesion in the top team to ensure follow-up.

There is real commitment to resolving the issues on the part of top management.

The organization is experiencing, or has recently experienced, some major change.

In order to show how this technique can speed the process of getting the information and acting on it, let us first look at three actual company situations where this approach has been successfully applied. Then we will examine both the positive results and the possible problems that could occur through the use and misuse of this technique. Finally, after a brief summary there are appendixes for the reader interested in a more elaborate description of the phasing and scheduling of such a meeting.

CASE EXAMPLE A

The initial application of the confrontation meeting technique occurred in 1965 in a large food products company. Into this long-time family-owned and closely controlled company, there was introduced for the first time a non-family professional general manager. He had been promoted from the ranks of the group that had previously reported to the family-member general manager.

This change in the "management culture," which had been carefully and thoroughly prepared by the family executives, was carried out with a minimum number of problems. The new general manager and his operating heads spent many hours together and developed a quite open problem-solving climate and an effective, cohesive team. Day-to-day operations were left pretty much in the hands of their immediate subordinates, while the top group focused on planning.

A few months after the change, however, the general manager began getting some information that indicated all was not well further down in the organization. On investigation, he discovered that many middle-level managers were feeling isolated from what was going on. Many were unclear about the authority and functions of the management committee (his top team); some were finding it very difficult to see and consult with their bosses (his operating heads); others were not being informed of decisions made at his management committee meetings; still othes were apprehensive that a new power elite was developing which in many ways was much worse than the former family managers.

In discussing this feedback information with his operating heads, the general manager found one or two who felt these issues required immediate management committee attention. But most of the members of the top team tended to minimize the information as "the usual griping," or "people needing too many decisions made for them," or "everybody always wanting to be in on everything."

The general manager then began searching for some way to:

Bring the whole matter into the open.

Determine the magnitude and potency of the total problem.

Give his management committee and himself a true picture of the state of the organization's attitudes and concerns.

Collect information on employee needs, problems, and frustrations in some organized way so that corrective actions could be taken in priority order.

Get his management committee members in better tune with their subordinates' feelings and attitudes, and put some pressure on the team members for continued two-way communications within their own special areas.

Make clear to the total organization that he—the top manager—was personally concerned.

Set up mechanisms by which all members of the total management group could feel that their individual needs were noticed.

Provide additional mechanisms for supervisors to influence the whole organization.

The confrontation meeting was created to satisfy these objectives and to minimize the time in which a large number of people would have to be away from the job.

Some seventy managers, representing the total management group, were brought together for a confrontation meeting starting at 9:00 in the morning and ending at 4:30 in the afternoon. The specific "design" for the day, which is broken down into a more detailed decription in Appendix A, had the following components.

1. Climate setting—establishing willingness to participate
2. Information collecting—getting the attitudes and feelings out in the open
3. Information sharing—making total information available to all
4. Priority setting and group action planning—holding work-unit sessions to set priority actions and to make timetable commitments.
5. Organization action planning—getting commitment by top management to the working of these priorities
6. Immediate follow-up by the top management committee—planning first actions and commitments

During the day-long affair, the group identified some eighty problems that were of concern to people throughout the organization; they selected priorities from among them; they began working on these priority issues in functional work units, and each unit produced action recommendations with timetables and targets; and they got a commitment from top management of actions on priorities that would be attended to. The top management team met immediately after the confrontation meeting to pin down the action steps and commitments.

(In subsequent applications of this confrontation meeting approach, a seventh component—a progress review—has been added, since experience has shown that it is important to reconvene the total group 4 to 6 weeks later for a progress review both from the functional units and from the top management team.)

CASE EXAMPLE B

A small company which makes products for the military had been operating at a stable sales volume of $3 million to $4 million. The invention of a new process and the advent of the war in Vietnam suddenly produced an explosion of business. Volume rose to the level of $6 million within 6 months and promised to redouble within another year.

Top management was desperately trying to (a) keep raw materials flowing through the line, (b) get material processed, (c) find people to hire, (d) discover quicker ways of job training, and (e) maintain quality under the enormously increased pressure.

There was constant interaction among the five members of the top-management team. They were aware of the tension and fatigue that existed on the production line, but they were only vaguely aware of the unrest, fatigue, concern, and loneliness of the middle manager and foreman groups. However, enough signals *had* filtered up to the top team to cause concern and a decision that something needed to be done right away. But, because of the pressures of work, finding the time to tackle the problems was as difficult as the issues themselves.

The entire management group agreed to give up one night and one morning; the confrontation meeting was conducted according to the six component phases described earlier, with phases 1, 2, and 3 being held in the evening and phases 4, 5, and 6 taking place the following morning.

CASE EXAMPLE C

A management organization took over the operation of a hotel which was in a sorry state of affairs. Under previous absentee ownership, the property had been allowed to run down; individual departments were independent empires; many people in management positions were nonprofessional hotel people (i.e., friends of the owners); and there was very low competence in the top management team.

The general manager saw as his priority missions the need to:

Stop the downhill trend.
Overcome a poor public image.
Clean up the property.
Weed out the low-potential (old friends) management.
Bring in professional managers in key spots.
Build a management team.
Build effective operating teams, with the members of the top-management team as links.

He followed his plan with considerable success. In a period of one year he had significantly cleaned up the property, improved the service, built a new dining room, produced an enviable food quality, and begun to build confidence in key buyers, such as convention managers. He had acquired and developed a very fine, professional, young management team that was both competent and highly motivated. This group had been working as a cohesive team on all the hotel's improvement goals; differences between them and their areas seemed to have been largely worked through.

At the level below the top group, the department and section heads, many of whom were also new, had been working under tremendous pressure for over a year to bring about improvements in the property and in the hotel's services. They felt very unappreciated by the top managers, who were described as ''always being in meetings and unavailable,'' or ''never rewarding us for good work,'' or ''requiring approval on all decisions but we can't get to see them,'' or ''developing a fine top management club but keeping the pressure on us and we're doing the work.''

The problem finally was brought to the attention of the top managers by some of the department heads. Immediate action was indicated and a confrontation meeting was decided on. It took place in two periods, an afternoon and the following morning. There was an immediate follow-up by the top management team in which many of the issues between departments and functions were identified as stemming back to the modus operandi of the top team. These issues were openly discussed and were worked through. Also in this application, a follow-up report and review session was scheduled for 5 weeks after the confrontation meeting.

Positive Results

The experience of the foregoing case examples, as well as that of other organizations in which the confrontation meeting technique has been applied, demonstrates that positive results—particularly, improved operational procedures and improved organization health—frequently occur.

OPERATIONAL ADVANTAGES

One of the outstanding plus factors is that procedures which have been confused are clarified. In addition, practices which have been nonexistent are initiated. Typical of these kinds of operational improvement, for example, are the reporting of financial information to operating units, the handling of the reservation system at a hotel, and the inspection procedures and responsibilities in a changing manufacturing process.

Another advantage is that task forces, or temporary systems, are set up as needed. These may be in the form of special teams to study the overlap in responsibilities between two departments and to write new statements and descriptions, or to work out a new system for handling order processing from sales to production planning, or to examine the kinds of information that should flow regularly from the management committee to middle management.

Still another improvement is in providing guidance to top management as to specific areas needing priority attention. For example, ''the overtime policy set under other conditions is really impeding the achievement of organization requirements,'' or ''the food in the employee's cafeteria is really creating morale problems,'' or ''the lack of understanding of where the organization is going and what top management's goals are is producing apathy,'' or ''what goes on in top management meetings does not get communicated to the middle managers.''

ORGANIZATION HEALTH

In reviewing the experiences of companies where the confrontation meeting approach has been instituted, I have perceived a number of positive results in the area of organization health:

A high degree of open communication between various departments and organization levels is achieved very quickly. Because people are assigned to functional units and produce data together, it is possible to express the real feeling of one level or group toward another, particularly if the middle echelon believes the top wants to hear it.

The information collected is current, correct, and "checkable."

A real dialogue can exist between the top management team and the rest of the management organization, which personalizes the top manager to the total group.

Larger numbers of people get "ownership" of the problem, since everyone has some influence through his unit's guidance to the top-management team; thus people feel they have made a real contribution. Even more, the requirement that each functional unit take personal responsibility for resolving some of the issues broadens the base of ownership.

Collaborative goal setting at several levels is demonstrated and practiced. The mechanism provides requirements for joint goal setting within each functional unit and between top and middle managers. People report that this helps them to understand management by objectives more clearly than before.

The top team can take corrective actions based on valid information. By making real commitments and establishing check or review points, there is a quick building of trust in management's intentions on the part of lower level managers.

There tends to be an increase in trust and confidence toward the top-management team and toward colleagues. A frequently appearing agenda item is the "need for better understanding of the job problems of other departments," and the output of these meetings is often the commitment to some "mechanism for systematic interdepartmental communication." People also report a change in their stereotypes of people in other areas.

This activity tends to be a "success experience" and thus increases total morale. The process itself, which requires interaction, contribution, and joint work on the problems and which rewards constructive criticism, tends to produce a high degree of enthusiasm and commitment. Because of this, the follow-up activities are crucial in ensuring continuation of this enthusiasm.

Potential Problems

The confrontation meeting technique produces, in a very short time, a great deal of commitment and desire for results on the part of a lot of people. Feelings tend to be more intense than in some other settings because of the concentration of time and manpower. As a result, problems can develop through misuse of the techniques.

If the top management team does not really use the information from its subordinates, or if there are great promises and little follow-up action, more harm can be caused to the organization's health than if the event were never held.

If the confrontation meeting is used as a manipulative device to give people the "feeling of participation," the act can boomerang. They will soon figure out management's intentions, and the reaction can be severe.

Another possible difficulty is that the functional units, full of enthusiasm at the meeting, set unrealistic or impractical goals and commitments. The behavior of the keyman in each unit—usually a department manager or division head—is crucial in keeping suggestions in balance.

One more possible problem may appear when the functional units select a few priority issues to report out. While these issues may be the most *urgent,* they are not necessarily the most *important.* Mechanisms for working *all* of the information need to be developed within each functional unit. In one of the case examples cited earlier, the groups worked the few problems they identified very thoroughly and never touched the others. This necessitated a "replay" 6 months later.

Summary

In periods of stress following major organization changes, there tends to be much confusion and energy expended that negatively affects productivity and organization health.

The top-management team needs quick, efficient ways of sensing the state of the organization's attitudes and feelings in order to plan appropriate actions and to devote its energy to the most important problems.

The usual methods of attitude surveys, extended

staff meetings, and so forth demand extensive time and require a delay between getting the information and acting on it.

A short micromechanism called a confrontation meeting can provide the total management group with:

An accurate reading on the organization's health.

The opportunity for work units to set priorities for improvement.

The opportunity for top management to make appropriate action decisions based on appropriate information from the organization.

An increased involvement in the organization's goals.

A real commitment to action on the part of subgroups.

A basis for determining other mechanisms for communication between levels and groups, appropriate location of decisions, and problem solving within subunits, as well as the machinery for upward influence.

Appendix A: Confrontation Meeting

Here is a detailed description of the seven components which make up the specific design for the day-long confrontation meeting.

PHASE 1.   CLIMATE SETTING (45 MINUTES TO 1 HOUR)

At the outset, the top manager needs to communicate to the total management group his goals for the meeting, and his concern for and interest in free discussion and issue facing. He also has to assure his people that there is no punishment for open confrontation.

It is also helpful to have some form of information session or lecture by the top manager or a consultant. Appropriate subjects might deal with the problems of communication, the need for understanding, the assumptions and the goals of the total organization, the concept of shared responsibility for the future of the organization, and the opportunity for and responsibility of influencing the organization.

PHASE 2.   INFORMATION COLLECTING (1 HOUR)

The total group is divided into small heterogeneous units of seven or eight people. If there is a top manage-

ment team that has been holding sessions regularly, it meets as a separate unit. The rest of the participants are assigned to units with a "diagonal slice" of the organization used as a basis for composition—that is, no boss and subordinate are together and each unit contains members from every functional area.

The assignment given to each of these units is along these lines: Think of yourself as an individual with needs and goals. Also think as a person concerned about the total organization. What are the obstacles, "demotivators," poor procedures or policies, unclear goals, or poor attitudes that exist today? What different conditions, if any, would make the organization more effective and make life in the organization better?

Each unit is instructed to select a reporter to present its results at a general information-collecting session to be held 1 hour later.

PHASE 3.   INFORMATION SHARING (1 HOUR)

Each reporter writes his unit's complete findings on newsprint, which is tacked up around the room.

The meeting leader suggests some categories under which all the data from all the sheets can be located. In other words, if there are seventy-five items, the likelihood is that these can be grouped into six or seven major categories—say, by type of problem, such as communications difficulties; or by type of relationship, such as problems with top management; or by type of area involved, such as problems in the mechanical department.

Then the meeting breaks, either for lunch or, if it happens to be an evening session, until the next morning.

During the break all the data sheets are duplicated for general distribution.

PHASE 4.   PRIORITY SETTING AND GROUP ACTION PLANNING (1 HOUR AND 15 MINUTES)

The total group reconvenes for a 15 minute general session. With the meeting leader, they go through the raw data on the duplicated sheets and put category numbers by each piece of data.

People are now assigned to their functional, natural work units for a 1 hour session. Manufacturing people at all levels go to one unit, everybody in sales to another, and so forth. These units are headed by a department manager or division head of that function. This means that some units may have as few as three people and some as many as twenty-five. Each unit is charged to perform three specific tasks:

1. Discuss the problems and issues which affect its area. Decide on the priorities and early actions to which the group is prepared to commit itself. (They should be prepared to share this commitment with their colleagues at the general session.)
2. Identify the issues and problems to which the top management team should give its priority attention.
3. Decide how to communicate the results of the session to their subordinates.

PHASE 5.   ORGANIZATION ACTION PLANNING
(1 TO 2 HOURS)

The total management group reconvenes in a general session, where:

1. Each functional unit reports its commitment and plans to the total group.
2. Each unit reports and lists the items that its members believe the management team should deal with first.
3. The top manager reacts to this list and makes commitments (through setting targets or assigning task forces or timetables, and so on) for action where required.
4. Each unit shares briefly its plans for communicating the results of the confrontation meeting to all subordinates.

PHASE 6.   IMMEDIATE FOLLOW-UP BY TOP TEAM
(1 TO 3 HOURS)

The top-management team meets immediately after the confrontation meeting ends to plan first follow-up actions, which should then be reported back to the total management group within a few days.

PHASE 7.   PROGRESS REVIEW (2 HOURS)

Follow-up [occurs] with total management group 4 to 6 weeks later.

Appendix B: Sample Schedule

9:00 A.M.   Opening Remarks, by general manager
Background, goals, outcomes
Norms of openness and "leveling"
Personal commitment to follow-up

9:10   General Session
Communications Problems in Organizations, by general manager (or consultant)
The communications process
Communications breakdowns in organizations and individuals
Dilemmas to be resolved
Conditions for more openness

10:00   Coffee

10:15   Data Production Unit Session
Sharing feelings and attitudes
Identifying problems and concerns
Collecting data

11:15   General Session
Sharing findings from each unit (on newsprint)
Developing categories on problem issues

12:15 P.M.   Lunch

2:00   General Session
Reviewing list of items in categories
Instructing functional units

2:15   Functional Unit Session
Listing priority actions to be taken
Preparing recommendations for top team
Planning for presentation of results at general meeting

3:15   General Session
Sharing recommendations of functional units
Listing priorities for top team action
Planning for communicating results of meeting to others

4:15   Closing Remarks, by general manager

4:30   Adjournment

Managing Conflict Between Groups

W. Warner Burke

When people work or live together, conflict is as inevitable as the chase that ensues when a cat sees a mouse, and, like the animals, we usually attempt to manage our conflicts by flight or fight. Since the 1950s, methods for managing conflicts more constructively have been developed by behavioral scientists, but such methods are used in a disproportionately small number of cases. Blake and Mouton (1961; 1962) have made a considerable contribution to the application of behavioral science to conflict resolution by taking the original research and theory of Sherif (Sherif, 1962; Sherif and Sherif, 1956) and applying it to organizations. A comprehensive explanation of this application has been published (Blake, Shepard, and Mouton, 1964) which provides strategies for improving headquarters-field relations, problem solving in labor-management conflict and intergroup dynamics in mergers. Their discussion of the Scofield case, a headquarters-field conflict, clearly illustrates the usefulness of this kind of organization development intervention. Moreover, Blake and Mouton (1968) have devoted one phase of their comprehensive approach to OD to intergroup development.

Why are these strategies and others (for example, Beckhard, 1969; Walton, 1969) not used more often? There is no doubt that they are needed for improving organizational effectiveness. In my experience, team building is the OD intervention most commonly used by practitioners, but, as every practitioner knows, team building is not, of itself, OD. Of course, dealing with conflict is not easy even if one is a third party.

Reprinted from John D. Adams (Ed.), *New Technologies in Organization Development: 2.* San Diego, Ca.: Organizational Associates, 1975. Used with permission.

Emotions are not only surfaced but are sometimes expressed in hurtful ways. The desire on the part of client and consultant alike to avoid these painful experiences no doubt provides one reason for the infrequent use of such interventions. Another reason may be our lack of knowledge about some specific procedures for managing an intergroup problem-solving meeting. Fordyce and Weil (1971) have provided some specific procedures (see for example, pp. 124–130), but their treatment of intergroup conflict is rather brief. Blake, Shepard, and Mouton's (1964) coverage of the Scofield headquarters-field conflict is comprehensive enough, but what if you do not have 6 days?

On the hunch that lack of knowledge about and experience with specific procedures for conducting an intergroup problem-solving meeting of a relatively short duration may account for what appears to be minimal use of an effective intervention, I have set for myself in this paper the objective of explaining in detail specific steps I take in conducting an "intergroup" when the time is limited to only two days. In providing the amount of detail that I do, I do not intend to present my procedure (which, after all, is a combination of many techniques I've learned from others) as *the way*. I simply want to explain what has worked for me and, as much as possible, provide the rationale for why I take certain steps.

I have used the procedure I shall describe with such groups as production and maintenance engineers from a company in the metals industry, medical technicians and physicians in a medical school–university hospital complex, and with manufacturing and engineering managers in an electrical products

319

plant. This last intergroup is the one I shall use as a case example for my explanation of the procedure.

Prior to Meeting

Some diagnostic work must be done before the meeting. This step is fundamental in practicing organization development (Burke and Hornstein, 1972). More specifically, the reasons in this case are not only to determine the need for such an intervention, but also (1) to give the consultant a "feel" for the situation and (2) to determine the clients' motivation for and commitment to a problem-solving meeting. If you find low motivation and commitment, my suggestion is to consider strongly calling the meeting off or simply not hold it if one had not been presumed. Frequently managers assume that the purpose of a meeting such as this one, or a team-building session for example, is for training and education. The consultant is going to "lay something on us." What must be made clear is that the objective of the meeting is to identify and work on real, nagging, and up to this point, unsolvable problems. Problem-solving work is difficult and tedious. The client must understand that the meeting is for work. *Consultants in OD make mistakes at this beginning point by allowing the client to place them in a teacher or trainer role and not in a role of facilitator and catalyst.* The consultant must emphasize that he cannot identify the issues and problems, much less solve them. The client must do this work, not the consultant. If the consultant determines that the objective for the meeting is not understood, then he must work to make it clear with a clear alternative being one of not holding the meeting, at least not the kind of meeting I describe in the article.

After determining that the diagnosis warrants an intergroup intervention, a general meeting of all concerned (the persons who will attend and do the work and those in the organizational hierarchy who are responsible for this client group) should be held on site prior to leaving for the meeting. This meeting should be called and conducted by the person (or persons) in the organizational hierarchy who is a common superior to the two groups. In the case example I am using, it was the plant manager to whom the heads of manufacturing and engineering reported. The purposes for the superior's calling this meeting are (1) of-

ficially to sanction the meeting; (2) for the boss (here, the plant manager) to present any mandates (what he hopes will be acomplished); and (3) to explain the "boundaries" or authority of the meeting. In other words, with this latter objective, the boss needs to say what decisions can be made, what actions can be taken, and what is "out of bounds." As the consultant, I follow the boss by then explaining, from my perspective, the purpose of the meeting and what the design will be. With respect to the purpose, I explain that we will not attempt to change anyone's personality or character structure but that our objectives are to discover what the actual problems are in the *interface* between the two groups and to plan action steps for correcting these problems.

Incidentally, in my experience with this intervention, most people have *not* had laboratory training nor have they participated previously in any kind of team-building process. I do not believe that either is a prerequisite for this intergroup design. These prior experiences would undoubtedly help but, with the kind of structure I use for this two-day meeting, neither is a necessity.

The Off-Site Meeting

Although this meeting could be held on location, the advantages of going off site are well known. Away from distractions, conditions are such that most energy can be directed toward the problem at hand, and during breaks, meals, and social time, the people usually remain together and continue working in some different ways than the work done during the "formal" sessions. These informal talks often facilitate the overall problem-solving process.

PHASE 1: IMAGE EXCHANGE (2 HOURS)

I like to begin a meeting of this kind with a brief description of other sessions I have conducted with other organizations. These examples (1) provide the client group with an overview of what they can expect and, therefore, reduce some of the ambiguity and anxiety, and (2) show that the consultant has done something like this before, again giving them some means of reducing counterproductive anxiety so that energy can be focused on the interface problems and not on the consultant and his design.

After my opening statement, usually no longer than 15 minutes, I divide the total group into their natural groupings. In this case there were six men in each group, engineering and manufacturing. Each of the two groups work separately for an hour and produce three lists on newsprint.[1]

1. How do we see ourselves? (It is frequently useful to include also a listing of how the group sees its responsibilities.)
2. How do we see the other group?
3. How do we think they see us? (In other words, each group is trying to predict the other group's second list.)

Their lists can be sentences, phrases, or one-word adjectives. Table 1 shows a sampling of what these two groups, engineering and manufacturing, produced. The rationale for conducting an image exchange is as follows:

The meeting begins on a note of personal involvement and discovery and not that of wrestling with problems at the outset.

Sharing perceptions usually takes care of some problems at the beginning. (For example, the engineering group believed that manufacturing saw them as intruding on their [manufacturing's] functions [see Table 1, no. 3, item f]. The manufacturing group didn't see them that way at all. This "perceived problem" was eliminated immediately.)

The exchange helps to sharpen what the real issues in the interface are.

I like to conduct the exchange of perceptions in the following order:

First, engineering (arbitrarily selected or they volunteer to go first) presents their list 1 (How do we see ourselves?).

Second, manufacturing presents their list 2 (How do we see them?).

Third, engineering presents their list 3 (How do we think they see us?).

Fourth, manufacturing presents their list 1.

Fifth, engineering presents their list 2.

Sixth, manufacturing presents their list 3.

The reason for this order is that it maximizes *exchange* (one group presents, followed by the other), and provides for quick feedback (for example, engineering reports on how they see themselves and this is followed with how they are seen). Engineering could present both their lists 1 and 3 followed by manufacturing's presentation of their list 2, and so forth for the remaining three steps in the procedure.

During this period of presentations, about an hour, the ground rule is that questions of *clarification only* can be discussed. This is not the time to debate differences or to take issue. The purpose of this phase is to present the data and to seek understanding.

PHASE 2: PROBLEM IDENTIFICATION (3 HOURS)

Phase 2 has four steps. Step one is to begin the task of identifying the problems that exist with the interface. To facilitate this step, I arrange for all six of the image exchange lists to be hung on the wall[2] so that the individuals can use the data for helping them to formulate their thoughts. This initial problem formulation is done by each person independently. About 30 minutes is required for this individual work. The rationale for this individual work at the outset of phase 2 is to legitimize and sanction independent thought, and maximize conditions for comprehensive coverage of problems. Since group work predominates in this type of design, some individuals may be inhibited in a group and the opportunity for independent work may be the primary mode for their contribution.

The second step is for the two groups to meet again separately and consolidate their individual work into a group list. By consolidation I do not mean to imply that the final group list will necessarily be shorter than the total for the individuals' list. It may be that little overlap occurs, although this is rare. It may also be that as a result of the group discussion other problems not previously thought of during the individual work become identified, a result that is common among groups that work effectively.

Step three consists of each group's presenting its problem list to the other. The purpose of this step is for each group to understand what the other group's

---

[1] The tools of the trade in OD are three: (1) a flip chart or easel with a newsprint pad, (2) felt markers in a variety of colors, and (3) masking tape. With these tools, OD practitioners can perform miracles!

[2] I refer to this particular step as "hanging up our dirty linens."

TABLE 1

Sampling of Image Exchange Lists Between the Engineering Department and the Manufacturing Group Within a Plant

---

List 1. *How Do We See Ourselves?*

Engineering

a) Stabilizing influence in the plant
b) Flexible but uncompromising
c) Cooperative
d) Competent but fallible
e) Strategy formulators
f) Creative

Manufacturing

a) Competent
b) Inexperienced
c) Error prone
d) Not cohesive
e) Creative
f) Hard working
g) Sensitive to criticism
h) Second class citizens

List 2. *How Do We See Them?*

Engineering (describing mfg.)

a) Unstable organization
b) Individually competent but not as a group
c) History oriented rather than forecast oriented
d) Unwilling to accept responsibility (they "call engineering")
e) Unwilling to compensate for others' errors
f) Not creative
g) Conscientious and industrious

Manufacturing (describing eng.)

a) Error prone
b) Competent technically
c) Unaware of mfg. problems
d) Do not have a sense of urgency
e) More responsive to marketing than to us
f) Unified as a group and consistent

List 3. *How Do We Think They See Us?*

Engineering

a) Poor knowledge of their function
b) Engineers live in an ivory tower
c) Know technical end but not tuned to mfg.'s needs
d) Error prone
e) Don't feel pressure of end dates for product shipments
f) Intrude on other functions
g) Overly restrictive requirements and tolerances

Manufacturing

a) Constantly changing
b) Error prone
c) Not quality conscious
d) Reactors rather than planners
e) Crisis prone
f) Unwilling or unable to follow drawings
g) Inflexible

---

perception is of the problems and what emphases each places on which issues. Again, only questions of clarification can be raised; debate is yet to come. In fact, I explain at the beginning of phase 2 that a ground rule will be that we refrain from dicussing any solutions to problems until we as thoroughly as possible identify and clarify what the problems are. The engineering department had a list of sixteen problems and issues and, coincidentally, manufacturing had sixteen as well.

The fourth step is one of consolidating the two lists. At this point, I ask each group to select two of their members to meet together for the purpose of consolidating the two lists. I ask each of the two groups to select two of their members for this task because (1) I obviously cannot do the job as effectively as they since I am not as familiar with the issues; (2) both groups' perceptions should influence the final problem list if accuracy of problem identification is to be achieved (people act according to their *perceptions* of issues, not according to the reality of the issues); and (3) neither group holds a high degree of trust for the other at this point, and equal representation, as well as choice in selecting who will perform the work, contributes to an abatement of suspicion.

These four individuals (here, two from engineering and two from manufacturing) take the two lists (thirty-two statements in all), eliminate overlaps, and restate the problems in as clear a way as possible. This temporary group works in public view while the others either observe or take a break. The consolidating work, depending on the total list of statements, of course, takes about 30 minutes. In the case example, the final list contained twenty items (see Table 2 for a sampling of these).

TABLE 2

Sampling of Consolidated Problem List from the Engineering and Manufacturing Intergroup Problem-Solving Session

---

Engineering does not feel responsible for understanding and using procedures; a lack of concern for details

Organizational inconsistencies—engineering is highly vertical and manufacturing horizontal

Lack of participation by the mfg. group at engineering level on long-range planning

Both units tend to be overly bureaucratic and inflexible; not responsive to one another's requests

Drawings and specs full of errors

Instability of mfg. organization; lack of depth and lack of experience

Frequent product and process changes; lack of advance communication on changes

Lack of mutual confidence

Engineering does not understand mfg.'s problems with the union

---

PHASE 3: ORGANIZING FOR PROBLEM SOLVING (30 MINUTES)

There are two steps in the third phase. First, each person selects from the total list of problems (twenty in all) the ones he sees as the most important. In the case example, I told them to select the top six. I chose the number 6 based on how I wanted to organize the remainder of the session. I suggest that they select these top problems according to one or both of the following criteria: (1) those that affect you the most, or (2) those that you believe need the most immediate attention. After each person makes his selection, I ask him to rank these top problems from most important to least. These rankings from everyone are tallied and the top group of problems (again the number was 6 in the case example) is selected as a function of the sum of the tallies of the rankings and, of course, the group's judgment.

The second step in this brief phase is for each person to make a first and second choice of the problem he would like to work on. Following these choices as much as possible, problem-solving groups are formed with half of each problem-solving group's members being from one of the organizational groups and half from the other. In the case of the engineering and manufacturing example of twelve persons, three cross-groups were formed of four members, two from engineering and two from manufacturing. The rationale for this way of organizing is the same as the reasons I outlined for step four of phase 2. Different perceptions influence the "shape" of the problems and both perceptions must contribute to the solving of the problems. Otherwise, the problems will remain, and no commitment to action steps on both parties' part will have been achieved. Moreover, the degree of misunderstanding and suspicion is reduced when the two groups have a chance to interact with one another toward a superordinate goal (Sherif and Sherif, 1956).

PHASE 4: PROBLEM SOLVING (4 HOURS)

The fourth phase is begun with a brief lecture on steps in problem solving. The lecture includes an explanation of force field analysis and how to use it in problem solving. I prefer to build the problem-solving steps around the force field analysis because the technique is (1) easy to understand and use, (2) instrumental in establishing specific objectives for change, and

(3) based on Lewin's theory of change which also provides the general theoretical frame of reference for organization development (Hornstein, Bunker, Burke, Gindes, and Lewicki, 1971). The seven steps I use are similar to others in use by applied behavioral scientists. Briefly, the steps[3] are as follows:

1. Problem identification.
2. Documentation—illustrations and examples of the problem.
3. Analysis of causes and establishing the objective for change: the force field analysis.
4. Selection of appropriate restraining force(s) to reduce. This step is based on the force field analysis conducted in the previous step. Selecting restraining forces for reduction is, of course, based on Lewin's principle of change, that is, reduction of restraining forces, as opposed to increasing driving forces, and develops less tension in the system and therefore less resistance to change.
5. Brainstorm ideas for reducing the restraining force(s).
6. Test brainstorming list for feasibility and make selections.
7. Plan action steps.

PHASE 5:   PROBLEM-SOLVING PRESENTATION (3 HOURS)

After completing the seven steps of problem solving for one of the problems selected, each group prepares a presentation of its work for the other groups. After each group's presentation, the other groups critique the presenting group's work with feedback and suggestions. The rationale for this phase is to: (1) use each group as a *resource* to all others; (2) *practice* what they will probably need to do when they return to their job (often presentations need to be made back "at the shop" to peers, subordinates, or superiors); and (3) *enhance motivation* (shared ownership) since each group is presenting to its peers.

If time permits, each group can take a second problem, usually their second choice from the original list of most important problems, and begin the problem-solving process (phase 4) again.

As a conclusion to the meeting, I make a brief state-

ment. It is usually something like, "Often when groups complete a meeting such as this, they take the attitude of 'we've done our work; now we'll go back to the shop to wait and see.' If your attitude is similar to this, then you'll wait and see nothing. Action must be taken by you if any change in the organization is to occur."

This statement is followed by a brief questionnaire of four items:

1. What are the advantages of following the kind of format (or design) we used during these two days?
2. The disadvantages?
3. To what extent do you believe anything will be different as a result of these two days? [The question is answered via a seven-point scale ranging from 1, "no difference," to 7, "to a great extent."]
4. What is your degree of optimism/pessimism about the "state" of your organization at this point in time? [This question is also answered on a seven-point scale ranging from 1, "high pessimism," to 7, "high optimism."]

The reason for asking the first two questions is to give me some feedback about the adequacy and relevance of the design. The purpose of asking the remaining two questions is quite another matter. I believe it is important to determine at this point in the meeting the "feeling state" of the client. People behave according to what they think *and feel*. If, for example, individuals believe that what they have done will amount to naught (a feeling of pessimism), then the problem-solving process will have been nothing more than an exercise. When I discover that pessimism is relatively high I then probe to try to discover why and if we can do anything about it.

For purposes of this paper, typical responses to the first two questions are the most relevant. Some responses to question 1 have been:

> Breaks down some barriers, may reveal feelings not previously known or understood.
>
> Working on real problems gives sense of purpose.
>
> Gets things going: gives you an idea of path to follow.
>
> Sets up actions and responsibilities for actions.
>
> It had the advantage of saving time and preventing disorganized discussion.
>
> Bringing things out in the open.

---

[3] For a fuller explanation see Burke and Ellis (1969). The present list of seven steps has been modified slightly from this previous explanation.

Allows criticism without taking it personally.

Helped to get problems down to "bite size."

Helped to formulate most troublesome problems.

Gave me more insight into other group.

Opens the door to honest communication with each other.

Reduces tension between the groups.

Some responses to question 2 have been:

The structure may keep some of the real issues hidden.

Image exchange may have been unnecessary for groups who know each other as well as we already do.

Aspects of total problem involving other management levels and other functions can't be covered adequately.

Restricted some significant division problems from being presented.

Some issues when discovered in the middle of the session may not be covered fully enough because backtracking is difficult.

Could cause hurt feelings, widen gulfs.

Can think of no disadvantages.

Naturally, groups' responses to questions 3 and 4 vary according to organization. Generally, people believe (but not strongly) that there will be a difference; the average is usually around 5 on the seven-point scale. Responses to the fourth question vary even more than those to the third question. This fourth question taps individual differences with respect to feelings more than the other questions.

To close the meeting, I report back to the groups their answers to the four questions and we discuss the implications. The primary purpose of this final process, as stated earlier, is to face the reality of people's feelings and that, in the final analysis, the extent to which action will actually be taken rests largely on individual emotion of motivation.

Follow-Up

Follow-up to an intervention such as this one may take a variety of forms. A must for the OD consultant, especially the internal practitioner, is to consult in whatever way appropriate with the problem-solving groups formed during the off-site meeting. For example, in the case reported above, a "progress report"

meeting of the entire off-site group was planned for one day 6 weeks later. I met with the group to help design and facilitate the meeting for this day. I recommended that I return for this meeting to help with the design but also to insure that the meeting would indeed be held.

Another follow-up activity to an OD intervention is to plan yet another intervention. As the experienced OD practitioner knows, an OD intervention sets in motion new and different organizational dynamics that call for further diagnosis and possible intervention as a consequence. With respect to the case example described in this paper, two additional interventions were planned. One was a team-building event for the head of manufacturing and his staff, and another was an additional intergroup problem-solving session for next lower levels of management in engineering and manufacturing.

In short, follow-up activities are planned and conducted as a function of the basic processes of OD, which is a continuous process of planned social interventions based on sound diagnoses.

Summary

So that the reader will not be lost in the details, I shall summarize this intervention for managing intergroup conflict by providing an outline of what I have described.

Prior to the meeting   General meeting of both groups with the relevant person(s) in the organizational hierarchy to establish objectives, boundaries of authority, and so on.

Phase 1   Image exchange—The two groups share their perceptions of themselves and one another according to three questions: (1) How do we see ourselves and our organizational responsibilities? (2) How do we see the other group? (3) How do we think they see us?

Phase 2   Problem identification—State the problems individually, consolidate individual work in the organizational grouping, groups present their list to one another, and these two problem lists are consolidated into one working list.

Phase 3   Organizing for problem solving—Individuals rank order the problem list from most important problem to least, then make a first and second choice as to the problem they want to tackle, and, finally, "cross-function" problem-solving groups are formed.

Phase 4 Problem solving—The cross-function work groups follow the seven steps of problem solving.

Phase 5 Problem-solving presentation—Each problem-solving group presents its work in terms of the content for each of the steps and their action plans.

Finally, it is important to obtain some assessment as to what the group thought about the meeting and their feelings about the future.

Conclusions

With respect to the advantages or strengths of this design for intergroup intervention, the quotes above from previous clients speak for themselves. These responses are fairly typical ones. The limitations of this design, in my opinion, are primarily in the area of structure. The format is quite structured and paced. This structuring and pacing is deliberate on my part due to the brevity of time. What is sacrificed, however, is the opportunity for people to think inferentially as opposed to deductively; in other words, to freewheel and possibly discover issues and solutions that would not likely occur in this tight design. Moreover, people are not quite as free to express their emotions as would be the case in a less structured design. With follow-up support, however, there are certainly opportunities to think in these ways following the workshop.

With all things considered, especially time, I believe this design is the most productive one, at least for the kinds of groups with which I have consulted. I also believe that this design has broader applicability to groups other than the ones with which I have worked, such as Blacks and Whites, headquarters-field, federal government and state government, school and community, and many others. The design would undoubtedly require modification according to the kind of groups in conflict.

References

Beckhard, R. *Organization Development: Strategies and Models.* Reading Mass.: Addison-Wesley, 1969.

Blake, R. R., and Mouton, J. S. *Group Dynamics—Key to Decision Making.* Houston: Gulf Publishing Co., 1961.

Blake, R. R., and Mouton, J. S. The Intergroup Dynamics of Win-Lose Conflict and Problem-Solving Collaboration in Union-Management Relations. In M. Sherif (Ed.), *Intergroup Relations and Leadership.* New York: Wiley, 1962, pp. 94–140.

Blake, R. R., and Mouton, J. S. *Corporation Excellence Through Grid Organization Development.* Houston: Gulf Publishing Co., 1968.

Blake, R. R., Shepard, H. A., and Mouton, J. S. *Managing Intergroup Conflict in Industry.* Houston: Gulf Publishing Co., 1964.

Burke, W. W., and Ellis, B. R. Designing a work conference on change and problem solving. *Adult Leadership,* 1969, *17,* pp. 410–412; 435–437.

Burke, W. W., and Hornstein, H. A. (Eds.). *The Social Technology of Organization Development.* Washington, D.C.: NTL Learning Resources Corp., 1972.

Fordyce, J. K., and Weil, R. *Managing with People.* Reading, Mass.: Addison-Wesley, 1971.

Horstein, H. A., Bunker, B. B., Burke, W. W., Gindes, M., and Lewicki, R. J. *Social Intervention: A Behavioral Science Approach.* New York: Free Press, 1971.

Sherif, M. (Ed.). *Intergroup Relations and Leadership.* New York: Wiley, 1962.

Sherif, M., and Sherif, C. W. *An Outline of Social Psychology* (rev. ed.). New York: Harper, 1956.

Walton, R. E. *Interpersonal Peacemaking: Confrontations and Third Party Consultation.* Reading, Mass.: Addison-Wesley, 1969.

A Union-Management Cooperative Project
To Improve the Quality of Work Life

John A. Drexler, Jr. and Edward E. Lawler III

This case describes the beginning of a quality of work life project in which we are responsible for the measurement activities. In this role we have attended meetings, read correspondence and documents concerning the project, conducted interviews, and administered questionnaires. The project is part of a programmatic effort jointly sponsored by the National Quality of Work Center (NQWC), Washington, D.C., and by the Institute for Social Research (ISR) at the University of Michigan. Before presenting the case, we will describe briefly the overall Quality of Work Program.

The Quality of Work Program

Efforts to improve the quality of work life in the United States have rarely involved organized labor.[1] Recognizing the need for joint union-management projects, Ted Mills, then of the National Commission on Productivity, developed during 1971 and 1972 a plan for joint union-management quality of work life projects. This plan called for a number of projects in which employees would become actively involved in designing and implementing organization change. It also involved an independent evaluation of the effects of the projects on indicators of both quality of work life and organizational effectiveness. In 1973, two cooperative projects were started as part of this program.

In 1974, Mills left the government to establish NQWC as an affiliate of ISR. NQWC took on the role of developing sites for joint union-management projects and for managing the action parts of projects. ISR took on the role of measuring the effects such projects have on individuals as well as on organizational performance and effectiveness.[2] Since the founding of NQWC, six additional cooperative projects have been started, so that at the present time eight are operational.

The program's goal is to improve the quality of work life. It attempts to achieve this through carefully measured organizational change projects in highly visible organizations. Independent measurement is included in order to facilitate learning about how quality of work life projects can best be done in order to provide a creditable record of results that can be an aid in dissemination. The program uses an intervention strategy which is intended to produce organization-wide improvements in the quality of work life. In all projects, commitment is required of key officials at all levels of the managerial and union hierarchies. This is ensured by establishing joint union-management committees at the top organizational level as well as at lower levels. This same structure is used to assist in dif-

Reproduced by special permission from *The Journal of Applied Behavior Science,* "A Union-Management Cooperative Project to Improve the Quality of Work Life" by John A. Drexler, Jr. and Edward E. Lawler III, Volume 13, Number 3, pp. 373–387, copyright 1977, NTL Institute.

[1] Exceptions to this are described by Weinberg (1976).

[2] The attitudinal data collected for these projects are described in the Michigan Organizational Assessment Package (1975), and the measures of organizational effectiveness are described by Mirvis and Macy (1976) and Macy and Mirvis (1976). The overall research design is described by Lawler (1977).

fusing project information through management and union organizations. Finally, the approach values the use of independent consultants whose orientation is to assist clients in designing and implementing client-driven changes.

Individual projects are designed to be multiyear efforts. After company and union members decide to proceed with a project, they then select a consultant or consultant team 'to fill the role of primary change agent. The consultant is hired for an 18 month period. Since the consultants' presence is limited to 18 months, they are expected to develop diagnostic and problem-solving skills among organizational members. Within the general guidelines that workplace changes must be jointly acceptable, any organization development strategy is appropriate. The measurement activities last for 3 years so that the long-term effects of the project can be determined.

MULTITIER COMMITTEE STRUCTURE
FOR SUPPORT AND DISSEMINATION

Projects may either be requested by the management or union or initiated by NQWC. The first step in most projects is to establish a joint top-level union-management group, in this case called the core committee. This committee commits itself to organizationwide change and it provides sanction, support, and visible commitment from the highest levels. Both parties sign a letter of agreement stating that either can withdraw from the project on 24 hours' notice. Consensus decision making is typically used both at this level and at lower levels as the project unfolds.

The core committee decides where demonstration projects will be conducted and does the initial screening of the independent consultants. It also decides how many other committees will be formed and where in the organization they will be positioned. In large organizations there are often two or more additional committees, at least one at the regional or division level and another at the workplace level. This multitier structure is used to assure support for projects in local workplaces by both the union and company hierarchies and especially to facilitate later dissemination throughout the union and the company. In all cases, a workplace committee is established to guide what will happen there. It determines its own goals and directions and selects an indepen-

dent consultant to work with it. In the present case, the workplace committee is called the joint site committee.

The National Processing Case

This case[3] involves a large international company and a large international union. So far, change activities have been centered in five plants. Four of the five plants produce different products that are part of a common product line, and the fifth provides finishing and shipping functions. Each of the four plants is highly interdependent with the finishing and shipping plant. The four production lines are really two sets of interdependent plants, the second plant of each set adding further value to the product made by the first. All five plants are located at the same physical location in one of the company's fourteen regions. Excluding persons working in a centralized maintenance crew, there are 385 persons working in these five plants. Approximately 90 percent of them are white males.

The international union, its local at the plants, and the company's management have had an adversary relationship over many years. The local has served as the employee representative at these plants for 26 years, and the company and this union have experienced a high grievance rate. Nevertheless, many union members say that the union's relationship with this company is better than the one it has with other companies in the same industry as evidenced by the fact that there has not been a strike originating in these plants since the mid-1960s. Older union members seem to trust the company's top management. They say that many of their problems are created by middle managers and not by top managers. The company president began his career as a line worker along with many of the persons who still work in one of the selected plants.

ENTRY PROCESS—ACHIEVING JOINT APPROVAL

An entry process of more than 14 months was involved in starting this project. Much of the early entry time

---

[3] Because this is an ongoing project, fictitious names and titles are used to prevent identification of the site and individuals involved.

was spent providing information to top management groups at the corporate level and to top union officials at the union's regional level. It was only during the last couple of months that significant activity took place at the five plants.

The first contact between NQWC and National occurred in late 1974 during a conference attended by a company internal consultant and an NQWC staff member. The consultant talked with the NQWC staff member and communicated to his home office what he learned about NQWC. His superior, a vice president for internal development, expressed interest and arranged a meeting among his staff, NQWC, and two executive vice presidents. National's managers were impressed and additional meetings between NQWC and several other company executives took place.

Finally, a meeting was arranged between NQWC and National's president. The president seemed willing to proceed with the project and delegated authority for it to an executive vice president. The president expressed hope that the program would eventually lead to companywide efforts. This was a decisive meeting in two respects: it firmed up the company's commitment to start the project but failed to gain the president's direct involvement in the project's development. The president's lack of involvement was and continues to be a source of concern, since it may cause problems in spreading the project throughout the company.

While the program was described by NQWC as being directed toward increasing both quality of work life and productivity, there is some indication that the company's interest in it was due to their desire to increase productivity. Some company documents written at this time refer to the project as a productivity improvement program, and quality of work life issues are mentioned in the context of how they ultimately will improve productivity.

Soon after being assured of the company's interest, NQWC initiated meetings with the two largest unions in National Processing. The smaller of the two unions, wary of management-directed "job enrichment" efforts elsewhere, showed little interest and decided not to participate. In the larger union, the international president was contacted, and the Quality of Work Program was described to him. NQWC carefully explained that if the union was interested in a joint

quality of work life project, one could be set up with National or with some other company. The international president was noncommittal and expressed some specific concerns, including how the project might affect the traditional adversary relationship between the company and the union. He also asked whether the project might result in a loss of jobs through organizational restructuring. NQWC explained that since the project would be jointly owned, no such change could occur without union sanction.

NQWC suggested that union officials independently contact the company and determine how committed it was to the project and how much it was using the project for purposes of increasing productivity.[4] The international president mentioned that contract negotiations with National were currently under way and that negotiations would have to be completed before the union could commit much time to this project.

In later discussions with NQWC, the company's vice president for internal development identified a regional union president who would turn out to be a key in establishing a project at National. The vice president said that the union regional president believed that NQWC had been involved in a similar project for another company in the same industry. The project was believed to have hurt the union; consequently, some union officials had doubts about NQWC's credibility. The NQWC representative contacted the regional union president and assured him that NQWC projects are not oriented exclusively toward management goals. Apparently convinced that NQWC could be trusted, the union regional president said that the union's international president told him he could proceed. The regional president, describing himself as "bold and eager for change," indicated his own willingness to proceed, noting, however, that he would have to obtain an endorsement from his executive committee. He suggested that NQWC wait several months until the contract negotiations were over before proceeding. NQWC agreed and said that the next

---

[4] NQWC views productivity increase motives as proper for a company and encourages companies to be open about it. Unions are told that, because projects are jointly controlled efforts, they need not fear a company's productivity motives.

step would be a meeting between National executives and him so that a joint decision could be made.

Once the contract negotiations were over, the union regional president had a meeting with his executive committee and introduced the notion of starting a quality of work project in one of the National locals. In order to help answer the questions that it thought would come up at this meeting, NQWC sent a union member from one of its other ongoing projects to the meeting. Questions were asked about the activities included as in projects, the effects the project would have on the contractual and adversary relationship with National, and whether participants could withdraw from the program if they wished. The presence of the representative from the other project was decisive in dealing with these questions. He provided examples of what could be done and reduced fears about possible negative effects on the contractual and adversary relationship. The meeting ended with a unanimous favorable vote and solidified regional union involvement in the project. At this point union enthusiasm was strong; a number of locals wanted to be chosen as the first project site.

The regional union president next accompanied an NQWC staff member to Europe to learn about the rising participative activity occurring there. The president toured various European plants and was particularly enthusiastic about quality of work projects after talking to some European practitioners.

In summary, NQWC spent much time and effort during the 14 month entry period bringing the project to a point where it had joint approval. It was achieved through many hours in meetings, soliciting the support of key officials from both parties. Usually, the parties expressed keen interest in a project but the interest was accompanied by a healthy caution. The company appeared to hope for productivity increases, and this was important in gaining its approval. The situation was more problematic on the union side. The union was concerned that its own power would be weakened and needed a number of assurances that it would not be harmed. It also needed education and exposure to an array of possible project activities before it was willing to agree to a project.

CORE COMMITTEE START-UP

Early in 1976, the top union officials and executive company officers joined together for the first joint Core Committee meeting. At this joint meeting, NQWC again reviewed the purpose and form of quality of work projects, and ISR described the kinds of measurement activities that would occur. Both parties expressed concerns about the measurement. Company representatives questioned why their own assessment staff could not perform the same functions. They were told that having independent assessors adds credibility to the project, and that using in-house skills might reduce the union's trust of the ongoing activities. The union was concerned about industrial engineers and whether time-and-motion studies would be part of the measurement package. The union was assured that this would not happen.

Another issue was the nature and manner of funding of the assessment work. It was decided that the money to support the assessment work was to be provided through the company's affiliated philanthropic foundation, while the cost of consultants would be paid for by the company through a no-strings-attached grant to NQWC. This financial structure ensured that third parties would control the distribution and allocation of funds for both the research and measurement.

The issue of membership on the Core Committee was also discussed. The company proposed that there be three management members: the executive vice president for operations, the executive vice president for administration, and the vice president for internal development. The union proposed their regional president and two regional vice presidents. It was also decided that the company vice president for internal development would act as recording secretary and project coordinator. The union regional president assumed the role of the committee's first chairperson, and it was agreed that an NQWC representative would continue to meet with the Core Committee in order to help the committee function effectively.

The next issue dealt with at the meeting was the selection of the particular workplace for the first demonstration project. Since NQWC previously had discussions about this with both the company and the union, this was a relatively short discussion. NQWC emphasized the need to avoid imposing the project on rank-and-file union members as well as on supervisory personnel. The union identified several acceptable locations, as did the management. A complex of plants in Fallsteppe, located in National's Hilltop Region, was acceptable to both. Since the union had already obtained a favorable reaction from its local leaders, the only thing needed was for the company to inform its local managers about the nature and scope of the project and to determine their interest. The company's executive vice president for administration expressed a strong preference that he personally introduce the project to the Hilltop Region managers who were responsible for the Fallsteppe location.

WORKPLACE START-UP

Approximately 6 weeks after the first Core Committee meeting, NQWC went to Fallsteppe for several weeks of meetings and activity that was decisive in establishing the workplace where the program would begin. First they met with the vice president for Hilltop Region, the personnel manager, and the manager of the Fallsteppe works. The Hilltop vice president was concerned about the commitment level of the company's top management. He described other development projects in which initially there was much encouragement from top management, but in which, after a short period of time, top management lost interest, leaving Hilltop with a project but little support. NQWC gave specific examples illustrating National's commitment and noted that the executive vice president planned to come to Fallsteppe the following week to brief the region's executive committee.

NQWC also mentioned that the local union president had already expressed some preference for beginning in a particular plant, Works #1. The Hilltop vice president explained that Works #1 would not be suitable because it was a money loser, and he expressed concern that the union might already be locked into the decision. NQWC reminded the vice president that selection decisions must be made by a joint region-level committee.

The same day NQWC met at the local union hall with several union officials to answer their questions. The union's regional president attended, as did the local president, two local vice presidents, and shop stewards from Works #1. The union officials were favorable to the idea of a project, and the first regional committee meeting was scheduled for the following day so that a specific workplace could be selected. This promised to be a crucial meeting since the union and

management had definite—but different—preferences about a site.

The next day at the first regional committee meeting the local union president described how he came to learn about the project and noted that the project had been received favorably by the union's local leadership. The company's regional vice president said that he saw the project as an opportunity to try a different approach for solving the problems of managing and working in an organization. Discussion progressed to the workplace selection. The company's regional vice president outlined the criteria suggested by NQWC and accepted by him: (1) a sufficient number of affected people to maximize the opportunity for change; (2) sufficient supervision levels to allow restriction or expansion of supervisory functions; (3) discrete rather than continuous-process operations to make it more feasible to experiment with job design; and (4) the presence of jobs which would allow workers to develop some discretion. He thought that most of the plants in Fallsteppe met these criteria.

One union representative asked whether the five plants that produced similar products could be involved. The company's regional vice president expressed concern about starting with too many plants and was dismayed that the union's position appeared to be firm. He noted that Works #1 was doing poorly in the market, and consequently it would not be a useful place to determine whether increased effectiveness and productivity would result. NQWC suggested having a single workplace committee with representatives from several plants and noted that subcommittees could be appointed to address problems of specific plants. The company vice president offered a compromise solution. He suggested that the project could start in Works #1 if the union agreed to expand the project to Works #2, a more profitable plant, soon after the project started. This was agreed to on the condition that the union first obtain approval from its members in Works #2.

Several days later NQWC and the local union president met with union officials from Works #2. The meeting lasted about 2 hours, and NQWC explained how the project would affect collective bargaining, the contract, grievance procedures, and seniority issues. Other issues related to what rank-and-file workers have to gain from the project and whether NQWC works with nonunion companies. NQWC used many examples from other projects to illustrate the kinds of activities that can occur during these projects. These union representatives decided that the project was worthwhile, and one of the officials spent much of his own time informing other rank-and-file workers about the project.

Two weeks later NQWC held meetings with the superintendents of Works #2 to inform them of the nature of the project. Foremen from all shifts attended this meeting and asked the same kinds of general questions asked elsewhere. They wanted to know what hourly workers were to get out of the project if the company gets increased production, how much nit-picking occurs at committee meetings, how the project coordinates people who have to interface with each other, and if the project would result in a loss of their authority or power. They also wondered whether they could really say that they did not want to participate.

JOINT SITE COMMITTEE

In late spring, 1976, after the initial visit by NQWC to Fallsteppe, the first meeting of the workplace committee was held. It was decided to call it the joint site committee. To ensure upper-level support of project activities and to provide linkages between committees, three union officials and two plant superintendents were made members of both the regional committee and the joint site committee. Union membership on the joint site committee was determined by different methods in each plant. A crew-type meeting was held in one plant, and another plant had a meeting at the union hall to elect its representatives. Persons were elected to or self-selected for committee membership. While every rank-and-file member was not involved in the selection process, the union members felt that the joint site committee was representative of a cross-section of work areas and shifts. Management personnel who expressed interest were appointed to the committee. At the first joint site committee meeting, there was further questioning of adequate representation, and additional foremen and hourly workers were appointed to the committee. One joint site committee member noticed that no women were present at the meeting, and committee members went out to recruit several women hourly workers. Although the decision made at the regional committee was to involve two plants, five plants were represented at the first joint site commit-

tee meeting. Most of the time at the first meeting was spent describing the project to committee members.

The second joint site committee meeting was scheduled for the following week. At this meeting the project and its measurement component were again described but there appeared to be little real understanding of it. At both meetings, concerns were expressed about the possible impact of the project on the traditional adversary relationship between management and labor and also about how individuals from nondaylight shifts could become involved in the project. It was mentioned that individuals who came in during their off shift, as well as those who had to come early or stay late, would be reimbursed for their time at their regular rates. The company and the union agreed to share the costs of this additional time. This decision extended the union's commitment to the project to a financial one. Plans were also made for the joint site committee to select the independent consultant team later in the week.

In summary, the start-up process was one that provided information to possible project participants about the nature and scope of quality of work life projects, that solicited commitment to the project by both management and union, that began a participative decision-making process through the use of consensus, and that ensured higher-level support and further dissemination by establishing a multitier committee structure with overlapping membership.

CONSULTANT SELECTION

The process for consultant selection was structured by NQWC so that the core and regional committees would screen candidates and the joint site committee would make the final selection. NQWC's role was first to screen potential applicants for the consultant job and then, since most members of these committees had little experience with consultants, to spend time briefing each committee on how to assess consultants. NQWC recommended the following criteria for consultant selection: (1) a person or team having some experience with labor and management relations; (2) a person or team providing a great deal of on-site presence; (3) the lead consultant being the person with the most on-site presence; (4) persons who could walk and talk on the shop floor; (5) a person or team able to explain adequately its approach and describe its skills; and (6) a team that valued using workplace expertise for designing change rather than one wanting to impose its own ideas on the client. A number of consulting groups applied to NQWC. Those not expressing a client-directed approach were screened out by NQWC immediately.

Four qualified consultant teams were recommended to and interviewed by the core committee. One was rejected outright. The core committee decided that it could live with the others if certain changes were made. (With one consultant team, for example, the academic member had to be removed.) When the regional committee met with three consultant teams, one was rejected because of its Eastern-establishment appearance and manner. Thus, the joint site committee had only two consultant teams left to interview. This seemed like a lack of choice to them, and they wanted to know how much control the core and regional committees would impose at later points in the project. NQWC explained why it was important for the core and regional committees to be comfortable with whatever consultant was chosen, as well as the importance of maintaining communication linkages with all committees.

The joint site committee had difficulty in deciding between the two remaining consultant teams because it liked both teams. It finally chose the one team that seemed best able to communicate with and relate to hourly workers. The team consisted of three white male consultants who work for a national consulting firm. The leader of the team is known for his previous work as a personnel manager and for his use of survey feedback methods, Scanlon plans, and team building. His approach to consulting can best be described as pragmatic and eclectic; he uses no one technique but, rather, a diagnostic approach, and he tries to build a consensus around changes.

Several biases were apparent in the core and regional committee interviews. The committees were antiacademic, antiyouth, and anti-Eastern establishment. Most members thought that people from these backgrounds would not be able to walk and talk on the shop floor (one consultant was asked whether he would wear his three-piece suit around the plant). Management members of the company also expressed concern about the ability of consultant groups to deal with organized labor. Management wanted to ensure that the consultant team would not be perceived as working solely for management. All three committees

expressed concern about whether the measurement and assessment program would interfere with the consultant's activities. Some consultants articulated reservations about their ability to be assessed by independent observers who did not understand their approach and techniques; other consultants welcomed the opportunity to work with the independent assessment team.

In summary, the consultant selection was a sensitive process. It reinforced the requirement for key person support by having the core and regional committees screen potential consultants first, but this resulted in some concern among joint site committee members about possible upper-level interference. The interviewing sessions were difficult for the consultant because committee members did not hesitate to ask hard questions. Finally, the critical characteristic for selection appeared to be the consultants' ability to relate to the clients at all hierarchical levels.

CONSULTANT ACTIVITIES

Once the consultant team was selected, it immediately began work. Through summer and fall, 1976, the lead consultant spent 3 or more days a week diagnosing the organization, meeting with workers, making the project visible, and building a team within the committee structures. In addition, an attitude survey was conducted as part of the independent measurement program. The results of this survey were fed back by the consultant and meetings were held to discuss them. A number of problems were identified in the areas of job design, training, safety, and communication; and some solutions have been implemented recently. Most of the activity to date has taken place in Works #1 and #2, with representatives from the other three plants observing the process.

Overall, through the end of 1976, progress on this project has been slow for three reasons. The first has to do with the structure of the joint site committee. Five plants were involved in the consultant selection process, and the joint site committee contains representatives from all five plants. This situation has had the effect of building up expectations that all five plants would be involved in the project. In fact, at a later regional committee meeting, the regional vice president was surprised to learn that there were persons from five plants actively involved. He had originally wanted only two plants and expressed dismay that the project had grown so large without his knowing about it.

A second reason is that the joint site committee has become bogged down in procedural issues. This committee wants to control the activities of the subcommittees that have been formed to deal with individual plants. This is not surprising since, during its start-up, this committee was told that it would have control over the project once it began. In addition, some union leaders have two reasons for wanting all problem solving done by the joint site committee. First, the union sees one plant as very independent and fears that this plant may get into contractual issues without regard for approval from other levels of union hierarchy. Second, the union leaders are worried that some people will miss out if specific activities start in only one plant. They feel that all can learn about the process only by including the entire joint site committee in it.

A third reason is that while joint site committee members have some knowledge of the project, rank-and-file workers through the plants have very little. To improve this situation, the joint site committee attempted to place bulletin boards in strategic places in the plants, but there was little follow-up. Lack of knowledge about the project was evident when the attitudinal survey was administered about 4 months after the joint site committee was formed. Few persons seemed aware of the project and the nature of its deliberations. This is not too surprising since the logistics problems in this site are substantial. The five plants involved cover a large land area, multiple shifts are involved, and many production jobs involve the operation of complex, noisy machines. The consultant team responded by making a concerted effort to inform persons throughout the plants about the nature of the project and by involving them in it through the use of the subcommittees.

The lead consultant has made some specific recommendations about how the committee structure could be changed. He has suggested that the roles of the regional and site committees are overlapping and has proposed that the site committee be disbanded and that its functions be assumed by the regional committee. In his model, the regional committee would serve in an advisory capacity for the project and would have as members managers and union officials ex officio. Each plant would have a committee that would deal

with its problems on an ongoing basis and would be more representative of the plant as a whole.

Resistance to the proposal was strong because the joint site committee union members were afraid that the plants might make decisions that would weaken the union or the contract. For example, people in one of the sites see the nature of the contract as constraining their efforts and would now like to suspend some of the contract provisions temporarily. This has reinforced the position of the stronger union members of the joint site committee that their committee should continue to serve as watchdog over lower-level committees. As a result, a compromise solution was accepted. Under it, the regional committee and joint site committee will continue to exist, and actions by subcommittees from each plant will have to be accepted by the joint site committee.

It seems apparent at this point that if significant change is going to take place in these five plants, something has to be done to free up the plants. Making this happen is the major challenge faced by the consultant team. If it does happen, there is a good chance that the changes will be disseminated to other parts of the company since the multitier structure is in place. The multitier approach was designed to insure that there would be support from all levels of management and the union for dissemination. These committees are continuing to meet and they already have established a new basis for communication between the union and management. Interestingly, NQWC has played a continuing role in the functioning of the core committee. The committee decided soon after the consultant was selected to continue to use NQWC as its consultant. Ultimately, the continued existence of the multitier structure depends on a success at Fallsteppe. It may well be 2 years or more before it can be known whether that success will be realized.

Implications for Theory and Practice

This is one of the most complex union-management cooperative projects that the NQWC/ISR program has undertaken and one of the most complex in the literature. It represents an effort to change the quality of work life in one of the largest companies in the United States, and it involves a major international union representing over 20,000 of the employees who work for the company. Thus, the potential for learning from it about large system change and union-management cooperation are appreciable. So far the major lessons relate primarily to *how such projects can be started*. Several years from now we should be in a position to talk about issues of workplace change.

In most union-management situations there are some pressures that favor the kind of project that was started in National Processing. However, the forces against it usually are stronger. The role of NQWC in this project was to reduce the negative forces so that a quality of work project could take place. Let us identify briefly the forces that were at work in the system and note how the NQWC model affected them.

REDUCING NEGATIVE FORCES

Both the top union and management officials were tired of the traditional adversary model because of its unproductive aspects. They both felt that work could be improved in many ways that would benefit both the union and management. However, these forces were more than offset by the forces favoring the traditional relationship. These include the different goals of the union and management, the lack of any model of or experience with successful cooperative problem solving, the desire of both parties to maintain a contract, the risk to both the union officials and company management in changing a relationship which brought them to power, and the time and cost required to change. NQWC reduced the forces against a quality of work project through a number of specific actions: it stressed that projects do not bring about the demise of collective bargaining, rather that they exist solely as an auxiliary to it; it specified common goals; it suggested a joint committee structure with consensus decision making; it suggested a letter of agreement with provisions for easy escape and joint ownership; and it introduced both the union and management to successful projects elsewhere. The net effect of all these activities was to make a project, directed at improving quality of working life, less threatening, more understandable, and more practical.

Role of third party. Would there have been a project in National if a third party like NQWC had not been active? It does not seem likely. National had attempted one many years earlier that was not successful. At the beginning of the present project, NQWC intervened by providing most of the communication and energy needed to get it started. Our conclusion is that a third party, at least in this instance, was essential for project start-up.

HOW AND WHERE TO FORM TIERS

The present case also illustrates some of the crucial structural issues that arise in large system change. The multitier structure that NQWC established has potential advantages in terms of dissemination and support, but it also may slow the initial progress at a site. It requires more approval and the formation and education of more committees than would a strategy that simply involved changes in a single plant. It also creates some difficult strategic problems: For example, how many committees should be formed and for how large a part of the organization should a committee be responsible? In the present case, committees were initially formed at three levels. It now appears that one of these committees (the joint site committee) may have been inappropriate and that change would have occurred more rapidly if a number of site committees had been formed. It is possible that with better analysis this could have been determined in advance. However, there is little theory or practice to guide this kind of entry process. Hopefully, out of this and similar projects, data will emerge on the efficacy of the multitier model and on how and where to form tiers. At this point, it can only be concluded that the model has proved to be a successful vehicle for starting such projects.

References

Lawler, E. E., III. Adaptive experiments: An approach to organizational behavior research. *The Academy of Management Review*, 1977, 2(4), pp. 576–585.

Macy, B. A., and Mirvis, P. H. A methodology for assessment of quality of work life and organizational effectiveness in behavioral-economic terms. *Administrative Science Quarterly*, 1976, *21*, pp. 212–226.

Michigan Organizational Assessment Package: Progress Report II. Ann Arbor: Institute for Social Research, The University of Michigan, August 1975.

Mirvis, P. H., and Macy, B. A. Human resource accounting: A measurement perspective. *The Academy of Management Review*, 1976, *1* (2), pp. 74–83.

Weinberg, E. Labor-management cooperation: A report on recent initiatives. *Monthly Labor Review*, April 1976, pp. 13–22.

Optimizing Team-Building Efforts

Richard Beckhard

The Problem of Energy

A tremendous amount of human energy in organizations is expended by participation in groups. In addition to the time spent in meetings exchanging necessary operating information, most management groups and work teams also spend a significant amount of time on issues such as future planning or improvement planning.

In the truly effective organization, most of the energy of the work force is available for doing and improving the work of the organization, and a minimum amount of energy is needed to maintain the human organization.

In trying to achieve this state, organizations devote considerable effort to improving the effectiveness of work teams. For example, such efforts form one of the major foundations in the Blake and Mouton Grid Organization Development Program. The programs of laboratory training are designed to help people improve the effectiveness of their collaborative work in group settings. Many team-building efforts conducted by internal and external organization development consultants are aimed at improving the effectiveness and working relationships of work groups.

The Purpose of Team Building

In recent years I have observed a number of team-development efforts and have lately come to the realization that there may be a discrepancy in priorities between those people in charge of teams

engaging in such efforts and those people who are facilitating them. Team leaders often consider their objectives to be improving work, setting priorities, or solving problems. Consultants, trainers, and helpers often see the prime purpose of the effort to be improving the workings of the group and/or the relationships of its members.

To help understand this more fully, I have developed a classification, in order of importance, of the reasons why teams or groups meet other than for the sharing of information. These are:

To set goals and/or priorities.
To analyze or allocate the way work is performed.
To examine the way a group is working; its processes, such as norms, decision making, communications.
To examine relationships among the people doing the work.

These purposes are usually operating in any team-development effort, but unless one purpose is defined as the primary purpose, there tends to be considerable misuse of energy. People then operate from their own hierarchy of purposes and, predictably, these are not always the same for all members.

In looking at the disenchantment of some managers and leaders regarding the amount of time spent on team-improvement activities in their organizations, I have noted that organization development consultants and trainers frequently are perceived by clients or team leaders as having a "universal" rank-order of the four purposes as follows:

The relationships among people
The way the group works together
The work
The goals and priorities

This perception is too often correct because the "orientation" of the organizational development consultant—his value system and much of his competence—probably is built around helping people work together in groups and is probably less related to the specific goal of an organization. However, if the perception is there on the part of the team leader, there probably will be a discrepancy between his preferred rank-ordering of priorities and his perceptions regarding preferences of the consultant.

It has also become clear that team leaders often tend to be inexplicit about their own rank-ordering. Therefore, the rank-ordering of the consultant may well be the controlling factor in a team-development effort. This is reinforced by the client's perception that the OD specialist is the expert. In such cases, the team leader tends to lean on the consultant for expert guidance and, in some cases, to give up his own responsibility for the effort.

Some Conditions for Effective Team Building

From the observations, I have developed a set of guidelines for team development:

The primary goal of a team development meeting must be explicit and well articulated.

This primary goal must be *owned* by the leader of the group and understood (hopefully, agreed to) by the work group members.

The leader's goal should be the condition within which third parties (consultants) work (i.e., the primary purpose is defined by the leader who sets the agenda and activities of the meeting).

If the consultant is working with a team, he should help the leader be explicit in defining and sharing the primary purpose.

The four goal categories probably will be dealt with in a particular activity but only as appropriate in relation to a primary purpose.

A Model for Team-Building Activities

The following model examines for each of the four primary purposes . . . four dimensions which would be considered:

Leader behavior
Member behavior

Outcomes
Third-party or consultant behavior

I will describe each of these dimensions in relation to each of the primary purposes and follow the description with a case illustration.

PRIMARY PURPOSE—SETTING GOALS OR PRIORITIES

Leader Behavior Issues

Are the work goals given (the leader's), or are they to be decided by the group?

Are the priorities a given or are they to be decided by the group?

How much freedom does the leader wish others to have in determining the agenda?

To what organization conditions, other goals, policies, etc., must these goals or priorities be related?

What preparation is necessary to optimize use of the resources of the members at the activity?

What are the leader's specific hoped-for outcomes for the meeting?

Member Behavior Issues

What behavior around the task is expected from members: Understanding? Decision making? Agreement to implement? Action plans?

What data are needed during the meeting, i.e., effects of alternative goals or priorities on members' work and the work of suborganizations?

Outcomes Possible

What is required from the meeting: A new statement of goals or priorities? Agreement to develop one?

What action plans and responsibilities for carrying out meeting outputs should be developed?

How will assignments of responsibilities be made?

What kind of feedback and checkpoints are or should be available?

Third-Party Behavior Issues. Some of the "process" questions that might be asked by a facilitator concern:

Clarity of the goal, i.e., agreement on priorities.
To what degree people are understanding each other.
Clarity of the ownership of the goals.
Awareness of consequences.
Commitment to action.

CASE

In a large consumer organization there were a number of departments with computer and information systems capabilities. These departments were combined into a new Management Methods Department, which was to provide leadership in applying the various technologies to requirements of the organization. It also was to provide support and assistance to a variety of users with respect to methods and hardware. A third mission was to provide an educational effort to increase the internal market of users.

The membership of the management team of this group comprised a variety of bases—some had worked together before, others had not. Each member had headed a specialty or specialists' group and had had his own "technological empire." The management group was asked to combine all these resources and develop a new kind of service organization.

The leader of the group wanted to introduce some new technologies which he knew would provide significant savings to some parts of the organization. He also was concerned with centralizing some hardware installations; with communicating the new department's capabilities and services to the rest of the organization; with upgrading both the amount and the quality of services provided; with developing some major new applications; and with creating a new image of helpfulness to the line managements of the business.

Having defined the primary purpose of the meeting as setting goal and mission priorities, the leader now needed to clarify his expectations around the first issue—were the priorities given or to be decided by the group? It became clear, by discussion, that the leader had preferences, but he really wanted consensus from this group on priorities and goals. He felt that all of his goals were interdependent; thus, it did not matter which one was worked first. Therefore, his first effort at the meeting was to convince the members that relative to their role expectations, he expected that this group would, as a group, determine the priorities of the various goals, set programs, and provide the resource management for carrying out the programs necessary to achieve the goals. The leader wanted a great deal of freedom to be shared among subordinates.

In the course of a couple of meetings, it became clear from discussions that there was also a need for exploration of the way the work was going to be done. Issues arose about how the group would handle decisions around priorities, how the information should flow between sections, and how the group norms regarding openness or leveling would be decided.

Some people were unclear about the leader's position on these issues but when his attitudes were shared, their confusion ended. He wanted all to have freedom to challenge goals and priorities.

Relationship problems surfaced which, after discussion, turned out to be goal problems. For example, one person in the group had held a job now held by another person in the group. Because they had different work priorities for that subsection, there was concern about the relationship between them. Discussion quickly cleared this up.

By treating the "how we work" and "relationship" questions as agenda matters to be dealt with as they got in the way of the goal-setting issues, the group was able to move quite rapidly toward actual setting of goals and priorities and to make action plans for following up.

PRIMARY PURPOSE—ANALYZING AND
ASSIGNING WORK

Leader Behavior Issues

Defining areas of work to be studied
Defining the current situation, i.e., where work and responsibility are located
Defining boundaries of his willingness to change
Defining roles he wants others to take in the meeting, i.e., suggestions, decisions, actions

Member Behavior Issues

An understanding of the areas of work to be allocated, the alternative possibilities, and the parameters of freedom to relocate work
Clear role expectations: What behavior is expected of them in the decision making?
Awareness of implications and costs of changing work
Payout for subordinates or members of changing allocations of work

Outcomes Possible

New work distribution

An action plan for communicating changes to others

Answers on costs, effects on compensation and rewards, effects on roles, titles, etc.

Action plan for follow-up evaluation of the changes

Third-Party Behavior Issues

Providing a method for working the issues, e.g., providing methods of analyzing work

Helping to clarify work boundaries

Getting the group to face action implications and to plan

Helping people understand each other

Raising issues of openness of communication within the group

CASE

The top management of a division of a large chemical organization is managed by a board composed of a chairman, two deputy chairmen, and ten members of the management board. The group functions as an executive board. Each member of the team except the chairman and deputy chairmen have functional responsibilities, such as manufacturing, engineering, and personnel. They also are responsible at the division level for some business area, e.g., serving as chairman of a wholly owned subsidiary.

Officially, the power of decisions rests centrally with the chairman. The remainder of the group had been perceived by its members as being mostly advisory. Actual functioning of the upper management of the organization was somewhat unclear. There were questions about the responsibilities of management board members acting in their functional capacities as opposed to their responsibilities as board members. There was considerable dissatisfaction with this ambiguity.

The chairman suggested having a team meeting to analyze realistically the tasks that needed to be performed by the board as a board; the tasks that were not getting performed; and the possibilities of delegating some tasks below board level to operating managers.

The method used was a review of the board agendas for the previous 6 months and an analysis of these agendas. This analysis provided three lists:

Things that the group did which absolutely must be done by them as a group

Work that was not being done that should be done by this group, e.g., long-range planning

Work that was being done by this group that could be done as well or almost as well by the same members operating in other roles or by other people

The analysis showed that between 25 and 30 percent of the work being done by this group could be done by others. There was a roughly similar amount of work that needed to be done that was not getting done.

The group examined its own attitudes and commitment toward turning over some major areas of work to other people. It explored the training, development, and changes of procedure that would be required for the transfer of work. It identified what this would mean in terms of rewards (who would be held accountable and responsible). The discussion also identified areas of personal development that the board or executive committee members needed in order to take on some of the work that they were not doing. It also provided some clarification of what the chairman expected of them. This discussion produced the need for further examination of some of the relationships between roles, particularly the roles between the deputy chairmen and the junior board members.

Outputs involved (1) a minor structural reorganization, (2) the delegation of a considerable amount of work, with full responsibility and accountability for its disposition, to the operating manager level, (3) the organization of a planning group within the board, and (4) a change of many of the practices of their board meetings.

PRIMARY PURPOSE—HOW THE GROUP WORKS

Leader Behavior Issues

Dissatisfaction with the status quo as a reason for wanting to change

Willingness to look at all data, styles, attitudes, titles, rewards, and processes

Willingness to be influenced

Self-realization by the leader that he is probably part of the relevant data

Methods for working the problem

Member Behavior Issues

The need for clear ground rules on voting; how much openness is allowed and the punishments or consequences of deviant behavior

The need to know what the boss's feelings are regarding present practices and possible changes

The need for a set of parameters of possibilities for change

The need for some readiness to work the problems

Outcomes Possible

Some new norms are possible.

Action plans regarding change procedures can emerge.

Some changed ownership in the management of certain processes, such as agenda planning, structure, decision making, and leadership, may result.

Third-Party Behavior Issues

Process interventions around issues are relevant, such as communication, decision making, norms, and leadership.

[The consultant] can provide methods for working the problems.

[The consultant] can help work issues such as those on listening, problem solving, role distortion, and projection.

CASE

In a large diversified organization, the personnel function had previously been managed by a director and several department heads, each of whom heads a function, such as employment, compensation, salary administration, benefits, training and development, industrial relations, and employee relations.

The heads of these groups were specialists. Their departments functioned as relatively independent staffs handling the particular function for which they were responsible. For general information-sharing—updating company policies and priorities and providing liaison with top management—there were "cabinet" meetings of the heads of departments with the director. However, there was no shared responsibility for or commitment to total management of the personnel function by the heads of the specific functions.

A new director moved in who believed that the personnel organization should be reorganized and redirected to focus around organization issues and human resources management issues rather than along the strict functional lines previously followed. For example, relations with employees involved not only the head of industrial relations but also the training and development people and the employment people. He also wanted to develop a management team in the personnel function that could locate the priority issues in the organization, and mobilize the total resources of the personnel staff and others in the organization to manage these priorities.

In his early weeks of the organization, he communicated these desires and priorities and received responses ranging from outright resistance to lip service approval. In most cases, people responded in a subordinate way to what they perceived to be commands.

The director really wanted to change the mode of working. He convened a meeting with the specific purpose of "taking a look at how we're working together"—what processes and procedures are used, and what processes, procedures, and systems will be necessary to move toward the kind of management of human resources that he required and desired. At the meeting, his statement of wishes immediately led to a discussion of how these decisions had been made, and how they were now being made by him, and how people hoped they would be made.

A second issue developed around communication and influence. A third issue was the director's leadership style and the differences between his style and that of the previous leadership. A fourth issue was what were the rewards and punishments for acting one way or another in this new situation.

As the group worked, it was able to examine thoroughly the various processes, procedures, roles, norms, etc., within which they worked, and to relate these to the defined goal of a coordinated management of the human resources function. This was a case where the goal was clearly to work on *how we work,* and specific plans for changing the way work was done in the organization became the case material and the validating point for the work on the primary purpose of the meeting.

PRIMARY PURPOSE—RELATIONSHIPS AMONG GROUP MEMBERS

Leader Behavior Issues

An awareness of the interpersonal issues in the group

A willingness to expose his own attitudes and biases

A willingness to be nonpunitive

Some assurance that group members see this activity as relevant

A willingness to change or to be influenced

Member Behavior Issues

Enough personal security to take some risks

A knowledge and belief that the leader has real interests in the process

Some confidence in the process and / or the third party

Some feelings of relevance of the activity

Some feelings of potency

Some willingness to expose feelings

Outcomes Possible

Increased understanding and acceptance of each other

Better listening

Some new norms, e.g., leveling, more information-based decisions

More feelings of ownership

More willingness to take risks

More willingness to confront conflict and work to resolve it

Third-Party Behavior Issues.   Interventions in this mode are most helpful around process issues.

Intervention process, i.e., communications, decision making

Protection of parameters of openness, confrontation, and so on

Modeling behavior, e.g., feedback

Objectivity as applied to the group's work

Nonjudgmental feedback

Resolution of interpersonal difficulties

CASE

A management group in a division of an organization had developed norms of openness, problem solving, and goal direction. The organization climate was quite open and free. The division was a high technology group with a number of extremely capable scientists whose whole background was entrepreneurial and professional. The management group was committed intellectually to building a participative, democratic organization. Obstacles toward achievement of this generally shared goal and value system were: (1) their own personal styles, and (2) the interaction among them. The group was able to be very open around technical problems, intergroup problems within the organization, and role problems. However, they were not able to deal with each other as people with different biases, interests, and styles. The norm of "nonconfronting" this kind of material was reinforced by the president, a brilliant executive, greatly admired by all the members of the team. He was a rational, sensible, analytically minded person who could keep the discussions rational and data-based. He managed, simultaneously, though inadvertently, to suppress much of the emotional data which were crucial and with which they needed to deal.

After a considerable amount of time working as a team—including outside developmental experiences by many individual members—a subgroup emerged which had a common goal of facing these relationship questions. It had enough potency to deal with both the president and colleagues. They suggested an extended meeting to have a thorough review of where they stood as *people* managing this business. The suggestion was accepted by all the members and the meeting was held.

At this meeting each individual received some feedback from all of his colleagues about his strengths and weaknesses as they perceived them, what bothered or pleased them about his behavior. Each individual could use this feedback any way he wished but there was no requirement for change. The feedback surfaced some historic issues that had been affecting the work of the group; for example, two people who had been competing throughout their careers maintained this competition in the group. They were perceived by all the others as sometimes robbing the group of their technical resource capability on the tasks because of their interpersonal relationship. It was agreed that the group would try to draw this to their attention whenever it arose in the future.

The feedback to the president by the team was accepted and generally understood by him. He acted on it to some degree; however, the main benefit of this feedback was that it freed the group to produce this kind of information in the future as needed. This became a norm of the group and was perhaps the single most significant result.

Here is a case in which interpersonal relationships of a group of responsible adults were impeding their doing what they all really wanted to do: effective work on goals and plans and effective management of their scientific capability in a humanized setting.

Summary

Work groups and teams spend a significant amount of man hours, in addition to their administrative information meetings, on group activities aimed at one of the following goals:

Establishing goals or priorities
Analyzing and distributing the work
Examining how the group works (procedures, processes, norms)

Examining the relationships among the group members as they work

There is a need for criteria for sorting out the rank-ordering of these purposes and for selecting *one* of them as a primary purpose.

The team leader must take responsibility for setting the specific core purpose of a meeting.

Third parties can make a major contribution in facilitating the work of such groups. Their help should be as process consultants within the core purpose defined by the client or team leader.

Managers can more or less systematically relate the primary purpose—goal setting, work planning, work relationships—to issues of leader behavior, member behavior, outcomes, and third-party or consultant behavior.

These options can help group leaders determine the goal of an improvement activity, the information needed to work the activity, an understanding of the kind of facilitation which might be helpful by a third party, and a clear commitment to some appropriate outcomes.

Conscious management of such team-building efforts can do much to utilize the human energy in organizationally and personally profitable ways.

Role Negotiation: A Tough-Minded Approach to Team Development

Roger Harrison

Behavioral science approaches to business have tended to focus on *alternatives* to power and politics in management and decision making, rather than directly upon the influence process. In the United States, for example, the sensitivity training approach has had quite a vogue. Managers are encouraged to abandon competitiveness and manipulation of one another in favor of open discussion of feelings, collaboration based on mutual trust, and egalitarian approaches to decision making. Various techniques (the T-group, the Managerial Grid) have been developed to bring about these changes.

In other approaches managers have been urged to change the motivational system, moving from reliance upon monetary rewards and punishments towards the development of more internal motivation based upon intrinsic interest in the job and personal commitment to meeting work objectives. Examples are programs of job enrichment and management by objectives. Still other practitioners have developed purely rational approaches to group problem solving (for example, Kepner Tregoe in the United States, and Coverdale in Britain).

In these approaches competition, conflict, and the struggle for power and influence tend to be explained away or ignored. They assume people will be collaborative and productive if they are taught how or if the barriers to their doing so are removed. These approaches may be called *tender-minded* in that they see power struggle as a symptom or a managerial *mistake* rather than as a basic and ubiquitous process in

organizations. The problem of organizational change is seen as one of releasing human potential for collaboration and productivity, rather than as one of controlling or checking competition for advantage and position.[1]

Consider some examples of problems with which I have met in my own consulting practice.

A product-centered system has been installed by a company which is organized along traditional functional lines. The product group includes representatives from the relevant functional divisions (sales, marketing, production, engineering, research, etc.). One group meets under the chairmanship of a product manager to review the commercial performance of the product and to plan capital expenditure, cost and production targets, pricing, and marketing strategy. In practice, however, some of the product managers call very few meetings and prepare the product plans without much input or consultation from the functional members of the group. The latter feel they have insufficient influence over the final target figures which they are called upon to meet and that the figures are frequently "unrealistic." Their performance frequently falls short of the target.

The production and engineering managers of a works have frequent disagreements over the work that is done by the latter for the former. The production manager complains that the engineering manager sets maintenance priorities to meet his own convenience and reduce his own costs, rather than to make sure

Reprinted from W. Warner Burke and Harvey A. Hornstein (Eds.), *The Social Technology of Organization Development*. San Diego, Ca.: University Associates, 1976. Used with permission.

[1] Of course this is not true of all behavioral approaches without exception. One in particular which has influenced my own thinking in the development of role negotiation is the confrontation meeting developed by Richard Beckhard some years ago.

production targets are met. The engineering manager maintains that the production manager gives insufficient notice of jobs which can be foreseen, and that the production operators cause unnecessary breakdowns by failure to carry out preventive maintenance procedures faithfully. The two men have aired their dissatisfactions with one another's performance from time to time, but both agree that no significant change has occurred.

A scientist in a development department complains of overly close supervision by his section manager. The manager is said by the scientist to intervene to change the priorities that he assigns to work, to interfere with his development of promising lines of enquiry, and to check up with insulting frequency to see that he is carrying out the manager's instructions. The scientist is actively trying to get a transfer to another section, because he feels he cannot do a proper job with so much hampering interference from above. When interviewed, the section manager says the scientist does competent work but is secretive and unwilling to listen to advice. He fails to let the manager know what he is doing and deviates without discussion from agreements the manager thought they had about how the work would be carried out. The manager feels he has to spend far too much time checking up on the scientist and is beginning to wonder whether his otherwise good work is worth the trouble which is required to manage him.

Each of these examples describes a problem involving the power and influence of one person or group over the activities of another. In each one, the objective of one or both parties is to gain increased control over the actions of the other, reduce control by the other over his own activities, or both at once. What is more, the participants themselves see the problem as one of influence and power. A consultant might tell them that their trouble was one of communication, or objective setting, or rational problem solving, and they would listen politely and perhaps try the approach suggested by the expert, but in their hearts they would still feel it was a question of who was going to have the final say, who was going to be boss.

Although my own development as a consultant was very much in the tender-minded tradition, I have increasingly come to feel that these managers are right. My growing conviction is that my clients have a more accurate mental map of the forces affecting them in their organizational lives than do my academic colleagues. This map usually charts power and influence and whether people are on their side or against them. On the map are indications as to whom one can be open and honest with and who will use the information against one. My clients do not chart an organizational world which is safe for openness, collaboration, creativity, and personal growth.

I do not mean to imply that the more optimistic behavioral science approaches to business are so naive as to claim the world is quite safe for the processes they try to promote. What I am concerned about is the failure to work with the forces which are in ascendance. In this paper I shall present a modest program for working with human problems in organizations which does work directly with issues of power, competitiveness, and coercion. The use of this method also involves an attempt to work from the clients' views of their problems and situations without making assumptions in advance about what their "real" needs are. This program is based on role negotiation, a technique which I have found useful in resolving differences and conflicts between managers and subordinates, between coworkers, and between different groups in an organization.

The name of the technique describes the process, which involves changing by means of negotiation with other interested parties the *role* which an individual or group performs in the organization. By an individual or group's role I mean the work arrangements he has with the others: what activities he is supposed to perform, what decisions he can make, to whom he reports and about what and how often, who can legitimately tell him what to do and under what circumstances, and so on. Some people would say that a man's job is the same as what I have called his role and I would partially agree with this, but what I mean by role includes not only the formal job description but also all the informal understandings, agreements, expectations, and arrangements with others which determine the way one person's or group's work affects or fits in with another's.

The basic approach of role negotiation has been successfully used with a wide variety of situations and clients: for example, a top management work team, a small teaching faculty, a large group of school administrators, superior-subordinate pairs, a special project team, etc. It has even proven useful in working with marital disagreements between husbands and wives, and I have come to regard it as a more or less universal tool for conflict resolution. The technique can be used with very small or quite large groups, although it is well to break down into subgroups if the size is over eight to ten. I have administered the technique with fifty or sixty people at one time, where they worked in smaller units which brought together those people who had the most to do with each other on the job.

The technique makes one basic assumption: that most people prefer a *fair negotiated settlement to a state of unresolved conflict,* and that they are willing to invest some time and make some concessions in order to achieve a solution. To operate the program, a modest but significant risk is called for from the participants: they must be open about what changes in behavior, authority, responsibility, etc., they wish to obtain from others in the situation. If the participants take the risk asked of them and specify concretely the changes desired on the part of others, then significant changes in work effectiveness can usually be obtained. I shall describe below a series of steps in this program. For the sake of illustration, we shall assume that a consultant is working with a work group of five to seven people which includes a manager and his subordinates, two levels in the formal organization.

Preparation

It goes almost without saying that no interference into the work relationships of a group or organization will be very successful unless the participants have confidence in the motives and competence of the consultant and are therefore willing at his behest to try something new and a bit strange. It also stands to reason that the consultant should know enough about the people, their work system, and their relationship problems to satisfy himself that the members of the group are ready to make a real effort towards improvement. No technique will work if the clients do not trust the consultant enough to give it a fair try or if the members of the group (particularly the high influence members) devote most of their effort to maintaining the status quo. In what follows I am assuming that this

confidence and readiness to work have been established. I realize that this is a rather large assumption, but these problems are universal in consulting and not peculiar to role negotiation. If anything, I have found that role negotiation requires somewhat less preparation than other team development techniques I have used.

Time and Place

If these basics are out of the way, then I try to get at least a day with the group away from the job location to get the role negotiation process under way. I have conducted half-day exercises, but they were more in the nature of demonstrations than actual working sessions. A 2-day session with a commitment to follow up in 3 to 4 weeks is about optimum. If the group is not felt to be quite prepared to undertake serious work, the session may be made longer with some trust-building and diagnostic activities in the beginning, working into the role negotiation when and if the group is ready for it.

The Consulting Contract

The first step in the actual role negotiation is *contract setting.* Its purpose is to get clear between the group and the consultant what each may expect from the other. This is a critical step in the change process. It controls and channels everything which happens afterwards. I work towards a contract with the following provisions, which it is helpful to get written down as a first practice step in the rather formal way of working which I try to establish.

1. It is not legitimate for the consultant to press or probe anyone's feelings. We are concerned about work: who does what, how, and with whom. How people feel about their work or about others in the group is their own business, to be introduced or not according to their own judgment and desire. The expression or nonexpression of feelings is not part of the contract.
2. Openness and honesty about behavior is expected and is essential for the achievement of results. This means that the consultant will probe for people to

be specific and concrete in expressing their expectations and demands for the behavior of others. Each team member is expected to be open and specific about what he wants others to *do more* or *do better* or *do less* or *maintain unchanged*.

3. No expectation or demand is adequately communicated until it has been written down and is clearly understood by both sender and receiver, nor will any change process be engaged in until this has been done.

4. The full sharing of expectations and demands does not constitute a completed change process. It is only the precondition for change to be agreed through negotiation. It is unreasonable for anyone in the group, manager or subordinate, to expect that any change will take place merely as a result of communicating a demand or expectation. Unless a team member is willing to change his own behavior in order to get what he wants from the other(s), he is likely to waste his and the group's time talking about the issue. When a member makes a request or demand for changed behavior on the part of another, the consultant will always ask what *quid pro quo* (something for something) he is willing to give in order to get what he wants. This goes for the manager as well as for the subordinates. If the former can get what he wants simply by issuing orders or clarifying expectations from his position of authority, he probably does not need a consultant or a change process.

5. The change process is essentially one of bargaining and negotiation in which two or more members each agree to change behavior in exchange for some desired change on the part of the other. This process is not complete until the agreement can be written down in terms which include the agreed changes in behavior and make clear what each party is expected to give in return.

6. Threats and pressures are neither illegitimate nor excluded from the negotiation process. However, group members should realize that overreliance on threats and punishment usually results in defensiveness, concealment, decreased communication, and retaliation, and may lead to breakdown of the negotiation. The consultant will do his best to help members to accomplish their aims with positive incentives wherever possible.

During the discussion of the contract, I try to help participants see that each member has power and influence in the group, both positively to reward and collaborate with others, and negatively to resist, block, or punish. Each uses his power and influence to create a desirable and satisfying work situation for himself. When this process takes place covertly, people often use a lot of time and energy in it unproductively. It is unproductive because people are unsure about others' desires and intentions. This makes it difficult to judge how a particular action will be responded to. We often judge others' wants and needs as though they were like our own. We do unto others as we would have them do unto us, and because they are not in all respects like us, our ignorance results in ineffectiveness. We make guesses about how others will respond to our attempts to influence their behavior, and when the guesses are wrong we have no option other than to continue the laborious process of trial and error, slowly building up our knowledge of what is and is not effective with each other person through a clumsy and not very systematic experimentation.

In stable, slowly changing organizational situations, this trial and error process may be satisfactory, because people do learn how to influence one another given a sufficient period of contact. When situations and personnel change more rapidly (over periods of months rather than years), then this most primitive learning process does not do the job fast enough. The more fluid the system, the more important it is to develop information rapidly which will permit people to influence one another effectively. I try to help my clients to see that if information about desires and intentions is equally shared, then they will all increase the effectiveness of their influence attempts. Then, when others try to influence them the proffered *quid pro quo* will be more likely to be one which they really want and need. The role negotiation is not only intended to have the effect of resolving current problems but also of increasing knowledge within the group of how effectively to influence one another. The intended effect is that the *total amount of influence of group members on one another should increase.* The consultant will so conduct himself that opportunities to increase one's influence within the system are as nearly equal as possible.

Diagnosis

The next stage is *issue diagnosis*. I ask each member to spend some time thinking about the way business is conducted between himself and the others in the group. What things would he change if he could? What things would he like to keep as they are? Who and what would have to change in order to improve things? In thinking about these things, I ask the members to focus especially on the things which might be changed to improve their own effectiveness, as these are the things I shall ask them to discuss and negotiate.

After they have spent 20 minutes or so thinking about these matters and perhaps making a few notes, I ask each member to take a set of issue diagnosis forms like the one in Exhibit 1. He is to fill out one issue diagnosis form for each other member, listing those things he would like to see the other person:

1. Do more or do better.
2. Do less or stop doing.
3. Keep on doing, maintain unchanged.

All of these messages are to be keyed to increasing the sender's own effectiveness in doing his own job.

These lists are exchanged so that each person has all the lists which pertain to his work behavior. Each member makes a master list for himself on a large piece of (flip chart) paper on which he shows the behavior which each other person desires him to do more or better, less, or continue unchanged (Exhibit 2). These are posted so that the entire group can peruse and refer to each list. Each member is allowed to question the others who have sent messages about his behavior, querying the what, why, and how of their requests, but no one is allowed a rebuttal, defense, or even a yes or no reply to the messages he has received. The consultant intervenes in the discussion to make sure that only clarification is taking place and that argument, discussion, and decision making about issues is not engaged in at this stage.

The purpose of this rather rigid and formal control on communication by the consultant is to make sure that the group does not have a negative problem-solving experience and that members do not get polarized on issues or take up extreme positions which they will feel impelled to defend in order to save face. Communication is controlled in order to prevent escalation of actual or potential conflicts. The strategy is to channel the energy which has been generated or released by the sharing of demands and expectations into successful problem solving and mutual influence. The consultant intervenes to inhibit hostile and destructive expression at this point and later to facilitate constructive bargaining and negotiation of mutually beneficial agreements. This initial sharing of desires and change goals leads to a point at which the team development process is most vulnerable, because if sufficient anger and defensiveness are generated by the problem sharing, the consultant will

---

EXHIBIT 1
Issue Diagnosis Form

Messages from Jim Farrell   *To* David Sills

1. *If you were to do the following things* more *or better,* *it would help me to increase my own effectiveness.*
   Be more receptive to improvement suggestions from the process engineers.
   Give *help* on cost control (see 2).
   Fight harder with the G.M. to get our plans improved.
2. *If you were to do the following things* less, *or were to* stop *doing them, it would help me to increase my own effectiveness.*
   Acting as judge and jury on cost control.
   Checking up frequently on small details of the work—asking for so many detailed progress reports.
3. *The following things which you have been doing help to increase my effectiveness, and I hope you will* continue *to do them.*
   Passing on full information in our weekly meetings.
   Being available when I need to talk to you.

EXHIBIT 2
Summary of Messages to James Farrell from Other Group Members

More or Better	Less or Stop	Continue as Now
Give information on project progress completion date slippage—Bill, Tony, David	Let people go to other good job opportunities—stop hanging on to your good engineers—Tony, Bill	Training operators on preventive maintenance—Henry
Send progress reports on Sortair project—Bill	Missing weekly planning meetings frequently—Jack, Henry, David	Good suggestions in meetings—Tony, Henry
Make engineers more readily available when help needed—Jack, Henry	Ignoring memos and reports re cost control—David	Asking the difficult and awkward questions—Tony, Jack
Keep better informed re plans and activities—David	Setting aside my priorities on engineering work—Henry, Jack	Willingness to help on design problems—Bill, Jack
Enforce safety rates on engineers when in production area—Henry	Charging time on Sortair to other accounts—David	Good quality project work—Bill, Henry, David, Jack
Push harder for the Sensitex project—David, Henry, Tony, Jack	Overrunning agreed project budget without discussing beforehand—David	

not be able to hold the negative processes in check long enough for the development of the positive problem-solving spiral on which the process depends for its effectiveness. It is true that such an uncontrollable breakthrough of hostility has not yet occurred in my experience with the method. Nevertheless, concern over the negative possibilities is in part responsible for my slow, deliberate, and rather formal development of the confrontation issues within the group.

Negotiation

After each member has had an opportunity to clarify the messages he has received, the group proceeds to the selection of issues for negotiation. The consultant begins this phase by reemphasizing that unless a *quid pro quo* can be offered in return for a desired behavior change, there is little point in having a discussion about it: *Unless behavior changes on both sides, the most likely prediction is that the status quo will continue.* (It can be argued that this is an extremely conservative point of view and that behavior does in fact change between men of good will simply as a result of an exchange of views. While I do not deny that this occurs, I do not assume it in my practice and I allow myself to be pleasantly surprised when it happens!)

Each participant is asked to indicate one or more issues on which he particularly wants to get some change on the part of another. He is also asked to select one or more issues on which he feels it may be possible for him to move in the direction desired by others. He does this by marking his own flip chart and those of the other members. In effect, each person is indicating the issues upon which he most wants to exert influence and those on which he is most willing to accept influence. With the help of the consultant the group then goes through the lists to select the most negotiable issues, those where there is a combination of a high desire for change on the part of an initiator and a willingness to negotiate on the part of the person whose behavior is the target of the change attempt. The consultant asks for a group of two or more persons who are involved in one such issue to volunteer for a negotiation demonstration before the rest of the group.

The negotiation process consists of the parties making contingent offers to one another of the form, "if you do X, I will do Y." The negotiation ends when all parties are satisfied that they will receive a reasonable return for whatever they are agreeing to give. The consultant asks that the agreement be formalized by writing down specifically and concretely what each party is

EXHIBIT 3

Final Written Agreement Between James Farrell and David Sills

---

Jim agrees to let David know as soon as agreed completion dates and cost projections look as though they will not be met, and also to discuss each project's progress fully with David on a biweekly basis.

In return David agrees not to raise questions about details and completion dates, pending a trial of this agreement to see if it provides sufficient information soon enough to deal with questions from above.

---

going to give and receive in the bargain (Exhibit 3). He also asks the participants to discuss openly what sanctions can be applied in the case of nonfulfillment of the bargain by one or another party. Often this involves no more than reversion to the status quo, but it may involve the application of pressures and penalties as well.

After the negotiation demonstration, the members are asked to select other issues they wish to work on. A number of negotiations may go on simultaneously, the consultant being involved at the request of any party to any negotiation. All agreements are published to the entire group, however, and questioned by the consultant and the other members to test the good faith and reality orientation of the parties in making them. Where agreement proves impossible, the consultant and other group members try to help the parties find further incentives (positive or, less desirably, coercive) which they may bring to bear to encourage agreement.

This process is, of course, not so simple as the bare bones outlined here. All kinds of difficulties can occur, from bargaining in bad faith, to refusal to bargain at all, to escalation of conflict. In my experience, however, group members tend to be rather wise about the issues they can and cannot deal with, and I refrain from pushing them to negotiate issues they feel are unresolvable. My aim is to create a beginning to team development with a successful experience which group members will see as a fruitful way of improving their effectiveness and satisfaction. I try to go no further than the members feel is reasonable.

Follow-Up

At the conclusion of a team development cycle as outlined above, I suggest that the group test the firmness of the agreements they have negotiated by living with them a while before trying to go further. We can then get together later to review the agreements, renegotiate ones which have not held or which are no longer viable, and continue the team development process by dealing with new issues. Hopefully, the group will eventually take over the conduct of the role negotiation activity and the consultant's role will wither away. This can occur when the group has developed sufficient control over the dangers, avoidances, and threats involved in the negotiation process that they no longer need third-party protection or encouragement. However, I do not claim any unusual success in freeing clients from dependence on my services. What I do find is that there is less backsliding between visits in teams I have worked with using this method than when I have applied more interpersonally oriented change interventions. The agreements obtained through role negotiation seem to have more "teeth" in them than those which rely on the softer processes of interpersonal trust and openness.

The Dynamics of Role Negotiation

Role negotiation intervenes directly into the relationships of power, authority, and influence within the group. The change effort is directed at the work relationships among members. It avoids probing into the likes and dislikes of members for one another and their personal feelings about one another. In this it is more consonant with the task-oriented norms of business than are most other behavioral approaches. I have found that groups with whom I have had difficulty working when I focused on interpersonal issues dropped their resistance and turned willingly to problem solving when I shifted my approach to role negotiation.

When I first developed the technique, I tried it out on a client group which was proving particularly hard to work with. They were suspicious and mistrustful of me and of each other and said quite openly that talking about their relationships was both "irrelevant to our work problems" and "dangerous—it could split the group apart.'' When I introduced role negotiation to them they saw ways they could deal with things which were bothering them without getting into touchy emotional confrontations they could not handle. They dropped their resistance dramatically and turned to work with a will which surprised and delighted me.

I have repeated this experience more than once. Clients seem more at home with problems of power and influence than they do with interpersonal issues. They feel more competent and less dependent upon the skill and trustworthiness of the consultant in dealing with these issues and so they are ready to work sooner and harder. I also find my own skill not so central to the change process as it is when I am dealing with interpersonal issues. The amount of skill and professional training which is required to conduct role negotiation is less than for more sensitive approaches.

That is not to say that role negotiation poses no threat to organization members. The consultant asks participants to be open about matters which are often covert in normal life. This requires more than the normal amount of trust and confidence. If it did not, these matters would have been talked about before the group ever got to the role negotiation.

There seems also to be some additional discomfort involved in writing down the changes one would like to see another make in his work behavior. Several times clients have questioned the necessity of doing this, and I suspect that some have avoided role negotiation altogether because this aspect made them uneasy. It is perhaps that one feels so exposed when his concerns are written out for all to see, and there is the fear that others will think them silly, childish, or odd (though this never seems to happen). If the matter comes up, I point out that one need not write down all concerns he has, but only those he would like to work on with others at this time.

Of course, role negotiation threatens people in one basic way it shares with any other process which really changes relationships. People are never quite sure they will personally be better off after the change than before. In the case of role negotiation, most of these fears are around losing power and influence, or losing freedom and becoming more controlled by others. There is particular resistance to talking openly about issues where one is trying for his own advantage to

manipulate another or when he feels that he might want to do this in the future. I think this is the main reason clients in role negotiation so often try to avoid the step of writing down their agreements. They feel if things are not down in black and white it will be easier later on to ignore the agreement if it becomes inconvenient. Also, writing down agreements is contrary to the aura of trust and good fellowship which some groups like to create on the surface and under cover of which they engage in quite a lot of cutthroat competition.

Role negotiation is, of course, no panacea for power problems in groups and between people. People may bargain in bad faith; agreements once reached may be broken; circumstances and personnel may change so that the work done becomes irrelevant. About all that can be said in reply is that these problems can exist in any group or organization. What role negotiation does is to try to deal with the problems directly and to identify and use constructively those areas of mutual advantage where both sides can benefit from discussion and agreement. These areas are almost always larger than people think they are, and when they find that they can achieve something for themselves by open negotiation which they could not achieve by covert competition, then the more constructive process can begin to grow.

The Economics of Role Negotiation

One disadvantage of most behavioral approaches to team development is that the level of skill and experience demanded of the consultant is very high indeed. Managers are not confident in dealing with these issues. Because they feel at risk they reasonably want to have as much safety and skill as money can buy. The demand for skilled consultants on interpersonal and group processes has created a shortage and a meteoric rise in consulting fees. It seems unlikely that the supply will soon catch up with the demand.

The shortage of highly skilled workers in team development argues for ''deskilling'' the requirements for effective consultant performance. I see role negotiation as a way of reducing the skill requirements for team development consultation. Preliminary results by internal consultants using the approach have been promising. For example, one management development manager teamed up with a colleague to conduct a successful role negotiation with his own top management. He reported that the main problem was getting up the confidence to take on the job. The team development session itself went smoothly. I cannot say whether this experience was typical; I suspect it was not. It does lead me to hope that role negotiation will prove to be practical for use by internal consultants without professional training in the behavioral sciences.

Summary

The following comments highlight the aspects of role negotiation which I believe commend it for use in team development and other face-to-face consulting situations in business.

Role negotiation focuses on work relationships: what people do and how they facilitate and inhibit one another in the performance of their jobs. It encourages participants to work with problems using words and concepts they are used to using in business. It avoids probing to the deeper levels of their feelings about one another unless this comes out naturally in the process.

Role negotiation deals directly with problems of power and influence which may be neglected by other behavioral approaches. It does not attempt to dethrone the authority in the group, but other members are helped to explore realistically the sources of power and influence available to them.

Also in contrast to some other behavioral approaches to team development, role negotiation is highly action-oriented. Its aim is not just the exposing and understanding of issues as such but the achievement of commitment to changed ways of working through mutually negotiated agreements. Changes achieved through role negotiation thus tend to be more stable and lasting than where such a commitment procedure is lacking.

All the procedures of role negotiation are clear and simple if a bit mechanical and can be described to clients in advance so they know what they are getting into. There is nothing mysterious about the technique, and this reduces clients' feelings of dependency upon the special skill of the consultant.

Role negotiation actually requires less skill from the consultant than some other behavioral approaches. I believe it is suitable for use, without lengthy special training, by internal consultants who are not themselves behavioral scientists. It can therefore be a moderate cost approach to organization change.

One final comment on the relationship between role negotiation and other behavioral approaches is in order. As mentioned above, my own development as a consultant was in the tradition of sensitivity training and other "soft" approaches to organization change. I believed then and still do that work groups can be effective and achievement-oriented and at the same time can support open and deeply satisfying interpersonal relationships among the members. What I do not now believe is that approaches at the interpersonal level can work well unless the ever-present issues of power and influence are first resolved to a reasonable level of satisfaction for the members. Role negotiation was not designed as a substitute for interpersonal approaches, but rather to fill this gap and provide a sound and effective base upon which to build more satisfying relationships. As a first or "basic" approach to team development, I think it is more appropriate than the more interpersonally focused methods, but I would hope that client groups would develop that commitment to their own growth and development which will eventually move them beyond role negotiation into deeper exploration of their own creative potential for integrating work and relationship.

A New Look at Managerial Decision Making

Victor H. Vroom

Introduction

While there are many differences in the roles that managers are called upon to play in organizations, all managers are decision makers. Furthermore, there is little doubt that their effectiveness as managers is largely reflected in their track record in making the "right" decisions.

Several scholarly disciplines share an interest in the decision-making process. On one hand, we have the fields of operations research and management science, both concerned with how to improve the decisions which are made. Their models of decision making, which are aimed at providing a rational basis for selecting among alternative courses of action, are termed *normative* or *prescriptive models.* On the other hand, we have, in the efforts of psychologists, sociologists, and political scientists, attempts to understand the decisions and choices that people do make. March and Simon were among the first to suggest that an understanding of the decision-making process could be central to an understanding of the behavior of organizations—a point of view that was later amplified by Cyert and March in their behavioral theory of the firm. In this tradition, the goal is understanding rather than improvement, and the models *descriptive* rather than normative.

Whether the models are normative or descriptive, the common ingredient is a conception of decision making as an information-processing activity, frequently one which takes place within a single manager. Both sets of models focus on the set of alter-

native decisions or problem solutions from which the choice is, or should be, made. The normative models are based on the consequences of choices among these alternatives, the descriptive models on the determinants of these choices. Alternatively, one could view the decision making which occurs in organizations as a social or interpersonal process rather than a cognitive one. A major aspect of the manager's role in the decision-making process is to determine which person or persons should take part in the solution of the problem or, to put it more broadly, which social process should be engaged in the solution of the problem or the making of the decision.

An example may be helpful in illustrating the difference. Let us assume that you are a manager who has five subordinates reporting to you. Each of these subordinates has a clearly defined and distinct set of responsibilities. One of these subordinates resigns to take a position with another organization. Due to a cost-cutting program recently initiated within the firm which makes it impossible to hire new employees, you cannot replace him with someone else. It will be necessary for you to find some way of reallocating the departing subordinate's responsibilities among the remaining four subordinates in such a way as to maintain the present workload and effectiveness of the unit.

The situation described is representative of many with which people in managerial positions are faced. There is some need for action—a problem exists and a solution or decision must be forthcoming. You, as manager, have some area of freedom or discretion (there are a number of possible ways in which the work can be reallocated), but there are also some constraints on your actions. For example, you cannot solve the

Reprinted by permission of the publisher from *Organizational Dynamics,* Spring 1973, © 1973 by AMACOM, a division of American Management Associations. All rights reserved.

problem by hiring someone from outside the organization. Furthermore, the solution adopted is going to have effects on people other than yourself (your subordinates are going to have to carry out whatever decision is reached).

Traditionally, efforts to understand or improve the process of decision making in situations such as this one would focus on the events which do (or should) take place within the head of the manager. If one's objectives were normative—i.e., to improve decision making—one might seek to develop an algorithm which would assure selection of the optimal set of work assignments from the total set of possibilities or to develop a set of heuristics (or rules of thumb) for reaching a satisfactory solution to the problem. If one's interests were descriptive, one could obtain from you a protocol of your thoughts as you generated and evaluated alternative solutions and, from such observations, attempt to formulate a model of your decision-making processes which could subsequently be tested against your behavior in other similar situations.

Underlying both approaches is the conviction that the manager is *the* problem solver or decision maker—that the task of translating problems into solutions is inevitably his task. In the alternative view of decision making as a social process, we see the manager's task as determining how the problem is to be solved, not the solution to be adopted. In the situation desribed, one can envision a number of possible decision-making processes that you could employ. You could make the decision by yourself and announce it to your subordinates; you could obtain additional information from your subordinates and then make the decision; you could consult with them either individually or collectively before making the decision; or you could convene them as a group and attempt to reach agreement on the solution to the problem. These alternatives vary in the amount of opportunity afforded your subordinates to participate with you in the solution of the problem.

As with what we have termed the *traditional way* of looking at the decision-making process, one can distinguish normative and descriptive questions. The normative questions concern the processes which should be used while the descriptive questions concern the decision-making process which is used.

About 4 years ago, Philip Yetton, then a graduate student at Carnegie-Mellon University, and I began a major research program in an attempt to answer these questions. A detailed presentation of this work may be found in our forthcoming book, *Leadership and Decision-Making*.[1] The purpose of this paper is to present an overview of our approach, methods, and major conclusions.

Toward a Normative Model

We began with the normative question. What would be a rational way of deciding on the form and amount of participation in decision making that should be used in different situations? We were tired of debates over the relative merits of theory X and theory Y and of the truism that leadership depends upon the situation. We felt that it was time for the behavioral sciences to move beyond such generalities and to attempt to come to grips with the complexities of the phenomena with which they intended to deal.

Table 1 shows a set of alternative decision processes which we have employed in our research. Each process is represented by a symbol (e.g., AI, CI, GII) which will be used as a convenient method of referring to each process. The first letter in this symbol signifies the basic properties of the process (A stands for autocratic, C for consultative, and G for group). The roman numerals which follow the first letter constitute variants on that process. Thus, AI represents the first variant on an autocratic process, and AII the second variant, etc.[2]

CONCEPTUAL AND EMPIRICAL BASIS OF THE MODEL

A model designed to regulate, in some rational way, choices among the decision processes shown in Table 1 should be based on sound empirical evidence concerning the likely consequences of the styles. The more complete the empirical base of knowledge, the greater the certainty with which one can develop the model

---

[1][Victor H. Vroom and Philip W. Yetton. *Leadership and Decision-Making*. Pittsburgh: University of Pittsburgh Press, 1976.]

[2] The absence of GI from the code is attributable to the fact that the list of decision processes used in this paper is a part of a larger set of such processes used in broader and more comprehensive models. A complete explication of the entire set of processes and of the models which use them may be found in Vroom and Yetton [1976].

TABLE 1
Types of Management Decision Styles

AI   You solve the problem or make the decision yourself, using information available to you at that time.

AII   You obtain the necessary information from your subordinate(s), then decide on the solution to the problem yourself. You may or may not tell your subordinates what the problem is in getting the information from them. The role played by your subordinates in making the decision is clearly one of providing the necessary information to you, rather than generating or evaluating alternative solutions.

CI   You share the problem with relevant subordinates individually, getting their ideas and suggestions without bringing them together as a group. Then *you* make the decision which may or may not reflect your subordinates' influence.

CII   You share the problem with your subordinates as a group, collectively obtaining their ideas and suggestions. Then *you* make the decision which may or may not reflect your subordinates' influence.

GII   You share a problem with your subordinates as a group. Together you generate and evaluate alternatives and attempt to reach agreement (consensus) on a solution. Your role is much like that of chairman. You do not try to influence the group to adopt your solution and you are willing to accept and implement any solution which has the support of the entire group.

---

and the greater will be its usefulness. To aid in understanding the conceptual basis of the model, it is important to distinguish three classes of outcomes which bear on the ultimate effectiveness of decisions. These are:

1. The quality or rationality of the decision.
2. The acceptance or commitment on the part of subordinates to execute the decision effectively.
3. The amount of time required to make the decision.

The evidence regarding the effects of participation on each of these outcomes or consequences has been reviewed by Vroom in *The Handbook of Social Psychology*. It was concluded that:

The results suggest that allocating problem-solving and decision-making tasks to entire groups requires a greater investment of man-hours but produces higher acceptance of decisions and a higher probability that the decision will be executed efficiently. Differences between these two methods in quality of decisions and in elapsed time are inconclusive and probably highly variable. . . . It would be naïve to think that group decision making is always more "effective" than autocratic decision making, or vice versa; the relative effectiveness of these two extreme methods depends both on the weights attached to quality, acceptance, and time variables, and on differences in amounts of these outcomes resulting from these methods, neither of which is invariant from one situation to another. The critics and proponents of participative management would do well to direct their efforts toward identifying the properties of situations in which different decision-making approaches are effective rather than wholesale condemnation or deification of one approach. (pp. 239–240)

Stemming from this review, an attempt has been made to identify these properties of the situation or problem which will be the basic elements in the model. These problem attributes are of two types: (1) those which specify the importance for a particular problem of quality and acceptance, and (2) those which, on the basis of available evidence, have a high probability of moderating the effects of participation on each of these outcomes. Table 2 shows the problem attributes used in the present form of the model. For each attribute a question is provided which might be used by a leader in diagnosing a particular problem prior to choosing his leadership style.

In phrasing the questions, technical language has been held to a minimum. Furthermore, the questions have been phrased in yes-no form, translating the continuous variables defined above into dichotomous variables. For example, instead of attempting to determine how important the decision quality is to the effectiveness of the decision (attribute A), the leader is asked in the first question to judge whether there is any quality component to the problem. Similarly, the difficult task of specifying exactly how much informa-

TABLE 2
Problem Attributes Used in the Model

Problem Attributes	Diagnostic Questions
A. The importance of the quality of the decision	Is there a quality requirement such that one solution is likely to be more rational than another?
B. The extent to which the leader possesses sufficient information/expertise to make a high-quality decision by himself	Do I have sufficient information to make a high-quality decision?
C. The extent to which the problem is structured	Is the problem structured?
D. The extent to which acceptance or commitment on the part of subordinates is critical to the effective implementation of the decision	Is acceptance of decision by subordinates critical to effective implementation?
E. The prior probability that the leader's autocratic decision will receive acceptance by subordinates	If I were to make the decision by myself, is it reasonably certain that it would be accepted by my subordinates?
F. The extent to which subordinates are motivated to attain the organizational goals as represented in the objectives explicit in the statement of the problem	Do subordinates share the organizational goals to be obtained in solving this problem?
G. The extent to which subordinates are likely to be in conflict over preferred solutions	Is conflict among subordinates likely in preferred solutions?

tion the leader possesses that is relevant to the decision (attribute B) is reduced to a simple judgment by the leader concerning whether he has sufficient information to make a high-quality decision.

It has been found that managers can diagnose a situation quite quickly and accurately by answering this set of seven questions concerning it. But how can such responses generate a prescription concerning the most effective leadership style or decision process? What kind of normative model of participation in decision making can be built from this set of problem attributes?

Figure 1 shows one such model expressed in the form of a decision tree. It is the seventh version of such a model which we have developed over the last 3 years [1970–1973]. The problem attributes, expressed in question form, are arranged along the top of the figure. To use the model for a particular decision-making situation, one starts at the left-hand side and words toward the right, asking oneself the question immediately above any box that is encountered.

When a terminal node is reached, a number will be found designating the problem type[3] and one of the decision-making processes appearing in Table 1. AI is prescribed for four problem types (1, 2, 4, and 5); AII is prescribed for two problem types (9 and 10); CI is prescribed for only one problem type (8); CII is prescribed for four problem types (7, 11, 13, and 14); and GII is prescribed for three problem types (3, 6, and 12). The relative frequency with which each of the five decision processes would be prescribed for any manager would, of course, be dependent on the distribution of problem types in his role.

RATIONALE UNDERLYING THE MODEL

The decision processes specified for each problem type are not arbitrary. The model's behavior is governed by a set of principles which are intended to be constant with existing evidence concerning the consequences of

[3] Problem type is a nominal variable designating classes of problems generated by the paths which lead to the terminal nodes.

FIGURE 1

Decision Process Flow Chart

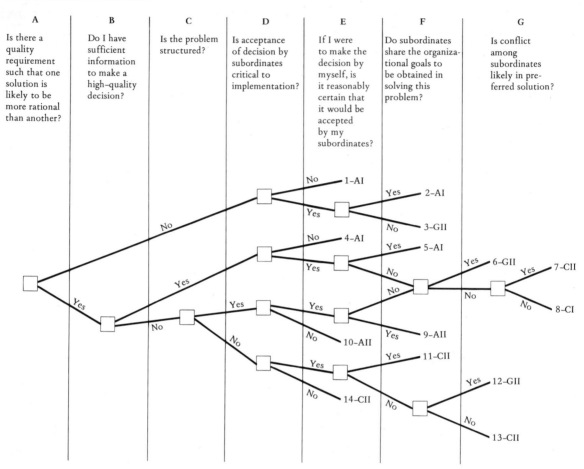

A	B	C	D	E	F	G
Is there a quality requirement such that one solution is likely to be more rational than another?	Do I have sufficient information to make a high–quality decision?	Is the problem structured?	Is acceptance of decision by subordinates critical to implementation?	If I were to make the decision by myself, is it reasonably certain that it would be accepted by my subordinates?	Do subordinates share the organizational goals to be obtained in solving this problem?	Is conflict among subordinates likely in preferred solution?

participation in decision making on organizational effectiveness.

There are two mechanisms underlying the behavior of the model. The first is a set of seven rules which serve to protect the quality and the acceptance of the decision by eliminating alternatives which risk one or the other of these decision outcomes. Once the rules have been applied, a feasible set of decision processes is generated. The second is a principle for choosing among alternatives in the feasible set where more than one exists.

Let us examine the rules first because they do much of the work of the model. As previously indicated, the rules are intended to protect both the quality and ac-

ceptance of the decision. In the form of the model shown, there are three rules which protect decision quality and four which protect acceptance. The seven rules are presented here both as verbal statements and in the more formal language of set theory. In the set theoretic formulation, the letters refer to the problem attributes as stated in question form in Table 2. A signifies that the answer to question A for a particular problem is *yes*; $\overline{A}$ signifies that the answer to that question is *no*; ∩ signifies *intersection*; = ▶ signifies *implies*; and $\overline{AI}$ signifies *not AI*. Thus, A ∩ $\overline{B}$ = ▶ $\overline{AI}$ may be read as follows: When both the answer to question A is yes and the answer to question B is no, AI is eliminated from the feasible set.

1. *The Information Rule.* If the quality of the decision is important and if the leader does not possess enough information or expertise to solve the problem by himself, AI is eliminated from the feasible set. (Its use risks a low-quality decision.) (A ∩ B = ▶ $\overline{\text{AI}}$)

2. *The Goal Congruence Rule.* If the quality of the decision is important and if the subordinates do not share the organizational goals to be obtained in solving the problem, GII is eliminated from the feasible set. (Alternatives which eliminate the leader's final control over the decision reached may jeopardize the quality of the decision.) (A ∩ $\overline{\text{F}}$ = ▶ $\overline{\text{GII}}$)

3. *The Unstructured Problem Rule.* In decisions in which the quality of decision is important, if the leader lacks the necessary information or expertise to solve the problem by himself, and if the problem is unstructured—i.e., he does not know exactly what information is needed and where it is located—the method used must provide not only for him to collect the information but to do so in an efficient and effective manner. Methods which involve interaction among all subordinates with full knowledge of the problem are likely to be both more efficient and more likely to generate a high-quality solution to the problem. Under these conditions, AI, AII, and CI are eliminated from the feasible set. (AI does not provide for him to collect the necessary information, and AII and CI represent more cumbersome, less effective, and less efficient means of bringing the necessary information to bear on the solution of the problem than methods which do permit those with the necessary information to interact.) (A ∩ $\overline{\text{B}}$ ∩ $\overline{\text{C}}$ = ▶ $\overline{\text{AI}}$, $\overline{\text{AII}}$, $\overline{\text{CI}}$)

4. *The Acceptance Rule.* If the acceptance of the decision by subordinates is critical to effective implementation, and if it is not certain that an autocratic decision made by the leader would receive that acceptance, AI and AII are eliminated from the feasible set. (Neither provides an opportunity for subordinates to participate in the decision and both risk the necessary acceptance.) (D ∩ $\overline{\text{E}}$ = ▶ $\overline{\text{AI}}$, $\overline{\text{AII}}$)

5. *The Conflict Rule.* If the acceptance of the decision is critical, and an autocratic decision is not certain to be accepted, and subordinates are likely to be in conflict or disagreement over the appropriate solution, AI, AII, and CI are eliminated from the feasible set. (The method used in solving the problem should enable those in disagreement to resolve their differences with full knowledge of the problem. Accordingly, under these conditions, AI, AII, and CI, which involve no interaction or only one-on-one relationships and therefore provide no opportunity for those in conflict to resolve their differences, are eliminated from the feasible set. Their use runs the risk of leaving some of the subordinates with less than the necessary commitment to the final decision.) (D ∩ $\overline{\text{E}}$ ∩ F = ▶ $\overline{\text{AI}}$, $\overline{\text{AII}}$, $\overline{\text{CI}}$)

6. *The Fairness Rule.* If the quality of decision is unimportant, and if acceptance is critical and not certain to result from an autocratic decision, AI, AII, CI, and CII are eliminated from the feasible set. (The method used should maximize the probability of acceptance as this is the only relevant consideration in determining the effectiveness of the decision. Under these circumstances, AI, AII, CI, and CII, which create less acceptance or commitment than GII, are eliminated from the feasible set. To use them is to run the risk of getting less than the needed acceptance of the decision.) ($\overline{\text{A}}$ ∩ D ∩ $\overline{\text{E}}$ = ▶ $\overline{\text{AI}}$, $\overline{\text{AII}}$, $\overline{\text{CI}}$, $\overline{\text{CII}}$)

7. *The Acceptance Priority Rule.* If acceptance is critical, not assured by an autocratic decision, and if subordinates can be trusted, AI, AII, CI, and CII are eliminated from the feasible set. (Methods which provide equal partnership in the decision-making process can provide greater acceptance without risking decision quality. Use of any method other than GII results in an unnecessary risk that the decision will not be fully accepted or receive the necessary commitment on the part of subordinates.) (A ∩ D ∩ $\overline{\text{E}}$ ∩ F = ▶ $\overline{\text{AI}}$, $\overline{\text{AII}}$, $\overline{\text{CI}}$, $\overline{\text{CII}}$)

Once all seven rules have been applied to a given problem, a feasible set of decision processes is given. The feasible set for each of the fourteen problem types is shown in Table 3. It can be seen that there are some problem types for which only one method remains in the feasible set, others for which two methods remain feasible, and still others for which five methods remain feasible.

When more than one method remains in the feasible set, there are a number of alternative decision rules which might dictate the choice among them. The one which underlies the prescriptions of the model shown

TABLE 3
Problem Types and the Feasible Set of Decision Processes

Problem Type	Acceptable Methods
1	AI, AII, CI, CII, GII
2	AI, AII, CI, CII, GII
3	GII
4	AI, AII, CI, CII, GII*
5	AI, AII, CI, CII, GII*
6	GII
7	CII
8	CI, CII
9	AII, CI, CII, GII*
10	AII, CI, CII, GII*
11	CII, GII*
12	GII
13	CII
14	CII, GII*

*Within the feasible set only when the answer to question F is yes.

in Figure 1 utilizes the number of man-hours used in solving the problem as the basis for choice. Given a set of methods with equal likelihood of meeting both quality and acceptance requirements for the decision, it chooses that method which requires the least investment in man-hours. On the basis of the empirical evidence summarized earlier, this is deemed to be the method furthest to the left within the feasible set. For example, since AI, AII, CI, CII, and GII are all feasible as in problem types 1 and 2, AI would be the method chosen. This decision rule acts to minimize man-hours subject to quality and acceptance constraints. . . .

SHORT- VERSUS LONG-TERM MODELS

The model described above seeks to protect, if relevant, the quality of the decision, to create any necessary acceptance of the decision, and to expend the least number of man-hours in the process. In view of its attention to conditions surrounding the making and implementation of a particular decision rather than any long-term considerations, it could be termed a *short-term model.*

It seems likely, however, that the leadership methods which may be optimal for short-term results may be different from those which would be optimal when executed over a longer period of time. Consider a leader who has been uniformly pursuing an autocratic style (AI or AII) and, perhaps as a consequence, has subordinates who cannot be trusted to pursue organization goals (attribute F) and who might be termed *yes men* (attribute E). An examination of the structure of the time-minimizing model reveals that, with few exceptions, the leader would be instructed by the model to continue his present autocratic style.

It appears likely, however, that the use of more participative methods would, in time, change the status of these problem attributes so as to develop ultimately a more effective problem-solving system. In the example given above, an autocratic approach would be indicated to maximize short-run benefits, but a higher degree of participation might maximize performance aggregated over a longer period.

A promising approach to the development of a long-term model is one which places less weight on man-hours as the basis for choice of method within the feasible set. Given a long-term orientation, one would be interested in the trade-off between man-hours in problem-solving and team development, both of which increase with participation. Viewed in these terms, the time-minimizing model places maximum relative weight on man-hours and no weight on development and hence chooses the style furthest to the left within the feasible set. A model which places less weight on man-hours and more weight on development would, if these assumptions are correct, choose a style further to the right within the feasible set.

Toward a Descriptive Model of Leader Behavior

So far we have been concerned with the normative questions defined at the outset. But how do managers really behave? What considerations affect these decisions about how much to share their decision-making power with their subordinates? In what respects is their behavior different from or similar to that of the model? These questions are but a few of those that we attempted to answer in a large-scale research program[4]

[4]This research program has been financially supported by the McKinsey Foundation, General Electric Foundation, Smith Richardson Foundation, and by the Office of Naval Research.

aimed at gaining a greater understanding of the factors that do influence managers in their choice of decision processes to fit the demands of the situation. Two rather different research methods have been utilized in studying these factors.

The first investigation utilized a method which we have come to term *recalled problems*. Over 500 managers from eleven different countries and representing a variety of firms were asked to provide a written description of a problem which they had recently had to solve in their managerial capacity. These varied in length from one paragraph to several pages and covered virtually every facet of managerial decision making. For each case, the manager was asked to indicate which of the decision processes shown in Table 1 they used to solve the problem. Finally, each manager was asked to answer the questions shown in Table 2 corresponding to the problem attributes used in the normative model.

The wealth of data, both qualitative and quantitative, served two purposes. Since each manager had diagnosed a situation which he had encountered in terms that are used in the normative model and had indicated the methods that he had used in dealing with it, it is possible to determine what differences, if any, there were between the model's behavior and his own behavior. Secondly, the written cases provided the basis for the construction of a *standard* set of cases used in later research to determine the factors which influence managers to share or retain their decision-making power. Each case depicted a manager faced with a problem to solve or a decision to make. The cases span a wide range of managerial problems including production scheduling, quality control, portfolio management, personnel allocation, and research and development. In each case a person could readily assume the role of the manager described and could be asked to indicate which of the decision processes he would use if actually faced with that situation.

In most of our research, a set of thirty cases has been used and the subjects have been several thousand managers who were participants in management development programs in the United States and abroad. The cases for use in the set were selected not randomly but systematically. We desired cases which could not only be coded unambiguously in the terms used in the normative model but which would also permit the assessment of the effects of each of the problem attributes used in the model on the person's behavior. The solution was to select cases in accordance with an experimental design such that they varied in terms of the seven attributes used in the model and variation in each attribute was independent of each other attribute. Several such standardized sets of cases have been developed, and over a thousand managers have now been studied using this approach.

To summarize all of the things that we have learned in the course of this research is well beyond the scope of this paper, but it is possible to discuss some of the highlights. Since the results obtained from the two research methods—recalled and standardized problems—are quite consistent, the major results can be presented independent of the method used.

Perhaps the most striking finding is the weakening of the widespread view that participativeness is a general trait which managers exhibit in different amounts. To be sure, there were differences among managers in their general tendencies to utilize participative methods as opposed to autocratic ones. On the standardized problems, these differences accounted for about 10 percent of the total variance in decision process observed. These differences in behavior between managers, however, were small in comparision with differences within managers. On the standardized problems, no manager has indicated that he would use the same decision process on all problems or decisions, and most use all five methods under some circumstances.

Some of this variance in behavior within managers can be attributed to widely shared tendencies to respond to some situations by sharing power and others by retaining it. It makes at least as much sense to talk about participative and autocratic situations as it does to talk about participative and autocratic managers. In fact, on the standardized problems, the variance in behavior across problems or cases is about three times as large as the variance across managers!

What are the characteristics of an autocratic as opposed to a participative situation? An answer to this question would constitute a partial descriptive model of this aspect of the decision-making process and has been our goal in much of the research that we have conducted. From our observations of behavior on both recalled problems and on standardized problems, it is clear that the decision-making process employed by a typical manager is influenced by a large number of factors, many of which are also utilized in the normative model. Following are several conclusions which are substantiated by the results on both recalled and standardized problems: Managers use decision processes providing less opportunity for participation (1) when they possess all the necessary information rather than when they lack some of the needed information; (2) when the problem which they face is well structured rather than unstructured; (3) when their subordinates' acceptance of the decision is not critical for the effective implementation of the decision or when the prior probability of acceptance of an autocratic decision is high; and (4) when the personal goals of their subordinates are *not* congruent with the goals of the organization as manifested in that problem.

So far we have been talking about relatively common or widely shared ways of dealing with organizational problems. Our results strongly suggest that there are some ways of "tailoring" one's approach to the situation which distinguish managers from one another. Theoretically, these can be thought of as differnces among managers in decision rules about when to encourage participation. Statistically, they are represented as interactions between situational variables and personal characteristics.

Consider, for example, two managers who have identical distributions of use of the five decision processes shown in Table 1 on a set of thirty cases. In a sense, they are equally participative (or autocratic). However the situations in which they permit or encourage participation in decision making on the part of their subordinates may be very different. One may restrict the participation of his subordinates to decisions without a quality requirement whereas the other may restrict their participation to problems with a quality requirement. The former would be more inclined to use participative decision processes (like GII) on such decisions as what color the walls would be painted or when the company picnic would be held. The latter would be more likely to encourage participation in decision making on decisions which have a clear and demonstrable impact on the organization's success in achieving its external goals.

Use of the standardized problem set permits the assessment of such differences in decision rules which govern choices among decision-making processes. Since the cases are selected in accordance with an experimental design, it can indicate differences in the behavior of managers attributable not only to the existence of a quality requirement in the problem but also in the effects of acceptance requirements, conflict, information requirements, and the like.

The research using both recalled and standardized problems has also enabled us to examine similarities and differences between the behavior of the normative model and the behavior of a typical manager. Such an analysis reveals, at the very least, what behavioral changes would be expected if managers began using the normative model as the basis for choosing their decision-making processes.

A typical manager says he would (or did) use exactly the same decision process as that shown in Figure 1 in about 40 percent of the situations. In two-thirds of the situations, his behavior is consistent with the feasible set of methods proposed in the model. Thus, in about one-third of the situations, his behavior violates at least one of the seven rules underlying the model.

The four rules designed to protect the acceptance or commitment of the decision have substantially higher probabilities of being violated than do the three rules designed to protect the quality or rationality of the decision. One of the acceptance rules, the Fairness Rule (rule 6) is violated about three-quarters of the time that it could have been applicable. On the other hand, one of the quality rules, the Information Rule (rule 1), is violated in only about 3 percent of occasions in which it is applicable. If we assume for the moment that these two sets of rules have equal validity, these findings strongly suggest that the decisions made by the typical manager are more likely to prove ineffective due to deficiencies of acceptance by subordinates than due to deficiencies in decision quality. Another striking difference between the behavior of the model and of the typical manager lies in the fact that the former shows far greater variance with the situation. If a typical manager voluntarily used the model as the basis for choosing his methods of making decisions, he would become both more autocratic and more participative. He would employ autocratic methods more frequently in situations in which his subordinates were unaffected by the decision and participative methods more frequently when his subordinates' cooperation and support were critical and/or their information and expertise required.

It should be noted that the typical manager to which we have been referring is merely a statistical average of the several thousand that have been studied over the last 3 or 4 years. There is a great deal of variance around that average. As evidenced by their behavior on standardized problems, some managers are already behaving in a manner which is highly consistent with the model while others' behavior is clearly at variance with it.

A New Technology for Leadership Development

The investigations that have been summarized here were conducted for research purposes to shed some light on the determinants and consequences of participation in decision making. In the course of the research, we realized that those managers who were contributing their time as subjects in the research were perceiving this investment as valuable in its own right and as contributing to their own learning and development. The fortunate coincidence of interest between the personal goals of the managers and our own research objectives both made the research task easier and began to suggest that the data collection procedures, with appropriate additions and modifications, might also serve as a valuable approach to leadership development. From this realization evolved an important by-product of the research activities—a new approach to leadership development based on the concepts in the normative model and the empirical methods of the descriptive research.

This approach is based on the assumption that one of the critical skills required of all leaders is the ability to adapt their behavior to the demands of the situation and that one component of this skill involves the ability to select the appropriate decision-making process for each problem or decision he confronts.

In Vroom and Yetton a leadership development program is described which is aimed at providing intensive training in that skill. It is not intended to "train" participants in the use of the model but rather to encourage them to examine their own leadership style and to ask themselves whether the methods they are using are most effective for their own organization.

A critical part of the program involves the use of a set of standardized cases, each depicting a leader faced with an administrative problem to solve. Each person is asked to specify the decision-making process that he would use if faced with each situation. His responses are processed by computer which generates a highly detailed analysis of his leadership style which is provided to him in the course of the program. The responses for all participants in the course are typically processed simultaneously, permitting the economical representation of differences between the person and other participants in the same program.

In its present form, a single computer printout for a person consists of three 15×11 inch pages, each filled with graphs and tables highlighting different features of his behavior. Understanding the results requires a detailed knowledge of the concepts underlying the model which has already been developed in one of the previous phases of the training program. The printout is accompanied by a manual which aids in the explanation of results and provides a suggested set of steps to be followed in extracting full meaning from the printout.

Following are a few of the questions which the printout answers:

1. How autocratic or participative am I in my dealings with subordinates in relationship to other participants in the program?
2. What decision processes do I use more or less frequently than the average?
3. How close does my behavior come to that of the model? How frequently does my behavior agree with the feasible set? What evidence is there that my leadership style reflects the pressure of time as opposed to a concern with the development of my subordinates? How do I compare in these respects with other participants in the class?
4. What rules do I violate most frequently and least frequently? How does this compare with other participants? On what cases did I violate these rules? Does my leadership style reflect more concern with getting decisions that are high in quality or decisions that are accepted?
5. What circumstances cause me to behave in an autocratic fashion? What circumstances cause me to behave participatively? In what respects is the

way in which I attempt to vary my behavior with the demands of the situation similar to that of the model?

When a typical manager receives his printout, he immediately goes to work trying to understand what it tells him about himself. After most of the major results have been understood, he goes back to the set of cases to reread those on which he has violated rules. Typically, managers show an interest in discussing and comparing their results with others in the program. Gatherings of four to six people comparing their results and their interpretations of them, often for several evening hours, were such a common feature that they have recently been institutionalized as part of the procedure.

It should be emphasized that the method of providing feedback to managers on their leadership style is just one part of the total training experience but it is an important part. The program is sufficiently new so that, to date, no long-term evaluative studies have been undertaken. The short-term results, reported in detail in Vroom and Yetton, look quite promising and can be summarized by the following comment written by one of the participants in an experimental version of the program:

> The (computer) output was perhaps the most informative personalized and comprehensive piece of relatively immediate feedback which I have ever received. I would venture to say that not many managers ever get a chance to confront their leadership style and scrutinize it. . . .It will indeed be unfortunate if we never consider the implications of how we treat our subordinates in the business world for the remainder of our careers.

Conclusion

As with participation in decision making, there are many concepts and applications developed within the social sciences, the utility of which is likely to vary with the situation. Decentralization, management by objectives, job enrichment, and sensitivity training are among the "treatments" frequently recommended as valuable but which are likely to have differential effects and to be of differential value under different conditions. In such instances, there are multiple consequences of each treatment, and estimates of their ability in a particular situation inevitably involve judgment concerning the value of each consequence and the probability of its occurrence in that situation.

The efforts reported in this paper rest on the conviction that social scientists can be of greater value in solving problems of organizational behavior if their prescriptive statements deal with the complexities involved in the phenomena with which they study.

The normative model described in this paper is but one small step in that direction. Some might argue that it is premature for social scientists to be prescriptive. Our knowledge is too limited and the issues too complex to warrant prescriptions for action, even those which are based on a diagnosis of situational demands. It is also true, however, that organizational problems persist and that their leaders cannot await the time for the behavioral sciences to perfect their disciplines before attempting to cope with them. Is it likely that models which encourage them to deal analytically with the forces impinging upon them would produce less rational choices than those which they now make? The criterion for social utility is not perfection but improvement over present practice.

Perhaps the most convincing argument for the development of normative models is the fact that in developing and using them their weaknesses can be identified. Insofar as their weaknesses stem from a lack of basic knowledge, this deficiency can be remedied through further research. A strong case can be made for the value of continued interplay between the worlds of practice and social science based on their potential contributions to one another.

Intervention

Edgar H. Schein

. . . One cannot completely separate the stages of data gathering and intervention. Both occur simultaneously: how one gathers data constitutes an intervention, and the kind of intervention one chooses will reveal new data derived from the reaction to the intervention. The separation of these two processes is, therefore, basically a matter of point of view or frame of reference. In this article I will focus on specific attempts to change organizational process by deliberate actions on the part of the consultant.

The interventions which a process consultant might make cannot be rigidly classified, but a broad categorization can be suggested.

1. *Agenda-setting interventions*
   a. Questions which direct attention to interpersonal issues
   b. Process-analysis periods
   c. Agenda review and testing procedures
   d. Meetings devoted to interpersonal process
   e. Conceptual inputs on interpersonal-process topics

2. *Feedback of observations or other data*
   a. Feedback to groups during process analysis or regular work time
   b. Feedback to individuals after meetings or after data gathering

3. *Coaching or counseling of individuals or groups*

From Edgar H. Schein, *Process Consultation: Its Role in Organizational Development*, pp. 102–122. © 1969 Addison-Wesley, Reading, Massachusetts. Reprinted with permission.

4. *Structural suggestions*
   a. Pertaining to group membership
   b. Pertaining to communication or interaction patterns
   c. Pertaining to allocation of work, assignment of responsibility, and lines of authority

The list is arranged in terms of a descending likelihood of use of the particular intervention. In other words, the kind of intervention I am most likely to make pertains to the group's agenda; the kind I am least likely to make is a structural suggestion. Actual solutions to management problems are not even listed because they would not be considered valid interventions in a process-consultant (P-C) model. If I permitted myself to become interested in a particular management problem in sales, marketing, or production, I would be switching roles from that of process consultant to that of expert resource. Once I have become an expert resource, I find I lose my effectiveness as a process consultant.

Agenda-Setting Interventions

The basic purpose of this type of intervention is to make the group sensitive to its own internal processes and to generate on the part of the group some interest in analyzing these processes. In the early stages of a project, I often find myself suggesting to a group that they should allocate fifteen minutes or so at the end of their meeting to review the meeting. I may suggest some dimensions such as how involved they felt, how clear communications were, how well member resources were used, and so on. If the group is willing, I have them fill in a postmeeting reaction form and tabulate their own data for further discussion. . . .

Out of process-analysis sessions there often arise two further issues, leading to further interventions. The group sometimes discovers that it has a variety of dissatisfactions with the manner in which it arrives at and processes its work agenda. I find myself at this point suggesting various ways by which the group can evaluate what to put on the agenda, how much time to allocate to each item, how to sort items in terms of importance or type of problem, and so on.

The other issue pertains to the matter of interpersonal process itself. The more interested the group becomes in its own workings, the more time it devotes to discussing this topic and the less time there is for its regular agenda. To deal with this dilemma I often suggest that process work could perhaps be done in depth by periodically allocating a whole meeting or some set block of time just to processes in the group.

Such meetings are often held away from the office at a motel or some other detached location, in order to permit the group to really work on group issues. I will not suggest this kind of meeting, however, until I believe the group is emotionally ready to handle a larger dose of process analysis. One of the frequent mistakes I have observed in colleagues' efforts to help organizations is an initial suggestion of holding a meeting to explore relationships and interpersonal issues. Such a meeting should not be scheduled without firsthand knowledge that members want it and are ready to deal emotionally with whatever issues might come up.

The final subheading under agenda-setting interventions concerns the matter of presenting relevant elements of theory about individuals, groups, and the management process. . . .

The key criterion for the choice of theory input is that the theory must be relevant to what the group already senses is a problem. There is little to be gained by giving important theory if the group has no data of its own to link to the theory. On the other hand, once the group has confronted an issue in its own process, I am always amazed at how ready the members are to look at and learn from general theory. . . .

Feedback of Observations or Other Data

FEEDBACK TO GROUPS

There are basically two types of circumstances which call for this type of intervention. Case 1 would be the situation where some group has agreed to a meeting in which interpersonal processes would be discussed and has further agreed to have the consultant survey the members of the group for their individual reactions and feelings. The feedback of the survey results then serves as the opening agenda for the meeting. Case 2 is the situation where a group has already learned to discuss interpersonal process and has developed a need to supplement such discussion with more personal kinds of feedback. . . .

It should be noted that in both types of situation there must be some readiness for active intervention or some consensus that feedback of observations or interview results would be a legitimate activity for the group to undertake. There is nothing more tempting for the process consultant than to leap in with his own observations as soon as he has picked up some data on an interesting issue. If the consultant is to maintain congruence with the P-C model, however, he must resist the temptation lest he put the group immediately on the defensive or undermine his own position by reporting something which does not make sense (or is unpalatable) to group members. The issue is not whether the observation is valid or not. The issue is whether the group is able and ready to understand and learn from the observation. Such ability and readiness must be built up before feedback can be useful. . . .

In giving either individual or group feedback from the interview summary, my role is to ensure understanding of the data and to stimulate acceptance of it, so that remedial action of some sort can be effectively undertaken. Once the expectation has been built that top management will do something, there is great risk of lowering morale if the report is merely read, without being acted upon in some manner. Incidentally, it is the process consultant's job to ensure that top management makes this commitment initially and that high-level officials understand that when the interviews are completed there will be some demands for action. If management merely wants information (without willingness to do something about the information), the process consultant should not do the interviews in the first place. The danger is too great that management will not like what it hears and will suppress the whole effort; such a course will only lead to a deterioration of morale.

The results of interviews (or questionnaires) do not necessarily have to go beyond the group which is interested in them. One of the simplest and most helpful things a group can do to enhance its own functioning is to have the consultant interview the members individually and report back to the group as a whole a summary of its own members' feelings. It is a way of hauling crucial data out into the open without the risk of personal exposure of any individual if he feels the data collected about him are damaging or that the analysis of such data will result in conclusions that are overcritical of his performance.

FEEDBACK TO INDIVIDUALS

This is an appropriate intervention when (1) some data have been gathered about the individual (by either interview or direct observation); and (2) the individual has indicated a readiness to hear such feedback. In the case where a number of subordinates have been interviewed, some of the comments they make will deal with their reactions to the boss's behavior. If the superior has agreed beforehand to listen to the others' reactions, it is quite appropriate for the consultant to describe the range of comments to him and to assist in interpreting the comments. If the consultant has been observing the boss in meetings, he can then add his own direct feedback and try to establish some relation between what he and the subordinates perceive. Sometimes there are no data from subordinates, only the consultant's observations. If the consultant feels that the manager is interested and shows a readiness to listen and learn, it is entirely appropriate for the consultant to share these observations.

In order for feedback to be effective, the consultant must be able to ask the right questions, observe the relevant behavioral events, and give the feedback in a manner which will facilitate learning on the part of the recipient. The behavior asked about or observed must be relevant to the task performance of the group and

to the goals of the total consultation project. The manner in which the feedback is given must reflect sensitivity to the blind spots or areas of defensiveness of the recipient. Feedback must be concrete, descriptive, verifiable, timely, and specific. The consultant must be prepared for defensiveness or too facile verbal acceptance, both of which imply a denial of the feedback. He must know how to impart potentially threatening information without demeaning the recipient. As I think back over my various consulting experiences, unquestionably the ones with the most disastrous results were those where I fed back "facts" without any concern for the feelings of the recipient. What then happened was that the facts were denied, and I was politely but firmly invited to terminate the relationship. . . .

Coaching or Counseling

The giving of feedback either to individuals or to groups almost invariably leads to coaching or counseling sessions. The manager may learn that he somehow fails to hear certain members of the group, that he does not give enough recognition for good performance, or that he is too unapproachable when the subordinate needs help. Inevitably his next question is, "How can I change my behavior to achieve better results?" Similarly, a group may learn that its members see the meetings as dull or unfruitful; inevitably the members then ask, "How can we make our meetings more interesting and productive?"

There are two cautions which the consultant must keep uppermost in his mind before answering the above questions:

1. Do not respond until you are sure that the group (or individual) has really understood the feedback and has been able to relate it to concrete observable behavior.
2. Do not respond until you are sure that the group member (or manager) has begun an active process of trying to solve the problem for himself.

If the consultant is not sure on point 1, he should continue to ask questions like: "What does that com-

ment mean to you in terms of how you see yourself?''
''Can you think of anything you do which might give
people that impression?'' ''What do you think the
giver of the comment was trying to get across to you?''

If the consultant is not sure on point 2, he can ask
questions like: ''Do you see anything in your own
behavior which you could change?'' ''What might
you do differently to create a different reaction?''
''Do you really want to change your behavior?''

If the consultant gets responses like ''I'm paying
you to give me advice,'' he must reassess the state of
the relationship and the readiness of the recipient of
the feedback to work on the problem area. If the feedback has been sincerely sought and has been
understood, it is most likely that the recipient will
have ideas and will share these with the consultant.
The consultant's role then becomes one of adding
alternatives to those already brought up by the client
and helping the client to analyze the costs and benefits
of the various alternatives which have been mentioned. . . .

There is a close similarity between interventions
which draw the group's attention to certain kinds of
process issues and what I choose to call *counseling* (or
coaching) types of interventions. One of the com-
monest opportunities to coach or counsel is to intervene when a particular event has occurred which is
typical of some problem that the group is trying to
overcome. At these times the consultant can be most
effective by pointing out what has just occurred and
inviting the group to examine the consequences. He is
giving feedback at a timely moment in order to help
the group to become more effective. . . .

Structural Suggestions

As I indicated at the outset of this article, this kind of
intervention is very rare, largely because it violates
some of the basic assumptions of the process-consul-
tation model. The consultant is rarely in a position to
suggest how work should be allocated, or communication patterns altered, or committees organized. The
most he can do is help the manager to assess the consequences of different alternatives, or suggest alternatives which have not been considered.

For example, in a company which had recently gone

from a functional to a product-line organization, I
noticed that communication among the functional
people (e.g., in marketing and engineering) had been
reduced very sharply. My intervention was designed to
draw attention to the fact that any form of organization has both strengths and weaknesses. Hence the
manager needs to make an effort to create informal
structures to compensate for the weaknesses created by
the formal structure. In this case, the company eventually adopted a committee structure which brought
the functional specialists together on a regular basis
and thus reduced the communication gap which had
resulted from the reorganization.

The consultant must make it quite clear that he
does not propose any particular solution as the best
one. However frustrating it might be to the client, the
process consultant must work to create a situation
where the client's ability to generate his own solutions
is enhanced. The consultant wants to increase
problem-solving ability, not to solve any particular
problem.

In my experience there has been only one class of exceptions to the above rule. If the client wants to set up
some meetings specifically for the purpose of working
on organizational or interpersonal problems, or wants
to design a data-gathering method, then the consultant indeed does have some relevant expertise which
he should bring to bear. From his own experience he
knows better than the client the pros and cons of interviews or questionnaires; he knows better what questions to ask, how to organize the data, and how to
organize feedback meetings; he knows better the right
sequence of events leading up to a good discussion of
interpersonal process in a committee. In such matters,
therefore, I am quite direct and positive in suggesting
procedures, who should be involved in them, who
should be told what, and how the whole project
should be handled. . . .

In conclusion, the process consultant should not
withhold his expertise on matters of the learning process itself, but he should be very careful not to confuse
being an expert on how to help an organization to
learn with being an expert on the actual management
problems which the organization is trying to solve.
The same logic applies to the evaluation of individuals: I will under no circumstances evaluate an

individual's ability to manage or solve work-related problems, but I will evaluate an individual's readiness to participate in an interview survey of his group or a feedback meeting. If I feel that his presence might undermine some other goals which the organization is trying to accomplish, I will seek to find a solution which will bypass this individual. These are often difficult judgments to make, but the process consultant cannot evade them if he defines the overall health of the organization as his basic target. However, he must always attempt to be fair both to the individual and the organization. If no course of action can be found without hurting either, then the whole project probably should be postponed. . . .

Career Development and Planning

Douglas T. Hall and Marilyn A. Morgan

Organizations can only be as flexible, adaptive, and creative as the people they employ. People bring organizations to life. If organizations are to be effective, their people must perform effectively. Therefore, to improve the functioning of an organization, it is necessary to maximize the development and utilization of its human resources. This essay will explore one avenue for the improved utilization of human resources: career development and planning.[1]

Why are careers important? Isn't the career the employee's own business—a private matter? Not really. For one thing, a person's career experiences and outcomes affect his or her performance, absenteeism, work quality, and turnover, all of which mean plus or minus dollars to the organization. For another, careers are a target for implementing equal employment opportunity. For many managers, in fact, career development and affirmative action are synonymous. For a

From "Career Development and Planning" by Douglas T. Hall and Marilyn A. Morgan in W. Clay Hamner and Frank L. Schmidt (Eds.), *Contemporary Problems in Personnel,* rev. ed. (Chicago: St. Clair Press, 1977), pp. 205–26. By permission of John Wiley & Sons, Inc.

[1] For further discussion of the issues raised in this essay, see D. T. Hall, *Careers in Organizations* (Pacific Palisades: Goodyear Publishing, 1976), and M. A. Morgan, "The Relative Impact of Job Histories on Career Outcome Variables," unpublished Ph.D. dissertation, Northwestern University, 1977.

The material in this essay was prepared under Grant No. 91-17-76-18 from the Manpower Administration, U.S. Department of Labor, under the authority of Title III, Part B, of the Comprehensive Employment and Training Act of 1973. Points of view or opinions stated in this essay do not necessarily represent the official position or policy of the Department of Labor.

third thing, one's work career is a major input to overall quality of life. People now have greater mobility and personal freedom than in the past, making it easier to achieve career fulfillment, which in turn puts more pressure on a person's employer to provide satisfying career opportunities. And, finally, given a sluggish, slow-growth economy, career opportunities have become more limited, making career planning more important if the person's career goals are to be met.

We will address three issues involved in career development. First we will present some basic concepts: What is a career and what constitutes development? Next, we will look at careers in the context of organizations. Finally, we will describe actions—both individual and organizational—which can facilitate career development.

Human Development Processes in Organizations

THE CAREER SUCCESS CYCLE

Let's start at the beginning, with the individual. Our basic assumption is that people seek rewards and positive reinforcement from their work. These rewards can be extrinsic, such as a pay raise or a pat on the back, or intrinsic, such as a feeling of worthwhile accomplishment. We will further assume that work behavior which is rewarded will tend to be repeated.

Our third assumption is that whenever possible people attempt to increase their sense of self-esteem and avoid lowering their self-esteem. One way people can enhance their self-esteem is through the development of their competence, which is the ability to act successfully in one's environment (White, 1959).

Lewin (1936) and Argyris (1964) have described the

conditions under which effective task performance will lead to increased self-esteem. For example, if (1) a woman sets a challenging goal for herself, and (2) the woman determines her own means of attaining that goal, and (3) if the goal is central to her self-concept, then she will experience *psychological success* upon attainment of that goal. This sense of personal success will lead to an increase in self-esteem. Since increased self-esteem is a powerful reinforcer, it will in turn lead to increased involvement in the task. This increased involvement will then lead the person to set additional goals in the same task area and to set higher levels of aspiration (Lewin, Dembo, Festinger, and Sears, 1944; Porter and Lawler, 1968). This success cycle is illustrated in Figure 1.

Simply put, this theory suggests that success breeds success. This cycle of events can be self-reinforcing and can be generalized beyond simple tasks to people's careers. When a man experiences a success cycle at work, he may develop great enthusiasm for the career area represented by the successful activity. He may talk about ''really finding himself'' or being ''turned on'' by his work.

Also shown in Figure 1 are some conditions in the work environment which feed in to the career success cycle. A challenging job makes it possible for the person to set difficult work goals. Autonomy on the job enables the person to determine his or her own means of attaining work goals. Support, help, and coaching from the boss and peers can be helpful in solving problems and maintaining work motivation. Feedback—information about how close the person is to attaining his or her work goals—is important in two ways. First, it helps the person direct his or her effort more effectively to improve performance. Second, it helps the person evaluate or confirm the level of performance that has been achieved. Unfortunately, in many jobs, performance standards are unclear and ambiguous, so that the person may not always know just what level of success has been attained unless external feedback is provided.

Research conducted at the General Electric Company illustrates how the career success cycle operates. In work planning and review sessions, employees who were given the most difficult goals (as opposed to either impossible or easy ones) showed the greatest gains in performance in later months (Stedry and Kay, 1962). People who participated in work planning and review sessions showed more positive work attitudes than people who received traditional performance appraisal sessions (in which the focus was on evaluating the person's performance). Key features of the work planning sessions were self-appraisal, mutual goal setting, and collaborative problem solving on how to

FIGURE 1
The Career Success Cycle

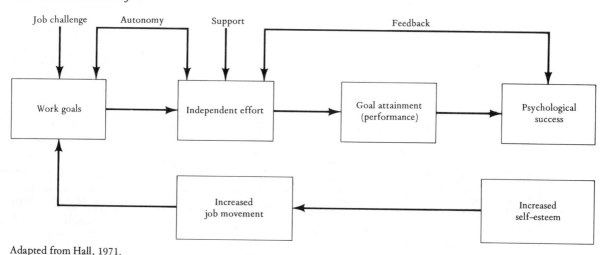

Adapted from Hall, 1971.

achieve future work goals (Kay and Hastman, 1966). Thus, in these GE studies, work performance and attitudes became more positive under two conditions necessary for psychological success: setting challenging self-relevant work goals and independent effort in attaining work goals.

It appears that the success cycle is more likely to be operative when there is a certain level of support, feedback, and autonomy in the climate of the organization. In a study of Roman Catholic parish priests, Hall and Schneider (1973) found that for priests who had high levels of autonomy and support (professional specialists), work satisfaction was related to intrinsic work satisfaction, which was in turn related to self-esteem. For people with low autonomy, the cycle appeared to be "short-circuited," and the person's self-esteem was unrelated to job attitudes. Apparently, a person's psychological reaction to a low-autonomy job is not to become less involved but to insulate his or her self-esteem from low job satisfaction. A study of students similarly found that the success cycle "works" better in an organization with high levels of support than in a lower-support organization (Hall and Hall, 1976a). Further evidence for the existence of the success cycles has been found among AT&T employees (Hall and Nougaim, 1968; Bray, Campbell, and Grant, 1974), students playing an executive simulation (Hall and Foster, 1977), and among operating employees in a government agency (Goodale, Hall, and Rabinowitz, 1976).

If a person insulates his or her self-esteem from the frustrations of an unchallenging job, what are the long-term effects of this adaptive and coping behavior? In the study of Roman Catholic priests referred to earlier, Hall and Schneider (1973) found that it was necessary for a man to spend 22 years as an assistant pastor (a job with extremely low autonomy and challenge) before becoming a pastor (a job with the opposite characteristics). Among pastors, work satisfaction was less related to work challenge and use of skills than it was for assistant pastors. It appears, then, that when people are deprived of opportunities for psychological success in an organization over many years, they may lose much of their desire to utilize conditions for psychological success when challenging work is finally made available. Thus, people's work abilities operate much like physical abilities: If you do not use them, you lose them.

CAREER STAGES: CHANGING NEEDS AND VALUES

What are the stages? Stages in human development are rather predictable, often stressful and trying (for the individual as well as others), and marked by potential for failure if mishandled.

A stage is a period of time in a person's life characterized by distinctive developmental tasks, concerns, needs, values, and activities. A stage is generally separated from the previous and subsequent stages by a role transition or status passage, and successful mastery of the developmental tasks at one stage is a necessary prerequisite to moving on to the following stage.

We tend to associate stages of development more with childhood than with adulthood. There are plenty of everyday terms available to describe life stages of children: infancy, childhood, preteen, adolescence, high-schooler, college student, and so forth. One reason for this is that there are more distinct statuses and status passages in childhood than in adulthood (starting grade school, becoming a teenager, getting a driver's license, graduating from high school, attaining legal age). The child's development is aided by the pacing which these clear passages provide.

The important passages and changes in adult life are harder to identify (Mills, 1970). Marriage and parenthood (and perhaps divorce) are often the last institutionalized role transitions a person moves through until retirement. Thus, the person must pace his or her development as an adult in terms of more subtle changes.

One guide for the pacing of adult development is the family and the life cycle of one's children. Since the passages of children are so clear, they can also serve to mark the parents'. In fact, an adult's development and social behavior may have more to do with the family life cycle than with his or her own age. As Cain has observed, "To be the father of a teen-age daughter elicits certain behavior patterns, whether the father be 30 or 70 years of age" (Cain, 1964, p. 289).

A second guide for pacing stages in adult development is the work career, which again may or may not be tied to age. As Hall has argued, "A lawyer or manager who is in the first permanent job following professional training (law school or business school), will probably be concerned about advancement and establishing a reputation among colleagues, whether he or she is 25 or 45" (Hall, 1976, p. 48). Let us examine the major career stages in some detail. (For an elaboration of the stages in adult development, the reader is referred to Gail Sheehy's [1974] *Passages*.)

A MODEL OF CAREER STAGES

Because the passages which mark adult life stages are less clear-cut than those of children, there is less agreement about just what are the main adult stages. However, enough work in different areas points in similar directions so that a tentative composite model can be constructed (see Figure 2; this model draws from the work of Donald Super, Daniel Levinson and associates, Erik Erikson, and that of the first author).

Erik Erikson (1963) describes the adolescent exploratory period as a stage of identity formation. Through personal exploration at a time when the personal stakes are not too high, the person clarifies his or her self-concept and intentions for a future career. Levinson, Darrow, Klein, Levinson, and McKee (1974) refer to this period as "getting into the adult world" (GIAW).

The most comprehensive statement of career stages comes from Donald Super (Super, 1957; Super and Bohn, 1970). Following a period of growth in childhood, the person goes through a period of *exploration,* in which self-examination, role tryouts, and occupational exploration take place. The final part of the exploration stage is a *trial* period, a time when a seemingly appropriate field has been selected, the person has found a beginning job and is trying it out as a life work. This trial period may involve several job changes as the person attempts to find a good fit between his or her work interests, needs, and skills, on the one hand, and the demands and rewards of a particular job, on the other.

It is ironic that what is a trial period to the individual (a perfectly natural, necessary stage of human development) translates into high turnover for the organization. This high turnover occurs among new employees, and since turnover costs money (in testing, interviewing, training), organizations usually try to keep turnover as low as possible. To this extent, then, at this point in the employee's career, the goals

FIGURE 2
An Integrative Model of Career Stages

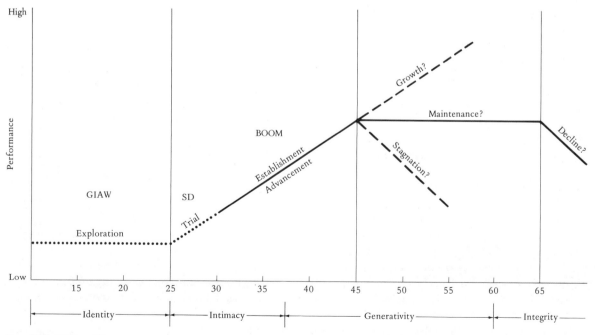

From Hall, 1976, p. 57.

of the organization and the developmental needs of the young employee are in conflict.

The next stage (between approximately ages 25 and 44) is termed *establishment* by Super:

Having found an appropriate field, effort is put forth to make a permanent place in it. There may be some trial early in this stage, with consequent shifting, but establishment may begin without trial, especially in the professions. (Super et al., 1957, pp. 40–41)

Once the person has settled into a particular job or field, establishment consists of achievement, performance, and advancement. Levinson et al. (1974) refer to the start of this establishment period as "settling down" (SD), and to the end of it, after one has severed ties with one's mentors, as "becoming one's own man" (BOOM). In terms of general human development, Erikson calls this a stage of developing intimacy. By intimacy, he means forming attachments and making commitments, to organizations and careers as well as to people (e.g., mates).

The forties mark the start of a *maintenance* stage, a midcareer plateau, according to Super: "Having made a place in the world of work, the concern is now to hold it. Little new ground is broken, but there is continuation along established lines" (Super et al., 1957, pp. 40–41). More recent writings, however, indicate that midcareer is not always the smooth plateau implied by Super. It can be a period of searching, reappraisal, depression, and redirection. Out of this midlife "crisis" can come either continuing growth or stagnation and early decline, depending on how successful the person is in confronting and overcoming the developmental tasks of this period. In a similar vein, Erikson describes midlife as a time for generativity, a concern for producing something meaningful to be left for the next generation.

The passages into the trial and establishment periods are fairly easy to define. Trial often starts when the person leaves school and starts to work. Establishment begins after the person decides to stay in one career field or job. Midlife is harder to pinpoint. (In fact, we do not even have a good descriptive term to use for it; we have to fall back on a chronological referent, midlife.)

Rather than one single transition point marking midlife, it seems to be triggered by a complex set of factors (from Hall, 1976):

Awareness of advancing age and awareness of death (the "psychology of turning 40")

Awareness of physical aging

Leveling off of career advancement; the person knows how many career goals have or will be attained

Search for new life goals

Marked change in family relationships (e.g., teen-aged children, a divorce)

Change in work relationships (e.g., now *you* are the boss, the SOB)

Growing sense of obsolescence (As Satchel Paige put it, "Never look back; someone may be gaining on you.")

Reduction in perceived occupational mobility

These changes occur gradually, in contrast to earlier abrupt transitions such as college graduation or becoming a parent. Therefore, the person may experience vague, generalized discomfort and restlessness which cannot be explained or tied down to one simple causal factor. In this sense, midlife may be more difficult to deal with than other stages because of its ambiguity, which in turn can aggravate its frustrations. Especially lucid popular descriptions of midlife experiences are found in Sheehy's (1974) *Passages,* Persig's (1974) *Zen and the Art of Motorcycle Maintenance,* and Heller's (1974) *Something Happened.*

The final stage is termed *decline* by Super. Reacting to the unattractiveness of this term, Super, who had just retired himself, commented, "You can call it what you want—the Golden Years, the Sunshine Years, whatever. But I'm there; take my word for it, it's decline!" (Super, 1973, personal communication).

Erikson refers to this final period with a more pleasant term, *integrity,* which is the feeling that the person is satisfied with his life, choices, and actions; he sees his life as having been meaningful and is willing to leave it as is. In terms of an organizational work career, this final stage involves the transition from membership in the organization to retirement and a new set of activities.

ORGANIZATIONAL CAREER MOVEMENT

Another way of analyzing career development is by tracking people's movements through organizations. This is in contrast to the model of career stages shown

FIGURE 3
Schein's Model of an Organization

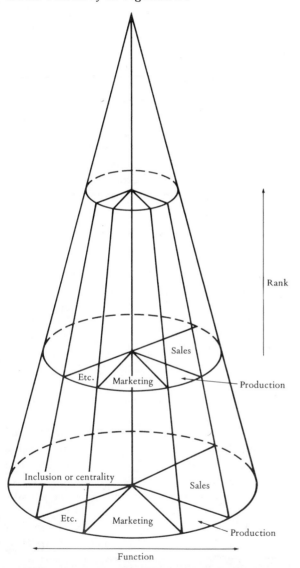

From Edgar H. Schein, "The Individual, the Organization, and the Career: A Conceptual Scheme." *Journal of Applied Behavioral Science, 7,* [1971]. Copyright 1971, NTL Institute.

in Figure 2, which shows the career in terms of changes in the person.

Schein (1971) has developed a model of organizational career passages, based on the conelike shape of an organization (shown in Figure 3). The three dimensions of the cone represent three types of moves the person may make in the organization:

Vertical—moving up or down represents changing one's rank or level in the organization.
Radial—moving more (or less) "inside" the system, becoming more (or less) central, part of the "inner circle," and acquiring more (or less) influence in the system.
Circumferential—transferring laterally to a different function, program, or product in the organization.

There are three types of boundaries which correspond to each type of movement.

Hierarchical. These separate the hierarchical levels from each other.
Inclusion. These separate individuals or groups who differ in the degree of their centrality.
Functional or departmental. These separate departments, or different functional groupings from each other.

Individuals pass through different types of boundaries in different stages of their careers. In the exploration and trial periods, the person passes through several inclusion boundaries, moving in and out of several organizations perhaps. Trial experiences may also contain many functional moves, as with trainees in a job-rotation development program. In the establishment-advancement stage, the person may have settled down into one function and is making hierarchical moves (e.g., promotions), as well as continuing to make inclusion moves (becoming more involved in and central to the organization). A midcareer plateau is just that, involving few changes or passages of any kind. And in decline, the main developmental task is to reverse the inclusion moves made earlier—that is, to move out of the organization.

These changes in organizational roles stimulate corresponding shifts in the identity and values of the job-holder and therefore are a strong means of organizational socialization:

These changes which occur during the course of his career, as a result of adult socialization or acculturation, are changes in the nature and integration of [the person's] social selves. It is highly unlikely that he will change substantially in his basic character structure and his pattern of psychological defenses, but he may change drastically in his social selves in the sense of developing new attitudes and values, new competencies, new images of himself, and new ways of entering and conducting himself in social situations. As he faces new roles which bring new demands, it is from his repertory of attributes and skills that he constructs or reconstructs himself to meet these demands. (Schein, 1971, pp. 308–9)

Now that we have an idea of what the person looks like over the course of a career, let's put the person in context—in the organization. How do organizational careers evolve?

People in Organizational Career Settings

For individuals, career planning means identifying major career goals and interim objectives so that one becomes more than a manager of his or her own career. Similarly, the organization needs to assume the responsibility for facilitating self-management of careers by assisting the individual in planning expected progress through the organization. It seems, then, that the implications of career development are best expressed in terms of the importance of the *management* of careers. Such a perspective allows us to view career planning or development as an ongoing process designed to help both the individual and the organization.

Two factors—*job characteristics* and *work-force composition*—are critical in career planning. First, the nature of the jobs through which the manager progresses is crucial. Since the elements of the model of psychological success consist of challenging goals, effort, performance, psychological success, self-esteem, and involvement, the job itself is an important trigger to a positive success cycle. Jobs should be designed and selected on the basis of the degree to which they provide the necessary factors to better assure psychological success.

Second, the nature of the current work force has an impact on career development. What happens when "nontraditional" workers occupy these enriched jobs in organizations? The current work force has been expanded in the last decade to include women and members of minority groups. With these new members selected, the organization must work to plan their advancement within organizational settings. Similarly, we are seeing increasing numbers of dual career couples. The problems and opportunities created by such situations are beginning to be explored by organizations.

THE NATURE OF THE JOB

The Initial Job.   The importance of the first assignment is often underestimated. Research in the area of early job challenge suggests that employees who receive especially challenging job assignments early in their careers do better in later jobs (e.g., Berlew and Hall, 1966; Bray, Campbell, and Grant, 1974).

Too often managers are afraid to give new employees any real responsibility until they have adjusted to the new work situation and have demonstrated their capabilities. Consequently, the initial job most often involves being assigned to a training program of some sort, working on a small or easy project, or serving as an assistant. The problem with the prove-yourself-before-we-give-you-any-responsibility philosophy is its self-fulfilling nature. How can an organization identify the capabilities and potential of a new employee if they begin by placing severe limits on the opportunities to perform? Most people can complete successfully a simple task or project. New employees can usually perform well as an assistant when they are told exactly what to do. It is difficult, however, to identify the limitations of individuals in such controlled assignments. Similarly, the individual is not provided the opportunity to "stretch" or use many of the skills developed in the years of schooling. He or she will often feel frustrated or bored by the routine nature of initial assignments. Thus, when organizations give low initial challenge and responsibility to new employees, they are actually "developing" low performance standards.

If initial career experiences have a continuing impact on the development of a person's career, then the entry-level job assignment is a crucial aspect of an employee's overall career planning effort. Organizations should analyze entry-level jobs in order to provide a meaningful, challenging experience for their new members. It is not easy to make these jobs more challenging, but such long-term payoffs as performance, commitment, and involvement make the effort worthwhile.

Some organizations believe in an initial period of job rotation. Rotation which sends an employee through a series of short-term, meaningless positions where he or she is nothing more than an observer of different parts of the organization will not provide the new hire with the necessary amounts of job challenge. However, it seems reasonable to expect that an entry-level assignment which relies heavily upon *planned job rotation* will be able to reconcile competing problems created by the dual needs of initial job challenge and training. Planned job rotations rely upon a series of meaningful job moves during the first 6 to 12 months of the employee's career. This set of jobs should be selected to encourage the development of skills essential to future job performance. Planned job rotations are an efficient means of providing the employee with a variety of meaningful experiences in a short time, as well as the opportunity to self-test working in different settings as part of a career development plan.

The Individual's Career Path.   The sequence of jobs through which an employee moves during a career constitutes his or her individual *career path* or *job history*. Research on the initial job assignment demonstrates the effect the first job has on the employee's overall growth and development. Consider the combined impact of a sequence of jobs on overall success over a 30 to 40 year career. Consider, for example, the potential paths to the job of store manager in a large retailing organization. The individual who moves through a series of jobs which provide him with increasing amounts of various job dimensions (e.g., challenge, variety, and functional area) will be better prepared to handle the responsibilities of store management because of it.

The career path or job history of an employee has a potentially stronger effect on overall development than any other experience or set of experiences in his or her career. A challenging job provides opportunities for varied experiences and skill development. Such experiences contribute to successful performance in the new job situation and are readily transferable to future situations. After performing well on a job, the employee has a better chance of moving on to another job which will provide opportunity for additional growth and development. Since most jobs have different characteristics, a variety of them encourages the development and use of varied skills. Movement through a variety of jobs increases the chances of career success, since performing well on one job will improve the chance of being assigned to a more demanding one. This means that a carefully planned sequence of job moves should be undertaken in an effort to assure levels of career success.

If job moves are to be used for growth and developmental purposes, care must be taken to use the career planning process effectively. The following steps are important:

Selection of a target job.   The individual must consider his or her career aspirations within the organization. In some cases the target job is determined by the nature of the business. For example, in retailing, likely target jobs would be store manager and head buyer. Similarly, the target job is often determined by the nature of the profession. In the case of academia, for instance, the target job is most often full professor.

Identification of the necessary skills and experiences. Although it is difficult to get accurate, objective information with which to identify the skills and experiences necessary to successfully perform the target job, job descriptions and analyses are probably the best sources of evaluative information. Individuals employed by organizations which have implemented the Hay System[2] have a definite advantage in this area since the characteristics of each job have been measured and can be used as an indication of skill requirements.

Identification of the necessary sequence of jobs. The following guidelines are useful in considering the sequencing of planned job moves which will provide the required levels of experience and skill development:

[2] The Hay System is a method of evaluating jobs by relying on factors that are common to all jobs in varying degrees. The system provides useful information about certain characteristics of each job by considering factors such as accountability, problem-solving opportunities, and technical skill requirements, and compares jobs to determine which contain more of these factors than others.

1. Select jobs which provide changes which are large enough to stretch skills and capabilities, yet small enough to be manageable.
2. Consider lateral moves as well as promotions, since moves at the same level often provide opportunities for skill development (e.g., change in function).
3. Allow for enough time to master the job but not so long an assignment that the performance of the job becomes routine.
4. Consider jobs which complement or supplement, not those which duplicate previous experiences.
5. Provide alternative moves or sequences (i.e., a contingency plan), since it is unlikely that the normal demands of the organization will allow for all the scheduled moves exactly as planned.

THE NATURE OF THE WORK FORCE: NONTRADITIONAL EMPLOYEES

Women and Minorities.   Five or so years ago a major organizational concern was to attract women and minorities into professional and managerial positions. The literature was full of cases describing the types of discriminatory practices common to most organizations. While there is still a concern for recruitment and selection, another issue is how best to assure the successful performance and advancement of women and minorities in organizational settings. The following comment from *Business Week* offers evidence of this problem.

> It took a decade of federal legislation, relentless agitation from the women's (and civil rights) movements, and seismic shifts in public opinion, but women (and minorities) are moving boldly into the mainstream of corporate management. The battle for equality in blue-collar and clerical jobs moved faster because bias was easier to prove. The far more complex struggle for equal status up the corporate ladder has taken longer and is far from over. But the big news is that women (and minorities) are making headway—slowly in the executive suite, faster at the lower rungs of middle management. (Nov. 24, 1975)

Career planning is recognized as an effective means of developing opportunities for minorities and women. Members of these groups need to plan their career moves very carefully in order to develop the necessary skills to assure successful performance in the more demanding jobs they will encounter as they move up the corporate ladder.

O'Leary (1974) identifies several factors which serve to inhibit the expression of upward occupational aspirations of women and could subsequently affect their overall career success: fear of failure, low self-esteem, sex role stereotypes, role conflicts, and the prevalence of the male managerial model. It is important that organizations consider these barriers to success in planning the career moves of women. Assignment to jobs which provide at least a minimal amount of support should be an important consideration. Support may take the form of good supervision, assignments which provide female peers or role models, and feedback on performance.

As with women's careers, careful career planning is important for the development of minorities. The challenge of integrating these employees into the work force is an issue being addressed by most organizations. Hence, variables affecting the careers of women and minorities seem to be an important area for future research.

Dual Careers.   Dual career couples are those in which both husband and wife pursue a full-time career. As more married women enter the work force, dual careers are becoming increasingly important factors for career management, because it is difficult to relocate one partner if the other is unable or unwilling to move. When both husband and wife have full-time careers, career flexibility decreases and planning becomes more crucial. The problem of dual career families is becoming increasingly common among young employees and must be dealt with by organizations.

For example, a large manufacturing firm in the Midwest recently experienced the following effects of a dual career situation. A very promising and also married young attorney had been working in its legal department for 5 years. Not only was he well respected in his own department but he had caught the attention of the company president and had been identified as one of several high-potential employees. During the couple's stay in the Midwest, the wife worked toward a Ph.D. in psychology. Upon receiving this degree she was offered an academic position in a prestigious university on the East Coast. Recognizing that such a position would be a very good way to start his wife's academic career, her husband requested a transfer to the eastern division of the firm. The head of the legal department and the president refused to consider the request. This attorney is now working for a competitor in the competitor's New York office and his wife is teaching at the eastern university.

This example suggests that the biggest problem created by dual career situations is job transfers. A transfer to another location means that the working spouse must relocate, too. If both husband and wife are employed by the same organization, both career moves are within the control of one organization. In the much more frequent situations where employment is by different organizations, there is the risk of either losing employees when one spouse is transferred or of being asked to arrange a transfer to the same location. An article in *Business Week* (Aug. 23, 1976) stated that working wives were the most critical factor in the unwillingness to move of male executives.

Similar dual career issues are found in recruiting employees. It is sometimes difficult to attract a person to an organization if its location does not provide career opportunities for the spouse. Organizations are often required to recruit both husband and wife or to help find a job for the spouse. The point is that the spouse's career opportunities increasingly affect the recruitment and advancement of today's employees. The issue, however, has not yet been realized by many organizations, but it seems destined to become a crucial organizational problem. Consideration of the spouse's career must be made in the career planning and development efforts or the organization runs the risk of losing many good employees.

Organizational Management of Careers

What, then can organizations do to manage employees' careers more effectively? We will now examine this critical, practical issue.

STAGE–SPECIFIC TRAINING

Much training in organizations is done across the board with large groups of employees. It may be aimed at all people at a particular job level or to all people about to enter a given job. This is reasonable. It is also reasonable that people in a given career stage,

or people about to enter a given stage, may also need training in how to deal with the developmental tasks of that stage. Unfortunately, this sort of stage-specific training is rarely done. What would such training entail?

Assessing Stages. First, it is necessary to have a way to identify who is at a given career stage. The time at which people move through various stages varies with the occupation and the organization. In most organizations there is usually some commonly accepted age at which advancement starts to level off. This could be taken as the start of midcareer. The trial period is easier to identify—people at this point are usually new employees in their first year or two. Establishment-advancement would probably span the second or third year of employment through the start of midcareer. Decline could be defined in terms of when people in the organization begin thinking about and preparing for retirement, perhaps 5 years before.

Once the stages have been defined, training needs can be identified. These can be broken down into two areas: task needs (dealing with job activities) and emotional needs (covering the feelings associated with career changes.) These needs are summarized in Table 1.

Trial Stage Needs. In the trial stage, the individual needs to be encouraged to spend some time in various job activities but with enough time spent in each activity so that challenge and success can be experienced. Self-exploration, through career assessment and planning exercises, should also be encouraged. On the emotional side, the person should be pressed to begin making choices and settling into an area of specialization. Even if the organization does not have a job-rotation training program, it would be a mistake to keep a young person in one function from the first day of employment without some opportunity to try some other areas.

Advancement Needs. In the establishment-advancement stage, job challenge is the critical need. The person needs to develop competence in some area of specialization. Technical training programs are especially important in this stage. A special effort should be made to develop creativity and innovation,

TABLE 1
Training Needs Within Career Stages

Stage	Task Needs	Emotional Needs
Trial	1. Varied job activities	1. Make preliminary job choices
	2. Self-exploration	2. Settling down
Establishment-advancement	1. Job challenge	1. Deal with rivalry and competition; face failures
	2. Develop competence in a specialty area	2. Deal with work-family conflicts
	3. Develop creativity and innovation	3. Support
	4. Rotate into new area after 3–5 years	4. Autonomy
Midcareer	1. Technical updating	1. Express feelings about midlife
	2. Develop skills in training and coaching others (younger employees)	2. Reorganize thinking about self in relation to work, family, community
	3. Rotation into new job requiring new skills	3. Reduce self-indulgence and competitiveness
	4. Develop broader view of work and own role in organization	
Late career	1. Plan for retirement	1. Support and counseling to see one's work as a platform for others
	2. Shift from power role to one of consultation and guidance	2. Develop sense of identity in extraorganizational activities
	3. Identify and develop successors	
	4. Begin activities outside the organization	

Adapted from Hall, 1976, p. 60.

since these qualities are usually at their peak in the early career years. After the person has developed specialized skills, the organization should avoid the temptation to keep the person in this area for too long. (Such a course is tempting because it would be a way of reaping a high return on the company's investments in the person's training, as, for example, when managers—especially sales managers—"capture" a good person and will not let that person advance.) After 3 to 5 years, the person should be moved into a new specialty, to prevent overspecialization and early obsolescence. On the emotional side, the advancing person needs to deal with strong feelings of rivalry and competition with peers. There may also be concerns about failure and about career-family conflicts which will call for opportunities to discuss them and emotional support from someone in the organization. Autonomy will be necessary to permit feelings of individual achievement and psychological success. An occasional "rap group" dealing with the stresses and conflict of expending high energy on success can be a beneficial way of dealing with these feelings.

Midcareer Needs. In midcareer, an individual's skills may need some updating if the person has not been rotated through new specialties at 3 to 5 year intervals earlier in the career. At this career point the person is doing less technical work and more administrative work. Harry Levinson (1969) posits that individuals should shift from being "quarterbacks" to "coaches" at this stage, and this calls for advanced training in human relations, communication, and management skills. Continued job rotation is still important to keep the person fresh and always learning. This is also a time when the person begins to identify more with the organization and can see his or her own work better in relation to the total organization's purposes. Seminars on company history, policies, and goals may be, ironically, better received by midcareer employees than by new employees, who usually get such material in their initial orientation sessions.

The emotional side of midcareer calls for an opportunity to talk with others about the feelings of midlife (anguish, reexamination of goals, limited time, restlessness, etc.). It also helps to encourage or help employees to do some life planning and re-relate their work commitments to family, community, and other involvements. Since advancement is leveling off, there may be need to redirect competitive energies, perhaps into the vicarious success of aiding subordinates' careers.

Late Career Needs. In the decline stage, it is important to begin planning for retirement, since good planning leads to a good transition. This means, in a sense, starting the career cycle again but now in the area of retirement activities (exploration, trial, establishment). After all, there is a *retirement career* to be planned for and managed, as well as the remaining work career. At the same time, the person must make arrangements to terminate the activities and responsibilities of the work career. This demands skills in identifying and developing successors, gradually involving successors in job activities and decisions. As the person plays a less active role in the organization, he or she can become more available as a source of consultation and organizational wisdom.

On the emotional side, there is a need to see how one's work has provided a foundation for the work of future generations of employees. There is a need to come to terms with one's overall work career and with the fact that it is ending. It is also important for the person to develop relationships and an identity outside the organization so that the end of employment is not seen as the end of his or her identity.

Why should an organization be concerned about the employee's planning for retirement? First, the late-career person can be a valuable resource in the development of younger employees *if* he has been well treated by the organization and is thus motivated to be helpful. Furthermore, younger employees are more likely to make commitments of time, energy, and involvement to the organization if they see that the organization maintains its interest in the development of employees through their later career stages (i.e., "If the organization treats pre-retirement employees well now, they'll probably treat me well, too").

CHANGING THE WORK ENVIRONMENT

Some of the stage-specific training we have just discussed can be done off the job in training facilities. As mentioned earlier, however, there is much potential for career development training inherent in the nature of the work environment. Let us quickly run down the different facets of the work environment (employee, job itself, boss, organization structure, and personnel policies) to see how it can be redesigned to foster employee career growth.[3]

Entry: Changing Employees Inputs. Young people just out of school and working on their first jobs often experience "reality shock"—that is, a job which falls far short of their expectations for experiences such as

---

[3] This material is based on Hall (1976b), pp. 151–65.

challenge, responsibility, autonomy, and feedback. There are two ways to reduce this expectation versus reality gap: either improve the experience or modify the expectations. One way to do the latter is for organizations to use *realistic job previews* (RJPs) in recruiting (Wanous, 1975). An RJP gives the negative features of a job as well as its positive ones (e.g., a telephone operator's job has low variety and close supervision as well as good pay and security). Realistic job previews seem to result in subsequent lower turnover, and they do not appear to hurt recruiting success (Wanous, 1975).

Another way of providing more realistic job orientations is to give students more training in job-related skills in educational systems, such as business and professional schools. Better links between educators and employers (e.g., through job internships, field projects, executive-in-residence programs) will help on this score, too.

Finally, better selection methods can be used by employers to get a better fit between employee and job. This does not necessarily mean luring the brightest or best-educated candidates. One manufacturing firm in Connecticut sharply reduced its reject rate and employee turnover when it started hiring people in the second quartile—an ability level which fit the routine assembly jobs much better than hiring the highest ability applicants.

Development Through the Job Itself. We have already heard about challenging initial jobs and career pathing as a way of building stretching experiences into the work environment. Employees should have several years to develop specialized competencies, but they should then be rotated into new activities every few years to prevent obsolescence. New job activities can force learning much more effectively than a whole string of university update courses.

Peer stimulation can be an excellent means of learning skills and positive work attitudes. Assigning the new employee to a work group or team of outstanding performers will pay dividends.

One of the largest areas of undeveloped potential for employee growth is feedback and performance appraisal. Feedback is essential in any kind of performance, and it is unfortunate that most of us "fly blind" on our jobs. We usually have to read in meaning to every subtle evaluative cue we receive from our bosses, and these inferences may be totally invalid. (That gruff "Hello!" this morning may have said more about his fight at home than about the report you turned in yesterday.) A simple, well-planned performance appraisal process (with a superior trained in how to do it) can be of the utmost value to the individual and the organization.

Finally, when you get good performance from an employee, do not let it pass unnoticed. As the work of many researchers shows, one of the simplest ways to increase the likelihood of occurrence of a behavior is to positively reinforce it. A word of recognition, a letter of congratulation, a pat on the back, a bonus—these are all ways to reward good performance and to encourage the performer to repeat it. Most of the time managers fail to respond to either good or poor performance—which in effect rewards poor performance and negatively reinforces good performance.

Changing the Superior's Role.   To involve the boss in career development, give her or him the skills necessary to be a good career developer. Skills such as performance appraisal, feedback, counseling, job design, and career plotting are fairly easy to develop in 2 or 3 day training sessions. One of the big reasons managers do not do more about career development is that they lack the skills for it.

Another way to utilize the boss for employee development is to assign new employees to outstanding managers who will set high standards of expected performance. Research has shown that people tend to perform at whatever level is expected (Livingston, 1969), which casts the manager in the role of organizational Pygmalion. Often new employees are assigned to bosses on a random basis; more care in the job assignment process costs little and has a high payoff.

Changing Organizational Structures.   The design of the organization shows up in the "fingerprints" it puts on people. A functional organization produces (possibly narrow) functional specialists. A product organization trains people who are loyal to their product (perhaps at the expense of concern for the firm's other products). A matrix structure (in which people work on cross-functional product teams) can combine the best of both orientations. It also offers two directions for moving people—to a new product but in the same function, or vice versa—which makes a person branch out a bit while still staying, to some extent, in familiar territory.

One of the reasons more effort is not placed on employee development is that this activity is often not rewarded. And it is not rewarded because it is hard to measure. Human-resource accounting is a way of measuring an organization's investments in people and the resulting returns. Therefore, as more companies develop human-resource information systems, this change can make the payoff to a manager for employee development more tangible (Hall, Alexander, Goodale, and Livingstone, 1976).

A third area of activity for many organizations is career planning services. These activities, designed specifically to stimulate career development, can range from very employee-oriented life planning (as at Continental Illinois Bank and The Travelers Insurance Companies, for example) through assessment center feedback (3M Company) to a combination of personal counseling, job design, and training bosses in career developing skills (AT&T). The range of these programs is wide, but though much activity is taking place, there is precious little evaluative research to help us separate the good from the god-awful.

Changing Personnel Policies. The final aspect of the work environment which can be altered to stimulate career development is the area of personnel policies.[4] For example, a policy of rotating managers through "people departments," such as personnel or organization development, can do as much to heighten line managers' sensitivity to employee development needs as can years of information campaigns. A policy of lifelong job rotation, as we have said before, can counteract obsolescence and maintain employee flexibility.

Another policy which can aid development is lateral and downward job transfers. Lateral interfunctional transfers can be a way of developing new skills without promoting the person. (If economic and organizational growth slows, promotion opportunities will diminish accordingly, and other movement possibilities must be explored.)

More controversial is the idea of downward transfers. The option of moving employees down (even if only temporarily) immensely increases an organization's degrees of freedom. Two conditions are important in reducing an outcry against demotions: (1) a guarantee that no one will take a pay cut; and (2) a guarantee that anyone who is moved down will never lose his or her job (a form of organizational tenure). One organization started a downward transfer policy by deliberately moving down two key and obviously successful vice-presidents in order to counter the belief that demotion means failure. The two VPs were assigned temporarily to "hot spots" in the organization, where they promptly shaped up ailing operations. The change also had the side effect of improving communications up to the other vice-presidents. The antidemotion norm is a tough one to buck, however, and in many organizations the benefits will not be worth the cost. However, it is worth thinking the unthinkable and at least considering the possibility of downward moves. Because of the ambiguity in the structure of most organizations, whether a particular move is a promotion or a demotion is often the subject of debate anyway.

One way to reduce the risks of promotions or cross-functional lateral moves is through fallback positions. A fallback position is identified before the transfer is made, and the organization and the employee agree in advance that if the transfer or promotion does not work out, the person will move to the fallback position with no stigma. This represents an acceptance by the organization that the transfer or promotion entails some risk and that the company is prepared to share in the risk and help resolve any resulting problems. Companies such as Heublein, Procter and Gamble, Continental Can, and Lehman Brothers have used fallback positions (*Business Week,* Sept. 28, 1974).

Another personnel innovation is organizational tenure. Using the university as a model, one Pennsylvania manufacturing company introduced a policy of evaluating new employees in two ways after their probationary periods. First, the standard retain-or-terminate decision was made. Then company management asked the question, "If we had to lay off 20 percent of our work force because of economic set-

---

[4] More detail on personnel policies to promote career development can be found in Hall and Hall (1976b).

backs, would this be a person we would let go (on the basis of performance)?'' If the answer was yes, the person would still be offered the job, but feedback about being in the lowest 20 percent would be given. (Many of the low 20 percent employees stayed on, and the feedback improved performance for some, in which case the ''contract'' was revised.) The top 80 percent employees also received feedback and were given a form of tenure in the organization. The active ingredient in this system, of course, is the feedback, which is probably more important than the tenure itself.

A final important personnel policy area relates to the dual career employee. As more women take up work careers (and assuming men continue to do so), and as long as men and women marry or live together, there will be increasing numbers of dual career employees in organizations. If an organization sees it as the couple's responsibility to cope with the stresses of dual career responsibilities, that organization runs the risk of losing, or failing to hire, talented, career-involved employees. A small interview survey conducted by Alison Martier, covering approximately thirty organizations in the Chicago area, identified the following policies for accommodating dual career employees:

1. Recognition of the existence of problems in dual careers
2. Help with relocation in the case of transfer of a spouse (or helping the spouse relocate if your employee is being transferred)
3. Flexible working hours (to facilitate child care)
4. Initiation of counseling for dual career employees
5. Family day-care centers
6. Improved career planning and counseling
7. A change in antinepotism rules (to make it easier for two members of the same family to work for the organization or perhaps the same unit in the organization)

These are preliminary approaches because we are at a preliminary stage in the recognition of dual career problems. As dual career employees who are now relatively young and low in power in most organizations rise to higher levels, more pressure for solutions will be generated. For this reason, the dual career issue has been called an ''organizational time bomb'' (Hall and Hall, 1976).

Planning for Your Own Career

A summary of the ideas presented in the preceding section is given in Table 2. This section is based upon the work of Schein (1964), Hall (1976c), and others. We will be talking about *typical career experiences,* but of course each person's career is unique, so don't panic if you do not like what you read here. We want to discuss your expectations, the company's expecta-

TABLE 2

Organizational Actions for Facilitating Career Development

Entry: changing employee inputs

1. Better links between school and work
2. Training students in job-related skills
3. Realistic job previews in recruiting
4. Better selection for person-job fit

Development through the job

1. Challenging initial jobs
2. Periodic job rotation
3. Colleague stimulation
4. Frequent feedback and performance review
5. Rewarding good performance

Changing the boss's role

1. Make bosses career developers
2. Train managers in job design and career planning
3. Reward managers for employee development

Changing organizational structures

1. Matrix organization structures
2. Accounting for human resources
3. Career planning services

Changing personnel policies

1. Rotation of managers through ''people departments''
2. Lifelong job rotation
3. Downward and lateral transfers
4. Tenure
5. Fallback positions for promoted employees
6. Support for dual career employees

Adapted from Hall, 1976, p. 177.

tions, how its members may perceive you, what you may experience in your first job, and how you can help yourself.

YOUR EXPECTATIONS

If you are typical, from your first job you will probably want opportunities for advancement, responsibility, interesting, meaningful, and challenging work, a chance to use your skills and educational training, security, and good pay. (In a Doonesbury cartoon, when Mark told his father that he was expecting these qualities in his first job, his father's response was, "In short, you have no intention of getting a job!")

WHAT THE COMPANY WILL EXPECT OF YOU

The company will expect you to have *competence* to get a job done—to identify problems and see them through to solutions. It will also expect you to accept *"organizational realities,"* that is, the need for stability and survival, informal power relationships, recognition of group loyalties, office politics, and the like. You will be expected to *generate and sell ideas.* This involves a wide range of human relations skills, such as translating technical solutions into practical, understandable terms, patiently overcoming resistance to change, and the ability to influence others. *Loyalty and commitment* may be important, especially in organizations with strong promotion-from-within policies. This loyalty may involve some sacrifice of parts of your personal life. *Personal integrity and strength* will also be highly valued as shown by your ability to stick to your own point of view without being a rebel, yet knowing how to compromise when necessary. Finally, the organization will look for your *ability to grow,* to assume responsibility and learn from mistakes (mistakes are expected, but not repeated mistakes).

HOW THE COMPANY WILL PERCEIVE YOU

How you are perceived naturally depends a lot on both you and the organization. The company may see you as overambitious and unrealistic in your expectations. You may seem too theoretical, too idealistic, or too naive and immature. You will probably lack experience. It may see you as too security-conscious and unwilling to take risks. You may have underdeveloped interpersonal skills, and you may have trouble selling your ideas. Overall, your boss and the organization may see you as a potentially *useful* resource who must be broken in first ("housebroken" in the words of some managers).

WHAT YOU WILL EXPERIENCE

The most common complaint of new graduates is *lack of challenge*—that is, underutilization of your skills and training. (But remember: You are being trained for managerial jobs 5 to 15 years off, not just for the first assignment.) Turnover is extremely high in the first year of employment, often around 50 percent. Because the actual job is so different from what you expected, you may experience reality shock.

To compound these problems, you may threaten your boss. Your starting pay may be uncomfortably close to his or hers, yet you may be young enough to be your boss's daughter or son. And you will be promoted above your present boss in a few years. And your boss may be a bit obsolete, threatened by your more recent skills and knowledge. And your boss may be going through a midcareer crisis, and so forth.

You may get little or no feedback on your performance. You may have trouble creating your own challenges, and your company training may be inadequate (in many companies, training is just a sink-or-swim process).

WHAT YOU CAN DO

The organization you work for and chance events have a lot of control over your career, but that control is not absolute. *Develop some career goals* and *do some career planning.* Many universities have counseling centers which provide excellent career planning services. A useful guide for self-management of careers is *What Color Is Your Parachute?* by R. N. Bolles (1974).

Career maturity involves the following career competencies: self-appraisal, obtaining occupational information, problem solving, planning, and choosing goals. Try to develop these skills.

Try to get realistic information about any organizations from whom you have offers. Research has shown that people with good information (positive and negative) about the company are more satisfied and are less likely to quit.

If you have a choice of offers, go for the most

challenging job. One of the best predictors of career success is the amount of challenge in your first job. In choosing your first job, challenge and potential for career growth should be more important than shorter term considerations such as salary or location. If you are stretched and pushed toward excellence in your first job, you will be more successful later and will have plenty of later offers with good salaries and locations.

Develop your communications and human relations skills. The most critical part of your job will be working with people, even if you are doing technical work.

Do not become overspecialized. It may be flattering to become the world's greatest expert on inflation accounting, but what happens to you when prices stabilize? To force yourself to keep learning and growing, move into a new area every 3 to 5 years. The time to begin fighting career obsolescence is now, when that obsolescence could be starting.

Finally, reassess your career periodically. Ask where you are headed and where you want to be, because the only way to get there from here is to know where "there" is.

References

Argyris, C. *Integrating the Individual and the Organization.* New York: Wiley, 1964.

Berlew, D. E., and Hall, D. T. The socialization of managers: Effects of expectations on performance. *Administrative Science Quarterly,* 1966, *11*, pp. 207–223.

Bolles, R. N. *What Color Is Your Parachute? A Practical Manual for Job-Hunters and Career Changers.* Berkeley, Calif.: Ten Speed Press, 1974.

Bray, D. W., Campbell, R. J., and Grant, D. L. *Formative Years in Business: A Long Term AT&T Study of Managerial Lives.* New York: Wiley, 1974.

Cain, L. D., Jr. Life Course and Social Structure. In R. Faris (Ed.), *Handbook of Modern Sociology.* Chicago: Rand McNally, 1964.

Erikson, E. H. *Childhood and Society.* New York: Norton, 1963.

Goodale, J. G., Hall, D. T., and Rabinowitz, S. A test of an integrative model of job involvement. Working paper, York University, 1976.

Hall, D. T. A theoretical model of career subidentity development in organizational settings. *Organizational Behavior and Human Performance,* 1971, *6,* pp. 50–76.

Hall, D. T., and Foster, L. W. Effects of goals, performance, and psychological success upon attitudes toward self, task, and career. *Academy of Management Journal,* 1977.

Hall, D. T., and Hall, F. S. What's new in career management? *Organizational Dynamics,* 1976b.

Hall, D. T., and Hall, F. S. The relationship between goals, performance, success, self-image, and involvement under different organization climates. *Journal of Vocational Behavior,* 1976a.

Hall, D. T. *Careers in Organizations.* Pacific Palisades, Calif.: Goodyear, 1976c.

Hall, D. T., and Nougaim, K. E. An examination of Maslow's need hierarchy in an organizational setting. *Organizational Behavior and Human Performance,* 1968, *3,* pp. 12–35.

Hall, D. T., and Schneider, B. *Organizational Climates and Careers: The Working Lives of Priests.* New York: Seminar (Academic) Press, 1973.

Hall, D. T., Alexander, M. O., Goodale, J. G., and Livingstone, J. L. How to make personnel decisions more productive. *Personnel,* 1976, *53,* pp. 10–20.

Heller, J. *Something Happened.* New York: Ballantine Books, 1974.

Kay, E., and Hastman, R. *An Evaluation of Work Planning and Goal-Setting Discussions.* Crotonville, New York: Behavioral Research Service, General Electric Company, 1966.

Levinson, D. J., Darrow, C., Klein, E., Levinson, M., and McKee, B. The Psychological Development of Men in Early Adulthood and the Mid-Life Transition. In D. F. Hicks, A. Thomas, and M. Roff (Eds.), *Life History Research in Psychopathology,* Vol. 3, Minneapolis: University of Minnesota Press, 1974.

Levinson, H. On being a middle-aged manager. *Harvard Business Review,* 1969, *47,* pp. 51–60.

Lewin, K. The psychology of success and failure. *Occupations,* 1936, *14,* pp. 926–930.

Lewin, K., Dembo, T., Festinger, L., and Sears, P. Level of Aspiration. In J. Mc V. Hunt (Ed.), *Personality and Behavior Disorders.* New York: Ronald Press, 1944.

Livingston, J. S. Pygmalion in management. *Harvard Business Review,* 1969, *47,* pp. 81–89.

Managers move more but enjoy it less. *Business Week,* August 23, 1976, pp. 19–20.

Mills, E. W. Career Development in Middle Life. In W. Bartlett (Ed.), *Evolving Religious Careers.* Washington, D.C.: Center for Applied Research in the Apostolate, 1970.

O'Leary, V. E. Some attitudinal barriers to occupational aspirations in women. *Psychological Bulletin,* 1974, *81,* pp. 809–826.

Persig, R. M. *Zen and the Art of Motorcycle Maintenance: An Inquiry into Values.* New York: Bantam Books, 1974.

Porter, L. W., and Lawler, E. E., III. *Managerial Attitudes and Performance.* New York: Irwin-Dorsey, 1968.

Schein, E. H. How to break in the college graduate. *Harvard Business Review,* 1964, *42,* pp. 68–76.

Schein, E. H. The individual, the organization, and the career: A conceptual scheme. *Journal of Applied Behavioral Science,* 1971, *7,* pp. 401–426.

Sheehy, G. *Passages: Predictable Crises of Adult Life.* New York: Dutton, 1974.

Stedry, A., and Kay, E. *The Effects of Goal Difficulty on Performance.* Lynn, Mass.: Behavioral Research Service, General Electric Company, 1962.

Super, D. E. *The Psychology of Careers.* New York: Harper & Row, 1957.

Super, D. E., and Bohn, M. J., Jr. *Occupational Psychology.* Belmont, California: Wadsworth, 1970.

Super, D. E., Crites, J., Hummel, R., Moser, H., Overstreet, P., and Warnath, C. *Vocational Development: A Framework for Research.* New York: Teachers College Press, 1957.

Up the ladder, finally. *Business Week,* November 24, 1975. pp. 58–68.

Wanous, J. P. Realistic job previews for organizational recruitment. *Personnel,* 1975, *52,* pp. 50–60.

White, R. W. Motivation reconsidered: The concept of competence. *Psychological Review,* 1959, *66,* pp. 297–323.

Value Dilemmas in Organization Development

Donald D. Bowen

Friedlander and Brown (1974) concluded their review of the status of organization development (OD) with the observation that "the future of OD rests in part on its values and the degree to which its practice, theory, and research are congruent with those values" (p. 335). The key value issue, they suggested, may be the conflict between the humanistic and democratic values of OD practitioners and the authoritarian, efficiency-oriented values of the managerial clientele most often served by OD consultants.

This paper will argue that value conflicts, perhaps even more than a dearth of research or techniques (although research difficulties are oft-cited constraints to development of the profession), currently limit further development of the theory and practice of OD. Value conflicts seem to be inherent in current conceptions of the consultant's function; resolving many of these conflicts may be facilitated by redefining the consultant's task along lines proposed by Argyris (1970) in his notion of intervention theory.

Value Dilemmas in OD Consulting

SITUATIONS IN WHICH THEY ARISE

The term *value dilemma* is used in a broad sense in this discussion; it is applied to any situation where there is internal conflict between the values or needs of different members of a consulting team or where the consultant's values or needs are inconsistent with those of

others involved in the consultation. The conflict may be experienced at either a conscious or unconscious level. Examples of value dilemmas are frequently mentioned in the literature. They arise, for example, when the consultant is used by the client to effect an end kept secret from the consultant, when higher management requests access to confidential information, when management unilaterally orders the installation of participative modes of supervision, or when the consultant discovers that the client practices blatant racism or sexism.

VALUE CONFLICT IN DIFFERENT APPROACHES TO OD

Friedlander and Brown (1974) have suggested a classification system for identifying the primary strategies of intervention employed by OD consultants. They differentiate between *technostructural approaches,* including strategies such as sociotechnical system design, job enlargement, and job enrichment, and *human processual approaches,* using such techniques as survey feedback, group development, and intergroup relations development.

Argyris (1970) has hypothesized that, compared to technostructural changes, human processual changes tend to involve situations that are more likely to create conflict for the consultant because they require greater deviance from existing norms, greater unfreezing of old behavior, development of a new self-corrective system, greater involvement of others in the change program, and greater personal and system discomfort. He has noted that the challenge to the consultant's skills and values may be overwhelming if the consultant's practice is not grounded in clearly articulated theory and values. The present discussion will focus on the value dilemmas of the OD consultant in human process interventions. To limit the perspective in such an arbitrary fashion may appear short-sighted, but if Argyris is correct, the dilemmas of consultancy should be more readily apparent in the context of human process consulting. Moreover, conclusions reached may also hold for technostructural practitioners to some extent.

HOW SERIOUS IS THE PROBLEM?

Tichy (1974) recently published data on the degree of inconsistency between values and actions among different types of change agents. Although his sample was small in size and not randomly selected, the results are disturbing. Of the four types of change agents studied, OD practitioners had the highest value-action incongruence. The nature of this inconsistency is informative: The OD consultants in Tichy's sample felt that *in theory* they should be working toward democratic, participative values, yet *in practice* they found themselves primarily concerned with helping to increase productivity and solve managerial problems. Tichy suggests that the significance of this finding is that it reveals a potential problem between OD consultants and management which hires them; as long as this value-action conflict persists, OD consultants will experience personal conflict and their interventions will be seen as internally inconsistent.

Practitioner concern over value conflicts seems to vary greatly. Some OD consultants probably evade the issues in the hope that someone else will resolve them. Some actually see their efforts as "value-free" and thereby deny the potential for conflict. One suspects, however, that most consultants encounter the problem far too often to ignore it.

The impact of value dilemmas on consultant effectiveness is perhaps most clearly seen in a common type of internal conflict described by Argyris (1970). Argyris has suggested that consultants usually have a strong need to experience competence. Faced with client resistance, the consultant may begin

> . . . focusing on pushing and controlling change, on manipulating the people, on taking more responsibility for the change, and thereby feeling the need to evaluate, interpret, and use inferred categories whose understanding depends upon knowledge of theory not available to clients. (p. 175)

The client may respond with greater resistance, thereby increasing the consultant's sense of frustration and causing the consultant to become more defensive and less effective in the face of impending failure. The consultant then experiences a decrease in energy and tolerance for stress and ambiguity, develops unrealistic goals for the consultant-client relationship, and feels an increased need for inclusion with and confirmation from the client.

One of the most important implications in Argyris's analysis is that the value conflicts experienced by the consultant will lead to changes in the consultant's own behavior, these changes will be perceived by the client, and the result will be a diminishing effectiveness of the consultant in subsequent intervention attempts.

If Argyris is correct in predicting that value conflicts decrease consultant effectiveness, even the most blasé and insensitive practitioner can ill afford to ignore the issue. Friedlander and Brown (1974) concluded that human processual approaches can generally be shown to improve attitudes but found practically no evidence that organizational effectiveness is improved. They suggested that one of the reasons for the lack of evidence for the impact of OD is the difficulty encountered in measuring the relevant variables. One also wonders, however, if the lack of evidence does not also reflect a reality that most interventions *do not succeed* in the long run. It is not hard to list numerous blue-chip firms that have become disillusioned with OD programs. It may be that consultant-client relationships deteriorate over time simply because clients sense that their consultants experience increasing difficulty in behaving in a manner consistent with the values espoused or implicit in the OD techniques employed.

Varieties of OD Value Dilemmas

Walton (1973, cited in Huse, 1975, p. 76) has concluded that ethical dilemmas can arise from five types of inconsistencies.

1. *An inconsistency may exist between the goals and strategies of the client and the values of the consultant.* This conflict is exemplified by the classic divergence already cited between the efficiency values

of the organization and the humanistic concern of the OD practitioner. Argyris (1970) has also devoted considerable attention to this type of conflict, noting that most consultations begin with the consultant being hired by one or a few individuals in the client system (e.g., the president or the top management group). Therefore one or more groups in the organization may indeed support the OD effort, but others will usually be indifferent or hostile. Moreover, if the consultant's values were not at considerable variance with the norms of the organization, what could the organization learn from the consultant?

2. *The client's actions in implementing the OD program may be inconsistent with the goals and values of the consultant.* The client may act out of ignorance or with forethought, but the former is probably more typical. For example, a vice-president in one organization became so convinced of the value of feedback for improving managerial performance that he held meetings with the people who reported to his subordinates to ask for evaluations of their bosses' performance. Because he excluded his immediate subordinates from these meetings, he generated substantial anxiety in the supposed beneficiaries of the feedback and jeopardized the entire OD program.

3. *There may be a difference between the consequences of the consultant's interventions and the consultant's personal values.* This type of dilemma is similar to the first, except that it is experienced after the fact rather than during the consultation. Thus potential for irreparable damage may be considerably more serious in this conflict situation.

4. *There may be a difference between the consultant's behavior and accepted professional standards.* If a well-developed, internally consistent theory of OD existed, it would provide a basis both for assessing and policing the activities of practitioners and for training prospective consultants. The present theory of OD is not always as helpful as it should be in resolving conflicts between professional norms and consultant needs. As already noted, the consultant is usually hired by one faction of the organization. This group becomes the natural ally and source of support for the interventionist at the beginning of the relationship. Most authorities agree, however, that the consultant's responsibilities are to work on behalf of the entire system, not for one group against another

(Argyris, 1970; Blake and Mouton, 1969; French and Bell, 1973; Huse, 1975; Steele, 1975). The capacity to serve the entire system requires, of course, that there be no irreconcilable conflicts of interest between groups or individuals within the organization. The validity of this assumption as a basic tenet of OD practice deserves reconsideration on the basis of simple practicality. This is not to deny Argyris's point that the consultant who does become caught up in the power struggles of the organization will quickly become ineffective. The consultant's problem is one of surviving in the system without developing contaminating alliances—a most difficult task.

5. *The consequences of an intervention may be inconsistent with values generally identified with OD.* If union critics are correct in their allegation that job-enrichment programs are fundamentally a form of speedup, consultants promoting these efforts may need to seriously reconsider the rationale for their activities.

Walton's (1973) dilemmas all involve conflicts between the consultant and others—clients, professional peers, or society in general. Argyris (1961, 1970) has focused more attention on the internal conflicts consultants experience, with special concern for the impact on the consultant's effectiveness. Value conflicts may occur when two or more of the consultant's values conflict with his or her needs. A similar problem may arise when practitioners collaborate in a team consultation. Steele (1975) has pointed to conflicts between the needs and values of team members as a common source of difficulty requiring constant, conscious attention within the team.

Further Strategic Difficulties

A number of chronic problems—some related to the conflicts already discussed, some not—emerge from study of OD theory and practice.

THE NECESSITY OF CONFLICT

One conclusion that is reached is that value conflicts in OD are inevitable and necessary. The five types of conflict cataloged by Walton (1973) all involve conflicts between the consultant and other groups. In some cases, improved theory and better training of practitioners would reduce the incidence or seriousness of these conflicts. Nevertheless, any situation involving more than one party, and particularly a situation in which one of the parties is engaged precisely because he or she subscribes to different values, is bound to produce conflict.

Most theories of OD emphasize, however, that conflict is not necessarily unproductive. Conflict creates more than obstacles; it also creates opportunities for learning, increasing one's competence, and contributing to the development of OD theory. The need for consultants to plan their work so that they are constantly learning and refining their skills has been increasingly stressed for individual development (Argyris, 1970; Argyris and Schon, 1974; Steele, 1975). In addition, such on-the-job learning from the value conflicts encountered may well prove to be the most valuable source of contributions to the general development of OD theory and practice.

CONSISTENCY AND COLLABORATION

Observation also suggests that for OD consultants, perhaps more than for any other professionals, consistency in values, needs, and behavior is itself a key value. There is an obvious reason why consistency is particularly important in OD practice. The consultant often develops the motivation to change in the client by surfacing the client's inconsistencies, and not surprisingly, the client then comes to expect the consultant to serve as the primary role model for more effective behavior.

One professional precept that is perhaps more honored in the breach than in the observance is that truly professional OD practitioners should always conduct research to evaluate their OD efforts. Moreover, in accordance with the principles of action research, evaluation should always be a joint effort involving both consultant and client. One can hardly quarrel with the aims of these prescriptions. A practical difficulty, however, arises from the fact that many clients do not care about such evaluations or do not know how to conduct meaningful research. They are unfamiliar with the techniques for determining the validity of measures; they are not likely to be conversant with factor analysis, multidimensional scaling, or similarly sophisticated statistical and other tools. The practitioner properly trained in the research methods of the behavioral sciences knows all too well how misleading an

evaluation can be unless the best possible strategies of research design and statistical analysis are used. The consultant's dilemma becomes one of deciding whether to allow the client a major role in planning the evaluation and thus accept a naive assessment, or whether to take the lead in designing the research and risk relegating the client to a distinctly junior status in the partnership. Argyris (1970) is probably correct in his argument that collaborative research is apt to produce more valid information; the argument here is not for deceptive, controlling research designs. On the other hand, even if the technical problems can be resolved, how can the consultant truly collaborate with a client system that may consist of several thousand people?

WITHHOLDING SERVICES

One of the most difficult value issues for interventionists is whether the practitioner is ever justified in unilaterally withholding his or her services from a client in need. Lippitt (1969) proposes that the real question for the consultant is the following: Given that some kind of change is going to occur, with or without your assistance, do you not have a responsibility to try to guide that change in the most constructive direction possible? Lippitt's point may be of greater relevance to the internal consultant or the consultant who already has an ongoing relationship with the client. Argyris (1970) takes an even stronger stand; he maintains that the responsibilities of professional OD practitioners to clients are analogous to those of medical doctors or lawyers, who are not permitted to refuse their services, at least in principle (although they often do in practice). Argyris argues that the very least the consultant must do is to provide ''first aid'' to the organization as long as rendering assistance does not compromise the consultant's values. Argyris offers an extreme example: Suppose the Ku Klux Klan asked for assistance? The KKK may be an organization that needs help more than others. If the Klan were genuinely interested in assessing itself and willing to commit itself to all that a valid assessment would entail regarding both itself and other groups, shouldn't the consultant be willing to help? If the Klan's objectives later proved to have been less than honestly stated, the consultant would be free to withdraw without having been compromised.

The arguments against allowing consultants to reject clients unilaterally are not trivial. Nevertheless, if this posture were adopted, most consultants would find compliance difficult. The best consultants have more requests for their services than they can fulfill; they must decide between clients on the basis of quick analyses of which clients are most likely to benefit from consultation.

Consultants must also consider whether refusing to deal with clients whose values are different from their own does not also imply that they are unwilling to question their own values and be as open to change as they ask their clients to be (Argyris, 1970). Actually, OD consultants are not likely to be asked to assist the Klan or the Nazi party. They are much more likely to experience the type of bind in which they discover during an ongoing relationship that the client shows signs that he is not going to change in the directions he claims he wants to go. At some point, the cues from the client become compelling. Consultants can never be absolutely sure, however, except in rare instances when the client reaches the same conclusions and a joint decision is made to discontinue the consultation. Even when both parties suspect the worst, the decision will be difficult if both have invested so much in the process that they are reluctant to admit failure.

Unraveling Some Knots

The value dilemmas described thus far are not easily resolved. Can anything be done? The remainder of this discussion will be devoted to an attempt to answer this question. The key to the solution, it will be suggested, is that many of the value dilemmas examined reflect how change agents define their role in relationship to their clients.

STANDARD DEFINITIONS OF OD CONSULTING

Let us begin by considering some of the definitions proposed by widely cited authorities in the field.

French and Bell (1973) define OD as

... a longe-range effort to improve an organization's problem-solving and renewal processes, particularly through a more effective and collaborative management of organization culture—with the assistance of a change agent, or catalyst, and the use of the theory and technology of applied behavioral science, including action research. (p. 15)

Lippitt (1969) speaks of organization renewal:

Organization renewal is the process of initiating, creating, and confronting needed changes so as to make it possible for organizations to become or remain viable, to adapt to new conditions, to solve problems, to learn from experiences, and to move toward greater organizational maturity. (p. 1)

Beckhard (1969) defines OD as

... an effort (1) *planned*, (2) *organizationwide*, and (3) *managed* from the *top* to (4) increase *organization effectiveness* and *health* through (5) *planned interventions* in the organization's "processes," using *behavioral science* knowledge. (p. 9)

And Golembiewski (1972) describes OD in part as

... a long-range effort to consciously introduce planned change into an organization in ways that involve its members, both in diagnosis of problems and prescriptions of change. (p. 114)

Although these definitions may differ in some respects, all explicitly or implicitly suggest that organizations *need* to change and that unless someone, usually the change agent, initiates or helps to initiate the needed change, the organization is not likely to move in the direction of becoming self-renewing, healthy, and effective. Thus, although OD practitioners and theorists generally agree that an OD consultation begins with a diagnostic phase, in a sense the diagnosis has already been made before the consultant sets foot inside the door. To question the usefulness of this approach does not imply doubt that most organizations would benefit from an improved interpersonal climate, a more organic organization, the use of more participative management techniques, and similar changes. The important issue is that accepted definitions of OD seem to orient the consultant toward a position that will *generate* value dilemmas and their ensuing practical difficulties.

THE PRIMARY TASK MODEL

Argyris (1970) has offered a conception of the consultant's function[1] that differs radically from those in

---

[1] Argyris's preference for the term *interventionist* rather than *change agent, facilitator,* etc., is clearly intended to differentiate his conception of the consultant's role from those generally found in the OD literature.

more general use. He defines the consultant's function in terms of three "primary tasks." First and most important is the generation of *valid information*. Second, helping the client system develop valid and useful information about its problems, the consultant prepares the organization to make *free choices* about how to proceed. The connection between these two functions is characterized as follows:

> In order to have free choice, the client has to have a cognitive map of what he wishes to do. The objectives of his action are known at the moment of decision. (p. 18)

Third, if the client has made a free choice, he will tend to have *internal commitment* to the decisions made.

> Internal commitment means the course of action or choice that has been internalized by each member so that he experiences a high degree of ownership and has a feeling of responsibility about the choice and its implications. (p. 20)

Argyris's formulation differs from that of other writers in that "change is not a primary task of the interventionist" (p. 21).

TOWARD THE RESOLUTION OF OD CONFLICTS

The value of Argyris's perspective becomes evident if some of the problems previously discussed are now reconsidered in light of his model.

The conflict between the humanistic values of the practitioner and the economic or political values of the client system ceases to be a disconcerting issue for the consultant who approaches the task with the following attitude: I am here to help this system develop valid information about how it functions. I cannot help them to be open to new information unless I am at least equally receptive. When we have the facts before us, we may both need to change our views. If the client chooses to ignore the information available, I am not compelled to go along with the client's interpretation. My primary allegiance is to valid information; my role as a consultant is not to defend my own values or to change the client's with respect to how this organization should function.

This position for the consultant is *not* value-free. It merely substitutes one set of values—criteria for the proper conduct of the consultation—for another set— preconceptions about the "good" organization and the necessity of change. There is substantial agreement that OD is inevitably value-laden (Huse, 1975).

The question is which set of values is more functional, both for helping the client and for promoting the growth of the consultant and the profession? Allegiance to valid information rather than to change or a particular normative concept of the organization encourages the consultant to approach the client system with fewer preconceptions of the type that are likely to make debilitating value dilemmas inevitable. If employees of a rigidly pyramidal organization are found to be experiencing real growth and satisfaction, then the commitment to valid information may lead the consultant to reassess his or her organizational theory rather than reject the data.

Conflicts that develop when overeager clients violate the goals and values of the consultant in misguided or premature attempts to implement a change program should be less likely to occur if the consultant and the client work out a contract based on the primary task model rather than on the accomplishment of prespecified changes. When change is the goal, both consultants and clients feel pressure to achieve the goal as expeditiously as possible. Argyris's primary intervention task model redefines the basic question to one of whether change is really necessary. As Albanese (1970) has noted, the truly healthy organization is not "change happy"; it recognizes that maintaining stability is sometimes more valuable than changing.

Consultation conceived in terms of Argyris's primary tasks is also less likely to lead to difficulties within the consulting team. If team members agree that it is not their fundamental job to initiate change or a particular type of change, then the questions that arise are likely to focus on the validity of the data or the analysis. In many cases, conflicts between team members can be resolved by designing procedures to verify or confirm the analysis.

Conflicts arising from inconsistency between the consultant's behavior and his or her own values seem, as previously noted, to originate in a need to feel competent in effecting change. The consultant comes to identify with change and assume responsibility for bringing it about. If the consultant's commitment to change exceeds the client's, resistance is generated and the consultant is tempted to react by coercing or manipulating the client. On the other hand, if the client develops a genuine commitment to change based on complete and valid information as Argyris defines it, the consultant will not feel compelled to motivate or control the client's behavior. The collaborative client-consultant relationship idealized in the norms of the OD profession should also be furthered when both parties are guided by valid information.

The problem of defining the client in an OD consultation is also more easily resolved within the primary task model. To undertake to serve the entire system always raises questions of where the boundaries of the system lie. Management usually has a narrower view than the consultant of who really has a legitimate interest in the situation. But when management and the consultant agree on the need for *valid information,* management concedes, in effect, that the consultant has a responsibility to seek out that information wherever it might be found. Operating from such a charter, the consultant has the opportunity to expand participation to all system members who can make a relevant contribution.

Finally, the primary intervention task philosophy sheds fresh light on the question of whether the interventionist, as a professional, is ever justified in unilaterally withholding his or her services. Clearly, saying no to a client who is unwilling to make a commitment to valid information and free choice is quite a different matter from refusing a request for help on the assumption that one's own values are superior to or different from those of the potential client.

Value dilemmas do not disappear under the primary task approach. Being confronted with an upsetting dilemma or paradox can provide a powerful impetus to change one's behavior (Lewin, 1958). Consultants who employ this principle to unfreeze their clients should be equally eager to seek paradoxes in their own behavior. Because the primary intervention task concept is a theory of consultancy rather than a theory of organizational processes, it is more likely to sensitize the consultant to dilemmas of a particular type, namely, those that present real opportunities for personal learning and for developing consulting skills and theory.

Issues in Research and Evaluation

When consultants concentrate on the generation of valid information, they feel less pressure to advocate a position or defend proposals from the attacks of skeptics. The primary task approach encourages clients and consultants to ask the same question: What must be done to insure the validity and completeness of our data?

Friedlander and Brown (1974) encountered frustration in assessing OD projects because of the difficulty of measuring the impact on organizational effectiveness. Traditional definitions of OD, which emphasize change as the central issue, require that OD be evaluated in terms of how beneficial were the changes that were made. If it is almost always futile to attempt to assess OD in these terms, it may prove more productive to focus research on more manageable issues. Within the more circumscribed primary task framework, the criteria of effectiveness fall into sharper focus. Did the client acknowledge the usefulness and validity of the data generated? Did the client's subsequent actions bear out his or her assessment? Can accurate predictions be made about further events within the client system? These are questions that the client and consultant may be able to answer more easily to their mutual satisfaction. And these are basic questions that must be answered in developing a theory of consultancy.

The OD Practitioner's Role in Change

One might infer from the discussion that the OD consultant should completely avoid taking part in the process of implementing changes in the client system. Such a position, however, would be neither practical nor desirable. The consultant is likely to have skills or information that the client system can use. Moreover, the process of changing, itself, is likely to produce additional valid information about the system, which must be monitored and fed back to the client. As the client begins to implement changes, there is a need to renegotiate the relationship with the consultant. If the consultant is to participate in the change process, what will his or her specific responsibilities be? Are these responsibilities defined in such a way that they advance rather than come into conflict with the primary intervention task activities, which are the consultant's first duty? Is it clearly understood that the client, not the consultant, is primarily responsible for both the process and the outcomes in implementing change?

One might also be tempted to infer that the consultant's responsibility ends with the collection and dissemination of valid information. Such an assumption leads to the untenable position that scientists are responsible only for the generation of knowledge and not for the use to which it is put. At some point, it is clearly unreasonable to expect OD practitioners as ''scientists'' to be responsible for the uses made of the fruits of their efforts. When knowledge becomes public property, scientists can do relatively little to control the uses made of their research findings by policymakers with whom they have no relationship. Within the consulting relationship, however, consultants can exercise substantial influence over the uses made of the data they generate. If a client adamantly insists on pursuing a project that threatens to injure the legitimate interest of others, the requirements of free and informed choice and internal commitment apply to all members of the client system, and the consultant not only can but should inform any members of the client system when impending decisions seem likely to jeopardize their interests. Interventionists have numerous opportunities to influence the direction of changes actually undertaken, and they have both the opportunity and the obligation to intervene in any situation where a client threatens to make unwarranted use of the data and knowledge produced in the consultancy.

Conclusion

In the preceding pages, a number of worrisome value dilemmas experienced by OD practitioners have been identified. These dilemmas reflect both inadequacies inherent in most current theories of consultation and problems encountered in the practical application of these theories. On the positive side, however, value conflicts seem to draw attention to the weaker links in OD theory and thus encourage the development of a stronger conceptual base. Such conflicts also serve to stimulate the learning and growth of practitioners if they are seen as opportunities, not merely obstacles.

The primary task model proposed by Argyris (1970) suggests elaborations that can be valuable in avoiding several particularly troublesome value dilemmas that inhibit the practitioner's capacity to be of assistance to the client system. Argyris's contribution has been to define the functions of OD consultants more clearly and to circumscribe their role, thereby reducing the tendency for consultants to approach their task with an orientation that is likely to generate value dilemmas of the less productive variety.

Perhaps the greatest single defect in almost all current concepts of OD is that they assume that change is necessary and desirable. They encourage the consultant to approach OD as a change agent, and, with the exception of Argyris's model, they thus imply that success as a consultant is a question of whether the consultant has been able to effect manifest change in the client system. A good doctor does not find something wrong with every patient, and OD professionals will experience fewer value conflicts if they define their functions so that they are not tempted to perform organizational surgery on every client. This new concept of OD, in which change is no longer primary, would appear to be the one crucial element that is needed to develop a viable theory of consultancy, a true theory which is more than an eclectic bag of techniques of change.

References

Albanese, R. Overcoming resistance to stability. *Business Horizons*, 1970 13 (2), pp. 35–42.

Argyris, C. Explorations in consulting-client relationships. *Human Organization*, 1961, *20*, pp. 121–33.

Argyris, C. *Intervention Theory and Method*. Reading, Mass.: Addison-Wesley, 1970.

Argyris, C., and Schon, D. A. *Theory in Practice: Increasing Professional Effectiveness*. San Francisco: Jossey-Bass, 1974.

Beckhard, R. *Organization Development: Strategies and Models*. Reading, Mass.: Addison-Wesley, 1969.

Blake, R. R., and Mouton, J. S. *Building a Dynamic Corporation Through Grid Organization Development*. Reading, Mass.: Addison-Wesley, 1969.

French, W. L., and Bell, C. H., Jr. *Organization Development*. Englewood Cliffs, N. J.: Prentice-Hall, 1973.

Friedlander, F., and Brown, L. D. Organization Development. In M. R. Rosenzweig and L. W. Porter (Eds.), *Annual Review of Psychology* (vol. 25). Palo Alto, Calif.: Annual Reviews, 1974.

Golembiewski, R. T. *Renewing Organizations: The Laboratory Approach to Planned Change.* Itasca, Ill.: Peacock, 1972.

Huse, E. F. *Organization Development and Change.* St. Paul, Minn.: West, 1975.

Lewin, K. Group Decision and Social Change. In E. E. Maccoby, T. M. Newcomb and E. L. Hartley (Eds.), *Readings in Social Psychology* (3rd ed.). New York: Holt, Rinehart & Winston, 1958.

Lippitt, G. L. *Organization Renewal.* Englewood Cliffs, N. J.: Prentice-Hall, 1969.

Steele, F. *Consulting for Organizational Change.* Amherst: University of Massachusetts, 1975.

Tichy, N. M. Agents of planned social change: Congruence of values, cognitions, and actions. *Administrative Science Quarterly,* 1974, *19,* pp. 164–182.

Walton, R. *Ethical issues in the practice of organizational development* (Working Paper No. 1840). Harvard Graduate School of Business Administration, May 1973.

The Role of the Consultant in Initiating Planned Change: A Case Study in Health Care Systems

Irwin Rubin, Mark Plovnick, and Ronald E. Fry

The basic purpose of this article is to consider the implicit strategies and assumptions an OD consultant tends to adopt in trying to initiate planned change in organizations. To do this, we intend to share some learning experiences we have had in trying to initiate a team development program for groups of interdisciplinary health care workers in numerous primary care settings.[1] Not having found ourselves succeeding in our efforts to initiate these programs, we were forced to reexamine what we felt were the relevant forces helping and hindering our success in these situations. We discovered that certain assumptions we were making were causing us to rely on inappropriate entry strategies. A rather dramatic shift in our strategies resulted, and in that process we became convinced that what we had learned was generalizable to the initiation of planned change in any setting.

Before we get to the specifics of our case, we would like you, the reader, to generate your own data base so you can relate our discussion to your own experiences. Reflect for a moment on a time when:

1. You were trying to initiate some planned changed effort.

From W. Warner Burke, ed., *Current Issues and Strategies in Organization Development* (New York: Human Sciences Press, 1977), pp. 324–354. Reprinted by permission.

[1] This chapter represents one part of a major effort, supported by the Robert Wood Johnson Foundation, to design and test educational programs focusing on the management of health care systems. (See Educational programs for health management: An overview. MIT/Sloan School Working Paper #617–72, September, 1972.)

The specific program being implemented was a self-instructional set of materials to lead a group through eight three-hour work sessions at no cost to the client. For more information, contact the authors at MIT/Sloan School of Management, 50 Memorial Drive, Cambridge, Massachusetts 02139.

2. You were convinced that you could help the client system with a problem it acknowledged.
3. For whatever reason(s), you failed to initiate or complete the activity (e.g., you terminated for some reason, you were not asked back, they never responded, etc.).

Now write down a list of reasons or factors which you felt led to this "failure."

If your list is anything like ours was, it contains more issues dealing with the client system, persons in the client system, and the environment around that system than it does issues about you, the consultant.

The major thrust of this article will be to share with you how we identified our "self-forces" in relation to the other forces we felt were blocking our successful initiation of a change effort. We will first describe our initial strategy for introducing and implementing a change program. Confronted with unsatisfactory results, we then had to experience what forces seemed to be affecting us as consultants. The body of the article is directed at this analysis, particularly at how we related to the forces identified and at the implications of this for our original strategies and assumptions.

The Technique of Scouting and Entry: An Initial Strategy[2]

Our initial behavior in trying to get planned change programs implemented in several health care settings was governed by a strategy which resulted from the following questions and assumptions:

[2] These two phases are part of a seven-phase model developed by Kolb and Frohman (1970): scouting; entry; diagnosis; planning; action; evaluation; and termination.

Question: Where in the system should we enter?

Assumption: Start at the top. (This led us to behave in ways that created contact with the official head(s) of these organizations as our clients.)

Question: Is there a felt need?

Assumption: The client knows most about his needs—which led us to behave in ways that:

1. Maximized the client's versus our own generation and sharing of valid information (i.e., being nondirective).
2. Maximized the client's free choice throughout the change process (i.e., being nondirective).

Question: How committed is the client to change?

Assumption: The client should be internally committed and his dependency upon us should be minimized—which led us to behave in ways that:

1. Facilitated the process versus doing it for the client (i.e., being nondirective).
2. Accepted client decisions versus "selling" the client (i.e., being nondirective).

It is important to note that when we started, we did not necessarily see a difference between the questions and the assumptions in the above strategy. We tended to adopt the assumptions as givens—almost automatic responses to the questions—as though the entire strategy were, in fact, a proven technique.

The specific interventions that resulted from this strategy consisted of:

1. Mailing an information blurb about our team development program to the heads of some thirty health care centers known to have some form of teams
2. Including in this initial mailing a set of guidelines for the client, to help him see if he had a need for team development, help him form a critical mass of internal people to manage a team development effort, help him decide which or how many teams should be offered the opportunity, etc.
3. Instructing the client to call us if he needed any help with the guidelines or would like more information, or, if he went through the guidelines, to call us for the team development materials

The results of this were not encouraging, to say the least. Over a period of 3 months, only two sites actu-

ally initiated team development programs.[3] Less than half a dozen sites responded at all to our mailing, and those that did were unable to use our input to initiate any change effort with or without the guidelines.

It was hard to set meetings with potential clients; appointments were cancelled frequently for unknown reasons or just forgotten.

It was even harder to have a group of people within the system meet with each other; usually, no one was capable of setting up such a meeting.

The potential client or client group was often unable to make any active decision regarding the initiation of a change project.

Client response to written memos, introductory material, or even telephone messages was sparse.

We believe that the above experiences resulted from a set of causal forces which exist within a health care organization, within the environment in which it operates, and within ourselves as consultants. These forces influence the process of getting in and getting started and ultimately influence the success of the relationship between the consultant and the organization. Specifically, these forces had to do with (1) the particular task that community health centers perform; (2) the client's internal resources—particularly those having to do with physicians; (3) the formal structure of these organizations; (4) the larger environment with which these organizations must interface; and (5) ourselves—how we reacted to all of these forces.

The Nature of the Task

There is a set of forces within a health care organization directly related to the nature of its primary task, which act as potential barriers to the successful initiation of a planned change effort. The task—the delivery of health care—is inherently vague and ambiguous, making it very difficult to set meaningful and measurable goals. Particularly in a ghetto setting where there is a focus on comprehensive health care (medical care plus housing, education, nutrition,

---

[3] Even these two sites were health centers at which we had had previous contact with physician administrators. These friends provided the driving force necessary to get the program started.

family planning, etc.), it is difficult to define and measure indicators of change and even more difficult to see any real signs of success. This is unlike industry where production (the task) is often more defined and measurable.

In addition, at a very basic level, a health care organization deals with issues of life and death. This fact adds anxiety and stress to the frustration created by not being able to know with any certainty if and when you are succeeding. These conditions have several implications for the initiation and implementation of planned change efforts. First, under such task-created anxiety, it is extremely difficult for a health care organization to develop a climate of experimentation and tentativeness which can facilitate the initiation of a change effort. In any system, an attempt to innovate raises anxiety. This is particularly so in health care, where a proposed change is very likely to involve at least some people, methods, or procedures which have direct interface with the patient (consumer). The organization message in this case is: "We are in a precarious state of affairs with respect to a very ambiguous, frustrating task. How can we risk upsetting this situation any further?"

In industry, for example, a proposal to do team building may raise less anxiety for two reasons: (1) the intervention is less likely to involve those who actually produce the product (assembly line workers versus management); and (2) even if the intervention does involve producers, it will have little direct effect on the product itself. In a health care situation, particularly where teams are delivering care, the same proposal is met with very high anxiety: the intervention directly involves the producers (health workers) and is very likely to alter the product (the way they function to deliver health care). Given the life and death nature of the task (product), any alteration might appear to have irreparable consequences. This can lead to an attitude of nonexperimentation.

In the face of uncertainty and anxiety, the health care organization demands concrete proof that a proposed change will or will not have certain effects. This manifests itself in a predictable set of questions or concerns: "Where have you done it before? How much will it improve health care? How can you guarantee it will not backfire? Have you ever worked in community health centers?" The consultant knows from his perspective that affirmative answers or promises to these queries are often inappropriate and sometimes impossible. What the organization is hearing from the consultant is the message: "Try a new 'something' which might yield better results." An industrial organization regularly conducts research and development and tends to be more experimental and willing to take risks. Health care organizations are not. They do not, for example, want to test and develop a drug on their patients. They want a proven solution which is ready to use.

If we replace the word *drug* in the above with *team building,* we can see that this attitude has spread beyond its appropriate point of focus. The organization seems frozen in terms of willingness to experiment with new organizational procedures, structures, etc., as well as being frozen, more appropriately, in terms of experimenting with new drugs and forms of patient treatment. This may be ironic in view of the fact that, given their ambiguous and frustrating task, most physicians in health care settings regularly operate from hunches and feelings. The irony becomes clearer if we distinguish between diagnosis and prescriptions. We have found that health workers are more likley to work from hunches when diagnosing a disorder than when prescribing a solution. Around organizational issues, they may agree with your diagnosis ("The team isn't working well together"), but disagree with your tentative solution ("We should try a pilot program in team development"). As we will discuss in detail later, the consultant needs to understand the "scientific" norms influencing physicians in particular to see further why experimental behavior is not considered appropriate.

What should a consultant do if he chooses not to take these signs of resistance as an indication that nothing can be done and that he should leave? First, he must be very aware of the paradox discussed above. Health care organizations are involved in a very turbulent, uncertain, and ambiguous task. They are, in a sense, in an unfrozen[4] climate with respect to the task. At the same time, they present a relatively frozen and static climate with respect to their attitudes toward

---

[4] See Schein's (1973) discussion of the three stages of change—unfreezing, change, and refreezing—based on Kurt Lewin's theoretical principles of change.

change. As a general rule, the consultant needs to be very careful about behaving in ways which increase anxiety and uncertainty, both of which are at a precariously high level already. He may, as we will discuss in detail later, need to be more of an expert than is normally required in other settings.

Of particular importance are his willingness and ability to learn to speak with people in health care organizations using their terms. Nowhere has the impact of our unique jargon been more clearly driven home than when we struggled painfully, for example, to communicate to community health workers "the simple concept of team development." We found it crucial to talk about their problems, their concerns, and *not* our methods or values, etc. Change objectives must be very specific. Elusive objectives like "helping you to function together," "smoother interpersonal relationships," etc., which we find so natural to use, only serve to increase the system's anxiety and uncertainty. The following scenario has been much more productive:

Question: Do you believe that you could deliver better health care if everyone better understood what everyone else expected them to do?
Answer: Yes! (hopefully)
Statement: We have some ways to help all of you better understand what you expect each other to do.

In other words, what for us as consultants might be most efficiently referred to as role negotiations (Harrison, 1972) may require a 5 minute explanation and discussion before any real understanding and commitment can be expected from the client.

The Nature of Internal Resources: The People

As we discussed above, the nature of the task of a health care organization mitigates initially against their willingness to adopt new solutions without proof. Related causal forces which result in resistance to change have to do with the attitudes of those who work in these systems. The attitudes and values of the professional physician predominate in these organizations and often pose problems for the change-oriented consultant.

One such attitude has to do with what we call the *preventive versus curative* mode of operation. With respect to the delivery of health care, many community health care delivery systems (community health centers in particular) adopt a curative (crisis-oriented) mode of operation. The problems in their patient populations seem so numerous and insurmountable (and indeed, in some cases they are) that virtually all of the health workers' efforts are invested in fighting immediate fires: "When a problem comes to our attention, we work to cure it." The alternative, which represents the stated ideal of most community health care organizations, is to strive to eliminate the conditions which caused the problems in the first place (via patient education, legislation, better housing, etc.)—the preventive mode. That this represents an ideal as yet to be reached is clear. Consequently, a majority of their directly related health care activities remains in the crisis care (curative) mode. Little effort is available for long-range planning, and investments in the future are hard to initiate. The paradox in this regard is clear: the longer one stays in a crisis management mode, the less time, energy, and resources there are to plan for the future.

Many factors contribute to the reinforcement of this attitude, including the nature of the task discussed earlier and certain environmental factors to be discussed later. Another important factor, related to the people focus in this section, is an understanding of what we call the *medical model* approach to problem solving.[5] As a function of education and professional socialization, physicians are trained to be experts at both diagnosis and prescription. The popular consultant posture of "we are here to help you work out answers to your own problems" is not one which fits easily with physicians and, hence, with a health care organization's dominant value system. Within the medical model, you involve the patient only indirectly in the diagnosis phase of problem solving and almost never in the prescription (choice of alternative action steps) phase.

Both the crisis mode and the medical model of change significantly influence the consultant's ability to gain the involvement and participation of the client. Involvement and participation by the client are

[5] Comparative models of styles of consultation, including the medical model, have been discussed and differentiated by Schein (1969).

felt to be essential in the successful initiation and implementation of a change effort. Meetings are scheduled and, with frustrating regularity, cancelled at the last minute or missed by several participants—"Something urgent came up!" One major reason for this, again stemming from the training and education of health workers, is their preference for practice (patient care) over administrative activities. The physician, for instance, is not trained to manage others or to administrate a clinic operation. When faced with choices, practice or research activities will usually come first. When forced to administrate, the crisis-oriented medical mode of problem solving will usually occur. Therefore, pressures will exist to have the consultant accept more of the responsibility to manage the change process than he might otherwise see as appropriate.

We have no simple recommendation on how to cope more successfully with the consequences of the above. Under certain conditions, it is clearly appropriate to confront the organization on issues of responsibility and commitment. Timing is obviously important, as in some cases all that will be accomplished is the creation of still another crisis to which the organization must respond.

Finally, with respect to internal resources, it is important to recognize that the community health center is a relatively new entity. As such, knowledge and experience of what is required to manage such an organization effectively are just beginning to develop. Consequently, there is a scarcity of people with the requisite knowledge and skills to manage such organizations. The resulting lower level of managerial sophistication reinforces the crisis orientation and short-range perspective discussed earlier.

In addition to the absence of required knowledge or experience, those who assume management positions are confronted with a host of other obstacles. First, the dominance of the physician (and related norms and values described earlier) in these settings often makes if very difficult to influence health workers if one is not an MD. Second, an administrator is likely to get little sense of achievement from his work because little useful feedback is forthcoming from health workers. This is an extreme but classic case of the situation wherein one only hears from people when they have a complaint about something; health workers generally lack appreciation or understanding of the nature of the administrator's work.

Third, there is an absence of clear paths of promotion. Where does one go after he has been chief administrator in a community health center? Finally, if the administrator is also an MD, he will experience conflict between loyalty to his physician peer group and the demands of organization management. Given all these obstacles, it is clear why it is difficult to recruit and retain sophisticated managers in these antiadministrative settings.

The Organization Structure: Power and Control

Who has what power? Most health care organizations are characterized by the existence of multiple power structures. For example, very often there exists a non-physician administrator whose primary responsibility is the acquisition and allocation of funds. His orientation is politicking with outside systems—gearing up for proposal writing and dealing with a diversity of city, state, and federal funding agencies. His major concern is what will look good to a provider of funds. Given the reality of his world, he has little motivation for anything which will not yield immediate outside visibility.

Operating alongside the administrator is a physician—the medical doctor—who is primarily concerned with issues of health care. If he is one of the socially minded new breed, he knows that quality health care is not equal to merely maximizing the number of patient contacts per health worker. To the administrator, however, this may be just the highly visible output measure he needs to keep funding agencies satisfied. In the absence of clearly defined lines of control between these two positions, the relationship between the people is strained and characterized by significant unresolved conflicts over who really has the power.[6]

This conflict and the resulting strained relationship

---

[6] We have found a somewhat opposite case to also result in similar conflicts. This is where the medical director is production-oriented—"Let's maximize patient visits"—and the administrator is more concerned with long-range planning and the implications of comprehensive health care. The important point, regardless of the specific individuals involved, is to recognize that the conflict is, at present, an inherent part of the system.

has consequences for others in the organization and subsequently for the consultant. A situation can result wherein various parts of the organization pick and choose allies. Very often, for example, support groups (x-ray, laboratories, records) will align themselves with the administrator, and deliverers will align themselves with the medical director. While we-they or intergroup problems are certainly not unique to health care organizations, when taken in conjunction with the other causal forces already discussed they result in additional complexities. The ''simple'' act of getting a team together to discuss a possible intervention (perceived to be an administrative matter) can be easy or difficult depending on who makes the request (administrator or physician) and to whom the request is made (entire team, team physician, team secretary, etc.) At a more general level, the ambiguous and conflicting nature of the power structure causes everyone to resist taking risks, particularly those involving the initiation of change efforts.

Added to this already difficult situation is the role of the community board. A representative group of people, somehow drawn from the community, are charged with the responsibility of overseeing—in a board-of-directors sense—the operation of their community health center. Little time or resources are available to train these people and to help them learn how to function effectively as a board. Consequently, they either find it difficult to function or they function in ways which may not be supportive of the health center itself. We have found several cases where the board members were predominantly and publicly concerned with expanding their individual power bases in the community and not at all with the delivery of health care. This creates more pressure on the administrators and medical directors, who usually have little ability to deal with this interface with the board. Thus, the consultant is confronted with a more complex and uncertain system. This is not usually the case with corporate boards, where the interface and division of roles between the board of directors and top management is clear and there is general commitment to common goals.

The need to recognize and deal with these complex power structures can be sharpened by briefly examining the anatomy of a failure we recently experienced.

The medical director of a community health center

became the entry point for initiating a discussion of a team-building program within the organization. After preliminary discussions with him, it was deemed advisable to involve a small group of influential people including, quite naturally, the administrator of the center.

A lengthy period of prolonged discussions, fraught with cancelled meetings, missed deadlines, etc., ensued. The medical director remained the prime contact, initiator, and mover within the system. Although the process seemed to be moving painfully slow, issues were being discussed and positive movement was occurring. Agreement had been reached (so it seemed!) by this group *as a group* to offer a team-building opportunity within the organization.

Then, suddenly, the process came to an abrupt halt. The administrator was asking the community board to request the medical director's resignation. Among the charges was ''his irresponsibility in promoting changes which would clearly bring the health care staff into conflict with one another and reduce the quality of patient care.''

What followed was a lengthy jurylike process in which the community board listened to witnesses from both sides. The consultant, rightly or wrongly, agreed to appear as an expert witness on health care organizations *and* less explicitly (but, nontheless, very clearly) to speak in defense of the medical director. The medical director was cleared of all charges. He waited for the administrator to resign or be asked to resign by the board. When this did not happen, the medical director quit. End of story, and end of a planned change effort at this particular center.[7]

While one could discuss this case from many points of view, several things are clear in retrospect. The medical director in our story was a deviant in terms of the predominant norms and values of that system. He was clearly not a deviant in terms of our predominant norms and values. Our own needs to succeed may well have blinded us from seeing the consequences of rely-

[7] Since the writing of this brief case description, events have occurred which further reinforce the need to be careful in dealing with the power structure. We have discovered that it was only from the ex-medical director's viewpoint that team development was dead. Other parts of the organization thought *we* had abandoned them because the medical director had resigned. Plans are in progress to resume the team development effort.

ing too heavily on the medical director. The community board was simply forgotten. No one within the organization mentioned them. We never thought to explore any linkages with them to gain their commitment and enhance their understanding of what was being considered.

Health care organizations, particularly community health centers, are not very structured organizations (in the formal sense, like organizations such as IBM and GM). The power structure and human interrelationships are ambiguous, diffuse, and generally highly strained and conflicting. The consultant trying to scout the system and negotiate entry needs to proceed very slowly and cautiously. He should be very careful to diagnose and involve all relevant parts of the diffuse and ambiguous power structure.

Being aware of and diagnosing the power structure will not, however, solve the entire problem. Even after the relevant groups or individuals are identified, pulling them together for any substantive decisions is difficult. From the consultant's point of view, it is crucial in many instances that consensus decisions be made around a number of issues. The very act of trying to accomplish such a decision-making process in and of itself represents a major intervention into many health care organizations. It can usually be assumed that in an industrial setting there is some legitimate authority (role position) that can schedule meetings with others. Because of the medical-administrative power struggle, such is not the case in many health care systems.

Very strong norms exist with respect to the handling of conflict. One can easily see that, given the anxiety generated by the difficulty and uncertainty of the task, the potential for the existence of conflict is high. Equally high is the perceived need to ignore or smooth over conflicts. In our failure example, one of the key charges against the medical director was the fact that he was, in effect, trying to bring conflict among the staff out into the open. When neither ignoring nor smoothing over is feasible, a forcing mode predominates wherein the physician generally has the last word.

The organization has little experience with collaborative problem solving and joint decision making. Decision making is primarily authoritarian, a circumstance due in part to the crisis orientation, in part to the scarcity of skilled managerial talent, and in large

measure to the dominant force of the physician's medical model in such organizations. As a result of prior training and experience, many MDs are accustomed to and comfortable with being solely responsible for major decisions. Within the context of a hospital operating room, such a posture is clearly essential and functional. Within a community health center, particularly around issues concerning the initiation and implementation of major changes, a very different mode of operation may be required.

One final area in which issues of power and control impact upon a consultant's ability to get started and work effectively in a health care organization has to do with who is helping whom. As we well know, few people feel particularly comfortable in the "one down" position of a client. They resist, fight, and are hesitant to own up to the fact that they may need help. In all likelihood, this issue is more extreme for professional helpers (health care workers and applied behavioral scientists) when they are clients. Nothing has more built-in defensiveness potential than one helper telling another helper he thinks he can help him!

The Wider Environment

While there may be little we, as consultants, or health care organizations can do in the short run about environmental forces, several are worth mentioning, as they have impact on the feasibility of initiating and implementing planned change. The more conspicuous of these forces are all related to the general issue of funding: Who is doing the funding? For what purposes (goals and objectives)? Under what conditions or constraints?

With the possible exception of private group practices, few health care organizations have the luxury of operating as highly autonomous units. In the case of a community health center, there is a community board involved. Most clinics and other health care organizations are tied closely to a hospital organization. Many hospitals are tied to academic organizations. And almost all of these systems are tied in varying degrees to multiple outside sources of funding.

Specifically with respect to community health centers, the present movement is toward more decentralized funding from multiple sources instead of centralized funding from HEW, OEO, etc. The nature of such current funding practices contributes to the uncertainty of the task of implementing planned change. Money (input) is allocated according to criteria which often have little to do with the delivery of health care, particularly comprehensive care (output). Output criteria, if they actually exist, usually appear in terms of patient contacts per physician, referrals per day, number registered, etc. Such short-run, numbers-oriented criteria may neither accurately reflect the needs of the patients nor assess the health workers' ability to meet those needs. The resulting dilemma for the consultant is clear. Unless a change effort can be clearly seen by administrators as helping to assure funding, they may resist it. But since criteria for funding are seldom related to comprehensive health care, the health workers are likely to resist a change effort unless they see it as being concerned with care-oriented criteria as well.

In addition, funding sources seldom legitimate the expenditure of funds for organizational development-type activities, as we would understand the term. Where a budget does exist, it is primarily for specific skill-training activities. What often results is a situation wherein, for example, the health care organization has extensive and costly educational equipment which may or may not be utilized at all. Even where the equipment is being used (as opposed to just collecting dust), it is probably being used in an environment where there is no coherent or systematic philosophy or plan for the development of human resources. Highly skilled people are then returned to an organization that has not made the changes necessary to utilize these resources more effectively.

Issues such as these have some very specific consequences for an outside consultant. In one center, for example, we were confronted directly by an outspoken physician with the question: "Where is the money coming from to pay you for your services?" The statement behind the question was clear: If we are paying out of our patient budget, the answer is *no!* In that instance, an outside foundation was funding the pilot intervention so we were judged acceptable. The dilemma became very clear when the foundation money dried up. The organization became very hesitant to continue prior activities or to engage in the initiation and implementation of new, previously agreed-upon programs. When someone else was making the investment, experimentation was more acceptable. When the organization itself had to make a financial investment, commitment dropped sharply. Getting started may well have been facilitated by the injection of outside funds but continuing required a higher and different level of commitment.[8]

Legislation is a final environmental force which can contribute to resistance to change. For example, HEW requires that a community board eventually manage a center. In reality, as we have noted previously, the board may have little concern for the delivery of health care. The result is that the organization may pay more attention to its relations with its board than other more meaningful measures of task performance in order to assure funding and licensing. Thus, the basic purpose of the organization becomes more complex and obscure, creating additional anxiety and frustration which contribute to increased resistance to change.

A Summary Perspective of Causal Forces

While the problems described above are in some sense unique to the health care field (particularly to comprehensive health care delivery), they can be generalized to be consistent with the models of organization commonly used in organization development. Viewing the series of obstacles described above in light of organization theory provides a more systematic understanding of the forces that we have found need to be managed in a planned change effort in health care systems.

One convenient organizational model developed by Leavitt (1967)[9] suggests several categories of subsystems within (and outside) organizations. These subsystems are continuously interacting to produce the phenomena we observe in organizations. Accord-

[8] We have no reason to believe that their hesitancy was caused by a feeling that the work was of no value. Getting in and getting started have proven to be difficult even in the situations where we are offering a pilot programmed team-development program at no financial cost to the organization in terms of consultant fees.

[9] Instead of or in addition to Leavitt's model, one could just as easily use the Lawrence and Lorsch (1967) framework of organization or the model described by Katz and Kahn (1966). The particular model is less important than the need for a systems perspective of organizations.

ing to Leavitt, the four primary subsystems of any organization are dynamics that have to do with (1) task, (2) structure, (3) technology, and (4) people. The system external to the organization Leavitt simply labels *environment*.

In our description of factors encountered in working with health care delivery systems, we were primarily describing forces associated with the task, structure, people, and environment as listed below:

Organization Factors in Health Care Delivery

1. Task
   a. Long-term versus short-term care (curative versus preventive)
   b. Specialty versus comprehensive care
   c. Medical versus health care
   d. Lack of relation between output (care) and input (funding)
2. People
   a. Training and socialization of professionals and nonprofessionals
   b. Norms and values: about health care, about management
   c. Styles: personality and cognitive
   d. Skills: health care and administrative
3. Structure
   a. Formal: lines of communication, authority, organization chart
   b. Informal: physician dominance of health care
4. Environment
   a. Community needs
   b. Legislative constraints
   c. Financial support: unpredictable and short-term; no investment in development

The Impact of These Causal Forces

The interactive nature of these forces presents a challenge to the consultant on two different fronts. On the one hand, the complex interdependent quality of these forces challenges the consultant to keep a large number of variables in mind when working in health care organizations. In this sense, planned change in health care organizations may differ from comparable efforts in other systems only in the amount of work required.

On the other hand, to the extent that these forces

represent given conditions unlikely to change in the short run, we also experience a challenge having to do with redefining ways a consultant can and should function in health care systems. In this sense, planned change in health care systems may not only be more work, it may also require different work than comparable efforts in other systems. Attitudes and assumptions may exist in our field (as we have argued exist among physicians, for example) which, if applied too rigidly and inflexibly, may result in a reduced ability to adapt and function effectively in health care systems.

Examples of Interdependence of Forces in Health Care Systems

With respect to the issue of keeping a large number of variables in mind, it is probably not sufficient to observe only that the life-and-death nature of the task in health care delivery influences people's attitudes in health care systems. In fact, the nature of the task varies from location to location (ghetto versus suburb) and from institution to institution (hospital versus neighborhood health centers)—in other words, the task varies with the environment and the technology.

More subtle is the recognition that the nature of the task is often defined by the nature of the people rather than vice versa, as when physicians (as a function of their training and socialization) insist on focusing on crisis care as opposed to preventive and/or comprehensive care.

As is the case with many of the large corporate organizations, the interaction between environment and the organization in health care is not strictly one way. Physicians, through their powerful lobbying agencies, have influenced legislation to the extent that they are afforded virtually unchallengeable control of our health care delivery systems. The desire to preserve this control combined with a trained indisposition towards administrative activities make for many of the organizational power and structure issues discussed earlier. Perhaps one of the most difficult phenomena to deal with is that within health care delivery, the task, formal structure, and environmental influences are all greatly determined by the nature of the people—by their training and by the social structure within the health care professions. The major result of this and the other problems discussed is that health care systems do not necessarily respond to strategies based solely on criteria of effectiveness and efficiency in performing their task—the delivery of health care. This type of interdependence demands that the consultant be able to diagnose and deal with health care organizations as very complex, fluid, rapidly changing open systems. In other words, he or she must first be able to identify and understand forces similar to those listed earlier and then examine how his or her own desires, motivations, and resources relate to the forces in order to take concrete steps to initiate change.

Implications for Scouting and Entry Strategies

Arranging the issues we discovered in working in health care delivery settings into a systematic organizational model has suggested several implications for developing strategies for organization interventions. The most general of these is that individual organizations do not have the type of control over themselves that is characteristic of private profit-making organizations. Powerful governmental control through statutes and funding and powerful professional norms and controls (both often incongruent with the task of meeting a community's health care needs) are major constraints in managing health care organizations. Inherent in this situation are several intervention dilemmas from the consultant's (e.g., the self-force) point of view.

1. Where in the system does the consultant enter?
2. How much free choice does he or she allow the client with respect to identifying problems and finding solutions? How much does the consultant inject himself or herself?
3. How much commitment does the consultant have? What is his or her motivation?
4. Whose needs are being met by the consultant's traditional demands for commitment (or how little commitment from the client is enough)?
5. Can consultants use power other than participative trust-based power (e.g., expert, positional, etc.)?

WHERE IN THE SYSTEM?

One of the tasks of scouting is to determine the most appropriate entry point in the organization. In health care delivery systems, it frequently appears that the entry point with the most leverage is outside the organization; that is, with the government, the funding agencies, or the medical schools and other training institutions. Indeed many people have chosen to focus their change efforts on these environmental factors.[10] However, if the goal is to provide more immediate assistance, it is necessary to focus on the health care organization with all the frustrations that are likely to result from the dysfunctional impact of the external reward system. In choosing points of entry within the organization, it has been our experience that maximum leverage is gained by working through a physician (not necessarily the medical doctor). Skeptical physicians listen to other physicians a good deal more than they listen to administrators, other health professionals, or, unfortunately, consultants.

However, because of the dual authority line present in many health systems, it is important not to overlook the nonmedical administrator. While in many cases a physician can go pretty far on his own, as in the example presented earlier, the uncommitted administrator can become an obstacle. Further, many administrators are personally sympathetic to the need for improved management of their organizations. Therefore, they are the best able to understand and appreciate OD strategies. Thus, they too need to be brought on board. It is important to remember in dealing with health systems that the absence of well-defined lines of authority often makes the old adage "start at the top" a somewhat ambiguous directive. Our experiences in neatly organized industrial organizations can easily lead us into misconceptions about where the top ought to be; what types of decisions the top can or cannot influence; and how much weight sanctions from the top carry with the producers.

FREE CHOICE, INTERNAL COMMITMENT— WHOSE NEEDS?

Among the more basic tenets behind much of our intervention strategy are the notions of valid data and free choice (Argyris, 1970). That is, the client should be aware of complete and true information about his

---

[10] One very notable example of such an environmental intervention is a program conducted by the MIT Sloan School of Management to provide change and management skills to the participating deans of the Association of American Medical Colleges.

organization and that his uncoerced decisions to participate in an intervention reflect his commitment to the need for and the particular strategy of change. In order to minimize client dependency on the consultant, consultants often interpret free choice as meaning they must minimize the use of expert power as a means of influence on the client.

What do we mean when we say free choice? What do we expect when we say internal commitment? We are not implying that these are unimportant questions to ask. We are suggesting greater flexibility around what constitutes an acceptable answer. For example, whose needs are we meeting by our tendency to avoid a high level of client dependency in the beginning of a relationship?

In the medical world, expert power is a way of life. When we deal with physicians, they act as patients and expect us to act as doctors. If we are really willing to take the client where he is at (as opposed to where we wish he were) and if we really believe we can be of help, why not tell him what we think he ought to do (write a prescription)?[11] We may need to provide considerably more concreteness in terms of steps to be taken than is appropriate in other settings.[12]

To reemphasize, we are not saying that issues of client dependence can be or should be ignored in health care systems. Such issues may, in fact, be more important in these settings. We may well need to view interdependence and independence as ideal states to be achieved other than as ideal conditions to expect at the point of getting started.

In addition, we suspect that many of us are reluctant to get involved in the day-to-day nitty-gritty management of change. We are all familiar with the glamorous "war stories" of successful confrontation meetings, etc. In health systems unused to effective management, it is often necessary for the consultant to get involved in such drab activities as scheduling meetings, insuring their attendance, and, in addi-

tion, managing their content. The consultant to health systems needs to be aware of his or her own resources (time, etc.) and motivations. To a certain degree, we may well be spoiled by the extent to which we have been able to maintain the position of elite outsiders[13] rather than being involved in the "dirty" day-to-day management of change.

FELT NEEDS—WHOSE?

Another issue facing the consultant in scouting the health care systems refers to the basic principle of felt needs. At the beginning of nearly every problem-solving, consulting, or change model there is a felt need. That is, the client system, having experienced a "hurt" or feeling a problem, is seeking help. In our experience we have found this to be the most effective way of entering an organization—being asked in.

However, we have also found that many health care organizations, though beset with organizational problems, are incapable of summoning a consultant. There are several reasons for this. First, though they are uncomfortable with a situation, they may not be aware that there is anything wrong or unusual about it. In many industrial organizations, for example, a crisis situation often unfreezes the organization and stimulates them to search for help to avoid future crises. In health care organizations, the crisis mode is the norm, not the exception—it is "the way things are in the business." Surprised health team members often comment: "Don't all teams work this way?" Second, health care organizations may suspect there is a better way to organize but do not know where to find the appropriate resources to help them. Third, though uncomfortable, they may choose to ignore "that administrative stuff." And, finally, being in the helping business themselves, they may find it difficult to ask for help.

For these reasons a consultant who is anxious to work at helping health care systems may have to initiate the contact and essentially market or create the felt need. This might require convincing skeptical administrators and physicians that (1) there is a better way to manage, (2) a consultant can help them to do so, and (3) it is worth their time, effort, and resources to try to change the way they are doing things.

---

[11] For a complete discussion of the impact of professional socialization on the helping relations particularly as it relates to physicians and the use of expert power to influence patients, see Friedson (1968).

[12] We cannot ignore the potential relevance of an intervention we have all made with other clients (other than ourselves) many times. "Perhaps they are resisting our process and not the content of our changes!"

[13] Our colleague, Ric Boyatzis, has labeled this phenomenon the *Lone Ranger* approach to consultation.

Summary: A New Entry Strategy to Accommodate Some Self-Forces

Based upon this analysis of forces hindering the initiation of effective change programs, we decided to alter our own behavior. We still considered the questions mentioned at the beginning but arrived at different behavioral solutions once we also considered ourselves and how we were relating to the other forces. Our new strategy was characterized by:

1. Active face-to-face selling of team concepts and our materials wherever we could meet with potential users—specifically the influential physicians who work on or with teams.
2. Less reliance on written guidelines and a you-call-us-when-you-are-ready posture.
3. A willingness to make in-person vists to a potential site to help sell or manage the implementation of the program.
4. Periodically calling up and checking on progress instead of waiting for a response.
5. Taking administrators out of the mangement role temporarily by making direct contact with members of teams as they went through the programs.

This strategy is still in use and has resulted in a "hit rate" of over 60 percent. That is, in over 60 percent of the sites we have contacted in this mode, one or more health care teams are going or have gone through a team development program.

To many of us this strategy may sound uncomfortable and unprofessional. In fact, to many consultants it represents a deviation from traditional professional roles—a role innovation (Schein, 1971). It represents a dramatic shift in the source and amount of influence the consultant brings to bear in a client relationship. Instead of relying comfortably on his professional title and its presumed status as a source of control (often the case when the client calls you), the consultant must rely more heavily on personal competence and the ability to communicate it (more like a sales-

person). Discomfort with this shift in roles stems primarily from the consultant feeling less control. It is the source of control which has changed, however, and has become more risky in a personal sense. The increased personal risk associated with this role innovation may be disconcerting to the consultant. But it may be that the relevance of this innovation is not limited to health care systems. To be effective change agents in any of today's complex organizational cultures may require us to consider ourselves as potential hindering forces in initiating change.

References

Argyris, C. *Intervention Theory and Method*. Reading, Massachusetts: Addison-Wesley, 1970.

Friedson, E. The Impurity of Professional and Authority. In H. S. Becker et al. (Eds.), *Institutions and the Person*. Chicago: Aldine, 1968. Pp. 25–35.

Harrison, R. Role negotiations: A Tough-Minded Approach to Team Development. In W. W. Burke and H. A. Hornstein (Eds.), *The Social Technology of Organization Development*. Fairfax, Virginia: NTL Learning Corp., 1972. Pp. 84–96.

Katz, D., and Kahn, R. L. *The Social Psychology of Organizations*. New York: Wiley, 1966.

Kolb, D., and Frohman, A. An organization development approach to consulting. *Sloan Management Review*, 1970, *12*(1).

Lawrence, P. R., and Lorsch, J. W. *Organization and environment: Managing differentiation and integration*. Boston: Division of Research, Graduate School of Business Administration, Harvard University, 1967.

Leavitt, H. *Managerial Psychology*. Chicago: University of Chicago Press, 1967.

Schein, E. H. *Process Consultation*. Reading, Massachusetts: Addison-Wesley, 1969.

Schein, E. H. Occupational socialization in the professions: The case of role innovation. *Journal of Psychiatric Research*, 1971, *8*, pp. 521–530.

Schein, E. H. Personal Change Through Interpersonal Relationships. In W. G. Bennis, E. H. Schein, D. E. Berlew, and F. I. Steele (Eds.), *Interpersonal Dynamics* (3rd ed.). Homewood, Illinois: Dorsey Press, 1973.